"Whether the Old Testament was authoritative for Christians was the first controversial question that confronted the early church. If only they had had access to this wonderful resource! Sadly, the Old Testament remains a stumbling block for many. Gignilliat and Thomas make what could easily be a crooked way straight, deftly attending to, and balancing, each book's literary integrity, place in the canon as a whole, and relation to Christ. Highly recommended!"

—**Kevin J. Vanhoozer**, Trinity Evangelical Divinity School

"This is one of those textbooks that won't be discarded at the semester's end but will be cherished as a valuable, lifelong resource. Gignilliat and Thomas introduce readers to the 'lay of the land' of the Old Testament, with a host of colorful charts, maps, and artwork. They also take readers beyond the typical boundaries of introductory textbooks by showing how the Old Testament texts echo through the canon and into reception history and theological discourse. This resource is a gift for both the classroom and the church!"

—**Elizabeth H. P. Backfish**, Jessup University

"In their *Reading the Old Testament as Christian Scripture*, Mark Gignilliat and Heath Thomas brilliantly illustrate the layered complexity of interpreting the Old Testament as Christian Scripture. Drawing on the full range of commentary, from Jerome and Augustine to the present, they engage both the beauty and the challenges of the Old Testament, always with an alertness to the questions posed by the modern Christian reader, and with helpful pointers to application. Their book-by-book introduction is enhanced by lavish illustrations from Christian art, informative sidebars, elegant and cultivated writing, and above all a deeply learned sensitivity to the particularities of the Old Testament books understood as witnesses to Christ."

—**J. Gordon McConville**, University of Gloucestershire (emeritus)

"It is often a challenge to find a textbook for the undergraduate classroom that will engage student attention, promote discussion, and effectively introduce the riches of the Old Testament. *Reading the Old Testament as Christian Scripture* does exactly this. It offers a clear and well-structured overview of biblical books, prioritizing attention to literary and theological content. True to its title, it reads the Old Testament as part of the Christian canon, pointing out canonical connections that link together books of the Old Testament and that link together the Old Testament and the New. Students will be very interested in the brief but insightful Reception History sidebars, which reflect on how Christian theologians have read these texts throughout the ages. Gignilliat and

Thomas have given us a textbook that will help to reinvigorate the witness of the Old Testament for the church through the classroom."

—**Aubrey E. Buster**, Wheaton College

"A beautifully produced volume, with artwork, diagrams, maps, sidebars, key verses, and discussion questions. This introduction is pitched to Christian undergrads (and perhaps, in some contexts, seminary students), from a broadly Reformed Protestant perspective. It aims to introduce earlier in students' study of the Bible a range of key insights arising from recent discussions about the biblical canon and the theological interpretation of Scripture. It will have wide appeal and, one hopes, extensive use."

—**Stephen B. Chapman**, Duke University

"If only I'd had this as my Old Testament textbook at university, I would have realized much earlier how to integrate theology and biblical studies, been more sensitive to and informed about the relationship between Jewish and Christian traditions, and become more nuanced in my understanding of scholarly discussions. Gignilliat and Thomas offer all these in a clear, helpful, accessible, and aesthetically pleasing format, so that students of Scripture can discover the God who reveals himself through the Old Testament."

—**Brittany N. Melton**, Regent College

"This is an outstanding resource. It is clearly presented with useful sidebars and images and with text that is economically stated and moves along, covering the important relationship between history, text, theology, and canon. *Reading the Old Testament as Christian Scripture* reminds me of a cross between the influential *Understanding the Old Testament* by Bernhard Anderson and the canonical introduction to the Old Testament by Brevard Childs. We are indebted to Gignilliat and Thomas for this fine collaborative effort. This book is sure to be seen in undergraduate and seminary classrooms. Bravo."

—**Christopher Seitz**, Wycliffe College, University of Toronto

"This theologically attuned and literarily sensitive introduction demonstrates how to read the Old Testament as Christian revelation. The authors situate the Old Testament in its historical environment and illustrate its ongoing cultural impact, but they never lose sight of the text of Scripture as a living word for those who are in Christ. They lead us into an interpretation that is life-giving for those who patiently read it alongside them. Highly recommended!"

—**Scott C. Jones**, Covenant College

READING *the* OLD TESTAMENT *as* CHRISTIAN SCRIPTURE

• READING •
CHRISTIAN
SCRIPTURE

VOLUMES AVAILABLE

——

Reading the Old Testament as Christian Scripture
Mark S. Gignilliat and Heath A. Thomas

——

Reading the New Testament as Christian Scripture
Constantine R. Campbell and Jonathan T. Pennington

——

Reading Wisdom and Psalms as Christian Scripture
Christopher B. Ansberry

——

Reading the Prophets as Christian Scripture
Eric J. Tully

——

Reading the Gospels as Christian Scripture
Joshua W. Jipp

——

Reading Paul as Christian Scripture
Constantine R. Campbell

——

READING *the* OLD TESTAMENT *as* CHRISTIAN SCRIPTURE

A LITERARY, CANONICAL, AND THEOLOGICAL SURVEY

MARK S. GIGNILLIAT
AND HEATH A. THOMAS

Baker Academic
a division of Baker Publishing Group
Grand Rapids, Michigan

© 2025 by Mark S. Gignilliat and Heath A. Thomas

Published by Baker Academic
a division of Baker Publishing Group
Grand Rapids, Michigan
BakerAcademic.com

Printed in the United States of America

Library of Congress Cataloging-in-Publication Data
Names: Gignilliat, Mark S., author. | Thomas, Heath, author.
Title: Reading the Old Testament as Christian scripture : a literary, canonical, and theological
    survey / Mark S. Gignilliat and Heath A. Thomas.
Description: Grand Rapids, Michigan : Baker Academic, a division of Baker Publishing Group,
    2025. | Series: Reading Christian scripture | Includes bibliographical references and index.
Identifiers: LCCN 2024027876 | ISBN 9780801098031 (cloth) | ISBN 9781493449316 (ebook) | ISBN
    9781493449323 (pdf)
Subjects: LCSH: Bible. Old Testament—Criticism, interpretation, etc. | Christianity and other
    religions—Judaism.
Classification: LCC BS2387 .G48 2025 | DDC 221.6088/2895—dc23/eng/20240725
LC record available at https://lccn.loc.gov/2024027876

Cover art: *Joseph and His Brother*, Albert Edelfelt (1877) / Artvee

Baker Publishing Group publications use paper produced from sustainable forestry practices and postconsumer waste whenever possible.

25   26   27   28   29   30   31   7   6   5   4   3   2   1

For our children in the prayerful hopes the God of the Bible captures their imaginations, affections, and loyalty.

Harrison, Isabelle, Simon, and Sophia Thomas

William, Jackson, Franklin, and Mary Grace Gignilliat

Contents

Acknowledgments

This book was a long time in coming, longer than either of us expected. We are glad to see it at the finish line and grateful for the many good colleagues and friends who helped to get it here. Indeed, it was a labor of love over an extended period of time. A special word of thanks goes to the good folks at Baker Academic. Jim Kinney shared the initial vision for this project and gave generously of his time, wisdom, and expertise, especially on the front end of the venture. Our good friend David Nelson, now at Baylor University Press, was a key and gracious figure during this phase as well, prodding us ever so kindly to get at it during the writing phase. After taking the baton from David, Brandy Scritchfield served the two of us in remarkable ways, and we think it's safe to say without her, this book would still be en route. Brandy is a gifted editor and a writer's friend. We remain grateful to her and the comfort of her little brick office that charmed us via Zoom. James Korsmo oversaw the production of the book to its printed form and became a wonderful companion and friend as we approached the finish line. His editorial eye, along with that of the very capable Wendy Widder Huisken, rescued us at several turns. We owe the two of them a debt of gratitude. Naturally, a book like this one could be written and rewritten again and again. The two of us have been at this project long enough to have shifted our views on things here or there. Nevertheless, we push this book off into an interpretive stream whose ripples and currents will never end, even into eternity.

We are grateful for the care and patience of our families, especially our wives. We dedicate this introduction to our children, some of whom have grown into adulthood in our time writing this book. In many ways, they are the book's target audience and represent the next generation of the faithful who are seeking God's thoughts in the pages of Holy Writ. God bless them as they amble through life's way. The attractions of the world sparkle and dazzle. We believe the living God of the Bible offers more: more beauty, more resplendence, more inspiration, more terror, and more forgiveness. We pray our children and those they represent will, like Moses, "turn aside and see this great sight" (Exod. 3:3 RSV).

Mark Gignilliat and Heath Thomas
August 5, 2024 (Ordinary Time)

Abbreviations

Old Testament

Gen.	Genesis		Eccles.	Ecclesiastes
Exod.	Exodus		Song	Song of Songs
Lev.	Leviticus		Isa.	Isaiah
Num.	Numbers		Jer.	Jeremiah
Deut.	Deuteronomy		Lam.	Lamentations
Josh.	Joshua		Ezek.	Ezekiel
Judg.	Judges		Dan.	Daniel
Ruth	Ruth		Hosea	Hosea
1 Sam.	1 Samuel		Joel	Joel
2 Sam.	2 Samuel		Amos	Amos
1 Kings	1 Kings		Obad.	Obadiah
2 Kings	2 Kings		Jon.	Jonah
1 Chron.	1 Chronicles		Mic.	Micah
2 Chron.	2 Chronicles		Nah.	Nahum
Ezra	Ezra		Hab.	Habakkuk
Neh.	Nehemiah		Zeph.	Zephaniah
Esther	Esther		Hag.	Haggai
Job	Job		Zech.	Zechariah
Ps(s).	Psalm(s)		Mal.	Malachi
Prov.	Proverbs			

New Testament

Matt.	Matthew		John	John
Mark	Mark		Acts	Acts
Luke	Luke		Rom.	Romans

1 Cor.	1 Corinthians	Philem.	Philemon
2 Cor.	2 Corinthians	Heb.	Hebrews
Gal.	Galatians	James	James
Eph.	Ephesians	1 Pet.	1 Peter
Phil.	Philippians	2 Pet.	2 Peter
Col.	Colossians	1 John	1 John
1 Thess.	1 Thessalonians	2 John	2 John
2 Thess.	2 Thessalonians	3 John	3 John
1 Tim.	1 Timothy	Jude	Jude
2 Tim.	2 Timothy	Rev.	Revelation
Titus	Titus		

Bible Versions

AT	authors' translation
CSB	Christian Standard Bible
ESV	English Standard Version
KJV	King James Version
LXX	Septuagint
NASB	New American Standard Bible (2020 edition)
NASB1995	New American Standard Bible (1995 edition)
NETS	New English Translation of the Septuagint
NIV	New International Version (2011)
NJPS	*Tanakh: The Holy Scriptures: The New JPS Translation according to the Traditional Hebrew Text*
NRSV	New Revised Standard Version
RSV	Revised Standard Version

General

AD	*anno Domini*, in the year of the Lord
BC	before Christ
ca.	circa
cf.	*confer*, compare
e.g.	*exempli gratia*, for example
esp.	especially
i.e.	*id est*, that is
OAN	oracle(s) against nations
r.	reigned

CHAPTER ONE

Introduction to the Old Testament as Christian Scripture

"The entire *history* of Israel was useless: away with it!"[1] Friedrich Nietzsche does not mince words with his startling claim about ancient Israel and their Scriptures. While most Christians affirm the Old Testament's canonical status, an element of Nietzsche's sentiment remains in many modern hearts and minds, even Christian ones. Christians read the covers on their Bibles, and they all say the same thing: Holy Bible. This description includes the Old Testament as part of our two-Testament **canon**, even when we might confess in our private moments that we find the Old Testament a strange pot of soup. How many of us, good intentions and all, have resolved to read through the Bible only to find ourselves exiting the back door once we hit Leviticus: sacrificial mechanics, purity laws, no shrimp? Is this stuff really useful? Is it really God's Word to humanity of all times? The Old Testament is a challenge.

But it is a challenge well worth the effort, and perhaps the challenge makes the Old Testament especially inviting, interesting, and fruitful. "To the hard of hearing," Flannery O'Connor claims, "you shout, and for the almost blind you draw

> **RECEPTION HISTORY**
>
> ### St. Augustine on Reading the Old Testament
>
> St. Augustine of Hippo, an important early-church theologian, confessed to the challenge of the Old Testament in the early days of his Christian faith. When preparing for his baptism, Augustine approached his bishop, Ambrose of Milan, and asked how best to ready himself for baptism. Ambrose encouraged Augustine to read Isaiah, for no **prophet** prepares for the gospel like Isaiah. Being the committed new Christian that Augustine was, he started reading Isaiah. He admits his immediate confusion: "But I did not understand the first passage of the book, and thought the whole would be equally obscure. So I put it on one side to be resumed when I had more practice in the Lord's style of language."[a]

1

Figure 1.1. Jesus, Moses, and Isaiah on a stained-glass window in the cathedral of Schwerin, Germany

large and startling figures."[2] O'Connor's description of her own shock-laden writing easily slides over as a fitting description of the Old Testament. Familiarity can breed contempt. When contempt, indifference, or boredom sets in, then a literary bullhorn is sometimes needed to rouse us from our religious slumbers. The Old Testament is this kind of bullhorn. It startles. It shocks. It comforts and confounds. It confronts our blindness and deafness with large and startling pictures. The book you are holding is an invitation to a wild and potentially life-altering encounter. Reader beware.

The Christian church has never operated without an authoritative collection of sacred Scripture that included the Old Testament. This basic fact makes Nietzsche's claim above clang in our theological ears. From Jesus and his disciples, to the early apostolic period, to the crucial **Trinitarian** debates of the fourth century, the Old Testament's canonical authority was assumed. When challenges to its authority arose, the luminaries of Christian orthodoxy rose to the challenge and reaffirmed the Old Testament's status as Scripture. Christian instincts through the centuries resist the diminishing of the Old Testament's canonical status, and for good reasons. Any encounter with Jesus Christ, the risen Lord—whether in the first or twenty-first century—demands an intense engagement with the Scriptures of Israel in order to realize who this Jesus actually was and is. 👥 📜

The book you are holding attempts to help you understand better what St. Augustine called "the Lord's style of language." This textbook does not pretend or seek to be exhaustive. Perhaps expressed better, we do not want this book to be exhausting. (Discerning readers know that no account of anything is ever exhaustive; we can put that fiction to bed.) Decisions regarding the book's content had to be made at every turn, so for the sake of clarity, in the next section we identify our interpretive instincts and organizing principles.

A Christian Introduction to the Old Testament

This introduction to the Old Testament is a Christian introduction. We assume this book will find its home in university and college classrooms, though we hope its range of reception goes beyond these settings. Many readers in today's intellectual climate accept the postmodern skepticism of **metanarratives**—that is, a resistance to all-encompassing theories about the complexities of human life, thought, and behavior.

However, this resistance to all-encompassing narratives or belief patterns is not the dismissal of metanarratives per se. No one can operate without some metanarrative(s) at work, without some organizing principle(s) for making sense of ourselves and our place in this world. Rather, the postmodern resistance is directed toward the dominance of one set of beliefs over against others, especially when autonomous reason is called in for support. The cultural manifesto of our day amounts to something like "You like tomato and I like tomahto. . . . Let's call the whole thing off."[3] We hear these sentiments all the time in today's public discourse.

This book is not a primer on postmodernism or the Zeitgeist of today's youth. Nor do the authors intend to huff over the sorry state of today's cultural climate. In fact, we feel quite the reverse. One positive outcome of the intellectual environment of our day is the clarification of our own intellectual and moral instincts: our metanarratives. We are all situated somewhere. Either consciously or subconsciously, everyone is working with some organizing principle(s) for how they understand the world and for how they read texts. We cannot escape our bodies or our minds.

RECEPTION HISTORY

"Scripture" in the New Testament

For Jesus and the apostles as well as early Christians, the appeal to "Scripture" is an appeal to the Old Testament. Readers can rightly extend Paul's claim about Scripture's inspiration and continued effectiveness (2 Tim. 3:16) to the whole Bible, but a first reading understands Paul as referring to the Old Testament. As Paul says elsewhere about the Scriptures of Israel, "For whatever was written in former days was written for our instruction" (Rom. 15:4 NRSV).

CANONICAL CONNECTIONS

Jesus in the Old Testament Scripture

Luke's Gospel links Jesus's postresurrection ministry with his exposition of the Old Testament. With the two disciples on the road to Emmaus and then with the rest of his disciples (Luke 24), Jesus offers an account of himself on the basis of Moses, the **Prophets**, and the Psalms. The Scriptures of Israel, or the Old Testament, provided the early apostolic community the theological ABCs for how to speak about the person and work of Jesus Christ.

All the throat clearing of the preceding paragraphs has a straightforward aim in mind. We want to make clear our "metanarrative," our location and place in the reading and reception of Israel's Scriptures. *We have a vested interest in the Old Testament primarily because of its status as Christian Scripture*. Our hope for this book is as broad a readership as possible. We aim to be hospitable and charitable to views that differ from ours. At the same time, we are attached to the object of our study by a shared confession of faith. We have a set of beliefs regarding the Old Testament's character and subject matter. Readers will sense these commitments from beginning to end. We cannot escape these commitments, nor do we wish to. Moreover, we hope that despite our interpretive instincts, those who do not share our Christian "metanarrative" may still benefit from our approach and presentation.

Old Testament or Hebrew Bible?

As the previous section makes explicit, we understand our subject matter as the *Old Testament* and will refer to the first part of the Christian canon as such. What may appear as an innocuous claim is actually quite contested. In biblical scholarship, the first part of the Christian canon is often referred to as the "Hebrew Bible." The title "Old Testament" carries with it antiquarian intellectual baggage or limits these sacred texts to a particular community of readers, whereas "Hebrew Bible" may avoid some of this baggage. On this score, a few matters are worth addressing.

First, the Old Testament is in fact a Hebrew Bible. Translators in the English Bible tradition from the King James Bible to the New International Version to the New Revised Standard Version work from a Hebrew (and in the case of a few sections, Aramaic) text. Especially in the Protestant translation tradition, the basic words, grammar, and syntax of the first part of the Christian canon is Hebrew in form. So, in a very real sense, the Old Testament *is* a Hebrew Bible. In our next section, we will return to this matter because it bears on how we structure the contents of the book you are holding.

Nevertheless, modern scholarship's resistance to the term "Old Testament" in favor of "Hebrew Bible" has multiple social and intellectual causes. Our concern is not to sort through these causes, but it is worth pointing out a potential hazard with the choice of the term "Hebrew Bible" over against "Old Testament." All acts of naming come with a set of stated or unstated ideas. Neither "Hebrew Bible" nor "Old Testament" is a neutral title.

Identifying the first part of the Christian canon as the Hebrew Bible may imply a closer proximity to the historical figures and institutions of that body of literature. A resistance to the title "Old Testament" marks a resistance to "Christianizing" this body of literature. For surely, Moses was no Trinitarian, and Jeremiah would not know Jesus of Nazareth if they met at a falafel stand in Jerusalem. From another vantage point, the term "Hebrew Bible" may seem to locate these sacred writings more closely with Judaism, the proper religious heir of these texts. When Christians take up their "Old Testament" they are in effect "reading someone else's mail." The choice of "Hebrew Bible" instead of "Old Testament" makes this matter clear.

Our approach to the first part of the Christian canon leans against the tendency to dislocate the sacred Scriptures of Israel from the communities of faith that cherish them. Modern approaches to Old Testament studies have yielded enormous interpretive fruit, fruit we will pick and eat all along the way through this volume. But modern literary and historical approaches also work with historicist instincts that tend to reduce the biblical texts and their "meaning" to a particular moment in historical time. The authors of this book find the historicist approach theologically anemic—and we will talk more about this in time. Admittedly, the fact that we even have our Bibles is a kind of historical question too. We believe we have our Bibles because their contents were recognized and received as sacred Scripture. This confession shapes how we read and receive the Old Testament.

We will turn to these matters more fully in our section below—"The Importance of Canon." At this point, we understand the Old Testament canon to anticipate readers who receive its texts as *sacred* and *authoritative*. This disposition to the material does not need to be at odds with "intellectual" or "scholarly" approaches. The church's reception of the Old Testament throughout its history bears witness to the happy commingling of these two perspectives. Nevertheless, the Old Testament as Christian Scripture resides most fittingly in contexts where confessions of faith and rigorous engagement with the biblical material are happily wed.

In this blissful nuptial arrangement, the language of "Old Testament" indicates something significant about the form of our Christian Bibles. The "old" in Old Testament should not connote a value statement about this portion of our Scripture, as in "Where are my *old* shoes? I have to cut the grass." In this frame of reference, the New Testament glimmers like a shiny, new car, while the Old Testament collects dust on the mantle like grandpa's wristwatch.

The language of "old" in Old Testament indicates that something had to come to an end before something new began. The history of God's dealings with Israel—the giving of the law and the thunder of the prophets—has

Judaism's Interpretive Lens

Everything we have said to this point has to do with the church. What about Jewish reception of the Old Testament? At a rudimentary level, **rabbinic Judaism** comes to the Scriptures of Israel with an interpretive lens as well. Christians read the Old Testament through the lens of a Trinitarian **rule of faith** or by means of the gospel revealed in Jesus Christ. The **synagogue** comes to the Scriptures of Israel through the interpretive lens of **Talmud** (the central text of rabbinic Judaism). Neither religious group reads the Scriptures of Israel outside an interpretive frame shaped by their respective communities of faith.

A Rule of Faith

Christian Bible reading is "ruled" reading. Christians read with a "rule of faith." Such a rule does not force the Bible against its own words. Rather, it functions as guardrails on the highway of Bible reading. Irenaeus illustrated the rule of faith in the second century with an instruction book from a mosaic artisan. If one orders a mosaic and the tiles arrive unarranged, then some guidebook is needed in order to put the mosaic together properly. Otherwise if you ordered a mosaic of a king, without the guide you might construct a fox or a dog. The rule of faith is a sort of guidebook for proper reading of the Bible's total witness, particularly as this relates to the identity of God as Father, Son, and Holy Spirit.[b]

T. S. Eliot and Scripture

Something of Scripture's religious character is affirmed in T. S. Eliot's following reflection:

> I could fulminate against the men of letters who have gone into ecstasies over "the Bible as literature," the Bible as "the noblest monument of English prose." Those who talk of the Bible as a "monument of English prose" are merely admiring it as a monument over the grave of Christianity. . . . The Bible has had a *literary* influence upon English literature not because it has been considered literature, but because it has been considered as the report of the Word of God.[c]

been written down and is now open to the future. In this future moment something new is about to break forth (Isa. 48:6). So, the Old Testament and the New Testament are fitted to each other around a common subject matter—namely, God's **revelation** of himself by the Spirit in the Son. When the Old Testament comes to the end of its material form, it anticipates God's redemptive activity in the world by his Son. But, and this is a crucial "but," the Old Testament is not merely instrumental in the sense that it gets us to Jesus Christ in the New Testament and then, as we remember Christopher Seitz describing it, falls back into the ocean like the booster rockets of a space shuttle. The Old Testament and its particular way of speaking continue as a witness to the one God Christians name as the Father, Son, and Holy Spirit.

"Old," then, does not mean settled, dusty, relegated to the attic with other interesting objects from a bygone era. The Old Testament is to the New Testament what breath is to life. You do not have the one without the other. Moreover, the Old Testament continues as a sacred and canonical body of Scripture. These ancient texts are the continued means by which God communicates his life-giving self to his people and the world. The Old Testament is "old" because its material form and "coming to be" had to end in anticipation of a new moment of God's self-unveiling. But it is precisely in its "oldness" that it continues to shape the way Christians understand our triune God and his redemptive mission for the universe.

Law, Prophets, and Writings

We had to decide in what order to present the material content of the Old Testament. We could present it in the form of our English Bibles. In this case, we would begin with the books of Moses, move to the historical books, then into the terrain of the poets and sages, and finish with the prophetic books. Malachi would have the last word. There is much to commend about this presentation of the Old Testament, including the simple fact that most readers know this ordering. 📖

We opted instead to present the Old Testament according to the ordering of the Hebrew canon—the **Law**, Prophets, and **Writings**, or **Torah**, **Nevi'im**, and **Ketuvim** (**TaNaK** in the Jewish tradition). Admittedly, this decision risks disorienting readers from a familiar pattern. However, this can have a positive outcome as well. Reading strategies that nudge us away from the overly familiar can provide new avenues of insight and appreciation. 📖

We do not follow this order of the canon simply to defamiliarize or disorient readers for the sake of new avenues of discovery. There are theological and interpretive issues at play in the ordering of the Old Testament according to its Hebrew schema. These issues bear some explanation.

The language "the Law and the Prophets" is shorthand for the fundamental form and authority of the Old Testament. Jesus, on the road to Emmaus, explains himself on the basis of the Law and the Prophets. Paul provides warrant for his gentile mission by appeal to the Law and the Prophets (Rom. 10:18–21). In fact, sometimes in the New Testament witness of Jesus, reference to

English Bible Order

Law/Pentateuch	History Books	Poetry & Wisdom	Prophets
Genesis	Joshua	Job	Isaiah
Exodus	Judges	Psalms	Jeremiah
Leviticus	Ruth	Proverbs	Lamentations
Numbers	1 Samuel	Ecclesiastes	Ezekiel
Deuteronomy	2 Samuel	Song of Songs	Daniel
	1 Kings		Hosea
	2 Kings		Joel
	1 Chronicles		Amos
	2 Chronicles		Obadiah
	Ezra		Jonah
	Nehemiah		Micah
	Esther		Nahum
			Habakkuk
			Zephaniah
			Haggai
			Zechariah
			Malachi

Public domain

Figure 1.2. Carpet page from the Leningrad Codex that artistically shows the tripartite division of the Tanak alongside the dedication

Hebrew Canon Book Order

Law	Prophets	Writings
Genesis	Joshua	Psalms
Exodus	Judges	Job
Leviticus	1 Samuel	Proverbs
Numbers	2 Samuel	Ruth
Deuteronomy	1 Kings	Song of Songs
	2 Kings	Ecclesiastes
	Isaiah	Lamentations
	Jeremiah	Esther
	Ezekiel	Daniel
	Hosea	Ezra
	Joel	Nehemiah
	Amos	1 Chronicles
	Obadiah	2 Chronicles
	Jonah	
	Micah	
	Nahum	
	Habakkuk	
	Zephaniah	
	Haggai	
	Zechariah	
	Malachi	

"the Law" seems to cover material beyond the five books of Moses alone (Matt. 22:36; 23:23; John 1:45; 10:34). "Law" can function as shorthand for all of Israel's Scriptures.

The Law and the Prophets are in internal conversation and mutually relate to each other in their canonical form. Though Genesis through Kings forms a history of Israel, there is a division between the end of Deuteronomy and the beginning of Joshua—the canonical seam of the Law and the Prophets. This canonical division does not subordinate the Prophets to the Law but maintains the integrity and reciprocity of both. The Law and the Prophets talk to each other, both in their coming to be and in their future reception.

Deuteronomy concludes with a portrait of Moses as a prophet like no other. This portrait links to a chain of prophetic activity after him (cf. Deut. 34:10–12; Jer. 1). Here too the connection between the Law and the Prophets comes from within the material form of the Old Testament canon. We will discuss these matters more fully in later chapters. Here we note that the language of "Law and Prophets" derives from the Old Testament itself. Moses and the prophets "need" each other for the total witness of God's self-revealing. The particular language of Law and Prophets forms the basic grammar for the Old Testament's self-understanding and presentation.

"What then of the Writings?" you might ask. The Writings demonstrate what faithful life looks like in light of the authority of the Law and the Prophets. Though not all Hebrew orderings place Psalms as the first book of the Writings, many do, including the medieval manuscript tradition behind nearly all English translations. The Psalms are located in the signal position of the Writings, and the first two psalms provide an entry point to the entire corpus. The themes of Psalm 1 and Psalm 2 reflect major focal points of the Law and the Writings: life shaped by Torah (Ps. 1) and existence in the kingdom of God (Ps. 2). (See the Psalms chapter for a fuller account of these two psalms.) In this account of the canonical shape of the Hebrew Bible, the Law and the Prophets form the basic building blocks for the entire Old Testament, including the Writings, which take their cue from the prior authority of these two.

Earlier we made a claim for the use of the title "Old Testament" over against "Hebrew Bible." Now, we seem to be taking with our left hand what we gave with our right. But such is not the case. Our opting for the title "Old Testament" locates our particular reading of these sacred texts in a believing community. Calling the Scriptures of Israel the Old Testament identifies our reading as a Christian exercise within the confessional framework of the Christian interpretive tradition. Nevertheless, such a claim in no way seeks to lessen the central role Israel plays as the means by which these sacred writings are collected and preserved (both for church and synagogue).

The apostle Paul speaks of Israel as the preservers and keepers of Israel's sacred traditions (Rom. 1:2–4; 9:5). Though Jews and Christians go their respective ways when interpreting the Scriptures of Israel, they share the same canonical collection as Old Testament or Tanak, respectively. If Jews and Christians were to go their separate ways about the canon itself, significant theological problems would arise with respect to the continuity of the one people of God.

Ordering this introduction to the Old Testament according to the structure of Law, Prophets, and Writings has numerous interpretive and theological benefits. Our decision for this traditional ordering is not meant to diminish the value of other canonical orderings. We have no hidden agenda to take away anyone's English Bibles. We have our own! Nevertheless, we believe the material content of the Old Testament in its given Hebrew form pressures us to read it according to this canonical shape. We hope that these "canonical lenses" for reading the Old Testament will generate new and interesting avenues of discovery and understanding for the reader.

RECEPTION HISTORY

Francis Turretin and the Hebrew Canon

The Protestant theologian Francis Turretin (seventeenth century) makes a claim for the priority of the Hebrew text along with its ordering and scope for theological reasons: "Nor should the canon of the Jews be distinguished here from that of Christians because Christians neither can nor ought to receive other books of the Old Testament as canonical than those which they received from Jews."[d]

RECEPTION HISTORY

Hugh of St. Victor and the Hebrew Canon

Hugh of St. Victor, a twelfth-century canon of the abbey of St. Victor, spoke of and interpreted the Old Testament according to its tripartite form. The Law, the Prophets, and the Writings ("Hagiographa" in Hugh's terminology), along with the books included therein, are the Old Testament of the Christian church.[e] Far from being a Protestant novelty, this affirmation of the Hebrew canon ordering has a long history in Western Christianity with St. Jerome (early fifth century) standing near the top.

The Importance of Canon: Form and Intention

The language and concept of "canon" is at the heart of our approach to the Old Testament. References to it litter previous paragraphs: canonical lenses, canonical shape, canonical authority, and so on. What does all this canon language mean? In this section, we turn to the significance of "canon" for reading the Old Testament as Christian Scripture. A brief description of canon will help frame our approach: *An appeal to canon*

The Heidelberg Catechism, Question 27

The Heidelberg Catechism dates to the sixteenth century and became a favored catechism of Reformed churches on the European continent.

27. *What do you understand by the providence of God?*
Providence is the almighty and ever-present power of God by which God upholds, as with his hand, heaven and earth and all creatures, and so rules them that leaf and blade, rain and drought, fruitful and lean years, food and drink, health and sickness, prosperity and poverty—all things, in fact, come to us not by chance but by his fatherly hand.[f]

entails a recognition of God's providential oversight of the compositional history, shaping, and collection of ancient Israel's sacred writings for future generations of readers. Much rides on this definition, so our attention turns now to clarifying what we mean by it.

A good deal of disagreement exists over the definition of "canon." We want to be clear about our understanding, even though scholars in the field continue to disagree over the definition and how much interpretive weight the term can handle. Canon is often understood as a property of Scripture that is external to it. In this case, it refers to a list of Scriptures determined to be authoritative by the synagogue or church. We might call this the "canon as list" model.

For our approach, canon is not an external property of Scripture determined by religious groups. Rather, the texts themselves bear witness to their authority or scriptural status. Their canonical status emerges from

Figure 1.3. Scene from Nicaea preserved in the central part of St. Sophia Cathedral. The Nicene Creed dates to the fourth century AD and stands as a touchstone of Trinitarian faith. The creed is cited every Sunday in churches around the world.

within the literature itself. The external "decisions" by ecclesial or religious bodies about canonicity—what texts are deemed "in" or "out"—derive from this primary reality. Canonical texts are recognized, not determined.

The Old Testament's canonical status arises from within the text itself. In this sense, the Old Testament appears to be aware of its own authoritative status. Moreover, a privileged standing is given to the Old Testament texts in the final form of their reception because the final form marks the end and goal of a providential history. Let us clarify what we mean by the "final form." The literary achievements of the Pentateuch in its five-book structure or Isaiah as a sixty-six-chapter whole or the entire collection of 150 Psalms—all these and more are the outworking of multiple processes of writing, collecting, arranging, expanding, and clarifying in a process leading to the text's final form. These compositional matters are complicated and provide the material for ongoing scholarly work (and disagreement!). Still, the approach of this book recognizes the final product of these literary achievements as the privileged form of these biblical texts, the texts received by Jews and Christians as canonical Scripture.

The Old Testament and History

The relationship between the Old Testament and history is an interpretive and theological trip wire. Over the last 250 years, biblical scholars have wrangled over this matter perhaps more than any other. An introduction like this one can only briefly address these complex yet fascinating issues. Again, we want to make clear our particular approach to this matter in the pages to follow, aware that not all share our interpretive commitments and equally aware of the mountains of secondary literature related to each point.

The Old Testament developed in historically and culturally conditioned times and places. How much of the Bible is culturally situated? Answer: all of it. The Bible affirms its connection to human history at every turn, and interpreters must attend to the cultural and historical texture of the Old Testament. Very basic matters such as the Northwest Semitic language of the Old Testament and the **Neo-Assyrian** influence on the Iron Age are

Reformed Theologian Herman Bavinck on Scripture

"We must all at one time or another have heard that **'higher criticism'** has systematically torn page after page out of the Bible. But the abuse of a thing does not make its usage an evil. If we are to understand the Scriptures in their totality and in their parts, it is of great importance to know exactly how gradually the Bible came into being and under what circumstances each of its books arose. On the long run such knowledge can only benefit the interpretation of the Word of God. We learn from it that the inspiration of the Spirit of God entered deeply and broadly into the life and thought of holy men of God."[g]

just a few aspects among many related to the study of the Old Testament. In our reading of the Old Testament texts, we hope to make responsible use of the many advances of modern biblical scholarship. Tools of biblical backgrounds—archaeological data, comparative religions, religious history, sociological concerns, geopolitical movements—do not drive our study but serve it, aiding and illustrating but not substantiating the texts before us. 📖

This study of the Old Testament focuses on texts. While affirming that historical events affect the text, we focus on the texts themselves and their presentation—or lack thereof—of such historical events. Our approach does not see the Old Testament texts as means of determining historical events *in themselves* apart from the way the texts frame the events. The fact that Samuel and Kings are in the Prophets tells us something about how we are to read these history books and what we are to expect from them. They are prophetic history and highly selective at that.

We are not seeking to drive a wedge between text and historical event. Israel's "own explicit assertions about Jahweh," to borrow a phrase from one of the twentieth century's more renowned Old Testament theologians, Gerhard von Rad,[4] assume the mighty and redemptive acts of God in history—that is, in time and space. Our modest aim is to remain clear about our object of study: the Old Testament in its given literary form.

Revelation and history relate to each other but in a proper order. One of the twentieth century's more important theologians, Karl Barth, turns a phrase worth pondering. He claims, "Revelation is not a predicate of history, but history is a predicate of revelation."[5] This obtuse phrase makes a straightforward claim. History as history or history as event has no independent status apart from God's revelation. Theologically speaking,

"God Is a Writer!"

The eighteenth-century German philosopher Johann Georg Hamann (1730–88) was a champion of the Christian faith. He was well aware of the swelling tide of **higher critical** readings of Scripture and wrote an essay on biblical interpretation that began by exclaiming, "God is a writer!"[h] Without the authorial role of God in biblical interpretation, the Old Testament and its people are lost in the cultural and historical complex of the ancient Near Eastern world.

we do not move from and through history or historical reconstruction to our account of God and his self-unveiling. The reverse is the case. We move from God's revelation of himself in his Son and his written word to our understanding of historical events and their importance. 👥

Revelation shapes our understanding of history. The Bible can be frustrating where we expect or want more historical or psychological data from the figures and events described. Think of the sacrifice of Isaac in Genesis 22. The text projects a dramatic

Figure 1.4. Mural from an Ethiopian Orthodox monastery in Bahir Dar

event, the horror of which paralyzes any reader. Yet the account in Genesis presents little emotion. God speaks an earth-shattering word to Abraham, who responds in obedience and faith. Isaac asks haunting questions. A knife is raised. An angel appears, and a tragedy is averted. As readers, we may fill in the dramatic gaps of the text: Abraham's tear-filled eyes and choked voice, Isaac's thoughts atop the altar, and so on. The biblical text itself is not interested in these dramatic details. These kinds of "frustrating" aspects of the biblical narratives are present in many accounts: Why did King Josiah die at the hands of **Pharaoh** Necho II at Megiddo? What was going on geopolitically to lead to this great tragedy? Why was Josiah at Megiddo in the first place? These are great questions, but the Bible seems less than interested in answering them. (See 2 Kings 23; 2 Chron. 35.)

The Bible is selective history, ordering itself according to the redemptive dynamic of God's relationship with his people Israel and the world. Affirming revelation's priority in our reading of the Bible's historical narratives turns our attention to the texts themselves and the narrative, poetic, and chronological choices they make. These choices may not always adhere to a strict linear account of history, instead being shaped by content or theology. The priority of revelation and a commitment to God's providential ordering of time are critical for reading the Old Testament in its own self-presentation.

Conclusion

This chapter is a kind of white-water guide's speech before anyone gets into the raft. It is probably not wise to push off into rapids without some sense of what is in store. We want readers to know where the authors are coming from interpretively, and we want to provide rationale for why the book is ordered the way it is. Many of the preceding comments demand fuller elaboration and argumentation, but that will have to await another day. Readers can breathe a sigh of relief. The fun of a white-water trip is not the guide's speech! It's time on the river.

In Flannery O'Connor's words, "large and startling figures" await the readers of this volume and, more importantly, readers of the Old Testament. Brevard Childs, a longtime and celebrated Old Testament professor at Yale Divinity School, was asked what he thought about a new Old Testament textbook that was selling a lot of copies. His response was off the cuff but loaded: "It's better than the Bible." Childs's concern is one we take seriously. This book will be worth our effort only if it excites and spurs readers to read the Old Testament for themselves. The Exploration sections of this volume intend to turn students to Scripture itself. We can promise readers one thing. This book is not better than the Bible.

This volume includes a number of different types of sidebars interspersed throughout the chapters. These sidebars serve as points of interest. They are not intended to be exhaustive (or exhausting) but rather suggestive of the kind of fruitful avenues readers of Scripture can pursue. They are teasers for what could become long conversations on a variety of interpretive matters. The kinds of sidebars are as follows: Canonical Connections, Theological Issues, Reception History, Historical Matters, and Literary Notes.

CANONICAL CONNECTIONS

Canonical Connections link the Scriptures, Old and New Testaments, in internal conversation.

THEOLOGICAL ISSUES

Theological Issues sidebars relate the text to some facet of Christian theology and/or practice.

RECEPTION HISTORY

Reception History sidebars provide examples of how the texts have been received in the Christian tradition.

HISTORICAL MATTERS

Historical Matters engage questions of textual background.

LITERARY NOTES

Literary Notes highlight aspects of the text's literary character and quality.

Christian Reading Questions

1. Christians are people of the book. Have Christians been people of the book from the beginning, even with Jesus and the early apostles? If so, how and why is this important?
2. Luke 24's account of the encounter on the road to Emmaus ignites the imagination. What does this account tell us about Jesus and his relationship to the Old Testament?
3. The term "Old Testament" can sound dusty and aged. What are some positive ways of understanding "Old" in "Old Testament," and why is this important?
4. Is the appeal to "canon" an external textual reality or something that emerges from within the texts themselves? Why is this important for the Christian faith?

CHAPTER TWO

Introduction to the Pentateuch

The five books of Moses, or the Pentateuch, form the first section of Israel's three-part canon: the Law, Prophets, and Writings. Readers of Scripture regularly conceive of this first section, often called the Law or Torah, in overly legalistic terms, as if it exists primarily to provide ancient Israel with a list of dos and don'ts. This perspective on the first part of the Old Testament canon suffers from too narrow a view of the Torah's reach.

Translating the Hebrew word *torah* as "law" has limitations, because the Torah contains narratives as well as legal codes. For example, the creation stories and the account of the Israelites leaving Egypt are in the Torah. "Torah" might be best translated as "instruction" or "teaching" rather than the more limited "law." Nevertheless, "Law" is a part of Christian discourse and reception of the Torah, so it is important for readers to understand that Torah reaches beyond legal concerns to a host of other matters, including but not limited to the following: the identity of Israel's God as creator of the world, the calling of the patriarchs, the redemption of Israel from Egyptian tyranny, the election of Israel, the giving of the law, and instructions for worship.

📖 🏺 👥

LITERARY NOTES

Broad Pentateuch Outline

Genesis 1–11	Primeval history
Genesis 12–50	Patriarchal history
Exodus 1–15	The exodus from Egypt
Exodus 16–18	Wilderness wanderings
Exodus 19–40; Leviticus; Numbers 1:1–10:10	Sinai instructions
Numbers 10:11–36:13	Wilderness wanderings
Deuteronomy	Sinai instructions expanded

Genesis's Storied Character

An aerial view of the Pentateuch reveals a continuous story of sorts. Genesis 1:1 takes us to the very beginning of the material creation. When readers arrive at the last chapter of the Pentateuch (Deut. 34), Moses is looking over the promised land from the heights of Mount Nebo before his impending death. A sequence of forward-moving time is evident in the Pentateuch from this aerial view. When readers, however, move from this bird's-eye view to the street level of the Pentateuch, this sense of sequential time becomes more difficult to see. For example, Exodus has many chapters of priestly instruction for the construction of the tabernacle, and Leviticus is not a story as such. Forcing all of the Pentateuch's material into a "storied form" meets challenges at almost every turn.

Figure 2.1. *The Tower of Babel* by Pieter Bruegel the Elder (1563)

(Forcing the whole of the Old Testament into a "storied form" runs into similar problems.) The five books of the Pentateuch demand attention as individual books in relation to each other. Each book requires readers to attend to its own theological and literary concerns.

Genesis ends with the account of Joseph, and Exodus begins with a brief appeal to this Genesis narrative. This gives Exodus continuity with the patriarchal history while moving the book toward its own objectives. Leviticus presents itself within the Sinai setting of the book of Exodus. At Sinai, Exodus concerns itself with the construction of the tabernacle and establishment of the priestly office, while Leviticus brings readers into the living dynamic of Israel's worship life. Origen, a second-century Christian interpreter, understood Leviticus as an invitation for the faithful of all time to encounter the living God. Origen's reading fits Leviticus's intention.

If an award existed for least read book in the Pentateuch, Numbers would win, hands down. Yet Numbers has its own literary concerns within the Pentateuch. Numbers focuses on laws within the camp of the wilderness generation, a generation on the move. The themes of march and conquest appear first in Numbers, with a priestly concern for the distinction between **holy** and profane rising to prominence. Numbers also presents the new generation toward the end of Israel's wilderness wanderings as they prepare to enter the promised land. It is this new generation who in Deuteronomy is instructed in its history of grace and call to obedience: what readers will come to identify as the basic structure of Israel's **covenant**

Figure 2.2. *The Coat of Many Colours* by Ford Madox Brown (1864/1866)

relationship with the Lord. As Deuteronomy 5:3 claims, "Not with our fathers did the LORD make this covenant, but with us, who are all of us here alive today" (ESV). This verse speaks volumes about the Pentateuch's understanding of the law and also signals the important place Deuteronomy holds at the end of the five-book structure. The law's divine purpose is not fixed in the past with our forefathers. The law's true purpose is in its ability to address every generation of the faithful (cf. Deut. 6:7). Each generation is brought before God to choose the path of life or death (cf. Ezek. 18).

A Grand Narrative or the Law and Prophets?

As mentioned in the introduction, we decided to present the Old Testament material according to its tripartite structure: Law, Prophets, and Writings. Within this framework, a break appears between Deuteronomy and Joshua.

Something occurs at this moment, marking a literary distinction between what comes before and what comes after. Deuteronomy ends the Pentateuch, and Joshua begins the Prophets.

From one vantage point, the great history of Israel unfolds in the Law and the so-called Former Prophets—Genesis through Kings. This grand narrative stretches from the creation of the world to Israel's exile to **Babylon**. Various critical theories have been offered to support the "grand narrative" theory. While this history is certainly present and has its merits, its presence does not do away with the important break occurring at the end of Deuteronomy and the beginning of Joshua, or the canonical division between the Law and the Prophets. What's at stake with this division?

Moses appears as the paradigmatic prophet in Israel's history, the standard-bearer of the prophetic tradition (Deut. 18). This portrayal of Moses relates the five books of Moses and the prophetic literature that begins with Joshua. They are in conversation with each other. Joshua becomes the leader of Israel once Moses passes off the scene. Yet Joshua does not carry on the Mosaic office as a kind of revived Moses. Joshua's relation to his predecessor is as caretaker of the Mosaic law and Moses's prophetic legacy. This servant-to-master relationship is evident in the descriptions of Moses and Joshua in Joshua 1. Moses is called the "servant of the LORD" (cf. Josh. 1:1), but the narrator describes Joshua as the servant of the Mosaic law (1:7–8). Joshua's leadership is defined by his courageous commitment to Israel's Torah as given by Moses: choose you this day whom you will serve (24:15).

In Joshua, then, the law of Moses is the authority by which righteous and faithful actions will be judged. Joshua's prophetic legacy as first within a larger prophetic corpus rests with his faithful reception of and adherence to the established authority of Moses in the Pentateuch. The covenant relation narrated in the Pentateuch remains the norm by which the biblical prophets evaluate Israel's faith and actions. The prophets stand before the leaders and people of Israel to remind them of Deuteronomy's promise of life or death. Like Joshua, they too put the choice to Israel: choose you this day whom you will serve.

Relationship, Land, and Offspring

The Pentateuch covers a lot of ground, and any attempt to reduce it to central motifs or themes runs into certain dangers. Yet it is helpful to have some idea of the material's overarching concerns, and the themes

Per-Åke Persson / Nationalmuseum / public domain / Wikimedia Commons

Figure 2.3. *Noah's Thank-offering* by Ester Almqvist

relationship, *offspring*, and *land* can be helpful. These themes will be worked out more fully in the chapters to come, so here we will be brief.

God establishes a covenant relationship with Abraham and his offspring in Genesis 12. A covenant is an agreement between two unequal parties, and it sets forth and clarifies the promises made and the means for maintaining a good relationship between the parties. When God establishes a covenant with Abraham's descendants at Mount Sinai under the leadership of Moses, the terms are simple and straightforward: I will be your God, and you will be my people (Exod. 6:7; Lev. 26:12). The Lord promises the gift of his presence with his people, and the promise of this gift, the light of God's countenance shining on them, is the soil from which life and human flourishing bud and grow. The covenant relation is one in which God promises to be near, dwelling in the very midst of his people.

The covenantal relationship between the Lord and Israel is founded and maintained primarily by God's election and love of Israel. The primacy of the Lord's electing grace and redeeming love are crucial because when the relationship comes undone because of Israel's covenant infidelity, it is the Lord's quickness to forgive and readiness to show mercy that sustain the relationship. To be sure, there are covenantal or relational responsibilities placed on Israel. Such is God's gift of the Torah or Law to his people, and it is why the Sinai traditions of law and instructions for worship fall properly under the category of relationship. But as Ezekiel the prophet reminds us, sounding a great deal like the apostle Paul in Romans 7, the law never had

Introduction to the Pentateuch 21

the ability to live up to its promises of life because humanity's enslavement to sin ensured this could not be the case (Ezek. 20:25).

The law sets forth a wise path for God's people. It is a covenantal gift with God's best intentions for the flourishing of his people. Yet Israel's long history of sin and its consequences reveals that the covenantal relation is lopsided in the direction of God's self-giving. Time after time, his necessary judgment opens up to the enduring character of his mercy and grace. Israel's prophetic history, as found in the books of Joshua, Judges, Samuel, and Kings, is one of struggle under the dynamics of the covenantal formula: I will be your God, and you will be my people. For the inverse is equally true, as the prophets from Isaiah to Malachi will warn. If you will not be *my* people, then you may not be a people at all. The Lord remains jealous of his people's singular loyalty to the Lord and the Lord alone (cf. Deut. 6:4).

The motifs of offspring and land develop from the motif of relationship. The Lord promises Abraham offspring, a people who would be blessed by the Lord for the benefit of the nations (Gen. 12:1–3). Isaiah will identify Abraham's promised offspring with the offspring of Isaiah's prophesied suffering servant (Isa. 53:10–54:3). The offspring theme weaves its way through the Pentateuch and the whole of the Old Testament as evidence of God's covenantal promises to Abraham.

The promise of land also emerges from the relational commitments God pledges to his people (Exod. 3:7–8; Deut. 1:8). Abraham was called to go to a place (Gen. 12:1). Israel sojourned in the wilderness on their way to a land flowing with milk and honey. God's people are not an abstract phenomenon but an identifiable people in an identifiable place. Yet the land itself was always to be viewed as a gift and not a possession (Deut. 8:10; 9:6). Because it was wrapped up in the details of the relationship between God and Israel, the land could be lost if the people disobeyed the covenant. In time, unfortunately, this is what happened under the foreign powers of Neo-Assyria and **Neo-Babylonia**. Yet, as is God's pattern of forgiveness, Israel returns to the land when divine providence moves the **king** of Persia to encourage the reestablishment of Judah's patterns of worship and national

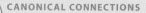

infrastructure. God's no of judgment yields to God's yes of mercy in time. But as the postexilic prophets indicate, Judah continues to struggle with covenant infidelity just as it had before the exile. The whole of the Pentateuch and the whole of the Old Testament open themselves to the future of God's severe and gracious dealings with Israel and the world.

Christian Reading Questions

1. What is the significance of thinking about "Torah" as a broader category than "law" or "legal codes"? Think about this with respect to a psalm like Psalm 1 that calls us to meditate on God's Torah day and night.

2. The Torah, or Five Books of Moses, stand in mutual relationship with the Prophets. How does this appreciation of the canonical shape of the Law and the Prophets aid reading and interpretation?

3. How do the categories of "land, relationship, and offspring" help one understand the Torah in all of its complex form?

4. Reflect on Psalm 136 regarding the religious implications of remembering God's mighty acts in history. How might this help you understand the importance of regular worship in church?

CHAPTER THREE

Genesis

Orientation

Why is there something and not nothing? Philosophers have been asking this question for a long time and answering it in various ways. While the question seems far removed from the concerns of everyday life, it lies near the center of our existence. Why *is* there something and not nothing? Why are we here and not nowhere? What holds together our physical existence in this universe?

These are life's big questions. In an age of distraction, we can inoculate ourselves against them, but even a surface reading of the Bible forces them back on us. The Bible can be like an undomesticated bull tromping through our living rooms. And when we open our Bibles to the very first page of its very first book—Genesis or "Beginnings"—these big questions are immediately addressed and answered. There is something and not nothing because God exists and because God speaks. The Bible makes a bold assertion right out of the gate: everything *is* because God *is*. *In the beginning God . . .*

Genesis is a remarkable book. It covers a vast expanse of history from the material beginning of the universe to the saving of the civilized world by one of Abraham's descendants, Joseph. In this span we encounter Adam and Eve, a cunning serpent, a murderous brother, a massive and devastating flood, giants, Babel's tower, and the profound redemptive grace God shows to the whole world in his covenant with Abraham and Abraham's offspring. Standard introductions to the book of Genesis divide it according to a natural break between Genesis 1–11 and Genesis 12–50. The first eleven chapters offer readers a **primeval history**, while the rest of the book narrows the focus to a narrative account of Israel's patriarchs. The twists and turns of Genesis are a literary thrill ride from beginning to end. For the overly familiar, a fresh pair of eyes is needed, while for those new to the scene, seat belts are a good suggestion.

The primeval history reaches back to the very beginning and provides explanations for those big questions of human existence raised at the beginning of this chapter. This first part of Genesis offers a perspective on how the world came to be. The technical term for this kind of perspective is **cosmogony**. Genesis records Israel's cosmogony, but most ancient Near Eastern cultures had their own cosmogony—their view on how the world came to be.

The Old Testament is not content merely to describe creation—for example, this is where and when the moon appears; here is why it gets cold in the winter; this is the reason the Gulf of Mexico does not swallow up Florida. The Old Testament goes beyond these kinds of descriptive explanations and provides an external and internal account for why our world is the way it is. In other words, the Old Testament provides a **cosmology**, and it does so with God or Elohim at the center of creation's cause and effect. As we follow the unfolding plot of our universe's genesis, readers find humanity as the apex of creation's reason for existence. Sadly, humanity's sin and rebellion against the Creator lead to creation's troubled and turbulent existence. There is no corner of the universe unaffected by the sin of Adam and Eve.

In the second section of Genesis, the patriarchal history, readers meet Abraham and learn of God's promises to him and his offspring for the sake of blessing the whole world (chaps. 12–50). This section begins with God's covenant with Abraham and then follows three generations of Israel's patriarchs:

The Election of Israel

The term "election" in Scripture refers to God's choice of Israel as his covenant people. His election of Israel does not stem from Israel's greatness or moral perfection but from God's self-giving love (cf. Deut. 7:7–10).

Abraham's descendants Isaac, Jacob, and Jacob's twelve sons—the twelve tribes of Israel. The patriarchs of Genesis precede the establishment of Israel as a nation-state in Exodus, where God rescues his people from slavery in Egypt and gives them the law through Moses at Mount Sinai. The patriarchs form the familial unit from which the nation will emerge, and the covenant God makes with Abraham is foundational to Israel's story.

While the Old Testament is a record of Israel's life with God, it does not begin with Abraham or God's covenant with him. Instead, it begins at the creation of the world and humanity's early struggles with sin and rebellion against the Creator. Israel's Scriptures make clear that Israel's God is no localized deity. Israel's God is at the beginning and makes the beginning possible. Israel's God is the Creator of heaven and earth. Though the Old Testament remains a witness to God's covenant relation with Israel—a covenant with irrevocable bonds (Rom. 11:29)—the first book of the Bible insists on the theological priority of creation. God's divine purposes are not limited in scope to Israel. The whole of creation is within the frame of God's creative and redemptive activities, and Israel's redemptive history is integral to the redemptive history of the whole world.

Before we turn to our exploration, we need to address one other matter about the identity of Israel's God. As mentioned in the introductory chapter, this book is an introduction to reading the Old Testament as Christian Scripture. This does not mean we will see Jesus in every verse, but it means we take into account that the Old Testament and the New Testament, though different, share in the same redemptive plan of God. Moreover, the one God whose name is Father, Son, and Holy Spirit is the same God of both Testaments.

Figure 3.1. *The Creation of the Animals* by Tintoretto (1550 or 1552)

Exploration—Reading Genesis

The Primeval History: Genesis 1–11

■ READ GENESIS 1–3 ■

T. S. Eliot concludes his oft-cited poem "The Hollow Men" with a haunting image:

> This is the way the world ends
> This is the way the world ends
> This is the way the world ends
> Not with a bang but a whimper.[1]

If Eliot is right about the end of the world, its beginning is the polar opposite. The world begins with a bang: "Let there be light!" The creation account in Genesis 1:1–2:3 is explosive.

Creation is not necessary. The triune God is sufficient within his own being, yet God creates the material world and its inhabitants as an act of kindness and grace. The world exists because God benevolently chooses to create. He does not have to.

Yet humanity is barely off the ground—literally!—before Adam and Eve rebel against their gracious Creator. In terms of literary space, the good order of creation before the entrance of sin lasts about two chapters. Genesis then spirals downward with sin's destructive force until God determines to destroy the world with the flood. The rebellion at the Tower of Babel and the dispersion of human languages conclude the primeval history, chapters that highlight humanity's sin against the Creator. They also reveal people's deep need for redeeming grace.

Two themes are central to these chapters. First, Israel's God is the creator of the whole universe. Everything in the material and spiritual universe is under God's gracious and just authority. Second, humanity's instinct is to rebel against the God who created them. The primeval history is marked by dissonance—chaos turns to cosmos when God creates, and cosmos yields to chaos when sin enters the door. The primeval history is a history of the tyranny of sin.

LET THERE BE LIGHT! GENESIS 1:1–2:3

Few chapters of the Bible generate more debate than Genesis 1. The reading here focuses where the text focuses and remains silent where the text is silent. Genesis 1 reveals a God who creates the world by the power of his Word and agency of his Spirit. Unlike gods in other ancient Near-ern creation accounts, Israel's God does not create the world by means of a

HISTORICAL MATTERS

Creation in the Ancient Near East

The Old Testament shares the conceptual world of its ancient Near Eastern setting. Observing similarities and differences between the accounts in the Old Testament and those of nearby cultures is instructive. For example, the Akkadian creation and flood myths—**Enuma Elish**, **Epic of Gilgamesh**, and the **myth of Atrahasis**—predate the Old Testament's narratives and share many of their literary features. In the Atrahasis myth, humanity is created for agricultural work in service of the gods. The gods send natural disasters, like a flood, at various times to control the population. In Enuma Elish, **Marduk**, a son of the gods and the epic's hero, wages war against **Tiamat**, the goddess of the sea (Tiamat's name is related to the Hebrew word *tehom*, or the deep, cf. Gen. 1:2). Tiamat embodies evil, and Marduk defeats her in combat. After blowing wind into her mouth and distending her body, he shoots her with an arrow. Then "he split her in two like a shellfish into two parts."[b] From these two parts of Tiamat's riven body, Marduk creates the heavens and the earth. It is easy to see significant divergences between the Old Testament's creation account and the cosmic battle of the Enuma Elish.

CANONICAL CONNECTIONS

The Cosmos as God's Temple

Verbal and thematic links between the creation account in Genesis 1 and the building of Israel's tabernacle/temple reveal the interconnectedness of creation and the sacred space/time of Israel's worship. (See Gen. 1:31; 2:1, 2, 3; and Exod. 39:32, 43; 40:33; Solomon took seven years to build the temple, cf. 1 Kings 6:38.)

These links suggest that the cosmos is God's temple and that the earthly tabernacle participates in the cosmic scope of creation's intended purpose: the worship and adoration of Israel's God and the extension of God's creative intent into the space and time of earthly existence. Moreover, the Creator's lordship over creation is not a fixture of the primeval past but is part of the earthly affairs of Israel's religious life. Temple and world complement one another, as Isaiah experienced: "Holy, holy, holy is the Lord Almighty; the whole earth is full of his glory" (Isa. 6:3).

cosmic battle among the deities. Rather, he speaks and the material world comes to be in an ordered arrangement. The "formless and void" (*tohu wabohu*; 1:2 NASB1995) primordial chaos is subdued into an ordered and meaningful cosmos. In terms of scientific mechanics, Genesis 1 does not offer much insight. Perhaps put better, Genesis 1 is uninterested in these kinds of modern discoveries. Genesis focuses on the agent of creation as Israel's God and concerns itself primarily with the *who* of creation, not the *how*.

Genesis 1 structures the first six days of creation in a clear pattern of correspondence (see table 3.1). The first three days describe the forms of the initial creation: light and dark, sky and water, fertile land and sea. The second set of three days (days four through six) orders this creation by filling each form with appropriate creaturely life—the sun, moon, and stars for day and night; fish and birds for water and sky; animals and humans for land. The literary effect on readers is one of order, intent, and meaning. No longer is chaos in charge. Creation is no longer "formless and void." The Creator speaks, and the created world does his bidding. Seven times in the first chapter of the Bible, God sees the work of his creation and calls it good. God's creation is good because it has purpose and harmony. Chaos has been subdued.

Table 3.1. The First Six Days of Creation

Day 1 (vv. 3–5)	Day 4 (vv. 14–19)
Light, separation of light from darkness	Celestial bodies: sun, moon, stars
Day 2 (vv. 6–8)	Day 5 (vv. 20–23)
Firmament (sky) separating waters above and below	Creatures of the water and creatures of the sky
Day 3 (vv. 9–13)	Day 6 (vv. 24–31)
Dry land	Land creatures and humans
Vegetation	Vegetation as food

The crowning achievement of God's creation is humanity on the sixth day. The narrative slows down on this day and intensifies its focus. The verb "create" (Hebrew *bara'*) from verses 1 and 21 appears again, testifying to the uniqueness of God's creative activity and forming a literary link back to creation's beginning. In the Old Testament only God "creates" (*bara'*), a testament to God's power to create from the sheer energy of his Word and without the aid of the material world. Human creative activity, our fashioning and forming, is on analogy to God's creative work. Still, our creative activities, especially in the visual and aural arts, depends on the creation God gave us and the wonders of the material world. In this sense, human creative activities operate at the level of "sub-creator" in the presence of God as *the* Creator.

God creates humans in his own image, indicating humanity's special position in God's creation. The exact nature of this image bearing is debated, in part because the text itself does not provide a clear explanation. Nor is image bearing a theme that weaves throughout the Old Testament, as themes of creation and chaos do (cf. Gen. 5:3). At the very least, image bearing involves two matters: humanity's oversight of God's creation as God's representatives (1:26) and humanity's relational orientation as observed in the male-female complementarity (1:27). Humans are made for relating to God and others. Human self-identity is grounded in relation to others and not in isolation: "It's not good for man to be alone" (2:18 NJPS).

At the end of the sixth day, God looks over his creation and calls it very good. Genesis 1 provides an external account, a kind of outward look in on God's creative activities and his ordering of the cosmos. Everything was ordered, good, proper, and harmonious—very much so. On the seventh day the work is finished and God rests. This is not God taking a break after a hard day's labor in the yard. Genesis 1 portrays the effortless activity of God in his creative labors; God is not tired on day seven. Rest is God's cessation from his labors. On the seventh day, God ceases his creative activity. God does not detach himself from creation but providentially oversees his finished work toward its redemptive end. 👥

CREATION AND FALL: GENESIS 2:4–3:24

Genesis 2:4 introduces a significant term within the overall structure of Genesis: *toledoth*. Occurring eleven times in the book, the formulaic word provides a handle for reading the final form of Genesis as a literary unity. Often translated "these are the generations of," the *toledoth* formula can introduce a typical genealogy: so-and-so begat so-and-so (5:1; 10:1; 11:10; 25:12; 36:1). *Toledoth* also introduces the most important narratives throughout the book: the creation of the world (2:4), the flood (6:9), Abraham (11:27), Jacob (25:19), and Joseph (37:2). In these occurrences, *toledoth* often introduces the family head (progenitor) of the people in the account that follows. For example, the Abrahamic narrative is introduced in Genesis 11:27 as follows: "These are the generations of Terah" (ESV; or "This is the account of Terah's family line," NIV). The focus of the text is on Abraham, but the ideas of kinship and genealogy are foundational to the development of Israel as a nation.

In light of these two functions—introducing genealogies or important narratives—*toledoth* may best be understood as "that which was produced by" or genealogical effects. This is the case in Genesis 2:4, which begins what is often called the second creation account: "This is the account of the heavens and the earth when they were created." The focus of the narrative that follows is not the creation of the heavens and the earth, as in Genesis 1. Instead, the Genesis 2 account turns inward and highlights what was engendered or produced by the creation of the heavens and the earth. What was produced by the creation of the heavens and the earth is humanity, revealing humanity as central to God's creative purposes.

Unlike the ancient Near Eastern myth of Atrahasis in which humanity is created for the sake of providing food for the gods, Genesis 2 reveals the enormous care and concern God has for people. God forms man from the dust of the ground and breathes life into his very being. God provides the Garden of Eden as a place for Adam's pleasure as well as profit. Adam is told to work the garden and take care of it (2:15). As surprising as it may sound, work or labor is not a product of the fall but is integral to the goodness of creation.

God also considers Adam's solitary state unhealthy and provides a suitable partner for him from his own flesh and blood. The sexual union of man and woman speaks to the sharing of flesh and the indissoluble bond of marriage. Eden was a place of beauty, pleasure, responsibility, and unfractured relations between humanity and God and between humans themselves. Adam and Eve "felt no shame" (2:25). This brief description of Adam and Eve in the Edenic state reveals something of the beauty and innocence of the prefallen world, the kind of innocence on display in C. S. Lewis's *Perelandra*, an imaginative depiction of a world unaffected by sin and rebellion. Sadly, Adam and Eve's innocence was not to last.

Genesis 3 moves the plot of the primeval history forward by introducing the cunning and crafty serpent. Distorting God's words, the serpent plants doubt in the woman's mind: "Did God really say . . . ?" (Gen. 3:1). She converses with the beast, and lured by his assurance that they would be like God, both the woman and the man eat the forbidden fruit. The beginning of the end is now upon humanity and all of the created order. Enslaved by pride, self-exaltation, and self-actualization, people have resisted hearing and following God's Word ever since. The innocent and shameless existence of Genesis 2 is lost, and sin distorts the goodness of God's creation. The rest of the primeval history gives evidence of how quickly and easily sin destroys.

Even within the tragedy of the fall, Israel's God displays his redemptive inclination. He moves toward the couple in their nakedness and shame and covers them with garments of skin. Even in judgment, the Creator preserves humanity and reveals his inclination to sustain and redeem. As readers discover throughout the Old Testament, a silver lining of redemptive hope is often found in the darkest moments of God's righteous judgments on humanity's sin.

After God pronounces the curse for sin, Adam names his wife Eve "because she would become the mother of all the living" (Gen. 3:20). In this name, he indicates his own affirmation of the mystery and profundity of life and the woman's role in perpetuating it despite the gloom of human rebellion. God promises that the offspring of the woman will in time bruise the serpent's head;

Mary, the New Eve

It was common in the early church to identify Mary, the mother of Jesus, as the new Eve. The apostle Paul refers to Christ as the second or last Adam (cf. 1 Cor. 15:22, 45), the one through whom all will be made alive. From Mary's womb comes humanity's ultimate hope and experience of life, resurrected life. In sharp contrast to Eve, this makes Mary "the mother of all the living" (cf. Gen. 3:20).

this human failure and rebellion will not determine humanity's destiny (3:15). There is hope for future redemption, even in Genesis 3's troubling realities of death. 🗒

SIN IS CROUCHING AT YOUR DOOR: GENESIS 4–11

The rest of the primeval history traces sin's devastating effects on humanity and the created order. It begins with the story of Cain and Abel, brothers who bring sacrifices to God. Cain brings an offering from his crops, and Abel brings a gift from his flocks. Without explanation in the text, God looks with favor on Abel's offering and rejects Cain's, but not Cain himself. Cain is angry, and God responds, "Why are you angry . . . ? If you do what is right, will you not be accepted?" (Gen. 4:6–7). Do what is right. This charge reminds readers of God's instructions to the man in Genesis 2 that he could eat from any tree in the garden but one (2:17).

God leaves Cain with a haunting warning: "Sin is crouching at your door; it desires to have you, but you must rule over it" (4:7). Sin lurks, awaiting opportunity, and in Genesis 4, it has its way with Cain. He is mastered by it and kills his brother. Confronted with his actions, Cain defends himself: "Am I my brother's keeper?" (4:9 NRSV). Cain's sin multiplies through subsequent generations, and by the end of Genesis 4, Cain's descendant Lamech boasts openly about his own acts of murder (4:17–24). 🗒

This sad story of Cain is not without God's gracious provision. Cain must live with the effects of his sin—being driven away from God's presence and where he had been living—but God protects and provides for him. Despite humanity's continued rebellion, the Creator continues to care for what he has made.

Public domain / Wikimedia Commons

Figure 3.2. *The Immaculate Conception and the Tree of the Science of Good and Evil* by Ercole Ramazzani (1573)

Genesis 6 introduces the time of the Nephilim, heroes of ancient folklore. The text reports that "the sons of God saw that the daughters of mankind were beautiful" and so "took" them for themselves (Gen. 6:2 NASB; cf. Gen. 3:6). This language echoes the description of Adam and Eve's sin in chapter 3, and this action of the sons of God mirrors the rebellious activity of Adam and Eve in chapter 3. They "saw" and "took." These mysterious figures, mostly likely semidivine figures we might associate with angels and demons, take up with the daughters of humanity in what appears to be a brazen effort to "make themselves like God." Adam and Eve grabbed after a similar promise. The spirit world and the human world share in their rebellion against the Creator. Creation's proper order has completely come undone, and God has had enough. "The LORD saw that the wickedness of humankind was great in the earth, and that every inclination of the thoughts of their hearts was only evil continually" (6:5–6 NRSV).

God's response to the world's rebellion is heartbreaking and tender. He is grieved. His heart is filled with pain. His decision to judge the world with the flood is not described in terms of fitful rage but brokenhearted sorrow. In Genesis 1, God saw his creation, and it was good (1:31). Now God sees his creation, and it is corrupt (6:12).

While the Nephilim of Genesis 6 may have been ancient heroes, Genesis 6 introduces a different kind of hero, a savior figure and righteous man named Noah (Gen. 6:9). From the midst of creation's rebellion there emerges a solitary figure, a new Adam, with whom God can hit the restart button.

God releases the waters of chaos, the primordial deep, the *tohu wabohu* of Genesis 1:2 ("all the springs of the great deep," Gen. 7:11, or the *tehom*). The scene is horrific and intended to strike terror in the hearts of readers. While modern people might enjoy the idea of a cruise on the open sea, ancient readers considered the waters or the deep pernicious and primordial. Monsters roam the deep. In the great flood of Genesis the waters of chaos are the waters of judgment unleashed; they are the undoing of creation.

When God tells Noah that the flood is coming "seven days from now" (7:4), the number is no accident. The seven days of creation are reversed. In

Figure 3.3. *Noah's Ark on Mount Ararat* by Simon de Myle (1570)

terms of literary space, the creation narratives take three chapters of Genesis, as does the flood narrative. This symmetry says something about the importance of the flood narrative to the overall telling of the primeval history and its relation to creation's undoing and new beginning.

God's redemption is evident in his saving of Noah and his family. It is important to see the redemptive motifs of this scene (cf. Isa. 54:9–10). The ark is salvation from the Lord's judgment, and God first makes a covenant with humanity in the flood narrative. God "remembers" Noah (Gen. 8:1);

CANONICAL CONNECTIONS

Old Testament Covenants

Readers encounter the term and concept of covenant throughout the Old Testament because it is foundational to YHWH's relationship with his people. A covenant (*berith*) is typically between two parties that are not equal partners, and it brings clarity to the nature of their relationship. Covenants are often accompanied by a sign: God's covenant with Noah came with a rainbow (or "bow of war," reminding humanity that God has put down his destructive bow); the covenant with Abraham comes with the practice of circumcision; and the Sinai covenant comes with the Sabbath as its sign.

The Old Testament summarizes the covenant between YHWH and Israel with the statement "I will be your God and you will be my people." Known as the covenant formula, this statement is beautiful in its simplicity.

Covenants usually included stipulations, the expectations that each party had of the other. The stipulations of God's covenant with Israel are detailed in the books of Exodus and Deuteronomy. The people were to obey his laws, and he would bless them. If they violated the terms of the covenant, they would be punished. As Israel's history reveals, God's people did violate the covenant, and the covenant relation came undone. Through the prophet Hosea, God told his people, "You are not my people and I am not your God" (Hosea 1:9 NRSV). Nevertheless, YHWH's commitment to his covenant with his people transcends all covenantal fissures.

The covenant with Noah after the flood has no stipulations. It is a purely unilateral covenant made by God with all humanity. His solemn commitment is no more total destruction from his hand (Gen. 8:21–22).

"remembering" is a term loaded with covenantal significance and appears again in Genesis and then throughout the Old Testament. God's remembering signals God's movement toward redemptive action. When the Lord remembers, his commitment to save is unstoppable. ⌇

In Genesis 8, the flood waters recede in an act of new creation. God sends his Spirit/wind (*ruach*) as he did in the creation account of Genesis 1 to push the waters back into place, removing chaos and restoring order (8:1; cf. 1:2). At the end of the chapter, God extends unprompted grace to all humanity. He promises to never again destroy the earth and all living creatures. But God makes this promise with full knowledge and understanding of the continued fallen nature of humanity; he promises even though "every inclination of the human heart is evil from childhood" (8:21). The compassionate and forbearing character of Israel's God is clear, and these attributes will be seen repeatedly throughout Israel's Scriptures.

As if on cue, the second Adam, Noah, and the beauty of the new creation come undone because of the continued presence of sin and human rebellion. These perpetual problems were not eradicated in the flood's waters. If anything, the flood serves to reinforce God's providential and redemptive commitment to humanity. In a scene that evokes shame, readers find Noah naked and drunk in his tent. Ham fails to cover his father and instead draws attention to it by informing his brother. The outcome of this scene is that Ham's offspring, the **Canaanites**, are cursed. Readers will meet the Canaanites again as Israel's story unfolds.

Genesis 10 maps world history by tracing the descendants of Noah through his sons, Shem, Ham, and Japheth. This record, the Table of Nations, identifies seventy nations or people groups and their territories. Of greatest interest in the narrative of Genesis, Shem's family line extends to Abraham and his offspring of promise, the people of Israel. The shape and course of civilization as we know it has been plotted with Noah's sons and their offspring.

The Table of Nations reveals God's intent to mark out national boundaries and identities. There is no mythological language in the table. It follows closely how early civilizations developed in time and place. In Genesis 11, however, one group in the region of Babylonia resists this divine order so that they would not "be scattered over the face of the whole earth" (11:4). As with the fall in chapter 3, the Tower of Babel story narrates humanity's pride and rebellion against its Creator. They organized their political and industrial efforts to build a tower so they "could make a name" for themselves (11:4). While they attempt to build something "up," God has to come "down" to see what the humans are doing, suggesting his immense power in the face of human limitations. In time, God will

The Tower of Babel and Pentecost

Many people draw a connection between the Tower of Babel narrative (Gen. 11) and the New Testament account of Pentecost (Acts 2). In Genesis 11, God comes down to have a look at what humanity is up to. The result of that "coming down" was the chaos of judgment. At Pentecost God comes down again by his Holy Spirit on those gathered in Jerusalem from around the world. Despite everyone's different languages, they are able to understand each other. The Spirit overcomes the confusion of languages, and in that unique redemptive moment, Babel's confusing effects are undone.

neutralize the pride of humanity by the remarkable humility of the incarnation. Here, however, readers see humanity's attempt to grab, self-exalt, and establish themselves in the face of the Creator's intent.

The Tower of Babel scene concludes the primeval history and leads into the patriarchal narrative and the Abrahamic covenant. With Abraham, readers will encounter God's redemptive means for drawing the whole of creation back to himself on the Lord's terms.

The Patriarchal History: Genesis 12–50

■ READ GENESIS 12; 15; 22; 32; 50 ■

The primeval history covers an enormous amount of time: from the creation of the world to the Tower of Babel. All of this history is compacted into twelve chapters of our Bibles. The story of the patriarchs—four generations of a single family line—fills thirty-eight chapters of Genesis. The proportions appear all off, and for good reason. The narrator of Genesis focuses on a distant descendant of Shem whom God calls to be the father of a great nation: Abraham. The story of Israel's beginning is set within the larger frame of God's creation and world history. From the macroview of the primeval history, the narrator turns to the microview of God's redemptive plan to restore creation to its original purposes.

The first subject of Genesis 12 is YHWH, the personal and revealed name of Israel's God. *Y-H-W-H* are the four Hebrew letters of the divine name and are often pronounced together as "Yahweh," though the exact pronunciation of the name remains a mystery. The name YHWH relates in particular to God's saving action in the exodus, an event the patriarchs experience in terms of promise but not fulfillment. More attention will be given to the divine name in the next chapter. The term "Elohim" or "God" appears most frequently in the Pentateuch when Israel's God, YHWH, is identified in contexts that range beyond the particularities of his established and revealed relationship with Israel. "In the beginning God [Elohim] created the heavens and the earth" (Gen. 1:1). Here in Genesis 12, YHWH, "the Lord" in most English translations, makes the initial move toward Abraham and is *the* defining subject of the patriarchal history.

The promises made to Abraham in Genesis 12:1–3 are worked out in detail later in Genesis 15 and 17. These later chapters express the call of Abraham and the promises delivered to him in terms of a covenant. God commits himself irrevocably to Abraham and his offspring. The terms of the promise are unilateral: I will make you a great nation, and I will bless you. I will bless those who bless you and curse those who curse you. The whole earth will experience divine favor, or blessing, because of you, Abraham (12:2–3).

Figure 3.4. *Hagar and Ishmael* by George Hitchcock

Go, the Lord tells Abraham. This remarkably brief command leads to the complete upheaval of Abraham's existence. Equally remarkable is the narrator's report of Abraham's response: "So Abraham went, as the Lord had told him" (12:4). That's it. God commands. Abraham believes and obeys. It is little wonder Abraham stands as the paragon of faith in Christianity and in Judaism and Islam as well. Abraham hears the command and promise of God and responds in belief and obedience. 📜

Within this opening story of the patriarchal narrative, three significant themes appear: offspring ("seed"), land, and covenantal relations. These themes weave through the Pentateuch and, more broadly, through much of Israel's Scriptures. First, the Lord promises Abraham offspring, a promise that has immediate and apparent challenges given Abraham's and Sarah's advanced age. Second, Abraham's offspring will be the beneficiaries of a promised land, even though the Canaanites were in the land at the time (Gen. 12:6). Finally, the covenant relation is initiated and maintained by God's promise and faithfulness, as will be evident throughout the Abrahamic narratives. The Abrahamic narratives conclude in chapters 22 and 23, coming full circle to these central themes. Genesis 22 renews the promise to Abraham's offspring after the offering of Isaac of **Mount Moriah**, while in Genesis 23 Abraham buys a burial plot for Sarah in the land of Canaan, the land of promise. Abraham does not yet possess all the land God promised, but Sarah rests in a small portion owned by Israel's patriarch.

The narrative clarifies and sharpens God's covenant with Abraham in chapters 15 and 17. God promises him offspring from "his own body," even though Abraham remains childless in his old age. In Genesis 15 Abraham believes, placing his confidence and hope in God's word. God credits as righteousness Abraham's faith or belief

CANONICAL CONNECTIONS

Abraham and the Sixth-Century-BC Exile

Exilic readers or hearers of the Abrahamic traditions—those who experienced the **Babylonian** captivity of the sixth century BC—must have understood their own story in relation to Abraham's. Abraham was called out by faith to leave Babylon (Ur of the Chaldeans) to go to the land of promise. Abraham's own story was one of wandering from exile toward the promised land.

in his promises (Gen. 15:6; cf. Rom. 4:18–24). In chapter 16, Abraham attempts to help God fulfill his promise, having a son with Sarah's servant Hagar. The birth of Hagar's son Ishmael creates great conflict, but God extends his protective grace over Hagar and Ishmael as well. When the promised son by Sarah finally arrives, they name him Isaac (Hebrew for "laughter"). The cosmic comedy of God's faithfulness to his promises plays loud and clear. From every natural vantage point, Isaac should not be. But he is, only because of the promises of God.

In chapter 17, Abraham responds to the covenant promises by obeying God's call to walk before him and be blameless (Gen. 17:1). God establishes a sign for his covenant with Abraham and his descendants, instructing that

LITERARY NOTES

Repeated Stories

Readers of Genesis may notice repetition of certain types of stories. For example, three times Genesis recounts the story of a patriarch moving south because of famine, then pretending his wife is his sister and narrowly escaping some murky moral waters when the local ruler wants the patriarch's wife (Gen. 12:10–20; 20; 26:1–12). At the end of each story, the patriarch leaves town unscathed and, strangely, better off than when he came.

Various explanations are offered for this literary phenomenon. Some critical scholars understand these stories as stemming from different literary sources that all borrowed from a common oral tradition. Literary approaches call these "type scenes" and consider them part of the Bible's literary artistry or poetry. Biblical authors can play with various features of the type scene for interpretive reasons. The recurrence of the basic elements of the theme witnesses to God's providence and the rhythmic ordering of Israel's history toward its redemptive end.

RECEPTION HISTORY

Abraham's Three Visitors and the Trinity

In Genesis 18 Abraham entertains three visitors, one of whom is said to be the Lord. This chapter provokes a wide range of interpretations in the Christian tradition. The fourth- and fifth-century theologian Augustine sees a Trinitarian dynamic in verses 1 and 2: "The LORD [YHWH]" appears to Abraham (v. 1), and he lifts his eyes and sees "three men" (v. 2). The singular divine being (v. 1) is juxtaposed to the three persons (v. 2), all within a single frame (see fig. 3.5). The **Reformer** Martin Luther offers a nuanced account of the three figures and affirms Augustine's "allegorical" reading. One cannot "prove" the Trinity by the Genesis 18 narrative, nor should one identify the three angels as the members of the Trinity in a simplistic way: "This is that." At the same time, Christian readers need not dismiss a Trinitarian reading in allegorical or figural terms, recognizing the doctrine rests on surer textual foundations than this one and is in accord with the mind of Scripture. John Calvin was slower to focus on this Trinitarian reading.[f] He focuses instead on Abraham's hospitality in this text (cf. Heb. 13:2). Two of the visitors do go into Sodom in chapter 19, creating some hurdles for a consistent Trinitarian reading.

THEOLOGICAL ISSUES

Manifestations of God in the Old Testament

Theologians may debate the "threeness" of Abraham's visitors in Genesis 18, but readers should not simply dismiss Trinitarian dynamics. Calvin, for example, resists the Trinitarian reading but insists on what we might call a christological reading. YHWH manifests himself in "angelic" or "human" form in the Old Testament, as in Genesis 18. In other words, it is not an offense to God's singular and undivided being to take on a material form. These manifestations in the Old Testament witness to the time when God takes on human flesh permanently in becoming a man, the man Jesus Christ (cf. John 1:1, 14). These Old Testament manifestations, therefore, are like lightning flashes on the hillside, revealing for a brief moment what will in time become a permanent and visible feature of God's identity.

they be circumcised. This sign is a symbol and reminder of the permanence of God's eternal covenant with Abraham and his son Isaac—"my covenant in your flesh" (17:13). Genesis 15 and 17 place faith and obedience in proper relation and order to one another. Theologically speaking, it is proper to speak of faith first. An assurance in the saving and redemptive promises of God is the soil from which genuine obedience can grow. When the ordering is reversed, obedience can become its own kind of Tower of Babel, seeking as it does to build one's way to God. 📖 👥 📑

The climax of the Abrahamic narratives is one of the most famous stories in Genesis—the offering of Isaac on Mount Moriah (Gen. 22). The focus of this dramatic and disturbing

Figure 3.5. *Icon of the Holy Trinity* by Andrei Rublev (1425)

scene fixes on Abraham's unquestioning obedience. In many ways, Lot is Abraham's foil, his narrative opposite. When Sodom and Gomorrah fall under the firestorm of divine judgment, God rescues Lot because of his familial connection to Abraham—"God remembered Abraham" (19:29). Yet when the cities are coming undone and Lot is rescued by angelic visitors, the narrative says, "And he lingered" (19:16). Not so with Abraham here in

Figure 3.6. *Sodom and Gomorrah* by John Martin (1852)

Faith, the Highest Passion

Søren Kierkegaard was a nineteenth-century Danish philosopher and theologian. *Fear and Trembling* is his reflection on Genesis 22. For Kierkegaard, Abraham's trust in God and his commands beyond what appears reasonable makes him a high-water mark of faith. Kierkegaard concludes this classic work reflecting on the statement "Faith is the highest passion in a human being."[9] Each generation must attend to their faith because each generation bears the responsibility for it. Faith is deeply personal and cannot passively rest on familial or societal dynamics.

Genesis 22 nor at his call in Genesis 12:1. Arise and go, and Abraham went as the Lord commanded. The Lord tells Abraham to sacrifice his son, and the next verse depicts Abraham saddling his donkey for the sacrificial journey. Abraham does not linger.

God's command that Abraham offer his son Isaac is difficult. Genesis 22 offers readers special insight into the unfolding events with the narrator's statement that God is "testing" Abraham (22:1)—a fact Abraham does not have. Adding to the difficulty for readers is the text's silence on Abraham's thoughts or his emotional state. Readers are left to fill in such gaps, none more poignant than the one that falls between Isaac's haunting question to his father, "Where is the lamb?" (22:7), and Abraham's response, "God himself will provide" (22:9). The simplicity of the narrative attests to two central features of God's test: (1) Will Abraham continue as a man of faith who places his confidence in God's promises despite the circumstances? (2) Will Abraham's faith lead to obedience?

Abraham raises the knife, but God stops it, providing a ram in Isaac's place and affirming Abraham in these two crucial facets of the test. 👥

This grueling narrative also symbolizes the faith and worship of Israel. Firstly, Abraham is offering Isaac up on Mount Moriah, the eventual location of the temple mount itself (cf. 2 Chron. 3:1). The sight remains a holy (and contested!) sight in Jerusalem to this day. Secondly, Abraham's offering of the ram God provides prefigures the ritual and moral purification rites of the future temple. Abraham is a paradigmatic Israelite even though he predates the founding of the nation. 👥

The Abraham narratives give way to the *toledoth* of Isaac in Genesis 25:19–35:29, which tells the story of Isaac's son Jacob. Isaac himself is underdeveloped as a patriarchal figure. In some sense, he is a literary prop providing the genetic link between Abraham and Jacob, the patriarch whose

Figure 3.7. *Sacrifice of Isaac* by Rembrandt (1635)

The Bound Isaac and the Crucified Christ

Christian interpreters have always seen a link between the bound Isaac (often called the "Akedah," or "Binding") and the crucified Christ. Melito of Sardis (second century AD) links Christ's crucifixion and Isaac's offering in several sermons. These kinds of readings are warranted and are not merely "sermonic." For example, both Isaac and Jesus move to their deaths as voluntary victims. And just as a ram took the place of Isaac, so Christ takes our place on the cross. In this imagery of substitution, the Akedah also links to the **Passover** (Exod. 12:1–28), where the lamb's blood stands in for the firstborn.

The New Testament use of the Akedah focuses on Abraham's faithfulness and God's faithfulness to "hand over" the son for the sake of our salvation (cf. Rom. 8:32). It also highlights Abraham's faith as an exemplar of Christian faith and obedience (Heb. 11:17–19; James 2:18–24). Abraham's statement "YHWH will see to it" (YHWH-Yireh) attests to his faith and faithfulness.

name will be changed to Israel. The story of Jacob is the largest section of the patriarchal history, and it is a story of conflict. Jacob first struggles with his twin brother, Esau. This struggle returns to the theme of sibling conflict in Genesis—a theme that begins with the story of Cain and Abel (Gen. 4) and culminates in the saga between Joseph and his brothers (Gen. 37–50). For his part, Jacob also comes into conflict with his trickster uncle Laban and even with God himself in a midnight wrestling match. Jacob's encounter with God forever changes him, his name, and the whole history of Israel. From Jacob, the twelve tribes of Israel are born.

The sibling rivalry between Jacob and Esau began in the womb, where their intense struggle prompted their mother, Rebekah, to ask God about them (Gen. 25:22). At birth Jacob came into the world holding on to Esau's heel and earning his name Jacob or "heel grabber" honestly (25:26). Jacob lived into his name; his devious ways characterize the Bible's recounting of his life. The second-born son, he convinces Esau to give him the firstborn's birthright, and he deceives his blind father, Isaac, into giving him Esau's firstborn blessing. Understandably, Esau hates Jacob (27:41), and Jacob flees for his life.

On his way to stay with family in Haran, Jacob has a life-changing dream. The portals of heaven open before him, and he sees a kind of heavenly ladder or ramp linking heaven and earth. Angels, heavenly messengers, descend and ascend as they carry out the Lord's tasks. At the head of the ladder is YHWH himself. The dream is glorious, terrible, and reassuring. YHWH speaks from atop the ladder and reaffirms the covenant he made with Jacob's father, Isaac (Gen. 26:24) and grandfather Abraham (12:1–3): a promise of offspring, land, and a privileged relationship with YHWH—"I am with you and will watch over you wherever you

CANONICAL CONNECTIONS

Barren Women in the Old Testament

The barren or childless woman plays an important role in the patriarchal history. Sarah, Rebekah, and Rachel all struggle with barrenness and look to the saving help of Israel's Creator God to open their wombs and give them children. Later, Samuel's mother, Hannah, pleads with God because of her barrenness. Births deemed impossible or improbable become the canvas for God's redemptive painting, taking that which seemed dead and giving new life to it. Isaiah 54:1 speaks of Jerusalem as a barren mother who in time has so many children her tent is about to burst. In the book of Isaiah, these children are the gift given by God to Jerusalem because of the Servant's suffering and death (Isa. 53:10, 54:1–3). Jerusalem did not produce these offspring. God provided them through his Servant. Barrenness as a theme attests to God's creative and saving power.

go" (28:15). The narratives that follow reveal continued conflict for Jacob, including his difficult and long ordeal with his uncle Laban. Laban promised his daughter Rachel to Jacob after seven years of labor, only to give him an unwelcome surprise on his wedding day: a different daughter than the one he loved (Gen. 29). After the marriage to Leah, Jacob eventually marries Rachel, but all told, Jacob works fourteen long years for two wives. Yet God's providence and grace are present through it all. The promises of God for Jacob and his offspring are sure and steadfast: "I am the LORD, the God of Abraham your father and the God of Isaac" (28:13 NRSV).

God is known to hurt his friends. The Lord wounds Jacob as well, yet in the wounding comes the transformation. The defining moment of the Jacob narratives is not the one Jacob assumed would be his *defining* moment: when he faces his brother after years of estrangement. That meeting goes well, in fact (Gen. 33). Esau and Jacob embrace in what appears to be a tender moment. Amicable as the encounter is, the brothers part ways. And that's that.

It is the night before this dreaded encounter that transforms Jacob, and Israel is born. Jacob sends his family across the Jabbok River and remains by himself. He encounters "a man," and they wrestle until daybreak.

Martin Luther describes this narrative as one of the strangest in the Bible (32:22–32). He is right. Who is the "man," and why do he and Jacob wrestle? How does a mere touch dislocate Jacob's hip? Why does Jacob demand a blessing? Enigmatic features pepper the scene from beginning to end, but one feature of the text is clear. This event has to do with Jacob's name. Observe the play on Hebrew words: Jacob (*Ya'aqob*) wrestles (*ye'abeq*) by the river Jabbok (*Yabboq*).

The heel grabber is at it again in this scene: "I will not let you go unless you bless me" (32:26). The disorienting aspect of the story is Jacob's prevailing over the "man," a "man" whom readers will discover is God in human or angelic form. Some Jewish interpretive traditions refuse to identify the "man" as God, but the "man" is God, and the encounter is a set-up. All the "man" has to do is touch Jacob's thigh, and his gait is permanently changed. This is no mere "man."

Scottish National Gallery / Wikimedia Commons

Figure 3.8. *The Vision after the Sermon* by Paul Gauguin (1888)

The conflict between Jacob and God allows for the dialogue of blessing between the two combatants. God asks Jacob a penetrating question: "What is your name?" (32:27).

"Jacob," comes the answer—the heel-grabber, the devious one.

"No longer," says the divine man. "You are now Israel because you strove with God and prevailed" (see 32:28). Jacob is now the one whose name reveals his true character as Israel's namesake. Israelites strive with God and refuse to let go of God and his promises.

Interestingly, Jacob returns the favor and asks God for his name (32:29). The Lord brushes off the question and does not answer. It is not that Jacob did not know the name YHWH. Rather, the author of the Pentateuch is creating a sense of anticipation about the divine name and its attachment to the redemptive event of the exodus. The next person in the Pentateuch to ask the Lord for his name is Moses before the burning bush (Exod. 3). The Lord's rebuff of Jacob's question offers a narrative insight: Jacob, that question is not for you yet in this redemptive moment; that question awaits a future time with Moses, my enslaved people, and a stubborn pharaoh. 🗞 👥

From the story of Jacob, Genesis turns to one of the Old Testament's most beloved stories: Joseph and his coat of many colors (Gen. 37–50). The Joseph narrative takes up significant space in Genesis, but it is not just about Joseph. Joseph's older brother Judah is also integral to the unfolding redemptive plot. Judah's tribe is the messianic tribe of promise—"The scepter shall not depart from Judah" (49:10 NRSV). Joseph does not play a role in the redemptive history to come, aside from his critical role in the survival of Abraham's descendants. Joseph himself is not included in the land allotments of the twelve tribes. Rather, his sons, Ephraim and Manasseh, share their father's allotment in the land (48:8–22). 🗞

CANONICAL CONNECTIONS

Hosea and Jacob's Wrestling with God

Hosea the prophet understands the Jabbok narrative of Genesis 32 as symbolic (Hosea 12:2–6). It reveals something about the character not just of Jacob but of Jacob's namesake, Israel, the covenant people of God. Hosea identifies the "man" as an angel and God at the same time. Moreover, for Hosea Jacob's wrestling match is a symbolic or figural presentation of Israel the nation at their best: weeping, repenting, and refusing to relinquish the promised blessings of God.

RECEPTION HISTORY

Luther and Calvin on Jacob's Wrestling with God

Martin Luther and John Calvin, in line with Hosea the prophet, understand Jacob's wrestling match as a symbolic account of the Christian life. When asked "What makes a theologian?" Luther's oft-repeated answer is "Anfechtungen," meaning "struggle, trial, conflict." Both Luther and Calvin see in the Jacob narrative a pattern of faithful struggle in the Christian's pilgrimage. Christians are not promised storm-free seas, but they are given gospel promises. In Jacob's story, Christians find their own: a dogged refusal to let go of God and his promises despite the current circumstances of life. The painting by Gauguin (see fig. 3.8) provides an evocative portrayal of the kind of participation in a biblical text Luther and Calvin suggest. These faithful women participate in the story by hearing God's word preached and prayerfully meditating on it. Calvin writes,

> Moreover, this passage teaches us always to expect the blessing of God, although we may have experienced his presence to be harsh and grievous, even to the disjointing of our members. For it is far better for the sons of God to be blessed, though mutilated and half destroyed, than to desire that peace in which they shall fall asleep, or than they should withdraw themselves from the presence of God, so as to turn away from his command, that they may riot with the wicked.[h]

Tamar in Messianic History

The story of Tamar and Judah in Genesis 38 does not make for easy reading. The subject matter startles and offends. Childless and vulnerable Tamar plays the prostitute to trick her father-in-law, Judah, into marital relations. The result is a child and Judah's praise of Tamar as "more righteous than I" (Gen. 38:26 NASB). The theme in Genesis 38 is the importance of offspring and Tamar's pivotal role in protecting the messianic line of Judah. Tamar is a Canaanite, one of those who must be driven out. Yet this Canaanite woman preserves Judah's royal line.

Later in biblical history another foreign woman will do the same: Ruth, the Moabitess. The genealogy at the end of Ruth makes clear the connection between Genesis 38 and Ruth. Tamar's son Perez fathered Hezron; Hezron produced Ram, and so on down to Ruth's son Obed, then Jesse and finally King David (Ruth 4:18–22). New Testament genealogy takes Tamar's action to its redemptive end with Jesus the **Messiah**, David's heir and offspring (Matt. 1:1–17).

The story of Joseph follows this favored son of Jacob as he's sold into Egyptian slavery and eventually, through a long and complex process, becomes vice-regent over the great and mighty Egypt. Joseph's narrative is open to a plethora of interpretations, including some discomfort in the Jewish interpretive tradition as it struggles to come to terms with this son of Jacob who has fully embraced Egyptian culture, including an Egyptian wife. One promising entry point into these narratives is to read them in conjunction with the Abrahamic promise in Genesis 12:1–3. God promises Abraham offspring who would be an instrument of blessing to all the nations; Joseph, a great-grandson of Abraham who rises to power in Egypt, is the means of saving many nations from famine. Joseph is a down payment, a making good on the covenant promises made to Abraham and reiterated to Isaac and Jacob: through Abraham's offspring the nations of the earth will be blessed. Moreover, Joseph's story witnesses to God's providence and the power of reconciliation. Few scenes in Scripture are as moving as the reconciliation scenes between Joseph and his brothers: "You intended to harm me, but God intended it for good to accomplish what is now being done, the saving of many lives" (50:20).

Genesis leaves us with the sons of Jacob in the land of Egypt and the covenant promises of God to Abraham regarding his offspring and the land open to future fulfillment. How will they enter the land God promised to Abraham? The book of Exodus links itself to these narrative and covenantal dynamics as it moves the plot forward.

Implementation—Reading Genesis as Christian Scripture Today

Reading Genesis is like running a marathon. By the time Joseph passes off the scene in chapter 50 and the twelve tribes of Israel have moved to center stage, readers need a moment to catch their breath. An enormous amount of ground has been covered. It is worth looking back to see the vistas and horizons of Genesis's literary scope. As Christian readers, we confess the Old Testament's continuing role in shaping our understanding of the one God we confess as Father, Son, and Holy Spirit. Genesis plays a signal role in the Old Testament's privileged place and continued influence on Christian theology.

The God of the Bible is Creator and Redeemer. In the primeval and patriarchal histories, Genesis emphasizes these facets of God's identity. God is Creator and Redeemer because of God's own singular will and desire to create the world and redeem it from the tyranny of sin. Nothing external to God's being demands or necessitates these creative and redemptive events. They are acts of self-giving, grace, and love. The creation of the world comes first in the Genesis account, and rightly so. The created world is not merely a vehicle or instrument for God's salvation of humanity. Creation has its own integrity, and its primary place in Genesis suggests redemption renews the whole disordered creation.

While creation cannot be reduced to this redemptive instrumentality, it stands that God's created world is the platform on which God will redeem humanity and the whole cosmos. God gives himself to space and time in order to be worshiped, known, and loved. All of these activities take place in the nitty-gritty details of the material world and human history. The promises made to Abraham and his offspring open up to the future as David's Son, who is God's Son, will enter the material world to redeem those who are captive to sin in order to make everything new.

KEY VERSES IN GENESIS

- In the beginning God created the heavens and the earth. 1:1
- Sin is crouching at your door; it desires to have you, but you must rule over it. 4:7b
- I will make you into a great nation, and I will bless you; I will make your name great, and you will be a blessing. 12:2

Christian Reading Questions

1. Read Genesis 1:1–2:4 and Psalms 8 and 19. How do these psalms engage the creation tradition?
2. What is the significance of the Bible beginning with the story of creation? How does this shape the way we think about God and the rest of what follows in the Bible?
3. How does sin act as an agent of chaos in Genesis 1–11?
4. How does the patriarchal history beginning at Genesis 12 address the problem of humanity's sin and rebellion?

CHAPTER FOUR

Exodus

Orientation

Exodus begins where Genesis leaves off. Jacob's twelves sons are now in
the land of Egypt. The first eight verses of Exodus link the patriarchal history of Genesis and the desperate events about to unfold for Abraham's
offspring (cf. Gen. 15:13). Even the book's first words resemble the *toledoth*
("these are the generations of") structure of Genesis: "these are the names
of" (Exod. 1:1). The sons of Jacob were "fruitful and . . . multiplied" (1:7
NASB), a phrase that echoes God's initial creative command to Adam and
Eve (Gen. 1:28). Jacob's offspring were growing strong and numerous, filling the land of Egypt. What appears in Exodus 1:7 as good news—God's
promise to Abraham that he would have numerous offspring is being
fulfilled—turns sour in the next verse: "A new king arose over Egypt who
did not know Joseph" (1:8 NJPS). *In Exodus, readers find Israel suffering
and no longer enjoying the benefits of Joseph's protection.*

Few books of the Bible excite the imagination like Exodus. Its stories of
enslavement and murder, political intrigue, a burning bush and a sea split-
ting wide open provide the foundation for Israel's existence as the people
of God. In Exodus, YHWH redeems his people from slavery, delivers them
from the aggressive hand of their enemies, and enters into a binding relationship with them through the giving of torah. At the same time, Exodus
problematizes this newly established relationship between the Lord and
Israel. The people worship a golden calf immediately after vowing allegiance to YHWH (Exod. 32–34), and their unfaithfulness to the covenant
creates uncertainty about their relationship with God. Can they continue as
the people of God? Is restoration possible and, if so, on what grounds? All

these dynamics and narrative tensions shape Exodus. Central to the book's redemptive and covenantal hope is God's revelation of his name, YHWH. *In Exodus, Israel encounters their living, redeeming, and sustaining God in the giving of his name.*

Many of the stories in Exodus are familiar, with the giving of the Ten Commandments (Exod. 20) near the top of the list. But the recipe for anointing oil may not be as familiar (30:22–24). There is also that scene where YHWH tries to kill Moses: a real bump on the narrative plane ride if ever there was one. An overview of Exodus may look as follows:

> Exodus 1:1–15:21—The exodus from Egypt
>
> Exodus 15:22–18:27—The journey to Mount Sinai
>
> Exodus 19–40—The Sinai instructions and conflict 🕮

Exploration—Reading Exodus

The Exodus from Egypt: Exodus 1:1–15:21

▨ READ EXODUS 1–15 ▨

In the first chapter of Exodus, "a new king arose over Egypt who did not know Joseph" (Exod. 1:8 NJPS). Whether this new king had never heard of Joseph or whether he dismissed Joseph and the importance of his role in Egypt's past are open to question. Whatever the circumstances of the king's lack of knowledge—willed or forgotten—Abraham's offspring are now a problem. The Israelites are too numerous, and the king considers them a potential threat. What do despots do with threats? They subjugate and control them by brute power. The new Egyptian king's actions are predictable but brutal nonetheless. He enslaves and oppresses them with increasingly hard labor. He "made their lives bitter" and "worked them ruthlessly" (1:13–14).

CANONICAL CONNECTIONS

Hosea and Israel's Relationship with God

The book of Hosea uses two dominant metaphors for God's relationship with Israel: marriage and sonship. Hosea 11:1 employs the exodus traditions this way: "When Israel was a child, I loved him, and out of Egypt I called my son." The paternal relationship YHWH has with Israel is a gift characterized by love. "I led them with chords of human kindness, with ties of love" (11:4). Yet, as Hosea heralds, Israel's whole history participates in the patterns established by the wilderness generation: the more I called, the more they went away (11:2).

Figure 4.1. *The Mother of Moses* by Simeon Solomon (1860)

Public domain / from Art in the Christian Tradition, a project of the Vanderbilt Divinity Library

The narrator does not name this new king. For the rest of Exodus 1–15, he is simply "Pharaoh." Given the place names and projects at Pithom and Rameses (1:11), an educated guess is that Pharaoh is either Seti I (1308–1290 BC) or Ramesses II (1290–1224 BC). The latter is the more likely candidate when Moses returns to Egypt and has his showdown with Pharaoh. Nevertheless, the narrative leaves Pharaoh nameless. Pharaoh holds a place; he's a figural representative of what might be called the anti-YHWH or the enemies-of-Israel party. In time, the **Assyrians** and Babylonians, the Greeks and Romans will all have their pharaohs too. The nameless one here becomes a type. Moreover, the fact that Pharaoh remains nameless while Israel's God makes his name known is a notable counterpoint.

Pharaoh's oppression of Israel turns murderous. When brutal servitude does not reduce Israel's growing population, he commissions the Hebrew midwives to do the unthinkable: murder all newborn sons in an effort to control the population. "But the midwives feared God" (Exod. 1:17 ESV). They defy Pharaoh's order and concoct a remarkable defense when questioned about their "failure." They say the Hebrew women are not like the Egyptian women. They are strong and have babies before the midwives can get to them. God blesses these midwives for their faithfulness, but Pharaoh's hostilities only increase. He orders the whole of Egypt to toss any newborn Hebrew son into the Nile.

Moses is born in the midst of this brutality. His parents have a problem on their hands when their "fine" baby boy appears (Exod. 2:2). The actual phrase is "And [his mother] saw him that he was good" (AT), in resonance with the goodness of God's creation in Genesis 1—"And God saw that it was good"

(Gen. 1:9, 12, 18, 21, 25; cf. 1:31). Exodus's story of redemption links to Genesis's story of creation. The two are fitted to each other.

Moses's parents place him in a basket, literally an "ark" (Exod. 2:3; cf. Gen. 6:14), to float down the Nile. Like Noah's ark was for Noah's family, Moses's little ark is the vessel of his salvation. In the midst of suffering and devastation, the hero of the story is rescued from the Nile and Pharaoh by none other than Pharaoh's own daughter. Moses's sister watches from afar and offers the baby's own mother as a nurse; in an act of kind and ironic providence, baby Moses is back in the arms of his Hebrew mother for a time.

Once grown, Moses kills an Egyptian who was "beating a Hebrew, one of his own people" (Exod. 2:11). The story moves quickly and leaves out a good deal of information. We do not know Moses's role in Pharaoh's house. We know nothing of potential tensions between him and Pharaoh's other sons (as in the famed dramatic plot of Cecil B. DeMille's *The Ten Commandments*). We also do not know how Moses came to understand his familial heritage: How does he know the Hebrews are "his own people"? Rather than answering these questions, the narrative moves us to the section's central episode, the moment when Moses meets God at the burning bush in Exodus 3.

A fugitive for murder, Moses flees to the desert of **Midian**, where he marries a woman named Zipporah. Moses meets Zipporah and her sisters, daughters of a **priest** named Reuel, at a well. This encounter is a type scene, like those of Jacob meeting Rachel (Gen. 29) and Abraham's servant meeting Rebekah, the wife of Isaac (Gen. 24). Moses's scene at the well links the narratives of Moses with the patriarchal narratives.

Between these events in chapter 2 and the burning bush in chapter 3 are three important verses: "Now it came about in the course of those many days that the king of Egypt died. And the sons of Israel groaned because of the bondage, and they cried out; and their cry for help because of their bondage ascended to God. So God heard their groaning; and God remembered His covenant with Abraham, Isaac, and Jacob. And God saw the sons of Israel, and God took notice of them" (Exod. 2:23–25 NASB). These verses describe a top-down view of the events from the perspective of Israel's God. The people groaned under the burden of their slavery. God heard these groans as prayers of despair, and God responds. Four verbs in this section mark God's actions and redemptive impulse to save. God heard. God remembered. God saw. God took notice. 📜

CANONICAL CONNECTIONS

Righteous Suffering

When Israel groans and cries out to God in its suffering, it does so as a type of the righteous sufferer. In Exodus 1–3, Israel suffers for no other reason than being Israel. The book of Psalms is replete with instances of Israelites' "crying out" (e.g., Pss. 22:2; 34:17; 88:1). Yet the exodus event itself—an event the Israelites of Exodus 1–3 have yet to experience—becomes the focal point of Israel's redemptive memory and future hope (cf. Pss. 77 and 78). God's mighty acts redeemed them in the past and will do so in the future, despite their current circumstances.

Readers of the Pentateuch have been waiting for Exodus 3, whether they realize it or not. Chapter 3 is a high-water mark in the unfolding narrative. More than this, it is a high-water mark in the Old Testament's abiding witness in the Christian canon. Any account of God's identity demands a close reading of Exodus 3. Jacob wrestled with God by the Jabbok River, forever altering his and Israel's identity. Yet even Jacob, the namesake of Israel, is rebuffed when he asks God for his name: "Why do you ask my name?" God replies without answering Jacob's question (Gen. 32:29). The answer awaits another moment in time, Moses's time. Now, with Moses, God is about to reveal the character of his name.

Exodus 3 has a mysterious quality. Moses enters into a sort of no-man's-land and comes to "the mountain of God" (3:1). The mountain of God is outside the range of Egypt and beyond the land of Midian. Israel's God is free and unfettered by any locality. Then Moses sees the striking sight of a bush in flames but not consumed by them. This flaming bush is the manifest presence of God on the divine mountain, Horeb. "Horeb" and "Sinai" are used interchangeably throughout the Pentateuch. Scholars offer varying accounts for why this is the case, but in Exodus 3 there is a linguistic link between the names. The Hebrew words for bush (*seneh*) and Sinai (*sinay*) sound similar, and it appears the narrative is aware of the connection. The **theophany**—appearance of God—that Moses experiences follows a pattern in the Bible as God reveals himself on a mountain, accompanied by physical wonders.

Exodus 3 contains a commissioning scene. Moses is called by the Lord for a particular task—leading the Israelites out of Egypt (3:9–12). The burning bush is itself a sign for Moses, marking the promise of God to do what he said and, in time, to bring Israel to this mountain in order to worship him. "I will be with you" is the divine promise and reinforces the relationship between the Lord as sending agent and Moses as the one sent (3:12). The prophetic book of Jeremiah uses similar language in the call of Jeremiah, suggesting the commissioning of Moses here puts him in close proximity with the prophetic office (cf. Deut. 18:18).

This commissioning scene is important, but what surrounds it is even more so—the unveiling of YHWH's identity. Who are you, Lord? What is your name? The angel of the Lord responds from the bush to Moses's questions because the bush itself is the physical manifestation of YHWH's presence: the eternal flame. The scene is holy and terrible and beautiful and inviting, all at the same time. The Lord identifies himself with the patriarchs of Israel's history, providing the covenantal and relational continuity of Israel in their current distress with the patriarchs who preceded them: Abraham, Isaac, and Jacob. Moses responds really the only way anyone could in the unmediated presence of the Lord: with fear. Yet the fear of the Holy One is a fear that both repels and fascinates, equally and simultaneously. Moses is afraid to look *and* he wishes to know more. What is your name? Who are you, Lord?

The revelation of the divine name in Exodus 3 needs to be read in concert with Exodus 6:2–9, where God reminds Moses of who he is, what he has promised, and what he will do for his people. Again, various literary and critical readings of these two texts offer explanations for the challenges presented. For example, God claims in Exodus 6:3 that the patriarchs did not know the name YHWH; they only knew God as El Shaddai (the mighty God). Reading Genesis shows this is not the case, where the name YHWH occurs in patriarchal stories (cf. Gen. 18). How do readers sort through this problem? One satisfying answer has to do with the oft-repeated phrase from Exodus 3:14, "I AM WHO I AM." This phrase is the answer God gives to Moses when he asks for God's name: "I AM WHO I AM. This is what you are to say to the Israelites: 'I AM has sent me to you.'" The very next verse says that "God also said to Moses, 'Say to the Israelites, "The LORD [YHWH], the God of your fathers—the God of Abraham, the God of Isaac and the God of Jacob—has sent me to you"'" (3:15). The narrator here blends the "I AM WHO I AM" of 3:14 with "YHWH" in 3:15 in such a way that the former helps us to understand the significance of the latter. Exodus 6:2–9 follows a similar pattern where the revelation of the name YHWH in verse 2 is followed by a covenantal history and the promise of redemption in the exodus. In these redemptive actions, God's name will be known in its full significance and character.

"I AM WHO I AM" reveals; it is not intended to conceal. God is not playing a linguistic cat and mouse game with Moses: "Who are you, Lord?" "I am who I am," God responds in a kind of no-answer or reticence to commit or come clean. "No, who are you really?" might be the proper response to such a reading. Rather, we might read "I AM WHO I AM" as "I WILL BE WHO I WILL BE." This reading recalls God's promise to Moses, "I will be with you" (Exod. 3:12). "I will be who I will be" speaks to the current redemptive moment and reveals the character of the divine name YHWH as specifically and uniquely related to this redemptive event. Who am I? What is my name? I am the God who will be your redeemer (3:16–18). I am the God whose name is revealed when I rush upon Pharaoh, the great enemy

Figure 4.2. *Landscape with Moses and the Burning Bush* by Domenichino (1610–16)

of YHWH and his people, and fight for my firstborn son, Israel. When the river Nile blushes red and the frogs croak in your ears. When the night hushes before the terror of my death angel while your firstborn sons rest securely in your arms. When you come to the sea and are trapped until you feel the wind split open a path before you. When all these mighty acts happen for you, then you will know who I really am. My name is forever linked to this redemptive moment: the exodus. It is not that the patriarchs did not know the divine name YHWH. But they did not know it in the character of this unique and redemptive moment. 📜

In many ways, the conflict between Pharaoh and YHWH is captured in the question, Whose firstborn son is going to live? It is a question with an edge to it, for in the battle between God and Pharaoh, someone's firstborn son is going to die. God instructs Moses to tell Pharaoh, "Thus says the Lord: Israel is my firstborn son, and I say to you, 'Let my son go that he may serve me.' If you refuse to let him go, behold, I will kill your firstborn son" (4:22–23 ESV). The relationship between YHWH and Israel is one of father to son. Israel is the object of YHWH's paternal love, and as the narrative continues, it will be the object of YHWH's fierce and protecting love: "Let my son go." 📖 👥

Pharaoh does not take well to this directive. He doubles down on his efforts to oppress God's people, and now they have to make bricks without straw. Moses views the whole thing as a disaster. He complains to God that he speaks in God's name, and Pharaoh's evil acts increase (5:22–23). The plan appeared straightforward, but as is often the case in God's redemptive plans, only God really knows the plan. In response, the Lord reinforces his initial commissioning of Moses (6:1–13), drawing Moses into a posture of faith and confidence in the promises of God.

Soon the Nile River turns a shade of color never seen before and dead fish appear on its surface. The plagues begin, and they have a stated goal—for the Egyptians and for the Israelites. Before Moses strikes the Nile, he is to tell Pharaoh, "By this you will know that I am the Lord" (7:17). With the arrival of the locusts, the Lord tells Moses that he is performing these signs so that the Israelites could tell their children and grandchildren about them, "that you may know that I am the Lord" (10:2). There is an intergenerational outlook attached to these signs and wonders in Israel's early history. The stories extend far beyond the moment itself. Tell these stories, the Lord says, to your children and your children's children. Let these foundational stories of my redemptive commitments to you, Israel, be part of your collective memory.

The plagues climax with the threat against the firstborn males and the first Passover for God's people. Passover (*pesach*) as a religious festival in Israel's history began as a matter of life and death. The people were to slaughter lambs and brush the blood over their doors so that the judgment would *pass over* their houses. Families were to eat the lamb for their Passover meal, but they

"A Bridegroom of Blood"

Strange scenes exist in the Bible, and they can confuse us. One of the more befuddling episodes is in Exodus 4 when YHWH tries to kill Moses. After the Lord calls Moses to bring the people out of Egypt and promises to be with him, Moses and his family are en route to Egypt when YHWH tries to kill Moses. Moses's wife, Zipporah, acts to save Moses, quickly circumcising their son. She calls Moses "a bridegroom of blood" (4:24–26). Elements of the text remain obscure. Why is the Lord angry with Moses? Why had Moses not circumcised his son? Is this why the Lord is angry? Does it have to do with Moses having a **Midianite** wife? The questions this text elicits are much longer than the text itself. However, one matter appears clear: the connection between the application of blood and the assuaging of the Lord's wrath. The terms used for blood and its application relate to the terms used for the application of blood at the Passover in Exodus 12.

RECEPTION HISTORY

"A Bridegroom of Blood" and Allegory

The hard parts of Scripture often provided the church fathers with a green light for allegorical interpretation, a way of finding deeper meaning in the words and imagery of the Bible. For example, the fourth-century bishop Gregory of Nyssa in his *The Life of Moses* reads Exodus 4:24–26 as an account of stripping pagan philosophy of its paganism in service of Christian thought. Two hundred years later, Maximus the Confessor reads the narrative as a symbolic account of the hard journey a Christian takes from vice toward virtue. The angel of death who attacks Moses seeks to rid him of his immobility in the pursuit of virtue. Immobility, for Maximus, is not neutral but necessarily moving away from virtue to vice.[c]

THEOLOGICAL ISSUES

The Exodus and Baptism

A symbolic relationship exists between Israel's redemption by water at the exodus and Christian baptism (1 Cor. 10:2). Israel's salvation at the Red Sea is the climax of the whole exodus event, including the plagues and Passover. The book of Psalms remembers God's covenant salvation at the exodus as central to Israel's religious life (cf. Pss. 77–78). Similarly, **Reformation** thought focuses on the importance of baptism in Christian formation and assurance. Baptism brings Christians into the very life, death, and resurrection of Jesus Christ. Baptism is God's move toward humanity, his saving activity.

Israel returned to the exodus again and again in their life before God. So too should Christians take heart and remember their baptism, remembering that God took the first move toward them in his saving actions in the person and work of Jesus Christ.

Table 4.1. The Plagues

1	Nile River to blood (7:14–24)
2	Frogs (7:25–8:15)
3	Gnats (8:16–19)
4	Flies (8:20–32)
5	Death of livestock (9:1–7)
6	Boils (9:8–12)
7	Hail (9:13–35)
8	Locusts (10:1–20)
9	Darkness (10:21–29)
10	Death of the firstborn (11:1–12:32)

were to eat with shoes on and staff in hand, ready to travel because the Lord would deliver them from slavery that very night. The blood over the doorposts, the consumption of the sacrificial offering, and the details of the table meal become part of the bodily ritual of Israel as it participates in its redemptive memories—a statute and memorial forever.

At midnight, the Lord struck Egypt, and the firstborn males of animals and people died. Only God's people with blood over their doors were spared. Pharaoh ordered the Israelites out of Egypt immediately.

God instructed his people to celebrate Passover every year, remembering his deliverance from slavery. The Passover itself is a blood ritual. We learn in Leviticus that life is in the blood (Lev. 17:11), and the application of the blood to the doorposts appears to represent the life that stands in the place of the firstborn. Where no blood is found, a life is taken. In this deadly encounter, YHWH's firstborn son lives. Pharaoh's does not. Another feast takes place with Passover, the Feast of Unleavened Bread. Beginning on Passover and then continuing for seven days, the people eat only bread without yeast and then

Figure 4.3. Inspired by the Passover, this plaque depicts a Christian marking the door with the Hebrew letter *tav* to signify God's protection.

culminate the week with a feast before the Lord.

Pharaoh suffers a tragic defeat at the hand of Israel's God. The children of Israel are liberated, but the battle is far from over. In a moment of rage, Pharaoh and his army chase after the Israelites and trap them at the Red Sea. With the sea in front and Pharaoh's army behind the people, the very presence of God in the form of a cloud descends between the two groups. God is in the midst of his people, despite their complaints: "Is it because there were no graves in Egypt that you have taken us away to die in the wilderness?" (Exod. 14:11 NASB). God had promised to be with them, and at the Red Sea the promise is tangible and visible. The Lord appears as the divine warrior that he is. God will fight for you, says Moses (14:14).

Figure 4.4. *Crossing of the Red Sea* by Cosimo Rosselli (1482)

And fight he does. God sends a wind to blow back the sea and dry the seabed; Israel coughs on the dust as they make their way through the judgment of the deep to the safety of the other side. When Pharaoh pursues, the judgment of the deep swallows him and his hordes alive. The narrative describes the scene in gruesome terms: "So the Lord saved Israel that day from the hand of the Egyptians, and Israel saw the Egyptians dead on the seashore" (14:30 NASB). What did Israel do in the face of God's redemptive power and grace? They believed (14:31). Then they sang (15:1–18).

The exodus from Egypt remains the defining event of Israel's relational and religious life before YHWH. Everything that follows in the narrative—the giving of torah, the failure with the golden calf, the grumbling and complaining in the wilderness, the tabernacle, the land—rests on the priority of this saving event. The exodus defines Israel as the object of divine grace and redemption. As the Song of Moses (15:1–18) rehearses, God and God alone is the saving figure of the exodus: "He has triumphed gloriously" (15:1 NRSV). What appeared as a hopeless defeat—Pharaoh behind the people and the sea

HISTORICAL MATTERS

The Sea in Exodus and the Ancient Near East

In the ancient world, the sea (Hebrew *yam*) often represents disorder. The mythological character of the sea appears throughout ancient Near Eastern religious texts and is often associated with a divine figure. The Canaanite god Baal wages war against Yam-Nahar (*yam* = sea, *nahar* = river) in an effort to bring about order and fertility. As we read in the previous chapter, the Babylonian god Marduk defeats Tiamat, the sea monster, and creates the world from her riven corpse.

While Exodus shows awareness of these religious traditions from the surrounding cultures, it goes its own way in terms of a more realistic or historical portrayal. YHWH is not fighting the sea monster in Exodus 14. YHWH stands before the waters and reveals his power as Creator and Redeemer in one fell swoop. Waters are often presented as judgment throughout the Old Testament—remember the chaotic waters of judgment in the flood. God protects his people from their enemies and the waters of judgment. The book of Psalms and the Prophets borrow mythological images of the sea for various rhetorical reasons, even in their description of the exodus (cf. Isa. 27:1; 51:9–11; Jer. 51:34). Nevertheless, in the exodus narrative, the enemy of God remains clear: Pharaoh. As miraculous as the exodus is, the literature is a realistic portrayal of God's historical activity in space and time.

CANONICAL CONNECTIONS

Warnings from Israel's History

As 1 Corinthians 10:1–13 makes clear, the believing and rejoicing community would not remain in this state:

> I do not want you to be unaware, brothers and sisters, that our ancestors were all under the cloud, and all passed through the sea, and all were baptized into Moses in the cloud and in the sea, and all ate the same spiritual food, and all drank the same spiritual drink. For they drank from the spiritual rock that followed them, and the rock was Christ. Nevertheless, God was not pleased with most of them, and they were struck down in the wilderness. (1 Cor. 10:1–4 NRSV)

Rejoicing turns to grumbling, and in time, grumbling turns to idolatry. The relation between grumbling and idolatry is inextricable. Thus, within the Scriptures, thanksgiving is idolatry's chief antidote.

THEOLOGICAL ISSUES

A Pattern of Grace

The exodus reveals humanity's need for greater redemption than the miraculous one at the Red Sea. Humanity needs redeeming grace from the oppressive power of sin. From its earliest pages, Scripture reveals a pattern of such grace: God judges the world because of sin in the chaos of the flood, sparing righteous Noah and his family. Yet sin continues to reign in the unfortunate scene with Ham and drunken Noah. The people of Israel in Egypt are spared by an unprecedented miracle of God. Yet the covenant relation will break down because of sin. The rejoicing in God's salvation at the Red Sea will not last but rather witnesses to the kind of rejoicing that will mark all God's people at the final exodus, the great day of the resurrection of the dead. Eternity will be flooded with songs rejoicing in the triumph of the Lion of Judah (Rev. 4–5).

in front of them—becomes the stage for God's stunning act of redemption. YHWH is the hero of the story.

The Journey to Mount Sinai: Exodus 15:22–18:27

From the Red Sea, the Israelites travel to Mount Sinai. The journey is a period of transition. Israel had seen the mighty power of God to save. Who could ever forget what happened to the sea, to Pharaoh's army? "When the waters saw you, O God, when the waters saw you, they were afraid" (Ps. 77:16 NRSV). For that generation of Israelites, the exodus was part of their collective religious memory. They saw it with their own eyes. They saw the waters cower before YHWH and gather themselves at attention. Unfortunately, human beings are funny creatures, with short-lived memories. We tend to live in the crisis of the moment, unable or unwilling to see it within a larger frame.

The exodus was yesterday. But today, we have no good water to drink (Exod. 15:22–26). Tomorrow, we will have no food to eat. The people were to be marked by faith and thanksgiving. They had seen God act. Instead, they struggle to believe in God's faithfulness, and they grumble. Nevertheless, God provides sweet water at Marah (Hebrew for "bitterness"). One night God provided quail, and every morning the heavenly mystery food appears—manna. God even brings water out of a rock for them to drink. Yet the people grumble, and Moses grows weary. He names one of their watering holes Massah and Meribah, meaning testing and strife in Hebrew. Instead of having faith, the Israelites test and prod and complain: "Is the LORD among us or not?" (17:7). The character of Israel's life before God becomes almost fixed at this point. The people are faithless, fickle, and incredulous. YHWH's character is also revealed; he shows remarkable patience and faithfulness as he provides for his people whatever they need.

Israel and the Amalekites

Israel's first holy war is waged against the Amalekites, a perpetual enemy of God's people in the Old Testament (Exod. 17:8–16). As with Pharaoh, God fights for his people by means of Moses's outstretched hands and staff. Unlike at the Red Sea, God makes use of human agents in this battle. The Amalekites are juxtaposed to the Midianites in Exodus 18, where Jethro, Moses's father-in-law, provides helpful advice for the political structuring of the Israelite community. Despite Jethro's hospitality and confession—"Now I know that YHWH is greater than all the gods" (18:11 AT)—the Midianites were in time an enemy of God's people as well (cf. Num. 22–24; Judg. 6–8).

Human Wisdom and Divine Revelation

The church fathers and Reformers focus on a particular challenge associated with Exodus 18. Why would Moses rely on the council of his father-in-law—the **wisdom** of human experience—when as a prophet he had access to divine revelation? The tension felt by interpreters is not a tension the Old Testament expresses. The division between sacred and secular was not a feature of Israel's existence, and wisdom from human experience could be received in concert with divine revelation. The book of Proverbs insists that the fear of the Lord is the beginning of wisdom, which provides the believing community the proper foundation for engaging and receiving human wisdom. Human wisdom cannot contradict the claims of revealed religion, but when wisdom is in concert with the fear of the Lord, it is a good gift of God's providential oversight of creaturely affairs and thought.

Manna and Jesus

The manna tradition appears in the Gospels—Matthew, Mark, Luke, and John. John identifies Jesus as the "living bread that came down from heaven" and understands Jesus as the bread of eternal life (John 6:51 NRSV). All four Gospels recount the story of Jesus feeding the five thousand with bread, presenting Jesus as the new Moses, feeding his people with God's word and physical bread (Matt. 14:13–21; Mark 6:30–44; Luke 9:10–17; John 6:1–15). Jesus as the new Moses signals the coming of the messianic age.

The Danger of Meribah and Massah

Psalm 95 presents Meribah and Massah as perpetual threats for the worshiping community. The psalmist calls on the people of God to worship and "kneel before the LORD our Maker; for he is our God and we are the people of his pasture, the sheep of his hand" (vv. 6–7 NRSV). The opposite of worship, the great impediment to life lived before God in joy and faithfulness, is the perpetual temptation of Meribah and Massah—testing God and complaining rather than trusting and remembering his saving grace.

Sinai Instructions and Conflict: Exodus 19–40

■ READ EXODUS 19–20; 32–34 ■

The brief journey to Mount Sinai functions like a prologue to the Sinai revelation. The people reach the mountain of God—Sinai or Horeb—where they will encounter God's holiness and gracious commitment to Israel as *his* people. In these chapters, the Lord sets out the shape and scope of his relation to Israel, a relationship marked by God's initiating and sustaining grace and Israel's commitment to worship YHWH and YHWH alone.

THE TEN COMMANDMENTS AND COVENANT CODE: EXODUS 19–24

The giving of the law with its moral and religious stipulations follows a rehearsal of God's redemptive activity: "You yourselves have seen what I did to the Egyptians" (19:4 ESV; cf. 20:1–2). The relation between the Lord and Israel is certainly one of grace and grace alone. At the same time, Israel's covenant obligations are essential to her existence and mission in the world. Put in other terms, Israel's actions have consequences.

Israel's election and redemption by the Lord come with responsibilities. Election has purpose—namely, for Israel to be a kingdom of priests (19:4–6). Israel's unique relation to the Lord as his "treasured possession" (19:5) displays to the world the ministry of YHWH. Therefore, Israel functions as a priest to the world (cf. Ps. 98:3). In this priestly identity, Israel mediates YHWH's presence to the nations by being and remaining in covenant fidelity with the Lord. This is what it means for Israel to be holy or set apart. Israel is called to be an example of how the Lord's relation with humanity was intended. The nation's separateness is for the sake of blessing the world (cf. Gen. 12:1–3).

The establishment of this covenant, the Mosaic covenant, has images associated with Old Testament theophanies: a thick cloud, thunder and lightning, fire and earthquake. Even more so, this theophany, this appearance of God at Sinai, becomes the symbolic standard for Israel's theophany traditions. God reveals his presence on the mountain, accompanied by physical signs and wonders. Moses, as Israel's prophet, intercessor, and representative of the people, makes his way up the mountain toward the very presence of YHWH. The giving of the law and making of the covenant happen with sensory overload. Little wonder the people "trembled" (Exod. 19:16).

After God's brief rehearsal of Israel's redemptive history in Exodus 20:1–2 (again, grace precedes the giving of the law), the Ten Commandments make their first appearance in the Pentateuch. These commandments have a privileged status within the Torah, appearing in their totality twice (Exod. 20:1–21; Deut. 5:1–21). Other texts refer to them (e.g., Exod. 31:18; Deut. 4:13; 10:4). Readers do well to remember the nature and occasion of these commands. They are not given in terms of eternal stipulations or laws but within the covenant community, in a specific relation between the Lord and his people. These divine imperatives form the

Table 4.2. Tables of the Ten Commandments in Exodus 20

First Table	Second Table
1. No other gods (v. 3)	5. Honor father and mother (v. 12)
2. No divine images (vv. 4–6)	6. No murder (value life) (v. 13)
3. No taking the Lord's name in vain (safeguard the honor of God's name) (v. 7)	7. No adultery (v. 14)
4. Keep the Sabbath (vv. 8–11)	8. No stealing (v. 15)
	9. No bearing false witness (v. 16)
	10. No coveting of neighbor's wife or possessions (v. 17)

foundation of God's initiating grace and redemptive actions. To modern ears, "law" comes with a certain amount of conceptual baggage, understood primarily as the establishment of boundaries by negative means. And while Old Testament law takes the negative form at times—"Thou shalt not . . ."—it should also be viewed positively as the means by which human relations with God are maintained and human beings can flourish.

Martin Luther on the First Commandment

Martin Luther's explanation of the first commandment in his Large Catechism is a classic and well-articulated account of what is at stake with the first commandment. Notice that for Luther the definitions for God and an idol are the same.

That is: Thou shalt have [and worship] Me alone as thy God. What is the force of this, and how is it to be understood? What does it mean to have a god? or, what is God? Answer: A god means that from which we are to expect all good and to which

we are to take refuge in all distress, so that to have a God is nothing else than to trust and believe Him from the [whole] heart; as I have often said that the confidence and faith of the heart alone make both God and an idol. If your faith and trust be right, then is your god also true; and, on the other hand, if your trust be false and wrong, then you have not the true God; for these two belong together faith and God. That now, I say, upon which you set your heart and put your trust is properly your god.[d]

Jesus's Summary of the Law

When the Pharisees ask Jesus about the greatest commandment, he answers as any good Jew would—with the Shema: "You shall love the Lord your God with all your heart, and with all your soul, and with all your mind." But Jesus adds the following, "And a second is like it: 'You shall love your neighbor as yourself'" (Matt. 22:37, 39 NRSV). The Pharisees did not ask Jesus about the second greatest commandment, but Jesus appears compelled to provide a fuller picture of the law. The love of God and the love of neighbor are properly

ordered one to the other. Love of God precedes love of neighbor and is the foundation for a proper ethic of neighbor relations. Jesus makes clear a central Old Testament concern: there is no love of God without love of neighbor. The two are necessarily conjoined and resist any disassembly. The Old Testament prophets especially reveal this to be the case, as they repeatedly indict God's people for claiming to love God but failing to love others (e.g., Isa. 58).

Apodictic and Casuistic Law

Scholars make a distinction between the two kinds of law given in Exodus 20–23. **Apodictic law** is a direct prohibition—"Thou shalt not . . ."—as found in the Ten Commandments. **Casuistic law**, or case law, follows an "if this . . . then that" pattern. In the Old Testa-

ment law, casuistic laws often begin "When you . . ." The so-called Covenant Code (Exod. 20:22–23:33) follows this pattern and details requirements necessary for daily life before God and neighbor. Casuistic law is the application of Torah to these kinds of concerns.

Numbering the Ten Commandments

Jews and most Protestants number the Ten Commandments differently than Roman Catholics and Lutherans. The difficulty of numbering comes in the command to have no other gods and the command against making divine images. Roman Catholics and Lutherans understand these as a single command. Thus, the prohibition of making images is not against images per se but against making images with the intent to worship them. Roman Catholics and Lu-

therans then distinguish two commands in the final instructions not to covet a neighbor's house, wife, and possessions: coveting another person's wife is lust (or adultery), and coveting another person's possessions is avarice. Jews and most Protestants read one command against coveting and understand the first two commands as separate commands. This separation explains in part why some in the Reformed tradition avoid icons and images in worship.

Broadly speaking, the Ten Commandments run along a vertical and a horizontal axis: the love of God (first table of the law) and the love of neighbor (second table of the law). The first command is foundational to the whole. On this command to "have no other gods before [or besides] me" the whole relationship between God and his people rests (Exod. 20:3). The Shema of Israel is at the very center of Israel's life lived before the Lord: "Hear, O Israel: The LORD our God, the LORD is one. Love the LORD your God with all your heart and with all your soul and with all your strength" (Deut. 6:4–5). The Shema also reinforces the foundational character of the first commandment—YHWH and YHWH alone. Without fidelity to the Lord *alone* as Israel's God, the whole of the covenantal relation vertically and horizontally falls apart. 👥 📜 📖 👥

THE GOLDEN CALF AND THE REVELATION OF THE DIVINE NAME: EXODUS 32–34

The book of Exodus relates a series of crises. Whether in Egyptian bondage or penned between Pharaoh's army and the Red Sea, Israel often appears in a hard place. Even after being miraculously freed from the threat of Egypt, Israel grumbles and finds ways to complicate their situation,

Public domain / Wikimedia Commons

understandable as the concern for food and water is. However, matters reach a boiling point when Moses ascends Mount Sinai and stays away a bit too long. While Moses is out of sight, the people break the first and second commandments. They construct a calf of gold and worship it as "your gods . . . who brought you up out of Egypt" (32:4). Moses's brother Aaron reveals the syncretistic (or blending of exclusive YHWH worship with idolatrous elements) nature of the event when he describes the feast day around the calf as "a feast unto YHWH" (32:5 AT). The future of the covenant relationship between the Lord and his people is at stake. Will the Lord continue to be their God and will Israel remain YHWH's people?

The covenant formula of the Pentateuch is a basic formula: I will be your God, and you will be my people (cf. 6:7). The positive construal of divine self-giving in this formula

Figure 4.5. *Moses Breaking the Tablets of the Law* by Rembrandt (1659)

has an unstated negative claim. It might go as follows: *If you will not be my people, then you may not be a people at all*. As readers will discover later in the Prophets, Hosea names his second child with Gomer, his adulterous wife, Lo-Ammi or "Not my people" (Hosea 1:9). The symbolism does not require explanation.

When God interrupts his fellowship with Moses on Mount Sinai because of the raucous cries of the people in their idolatry, he says, "Go down, for *your* people, whom you brought up out of the land of Egypt, have corrupted themselves. . . . I have seen this people, and behold, it is a stiff-necked people" (Exod. 32:7, 9 ESV, emphasis added). God's use of the distancing pronoun "your" instead of "my" as in the covenant formula is significant. The covenant relationship is on the line. The situation is so serious that God suggests that he wipe out the people and start over with Moses. Moses intercedes on their behalf, and God does not destroy the people (32:10–14). But the threat was real because the Ten Commandments come in either-or terms: either you obey or you aren't my people. Israel chose "or." So, when Israel surrounds the golden calf and worships it, they show themselves to be "not God's people." How can the covenant relation continue in the face of Israel's unfaithfulness?

It is in this story—the golden calf debacle and the Lord's description of the people as stiff-necked—where the revelation of the divine name appears again. Moses asks to know God's ways (33:13), and the Lord obliges with the self-giving of his presence and an explanation of his own name, YHWH. How is the covenant relationship maintained in light of Israel's stiff-necked and hell-bent propensity to sin? Because of the character of Israel's God as revealed in his name.

YHWH descends to Moses and gives Moses an exposition of his name: "The Lord, the Lord, the compassionate and gracious God, slow to anger, abounding in love and faithfulness, maintaining love to thousands, and forgiving wickedness, rebellion and sin. Yet he does not leave the guilty unpunished; he punishes the children and their children for the sin of the parents to the third and fourth generation" (34:6–7). Benno Jacob (1862–1945), an important scholar in the Jewish interpretive tradition, refers to these attributes as "the famous thirteen Talmudic attributes,"[1] or thirteen *middoth* (attributes). Getting to the number thirteen remains a challenge, but Jacob, in conversation with others, settles on the list in table 4.3.

Table 4.3. Thirteen Middoth

1	God of mercy
2	Grace
3	Long-suffering/patient
4	Full of steadfast love (*hesed*)
5	Faithful
6	Visiting steadfast love (*hesed*) to the thousandth (generation)
7	Forgiving iniquity
8	Forgiving rebellion
9	Forgiving sin
10	Visiting sins of fathers to sons
11	Sons to sons (second generation)
12	Visiting sins of the fathers to the third (generation)
13	Visiting sins of the fathers to the fourth (generation)

The Lord Passes before Moses

Exodus 34:6 says, "And the Lord passed by before him, and proclaimed . . ." Rabbi Yohanan commented:

> Were it not explicitly written in the verse, it would be impossible to say this, as it would be insulting to God's honor. The verse teaches that the Holy One, Blessed be He, wrapped Himself in a prayer shawl like a prayer leader and showed Moses the structure of the order of the prayer. He said to him: Whenever the Jewish people sin, let them act before Me in accordance with this order. Let the prayer leader wrap himself in a prayer shawl and publicly recite the *thirteen* attributes of mercy, and I will forgive them.[e]

The Divine Attributes in the Prophets

The Minor Prophets (Hosea–Malachi) appeal to the divine attributes of Exodus 34 at various times (e.g., Joel 2:12–14; Jon. 3:9–10; 4:2; Mic. 7:18–20; Nah. 1:2–3). These attributes are, in part, an answer to the invitation at the end of Hosea to know and discern the ways of the Lord (Hosea 14:9). Discerning the Lord's will and ways involves coming to terms with God's being and character as merciful and severe. The prophets' repeated invitation to repent is predicated on a central feature of God's being—namely, he is quick to forgive and always shows mercy to the repentant.

What these attributes reveal is that YHWH is merciful and severe, a God of gracious patience and willingness to forgive and a God whose justice does not overlook sin indefinitely and will indeed bring judgment. Both mercy and severity stem from the singularity of God's being and are not in competition with each other. Still, the disproportionate relation in the *middoth* between mercy and severity is marked: visiting steadfast love to the thousandth generation and sins down to the fourth generation. In theological terms, God is gracious and patient; his quickness to forgive is his ordinary property, his disposition. His judgment, though real and threatening, is his alien work, whose purpose is restorative, not punitive.

After the revelation of the divine name in Exodus 34, Moses intercedes for the people again, asking the Lord to forgive their sins. And the Lord does exactly that and then renews the covenant with his people (34:10–28). How can the covenant endure even when the people have broken their covenant obligations? Because of the character of the Lord as revealed in his name. Because God is quick to forgive. He runs off the front porch to meet his wayward son when he returns home in repentance. It is his character to do so. In overly simplistic terms, it comes easy for the Lord to forgive. It is in his nature. It is revealed in his name.

INSTRUCTIONS FOR WORSHIP: EXODUS 25–31 AND 35–40

After establishing the covenant at Sinai, the Lord gives very specific instructions regarding the Israelite cult—its worship, tabernacle, and priesthood. Exodus seems to stutter with these instructions: chapters 35–40 appear as a repetition of the material already presented in chapters 25–31. However, these two blocks of cultic instruction complement each other. The first reveals the instructions for worship given by the Lord to Moses. The second block witnesses to the carrying out of the instructions. In terms of literary space, a great deal of attention is given to these cultic concerns, revealing the important intersection of worship and all of life lived before the Lord.

The tabernacle was the place of God's presence among the people. "Tabernacling" or "dwelling" represents the Hebrew verb *shakan*, from which the word "Shekinah" stems. God's presence is not bound to the tabernacle, and moral pollution and covenant infidelity can lead to God's abandonment of the tabernacle or, in time, the temple (cf. Ezek. 10:18–22; 43:1–7). Still, the tabernacle itself and the careful details of its construction and maintenance witness to God's gracious promise to be with his people. This promise is at the heart of the Old Testament's theological description of the Lord's gracious relation to his people. *I will be with you—Immanuel.* God's presence is always a gift and is never constrained by human rituals. At the same time, the relationship can be impaired and threatened when the people of God turn away, seeking after alternative gods as the worship of the golden calf reveals. (See the sidebar "The Cosmos as God's Temple" in chap. 3.)

Table 4.4. Overview of the Tabernacle Instructions

25:1–7	Materials for the tabernacle's construction
25:8–9	The purpose of the sanctuary
25:10–40; 30:1–10, 17–21	The furnishings
26:1–37	Architectural details for the tabernacle
27:1–8	The bronze altar
27:9–19	The tabernacle's courtyard
27:20–21; 30:11–16, 22–38	Instructions for lamp and anointing oil
28–29	Instructions for the priesthood and sacrifices
31:1–11	Builders selected
31:12–18	Sabbath instructions

Figure 4.6. Replica of the tabernacle

LITERARY NOTES

Creation and the Tabernacle

Exodus 25–31 contains seven sets of instructions about the tabernacle from the Lord to Moses. Each begins with "the Lord said to Moses" (25:1; 30:11, 17, 22, 32; 31:1, 12), and the section culminates with instructions for the Sabbath (31:12–17). The tabernacle plays an eschatological role for God's people, much like the seventh day of creation. The tabernacle was the promise of life in the midst of death, a forward-looking intimation of hope when the seventh day of God's creation becomes every day for the faithful.

CANONICAL CONNECTIONS

Jesus and the Tabernacle

In John's Gospel, Christ's incarnation is presented in terms of the Word becoming flesh and "dwelling" among us (1:14). The term "dwelling" in John 1 intentionally echoes the tabernacle language of the Pentateuch and the Shekinah glory of God filling the tabernacle in the midst of God's people. In Christ, the glory of God dwells with his people in the person of the Son, the very tabernacle/temple of God's presence. The tabernacle/temple ministered God's presence in a sacramental way via the physical materials of the structure itself. In this sense, the tabernacle could never be called God, but it was the instrument of God's indwelling. Jesus, on the other hand, was God in their midst.

Implementation—Reading Exodus as Christian Scripture Today

Exodus is foundational to the Old Testament's theological presentation. Central to this presentation is the revelation of the divine name, YHWH. The Lord's name as it reveals his character occurs with the exodus and the events surrounding it. The Lord promises to be with his people, in their very midst. He does so by the material means of a tabernacle, priesthood, and sacrificial system to mediate the presence of the Lord in the midst of the Lord's people. The golden calf fiasco almost brought an end to the relationship between the Lord and *this* people. Yet the Lord is merciful and gracious and quick to forgive, as his name reveals (Exod. 34:6–7). The book of Exodus reveals the Lord as merciful and severe, and it bears witness to God's eternal identity with his people for all time.

KEY VERSES IN EXODUS

- Moses said to God, "Suppose I go to the Israelites and say to them, 'The God of your fathers has sent me to you,' and they ask me, 'What is his name?' Then what shall I tell them?" God said to Moses, "I AM WHO I AM. This is what you are to say to the Israelites: 'I AM has sent me to you.'" God also said to Moses, "Say to the Israelites, 'The LORD, the God of your fathers—the God of Abraham, the God of Isaac and the God of Jacob—has sent me to you.'" 3:13–15
- Then say to Pharaoh, "This is what the LORD says: Israel is my firstborn son, and I told you, 'Let my son go, so he may worship me.' But you refused to let him go; so I will kill your firstborn son." 4:22–23
- That you may tell your children and grandchildren how I dealt harshly with the Egyptians and how I performed my signs among them, and that you may know that I am the LORD. 10:2
- "You will be for me a kingdom of priests and a holy nation." These are the words you are to speak to the Israelites. 19:6
- And he passed in front of Moses, proclaiming, "The LORD, the LORD, the compassionate and gracious God, slow to anger, abounding in love and faithfulness, maintaining love to thousands, and forgiving wickedness, rebellion and sin. Yet he does not leave the guilty unpunished; he punishes the children and their children for the sin of the parents to the third and fourth generation." 34:6–7

Christian Reading Questions

1. Why is the exodus so important to the covenantal history of Israel?
2. What is the significance of God linking his name to his redemptive actions? How does this become especially significant on the other side of the golden calf episode?
3. Why is it important that Moses rehearses Israel's redemption story before giving the Ten Commandments?
4. The tabernacle offers the promise of God's presence. How does the tabernacle help us think about the importance of the person and work of Jesus Christ?

CHAPTER FIVE

Leviticus

Orientation

Most "read through the Bible" plans get hung up in Leviticus. It is, after all, extraordinarily strange to modern ears. Sacrifice, rituals, priests and sprinkling, impurity, **clean** and **unclean**, tabernacles and **holiness**—it all is too much! And from a Christian reader's perspective, if one has abandoned the Old Testament because we have Jesus and so don't need it anymore (as some Christians unhelpfully assert), then Leviticus will seem all the more irrelevant.

Despite its oddity and seeming irrelevance, Leviticus is life giving and good for those who patiently and intentionally read it. This is because

RECEPTION HISTORY

Marcion and the Old Testament

The early Christian leader Marcion (ca. 85–160) viewed the Old Testament, with all its legal regulations, sacrifice, and violence, as something other than Christian Scripture. In fact, he excised the entire Old Testament from Scripture and abandoned it utterly. Other Christian leaders recognized Marcion's grave error, and they argued for the Old Testament as Christian Scripture, preserving the oddity—and theological richness—of books like Leviticus.

RECEPTION HISTORY

Anti-Semitism and Christianity

Sadly, anti-Semitism recurs throughout history, and Christianity has sometimes contributed to it. Christianity has witnessed anti-Semitism in its ranks because of (1) a general view that the Mosaic law is ineffective and thereby needs to be replaced with Christian teaching, (2) a view that the Jewish nation gives way to the Christian church, or (3) a view that the Jewish people killed Jesus. As early as the second century AD, Justin Martyr, in his *Dialogue with Trypho* (a Jew), disparaged the Jewish people and the law of Moses as irrelevant for the Christian church. He argued that the law was given as a means to constrain a willful and sinful people but should be abandoned in the light of Christ. Moreover, Justin Martyr provided a pathway for the Christian church to abandon its Jewish roots, Jewish Scripture, and identity as emerging from the heritage of the Israelite identity. Christianity, however, is nourished by the spring of the Old Testament, and Jesus's command to love our neighbor (Matt. 22:39) reminds Christians of their commitment to stand against anti-Semitism.

Leviticus begins to answer big questions for God's people. Let us mention three key questions:

1. In light of what has gone wrong in Israel's relationship with God, how shall God's people manage sin in their community?
2. In light of how Israel is called to be a kingdom of priests and a holy nation belonging to God (Exod. 19:6), how should Israel live in their world with purpose in their covenantal relationship with YHWH, their God and King?
3. How shall Israel differentiate itself from the rest of the nations?

1. How Shall God's People Manage Sin?

In light of what has gone wrong in Israel's relationship with God, how shall God's people manage sin in their community? We saw how God responded to Israel's disobedience in Exodus 32; he preserved them amid judgment and death. In Leviticus, sin will be managed through the sacrificial system. For Christian readers, Leviticus reinforces the grave problem of sin and prepares readers for the extraordinary sacrifice made by Jesus on the cross.

2. How Should Israel Live in Their World?

In light of how Israel is called to be a kingdom of priests and a holy nation belonging to God (Exod. 19:6), how should Israel live in their world with purpose in their covenantal relationship with YHWH, their God and King? Leviticus's response is through a holy communal life. Holiness in the camp is key to understanding what kind of life God requires of his people, both in ancient Israel and in the church today.

CANONICAL CONNECTIONS

Holiness for the Christian Church

Holiness is just as important for Christian readers as it was for the Israelites. Devotion to God and, thereby, a denial of anything that is contrary to God's ways are what it means to follow God. It is no surprise the apostle Peter uses the language of Leviticus 11:44–45 and 19:2 to instruct the Christian church: "Like obedient children, do not be conformed to the desires that you formerly had in ignorance. Instead, as he who called you is holy, be holy yourselves in all your conduct; for it is written, 'You shall be holy, for I am holy'" (1 Pet. 1:14–16 NRSV).

RECEPTION HISTORY

Origen on Leviticus

One of the earliest commentators on Leviticus was the controversial Christian bishop Origen of Alexandria (185–ca. 254). He reads Leviticus as presenting, in advance, a living picture of the full reality of life that would come in Jesus Christ. Leviticus must be understood through the letter (realities pertaining to Israel) but crucially through the spirit (realities pertaining to Jesus disclosed in Scripture) (see 2 Cor. 3:6).

Such, therefore, is what we now find as we go through the book of Leviticus, in which sacrificial rites, the diversity of offerings, and even the ministries of the priests are described. But perchance the worthy and the unworthy see and hear these things according to the letter, which is, as it were, the flesh of the Word of God and the clothing of its divinity. But "blessed are those eyes" which inwardly see the divine spirit that is concealed in the veil of the letter; and blessed are they who bring clean ears of the inner person to hear these things.[a]

Leviticus may answer big questions, but its literary style differs from that of Genesis and Exodus. Leviticus's narrative of events at Mount Sinai slows down to focus on details about ritual, holiness, and living well before God. 📖 📖 📖

Leviticus also projects a world of ritual and expects the reader to understand it. At its most basic level, **ritual** is a regular symbolic action designed to communicate or inculcate something about reality. Ritual is a divine gift by which God opens Israel up to knowing and experiencing reality in ways not otherwise understandable or experiential. Rituals—such as organizing the camp a particular way, offering sacrifices in particular ways, and organizing time according to a rhythm in the calendar—shape Israel to know realities about their God and their world, indeed *themselves*, as participants in the scope of divine action.

Leviticus was written in a context where ritual space, time, and states made sense to readers. In the modern world, the sensibility of ritual as depicted in Leviticus is not as clear. Therefore, it is necessary to look at the ritual world of the text to understand how God communicates through it.

RITUAL SPACE: THE CAMP AND TABERNACLE

Leviticus depicts a world in which Israel's space was ritualized. Israel's camp surrounded the tabernacle, which was holy and central to the people's place. It looked like the representation in figure 5.1, according to Numbers 2. The tabernacle sat in the middle of the camp, and the Levitical priesthood surrounded the tabernacle. The twelve tribes of Israel were arranged around the priests. The high priest and Moses arranged themselves to the east, where the entrance to the tabernacle was located. Likewise, the tribe of Judah was set to the east. The morning sun rose in the east, illuminating the people, priests, and entrance to the tabernacle each day.

LITERARY NOTES

Narrative Pacing in Leviticus

Exodus draws attention to the events surrounding Israel's deliverance from Egypt and journey toward the promised land. The events cover a good bit of time and vary in setting: from Egypt, to the sea, to the wilderness. By contrast, the entirety of Leviticus is set at Mount Sinai. The narrative focuses not on the great events of salvation but on the giving of the laws, statutes, and ordinances by God, offering a clear and deliberate recounting of these laws and instructions.

LITERARY NOTES

Leviticus Following Exodus

The opening words of Leviticus in the Hebrew text are translated "Then he called to Moses, and YHWH spoke to him from the tent of meeting" (Lev. 1:1 AT). No explicit subject is identified for the opening verb, but it connects to the end of the book of Exodus and continues its story: "So the cloud of the LORD was over the tabernacle by day, and fire was in the cloud by night, in the sight of all the Israelites during all their travels" (Exod. 40:38).

This is why it is appropriate to translate the opening line of Leviticus as most English translations do: "Then YHWH called to Moses and spoke to him from the tent of meeting." From Exodus to Leviticus, the narrative slows down considerably, focusing time and action at Mount Sinai, around the tabernacle. Central to the narrative is God's holiness and how the people relate to God, to one another, and to the nations surrounding them. God continues to speak to Moses at Sinai, and he delivers the content of Leviticus through Moses to Israel.

LITERARY NOTES

The Structure of Leviticus

Leviticus 1–10: Regulations for sacrifices, people, and priests

Leviticus 11–15: Regulations regarding impurity, sin, and their treatment

Leviticus 16: Day of Atonement

Leviticus 17–27: Regulations regarding how to live as God's people in God's land

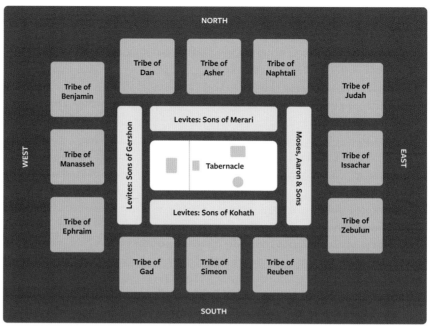

Figure 5.1. Arrangement of the Israelite camp from above

The tabernacle sat in the center of the Israelite camp, serving as its holy sanctuary. The holiest place (holy of holies) rested in the center of the tabernacle, with the ark of the covenant specially arranged within the holy of holies. According to Exodus 25:10–22, the ark of the covenant was the gold-plated chest that stored the tablets of the commandments of YHWH. Arranged on top of the ark of the covenant was the "mercy seat" (sometimes translated as "atonement cover"), the lid of the ark of the covenant. The mercy seat was beautiful and intricate, with the wings of angelic figures bent toward one another; the high priest would sprinkle sacrificial blood on the mercy seat on the day of atonement, making peace between God and Israel annually (Lev. 16:13–14). Thus, we see the camp arranged from holiest (tabernacle) to holy (priests) to **common** (the people of the tribes). The arrangement of the camp testified to the holy God of Israel. As God created a world that is ordered and good, so Israel's camp is ordered according to the four directions of the compass with God's tabernacle set in the center of it all. In terms of ritual space, God is at the center of Israel's journey in the wilderness.

Sacred spaces within the tabernacle symbolically reinforce the significance of space. Only the high priest could enter the holiest place, and only at special times. Consecrated priests could serve in the holy place, where the table of showbread, the altar of incense, and the golden menorah resided.

Common Israelites (nonpriests) could not enter the tabernacle complex but had to pass their sacrifice to the priest at the entrance. He would take it

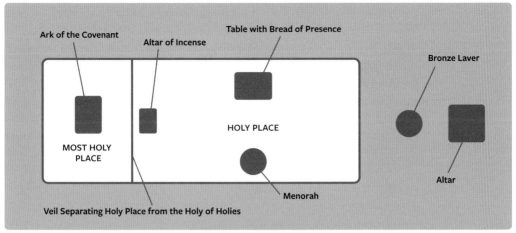

Figure 5.2. Israel's tabernacle from above

inside for ritual slaughter and offering. Outside the camp was beyond the confines of Israel's sacred space. Thus, the tabernacle and camp of Israel illustrate an ascending scale of holiness.

Upon entering the camp, one would witness a visual symbol of this ascending scale of holiness pointing to the center of it all: the most holy place where YHWH dwells. This visual and spatial representation depicts the

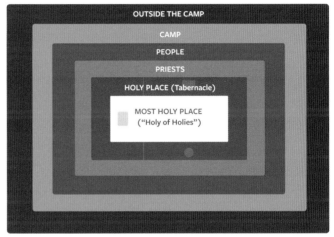

Figure 5.3. Ascending scale of holiness in the camp of Israel

theological reality of Israel's consecration to YHWH and the utter holiness of YHWH as Israel's covenant king. All of life pointed toward the meeting place between God and humanity: the tabernacle, with Israel's God at the center of it all.

RITUAL TIME: SABBATH, FESTIVALS, AND SACRIFICE

YHWH instructed Israel to follow a ritually ordered rhythm of life. For six days, they were to work and then have one day of rest (Sabbath), which is a day regarded as a sacred assembly for worship and enjoyment of YHWH. This seven-day rhythm derives from the order of creation: God created on six days and rested on the Sabbath day, which God consecrates (Gen. 1). Leviticus reiterates this design for time in Leviticus 23:3 by extending it into the festival seasons.

Thus, Israel's regular rhythms reflect God's creative design and testify that God has created the world good. The seasons and festivals remind God's people of God's provision of **atonement**, and they reinforce Israel's unique story with God and their covenant. Time itself bends to the purposes of knowing God and understanding humanity's relationship with their Creator.

RITUAL STATES: HOLY AND COMMON, CLEAN AND UNCLEAN

Perhaps one of the most complex and confusing elements of the ritual world of Israel is its ritual "states." Leviticus conveys ritual states by calling things holy, clean, unclean, and common (sometimes "profane") to identify the state of people, places, or things before God.

Common—In Leviticus 10:10 priests are to "distinguish between the holy and the common, between the unclean and the clean." Thus "common" likely denotes the neutral ritual state (a baseline of sorts), and common things are divided into two types: the clean and the unclean.

Clean—Most common things are "clean," which means "pure" and qualified for normal use. If a person who has skin disease (and is thereby unclean) becomes well and follows prescribed rituals, the priest can pronounce that person "clean," just as a modern doctor would say a sick person is back to normal.

Unclean—By contrast, being unclean means that the person, place, or thing is unqualified for normal use. Uncleanness is the inverse of cleanness. It depicts some abnormality when compared with normal function or usage. A unique feature of uncleanness is that it can sometimes be contagious. Things that come into contact with skin disease or things that have touched corpses—both of which are "unclean"—become unclean by virtue of contact with them (see Lev. 11–15; Num. 19). However, not all items that are unclean are contagious.

Holy—Ritual holiness means something or someone has been set apart by God for a particular task or function. Common, clean things can be made holy through ritual acts of sanctification. Unclean things cannot be made holy. Holiness, then, is a ritual state that is opposed to uncleanness. Unclean things or people cannot be mixed with holy things or people. This is the reason people afflicted with permanent skin disease (and thereby perpetually unclean) are set outside the camp of Israel. This safeguards the holiness of the camp.

Ritual states can move from common and clean to common and unclean. Unclean things can be made clean through cleansing rituals to return to the state of being clean. Alternatively, common and clean things can move to a ritual state of holiness through rites of sanctification, making them fit for special use, especially at the sanctuary. However, holy things can be profaned due to sin and thereby made common and, possibly, unclean as well.

The ritual world of holy and common, clean and unclean reflects for Israel significant truths:

1. God is holy.
2. Holiness is a property of God, but holiness can be a gracious, divine conferral on a person, place, or thing by God, who alone makes them holy (the English word for this Hebrew concept is "sanctified").
3. Uncleanness testifies to something being abnormal in the world that needs to be addressed.
4. Ritual uncleanness of a person, place, or thing can be altered by virtue of divine action and/or prescribed ritual action.
5. Divine grace is operative in the face of abnormality and sin.

Further, ritual states are conceptualized according to what is "normal" and "abnormal." Leviticus pictures God as the source and force of

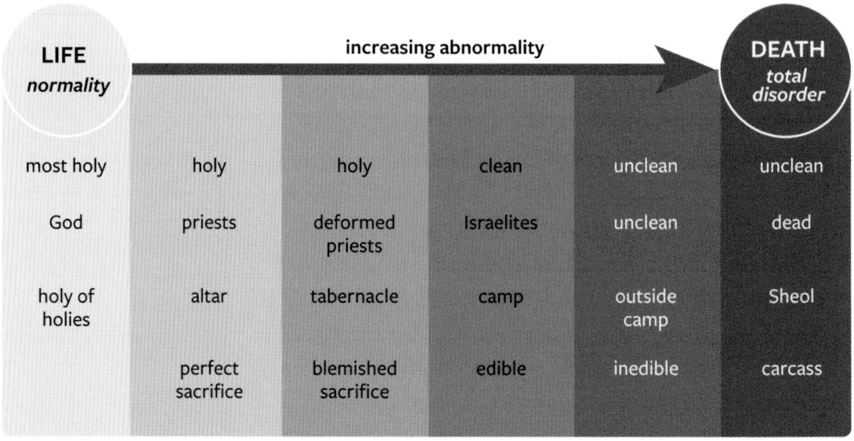

LIFE normality		increasing abnormality			DEATH total disorder
most holy	holy	holy	clean	unclean	unclean
God	priests	deformed priests	Israelites	unclean	dead
holy of holies	altar	tabernacle	camp	outside camp	Sheol
	perfect sacrifice	blemished sacrifice	edible	inedible	carcass

Figure 5.4. Life and normality, death and disorder in Leviticus's ritual world

life for all things. When Israel worshiped their God, they worshiped the God of life and vitality rather than a deity of death. Death is opposed to the vitality of God and represents disorder and desacralization. Prescribed rituals that purified uncleanness and addressed unholiness, as odd as they may sound to modern ears, nonetheless testified to Israel of the victory of the God of life.

3. How Shall Israel Differentiate Itself?

The third big question Leviticus answers is, How shall Israel differentiate itself from the rest of the nations? Leviticus's response is through sacrifices; distinctive dietary laws, calendar of worship and celebration, and agriculture laws; an economy of care rather than pure profit; and a religious system to regulate and manage holiness and purity among the people of God so they can display the glories of their God to the world.

One final note on the ritual world of Leviticus. If one wonders why these rituals and this ritual world were necessary, the answer is found in the narrative from Genesis to Leviticus. Sin, the great problem that brings death (Gen. 3), must be addressed for God's people to live in God's land. Sacrifices and rituals testify to God's management of sin and death. 🔲

The ancient "clothing" of sacrifice and rituals may not be the "clothing" we would wear today, but sacrifice and rituals were common in the ancient world. They were understood. The ritual space and

THEOLOGICAL ISSUES

Are Uncleanness and Impurity Related to Sin?

A major question for theologians turns on whether ritual impurity or uncleanness can be correlated to specific sins. Most would argue that ritual impurity simply reflects the inability of an individual to worship at the sanctuary until the impurity has been purged or cleansed. Thus, ritual impurity has nothing to do with specific sins of the people. For example, handling a dead body for burial makes that person ritually impure, even if there is no sin attached to the act. Moral impurity, however, is willful sin committed against God, either of omission (what one ought to have done but did not do, and thereby is sinful) or commission (what one did that is sinful).

Nonetheless, when we reflect on how ritual and moral impurity appear in the Old Testament, both are in the context of the sanctuary and need specialized rituals to maintain Israel's relationship with YHWH. Thus, the very existence of the sanctuary highlights the regular and persistent problem of sin and relationship management, even if ritual impurity cannot be necessarily connected to specific sins as can moral impurity.

ritual times, though unique to Israel, fit broadly within the world of temples and sacrifice and sacred time witnessed among the ancients. God opens Israel's eyes to their problems and the solution through the world of ritual evident in the Old Testament.

Exploration—Reading Leviticus

Regulations for Sacrifices, People, and Priests: Leviticus 1–10

■ READ LEVITICUS 1–10 ■

God delivers to Moses the instructions for all of Israel regarding who should offer sacrifices, when and where they should make these sacrifices, how the sacrifices are accomplished, and why they should make sacrifices.

Who	The men of Israel and the priests
When	Various times and seasons
Where	The tabernacle (and later, the temple)
How	Prescribed processes of ritual purification and slaughter
Why	To express the bond between Israel and YHWH, including celebrating YHWH's provision for Israel and seeking atonement for sin or guilt

Sacrifice was necessary to bring atonement (1:4). As Leviticus 4:26 states, "Thus the priest shall make atonement [*kipper*] on his behalf for his sin, and he shall be forgiven" (NRSV). The English word "atonement" translates the Hebrew word *kipper*. In Leviticus, *kipper* can mean one of two things, and this helps us understand what atonement is and what it does. "Atonement" means both (a) payment or ransom for sin and (b) purification from uncleanness or impurity.

ATONEMENT AS RANSOM

In the first case, atonement is a kind of payment of a ransom (through sacrifice) for the sin of the guilty party (sinner) to the offended party (God).[1] God has been offended by the Israelites' sin, and the sacrifice pays the penalty of sin so that the covenant relationship with God is reconciled.

The necessity of atonement shows that breaches *will* occur in the relationship between God and Israel. God expects that Israel will not—cannot—be perfect and sinless. Out of divine grace and patience, God provides a mechanism for Israel to manage their sin so their relationship with God will be healthy and good.

Interestingly, the sacrifices are given by the people, which attests to the fact that humans effect relational breach with God (through intentional or unintentional sin) and not the other way around. However, Leviticus helps us to understand that God's role in atonement is essential.

We might think that sacrifice is what people offer to God. From a certain perspective, that is correct: Israel gives sacrifices on the altar through the priests. But in fact, we must recognize that sacrifice is about what *God offers to Israel*: atonement. Atonement is fundamentally about God giving sinful Israel reconciliation and forgiveness so that they might fulfill their covenantal identity as a "kingdom of priests and a holy nation" (Exod. 19:6).

ATONEMENT AS PURIFICATION

In the second case, atonement appears in contexts of ritual purification. Many argue that atonement is *really* about purification or purgation of the effects of impurity. The Hebrew word *kipper* shows up in places like Leviticus 16:13, where cleansing and purification language appears as well. Thus, atonement can also indicate a kind purification: a washing or cleansing to remove ritual impurity. Leviticus 11–15 depicts the importance of purity among the people, the priests, and the sacrifices.

Although some scholars lean toward one or the other aspect of atonement, the text allows us to recognize atonement as either payment or purification. Atonement entails both a ransom *and* a purification.[2]

Leviticus shows how sinning against another human being is also a sin against God. For example, Leviticus 6 stipulates that when one defrauds one's neighbor by robbery, deceit, or lies, the guilty party must address both the fraud of neighbor as well as the relational breach with God. The guilty party pays a penalty to the defrauded party and then offers a reparation offering (sometimes translated as "guilt offering") to God. In this way, Leviticus exposes a double love for Israel's life: a love of God (Deut. 6:5) and a love of neighbor (Lev. 19:18).

CANONICAL CONNECTIONS

Jesus and the Greatest Commandment

Jesus taught that the entire Israelite law (cultic law included) can be distilled into two basic tenets: love of God and love of neighbor (Matt. 22:36–40; Mark 12:28–31; Luke 10:25–28). Jesus saw these two tenets, drawn from Deuteronomy 6:5 and Leviticus 19:18, as the hinge on which the Old Testament teaching turns.

The rituals for atonement were an orchestrated affair, and the impression given by Leviticus 1–10 is that sacrifice was a bloody business. The offerings were prepared and given to God and prepared for the priests according to specific instructions. Amid the slaughter of the animals, blood was spilled, sprinkled, or burned, but never eaten. Why does the text focus so much on blood? There are two reasons:

1. Blood is sacred and life giving, as we see in Leviticus 17:13, 14: "The life of every creature is its blood."

2. Blood is a powerful ransom for sin and detergent for impurity (Lev. 17:11–14): "It is the blood that makes atonement for one's life" (17:11). Whether for sin or impurity, blood makes atonement. 📜 🏺 🏺

Regulations Regarding Impurity, Sin, and Their Treatment: Leviticus 11–15

▦ READ LEVITICUS 11; 13–14 ▦

From the regulations regarding sacrifice in the first part of the book, Leviticus turns to the world of purity and impurity and of priestly discernment. The regulations in chapters 11–15 span the gamut of Israel's life and regulate how God's people shall remain fit for service in God's kingdom.

Leviticus 11 describes the different foods that Israel can and cannot eat. These regulations are known as kosher laws, or laws that differentiate clean versus unclean animals. Like the ritual world described above, the ways in which Israel eats differentiates them from other nations. The food regulations include all animal groups: (1) large land animals (11:2–8), (2) water animals and fish (11:9–12), (3) birds (11:13–19), (4) flying insects (11:20–23), and (5) smaller land animals (11:41–42). Separation of clean and unclean, edible and inedible is vital to depict God's order and design in creation, separate Israel from the nations, and show how even Israel's diet reflects their covenant relationship to God.

Often these dietary laws, because they differentiate "clean" and "unclean," are thought to reflect healthy versus unhealthy food. Alternatively, they are thought to reflect different levels of human loathing regarding the animals, in the sense that some animals (like pigs or oysters) are disgusting while others (like sheep or locusts) are not disgusting

CANONICAL CONNECTIONS

Acts 15

In the early days of Christianity, non-Jews (known as gentiles) began following Jesus as the Messiah alongside the Jewish followers of Jesus. One of the key questions that gripped the church was whether gentiles had to convert to Judaism and adhere to Jewish law to be faithful followers of Jesus. Would gentiles be required to follow all the laws, including laws like Leviticus 17:11–14, which prohibits eating the blood of animals? A group called the Jerusalem Council met to discern what should be done. Peter told the council that God had "cleansed [the gentiles'] hearts by faith" (Acts 15:9 ESV) and had given the Holy Spirit to both Jews and gentiles. It was decided that gentiles were not required to follow the laws of Judaism, except for the following specific requirements: "Abstain from what has been sacrificed to idols, and from blood, and from what has been strangled, and from sexual immorality. If you keep yourselves from these, you will do well" (15:29 ESV).

HISTORICAL MATTERS

Sacrifice in the Ancient World

Sacrifices may seem strange to modern readers, but offerings and sacrifices were not uncommon in the ancient world. Ancient Near Eastern people offered food and drink to their deities. Sacrifice of animals to appease the gods was a common feature in Egypt, Mesopotamia, and ancient Greece. Israel sits within this ancient Near Eastern context, but its theological focus on YHWH and blood sacrifice as a management for sin is distinctive. Only Israelite sacrifice systematically applies blood as a ransom or payment for the life of the offerer and a purification for the altar and sanctuary.[c]

but good for food. But the relative healthiness or sense of disgust has little to do with the dietary laws. Rather, it appears that the laws attempt to reflect boundaries within a taxonomy, albeit in an incomplete way. So, catfish are prohibited as food because they do not fully fit the grouping of fish: they swim in the water and have fins and gills, but they do not have scales.

HISTORICAL MATTERS

Offerings and Sacrifices in Leviticus

Name	Purpose	Kind of Offering	Nature of Offering	Actions of Offerers	Actions of Priest	Kinds of Sin Managed
Burnt offering (*'olah*) (Lev. 1:3–17; 6:8–13)	Atone for basic human sinfulness	Male without blemish from herd (cattle), flock (sheep/goats), or two birds	Completely burned	Brings offering; places hand on head; slays, skins, cuts in pieces	Generally offers *'olah* twice daily. Accepts offering; throws blood against altar; places pieces on fire; washes entrails and legs	Breach between God and Israel. Brings atonement (Lev. 4), acceptance by God (1:3), and consecration for service; ideally, it expresses complete devotion to the Lord
Grain offering (*minhah*) (Lev. 2; 6:14–23)	To secure or retain goodwill	Fine flour cakes or wafers, or firstfruits, anointed with oil, frankincense, salt, but no leaven or honey; usually accompanied by animal sacrifice	Token given by offerer and burned by priest	Brings offering; takes handful of grain or cereal	Receives handful and burns it; priests and sons eat the remainder	None—the offering is a gift of consecration to God
Fellowship offering (*shelamim*) (Lev. 3; 7:11–21, 28–36)	To render praise to YHWH for his goodness	Male/female from herd (cattle) or flock (sheep/goats) without blemish	Fatty portions burned; remainder eaten	Brings offering; places hand on head; slays, skins, cuts in pieces; eats of remainder (same or next day); this is an expression of communion for the people, priests, and God	Accepts offering; throws blood on altar; burns fatty portions; eats of remainder (same day); this is an expression of communion for the people, priests, and God	None—the offering is a celebration of peace between God and humanity. It is an expression of praise and communion.
Purification offering for sin / "sin offering" (*hatta't*) (Lev. 4:1–5:13; 6:24–30)	To atone for a specific unwitting sin (except see Num. 19) and atone for specific cases (cf. Lev. 5:1–5); forgiveness after the sacrifice is offered	*Priests:* a bull *Congregation:* young bull *Ruler:* male goat *General populace:* female goat/ sheep *Poor:* two birds *Destitute:* flour	Fatty portions burned; remainder eaten (except see Num. 19); hide, offal, head, and shanks burned outside the camp	Confess sin (Lev. 5:5); brings penalty (*'asham*) offering to the Lord for sin (elders do so for congregation, but see Num. 19 for an exceptional *hatta't* sacrifice)	Accepts offering; throws blood against altar; burns fat, etc. on altar, but burns offal, hide, etc. outside camp; eats meat. But if own sin is included, portion burned outside camp rather than eaten.	Unintentional sins like not giving testimony, unwitting touching of unclean thing, unwitting touching of uncleanness belonging to humans, rash oaths

Fish fit for food have scales. Likewise, lobsters may be delicious but they are not clearly fish with scales and fins. Likewise, oysters are sea creatures without fins or scales and therefore are unfit for food. For birds, the rabbis believed that forbidden fowl were designated as such because they were birds of prey, but this is unclear. This rationale works only so far for the animal

Name	Purpose	Kind of Offering	Nature of Offering	Actions of Offerers	Actions of Priest	Kinds of Sin Managed
Reparation offering / "guilt offering" (*'asham*) (Lev. 5:14–6:7; 7:1–10)	To atone for a sin requiring restitution or a breach of faith; forgiveness from God and reconciliation	Like *hatta't* offering (plus any specified restitution)	Like purification offering	Like purification offering (plus specified restitution)	Like purification offering (plus specified restitution)	Manages sins against both God and neighbor (hence sacrifice and restitution)
Praise offering (*todah*, a kind of *shelamim*) (Lev. 7:12–15; 22:29)	For a blessing received	Male/female or flock without blemish from herd, plus fine flour cakes/wafers anointed with oil	Token given by offerer for a received blessing: animal sacrifice and flour cakes/wafers given to priests	One portion belongs to the priest; the rest belongs to the Lord	Receives the animal and burns the offering of the *shelamim*; eats the prescribed portion	None—a gift of peace
Vow offering (*neder*, a kind of *shelamim*) (Lev. 7:16–21)	In fulfillment of a vow	Male/female from herd or flock without blemish, plus fine flour cakes/wafers anointed with oil	Token given by offerer for a received blessing: animal sacrifice and flour cakes/wafers given to priests	One portion belongs to the priest; the rest belongs to the Lord	Receives the animal; burns the offering of the *shelamim*; eats the prescribed portion	None—a gift of peace
Freewill offering (*nedabah*, a kind of *shelamim*) (Lev. 7:16–21)	Spontaneous praise to God	Male/female from herd or flock without blemish, plus fine flour cakes/wafers anointed with oil	Token given by offerer for a received blessing: animal sacrifice and flour cakes/wafers given to priests	One portion belongs to the priest; the rest belongs to the Lord	Receives the animal and burns the offering of the *shelamim*; eats the prescribed portion	None—a gift of peace
Exile (Lev. 26:27–39)	Stipulation for defiant sin against God— dispositional and willful rejection of God's ways	Unique and most severe of all offerings; the people themselves become the offering before God	God's people disciplined seven times for their sin; cannibalism; destruction; divine rejection (v. 30); rejection of *'olah* sacrifices; scattering among the nations	Exiled and scattered; confession of sin of uncircumcised hearts; humility; exile serves as penalty for sin	Exiled and scattered; confession of sin of uncircumcised hearts; humility; exile serves as penalty for sin	Defiant sin against God; part of a four-fold intensification of punishment against willful sin (cf. Lev. 26:14–20, 21–22, 23–26, 27–39)

Note: The *'olah*, *hattat*, and *'asham* sacrifices take place once guilt has been established and admitted. Yet if God's people do not admit their sin, then the stipulation of the exile, recorded in Lev. 26:27–39, takes hold to manage this act of defiant sin. In other words, priestly legislation has no sacrificial means to deal with defiant sin. Even the Day of Atonement ritual (Lev. 16) is a general sacrifice that atones for the priests and populace in general, and they admit sin (16:21) as well as practice self-denial (16:29) in recognition of their sin. Atonement for defiant sin, where sin is not admitted in some way, is achieved through exile. Still, exile is not an annulment of Israel being God's people as much as it is a disciplinary action, designed to reconcile God's people and to renew their own identity before God (cf. 26:40–45).

Figure 5.5. Egyptian relief of a sacrificial scene in Mastaba of Mereruka (Saqqara, Egypt)

groups, however, and the reason for some of the distinctions between clean and unclean remains unclear.

Leviticus 12–15 speaks to different ways of addressing impurity of individuals. Impurity prevents one from worshiping at the tabernacle and therefore threatens the ability of individuals and the community to be fit for service as God's people. Chapter 12 details dealing with the impurity of childbirth and what should be done at the tabernacle in worship after the birth. Chapters 13–14 deal specifically with priests diagnosing and prescribing purification rituals for skin diseases. The problem with skin diseases—whether small or great—is what they represent: a diminishment of wholeness and an indication of something that is fundamentally wrong in the world. The rituals prescribed for those with skin diseases reflect a view that is ritually governed. Skin disease reflects abnormality and inability to associate with the normal ways of life. Therefore, those with skin disease are physically moved outside the normal patterns of life until their skin disease is rectified and its absence is confirmed by the priest. After healing, the afflicted person can then ritually move to the normal patterns of life. These are ritual movements from regular life to disordered or abnormal life because of skin disease to renewed life confirmed with ritual.

Ultimately what lay under threat with impurity and uncleanness is the holiness and sanctity of God, whose presence was central to the people at the tabernacle: "You must keep the Israelites separate from things that make them unclean, so they will not die in their uncleanness for **defiling** my dwelling place, which is among them" (Lev. 15:31). Israel's uncleanness and impurity is not dangerous for them because it is unhygienic or unhealthy. Rather, it is dangerous and lethal

Figure 5.6. Sacrifice of a young boar with kalos inscription (ΕΠΙΔΡΟΜΟΣ ΚΑΛΟΣ); tondo (circular painting) from an Attic red-figure cup (ca. 510–500 BC)

because it somehow defiles God's sacred places. Because God will not tolerate any diminishment of his holiness, those who remain unclean without ritual conversion to cleanness or purity will "die in their uncleanness." Separation from impurity, and dealing with impurity once it obtains, is vital for the ritual world of Israel.

The Day of Atonement: Leviticus 16

■ READ LEVITICUS 16 ■

After these food laws, we turn to the Day of Atonement ritual in Leviticus 16. This ritual is distinct from other sacrifices and represents the key festival in Israel's calendar. This is because the Day of Atonement provides atonement for Israel's inadvertent sins.

The ritual is different from the others, as only the high priest (Aaron) can go into the most holy place of the tabernacle and make an offering. Aaron must provide a sin offering for himself and his family. Then he can mediate between God and the rest of Israel. He is then to bring two goats for offering: one for YHWH and the other as the "scapegoat." The sacrificial goat is a sin offering for the people, and Aaron is to offer its blood on the mercy seat of the ark of the covenant and in front of it. As Aaron does this, the goat's blood makes "atonement for the Most Holy Place because of the uncleanness and rebellion of the Israelites, whatever their sins have been. He is to do the same for the tent of meeting, which is among them in the midst of their uncleanness" (Lev. 16:16).

In the ritual concerning the "scapegoat," Aaron lays both hands on the head of the goat and is to "confess over it all the wickedness and rebellion of the Israelites—all their sins—and put them on the goat's head" (Lev. 16:21). After this, Aaron sends the goat away into the wilderness under the direction of a specific person. The rationale for the scapegoat probably involves the nature of the sin it addresses: intentional sins. They must be transferred to the animal as a substitute and sent away from the camp into the wilderness.

The text stipulates that this second goat "will carry on itself all their sins to a remote place; and the man shall release it in the wilderness" (Lev. 16:22). Both goats deal with sin: the goat for YHWH is a sin offering for the people that is killed, and its blood cleanses the ark, holy place, most holy place, altar, and shrine; the scapegoat bears the intentional sins of the people and carries them away from the camp. Various ritual washings for all parties ensue, as well as ritual burnings of various parts of the sacrifices. The rationale for the Day of Atonement is straightforward: "Atonement is to be made once a year for all the sins of the Israelites" (16:34). When it

Tertullian and the Day of Atonement

The church father Tertullian understands the two goats associated with the Day of Atonement to relate to the nature of Jesus:

If I may offer, moreover, an interpretation of the two goats which were presented on the "great day of atonement," do they not also figure the two natures of Christ? They were of like size, and very similar in appearance, owing to the Lord's identity of aspect; because He is not to come in any other form, having to be recognized by those by whom He was also wounded and pierced. One of these goats was bound with scarlet, and driven by the people out of the camp into the wilderness, amid cursing, and spitting, and pulling, and piercing, being thus marked with all the signs of the Lord's own passion; while the other, by being offered up for sins, and given to the priests of the temple for meat, afforded proofs of His second appearance, when (after all sins have been expiated) the priests of the spiritual temple, that is, the church, are to enjoy the flesh, as it were, of the Lord's own grace, whilst the residue go away from salvation without tasting it.[d]

happens, all should celebrate that it deals with the intentional sins of the people.

Regulations for Living as God's People in God's Land: Leviticus 17–27

■ READ LEVITICUS 19 ■

Leviticus 17 and 18 discuss appropriate slaughter of animals and include diverse laws about appropriate and inappropriate sexual relations. Leviticus 19 contains an array of instructions, ranging from how Israel should provide for the stranger in their midst by not harvesting the corners of the field to not insulting those with physical disabilities. It describes what clothes a person should wear and how one should plant trees, care for others, breed animals, speak to one another, and exercise justice in the land.

Leviticus 19 is significant in the way it promotes a society of love and respect. In addition to prescribing care for the most vulnerable and physically disabled, it prescribes love for fellow Israelites *and* for resident aliens in the land:

Do not seek revenge or bear a grudge against anyone among your people, but love your neighbor as yourself. I am the LORD. (19:18)

Figure 5.7. William Holman Hunt, *The Scapegoat* (ca. 1854–55)

The foreigner residing among you must be treated as your native-born. Love them as yourself, for you were foreigners in Egypt. I am the LORD your God. (19:34)

Love is more than an emotion; it is an act of covenant devotion. Thus, the native-born Israelite and the resident alien (non-native) demand the same care and commitment. Israel is to be indiscriminate in the way they care for people: all are worthy of

Table 5.1. Ritualization of Time in Israel

Holy Times and Festivals	Text	Purpose of Celebration	Common Times (based on Jewish / Gregorian Calendars)
Weekly Sabbath (seventh day)	Lev. 23:3	Rest as God rested (Gen. 2:2–3)	Common weekdays (days 1–6)
Feast of Unleavened Bread/Passover (*pesach*)	Lev. 23:4–8; Exod. 12	Divine deliverance from Egypt	14 Nisan / March–April
Festival of Weeks (Shavuot/Pentecost)	Lev. 23:9–22	Divine provision in the harvest	6 Sivan / May–June
Day of Atonement (Yom Kippur)	Lev. 16; 23:26–32	Divine atonement for national sin	10 Tishri / September–October
Feast of Tabernacles (Sukkoth)	Lev. 23:33–36	Divine provision in the wilderness	15–21 Tishri / September–October
Sabbath Year	Lev. 25:4–7	Divine renewal of the land while it rests from agriculture	Common years (years 1–6)
Jubilee Year (seventh Sabbath Year)	Lev. 25:8–17	Return of land to original owners; release of indentured people	Non-Jubilee years (49 years)

covenant fidelity and love. The rationale? As God cared for Israel, so Israel should go and do likewise for others.

Leviticus 20 provides instruction about false worship and sexual immorality. Amid these laws is Leviticus 20:7–8, which provides the rationale for Israel's holiness: "Consecrate yourselves and be holy, because I am the LORD your God. Keep my decrees and follow them. I am the LORD, who makes you holy." Leviticus 21–25 provides instructions for God's people regarding holy things and holy seasons (see table 5.1). Time is ritually set for a rhythm of devotion to God.

The book concludes with a summary of blessings for obedience and curses for disobedience in Leviticus 26. In disobedience God's people will be exiled from the land that God has given them. When Israel is in the far country of their sin and confesses to God—"when their uncircumcised hearts are humbled and they pay for their sin"—God promises that he will

CANONICAL CONNECTIONS

The Covenant Formula

Leviticus 26:12–13 affirms that YHWH would be Israel's God and Israel would be the people of YHWH. Verse 12 indicates that YHWH will "walk among" Israel and be their God, and Israel will be God's people. This formulaic expression ("I will be your God and you will be my people," v. 12) reinforces the covenant between God and Israel. It is not a contract but rather a relational priority based on God's commitment to Abraham and his descendants. This notion occurs throughout the Torah (e.g., Exod. 6:7; Deut. 4:20; 7:6; 14:2; 26:16–19; 27:9; 29:13), and it is pervasive through the Prophets and Writings.

The phrase describing YHWH "walking" among the people of God in Leviticus 26:12 echoes God "walking" with Adam and Eve in the Garden of Eden (Gen. 3:8). Whereas Genesis 3:8 reveals a rupture of the relationship due to sin, the regulations and sacrifices in Leviticus enable God's people to walk with God once again. This phrase reminds God's people they can walk in deliverance from bondage. The narrative identity of Israel being delivered from Egypt tells God's people that they are powerless but have been delivered by God to walk in freedom rather than live under oppression. This phrase also reminds God's people they are delivered for a purpose—namely, to be holy for God is holy. God's people are set apart to be a kingdom of priests and a holy nation. God wants Israel, those he delivered from Egyptian bondage (Exod. 19:4–5), to represent his holiness to the nations all around: teaching the nations about God and interceding for them, fitting to the role of priests.

remember the "covenant with Jacob and my covenant with Isaac and my covenant with Abraham, and I will remember the land" (26:41–42). The exile draws God's people to repentance and confession and uniquely "pays" for their sin. In this way, God's people in exile act as a strange sacrifice. The end of the book casts an ominous note on the efficacy of the management of sin through sacrifice in the book. Exile is coming.

Implementation—Reading Leviticus as Christian Scripture Today

What does it mean to read this book as Christian Scripture? At a basic level, Leviticus is about laws regarding ritual, land, and moral demands like loving God. Understanding this fact, but recognizing the challenge of obeying laws related to Israel's government or ritual worship, some Christians divide the Old Testament law into three kinds: civil or judicial laws (laws relating to the governance of Israel and their life in the land), ceremonial laws (laws relating to sacrifice and specific ritual ceremonies), and moral laws (laws relating to loving God and neighbor).

Under this framework, the laws that are timely for ancient Israel (civil/judicial laws and ceremonial laws) as they lived in the land are no longer valid, but the timeless moral laws (e.g., Lev. 19:18 or the Ten Commandments) remain valid for Christians today. Christians avoid civil and ceremonial laws and only hold to the moral law, which Jesus affirmed by upholding the "greatest commandment" on which hangs the entirety of the Old Testament teaching (Matt. 22:36–40).

The problem with this view is that it is untenable. All laws in the Old Testament are moral, if we mean that these laws help Israel to live out what it means to love God and neighbor. How does one read Leviticus 19:18 as a moral law and the other laws in the chapter as something else? A better way to read these laws is to understand that the laws recorded in the Old Testament do the following:

1. Disclose the holy God who is worthy of worship
2. Disclose what it meant for God's holy people to worship YHWH in the land
3. Disclose a virtuous way of life for YHWH's people, shaping them for good
4. Disclose the problem of Israel's sin and detail remedies for managing sin through sacrifice
5. Disclose a need for a permanent remedy for sin, preparing the way for the coming of Jesus Christ

More fundamentally, Leviticus presents a liturgically shaped life. This great wisdom instills rhythm to a life lived well before God. The Christian tradition has taken this deep and fundamental insight and applied it to a liturgically shaped life in the light of Christ. The two great festivals of the Christian calendar, Easter and Advent, anticipate the life found in Christ and the way of Christ. Liturgical structures in worship, celebration of festival versus ordinary time, and celebration before the Lord in the gathered community, as well as regular confession and repentance, remind the church of their past, present, and future hope. Christ and his sacrifice and resurrection stand central to it all, empowering God's people for the world.

In the final Passover with his disciples, Jesus leads his disciples to eat the prescribed meal. He breaks the unleavened bread, takes a cup of wine, and says, "This is my blood of the covenant, which is poured out for many. . . . Truly I tell you, I will not drink again from the fruit of the vine until that day when I drink it new in the kingdom of God" (Mark 14:24–25; cf. Matt. 26:26–30; Luke 22:14–20).

This is, by any account, a strange scene and a unique statement. Jesus's own body and blood will satisfy God so that he will pass over his judgment. In Mark 14:22–25, the blood of Jesus, which is "poured out," is a sign of the covenant and also an indication of Jesus's sacrifice, which would provide atonement. When we reflect on this point in the context of the covenant story of Scripture, we see that Jesus believes that his sacrifice offers atonement for sin. His blood covers sin and makes it possible for reconciliation with God. ⌇

Hebrews and Leviticus

The book of Hebrews argues for the superiority of Christ to matters of the old covenant. In chapter 9, the author of Hebrews compares Jesus to the priesthood and sacrificial system outlined in Leviticus:

> But when Christ came as high priest of the good things that are now already here, he went through the greater and more perfect tabernacle that is not made with human hands, that is to say, is not a part of this creation. He did not enter by means of the blood of goats and calves; but he entered the Most Holy Place once for all by his own blood, thus obtaining eternal redemption. The blood of goats and bulls and the ashes of a heifer sprinkled on those who are ceremonially unclean sanctify them so that they are outwardly clean. How much more, then, will the blood of Christ, who through the eternal Spirit offered himself unblemished to God, cleanse our consciences from acts that lead to death, so that we may serve the living God! (Heb. 9:11–14)

Themes expressed in this chapter—the problem of sin, sacrifice as a way to atone and sanctify Israel for service to the Lord, the need of blood to redeem and purify—all find their significance in the utterly unique sacrifice of Jesus. His shed blood was sacrificial and atoning.

The difference, of course, is that the sacrifice of Jesus is understood as the final sacrifice. The writer of Hebrews says that Jesus "has appeared once for all at the culmination of the ages to do away with sin by the sacrifice of himself. Just as people are destined to die once, and after that to face judgment, so Christ was sacrificed once to take away the sins of many; and he will appear a second time, not to bear sin, but to bring salvation to those who are waiting for him" (Heb. 9:26–28). The logic of Hebrews 9 is clear. Those who follow Jesus and have received the forgiveness offered by his sacrifice are now called to "serve the living God," just as Israel was called to do (9:14).

The apostle Peter uses the language of Leviticus to define how the church ought to conduct their lives (1 Pet. 1:15–16). Peter's use of holiness commands from Leviticus (Lev. 11:44, 45; 19:2) helps the church understand that holiness—a life set apart for God, or being "fit for service" (Luke 9:62)—is not an antiquated demand from an irrelevant book but rather a continuing call for the people of God.

KEY VERSES IN LEVITICUS

- This is a lasting ordinance for the generations to come, so that you can distinguish between the holy and the common, between the unclean and the clean. 10:10
- Do not seek revenge or bear a grudge against anyone among your people, but love your neighbor as yourself. I am the Lord. 19:18
- Consecrate yourselves and be holy, because I am the Lord your God. Keep my decrees and follow them. I am the Lord, who makes you holy. 20:7–8

Christian Reading Questions

1. As holiness is differentiated in relation to God, land, and people, offer a theology of holiness according to Leviticus.
2. What is atonement in Leviticus, and why is it important for the covenant bond between YHWH and Israel?
3. What is the purpose of the sacrificial system and why is it necessary and good for Israel's life?
4. What are the essential theological elements of Leviticus's presentation of Israel's God?
5. How does the New Testament interact with Leviticus in its presentation of Jesus?

CHAPTER SIX

Numbers

Orientation

Transitions mark the book of Numbers, including shifts of place, leadership, and generations. Israel moves from Egypt to Sinai to Kadesh and then to Moab. Moses, Aaron, and Miriam lead Israel in Numbers, but by chapter 20 we discover Joshua and Caleb will lead Israel into the land of Canaan. Finally, because of Israel's disobedience and lack of faith, the text describes the first generation's death in the wilderness and the rise of the

LITERARY NOTES

Why Is It Called "Numbers"?

The Hebrew title of Numbers comes from a word in the first verse of the book, *bemidbar*, which translates as "in the wilderness" (Num. 1:1). So where did the English title, "Numbers," originate? It comes from the Latin title *Numeri*, following the earlier Greek title *Arithmoi*. The Latin and Greek titles probably point to the various censuses in the book (Num. 1–4; 26).

"In the wilderness" better represents the content of the book, as Israel navigates the wilderness from Sinai to the plains of Moab during the span of forty years. In their traverse, the first generation, those who witnessed Israel's miraculous deliverance from Egypt, passes away, and the second generation arises to enter the promised land.

Theologically, the title "in the wilderness" can be understood as the Christian journey of faith: from the struggle in the wilderness of sin to the threshold of promised hope before God. Life is a struggle, but God provides and prepares for our future hope.[a]

RECEPTION HISTORY

Origen on Numbers

The early Christian interpreter Origen read the book of Numbers as illustrating the journey of the life of faith. Numbers depicts a "double exodus": an exodus from the life of sin without Christ and an exodus from the earthly plane to the glories of heaven. In Origen's homily on Numbers 33, the forty-two stages of Israel's journey from Egypt through the wilderness illustrate the spiritual journey toward enlightenment as well as the forty-two generations leading to Jesus Christ.

"[We] said that in a spiritual sense there can be a double exodus from Egypt, either when we leave our life as gentiles and come to the knowledge of divine Law or when the soul leaves its dwelling place in the body. Therefore, these stages [in Num. 33:1–2], which Moses now writes down 'by the Word of the Lord,' point toward both."[b]

second generation who will enter the land of promise. Life changes in the wilderness.

Exploration—Reading Numbers

Preparation in the Wilderness of Sinai: Numbers 1:1–10:10

▓ READ NUMBERS 2–3 ▓

Numbers 1–4 depicts several censuses that establish the narrative moving forward: the general census of the people (Num. 1) and the censuses of the Kohathites (4:1–20), Gershonites (4:21–28), Merarites (4:29–33), and Levites (4:34–49). The censuses surround the description of the camp's organization in Numbers 2–3, reflecting the ritual centrality of the priesthood and tabernacle for Israel.

The tabernacle maintained Israel's holiness before God, and therefore governed Israel's journey from Egypt through Kadesh to the plains of Moab. God's presence was central to the camp, and the emphasis on the Levitical families surrounding the tabernacle in Numbers 2–3 highlights the continuing need for holiness on the journey to the land of promise. Ritual space that preserves and promotes Israel's holiness before God sets an expectation for how Israel is to respond to God in the rest of the book, but it also foreshadows how Israel will fail in their holiness before God throughout their wilderness journey.

Numbers 5 presents laws regarding uncleanness and ritual separation for leprosy, underlining Israel's call to be holy and to preserve God's holiness among them. Laws regarding restitution and alleged unfaithfulness, which require purification and atonement, are prescribed

The Structure of Numbers

Geographical Structure

Numbers is organized into three major units, governed by geographical change:

> Numbers 1:1–10:10: Preparation in the wilderness of Sinai
> Numbers 10:11–20:21: From Sinai to Kadesh, wandering
> Numbers 20:22–36:13: From Kadesh to the plains of Moab

Chronological Structure

The book covers forty years from Sinai to Moab. The three sections of the book are not balanced in terms of chronology, a challenge that confounds many readers:

> Numbers 1:1–10:10: approximately nineteen days
> Numbers 10:11–20:21: approximately thirty-eight years
> Numbers 20:22–36:13: approximately five months

Israel's complaint (Num. 11:1–15) and rebellion (20:1–13) frame the central section of the book, and the Korahite rebellion marks its middle (chaps. 16–17). Thus, the book offers an overall negative portrayal of Israel in the thirty-eight years of wandering. God's gracious intervention contrasts Israel's negative portrayal. God disciplines and preserves Israel despite their rebellion against their covenant Lord (14:18–25).

Figure 6.1. Representation of Origen writing, *Origene autore*, from Schäftlarn Manuscript (ca. 1160), in *Numeros homilia XXVII*

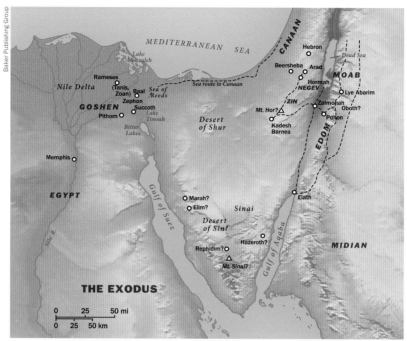

Figure 6.2. Israel's exodus and wilderness wanderings

in Numbers 5 as well, reinforcing the theology of holiness presented in Leviticus.

Numbers 6–10 presents holiness as specific kinds of consecrations to YHWH. Numbers 6 includes the law of the Nazirite. Nazirites are men or women who vow to consecrate themselves to God for shorter or longer periods of time. Nazirites avoid consuming alcohol, vinegar, fresh or dried grapes, grape juice, grape skins or seeds; shaving their head; and touching a corpse. It is unclear why these items are forbidden, but in their asceticism, Nazirites dedicate themselves to the Lord amid the people. Their devotion is public and not hidden, another example of service to YHWH, a theme that emerges in these chapters.

Public consecration depicted in Numbers 6 concludes with the "priestly blessing." It reads:

> The LORD said to Moses, "Tell Aaron and his sons, 'This is how you are to bless the Israelites. Say to them:
>
>> "'"The LORD bless you
>>   and keep you;
>> the LORD make his face to shine on you
>>   and be gracious to you;
>> the LORD turn his face toward you
>>   and give you peace."'"
>
> "So they will put my name on the Israelites, and I will bless them." (6:22–27)

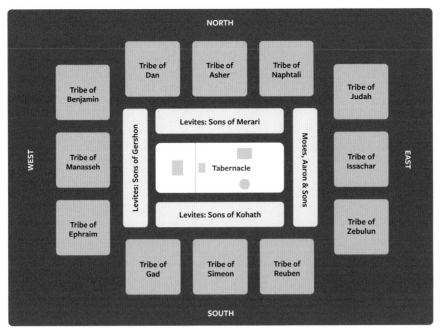

Figure 6.3. Arrangement of the Israelite camp from above (Num. 2–3)

In this poetic formula, God blesses the people through the priests. The blessing's power and efficacy derive from the Lord, and the priest is merely a conduit of divine blessing. So we see God always on the move *toward the people*. Israel cannot earn, nor do they deserve, God's blessing. Instead, the power of the blessing comes from the gracious initiative of YHWH.

Taken within the covenant story in the Pentateuch, the priestly blessing shows how YHWH continues to bless the world through Israel, and Israel is affirmed as the mediator of divine blessing that originated in Abraham (Gen. 12:2–3).

Israel's covenant relationship with YHWH is typified by the "name" God puts on them (Num. 6:27). God's name on Israel reflects the covenant relationship between his people and their God. Israel bears the very name of God in relationship with their covenant Lord—they are not their own, nor are they on their own. God's presence and blessing and name go with them in their journey to their promised home.[1]

Preparation and consecration continue in Numbers 7–10, where the text details specific sacrifices and offerings for Israel's leadership. These offerings are meant for the consecration of the altar, and they provide the materials necessary to begin regular sacrifices at the tabernacle (7:1–88). Each of the twelve tribes of Israel gives toward the dedication, and the

The Priestly Blessing

Two tiny silver amulets dated to the sixth century BC were discovered in excavations at Ketef Hinnom in Jerusalem. They are not large (only a few inches in length), but they contain the earliest inscription of biblical text known to exist. These silver amulets have portions of the priestly blessing of Numbers 6:22–27, particularly verses 24–26: "The LORD bless you and keep you; the LORD make his face to shine upon you, and be gracious to you; the LORD lift up his countenance upon you, and give you peace" (NRSV).

More than a token or talisman, these amulets rehearse for their owners their devotion to YHWH and remind them of YHWH's divine commitment to them.

Figure 6.4. "Priestly Blessing" on silver amulet, Israel Museum, Jerusalem (sixth century BC)

Gary Todd/ CC 0 / Wikimedia Commons

gifts are facilitated by the leadership of each tribe. The people are prepared for their purpose as the people of YHWH. They are set apart for service to God and to be a blessing to the nations.

Numbers 8 presents the consecration of the Levites, priests who minister before the Lord to mediate for the people of Israel. Levites serve at the tabernacle, accomplishing tasks we might consider menial and mundane (slaughtering animals and managing the daily operations of the tabernacle) as well as tasks we might consider honored (like ministering before YHWH in the holy place). In fact, *all* tasks are honored as God has set the Levites apart for service to God and the people.

After the people and priests are consecrated, the narrative turns to the regulations concerning the Passover celebration (9:1–14). The co-text to this instruction is, as we have seen, Exodus 12:1–30. Israel is to celebrate the Passover annually (14 Nisan / March–April). Passover commemorates Israel's deliverance from Egypt and draws God's people into a story of divine redemption. In its celebration Israel embraces a communal rhythm of remembrance and celebration. If God has delivered in the past, God is reliable to deliver in the present and the future!

Numbers 9 concludes with a description of the divine presence over the tabernacle in the form of a cloud by day and a pillar of fire by night (9:15–16). It retells the story of Exodus 40:34–38, where the cloud that covers the tabernacle is called the "glory of YHWH." The pillar of cloud and fire functions as a visible reminder of the presence of YHWH at the tabernacle: where YHWH's presence goes, the people should follow. The pillar of cloud and fire also visibly establishes a connection between heaven (the abode of God) and earth (the abode of humanity). When Israel meets with God at the tabernacle and follows divine direction in the cloud and fire, they engage the nexus point where heaven and earth meet. In this way, the transcendent God of creation meets with the people of Israel. The tabernacle, fire, and cloud make God visible and approachable so the people might meet with the divine. One scholar provocatively identifies the tabernacle as being like the body of God: where it goes, the people follow; it is the place where God appears and speaks and forgives and hears prayers and the

Figure 6.5. *The Israelites Led by the Pillar of Fire by Night* by William West (ca. 1845)

people see God.[2] Because of God's presence in the pillar of cloud and fire at the tabernacle, Israel has become "followers of a God who is on the move, in whose service true freedom and joy are to be found."[3]

These comments remind us that Israel is bound for a destination: the land God has promised them. In light of this, Numbers 10:1–10 details a seemingly insignificant detail: the silver trumpets. These are to be blown to bring the people of Israel together and then are blown to break camp and travel to the next destination. These trumpets are also blown at the appearance of an enemy threat and at the appointed festivals. When the trumpets are blown, God's people would be reminded of God's preparation for the journey of life, protection in times of trouble, and provision in times of celebration.

From Sinai to Kadesh, Wandering: Numbers 10:11–20:21

■ READ NUMBERS 16–20 ■

Immediately after the information regarding the silver trumpets, the narrative reports that Israel sets out in a prescribed manner. At the head of the procession is the tribe of Judah, leading the rest of the Israelites (Num. 10:14). The cloud lifts from the tabernacle, and Israel follows. Interestingly, whenever the cloud proceeded and the ark of the covenant processed, Moses was to offer this poetic proclamation: "Rise up, Lord! May your enemies be scattered; may your foes flee before you" (10:35). Whenever the cloud stopped and the ark stopped, Moses was to proclaim: "Return, Lord, to the countless thousands of Israel" (10:36).

Numbers 11–14 jars against the proclamation of divine presence and protection in Numbers 10:35–36 and exposes how quickly Israel devolves into complaint, jealousy, and rebellion despite divine provision. Numbers 11 recounts Israel's immediate complaint about their perceived misfortune and a desire for meat. They complain about the manna God had provided since Sinai (Exod. 16:31–35). "Manna" in Hebrew means "what is this stuff?" and was divine food provided in the wilderness. Instead, what Israel wants is the food they had in Egypt, or at least some meat to consume. By highlighting the food of Egypt, the narrative casts Israel's desires as looking back to the former way of life rather than focusing on the journey toward the promised land with God.

In Numbers we see a pattern of divine faithfulness (Num. 1–10) followed by Israel's ill-tempered behavior. The story of Numbers up to this point presents God as being for Israel, providing for Israel, and carrying Israel to the land sworn to the patriarchs. Following this provision, Numbers 11, 14, 16, and 21 reveal how complaint, grumbling, jealousy, and rebellion spring up among the Israelites (see table 6.1). In each of these incidents, Israel rebels against God and divine leadership. Numbers 11 exposes Israel's lack of faith in divine provision. Numbers 12 reveals jealousy and possibly racism infecting the leadership of Israel. Miriam and Aaron (Moses's siblings) complain that he has married a "Cushite" woman; Cush is often thought to be the southern region of Egypt, or even Ethiopia. Their complaint reveals a negative attitude toward Moses's wife because of her kinship group, her ethnicity, or the fact that she was a non-Israelite. This is why we say that possibly racism is shown against Moses and Zipporah.

Table 6.1. Israel's Rebellion against God

Numbers 11	Israel complains about their journey and their lack of meat.
Numbers 12	Miriam and Aaron become jealous of Moses and speak against Moses's wife, Zipporah, who is a Cushite and most likely a Black woman.
Numbers 14	After the spies survey the land, Israel decides not to enter and complains against God's provision of the promised land.
Numbers 16	Priests under Korah revolt against Moses and Aaron's divinely appointed leadership.
Numbers 20	Israel revolts against God because of a lack of water in the desert.
Numbers 21	Israel rebels against God because they are impatient to get to Canaan.

Numbers 14 reveals how the people doubt God's ability to carry them into Canaan safely. In Numbers 16, jealousy again marks the leadership of Israel; however, in this case the priestly tribe of Korah is guilty. The Korahites want to do what Moses and Aaron did rather than what God had provided for the Korahites to do.

Numbers 17–18 affirms Aaron's leadership, when his staff is brought before the ark of the covenant along with the other walking staffs of the leaders of Israel. The leader whom God chooses from the

Figure 6.6. *Moses and the Messengers from Canaan* by Giovanni Lanfranco (1621–24)

bunch would see his staff sprout. Aaron's staff buds, sprouts, and produces almonds. Interestingly, Aaron's priestly leadership serves as a warning against Israel's complaint and rebellion (17:10). With Aaron's leadership affirmed, Numbers 18 presents the roles and responsibilities of the priests, who will serve under Aaron.

Numbers 20 exposes Israel's lack of faith in divine provision for water. And finally, Numbers 21 reveals a fundamental lack of trust in God's way and God's timing as Israel becomes impatient following God's presence in the cloud and pillar of fire, desiring to arrive in Canaan on a quicker route and timeline.

Each rebellion reveals a lack of trust and understanding of YHWH, Israel's deliverer, protector, guide, and provider. Of course, Israel's story serves as a model for the human story. Although Exodus and Numbers both display YHWH's unrivaled care and protection for Israel, Israel displays a tendency to forget God's beneficence and defense. At every turn, God provides water in the desert, food in the wilderness, protection from enemies, and pathways on which they can walk in their journey to the land of promise.

Figure 6.7. *Moses and His Ethiopian Wife Sephora* by Jacob Jordaens (1650)

Figure 6.8. *Aaron's Rod in Bloom* by a master of the Marienkirche Stained-Glass Panels, Germany, at the State Hermitage Museum, St. Petersburg (late fourteenth century)

It is no wonder, in light of the rebellion and subsequent divine punishments and death in Numbers 11–20, that Numbers 19 depicts a law about purification from corpse contamination. Of course, purification from corpse contamination is necessary because death is the ultimate agent that defiles Israelites. Death is diametrically opposed to YHWH, the God of life. Contamination from being exposed to a corpse defiles Israelites, preventing them from worshiping at the sanctuary. (For reference, see fig. 5.4 in our chapter on Leviticus.)

Purification from corpse contamination comes by sprinkling ashes of a perfect red cow on affected people, places, and things. In Numbers 19, Eleazar, son of the high priest, accompanies a group outside the camp of Israel, and they kill the red cow. They burn up the cow outside the camp— her body, entrails, fat, kidneys, blood, and even dung—everything. Red cedar, red yarn, and hyssop (a reddish plant) also are thrown into the fire. The ashes of these objects are deposited in a clean place outside the camp. The second half of Numbers 19 presents three cases in which these ashes would be used to purify from contamination. The first case (vv. 11–13) is general and prescribes how the ashes should be manipulated whenever anybody touches the corpse of a human being. The second case is more specific, detailing the procedure when anyone touches a corpse in a tent, presumably *inside* the camp. The third case portrays the procedure when anyone comes across a corpse *outside* the camp—in a field, a battlefield, or a graveyard.

The ritual cleanses from such exposure. The affected Israelites would present themselves to a priest, who would take ashes of the red cow, mix them with running water (not cistern water, but spring water or river water, any source of water that flows naturally) and then dip a hyssop branch into the paste and sprinkle it on the affected person, tent, open pots, furnishings, and so on. The affected person undergoes this sprinkling on the third and seventh days. If the sprinkling is not done, the person will be sent out of the camp because they have defiled God's sanctuary.

The problem of death reminds God's people that something is terribly wrong among them. Death is the ultimate disorder for Israel, both ritually and existentially, perpetually casting its shadow over them. However, Numbers 19 testifies to God's gracious provision to care for his people so they might relate with the divine at the sanctuary, even in the face of death. Without the ritual, impurity would prevent communion with YHWH at the sanctuary. By giving this law to Israel, God provides more than food, water, and guidance in the wilderness. YHWH offers a pathway to continued communion, even in the face of death.

The problem of death persists in Numbers 20, as does the persistent challenge of rebellion against God's word. In Numbers 20:6–13, Moses and Aaron disobey the Lord's command to order the rock to produce water for the people. Instead of commanding the rock, Moses strikes it with his rod (v. 11) as he had done at Meribah (Exod. 17:1–7). This disobedience against God's clear command is equated with unbelief, a failure to honor God as holy before his people, and then rebellion against God's word. This lack of faith and rebellion against God's word threatens the entire camp as it infringes on the very sanctity of God. Because Moses and Aaron did not trust God, the brothers are given a terrible sentence: they will not enter God's promised land. Aaron dies almost immediately after this act of faithlessness (Num. 20:23–29). The rationale given for his death appears in verse 24: "because you [plural, indicating both Moses and Aaron] rebelled against my word concerning the waters of Meribah" (AT).[4] Aaron's punishment in the narrative foreshadows Moses's coming death, an event explicitly declared in Deuteronomy and related directly to the incident at Meribah (Deut. 32:50–51). For the reader, this narrative explication of disobedience against God's clear command serves as a powerful *negative* example, certainly for the leaders of Israel but also for the entire populace.

From Kadesh to the Plains of Moab: Numbers 20:22–36:13

■ READ NUMBERS 21–24 ■

Divine discipline for Israel climaxes in Numbers 21. God's people experience victory over the Canaanite king of Arad (anticipatory of Israel's possession of the land of Canaan), and then they complain against God when the divine presence leads them around Edom on the way to the promised land. Preferring their own timing and route instead of God's (presumably the pillar of cloud and fire still guide them), they complain about God leading them to die in the desert when really all God has done is to provide food and water, protection and provision in the wilderness. Their impatience and complaint are met with divine anger and punishment.

God sends poisonous serpents that bite many Israelites, and they die. Confessing their sin, they ask God for deliverance from the snakes. Moses prays for Israel, and God directs Moses to construct a snake made of copper (perhaps bronze), set it on a pole, and then erect the snake in the sight of Israel. When Israelites were bitten by the serpents, they would look at the serpent standard and live (Num. 21:1–9). 𐤔 𐤏 𐤔

Figure 6.9. Serpentine cross sculpture on Mount Nebo, Jordan

Numbers 1–21 provides several examples of Israel's complaining against God in the wilderness. When these are compared with complaint

CANONICAL CONNECTIONS

The Bronze Serpent and Jesus

The Gospel writer John draws an analogy between Jesus's crucifixion and the story of the bronze serpent in Numbers 21: "Just as Moses lifted up the snake in the wilderness, so the Son of Man must be lifted up, that everyone who believes may have eternal life in him" (John 3:14–15).

HISTORICAL MATTERS

Ancient Images, Talismans, and Amulets

God's command in Numbers 21 about the bronze snake may seem strange to us, but in the ancient world people looked at or wore images, talismans, and amulets to be healed. In Egypt amulets of serpents were meant to channel the power of the snake or protect against the power of a snake bite. Images, amulets, and talismans appear from 3000 to 300 BC, indicating the persistence of the idea.

From a biblical perspective, creatures do not have power to heal or stave off death: only Israel's creator holds that power. However, Numbers 21 resonates with the notion that looking at a totem staves off death and divine punishment. Israel's looking at the bronze snake is an act of obedience and deep faith in YHWH: Would they obey YHWH's command to look at the copper snake and live . . . or not?

CANONICAL CONNECTIONS

Copper Serpents and Golden Mice

The story of the Philistines capturing the ark of the covenant in 1 Samuel 5–6 says that God unleashes a plague of tumors on the Philistines for their action (1 Sam. 5:9, 12). The Philistines remedy their affliction by crafting five golden tumors and five golden mice, believing this costly talisman would ward off the tumors. The golden

tumors and golden mice represent the five major cities of Philistia (Ekron, Gaza, Ashdod, Ashkelon, and Gath) and their leadership and serve as a "guilt offering" (6:4) to spare them further death. It is easy to recognize the affinity between this story and Numbers 21 in their shared use of talismans counteracting mortal threat.

	Numbers 21	1 Samuel 5–6
Metal	Copper	Gold
Object	Serpent	Mice and tumors
Offending nation	Israel	Philistia
Manipulation of talisman	Placed on a pole	Placed within a box on a cart
Offending party action	Look at the serpent	Carry the box with objects through Philistia back to the Israelite camp
Intended effect	Ameliorate divine wrath and preserve Israelite lives	Ameliorate divine wrath and preserve Philistine lives

speeches in Exodus, one notes a pattern of Israel's complaints and God's responses in the books. 📖 ✝

This final section in the book depicts an extraordinary affirmation of God's blessing of Israel despite their rebellion, particularly in the story of Balaam and Israel (Num. 22–24). In this passage, Balaam is hired by Balak, king of Moab, to curse Israel. Balaam offers four oracles, and instead of cursing Israel, he blesses them. Balaam's story of blessing Israel draws the reader back to the priestly blessing of Numbers 6, reminding us that God's

Complaint Speech in the Pentateuch

The theme of complaint looms large in Exodus and Numbers. The people "complain" or "grumble" or "weep" about their situation. They lodge their complaint against Moses and/or Aaron, and then God responds. In Exodus the response is positive, but in Numbers, the divine response is negative: God judges Israel's complaint in Numbers where he did not in Exodus. Numbers 14 goes so far as to indicate the first generation would not enter the promised land, and Numbers 20 reveals Moses will not either. Everyone from the generation of Moses, Aaron, and Miriam will die in the wilderness. The second generation will enter, and God's purposes will be accomplished with Israel through that generation.

	People "complain"	People speak to Moses/Aaron	Speech to Moses/God	Speech to Moses/Aaron equated to speaking to God	Positive divine response	Negative divine response (punishment)	God's anger burns
Exodus 4:14					X		X
Exodus 5:22–23					X		
Exodus 6:30					X		
Exodus 16:2–3	X	X		X	X		
Exodus 17:3	X	X		X	X		
Numbers 11:1–3	X	X		X		X (God's fire consumes outlying parts of the camp)	X
Numbers 11:4–35	No, but weeping over lack of meat	X		X		X (plague)	X
Numbers 14; esp. 14:2, 27, 36	X	X		X		X (pronouncement of death of first generation)	
Numbers 16; esp. 16:11, 41	X	X		X		X (plague)	
Numbers 20:1–13	X	X		X		X (Moses/Aaron disallowed into promised land)	X
Numbers 21:4–9	No, but "spoke against"		X			X (snakes; death of the people)	

desire for his people is blessing, not cursing. The text indicates those who embrace Israel's God will experience blessing as well. On a full-scale reading of Genesis–Deuteronomy, this focus on divine blessing of Israel makes sense. God blessing a particular people (Israel) is the divine means of blessing the universal (all nations), as detailed in Genesis 12:3: "I will bless those who bless you, and whoever curses you I will curse; and all the peoples of the earth will be blessed through you."

Interestingly, even after YHWH provides blessing for Israel, they rebel against him through idolatry at Baal Peor (Num. 25). Idolatry in this passage is described as "yoking" oneself to another deity instead of YHWH, a unique expression here (25:3). One person who rejects such activity is Phinehas, Eleazar's son. He is the grandson of Aaron and therefore a priest. The text says he impales his fellow Israelite and a Midianite woman as an act of zeal for God. While it is difficult for modern readers to hear, the text

---

THEOLOGICAL ISSUES

Is God Capricious?

In light of the divine responses to Israel's complaints, one may think God is capricious: one cannot know if God will be angry or gracious, so complain at your peril! However, a close reading of the complaints in Exodus and Numbers reveals something startling. God's different responses to complaint between Exodus 15–18 and Numbers 10–25 are explainable by the covenant established between God and Israel. Before Sinai, God's people had not received God's instruction or God's continued protection. But once the covenant with YHWH is established, defiant sin against God's provision and instruction—typified by complaints in Numbers—demands divine judgment.[c] Numbers shows us when complaint is inappropriate in the life of faith: when complaint means rejecting the responsibilities of the covenant relationship with God.

THEOLOGICAL ISSUES

Messiah in Balaam's Blessing

In Balaam's blessing, Numbers 24:17–19 depicts a "star" (24:17) and "ruler" (24:19) that will come from Israel in the distant future. This prophecy is matched with Jacob's blessing and the rise of Judah in Genesis 49:9–12, where the "scepter will not depart Judah" (49:10). In other words, these texts speak to a coming ruler for Israel from the tribe of Judah. Later Jewish tradition (e.g., Dead Sea Scrolls [Testimonia (4QTest) 9–13]; Targum Onqelos) also considered Numbers 24:17–19 messianic. Christian tradition viewed the messianic identity to refer to none other than Jesus the Messiah.[d]

HISTORICAL MATTERS

Balaam and Deir 'Alla

Balaam, a non-Israelite prophet, appears in archaeological evidence from Deir 'Alla, where an eighth-century-BC inscription depicts the actions of Balaam, son of Beor, a "seer."[e] Balaam undergoes a vision in the night in which the gods come to him and he sees a divine being like El, the Canaanite high god of the pantheon. The vision describes impending doom, and upon hearing it Balaam weeps, fasts, and proclaims to the people the vision.[f] Balaam's message presents a dark and topsy-turvy world of doom. In their power the gods have decreed an inversion of the natural order of things, and Balaam must communicate this dire news. There is mention of action against the king ("I have punished the king"), but the identity of the king or his people remains unclear. This dark and ominous word of doom comes to Balaam unsolicited. The text says, "The gods came to him during the night," and he must face their word of doom. In the night vision, El sits as the high god of the pantheon of "gods," and the text indicates that Balaam responds to the entire weight of their message.

indicates his action prevents further destruction among his people, and so it was a protective action. It is remembered as such, for instance, in Psalm 106:30.

After recounting the disaster at Baal Peor, the text turns to the second census in the book, indicating a new start for Israel. This census focuses on those who are twenty years old and older, "everyone in Israel able to go to war" (Num. 26:2 NRSV). Those who would die in the wilderness are not included in this census, which attends to Israel's second generation, those who will take the land.

Figure 6.10. Hathor amulet (ca. 1086–332 BC)

Chapter 27 reinforces this emphasis on the second generation and the new focus for Israel with the inheritance allowance for the daughters of Zelophehad (27:1–11) and the appointment of Joshua as Moses's successor (27:12–23). The text describes a situation in which the father of the family group (Zelophehad) dies, and his heirs are daughters rather than sons. God grants each family group and tribe parcels of land as a divine gift, as is described in Joshua 13–21. The problem, of course, is in the fact that the patrimonial inheritance of the land goes through the lineage of sons in the ancient world. But here, the daughters of Zelophehad appeal to Moses and request that in a situation in which the patriarch dies, land can be given to daughters rather than divided up among other tribes. In this ancient patriarchal society, the text speaks to the inheritance rights of women as they go into the promised land, which represents a democratizing tendency compared to Israel's ancient Near Eastern neighbors. This emphasis recurs at the end of the book, which returns to the daughters of Zelophehad, providing instruction for inheritance rights as God's people enter the land (36:1–13).

Joshua's succession (27:12–23) reminds Israel that Moses will die outside the land and new leadership is needed, but more than that point, it indicates that God's people are moving out of the wilderness. The book concludes on the brink of the promised land, on the plains of Moab just opposite the city of Jericho (33:48). Israel is reminded to live as a worshiping community, with attention given to how to make offerings to God, celebrate the Passover, and celebrate the festival calendar (chaps. 28–29). Further, after a summary review of the wilderness travels in Numbers 33, Moses instructs Israel how to be a people who follow God's commandments as they enter the land and set up its administration (chaps. 30, 32, 34–35). The book reveals how this worshiping, obedient community will live in conflict with the nations, indicated by the war with Midian (chap. 31) but also with themselves, indicated by the instruction regarding cities of refuge and instructions concerning blood vengeance.

Numbers 35:1–8 designates forty-eight cities throughout the land to the Levites, because they have no tribal allotment given by God. These cities, then, would provide homes for the Levites as they ministered to the people of God. Numbers 35:9–34 describes the first avenger (not Captain America!)—the "avenger of blood." This passage also stipulates that six of the forty-eight Levitical cities would be designated as "cities of refuge," which afforded safe harbor for those who accidentally killed another Israelite without malicious intent (what today we sometimes call "manslaughter"), protecting them from blood vengeance. Otherwise, ancient practices allowed the bereaved family to kill the offending person (blood vengeance) by means of the "avenger of blood." A life for a life, otherwise known as lex talionis, a law of retribution that emphasizes equal measure where the punishment fits the crime: "an eye for an eye, a tooth for a tooth" (cf. Exod. 21:23–24; Lev. 24:17–20; Deut. 19:21). Cities of refuge also protected the offending party and their family against the avenger of blood going beyond the law of equal measure. For instance, the avenger of blood could not execute the offending party's entire family for inadvertent manslaughter. So, the cities of refuge offer divine compassion alongside divine justice for God's people.

Implementation—Reading Numbers as Christian Scripture Today

Israel has journeyed with God in the wilderness and approaches the promised land with threats of division and death from both within and without. Their ancient journey mirrors the modern life journey today as we live before God—*coram Deo*. In its presentation of Israel's life, and thereby our own journeys, Numbers concludes with extraordinary insight: although God's people are entering God's land under God's rule, their entry is not idealistic or idyllic. Numbers reveals life is neither idealistic nor fatalistic. On the one hand, the journey with God in the wilderness of the present world is marked with both brokenness and blessing. There is brokenness today in the sense of leadership failures, just as there was among the Israelites (Num. 20). Jealousy, racism, and envy transpire in the present world, just as they did in the broken community of Israel. Numbers portrays the real world rather than fantasy or idealism.

And yet, on the other hand, amid the brokenness Israel still journeys with God. Blessing is YHWH's

THEOLOGICAL ISSUES

Coram Deo

This Latin phrase emerges from Jerome's Latin translation of the Bible for the common good, called the Vulgate (ca. AD 405). Literally, *coram Deo* means "in the presence of God" or "before God." Its meaning is captured in Psalm 56:13: "For you have delivered me from death and my feet from stumbling, that I may walk before God in the light of life." Walking before God (*coram Deo*) is what it means for Israel to live as God's people in the promised land. More fundamentally, *coram Deo* is a fitting way to understand what it means to be human.

desire for Israel. The Aaronic blessing for the people in Numbers 6:22–27 testifies to the blessing of the created world (even in the wilderness) because God has made it so. It is YHWH's desire to continue the blessing of Abraham (Gen. 12:2–3) through the family of Israel. Israel is called to embrace divine blessing genuinely, even if they wander from YHWH's call. Joshua's and Caleb's devotion to YHWH (as well as that of Phinehas in Num. 25) in the face of opposition reinforces the genuine choice to follow YHWH's call for blessing.

Numbers cannot be described as fatalistic. Although Israel has rebelled in their journey in the wilderness and the first generation dies as a result, the opportunity for divine blessing is always available and open for the second generation. Still, God's desire for blessing is balanced with the recurrent rebellion and complaint of Israel in the wilderness, especially among the first generation. Corporately Israel embraces a broken blessing rather than a fully orbed faith in God's ability to care for, provide for, sustain, and guide them.

Do we, as modern readers, fare any better? Life before God is marked by lack of trust in divine guidance, provision, and care, even if God has demonstrated that all are secured and available to us. The question, then, turns on who provides life for ancient and modern pilgrims on the journey of faith.

Numbers also lifts up YHWH the God of life. YHWH gives and sustains life; this is particularly displayed in Numbers 19's law of the ritual for

purification from corpse contamination. On the one hand, this passage presents theology beautifully: YHWH expresses passion for life and humanity's problem with death. On the other hand, we must also say that the law itself anticipates an ultimate solution to the problem of death. The law was given in a world in which people could understand the Lord. Sacrifices and ceremonies like Israel's abounded in the ancient Near East, but this law does not prescribe a solution that provides an end to death itself. Sprinkling always needed to be given, and sin offerings had to continually be burned. The law provides symbols for dealing with death, but it does not provide an ultimate response for the *defeat of death*. But God knew that, and the law presupposes that. The law *anticipates* God's final response to death and its final defeat.

KEY VERSES IN NUMBERS

- Take a census of the whole Israelite community by their clans and families, listing every man by name, one by one. 1:2
- The LORD bless you and keep you; the LORD make his face shine on you and be gracious to you; the LORD turn his face toward you and give you peace. 6:24–26
- I see him, but not now; I behold him, but not near. A star will come out of Jacob; a scepter will rise out of Israel. He will crush the foreheads of Moab, the skulls of all the people of Sheth. 24:17

Christian Reading Questions

1. How does the idea of "journeying" with God help us understand the importance of Numbers?
2. Why does God get angry with the Israelites when they complain in Numbers but not get angry with them in Exodus?
3. How does the theme of divine blessing appear in Numbers, and why is it important?
4. How can we understand Numbers as Christian Scripture?

CHAPTER SEVEN

Deuteronomy

Orientation

God's people have made their way to the borders of the promised land. They stand on the plains of Moab looking westward across the Jordan River into the land that God swore to give Abraham, Isaac, and Jacob. This second generation is at a moment of great decision: Will they step into the promise of God's best for them, or will they be like the first generation who

LITERARY NOTES

The Structure of Deuteronomy

A complex book, Deuteronomy can be understood as (1) a set of three discourses by Moses and (2) as a distinctive covenant between God and Israel. On the first reading, the three speeches are identifiable by the particular phrases in the book:

- Discourse 1: Deuteronomy 1:6–4:43
  - This discourse is marked with an introduction: "Beyond the Jordan in the land of Moab, Moses undertook to expound this law as follows . . ." (1:5 NRSV).
  - Moses recounts the story of Israel in the wilderness and reminds God's people both of their rebellion and sin and of God's miraculous provision in leading them to the plains of Moab, where they receive Moses's instruction. In this compressed retelling of the book of Numbers, Israel is reminded of who they are and, more importantly, who God is and who he has made them to be: his special people chosen to be a blessing to the world.
- Discourse 2: Deuteronomy 4:44–28:68
  - This discourse is introduced by the phrase, "Now this is the law that Moses set before the Israelites . . ." (4:44 NRSV).

- Moses discloses to the people the laws, statutes, and ordinances they are to obey as they live as God's people in God's land under God's rule. This section takes the form of stipulations of an ancient covenant with God. The exact form of the covenant is similar to some ancient suzerain-vassal treaties in Assyria and (earlier) Hittite treaties. In the covenant, God serves as the suzerain who initiates the relationship with Israel, and Israel is the vassal who commits themselves to love their Lord.
- Discourse 3: Deuteronomy 29–31
  - This discourse is introduction by the phrase, "These are the words of the covenant that the LORD commanded Moses to make with the Israelites in the land of Moab, in addition to the covenant that he had made with them at Horeb. Moses summoned all Israel and said to them . . ." (29:1–2 NRSV).
  - This final speech closes the sermons of Moses. In this final speech, one sees the succession of Joshua as the leader of Israel after Moses.
- Conclusion: Deuteronomy 32–34
  - The book concludes with the Song of Moses (32:1–43) and Moses's final benediction and death (chaps. 33–34).

Vassal Treaties

As a covenant text, Deuteronomy exhibits similarities to ancient Near Eastern vassal treaties, in which the greater party enjoins a lesser party to fidelity. There is debate as to whether Deuteronomy follows ancient second-millennium-BC Hittite suzerain-vassal treaties or later seventh-century Assyrian vassal treaties like those of Assyrian king Esarhaddon (ca. 672 BC). For our part, we recognize that Deuteronomy exhibits characteristics consonant with the Hittite treaties, but we recognize as well that the vassal treaties of Esarhaddon share language with Deuteronomy 6, 13, and 28.

Vassal Treaties and Deuteronomy

Both Hittite treaties and the Assyrian vassal treaties of Esarhaddon impose covenant stipulations on the vassal party. Several elements are standard in this form:

1. *Title/preamble:* names the parties involved (Deut. 1:1–5).
2. *Historical prologue:* traces past relations between the parties (present in Deut. 1:6–4:49 but absent in the vassal treaty of Esarhaddon).
3. *Stipulations:* laws or requirements given by the suzerain to be kept by the vassal as the terms of the covenant (Deut. 5–26).
4. *Deposit and reading:* the deposition of the covenant in an appropriate place as well as the periodic reading of the covenant (deposit: Deut. 31:9, 24–26; reading: Deut. 31:10–13).
5. *Witnesses:* those who attend the making of the treaty/covenant (Deut. 30:19; 31:26; 32:1).
6. *Sanctions:* blessings and curses to be imposed by the superior party, including revocation of the covenant, should the vassal fail to keep its terms. This type of treaty/covenant contains a list of blessings and curses attendant to its ratification and maintenance by the vassal (Deut. 27, 28, 30).

missed their inheritance? Moses calls God's people to choose faithfulness to God rather than shrink away from faithfulness. The book of Deuteronomy is that call. 📖 🏺 🏺

Deuteronomy shares characteristics with ancient Near Eastern covenants and likely should be understood as a covenant text that *reaffirms* the covenant at Sinai (Exod. 19–24). But if that is true, we must consider again what a covenant is.

The language of covenant is strange, and perhaps we understand it like a contract. Contracts are arrangements between two parties in which goods and services are agreed on and supplied, with certain stipulations detailed "in the fine print" (e.g., pay money and receive a certain service). For instance, consider a smartphone contract. Someone who purchases a smartphone from a provider goes to the store, sets up a contract, pays the bill, promises to continue paying the monthly bill for service, and then leaves with a new phone.

Prior to entering the store, the buyer had no preexisting relationship with the provider. The contract establishes the relationship. If the smartphone owner does not pay the monthly service charges, then the contract is forfeited. The services to the smartphone are terminated for good. The relationship, as defined by the contract, is over.

Osama Shukir Muhammed Amin FRCP(Glasg) / CC BY-SA 4.0 / Wikimedia Commons

Figure 7.1. A clay tablet portion of the Akkadian Kadesh Treaty (ca. 1269 BC), Boğazköy, Turkey. Museum of the Ancient Orient, Istanbul, Turkey.

Is this how Israel's covenant with God works? In short, no. God's covenants are not contracts. Covenants that are made by God are different from a smartphone contract for many reasons. We identify just three. First, God's covenants are not impersonal business contracts. The covenant with Israel is

Figure 7.2. The plains of Moab

personal and familial: it is built on a relationship with Abraham and the patriarchs. This covenant incorporates Israel into the family of God. Second, God's covenant with Israel is guaranteed by God himself rather than Israel's fidelity (or lack thereof). God swears to keep the covenant because God initiated the covenant and ensures its success. Third, God's covenants are rooted in his creative and gracious action. Israel did not earn their covenant status due to their rights, power, or holiness (Deut. 7:7–8; 9:5–7). Rather, it is because of God's gracious and creative action that Israel stands before God to be a covenant people.

Exploration—Reading Deuteronomy

Rehearsing Israel's Story: Deuteronomy 1:1–4:43

■ READ DEUTERONOMY 1–4 ■

The opening chapters of Deuteronomy rehearse Israel's journey from Sinai or, as Deuteronomy identifies the mountain, "Horeb" (1:6), to the plains of Moab. Moses recapitulates the story of Israel to great effect:

Deuteronomy 1:9–18	=	Exodus 18:13–27
Deuteronomy 1:19–46	=	Numbers 13–14
Deuteronomy 2:1–7	=	Numbers 20:14–21
Deuteronomy 2:8–3:20	=	Numbers 21:21–35
Deuteronomy 3:21–29	=	Numbers 25:1–9

At each turn, we see God's faithfulness despite human waywardness. Israel's infidelity to God at Kadesh Barnea and Baal Peor prevents Moses and the first generation of Israel from going into the land (1:37–38; 3:26–27).

The second generation will go in (1:35–36, 38). Because of unfaithfulness in the wilderness, the generation that experienced the deliverance from Egypt will die out. Moses calls on the second generation to obey the demands of their covenant relationship (4:5–8).

Israel's obedience in their covenant relationship was to be a beacon of wisdom to the surrounding nations and evidence of the power of the God they serve. In this way, Israel's covenant blessing by God would become an invitation to the nations, a theme that the prophets will later develop further (cf. Isa. 2:2–4; Mic. 4:1–5).

Covenant obedience requires allegiance to God *alone*. Deuteronomy 4:15–40 warns Israel against worshiping other deities as they enter the promised land, and they should particularly avoid worshiping the heavens or hand-fashioned idols. In Israelite understanding, the work of human hands (idols) or creation (sun, moon, and stars) cannot be God! There is only *one* God, the one who made the heavens and the earth (Gen. 1). Deuteronomy 4:35–40 summarizes Israel's covenant obligations to their divine deliverer and creator. The one who made heaven and earth is the one who calls Israel to keep God's decrees and commandments so that they might live long in the land.

The Stipulations, Decrees, and Laws: Deuteronomy 4:44–28:68

■ READ DEUTERONOMY 5–11; 16–18; 23–26 ■

In the second discourse, Moses recounts the stipulations, decrees, and laws for Israel as they live in the land that YHWH provides for them. What follows in Deuteronomy 5:6–21 is the Ten Commandments with some modification from Exodus 20:1–18. First, God speaks from the fire on the mountain in Exodus, whereas in Deuteronomy Moses speaks to Israel from the plains of Moab. There are other differences as well. Both accounts offer

CANONICAL CONNECTIONS

The Sabbath Command in Exodus and Deuteronomy

Exodus 20:8–11	Deuteronomy 5:12–15
"Remember the Sabbath day by keeping it holy. Six days you shall labor and do all your work, but the seventh day is a sabbath to the LORD your God. On it you shall not do any work, neither you, nor your son or daughter, nor your male or female servant, nor your animals, nor any foreigner residing in your towns. For in six days the LORD made the heavens and the earth, the sea, and all that is in them, but he rested on the seventh day. Therefore the LORD blessed the Sabbath day and made it holy."	"Observe the Sabbath day by keeping it holy, as the LORD your God has commanded you. Six days you shall labor and do all your work, but the seventh day is a sabbath to the LORD your God. On it you shall not do any work, neither you, nor your son or daughter, nor your male or female servant, nor your ox, your donkey or any of your animals, nor any foreigner residing in your towns, so that your male and female servants may rest, as you do. Remember that you were slaves in Egypt and that the LORD your God brought you out of there with a mighty hand and an outstretched arm. Therefore the LORD your God has commanded you to observe the Sabbath day."

the same ten commands, but Deuteronomy significantly expands the fourth command (Sabbath). The rationale for the command in Exodus derives from God's role as creator. The rationale for the command in Deuteronomy derives from God's role as deliverer. 📜

Repeating the Ten Commandments in Deuteronomy enables Israel to reflect on their covenantal story in the economy of the human story. God's people have been delivered from Egypt to be a blessing to the whole of humanity.

God's work with Israel, retold in Deuteronomy, presents the divine response to the problem of the sinful world expounded in Genesis 1–11. The creator God and covenant Lord calls and causes Israel to thrive and multiply whether in Egypt, in the wilderness, or in the land of promise, echoing and fulfilling the command to humanity at creation, "Be fruitful and multiply" (Gen. 1:28 NRSV).

Deuteronomy's language reminds Israel that *God* has multiplied them (Deut. 1:9–10; 6:3; 7:13; 8:1, 13; 11:21; 13:17; 30:16). God's gift of "multiplication" for Israel is such that their number might be compared to the number of the "stars in the sky" (1:9–10; 10:22), a phrase that echoes the divine promise to the patriarchs (Gen. 15:5; 22:17; 26:4). Israel will be God's agent of blessing and multiplication. The story of a broken world will be countered with the story of God's work in Israel.

God is Israel's deliverer from that "iron furnace" of Egypt (Deut. 4:20 NASB), which is also described as a "house of slavery" (5:6; 6:12; 8:14; 13:5, 10 NASB). God sustains and preserves this people in spite of their sin and rebellion and gives them life by miraculous provision of food and water in the wilderness (8:15–16). God prepares a place in which they shall live (6:10–11; 7:1–2). God gives Israel the law, by which they shall live long in the land as they love the Lord their God with all their hearts (6:5).

The command to love in Deuteronomy 6:4–5 is known as the Shema and great command: "Hear, O Israel! YHWH is our God, YHWH alone! You shall love YHWH your God with all your heart and with all your soul and with all your strength" (AT). The command reminds Israel that obedience to God (by obeying the law) is not a heavy burden; it is an act of love and covenant devotion.

The Shema reminds Israel that God alone is worthy of worship. No other rival deities are worthy of worship. In light of the problems Israel has faced thus

Public domain / Wikimedia Commons

Figure 7.3. Frontispiece for the book of Deuteronomy, folio 50 recto of the Bible of San Paolo fuori le Mura

far with idolatry, reminding Israel of this fact is crucial. Because of YH-WH's covenant commitment, Israel is required to avoid all idolatry and sin and stay true to their covenant commitment in an act of covenant devotion: love. Their devotion should penetrate every aspect of their communal life: heart, soul, and strength.

Deuteronomy 6:4 details YHWH's commitment to Israel, reminding them of what he has done for them by delivering them. Deuteronomy 6:5 then expresses how Israel should respond to YHWH's commitment to them: God's people are commanded to love YHWH in all of life. This love is not limited to an emotion; rather, to "love" YHWH corresponds to a total devotion to Israel's God in the covenant bond. In this way, the Shema

THEOLOGICAL ISSUES

The Shema and the Uniqueness of God

Deuteronomy 6:4–5 is a profound theological disclosure of Israel's God. Who God is demands Israel's attentiveness, thus the command to "hear, O Israel!" The Shema appears with two parallel verbal commands that disclose the identity of YHWH and that define the shape of Israel's obedience to YHWH. In this way, the Shema can be arranged poetically:

Hear, O Israel!
    YHWH is our God,
    YHWH alone!
You shall love YHWH your God

with all your heart
and with all your soul
and with all your strength. (AT)

The reality of God is disclosed in the two lines that describe God: YHWH is Israel's ("our") God, and YHWH alone serves this capacity as the covenant God of Israel. English translations differ in their rendering of the last half of Deuteronomy 6:4 because of the flexibility of the Hebrew language. It can be translated in several ways: "YHWH is our God, YHWH is One" or "YHWH, our God, YHWH is One." The most likely candidate for translation of the Hebrew, however, is how we have rendered it: "YHWH is our God, YHWH alone!"

RECEPTION HISTORY

The Greek Translation of the Shema

Greek translations of Deuteronomy, sometimes called the Septuagint, render the Shema as follows: "Hear, O Israel: The Lord our God is one Lord. And you shall love the Lord your God with the whole of your mind and with the whole of your soul and with the whole of your power" (6:4–5 NETS).

The accent of the Greek translation is on the "oneness" of God, highlighting the monotheistic reality of Israel's God. Moreover, the divine name YHWH is translated by the generic title "Lord" in the Greek (kyrios).

CANONICAL CONNECTIONS

Deuteronomy 6:4 and 1 Corinthians 8:4

Paul uses the Shema in 1 Corinthians 8:4 to argue that food offered to idols is not a problem in reality: "About eating food sacrificed to idols, then, we know that 'an idol is nothing in the world,' and that 'there is no God but one'" (1 Cor. 8:4 CSB). Paul highlights the uniqueness of Israel's God, as well as the demands God's call makes on Jesus's disciples. For the sake of argument, Paul says that even if there were other gods (there are none), any supposed rival deities would not be what God the Father and the Lord Jesus Christ (who are "one," echoing Deut. 6:4) are in actuality: God. Paul links God

the Father and the Lord Jesus Christ, recognizing Jesus and God are the same God: "For Paul, Jesus is not just simply equated with Yhwh without remainder; rather, Jesus is somehow the unique manifestation of Yhwh (Israel's one god)."[a] Because of this, food offered to idols is not offered to real deities. Paul then uses Deuteronomy throughout the chapter to reinforce covenant obedience, avoiding sin and immorality, and devotion to God alone. The echoes of Deuteronomy's theology resound in Paul's teaching.[b]

prioritizes the grace of YHWH but necessitates and envisions human commitment to YHWH as the appropriate response to divine grace.

Deuteronomy 7–8 instructs Israel on how they should immediately go in and drive out the nations that inhabit the land. Further, when they arrive in the land, they are not to forget YHWH and then fall into idolatry. Deuteronomy 9 rehearses the story at Sinai and its call for Israel to remember God. In worshiping the golden calf at Sinai, Israel forgot God and threatened their very existence. Only Moses's mediation preserved them. Moses reminds the people that God gave him tablets of instruction (Deut. 10), and then he again calls Israel to devotion, to love the Lord with their heart and soul and to observe the laws that God gives for their own good (10:12–13).

To fear God means demonstrating awe and devotion to God in all of life. It means walking with God, loving God, and serving God with everything that one has. Israel loves YHWH by observing the divine instructions. These commands are not burdens; rather, they are for Israel's own good. This call for love and obedience is given further accent in Deuteronomy 11. There, as in Leviticus 26, blessing lay before Israel for obedience and a curse for disobedience.

Specific stipulations or "laws" described in general terms in Deuteronomy 6–11 appear throughout chapters 12–26. The laws complement what is in Exodus–Numbers and, in some cases, diverge from them. Deuteronomy envisages community life lived *in the promised land* rather than in the wilderness, which could account for some discrepancies between laws.

LITURGICAL FRAMEWORK OF WORSHIP AND REJOICING

These chapters contain a set of instructions (torah) that Israel is to embody as they live in God's land under God's rule. This way of life could be seen as a kind of legalistic burden, but it should not be. Language of "rejoicing" before the Lord recurs in the legal material in Deuteronomy 12–26 (see esp. 12:7, 12, 18; 14:26; 16:11, 14; 26:11; cf. 27:7). In fact, Deuteronomy 12:7 and 26:11 bookend the legal material with instruction for rejoicing and celebration before YHWH. This framing of "rejoicing" language tells us about Israel's life and Israel's law: they are something to be celebrated! With the frame of 12:7 and 26:11, and the "rejoicing" language throughout

Theology of the Land in Deuteronomy

Deuteronomy's moral vision is bound to the land, particularly the land of Canaan. The land is a gift given by YHWH (Deut. 9:6; 27:3), and Israel is the steward of that gift. Israel's privilege and moral responsibility are to live well in God's land. In this sense, Deuteronomy's moral vision is more than an abstract set of ethics—it is always "earthy." How Israel farms, how they harvest, how they treat the most vulnerable within their society, and how they worship are all part of the moral vision of Israel. In short, Israel is to steward the land as a gift and the place of divine abundance. However, the land becomes a threat for Israel when they compromise faith and disobey YHWH's commands, failing in the moral vision the land demands. If Israel fails in their stewardship of people and place, the land becomes a place uninhabitable, and Israel is exiled from it (28:15–68).

the legal material, it becomes clear that, far from being a burden, God's law is good, and it is a delight!

Israel's view of life is shaped by a liturgical framework of worship and rejoicing, and within that worshipful community the law in Deuteronomy 12–26 addresses different facets of communal living. This life includes regular communal celebrations and proper worship (chaps. 14–16); authority structures present in society, such as **judges** and rulers (chaps. 16–18); laws regarding human relationships and warfare (chaps. 19–22); instruction on sexuality (chap. 22); and various laws dealing with other aspects of community life (chaps. 23–26). The law's expansive (but not exhaustive) presentation reveals that for Israel the "good life" is not marked by

RECEPTION HISTORY

The Not-Good Law

"So I gave them other statutes that were not good and laws through which they could not live" (Ezek. 20:25). God speaks these words to Israel at the time of their exile in Babylon (586–515 BC) to remind them of the ways that they rebelled against the stipulations of their covenant relationship with YHWH. Ezekiel's reference to "not good" statutes does not contradict Deuteronomy's teaching about the law being good as much as it reflects how Israel rebelled and experienced covenant curse. As a result, Israel did not live in the land and experienced exile.

THEOLOGICAL ISSUES

The Law Is Holy, Righteous, and Good

Modern readers, especially Christian readers, may wonder how the apostle Paul could claim "the law is holy, and the commandment is holy, righteous and good" (Rom. 7:12). The reason is found in Deuteronomy. The law is a gift from a gracious God who helps Israel understand (1) persistent human sin in Israel's history and future, (2) divine grace in managing sin through sacrifice and the giving of law, (3) consequences for faithfulness and faithlessness, and (4) divine grace beyond Israel's faithlessness.

RECEPTION HISTORY

Calvin's Three Uses of Law

The Reformer John Calvin identified three uses for the Old Testament law:

Use 1: God's law exposes human sin and drives toward divine grace.

Thus the Law is a kind of mirror. As in a mirror we discover any stains upon our face, so in the Law we behold, first, our impotence; then, in consequence of it, our iniquity; and, finally, the curse, as the consequence of both. He who has no power of following righteousness is necessarily plunged in the mire of iniquity, and this iniquity is immediately followed by the curse.[c]

Use 2: God's law curbs sinful action by the threat of punishment.

The second office of the Law is, by means of its fearful denunciations and the consequent dread of punishment, to curb those who, unless forced, have no regard for rectitude and justice. Such persons are curbed not because their mind is inwardly moved and affected, but because, as if a bridle were laid upon them, they refrain their hands from external acts, and internally check the depravity which would otherwise petulantly burst forth.[d]

Use 3: God's law is a delight to the redeemed.

The third use of the Law (being also the principal use, and more closely connected with its proper end) has respect to believers in whose hearts the Spirit of God already flourishes and reigns. For although the Law is written and engraven on their hearts by the finger of God, that is, although they are so influenced and actuated by the Spirit, that they desire to obey God, there are two ways in which they still profit in the Law.[e]

Figure 7.4. Mosaic of Moses and the Torah in the Old City of Jerusalem, Israel

a separation between secular and sacred, as we may think today. Torah's instructions speak to challenges of Israel's communal life.

A mosaic in Jerusalem's Jewish quarter offers a conception of the torah (see fig. 7.4). Moses holds aloft the torah in a scene that tells Israel's story and envisions Israel's life: worship, slavery, farming, deliverance, judiciary, and so on. The imagery is precise: the Torah scroll is set at the pinnacle of the mosaic, as if it has a word to say to all that lay below it: from the most basic need of life (water) to the natural world to human industry. Social inequities are displayed by Egyptian pyramids and Israel's slavery. The twelve tribes of Israel, represented in a circular image, surround a menorah, representing Israel and worship. This stunning mosaic illustrates Deuteronomy's view of its legal material: God's instruction (torah) speaks to *all of life.*

Israel is to recognize the majesty and goodness of God *in all of life.* All of life belongs to God: work, family, sex, friendships, farming, and even the organization of society. Israel's obedience to God's law exhibits their love and worship of God. As strange as it might appear to modern readers, Israel's obedience to God's instruction is neither empty legalism nor worthless ritual. The instructions of Deuteronomy 12–26 contextualize for Israel in God's land their love of God, which is matched with a deep love and care for their neighbor.

HISTORICAL MATTERS

God's Name, Places, and People

The place formula in Deuteronomy emphasizes the importance of God's name set on sacred space. The name placement signifies that place uniquely belongs to him. Ancient Near Eastern peoples inscribed the name of their deity on the foundation stone of the shrine they constructed to that deity. In Deuteronomy God may be commanding Israel to inscribe the divine name on the foundation stone of the shrine, signifying the shrine belongs to YHWH alone. Alternatively, it may be inscribed elsewhere, as one finds of other deities in ancient Near Eastern temples.

Misusing God's Name

The idea of God placing the "Name" on the shrine may recall the third command in the Ten Commandments: "You shall not misuse the name of the Lord your God, for the Lord will not hold anyone guiltless who misuses his name" (Deut. 5:11). Normally, we take this misuse of the name of God to be swearing or cursing. However, the verse could be translated, "You shall not bear the name of the Lord your God to no good purpose" (AT). If this is accurate, then the command against misuse of God's name means more than just misusing your lips with an oath or curse. The command means that God has put the divine name on the people, who bear that name. Because of their covenant commitment, they belong in relationship to God. If they live in a manner that does not reflect the majesty and glory of YHWH's name appropriately—or they bear God's very name on their lives "in vain" or "to no good purpose"—then they are in violation of their relationship with God. Bearing God's name means that Israel is a people reflecting the glory of God and belonging to God.[f]

Ten Commandments as an Organizing Principle

The Ten Commandments of Exodus 20 and Deuteronomy 5 serve as a general organizing principle for the legal code of Deuteronomy 12–26. A close inspection of the laws and their correlation to the Ten Commandments reveals how this is the case.

Deuteronomy 12–13	Purity of worship instructed in these laws reflects commands 1–3 and their injunction to worship God alone.
Deuteronomy 14:28–16:17	Sabbath (command 4) is reflected with the emphasis on holy rhythms of Israel's communal life and the care for the poor.
Deuteronomy 16:18–18:22	Honoring parents (command 5) is reflected in the laws regarding proper authority (prophets, priests, judges, and kings).
Deuteronomy 19:1–21:9	Prohibition of murder (command 6) is reflected in the opening and concluding laws in this section.
Deuteronomy 22:13–30	Prohibition of adultery (command 7) is reflected in the laws dealing with sexual offenses and sexual sin.
Deuteronomy 23–26	Prohibition of theft and covetousness (commands 8 and 10) are reflected in the laws regarding care and compassion, especially of the weak and poor in Israel's community.

This literary arrangement reveals the ethical vision of the Ten Commandments and the ethical vision of Israel's life. Israel's laws were not arbitrary but exhibited moral foundation and entailed a moral vision.

While it would take us too far afield to dig deeply into all the laws, it is worthwhile looking closely at some that will help us better understand the Old Testament books that follow. Deuteronomy sets the stage for how Israel should live in the land, and the Former and Latter Prophets (Joshua–Malachi) provide an extended comment on and assessment of how Israel has responded to their covenant commitment to God expressed in Deuteronomy.

CENTRAL SANCTUARY AND PROHIBITION AGAINST IDOLATRY

Language of worshiping God at the central sanctuary opens the legal material in Deuteronomy 12–26, and it is repeated some twenty-five times in the book as a kind of "place formula," with some variation: "the place the Lord your God will choose from among all your tribes to put his Name there for his dwelling" (12:5; see also 12:11, 14, 18, 21, 26; 14:23, 25; 15:20; 16:2, 6, 7, 11, 15, 16; 17:8, 10; 18:6; 26:2; 31:11). This phrase says several things about the central sanctuary.[1]

1. God chooses the central place of worship. This implies God's election of the place for God's purposes, much like God has chosen Israel for a purpose. The central sanctuary is not "won" by the people so that one tribe can exert a power claim over others. God's divine choice of place belongs to him and to no others. God dwells in the central sanctuary in a particular way, receiving the festival worship, sacrifices, and celebrations of the people. The goal of pilgrimage to the sanctuary is "rejoicing" before the Lord as a community celebration.

2. The central sanctuary is located in the tribal allotments in the land, detailed in Numbers 34. Thus, the central sanctuary fits within the covenantal purposes of Israel: God's people, worshiping in God's land, under God's rule.

Figure 7.5. Shamash, the sun god, Sippar, Early Iron Age, ca. 870 BC, plaster cast of limestone original, Oriental Institute Museum, University of Chicago

3. God's "name" will be placed in the central sanctuary, which implies both his covenantal commitment to his people and place as well as divine ownership. Both people and place represent God and God's very "name." By placing the divine name on the central sanctuary, God validates *this* place as a proper place, instead of other places, to worship God.

The central site does not *necessarily* mean Jerusalem, because God can be worshiped anywhere he chooses. Before the monarchy in Israel, Shiloh served as the place for the central sanctuary (2 Sam. 1). Still, as the story of Israel progresses, God selects Jerusalem for the sanctuary under the reign of King David (2 Sam. 6–7).

LEADERSHIP LAWS

The leadership laws in Deuteronomy 16:18–18:22 offer a helpful example of how Israel's law is different, democratizing, and devoted to the worship of God alone. The idealized portrait of leadership in this section provides a helpful grid by which to assess leadership that emerges in Joshua through Kings as well as in the Latter Prophets and Writings. From 4000 to 300 BC the Near Eastern context exhibits kings, prophets, priests, and judges, who governed the social structures of the ancient world.[2] But Israel's leadership laws subvert existing leadership structures in their ancient

Near Eastern context, and they reinforce the covenant obligations of Israel to their God.

Judge (16:18–20): Deuteronomy stipulates four expectations of judges in Israel:

1. Judges are appointed throughout all towns in Israel to judge the people with "righteous judgment" (16:18 NASB).

2. Judges are to be impartial and provide justice to all peoples in the land (16:19a).

3. Judges are to shun all bribes or means of rigging the judicial process (16:19b).

4. Judges are to pursue "justice and justice alone" rather than anything else such as money, power, kingship, or women (16:20). By pursuing justice and justice alone, Israel's judges emulate the just judgment of God, whose justice Deuteronomy extols without compare: "He is the Rock, his works are perfect, and all his ways are just. A faithful God who does no wrong, upright and just is he" (32:4).

By pursuing and executing justice, the judge imitates the very faithfulness and justice of God. Therefore, impartiality is a requirement for the judge, so that all the people in the land (including the most vulnerable: widows, orphans, resident aliens/immigrants; cf. 24:17; 27:19) receive fair judgment and justice in their communities. Any means of rigging the judicial system by bribery or any form of unseemly compensation are to be avoided at all costs.

Judges are to appear throughout the land of Israel, reinforcing the pervasive call for justice. Justice should not be localized to only one or two central places while the remainder of the land is lawless and without restraint. Rather, thorough judicial representation throughout the towns and cities is designed to create a community of justice, fair-dealing, and peace.

King (Deut. 17:14–20): The law code in Deuteronomy details five stipulations for kings in Israel:

1. The king is to be chosen by God and appointed by the people (17:15).

2. The king is to be from among the Israelites and be a native Israelite (17:15).

3. The king must show restraint in acquiring horses (military), wives (international treaties), and silver/gold (money) (17:16–17).

4. When ruling, the king must write a copy of the law in the presence of the Levitical priests, and he is to obey and read it his entire life in order that he will fear God, observe God's instruction, and obey the statutes (17:18–19).

5. The king is to keep his heart humble, grounded, and obedient to God's law by doing number 4 above (17:20).

The law of the king reveals that the king is not divine or semidivine but rather a regular Israelite (one from among the Israelites). Moreover, Israel's king cannot raise a strong army or cavalry (amassing horses), presumably limiting royal conquest and imperial power since kings in the ancient world raised cavalries for the purpose of imperial expansion. Theologically, the king should embrace that his place is the promised land, the divine land grant given by God to Israel. The other nations have their lands that do not belong to Israel. Recognizing this, Israel's king is to content himself with what God provides. The king cannot aggrandize his royal line or legacy by expanding beyond the limits God has provided. This royal limit subverts the regular royal practices of Assyria, Babylon, Egypt, and other nation-states around Israel.

Moreover, the king cannot make significant international treaties by gaining a large harem of wives and concubines. This law makes strange sense: in those days, a king would secure power through international alliances, and alliances were forged in marriage between royal houses. Peace and prosperity were secured through the international prowess and craftiness of the king. Another problem of this, of course, was that the gods of the nations did not cohere with Israel's worship of YHWH alone. Intermarriage with other royal houses threatened to diminish the king's covenant loyalty to

Kings in the Ancient Near East

Kings governed their people and usually gave laws, as in the famous example of the law code of King Hammurabi of Babylon (r. 1795–1750 BC). They ruled their lands under the authority of their patron deity, often with religion co-opted for royal purposes. For example, the annual New Year's festival (the Akitu festival) celebrated the new year and reestablished the reign of the king under divine authority.[h]

Figure 7.6. Hammurabi law code

Israel's God. Rather, Israel's king should trust in God alone for security and provision and not international politics.

Note also that the king should not have great wealth in gold or silver. There were two primary ways in which a king grew his wealth in the ancient world: taxation and conquest. By limiting the wealth of the king, this law prevents exploitative taxation of Israelites for the crown as well as prevents imperial expansion through conquests and pillaging of nation-states surrounding Israel. The law eviscerates regular royal practices in the ancient world and provides a different vision of royal leadership: service, sustainability, and security by reliance on God.

Finally, the king cannot operate free from Israel's people. The law of the king democratizes royal authority into a balance of powers rather than affirming unilateral royal power. The admonition for the king to keep a copy of the law and be taught by the priests essentially creates a balance of power between royal and religious leadership in the land. God's law becomes the wisdom of Israel's king, keeping him humble and reliant on God while subservient to God and the Lord's priests.

Figure 7.7. Priest-king or deity, Hittite, North Syria (early seventeenth century BC)

Priest (18:1–8): Deuteronomy gives five requirements for priests in Israel:

1. They (the tribe of Levi) are to have no tribal inheritance or "portion" from the Lord. Rather, God will be their inheritance (18:1).
2. They will not work a tract of land for food, but rather they will eat sacrificial offerings as their inheritance (18:1).
3. The priest is to receive from those worshiping at the chosen place certain portions of the sacrifice (shoulder, jaws, and stomach) and the firstfruits of grain, wine, oil, and wool (18:3–4).
4. The priest is chosen by God to minister before God on behalf of the people (18:5).
5. The priest is free to leave his own towns and villages and go to the place the Lord chooses (18:6–7).

The law of the priest reveals an economy of care. Because the priests do not have a land allotment among the tribes of Israel, they cannot grow their crops and provide food for their tribe. Recognizing this fact, Israel's regular worship at the central sanctuary provides the grain, oil, wine, and meat necessary for priestly sustenance. God has created a system in which Israel's regular worship provides for the good of all, because if the priests die out, then Israel has no mediators to stand in the gap between them and

God. Then sacrifices cannot be received or offered. If the priests are not present for the people, then atonement cannot be gained, and Israel cannot be sanctified for service. By God's economy of care through the sacrificial provisions, the priests depend on the people for their sustenance and life, and the people depend on the priests for sacrifice, prayer, and instruction. 🕭

In this way, the priesthood in Israel was designed to be a system of care and sanctification for the people rather than a system of power to exploit the Israelites of their goods. By way of contrast, priests in Egypt were significant landholders and, therefore, wealthy elites who could exploit the poor. The law of the priest in Deuteronomy provides a subversive word to such practices. The priesthood is dependent on the faithfulness of the people, and the people are dependent on the faithfulness of the priests. This economy of dependency and care opens the possibility for mutuality and shared concern, truly an opportunity to love one's neighbor as oneself.

Prophet (18:9–22): Deuteronomy lays out seven requirements for prophets in Israel:

1. The true prophet is to be like the rest of the nation—loyal to God ("blameless before the LORD your God," 18:13) and staying true to worship of him (18:9–14).
2. The true prophet is to be like Moses— from among "fellow Israelites" (18:15).
3. The true prophet mediates between God and the people. Differently from the priest, the prophet serves the function of speaking God's word rather than administering sacrifices (18:18).

Figure 7.8. Procession to an altar to sacrifice a lamb, accompanied by the flute and lyre; the dedication to the Charites; painted wooden plaque found near ancient Sikyon, in Corinthia (ca. 540–530 BC); National Archaeological Museum of Athens

Figure 7.9. A religious ritual scene on a plaque, a naked male with libation before a seated Mesopotamian god; from southern Iraq (Nippur?); early Dynastic period, ca. 2600–2300 BC; Ancient Orient Museum, Istanbul, Turkey

4. The true prophet speaks *only* the words and message that God has given (18:18, 20).

5. The true prophet is authoritative in his speech, due to the fact that his words are God's words (18:19).

6. The prophet is accountable to death for speaking anything other than God's word (18:20).

7. The true prophet will be recognizable on the basis that the prophecy is fulfilled (18:22). On this point, note the relationship between Deuteronomy 18 and Deuteronomy 13.

The law of the prophet concludes this section on leadership. Like priests, the prophet is to be set apart for service and be "blameless" before God (18:13). Like the king, the prophet is a fellow Israelite and not divine or semidivine. A prophet is known not for eloquence of speech but rather for delivering the messages of the Lord. The prophet speaks God's messages regardless of the benefit—or lack thereof—that message might bring the messenger. In this way, the prophet can speak to kings, other prophets, leadership, or regular Israelites. The prophet is not bound by other people, only by the burden the Lord gives.

We shall see that some prophets in Joshua–Kings sometimes speak what is expeditious and beneficial for them rather than what God calls them to speak. The law of the prophet reminds God's people that the prophet is not a puppet of the royal court, present to legitimate any whim of the crown. Rather, the prophet of God speaks God's truth to power, often at the cost of their own lives (see the story of Jeremiah!). This commitment to God rather than the royal court subverts the traditional role of the prophet in the ancient world. In Babylonia and Assyria, for example, prophets existed to rubber-stamp the desires of the king rather than speak truth to power.[3]

REAFFIRMATION OF COVENANT IDENTITY

In the conclusion of Deuteronomy's legal material, Moses reaffirms God's call on Israel's life. The summary statement in Deuteronomy 26:16–19 closes the stipulations of the covenant, reminding God's people to follow his instructions, observing them with all their heart and soul, an echo of the Shema. The themes from Deuteronomy 1–11 and 12–26 find their accent in 26:16–19. The Ten Commandments, the laws, covenant love, and the call to "Hear!" or "listen" to the Lord are all here. Moses even draws Israel back to their covenant identity disclosed in part in Exodus 19:4–6: they are his treasured

Figure 7.10. Plaster-covered tablet from Lahun, Middle Kingdom of Egypt, Twelfth Dynasty

possession and a holy people belonging to God; they have the covenant promise and high honor among all the nations.

After this Moses and the elders instruct the people to write down these covenant commands and instructions on plaster-coated tablets and set them up on Mount Ebal once they enter into the promised land (27:1–10). Then, Deuteronomy 27:11–26 stipulates how the Levites are to utter curses on anyone who disobeys the demands of the covenant. The idea is that as soon as they enter the promised land, they are to reaffirm in the land what they received outside the land.

How would Israel do in their devotion to God? The terms of the covenant in Deuteronomy 28 present various blessings for obedience and curses for disobedience. These blessings and curses give the audience a decision to make: Will they embrace "this law" or not? It is true that curses far outweigh blessings in this material, indicating that an expectation of Israel's covenant breach looms darkly on the horizon of the book.

Renewal of the Covenant and Leadership Succession: Deuteronomy 29–31

■ READ DEUTERONOMY 29–31 ■

This section emphasizes the renewal of the covenant, which may be considered as necessary in light of the anticipated failure of the people of Israel to obey the terms of the covenant. So Deuteronomy 29 recounts the renewal of the covenant, which is followed by a distinctive offer of life and death in Deuteronomy 30. God's call to Israel's obedience is clear for the generation listening to the speeches of Moses.

Figure 7.11. *Moses sieht das Gelobte Land vor seinem Tode* (Moses sees the promised land before his death), by Lesser Ury (1928)

Paul Reads Deuteronomy 30 Christologically

"Moses writes this about the righteousness that is by the law: 'The person who does these things will live by them.' But the righteousness that is by faith says: 'Do not say in your heart, "Who will ascend into heaven?"' (that is, to bring Christ down) 'or "Who will descend into the deep?"' (that is, to bring Christ up from the dead). But what does it say? 'The word is near you; it is in your mouth and in your heart,' that is, the message concerning faith that we proclaim: If you declare with your mouth, 'Jesus is Lord,' and believe in your heart that God raised him from the dead, you will be saved" (Rom. 10:5–9; cf. Deut. 30:14).

God's people are drawn to choose the Lord by obeying his torah, and thereby receiving life. The call to obedience and the life YHWH offers is not too difficult for them that they have to go to the heavens and ask God to bring it to them (30:12) or so distant from them that they need to cross the sea to get it (30:13). "No, the word is very near you; it is in your mouth and in your heart so you may obey it" (30:14).

Deuteronomy 30:15–20 is unambiguous, especially in verse 19: "Now choose life, so that you may live, you and your offspring" (AT). The following verse clarifies the nature of the choice: "to love YHWH your God, to obey his voice, and to cling to him. For he is your life and the length of your days" (30:20 AT). Deuteronomy 30:1–20 draws Israel to the point of choice, today. When (and if) God's people embrace the choice of life, God is "near" to them, a point recognized in the intertextual connections between Deuteronomy 4:5–8 and 30:14. If Israel keeps the word that is given them (30:14), he will be near to them (4:5–8). God's offer in Deuteronomy 30 is a genuine choice of life or death for Israel. They are called to "choose life." As they do, God will reside among them. If they do not, they will experience death outside the land. The nations will look and see what Israel has chosen, whether life or death (29:23–28).

The book follows this call to "choose life" with three elements: the leadership succession of Joshua for Moses (Deut. 31:1–8, 14–15, 23), the command to write down the law for Israel on a scroll that should be preserved for the people of God as they go into the land (31:9–13, 24–29), and the command for Moses to compose a final song (31:16–22, 30).

The Conclusion: Deuteronomy 32–34

■ READ DEUTERONOMY 32–34 ■

These final chapters include the book's conclusion and the death of Moses. Chapter 32 is typically known as the Song of Moses. It is complex, extraordinary poetry that tells the story of God's work with Israel, which is then complemented by Moses blessing the people by tribes in Deuteronomy 33. The song and the blessing draw together themes of YHWH's greatness and transcendence as well as the election and blessing of Israel in God's purposes.

Finally, Deuteronomy closes with Moses's death (34:1–12). Three speakers in the book describe Moses's death: Moses (1:37–38; 3:26–27; 4:21–24; 31:2, 27–29), the narrator (34:5), and God (31:14, 16; 32:50–51; 34:4; cf. 3:26–27; 31:2). In Deuteronomy 1:37; 3:26; and 4:21, Moses explains that he will die outside the land because of Israel's rebellion against YHWH. Interestingly, in Deuteronomy 32:50–51, God connects Moses's death to disobedience and not consecrating God's name (cf. Num. 20:12, 24 and 27:12–14). Understood with either rationale, Moses dies on Mount Nebo on the eastern side of the Jordan River.

This final chapter in Moses's life honors him in a way like no other: "No prophet has risen in Israel like Moses, whom the LORD knew face to face, who did all those signs and wonders the LORD sent him to do in Egypt—to Pharaoh and to all his officials and to his whole land. For no one has ever shown the mighty power or performed the awesome deeds that Moses did in the sight of all Israel" (34:10–12). Still, a note of sadness lingers as a warning for God's people in the death of Moses: disobedience to God's command brings death. 👥

Figure 7.12. Marble sculpture *Moses* by Michelangelo Buonarroti in Basilica of San Pietro in Vincoli, Rome (1513–15)

Figure 7.13. Floor mosaics inside the Basilica of Moses, Mount Nebo, Jordan

RECEPTION HISTORY

Gregory of Nyssa, *The Life of Moses*

Gregory of Nyssa, a fourth-century church leader from Cappadocia (modern-day Turkey), was inspired to explore the life of Moses in the Pentateuch as a way to inculcate virtue in the Christian life. He discusses two aspects of the Scripture, the *historia* (the literal sense) and the *theoria* (the spiritual sense): "I think there is no need to prolong the discourse by presenting to the reader the whole life of Moses as an example of virtue.... What then are we taught through what has been said? To have but one purpose in life: to be called servants of God by virtue of the lives we live."[i]

Implementation—Reading Deuteronomy as Christian Scripture Today

"All roads lead back to Deuteronomy," or so one of our doctoral supervisors told us. By this he meant that Deuteronomy is the conclusion to the Pentateuch, the hinge to the Prophets, and the framework for what it means to be the people of God. The realities of God's mission, divine election, God's grace, God's name, and the future all find their place in the book. YHWH's call for human choice and covenantal obedience is the very core of the book's theological message. So it is not surprising that all roads lead to this book. Further, Deuteronomy is one of the "big three" most cited Old Testament books in the New Testament, alongside Isaiah and the Psalms. This is because of the significant number of key texts in Deuteronomy that frame life before God in the New Testament (like the Shema).

To read Deuteronomy in its fullness—with the richness of its theological vision in view—is to read the book as Christian Scripture. Let us unpack how the theological richness frames our understanding of God.

God makes a redemptive community for himself and sends that people on a mission to make him known. Israel's life before God becomes a witness to the nations, and the *missiological* significance of Deuteronomy comes to the fore. In Deuteronomy's covenantal structure, we see God's unique call to Israel to shine the light of Israel's God to all around them. Israel's election by God, then, is not for themselves as much as it is for the sake of God's glory and the sake of the nations around them. In Israel's obedience, God would be glorified and the nations would see the uniqueness of God. However, Deuteronomy 28 reveals that in Israel's disobedience, God would still achieve his purposes through them: the nations would see Israel exiled because of the holiness of God.

In addition to the missiological identity of Israel, Deuteronomy displays the radical *grace* of God. Grace is demonstrated by bringing the second generation to the threshold of promise on the plains of Moab. What was for the first generation, who died in the wilderness, will be for the second generation and the children that follow. God is providing a rich and fertile land from which they will shine God's light among

---

THEOLOGICAL ISSUES

The Missiological Identity of Israel

Like other ancient Near Eastern peoples, Israel's identity was defined by their deity (YHWH), their God-given and protected land, and their status as a people belonging to that land and that God. God-land-people forms the heart of Israel's identity. Because of their covenant with YHWH, Israel is the agent of blessing through whom all the earth will find blessing. Israel is a paradigm for what humanity should be as they obey God's instruction and do good works for which they were created. In this way, the story of Adam and humanity progresses in the story of Israel. Israel represents new humanity in the promised land. As they live well on God's land, they shine God's light among the nations. Even after Israel's rebellion and exile, God will draw them back to their proper relationship and place them in the land once again: "The Lord your God will circumcise your heart and the hearts of your offspring to love the Lord your God with all your heart and soul, in order that you will live" (Deut. 30:6 AT). God will achieve his purposes through his people, so the world will know the God of covenant and creation.

the nations. Even in the face of Israel's sin, God's grace preserves them and brings them back after the exile. In all of this, God's grace rises to the forefront of the book, despite human frailty. Future hope becomes an expression of that grace: God will bring his people back home. This is the extraordinary outworking of divine love and grace.

This same grace is what God demonstrates to a wayward world in the radical gift of his Son, Jesus Christ, as the means of forgiveness and redemption. It is God's grace that leads people to repentance. It is God's love that motivates the sending of the Son. It is God's grace that motivates Jesus's mission and invites the church to live as people of grace (Eph. 2:4–10).

KEY VERSES IN DEUTERONOMY

- Hear, O Israel: The Lord our God, the Lord is one. Love the Lord your God with all your heart and with all your soul and with all your strength. 6:4–5
- And now, Israel, what does the Lord your God ask of you but to fear the Lord your God, to walk in obedience to him, to love him, to serve the Lord your God with all your heart and with all your soul, and to observe the Lord's commands and decrees that I am giving you today for your own good? 10:12–13
- See, I set before you today life and prosperity, death and destruction. For I command you today to love the Lord your God, to walk in obedience to him, and to keep his commands, decrees and laws; then you will live and increase, and the Lord your God will bless you in the land you are entering to possess. 30:15–16

Christian Reading Questions

1. Compare and contrast the Ten Commandments in Deuteronomy and Exodus.
2. What is the Shema, and what is its significance?
3. Explain how Deuteronomy can be understood as a covenant.
4. How would you describe the theology of Deuteronomy?
5. What is the significance of the ending of Deuteronomy?

CHAPTER EIGHT

Introduction to the Prophets

Theophanes the Greek, a famous iconographer in the fifteenth century, created a masterpiece in his *Transfiguration of Jesus* (see fig. 8.1). The work is drawn from a strange and wonderful story of Jesus being transfigured on a high mountain before the disciples (Matt. 17). In the story, Jesus's appearance is brilliant and his face shines. The text also depicts Jesus talking with two significant figures from the Old Testament: Moses and Elijah (Matt. 17:3).

Theophanes illustrates the story with Jesus elevated at the center and speaking with the two Old Testament figures to the right and left. His disciples are below, confused, and their attempt to make sense of the moment resonates with modern readers. One question that surely surfaces is, Why Moses and Elijah? What is their significance?

Moses and Elijah represent the first and second great prophets of the Old Testament. Moses is associated with the Torah as the great lawgiver, and he is the exemplar for all other prophets (Deut. 18:15–18; 34:10). Elijah is the prophet whose life stories echo those of Moses, as indicated in the sidebar "Parallels between Moses and Elijah." And Elijah is the central prophet in the book of 1–2 Kings. Together, Moses and Elijah represent God's instruction and prophecy in the Old Testament. 📜

The influence of Moses and Elijah was so great that by the time of Jesus, the two Old Testament figures were expected to return to usher in the new age of God's reign. This teaching is captured in the later teaching of the rabbis, particularly in Deuteronomy Rabbah. 👥

In Deuteronomy Rabbah, Moses and Elijah appear together on the "day of the Lord," a prophetic event in which God reveals himself in judgment against the wicked and with salvation for the righteous. A reasonable interpretation of Moses's and Elijah's appearance in Matthew 17 is that God's day of salvation and judgment has come with the ministry of Jesus.

Figure 8.1. *Transfiguration of Jesus*, icon by Theophanes the Greek (fifteenth century), Tretyakov Gallery

Jesus is the prophet like Moses. Jesus is the prophet who ushers in the day of the Lord. God says to the disciples, "This is my beloved Son, with whom I am well pleased; listen to him" (Matt. 17:5 ESV).

The Prophets (Nevi'im) as a Canonical Group

The appearance of Moses and Elijah in Matthew 17 draws together figures from the first two sections of the Old Testament: Torah (Moses) and Prophets (Elijah). We have explored the Torah in the preceding chapters and now turn to the canonical group called the Prophets (Hebrew: *nevi'im*). By "the Prophets" we mean the books

RECEPTION HISTORY

Moses and Elijah on the Day of YHWH

Jewish rabbis highlight the significance of Moses and Elijah by reflecting on biblical texts that mention them. Their oral teaching regarding these Old Testament figures appears in Deuteronomy Rabbah, a collection of rabbinic instruction. The oral instruction behind Deuteronomy Rabbah is said to go back centuries, but the book itself was compiled in the medieval period, perhaps sometime between the sixth and seventh centuries. The rabbis depict God speaking to Moses, saying: "'Moses, I swear to you, as you devoted your life to their [Israel's] service in this world, so too in the time to come when I bring Elijah, the prophet, unto them, the two of you shall come together.' At that time he will come and comfort you, as it is said, Behold I will send you Elijah the prophet. . . . And he shall turn the heart of the fathers to the children (Mal. III, 23 f)."[a]

of the Old Testament from Joshua through Malachi. We shall refer to these texts as Prophets or prophetic books.

In the Hebrew ordering of the Prophets, these books are divided into two subunits: the Former and Latter Prophets. The Former Prophets correspond to the narrative of Israel from their entry into the promised land (Joshua) to the dissolution of the monarchy and exile from the promised land (2 Kings). The Latter Prophets focus on specific prophetic ministries in that larger storyline of Israel and beyond: from the eighth and seventh centuries BC (e.g., Isaiah, Hosea, Amos, Micah, and Zephaniah) to the exile in the sixth century BC (e.g., Ezekiel) to the restoration in the sixth to fourth centuries BC (Zechariah, Haggai, and Malachi).

The Prophets (Nevi'im)

Former Prophets	Latter Prophets
Joshua	Isaiah
Judges	Jeremiah
1–2 Samuel	Ezekiel
1–2 Kings	The Twelve (Minor Prophets)

In their original scrolls, 1–2 Samuel was one book rather than two, as we have in English Bibles today. The same is true of 1–2 Kings.

In the Former Prophets (Joshua–Kings) narrative material predominates. This grand narrative continues from the first five books of the Old Testament and picks up the story of Israel at its entry into the promised land (Joshua), to the rise of the judges as charismatic leaders in the land (Judges), to the transition to monarchy and particularly the Davidic dynasty (1–2 Samuel). The book of 1–2 Kings recounts the rise and fall of David's dynasty, as the united kingdom of David and his son Solomon divides into the Northern Kingdom of Israel and the Southern Kingdom of Judah. Finally, 2 Kings recounts the demise of the Northern Kingdom (722 BC at the hands of the Assyrian Empire) and of the Southern Kingdom as well (586 BC at the hands of the Neo-Babylonian Empire). The corpus concludes with a glimmer of hope: the Babylonian king Evil-Merodach (son of Nebuchadnezzar) enters into some sort of negotiations with the exiled last king of Judah, Jehoiachin, and elevates him to prestige in Babylon (2 Kings 25:27–30). It is only a glimmer of hope, however, as God's people have been exiled from their homeland and live as strangers in a foreign land.

It might be hard to link this narrative of Israel with prophecy. Often, these books are described by another name: historical books. However, it would be wrongheaded to distinguish history from prophecy in the Old Testament. Old Testament history writing was not like modern history writing. While these biblical books are designed to convey significant facts, figures, dates, and events, they do something much more for the reader.

The books of Joshua–Kings tell the story of God's purposes with Israel and Israel's response to God. This story is told so that God's people may understand their God, as well as what he has done and will do to accomplish his purposes in the world through Israel. These texts connect events from the past to events in the present and even in the future. By linking events in this way through the story in the Former Prophets, these books order time according to the purposes of God. The story is theological and instructive so we can understand God and the human story in relation to God.

Even as Joshua–Kings continues the primary story of Israel from Genesis through Deuteronomy, the narrative offers many negative examples for God's people to study and from which they may learn. These texts also provide exemplars of God's faithfulness, judgment, and forgiveness by which God's people can come to a deeper communion with God.

Another feature of the prophetic books comes in the Latter Prophets—namely, the inclusion of the twelve Minor Prophets as a large anthology of prophetic texts that serves as a kind of conclusion to the entire corpus of the Prophets.[1] The twelve Minor Prophets, Hosea–Malachi, originally fit on one scroll and, in some way, should be understood as one book.

The book of Malachi brings both the Minor Prophets and the Prophets as a whole to an end with two conclusions. The first appears in Malachi 4:4: "Remember the teaching of my servant Moses, the statutes and ordinances that I commanded him at Horeb for all Israel" (NRSV). God's people are called to remember God's instruction once again, this time as Israel reflects on its historical inability to keep the law and its need to depend continually on God's grace and love toward them despite their failure. Malachi 4:4 requires God's people ultimately to depend on God's saving work with their whole being in faith *despite* their waywardness (cf. Deut. 30:1–10).

This lesson draws together human obedience and divine activity in the heart and life of God's people. Obedience to God's instruction, captured in the term "remember" in Malachi 4:4, reinforces God's unchanging command for devotion, recognizes Israel's

CANONICAL CONNECTIONS

Deuteronomy and Malachi

"Horeb" in Malachi 4:4 recalls the second giving of the law in Deuteronomy, as Horeb is the name for Sinai in Deuteronomy. Thus, the last book of the Prophets draws us back to the last book of the Torah.

Deuteronomy, the last book of the Torah	Moses, Horeb, laws
Malachi, the last book of the Prophets	Moses, Horeb, laws

Malachi places the reader at Sinai/Horeb again. The reader, like Israel at Sinai or Israel on the plains of Moab, once again is responsible for observing "statutes" and "ordinances" that the first generation, as well as the second and subsequent generations, failed to keep (cf. Deut. 5:2–5).

(and the reader's) own story of sinfulness, and yet invites Israel once again to trust that God will enact change within the very heart of Israel by his gracious action.

The second conclusion to the Prophets occurs in Malachi 4:5–6, a text that frames future hope: "See! I am sending to you Elijah the prophet before the great and terrible Day of the Lord comes. And he will turn the heart of fathers to their sons, and the heart of sons to their fathers, lest I come and I strike the land with a curse" (AT). We saw this text as important for the rabbis in Deuteronomy Rabbah, connecting Moses and Elijah. This second conclusion correlates the coming of Elijah the prophet with the call to remember the instruction of Moses in Malachi 4:4. Thus, Moses and Elijah represent the great prophets of the periods of the exodus (Moses) and the early monarchy (Elijah). Canonically, Moses and Elijah serve as shorthand for the "Torah and Prophets," the two subsections of the tripartite Hebrew canon: the Torah (Moses) and the Prophets (Elijah).

The first and second conclusions of Malachi, then, provide canonical connection by drawing together past ("Torah of Moses") and future (a new "Elijah, the prophet"). Remembering the instruction of Moses (Torah) is not just about remembering what God has done with his people in previous generations; the wise reader will correlate God's work in the past to what God will do in the future, when Elijah the prophet comes to usher in the day of the Lord. This future Elijah recapitulates the prophetic work for God's people in the future day.

The book of Malachi concludes by highlighting the prophet God will raise up before the coming day of salvation and judgment. In this way, a future-oriented, eschatological focus appears at the end of the book of Malachi, the end of the Minor Prophets, and the end of the Prophets. This eschatological focus centers on the day of the Lord, where God is revealed in judgment and salvation heralded by the coming of the prophet Elijah. When Elijah comes, the day of the Lord is not far behind!

Prophetic Books

The words of the prophets in various times and places from the early monarchy (1000 BC) to the late Persian period (400 BC) were received and compiled into the books of the Former and Latter Prophets. The collection, revision, and compilation of prophetic books by the prophets took place over centuries, as we see, for example, in the creation of

Figure 8.2. Oldest stained glass window of the prophets in Europe; *from left to right:* Moses, Hosea, Daniel, Jonah, and King David (ca. after 1132); Augsburg Cathedral, Germany

the Minor Prophets, which span from the eighth century to the fifth century BC. It is apparent that the prophetic books do not give a video-like chronological recording of the events of the past. They are occasional, they bring together different bits of historical and poetic material, and they are crafted to proclaim theological messages in their canonical form.

One interesting feature of the prophetic books is that the original life situations and settings of the prophets sometimes lose focus as they take shape in their canonical form. For this reason, the focus of interpretation is the *book* rather than the reconstructed life situations of the prophet. One way to conceptualize this is that the life of the prophet is like a single pane in a stained glass window. The whole window is the book that bears the prophet's name, but this or that action, speech, or message is sensible only when interpreted within the book as a whole. Moreover, the lives of the prophets are illumined by the light that God shines through their stories.

This point is evident, for example, in the preaching of Jeremiah, where the central theme of the book is found in God's message to the prophet to preach: "See, today I appoint you over nations and kingdoms to uproot and tear down, to destroy and overthrow, to build and to plant" (Jer. 1:10). Different moments in the life of Jeremiah are drawn together in the book to expound on (or illumine) God's central message. Jeremiah's actions at different points in his life testify to this theme found in the book.

A second feature of the prophetic books is that the individual books should be interpreted within the larger corpus of the Prophets. We see this clearly in the twelve Minor Prophets. Each individual Minor Prophet displays an integrity all its own, but these individual books ought to be correlated and interpreted with their overall messages as well. Literary features within—and across—the books give guidance on how to do that. For example, the presentation of Nineveh's repentance in the book of Jonah is counterbalanced by Nahum's depiction of Nineveh's waywardness. In both books, God displays his commitment to both compassion and justice.

The "Grace Formula" in the Minor Prophets

"YHWH, YHWH, a God merciful and gracious, slow to anger, and abounding in steadfast love and faithfulness, keeping steadfast love for the thousandth generation, forgiving iniquity and transgression and sin, yet by no means clearing the guilty, but visiting the iniquity of the parents upon the children and the children's children, to the third and the fourth generation" (Exod. 34:6–7 AT).

This expression from Exodus, sometimes called the "grace formula," is evident in Joel 2:13, where God's compassion/graciousness drives the prophetic call to repentance. It is also evident in Jonah 4:2 when Jonah laments the mercy and grace of God as well as the fact that God is slow to anger and abounding in steadfast love. However, the other books that use the formula incorporate fewer elements. Micah 7:18–20 says YHWH forgives, passes over transgression, and delights in showing steadfast love. Nahum 1:3 emphasizes God is slow to anger but does not clear the guilty of their sin—and Joel 2:13 and Jonah 4:2 reaffirm God being slow to anger. In the Minor Prophets, Exodus 34:6–7 emerges at various points, and where these verses appear is theologically significant.[b]

The grace formula in the Minor Prophets offers an extended theological rationale for divine judgment and salvation as God deals with Israel and the nations. God's identity in these books is consistent with the revelation of the divine identity in Exodus: gracious, merciful, patient, and willing to forgive by divine grace. Still, divine justice governs divine action, so divine patience is met with God's justice, ensuring he will not clear the guilty. God will execute justice whether the guilty are within Israel or the nations (Joel 2:13; Nah. 1:3). God will display compassion, forgiveness, and grace, whether to Israel (Mic. 7:18–20) or the nations (Jonah). What God requires of Israel (Joel) or the nations (Jonah) for forgiveness is repentance.

Thus, the canonical location of Jonah and Nahum reveals something of the identity of God. With its focus on divine compassion and relenting over sin, Jonah leads us to recognize the grace of God on all nations, especially on those who turn to God in repentance as did the Ninevites. However, in Nahum, divine compassion is met with a strong view of divine justice, wherein exploitation and greed are set to rights in the judgment of God, again directed at Nineveh. Both divine compassion and divine justice emerge from the canonical placement of Jonah and Nahum, following the compassion-first formula in Exodus 34:6–7.

Prophets in Israel

Myriad individuals serve as "prophets," spokespeople for God. Old Testament prophets, like their ancient Near Eastern equivalents, speak for deities. Israel's prophets proclaimed messages given to them by Israel's God. Prophets from other ancient Near Eastern countries (such as Assyria, Babylonia, Syria, Edom, and Phoenicia) spoke on behalf of the many gods in the ancient world. We find early evidence for prophecy in regions of the ancient Near East from roughly 2500 BC to 400 BC.[2] These regions include the regions of the Tigris and Euphrates Rivers (upper and lower Mesopotamia) to the land of Canaan on the Mediterranean Sea.

The prophet associates closely with the divine. As a result, prophets belong to a broader group of people sometimes called diviners. The task of diviners was discerning—or divining—the will of the gods. Ancient

HISTORICAL MATTERS

Mari Archives and Prophecy

The city-state of Mari sat on the west bank of the Euphrates River and was influential in northern Mesopotamia, at least until Hammurabi of Babylon destroyed the city (1760–1757 BC). For twelve hundred years, Mari was a cultural influence, evidenced by the roughly fifteen thousand tablets unearthed by archaeologists in the 1930s. These tablets give a picture of ancient Mesopotamian prophecy.

Near Eastern diviners fell into different groups according to their specialties. There were "technical diviners," or those who trained in specific skills—such as interpreting dreams (dream divination) or examining the entrails or livers of animals (haruspicy and extispicy) or interpreting movements of the heavens (astrology). It was thought that examining entrails, the heavens, or dreams enabled diviners to determine the will of the gods and good or bad omens. The counterparts of tech-

Figure 8.3. Cuneiform clay tablets from Amorite kingdom of Mari (first half of second millennium BC), Ancient Near East Gallery, Louvre Museum, Paris, France

nical diviners were "intuitive diviners." Intuitive diviners did not need special training in astrology or haruspicy or other skills. They received divine messages directly and conveyed them to individuals or groups.

Israel's prophets stand within the stream of intuitive diviners, and in some ways, they look like prophets in other ancient Near Eastern nations. Still, despite similarities, Israel's prophets and prophecy diverge from their neighbors as well.

First, whereas other ancient Near Eastern prophets manifest primarily as technical diviners, Israel's prophets present primarily as intuitive diviners. While some Israelite prophets dream dreams or sometimes interpret them (e.g., Zechariah, who experiences dream-visions; Daniel, who experiences and interprets visions and dreams), the preponderance of evidence from Joshua

Figure 8.4. *The Six-Winged Seraph* by Mikhail Vrubel (1904)

Gary Todd / CC 0 / Wikimedia Commons

Public domain / Wikimedia Commons

HISTORICAL MATTERS

Taxonomy of Diviners in the Ancient Near East[c]

```
                            diviners
                   /                      \
        technical diviner            intuitive diviner
         /          \                   /          \
dream interpreter  augury,          dreamer      prophet
                   extispicy, etc.
```

Figure 8.5. Taxonomy of diviners in the ancient Near East (following Stökl)

Mukannishum to Zimri-Lim, King of Mari

Mukannishum wrote to Zimri-Lim, king of Mari (1776–1761 BC), about the act of a prophet of the deity Dagon on his behalf. The prophecy encourages Zimri-Lim not to fear Babylon. "A prophet of Dagan of Tutt[ul] arose and spoke as follows: 'Babylon, what are you constantly doing? I will gather you into a net and . . . The dwellings of the seven accomplices and all their wealth I give in the hand of Zimri- L[im]."'[d] Unfortunately, this encouragement was misplaced, as King Hammurabi of Babylon destroyed Mari by 1759 BC.

CANONICAL CONNECTIONS

False Prophecy in Jeremiah

"Do not listen to what the prophets are prophesying to you; they fill you with false hopes. They speak visions from their own minds, not from the mouth of the Lord. They keep saying to those who despise me, 'The Lord says: You will have peace.' And to all who follow the stubbornness of their hearts they say, 'No harm will come to you'" (Jer. 23:16–17).

LITERARY NOTES

Terminology for Prophets

The Old Testament has several terms for prophets: "prophet" (nebi' or nevi'), "seer" (ro'eh), and "visionary" (hozeh).[e] Two of these terms are used together in 1 Samuel 9:9 ("seer" and "prophet"). This different terminology in 1 Samuel 9:9 may indicate different functions. "Seer" (ro'eh) might refer to an intuitive diviner instead of a technical diviner, the "seer" (ro'eh) could have been an independent prophet affiliated with prophetic groups or guilds called the "sons of the prophets" instead of the royal court. The "visionary" (hozeh) was likely a diviner in the royal court, and "prophet" (nebi') is a generic term that encompassed the work of both "seer" (ro'eh) and "visionary" (hozeh) (perhaps other activity as well).[f]

through Malachi indicates that prophets in Judah and Israel received messages from God and then delivered those messages to individuals or groups. This describes the ministries of Isaiah, Jeremiah, Ezekiel, Habakkuk, Malachi, and the other prophets as well as the ministries of prophets mentioned in Joshua–Kings. These messages often appear with formulaic prophetic expressions, such as "the word of the Lord," "thus says the Lord," and "the Lord's declaration."[3]

Second, in Israel prophets speak YHWH's messages. Deuteronomy 13 and 18 are clear about the allegiance of the true prophet to speak the word of God and the word of God only. In other nations of the ancient world, prophets (whether technical or intuitive diviners) were mouthpieces for, and co-opted by, the royal court more than they were spokespeople for their god(s). For example, Old Babylonian and Neo-Assyrian sources indicate prophecy was a tool used to legitimize and advance the interests of the king through the will of the deity (whether Bel, Ishtar, Nabu, El, Shamash, Sin, Marduk, or another Mesopotamian deity).

Mesopotamian prophets did not provide a significant critique of royal actions or ambition, and divination especially was designed to affirm royal policy rather than counteract it. The Old Testament tells the story of prophets who follow the tendency of their neighbors: "guns for hire" in the interests of the royal court. However, these prophets are decried for leading the people astray and into sin.

By contrast, true prophets were called to speak the word of the Lord alone. They were not to be co-opted by state power or coerced by special interests. This is why suffering is a regular feature in the life of prophets.

Gender of the Prophets

There were both male and female prophets in Israel. The "major" prophets (Isaiah, Jeremiah, and

Ezekiel) were male, as were the twelve "minor" prophets (Hosea, Joel, Amos, Obadiah, Jonah, Micah, Nahum, Habakkuk, Zephaniah, Haggai, Zechariah, and Malachi). However, female prophets appear in texts that belong to nearly every stage in Israel's story.

During the time of the exodus from Egypt, Miriam (Moses and Aaron's sister) appears as a prophetess: "Then Miriam the prophet, Aaron's sister, took a timbrel in her hand, and all the women followed her, with timbrels and dancing. Miriam sang to them: 'Sing to the LORD, for he is highly exalted. Both horse and driver he has hurled into the sea'" (Exod. 15:20–21). Miriam leads God's people to celebrate God's victory over Egypt and Pharaoh in their miraculous deliverance.

Figure 8.6. Prophetesses Miriam, Deborah, and Judith, in Alsace, Bas-Rhin, Église protestante Saint-Pierre-le-Jeune de Strasbourg, France

In the days of the judges, prior to the monarchy, Deborah is identified as a prophet (Judg. 4:4). Deborah was both prophet and judge, speaking the word of the Lord and leading God's people. Her story has been an inspiration for artists as well as women and men throughout Christian history. 👥

In Isaiah 8, the prophet Isaiah conceives a son with his wife, a "prophetess" (Isa. 8:3). This unnamed prophetess served during the reign of Ahaz in eighth-century-BC Judah. In the period of the late monarchy in Judah, the prophetess Huldah plays a crucial role in the discovery of the law scroll during the reign of Josiah (2 Kings 22:14–20). When the leaders come to her, Huldah speaks the word of God in terms consistent with the oracles of judgment and salvation one finds in the prophetic books and using the same kind of formula, "Thus says the LORD" (cf. 2 Kings 22:15, 16, 18, 19).

In the book of Joel, God provides a **salvation oracle** for the future in which *all* will prophesy with the power of the Spirit of God, both men and women, young and old: "And afterward, I will pour out my Spirit on all people. Your sons and daughters will prophesy, your old men will dream dreams, your young men will see visions. Even on my servants, both

Prophetic Guilds

Sometimes prophets gathered in groups or "guilds." This may be what is meant by the biblical language "sons of the prophets" (e.g., 1 Kings 20:35; 2 Kings 2:3–15; 4:1, 38; 5:22; 6:1 NASB). A prophetic group in 1 Samuel 10:5, 10 is called "a procession of prophets." These prophets used musical instruments and demonstrated ecstatic frenzy. A group of prophets in 1 Samuel 19:20, who appear with Saul and with whom the narrator compares him, likely are diviner-ecstatics and are called "the company of the prophets" (NASB). This company of the prophets does not use instruments but does go into an ecstatic frenzy, as in 1 Samuel 10:5, 10.

LITERARY NOTES

Basic Types of Prophetic Speech

Prophetic utterance: Often the phrase "the Lord's declaration" appears in the beginning, middle, or end of a prophetic message.

Messenger speech: Often the phrase "thus says the Lord" or "says the Lord" accompanies a prophetic speech. It signifies God's speech to the prophet and the prophet's self-identification as the spokesperson and messenger for God. The messenger speech suggests a word-for-word disclosure of God's message to the audience through the prophet.

Judgment oracle: This is a primarily negative pronouncement of God's action or disaster on individuals, groups, or nations.

Oracle against nations: A kind of judgment oracle, this type of speech is directed against foreign nations that threatened Israel or Judah.

Lawsuit text: This is a text that takes the form of a legal accusation against a party, with YHWH as prosecutor and judge. These often function with judgment oracles.

Salvation oracle: Counterpart to the judgment oracle, this is a message of restoration or salvation by YHWH.

Messianic oracle: This variation on the salvation oracle offers hope in terms of a future anointed king appointed by YHWH for justice and deliverance.

men and women, I will pour out my Spirit in those days" (Joel 2:28–29). In this vision, prophecy is dispensed democratically among the people, and the Spirit of God is poured out.

Actions of the Prophets

People like Abraham (Gen. 20:7), Moses (Deut. 34:10), Aaron (Exod. 7:1), Miriam (15:20), Deborah (Judg. 4:4), Samuel (1 Sam. 3:20), and Gad (22:5) are prophets because they receive a word from God and then share that message with others (Exod. 7:1; cf. Deut. 18:15–22). Prophets disclose God's hidden will to those unable to see it (Amos 3:7). The prophets of Israel speak the word of YHWH. This is true throughout Israel's history in the Old Testament.

In the monarchy and after, prophets used two primary modes of speech: **judgment oracles** and salvation oracles. Judgment oracles pronounce divine judgment against different parties: prophets, priests, king, the royal house, God's people, or other nations. Conversely, salvation oracles pronounce divine deliverance for different parties: prophets, priests, king, the royal house, God's people, or other nations. The prophets used a wide variety of speech types to deliver their oracles.

Sometimes the prophets deliver their messages in unusual ways. The most unusual is sign acts, when the prophet is called by God to enact or perform a message instead of simply speaking it. These living testimonies from the prophets disclose the message of the Lord. More recent scholarship has recognized that the prophets were embodied performers (or "performance artists") of the word of God.[4]

Who Could Be a Prophet?

Prophets could come from anywhere and from any social stratum in the land. For example, Isaiah

Sign Acts of the Prophets

	Divine Command	Reason for the Action
Isaiah	Name children: "Shear-Jashub" (Isa. 7:3), "Immanuel" (Isa. 7:14), "Maher-Shalal-Hash-Baz" (Isa. 8:3)	To signify God's presence ("Shear-Jashub" and "Immanuel"); to signify divine judgment ("Maher-Shalal-Hash-Baz")
	Go around naked (Isa. 20:1–4)	To signify God's judgment
Hosea	Take a wife (Hosea 1:2–3)	To signify the covenant relationship
	Name children: "Jezreel" (Hosea 1:4), "Lo-Ruhamah" (Hosea 1:6), "Lo-Ammi" (Hosea 1:9)	To signify judgment
	Buy back a woman (Hosea 3:1–5)	To signify God's redemption
Jeremiah	Buy, bury, then wear soiled undergarments (Jer. 13:1–11)	To illustrate the uncleanness of the people
	Do not marry or attend funerals/ feasts (Jer. 16:1–9)	To illustrate the coming destruction of Judah
	Shatter pottery (Jer. 19:1–13)	To illustrate the shattering of Judah
	Wear a yoke (Jer. 27–28)	To illustrate submission to Babylon
	Purchase a parcel of land just before invasion (Jer. 32:6–15)	To illustrate the hope of God's people and land beyond the exile
	Offer wine to the Rechabites (Jer. 35)	To contrast Rechabites to the faithlessness of Judah
	Hide stones in wall (Jer. 43:8–13)	To illustrate coming invasion and foreign rule
	Send Seriah a scroll that is thrown into the Euphrates River (Jer. 51:59–64)	To illustrate the coming demise of Babylon
Ezekiel	Go speechless (Ezek. 3:24–27)	To illustrate Ezekiel's inability to speak prophetic words of rebuke or to call Judah to repentance
	Lie on side for 390 days (Ezek. 4:4–6)	To illustrate the sins of Israel
	Lie on other side for 40 days (Ezek. 4:4–6)	To illustrate the sins of Judah
	Draw Jerusalem on a brick and lay siege to the brick (Ezek. 4:1–3)	To illustrate the siege of Jerusalem
	Eat rationed portions of food (Ezek. 4:9–17)	To illustrate the siege of Jerusalem
	Cut hair and divide it in three portions; burn, chop, and scatter it (Ezek. 5:1–4)	To illustrate the ways in which the people of Judah will be burned, chopped, and dispersed by Babylon
	Do not mourn death of wife (Ezek. 24:15–24)	To illustrate the certainty of exile and judgment and the way God's people should respond to it
	Bring together two sticks (Ezek. 37:15–28)	To illustrate future hope and the reunification of Israel and Judah

likely belonged to the royal court in Jerusalem, as he was familiar with it and had access to it. Jeremiah was a priest, as was Ezekiel. Deborah was a prophet and a judge. Miriam was a singer and a prophet.

Prophets can be rich people, poor people, people in urban or rural contexts, priests, or everyday people—the biblical material presents a myriad of options. Amos was a shepherd from Tekoa and had no formal training in prophecy (not the son of a prophet, Amos 7:14). Habakkuk, like Isaiah, may have been an urban priest, as he was familiar with the temple in Jerusalem. Haggai lived in Judah under a Persian occupation force, as did Zechariah. The prophets came from diverse backgrounds, were not restricted to a specific social class, and were called by God to prophesy at many different times.

Covenant Enforcers

More than anything, prophets served as "covenant enforcers," holding Israel to God's call and election as a "kingdom of priests and a holy nation" (Exod. 19:6).[5] To read the prophets is to see how the prophets interpret the terms of the covenant with God for Israel and how the prophets depict the outcomes for covenant breach.

The prophets are hard on God's people, but they are this way because Israel's relationship with God and their representation to the world are at stake. God chose Israel for relationship, but Israel and Judah threaten that relationship and prevent communion with God by their sin. Any breach of covenant relationship with God is not good or life giving. Rather, to move away from God is to move toward death. The covenant enforcers call God's people to remember their first love, the one who delivered Israel out of Egypt for communion and purpose in the land through the covenant at Sinai (Exod. 19–23), a covenant reaffirmed on the plains of Moab (Deut. 27–30) and affirmed again in the covenant renewal ceremony at Shechem (Josh. 24).

Figure 8.7. Icon of Jeremiah the prophet, exhibited at the Museum of Byzantine Culture, Thessaloniki, Greece

The prophets are also hard on the people because God chose Israel to be a "kingdom of priests and a holy nation" (Exod. 19:6). Israel's responsibility was to mediate between God and the nations, teaching the nations God's instruction and praying for the nations. This was their priestly duty as God's people. But priests had to be holy, and holiness meant being fit for service in the terms of the covenant. Israel was to embody God's righteousness by following the instruction of God as they lived well in the land God gave them. When they did, the nations would observe Israel and wonder at them and their God. When Israel did not follow the stipulations of the covenant, the prophets called Israel back to faithfulness because Israel's election was for a purpose: they were blessed by God to be a blessing to the nations.

As readers of the Prophets, then, we must know the foundation of their preaching: the instruction of God in the covenant. The specifics of covenant stipulations can be found in Exodus–Deuteronomy. However, the prophets recall the stories of Genesis often in their prophecies. As a result, one of the ways we begin to understand the prophetic critiques is to know the story in which the prophets are bound: the story from creation to the threshold of the land of promise. Only then will we be able to fully grasp their messages.

How to Read the Prophets as Christian Scripture

The Old Testament prophets declare God and his ways. God spoke through the prophets and prophetic books to reveal himself as the one God who creates and makes covenant and to show how all of creation relates to this God. In the light of human rebellion, the prophets reveal how God has gone on a reclamation project to establish his reign in the world. God's people, Israel, are central to that plan.

The prophets address how God will rule among his people in his land and how Israel refuses to allow God's rule. Analogous to modern prophetic voices in America who advocate justice and social reform as Dr. Martin Luther King Jr. did in the civil rights movement, prophets in Israel called God's people to justice (Amos 5:24; Mic. 6:8).

The prophets speak to a fundamental challenge for Israel, highlighted in the narrative of Joshua–Kings: Israel needs divine redemption, and the nations need that redemption as well. The prophets anticipate that redemption and God's consummate reign with his definitive work in a new covenant (Jer. 31) with a Suffering Servant (Isa. 53), among other beautiful images (Isa. 2; Mic. 4). Thus, the prophets exclaim the radical grace of YHWH for Israel and the nations, revealed ultimately in a future work of redemption.

The New Testament testifies that this work of God, anticipated in the prophets, is found in Jesus. The writer of Hebrews says, "In the past God spoke to our ancestors through the prophets at many times and in various ways, but in these last days he has spoken to us by his Son, whom he

Public domain / Wikimedia Commons

Figure 8.8. Martin Luther King Jr. addresses a crowd from the steps of the Lincoln Memorial

Ignatius of Antioch (ca. AD 35–110) on Jesus and the Prophets

"But as for myself, the archives are Jesus Christ, the sacred archives are his crucifixion, his death, his burial and his resurrection, and the faith which is through him: in these I wish to be justified by your prayers. . . . But something special comes with the Gospel: the coming of the Savior, our Lord Jesus Christ, his passion, and his resurrection. For the beloved prophets proclaimed him, but the gospel is the completion of immortality."[h]

appointed heir of all things, and through whom also he made the universe" (Heb. 1:1–2). These verses affirm that Jesus is the true prophet who discloses the purposes of God. If God spoke through the prophets in the past, he gave his people the sure and true final prophet in his Son, Jesus. In Jesus's own day, most people rejected him. Still, the crowds became ever more aware that this person was a true prophet, a spokesperson for God (Matt. 21:11; cf. 16:14).

Jesus spoke of God's salvation coming through repentance and belief in Jesus's reign as well as of God's judgment if people reject that reign. In this way, Jesus draws attention to themes already disclosed in Judges and Isaiah, among others. As we saw at the beginning of this chapter considering the transfiguration, Jesus is understood as the final prophet and ultimate Word from God. Jesus is the One of whom the Father said, "This is my beloved Son, with whom I am well pleased; listen to him" (Matt. 17:5 ESV).

KEY VERSES IN THE PROPHETS

- Formerly in Israel, if someone went to inquire of God, they would say, "Come, let us go to the seer," because the prophet of today used to be called a seer. 1 Sam. 9:9
- Surely the Sovereign Lord does nothing without revealing his plan to his servants the prophets. Amos 3:7
- He has shown you, O mortal, what is good. And what does the Lord require of you? To act justly and to love mercy and to walk humbly with your God. Mic. 6:8

Christian Reading Questions

1. Identify and explain the Prophets as a canonical unit.
2. What is the role of the prophet in the Old Testament?
3. What did prophets do, and how do Israel's prophets compare and contrast with other prophets in the ancient Near East?
4. Explain how the Prophets relate to the Pentateuch.
5. How do Moses and Elijah cohere in the Old and New Testaments? What is the significance of their appearance at the transfiguration of Jesus?

CHAPTER NINE

Joshua

Orientation

"Moses my servant is dead." This sentence from the second verse of Joshua makes a great deal clear about the book in its redemptive and canonical moment. The book of Joshua is about Israel *after* Moses. At the same time, Israel is still living in view of Moses's continuing authority and legacy. Joshua steps into the leadership void left by Moses. In some senses, Joshua is the new Moses, but in more substantial ways, he is not. Joshua's leadership role within Israel is defined by his reception of Moses's continued authority in the law he left; though Moses is dead, he continues to speak. Joshua's leadership is in service of this Mosaic legacy, and Joshua's characterization in the book attests to the nature of his leadership in light of Mosaic priority.

Joshua is a bridge book. It builds on the foundation of the Torah and moves into the promised land, following Israel's historical movement forward in time. These are the days of Israel before the establishment of the

Figure 9.1. View of promised land from Mount Nebo in Jordan

Ccinar / Shutterstock

Joshua as a Prophet

Joshua fulfills the role of prophet spoken of by Moses in Deuteronomy 18:15–18. He appears as one who delivers the word of the Lord given to him. The prophets often make use of the phrase "Thus says the LORD," revealing the role of the prophet as covenant mediator. Readers will discover this phrase at almost every turn in the books of Isaiah–Malachi. In Joshua, the phrase is found on the lips of Joshua (7:13; 24:2). Joshua's identity as a prophet has implications for this section of the Old Testament canon because Joshua is the first book of the Prophets. The prophetic history in the narratives of Joshua–Kings orients itself to the concerns of the Pentateuch, most especially the book of Deuteronomy. When Joshua ends the book with his call, "Choose for yourselves this day whom you will serve," he echoes the internal claims of Deuteronomy: choose life (Josh. 24:15; cf. Deut. 30:19).

Joshua and Deuteronomy

The close links between the books of Joshua and Deuteronomy have long been observed by interpreters. The covenant stipulations for life and death in terms of covenant loyalty, the promises of entry into the promised land now fulfilled (Deut. 12:9–10), and the continuing Mosaic legacy all indicate the beginnings of Israel's history in the land as rooted in the theological dynamics of Deuteronomy and the Pentateuch more broadly.

Figure 9.2. *The Angel Appearing to Joshua* by Gustave Doré

Public domain / The Holy Bible containing the Old and New Testaments

monarchy and then the division of the kingdom into its northern (Israel) and southern (Judah) regions. There is no Saul, David, or Solomon yet. The Torah had set out the nature of the covenantal relation between YHWH and Israel. The Lord is jealous for the loyalty of his people: "Hear, O Israel: the LORD our God, the LORD is one [or the Lord alone]" (Deut. 6:4 AT). No others. Me alone. At the very heart of the covenantal relationship is not a call to moralistic perfection but a call to exclusive loyalty to Israel's God alone: YHWH and no other. Human flourishing and communal joy stem from the exclusive character of Israel's worship of YHWH. As the Ten Commandments remind us, when the first commandment comes undone, the rest quickly follow.

In time, the covenant relation will be unrecognizable. The book of Judges, immediately after Joshua, illustrates the pattern of sin's downward spiral. This pattern will continue into the books of Samuel and Kings until both Northern and Southern Kingdoms fall to foreign empires (Israel in 722 BC; Judah in 586 BC). But not yet. Joshua and the wilderness-wanderers-turned-possessors-of-the-promised-land are testimony to a golden age of Israel's past. This is a time when the covenant was obeyed and the people were living into God's promises and enjoying the human flourishing that came along with covenant faithfulness to YHWH.

Exploration—Reading Joshua

The book of Joshua falls neatly into two parts. After the introductory chapter, the first section of the book (chaps. 1–12) focuses on the conquest of the land, with the second part of the book (chaps. 13–22) outlining the allotment of the land to the tribes of Israel. The final two chapters conclude with Joshua's charge to the elders of Israel and the entire people to remain faithful to the covenant (chaps. 23–24).

The Promises of God and the Conquest of the Land: Joshua 1–12

■ READ JOSHUA 1–4 ■

The first chapter of Joshua paints a picture of the new environment Israel inhabits. The years of wilderness wandering have come to an end. The promise of a future land for Abraham's offspring rests on the near horizon of fulfillment. This promise was not spiritualized away but remains a concrete gift of God to those in covenant relation to him. Joshua charges Israel to be strong and courageous. This kind of charge makes sense in light of the military campaigns awaiting them, but the call to strength and courage is not based on Israel's military prowess or brute capabilities. The charge rests on God's promise to be with them, as he had been with Moses: I will be with you to deliver you (Exod. 3:12; Josh. 1:5). Joshua 1:5–9 establishes three interdependent emphases: (1) strength and courage, (2) the promise of God's presence, and (3) attending to the law given to Moses.

Joshua 1 lays claim to the promises of God. The promised land is exactly that, the *promised* land. Joshua steps into the leadership with full

Figure 9.3. *Joshua Passing the River Jordan with the Ark of the Covenant* by Benjamin West

assurance of the promises given to Israel by God through Moses: "Remember the word that Moses the servant of the LORD commanded you" (Josh. 1:13 NRSV; cf. Deut. 12:9–10). Readers do not have to strain to see a central theme of Joshua. Israel's religious and national health rests on the authority and supremacy of the Lord, his promises, and his instructions. Israel's long history that ultimately leads to exile will reveal the nation's struggle to come to terms with these most important theological matters.

Israel's early history repeats certain patterns. In Joshua 3, Joshua crosses the Jordan River in ways reminiscent of the exodus event and the crossing of the Red Sea. In Joshua 2, the people of Israel send spies into the land of Canaan as they did back in Numbers 13–14. The first attempt at sending spies into the land did not end well. Of the twelve spies sent, only two—Joshua and Caleb—announced their confidence in the Lord's ability to give them the victory. Everyone else cowered in fear, and this fear spread like a toxin through the camp. Israel's unbelief led to their forty-year detour through the wilderness. Now, Israel has come full circle, situated outside the land while two spies scout out the enemy.

The spies go to the city of Jericho, where they stay with a prostitute named Rahab. Rahab's house was part of the city wall and was most likely in a discreet locale, given the nature of her trade. All these factors made her house an ideal location for

RECEPTION HISTORY

Rahab's Profession among Interpreters

In John Calvin's commentary on Joshua, he challenges certain readings of the Rahab narrative that describe her profession as simply the "keeper of an inn." There are obvious reasons why Rahab's profession as a prostitute causes some interpreters in the Jewish and Christian traditions to blush. But Calvin insists on reading the text for what it says and for celebrating the grace of God in Rahab's life. The nature of Rahab's profession only makes the brilliance of God's grace more luminous.

espionage. Nevertheless, news of the spies reaches the king of Jericho, who hurries to ferret out the spies from Rahab's home. Rahab, however, proves faithful. Put in terms of Joshua 1, Rahab is "strong and courageous." She provides cover for the two spies by offering a completely plausible story, given her profession: "Yes, the men came to me, but I did not know where they had come from." She said they had left, and the king had better pursue them quickly to have any chance of catching up to them (2:4–5).

Rahab acts in faithfulness when she hides the spies on her rooftop, diverting those seeking their harm. Why would she do this? Why would she endanger herself on their behalf? What's the source of her "strength and courage"? Reports of the mighty deeds of Israel's God, the Lord Almighty, have reached her ears. The stories of the exodus, some forty years old, have gone throughout the land, and the people of Jericho are afraid. Rahab is afraid too, but her fear leads her to faith: "for the LORD your God is God in heaven above and on the earth below" (2:11). Rahab puts her full confidence and trust in Israel's God to save and redeem. The result of her faith is the salvation of her entire family when the onslaught begins. Rahab is a testimony to the outstretched arm of the Lord to all, even Canaanites, who turn to him in faith and devotion.

When the spies return to Joshua, they bring a clear message: Jericho is ours. Joshua and the people set out for Jericho, camping for three days at the Jordan River. At the Red Sea, the Lord made use of Moses's staff and a strong wind. Now, the Levites carry the ark of the covenant on their shoulders as they step into the waters of the Jordan. Once their sandals touch the water, the Lord makes a path for them to the other side.

Remembering the surprising and saving deeds of the Lord is a central tenet of Old Testament faith. The Psalms are replete with calls to remember the mighty acts of the Lord (cf. Ps. 77). Deuteronomy gives an account of the law in chapters 5–6, along with a call for parents to teach their children the law, day and night. When the children ask the meaning of these laws, Deuteronomy tells us, the answer is

THEOLOGICAL ISSUES

Gentiles and the Divine Name

Rahab is a gentile who places her saving hope in Israel's God, YHWH. The names of God within the Pentateuch—Elohim and YHWH—move from a general claim about the Creator of the world to the personal and revealed name of Israel's God, YHWH. God's giving of his name YHWH to the people of Israel is a gift specifically targeted at Israel. Yet here Rahab, the Canaanite, like the sailors on Jonah's boat in Jonah 1, calls out to YHWH. Rahab's use of the divine name in her confession reveals her proper place in the covenant community of Israel.

CANONICAL CONNECTIONS

Rahab's Place in the Canon

The Gospel writer Matthew lists Rahab as the mother of Boaz, the great-grandfather of King David in his genealogy of Jesus (Matt. 1:5; cf. Heb. 11:31; James 2:25). What a remarkable testimony to God's triumphant grace to find Rahab in the most important genealogy of all time.

CANONICAL CONNECTIONS

Crossing the Red Sea and the Jordan River

The Hebrew word for sea is *yam*, and the Hebrew word for river is *nahar*. Psalm 66:6 appears to bring together the crossing of the Red Sea (*yam*) in Exodus and the crossing of the Jordan River (*nahar*) in Joshua. "He turned the sea [*yam*] into dry land, they passed through the waters [*nahar*] on foot—come, let us rejoice in him." Though different historical moments, both events share in the same imagery and saving significance.

a retelling of Israel's salvation story in the exodus (cf. Deut. 6:20–25). Adherence to the law is an invitation to remember God's salvation. The pattern continues in Joshua as well. Once on the far side of the Jordan, after the display of God's mighty power to make a way for his people, Joshua establishes a memorial in the Jordan River (Josh. 4:9). Twelve large stones,

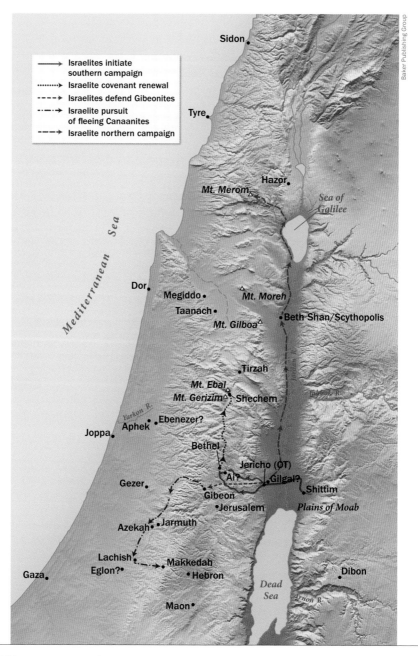

Figure 9.4. Map of locations in Joshua

one from each of Israel's tribes, are also carried to Gilgal on Jericho's eastern side and placed together as a "memorial forever" (4:7 NRSV). Why a memorial? Again, the stones serve the purpose of eliciting questions from children: "Father, what are these stones all about?" The question provides parents a platform to remind their children and their children's children of God's saving actions.

The possession of the land is fully at hand. Chapter 5 clarifies a few necessary matters before the forward advance. It begins by setting the stage: the Canaanite kings are melting with fear. They have "no spirit" to fight (Josh. 5:1 NASB). Fruit of victory is ripe for plucking. But before this can take place another matter needs attention. Because of the unfaithfulness of the wilderness generation, the male Israelites born during those decades were left uncircumcised. Joshua remedied this situation at Gilgal (5:8). Another matter addressed in Joshua 5 is the celebration of Passover. This event must have been a great encouragement for the Israelites as they remembered God's saving deeds at the exodus in anticipation of his doing so again. Following this celebration, God's provision of manna stopped because the people were able to get food from the land.

Before the fall of Jericho in chapter 6, Joshua has a strange encounter with a "man" standing before him with a drawn sword. The "man" reveals himself as the commander of the Lord's armies. Readers might recall Jacob's midnight encounter with a "man" by the Jabbok River (Gen. 32). Joshua asks his visitor, "Are you for us or for our enemies?" (Josh. 5:13). Surely the answer should be "I'm for you," but instead the reply is "Neither" (5:14). The "man" is for the Lord. Before Israel begins to conquer the land, this encounter makes something very clear: The question Israel is to ask is not "Is the Lord on our side?" The more necessary question is "Are we on the Lord's side?" The Lord will fight for them as their divine warrior, but as chapters 6–7 will reveal, Israelite faithfulness to the Lord is the guarantee of victory, regardless of the enemy's strength.

What follows in the narrative of Joshua are accounts of the fall of Jericho (chap. 6) and Israel's defeat at Ai (chap. 7). These two stories balance each other and illustrate the importance of Joshua's encounter with the commander of the Lord's army in chapter 5: Who is on the Lord's side?

Figure 9.5. Battle of Jericho as depicted in Bible de Saint-Jean d'Arce

The Battle of Jericho reveals God's faithfulness to Israel. Joshua 6:2 claims that, from the Lord's perspective, the battle was won before it even began. God commands the people to march around the city once a day for six days. Priests carrying the ark of the covenant lead the march, witnessing to the promise of God's presence with the people. On the seventh day the Israelites march around Jericho seven times while the priests blow trumpets. After a long blast and a loud shout, the city walls tumble down as an act of God's saving intervention. The Israelites capture the city, saving Rahab and her family because of her faith in YHWH, the God of Israel.

The "battle" of Jericho was not much of a battle at all. A seven-day march around the city is not the mark of military prowess but of a faithful God and a faithful people. The seven-day march echoes the seven days of creation; this battle was the work of Israel's warrior king, the Lord himself. The story concludes with an important and revealing statement: "So the Lord was with Joshua" (6:27).

God gave strict instructions regarding the destruction of Jericho. All the silver, gold, and valuables were set apart as sacred to God, and everything else was to be destroyed (6:19, 21, 24). Known as *herem* warfare—translated as "the ban" (NASB) or "the devoted things" (NIV, NRSV)—this kind of warfare flows from YHWH's exclusive claim on Israel: "The Lord, our God, the Lord alone" (Deut. 6:4 AT). What appears as drastic and severe—the total annihilation of a people group—attests to God's concerns to keep Israel pure from the moral corruption of the surrounding Canaanite cultures. And yet readers do well to remember God's gracious kindness to the Canaanite Rahab, who put her faith in YHWH and was spared. *Herem* warfare was not Israel's "foreign policy" or the normal state of affairs. It was part of a unique moment in Israel's history, as God sought to protect Israel from the idolatrous sin of the Canaanites (Deut. 20:16–18). Readers may also have to allow for some hyperbole or exaggerated speech about the extent of *herem* in Joshua 6–12. One example is Israel's destruction of Hebron. Joshua 10:36–39 speaks of Hebron's complete destruction, but Joshua 15:13–15 narrates Caleb having to deal with residual problems there. The book of Joshua lives in the tension of these two pictures:

complete destruction of the Canaanite cities and the necessity of continued action against the Canaanite cities. If the book of Joshua has no trouble with this narrated tension, then neither should we. The exaggerated speech is not disingenuous or a fabrication. Rather, it attests to the exclusive claims of YHWH on the people. Moreover, *herem* warfare did not promise the spoils of war to the combatants, as most wars of this time did. Soldiers risking their lives in combat were often motivated by these spoils—"To the victor go the spoils." But the Lord forbade Israelite soldiers from participating in such looting. The conquest of the land was the Lord's war, and the spoils of war were dedicated to God.

In the Battle of Jericho, however, the temptation to loot proved too much for Achan. Chapter 7 describes Achan's sin with an all too familiar pattern: he "saw," he "coveted," he "took" (7:21). As with Adam and Eve, the fruit was before him, and he "took" it. The consequences of the sin, like that of Adam and Eve's, was death—his own as punishment and that of his fellow Israelites in the Battle of Ai.

Achan's sin was secret until Israel's second battle, the Battle of Ai. Joshua is so confident in this battle, he does not even send his whole army, just a few squadrons. But Israel is soundly defeated, and when Joshua complains to God about the turn of events, God tells him there is sin in the camp. Achan is to be destroyed because "he has violated the covenant of the LORD and has done an outrageous thing in Israel" (7:15).

Once Achan's sin has been dealt with, Joshua and his army are ready to face Ai again. The result of this battle is victory (Josh. 8). What was the difference? Exclusive loyalty to the Lord and his instructions. Again, readers are uncomfortably aware that the whole of Joshua concerns itself with the complete and total dedication of everything to the Lord: the people of Israel, the land, the surrounding nations— all are the Lord's. Israel's faithfulness to the Lord's claims on them assured them of their conquest. In a

Mount Ebal in Deuteronomy and Joshua

After the destruction of Ai, Joshua holds a covenant renewal ceremony on Mount Ebal (Josh. 8:30–35). An altar was built, the law was recopied, and Joshua read the entire Mosaic law to all the people, including the sojourners among them like Rahab. This scene fulfills the commands Moses made in Deuteronomy 27:2–8.

condensed narration, the remaining chapters in the first part of Joshua narrate the rest of Israel's conquest of the land (chaps. 10–12).

Settling in the Land: Joshua 13–24

■ READ JOSHUA 22–24 ■

The second half of Joshua is not easy reading. Obscure place names and territorial boundary markers fill the pages, and a natural response from today's

Figure 9.6. Map of Israel's tribal distribution

Baker Publishing Group

readers is to skip past them. Nevertheless, it is important to have a sense of what is taking place in these chapters. A significant amount of Old Testament textual space is given to the second half of Joshua. The Old Testament considers these chapters and their details important. Why? Because so much of what precedes Joshua in the Pentateuch comes to fruition here (cf. Deut. 7:18–24; 30:20). The promise given to Abraham regarding a land for his offspring meets its moment of fulfillment. The tribes who represent the great-grandchildren of Abraham and the offspring of Jacob are now allotted their space and place. The lots for each tribe's land were cast by Joshua, Eleazar the priest, and the heads of the tribes. Once the lot was cast, the land inheritance was distributed to the tribes. The details of the inheritance allotment continue tribe by tribe, excluding the Levites, who are given no land possession but inherit the Lord himself as they dedicate themselves to worship and priestly ministry (Josh. 13:33).

In the final two chapters of the book, Joshua gathers the leaders of the tribes and reminds them of God's faithfulness to them (chap. 23). The lands may be distributed to the tribes, but the work of possession continues. Joshua gives these leaders a gift of clarity regarding the situation: "You yourselves have seen everything the LORD your God has done to all these nations for your sake; it was the LORD your God who fought for you" (23:3). The book began with a call to courage, and so too it ends. The courage Joshua calls for is the courage to obey God's word as given through Moses: "Be very strong; be careful to obey all that is written in the Book of the Law of Moses" (23:6). There are dangerous temptations at every turn with the religious and moral culture of the Canaanites still present. Be careful, Joshua warns. The Canaanite gods must be resisted. Remember, God brought you to this moment by his own power and presence. Yet God's power and presence are gifts and never possessions. The warning comes in verse 12: "But if . . ." If you turn away, then these gifts may be rescinded. The whole future of Israel's life with God

CANONICAL CONNECTIONS

Casting Lots in Joshua and Acts

Is the distribution of the land decided by the casting of lots, or in our terms, dice? The Israelites under Joshua believed these matters were in the hands of the Lord and, as in Proverbs 16:33, understood the casting of lots as under God's control. On a more practical side, the casting of lots removed the political dimension of such an important decision, providing impartiality at some level. In the New Testament the apostles cast lots to replace Judas Iscariot among the twelve. This casting of lots in the book of Acts echoes this event in Joshua, as the "twelve" apostles extend God's land promise to the whole world (Acts 1:8).

CANONICAL CONNECTIONS

Did the Tribes Possess the Land or Not?

A tension exists in these chapters of land distribution. The land is apportioned to the respective tribes as their inheritance, yet residual problems remain as possession of the land entails continued struggle with the previous inhabitants. There is a sense of possession and nonpossession at the same time. One aspect of this tension may be a continued reminder to God's people that the land was not theirs by right but by gift/inheritance, by the Lord's continued presence as their warrior. Continued faithfulness was necessary for the maintaining and possession of the land, as Deuteronomy reminds again and again. The prophet Micah later says the loss of the land is due to Judah's unfaithfulness (Mic. 2:4–5). No one, according to Micah, will be left to divide the land by lot. The promise in Isaiah of a new heavens and a new earth moves the land promise into a more global and eschatological view (Isa. 65–66).

is laid bare in these chapters. Will Israel remain faithful to YHWH and YHWH alone? Readers know the answer is unfortunately no.

From his charge to the elders of the land, Joshua turns to the people at large (chap. 24). He reminds them of the history of their salvation. From Abraham's **polytheistic** beginnings to Israel's presence in the promised land, the Lord had given himself to Israel as their God. The story of salvation was a motivation for fear and fidelity to YHWH as Israel's God alone. Israel's existence comes down to one question: Will you forsake YHWH for other gods? (24:19–20). The people shout, "No!" (24:21). With a passionate appeal, Joshua calls the people to destroy any gods they had kept, giving their hearts solely to the Lord. Again, the people respond, "We will serve the Lord our God and obey him" (24:24). It is a powerful scene at the end of Joshua. The Lord had redeemed his people and fought for them. The promised land is now occupied, and the people's hearts and minds are filled with hope and gratitude to their God. But such is the nature of the human heart and its struggle with sin that before long, everyone would be doing what was right in their own eyes (Judges).

Implementation—Reading Joshua as Christian Scripture Today

Along the coast of northern France and nestled on a ridge above the roaring coastline rests a hallowed site. Rows upon rows of white crosses mark the final resting place for thousands who gave their lives in the Battle of Normandy during World War II. Just below these crosses, waves crash onto Omaha Beach, transporting visitors back to one of the United States' defining moments in its relatively short history: D-Day. Those crosses stand as a perpetual reminder of the greatest of national heroics and sacrifices made in a hellish quest for liberation. Those crosses remind many Americans of a golden age in our history, even though that age also exhibited the struggles of human existence.

In many ways, the book of Joshua takes readers back to a golden age of Israel's past. This age too was marked by bravery and heroics—"Be strong and take courage!" Yet the heroics did not rest on Israel's military prowess but on the promise of Israel's God to fight for his people. The people trusted God and acted in covenant fidelity to the Lord. They put away foreign gods to keep the first commandment and adhere to the call of the Shema (Deut. 6:4). The people were indeed God's people, and YHWH was their God. As their God, YHWH fought for them and gave them the land he had promised to Abraham their forefather. The golden age would be short-lived, though there would be episodes of it again in the future—such as the Solomonic era and the renewal of the covenant in Josiah's day. Yet Israel's history in the land would be a history of loss, with Joshua as a canonical reminder from generation to generation of that special time "back then" in order to inspire hope for a future day like unto it.

KEY VERSES IN JOSHUA

- Be strong and very courageous. Be careful to obey all the law my servant Moses gave you; do not turn from it to the right or to the left, that you may be successful wherever you go. Keep this Book of the Law always on your lips; meditate on it day and night, so that you may be careful to do everything written in it. Then you will be prosperous and successful. Have I not commanded you? Be strong and courageous. Do not be afraid; do not be discouraged, for the LORD your God will be with you wherever you go. 1:7–9
- Be very strong; be careful to obey all that is written in the Book of the Law of Moses, without turning aside to the right or to the left. Do not associate with these nations that remain among you; do not invoke the names of their gods or swear by them. You must not serve them or bow down to them. But you are to hold fast to the LORD your God, as you have until now. The LORD has driven out before you great and powerful nations; to this day no one has been able to withstand you. One of you routs a thousand, because the LORD your God fights for you, just as he promised. So be very careful to love the LORD your God. 23:6–11
- And the people said to Joshua, "We will serve the LORD our God and obey him." 24:24

Christian Reading Questions

1. Joshua is the golden age of Israel's history. But it did not last long. What does this tell us about the human heart and its need?
2. The great triumphs of Joshua are all due to God's powerful aid. How does looking to the past help believers in the present?
3. How does the book of Joshua present complete and total loyalty to the Lord God? How does this relate to a Christian understanding of following Jesus?
4. On what basis are the people encouraged to be "strong and courageous"? How can such promises bolster the life of faith?

CHAPTER TEN

Judges

Orientation

Have you ever started reading a book, only to find that it was too difficult to finish? Maybe it was too violent or scary or just plain boring. The book of Judges is not boring, but it does include scary and violent parts. The reason for its gruesome content is because of its central message: the long-term outcome of disobedience to God is disaster. More specifically, Judges shows what it looks like when Israel becomes like the nations around them. It exposes in lucid detail the downward spiral into sin.

In many ways, the book is monstrous. But even monstrous books like Judges can be valuable when they hold a mirror to the world as it is rather than offering a utopian view of the world as we want it to be. We discover, by negative example, the kind of people and communities we *don't* want to be.

The book begins with Israel united in the land, and it concludes with Israel in a civil war. The book also presents an interesting structure, in which the ending takes us back to the beginning, in a kind of circle. This gives the effect of return: Israel is in the same state at the end of the book as they were at the beginning—only worse. One understands this only by exploring the repeated elements of the book. 📖

This cyclical structure is seen in repeated elements in Judges 1–2 and Judges 19–21.[1] In Judges 1 and 20 the Israelites gather together for war and inquire about leadership. The tribe of Judah is identified as the leader in both cases. The first inquiry (Judg. 1) concerns going in to take the land, and the second (Judg. 20) concerns going in to destroy

📖 LITERARY NOTES

The Structure of Judges

1. Introducing the cycle (1:1–3:6)
2. The judges in the cycle (3:7–16:31)
3. The epilogue and no king (17:1–21:25)

Benjamin. The Israelites weep over judgment in Judges 2:4–5 and 21:2–4. In 2:4–5, they weep over God's judgment against their failure to drive out nations, but in 21:2–4, they weep over their success of attacking the tribe of Benjamin! Repetition between texts drives home the horrible reality borne out in the book: Israel is committed to destroying themselves rather than driving out the nations.

Finally, we see the repeated elements of Jebus/Jerusalem in Judges 1 and 19. In Judges 1, the tribe of Benjamin fails to drive out the Jebusites from their city (Jebus/Jerusalem), and they remain there (1:21). In Judges 19, the Levite and his concubine travel past Jebus/Jerusalem because it is a city full of foreigners (19:10) and then go to Gibeah, a city of Israelites, where trouble and horrors break out. They would have been safer and better off staying among the Jebusites in Jerusalem rather than among Israelites in Gibeah, considering the crimes that Israel commits there. The structure is circular, and it reveals the end of the book is like the beginning, only worse.

Exploration—Reading Judges

Introducing the Cycle: Judges 1:1–3:6

■ READ JUDGES 1–3 ■

The book of Judges opens with a question of leadership. Israel's first and second generations were marked by the leadership of Moses and Joshua, respectively. Joshua's impending death leaves no successor, creating a vacuum of leadership. This is a significant problem, because the book of Joshua concludes with not all the promised land under the control of Israel.

In Judges 1, the tribe of Judah is chosen rather than an individual to lead the people in this transition period. God empowers Judah to take their tribal allotment, but other tribes are not as

Judges in Deuteronomy and Kings

Leadership is a major theme in the book of Judges, and it drives us to ask about the group of leaders in the book called "judges." What is a "judge"? The Hebrew word is *shophet*. In our culture, we think of a judge in narrow terms, as someone who issues a legal decision in a court of law. In the Old Testament, that idea sometimes fits what a *shophet* is. Deuteronomy clarified the role of a *shophet* as a public official who provides legal rulings (Deut. 16:18–20). However, the meaning of the term is likely broader in the Old Testament, wherein a judge exercises some sort of authority and decision-making, like a municipal governor or leader.

THEOLOGICAL ISSUES

YHWH as Judge

Despite the English title of the book of Judges, the only named individual who is described with the Hebrew noun "judge" (*shophet*) in the book of Judges is YHWH. Jepthah speaks of "YHWH the judge" (11:27). Thus, YHWH is the ruler, adjudicator, and deliverer of Israel.

LITERARY NOTES

Judges as Charismatic Saviors

The Hebrew verb "to judge/govern" (*shaphat*) appears with leaders we translate as "judges" in the book of Judges. These individuals generally do not give legal rulings about disputes as in Deuteronomy or Kings. Rather, they exhibit charismatic (Spirit-led) qualities of leadership, save Israel from oppression, and then lead the people for a while. Interestingly, the narrative does not focus on the ways leaders like Deborah, Ehud, Gideon, or Samson governed their people. Rather, the focus of the narrative is how these leaders were used of God to deliver the people. For this reason, in the book of Judges, a "judge" is more like a "savior" or "deliverer." God raised up these deliverers in moments of crisis and oppression, and they brought relief from foreign oppression and provided temporary peace. In the book of Judges, the judges are charismatic deliverers.

successful: Manasseh, Benjamin, Zebulun, Asher, Naphtali, Dan. The outcome of this failure is a word of judgment that sets the stage for the book. Speaking for God, an angel appears to the people, saying, "I brought you up out of Egypt and led you into the land I swore to give to your ancestors. I said, 'I will never break my covenant with you, and you shall not make a covenant with the people of this land, but you shall break down their altars.' Yet you have disobeyed me. Why have you done this? And I have also said, 'I will not drive them out before you; they will become traps for you, and their gods will become snares to you'" (2:1–3).

This statement introduces the problem of the book. Israel's disobedience to God's word and their failure to drive out the inhabitants of the land lead them to idolatry (cf. Deut. 7). This generation under the leadership of Judah represents a generation after Moses and Joshua, and the text says that this third generation "knew neither the Lord nor what he had done for Israel. Then the Israelites did evil in the eyes of the Lord and served the Baals. They forsook the Lord, the God of their ancestors, who had brought them out of Egypt. They followed and worshiped various gods of the peoples around them" (Judg. 2:10–12).

Israel's rebellion generates a divine response in the "cycle" presented in Judges 2. We have seen in the circular structure of the book of Judges that repetition at various levels in narrative is a vital technique in the Old Testament to teach us about humanity and God. Repeated phrases occur through the progression of the narrative and reinforce or deepen our understanding of divine or human action. Entire scenes may be repeated to help us understand the virtue or vice of the people in the narrative, or to understand God better. Repetition of phrases and scenes in the book of Judges characterizes the cycle of Israel's sin and God's response. In this cycle we feel the people of God going "round and round" in circles on a downward trajectory of sin. 📖

Figure 10.1. The cycle of sin and salvation in Judges

1. Israel sins against God
2. God raises an oppressor
3. Israel cries out to God for help
4. God delivers by a judge
5. Period of peace under the judge

The Cycle of Sin and Salvation

1. The Israelites rebel against God (2:10–13).
2. God raises up an oppressor (2:14–15).
3. The Israelites cry out to God (2:15, 18b).
4. God raises up a deliverer (2:16–18).
5. God provides peace under the judge for a time (2:18–19).

On the one hand, the cycle reveals Israel's proclivity toward sin and rebellion against YHWH. When they fail to follow God, God raises up oppressors. These oppressors create havoc for the Israelites, who then cry

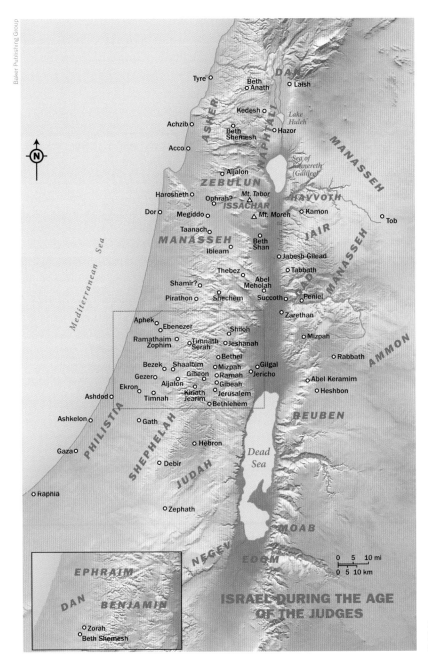

Figure 10.2. Map of Israel in the time of the judges

Who Are the Canaanites?

Judges warns Israel against making covenants with the Canaanites because God's people would then pursue the gods of the Canaanites (like Baal and Ashtoreth in Judg. 2:11–13). But who are the Canaanites? "Canaanite" describes those peoples living in the land of Palestine, including Jebusites, Amorites, Philistines, Perizzites, Sidonians, Hittites, and Hivites. The text depicts these nations as inhabiting the land that God has given Israel as a divine land grant. The Canaanites were polytheists, and their devotion to their gods was a "snare" for Israel (2:3).[a]

out to God for help. Each time, God raises up a judge to deliver Israel and bring them back into their proper covenant relationship. Peace ensues under the leadership of each judge until the cycle starts again when Israel sins.

On the other hand, a pattern of grace and deliverance in the book of Judges echoes the story of God's deliverance of Israel from Egypt. Each act of deliverance from an oppressor in Judges "should be understood as a sort of new exodus, God's gracious deliverance of the people from an oppressive, death-dealing situation."[2] In this way, divine grace and mercy, despite human sin, appear as a golden thread in the dark narrative

Canaanite Pantheon

Canaanite gods exerted authority over the natural world, human skills and culture, and even life and death. The gods El and Asherah procreated various sons and daughters, who were divine beings as well. Baal, Asherah, and Astarte provided rain and fertility. In an agrarian society, rain and crops were essential to life. It is not surprising Israel would be tempted to pursue these fertility deities like the nations around them. After all, their world did not display the secular/sacred distinctions of the modern world. The totality of Canaanite existence was haunted with the divine. In theological terms, Israel was tempted to worship a created thing rather than their Creator, YHWH.

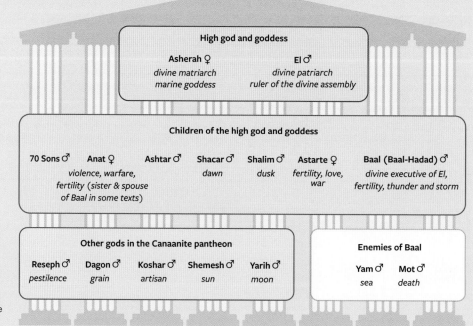

Figure 10.3. The Canaanite pantheon

tapestry of Judges. In this chapter, we will highlight several aspects of Judges that help us get a better handle on the theology of the book.

The Judges in the Cycle: Judges 3:7–16:31

THE FIRST JUDGES: JUDGES 3:7–11

The accounts of three judges open the book, with a significant amount of violence and bloodshed. Othniel (Judg. 3:7–11) delivers Israel from the oppression of Cushan-Rishathaim, king of Aram Naharaim (a kingdom in northwest Mesopotamia). Othniel is Caleb's nephew, linking the first judge to the Joshua-Caleb leadership generation that followed Moses. After Othniel's victory, the land enjoys a forty-year peace (3:11). After Othniel, Ehud leads Israel to victory over Moab (3:12–30). Ehud pretends to offer tribute to the Moabite king, Eglon, whom the text describes as very fat. Ehud plunges his knife into the king's stomach and escapes. Israel enjoys eighty years of peace (3:30). Shamgar's treatment is very brief; he defeats the Philistines (3:31). 🏺 🏺

DEBORAH AND BARAK: JUDGES 4–5

▓ READ JUDGES 4–5 ▓

After the first three judges, the narrative slows down with the violent story of Deborah and Barak (Judg. 4–5). Deborah is a prophetess and judge, and she governs under a palm tree. She is a faithful follower of God and encourages Barak, her coleader, to go to war against King Jabin of the

Figure 10.4. *Ehud, a Clever Leader, Deborah, a Prophetess*. Old Testament miniatures with Latin, Persian, and Judeo-Persian inscriptions. Paris, France (ca. 1244–54).

Canaanites. Their victory is due to God's intervention: "At Barak's advance, the LORD routed Sisera and all his chariots and army by the sword, and Sisera got down from his chariot and fled on foot" (4:15). Sisera flees and hides in the tent of Jael, an ally's wife (4:17). While Sisera sleeps in the tent, Jael drives a tent peg

Figure 10.5. *Jael and Sisera* by Artemisia Gentileschi (1620)

through his head, a scene that has captured the imagination of countless artists. The text makes clear who wins the victory: "On that day God subdued Jabin king of Canaan before the Israelites" (4:23).

Judges 5 is a song written in ancient Hebrew poetry that recognizes God's divine power in deliverance.[3] The poem refers to Sinai in its opening praise of YHWH as the divine warrior, connecting the song to God's deliverance of Israel in the exodus to worship at Sinai (5:4–5). Then Judges 5 portrays details omitted from the story in Judges 4 and invokes blessing for Jael, who killed Sisera (5:24), presumably in obedience to the Lord's command for God's people to fight Jabin and, thereby, Sisera. The poem concludes with a curse and a blessing: "So may all your enemies perish, LORD! But may all who love you be like the sun when it rises in its strength" (5:31). The question, of course, is whether the judges who follow will love YHWH.

FROM GIDEON TO SAMSON: JUDGES 6–16

◼ READ JUDGES 6–9 ◼

The answer to the question of whether the judges will love YHWH is in three extended narratives focusing on the lives of Gideon and his son Abimelech (Judg. 6:8–9:57), Jephthah (10:6–12:7), and Samson (13:1–16:31). Unfortunately, each of these figures loves something other than YHWH, as the narrative bears out.

This section opens by describing an unnamed prophet who appears in Judges 6:7–8. True to the pattern of "the cycle," Israel cries out to God because of their oppressor, this time the people of Midian (v. 7). Although we would expect God to raise up a deliverer, we find a strange insertion of the unnamed prophet who declares essentially a word of judgment in response to Israel's cries for help. "This is what the Lord, the God of Israel, says: I brought you up out of Egypt, out of the land of slavery. I rescued you from the hand of the Egyptians. And I delivered you from the hand of all your oppressors; I drove them out before you and gave you their land. I said to you, 'I am the Lord your God; do not worship the gods of the Amorites, in whose land you live.' But you have not listened to me" (6:8–10). Here, the prophet is a spokesperson of judgment. There is no real complexity to his characterization, and he serves as an agent to carry the narrative forward. Gideon, by contrast, is quite complex, a full-fledged character! He is the first of three flawed judges in the narrative: Gideon, Jephthah, and Samson.

It is clear why Midian oppresses Israel, at least from the perspective of the narrator and the prophet in Judges 6:1–10. But not for Gideon. Immediately after presenting the words of the unnamed prophet, the narrative says an angel of the Lord appears to Gideon and proclaimed YHWH's presence with him. Gideon responds, "If the Lord is with us, why has all this happened to us? Where are all his wonders that our ancestors told us about when they said, 'Did not the Lord bring us up out of Egypt?' But now the Lord has abandoned us and given us into the hand of Midian" (6:13).

The angel pronounces an unexpected affirmation that contrasts with Gideon's confusion: "The Lord is with you, mighty warrior" (6:12). God has raised up Gideon for a purpose, but he does not see it immediately. YHWH has raised Gideon to deliver God's people from their oppression, true to the role of the judge. But why has Gideon been chosen? The rationale is unclear. The reason for God's selection of this judge, of any judge, belongs solely in the mind of God.

Gideon is unsure about this call to be a deliverer and asks God for a sign that it really is God who is speaking to him. God does so by using the angel to light the sacrifice on fire with a staff. Upon seeing the act, Gideon exclaims, "Alas, Sovereign Lord! I

LITERARY NOTES

What Is Characterization?

Biblical narrative utilizes complex characterization in Judges. Characterization is a way to describe how characters in biblical narrative are portrayed. We do not find full details in narrative, but what narrative we do have is important. Adele Berlin divides characters into three types:

1. Full-fledged characters display emotion and inner thoughts. Still, their actions and the motivations that govern them are often left for the reader to discern.
2. Types are idealized figures, like the "villain" or the "hero." Narrative also uses character types to advance the story along.
3. Agents are characters necessary for the plot to advance.[b]

THEOLOGICAL ISSUES

The Angel of YHWH

One of the ways that God manifests himself in the Old Testament is through the "angel of the Lord" (the angel of YHWH). The angel of the Lord is not necessarily a luminous figure with a halo and wings, as we find in artwork. The angel of the Lord is a messenger of God who speaks the words of God. In the Old Testament, characters like Gideon speak to the angel of the Lord as if they are speaking to God. They often address the angel as "lord," but this is not a recognition that the angel of the Lord is divine or on par with YHWH. From the perspective of the speaker (in this case, Gideon), the angel of the Lord is like God. To see an angel is to see a manifestation of the divine. However, the angel is likely a messenger of YHWH, not YHWH himself.[c] Angels are heavenly messengers, often indistinguishable from normal human beings, who speak for God or do specific work for God or reveal something about God's plans or designs.

have seen the angel of the LORD face to face!" (6:22). He builds an altar on the place to commemorate the experience.

Gideon's request for a sign may seem unusual and may even appear pious. This act could be interpreted as an act of humility or deference, even worship, to the Lord. In fact, it is not. The narrative reveals Gideon's reticence to respond to God's call to deliver with another request that God give him a sign, this time using a fleece (6:36–40). Unsure if God will give him victory in battle, Gideon asks God for a sign to make dew appear *only* on a fleece on the ground, with the rest of the ground dry. God does as he asks. Then Gideon asks for the reverse: ground wet, fleece dry. God responds by doing so, and the story ends—as if to say, God did his part, now what will Gideon do? Will he fulfill the call?

Gideon does respond in Judges 7 and prepares to fight the Midianites near the hill of Moreh in the Jezreel Valley. God tells Gideon his army is too big: "I cannot deliver Midian into their hands, or Israel would boast against me, 'My own strength has saved me'" (7:2). Through a selection process, God reduces the number of Israelite warriors, decreasing the Israelite army from thirty-two thousand warriors to three hundred (7:3–8). God's people miraculously win the battle and pursue the Midianites and their kings. When Gideon's troops arrive at the town of Sukkoth across the Jordan River, the Israelites there refuse to help his army with supplies or food in their pursuit. After Gideon eventually captures the fleeing Midianite kings, he goes after the people of Sukkoth for refusing to help him and his troops. He humiliates the elders of Sukkoth, pulls down a large tower, and kills the men of the city (8:16–17).

Figure 10.6. *Gideon's Sacrifice* (Judg. 6:19–24) by Ferdinand Bol (1640)

The narrative then shifts to issues of kingship in Israel. Upon Gideon's great victory, the Israelites say to him, "Rule over us—you, your son and your grandson—because you have saved us from the hand of Midian" (8:22). Gideon refuses: "I will not rule over you, nor will my son rule over you. The LORD will rule over you" (8:23).

Gideon's response seems pious, but appearances can be deceiving. Although Gideon says he wants God to be king, Gideon's son is called Abimelech, which in

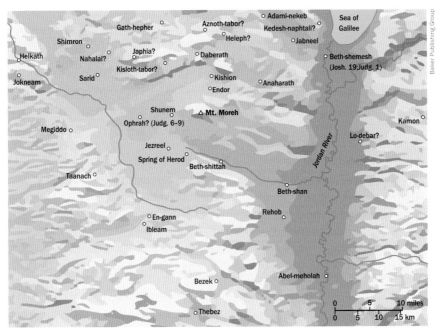

Baker Publishing Group

Figure 10.7. Map of Jezreel Valley with Mount Moreh

Hebrew means "my father is king." The name of Gideon's son subverts Gideon's pious statement, and what the narrative *shows* is that Gideon is trying to be king, despite what he says. He wants to build his own kingdom rather than YHWH's kingdom. The next actions in the narrative reveal Gideon's desire for kingship: he asks for tribute from the Israelites, much like a king would require tribute from his subjects. Gideon then fashions the tribute of gold into the form of an ephod, a garment only worn by priests (Exod. 28:6–14). Gideon's ephod is more likely an image or an idol, not a garment. The Israelites then worship Gideon's ephod (Judg. 8:27).

Gideon's story concludes with his kingdom and dynasty established at the expense of YHWH's rule and under conditions of idolatry. Although Gideon did some good things, his leadership was fraught with selfishness and idolatry. The rule of his son Abimelech continues Gideon's downward trajectory. Abimelech's leadership is marked with murder and mayhem, and he dies in ignominy (Judg. 9).

THEOLOGICAL ISSUES

The Spirit of YHWH in Judges

YHWH's "Spirit" appears regularly in the book (Judg. 3:10; 6:34; 11:29; 13:25; 14:6, 19; 15:14). What does this mean? The Hebrew term for "spirit" is the same word that can be translated "wind," the Hebrew word *ruach*. Context helps us determine which nuance is required. The language of the "Spirit" in Judges likely means that the empowering presence of God rests on the judges and enables them to accomplish certain tasks. We find this in other Old Testament texts as well (1 Sam. 10:10; Isa. 61:1). YHWH is known by his Spirit active in the lives of those he raises up for his purposes. In the New Testament, God fills believers with the Spirit of God to do powerful acts (Rom. 15:19; 2 Tim. 1:7).

RECEPTION HISTORY

Cyril of Jerusalem (ca. 315–86) on the Spirit in Judges

"In the might of this Spirit, as we have it in the Book of Judges, Othniel judged; Gideon waxed strong; Jeptha conquered; Deborah, a woman, waged war; and Samson, so long as he did righteously, and grieved Him not, wrought deeds above man's power."[d]

Gideon and Abimelech are followed by judges Tola and Jair, but the next major judge is Jephthah, who delivers Israel from the oppression of the Ammonites. Jephthah is described as an unexpected leader, whose family history is a bit suspect and who leads a gang of scoundrels. Nonetheless, God gives his Spirit to Jephthah to deliver Israel from Ammon (11:29). At this point in the narrative Jephthah makes an unwise vow. He says to YHWH, "If you give the Ammonites into my hands, whatever comes out of the door of my house to meet me when I return in triumph from the Ammonites will be the LORD's, and I will sacrifice it as a burnt offering" (11:30–31). 🔲 👥

As with the other judges, God delivers his people through the leadership of Jephthah, but his vow makes his victory unsatisfying. The reader wonders, What will the victory cost Jephthah? What could he think would come out of his house, *except his family*? And sure enough, when Jephthah returns home triumphant, "Who should come out to meet him but his daughter, dancing to the sound of timbrels! She was an only child. Except for her he had neither son nor daughter" (11:34).

Jephthah realizes what he has done and tears his clothes in grief. But he goes through with his vow, a rash vow though it may be (11:39), and his victory over Ammon recedes into the background.

Jephthah's vow, according to God's instructions in the law, need not be fulfilled, as he has uttered what could be considered a rash vow (Lev. 5:4–13). He could have recognized his sin and offered a substitute sacrifice for his stupidity. He also could have incurred the wrath of God himself, breaking the vow at the cost of his own life. Additionally, instead of killing his only child, he could have devoted her to the Lord for service at the sanctuary (Lev. 27). She could have served the Lord rather than be killed by her father. The fact that Jephthah believed God would want him to sacrifice his own daughter reveals his lack of character or commitment to God's word. After all, human sacrifice is forbidden by God (Lev. 18:21; 20:2–5). Jephthah's rash vow and horrific sacrifice serve as a bellwether for the remainder of his leadership. It ends badly.

The same can be said of Samson, perhaps the most famous of all the judges, who delivers Israel from the Philistines. Different from many judges who were unlikely leaders (Deborah, a woman; Ehud, left-handed; Shamgar, likely a foreigner; Gideon, fearful and corrupt; Jephthah, a scoundrel), Samson looks the part. He is a Nazirite—one devoted to God (Num. 6:1–21)—and he has Spirit-endowed successes early in his leadership.

However, as we have seen, Judges is subtle in the way it shows questionable action rather than saying it outright. Samson breaks God's law regularly, but perhaps nowhere more clearly than in his desire for a romantic relationship with a Philistine woman (Judg. 14:2–3). This sets the stage for the rest of Samson's story. Intermarrying with foreign peoples of the promised land was forbidden because of its capacity to lead God's people to idolatry (Deut. 7:3–6). Nonetheless, Samson wants the Philistine woman and tells his father, "Get her for me. She's the right one for me" (Judg. 14:3).

A closer translation of Samson's words from the Hebrew text in Judges 14:3 is "Take her for me. For this is right in my eyes." Samson's phrase is eerily like the repeated refrain of Judges 17 and 21 (17:6; 21:25): "There was no king in Israel and everyone did what was right in their own eyes" (AT). The counterpoint to this phrase is God's perspective in the cycle throughout Judges: Israel did what was evil in YHWH's eyes (3:7, 12; 4:1; 6:1; 10:6; 13:1). Comparing the two perspectives (God's and Samson's) reveals that Samson's moral compass is governed by his "own eyes" rather than what is right in God's eyes. His own morality trumps God's moral standards of right and wrong.[4]

Figure 10.8. Samson fountain on the Kramgasse in the Old City of Bern, Switzerland, built in 1544 by Hans Gieng

Samson's story follows the pattern of the judges before him, on a downward spiral to sin and loss. Samson does miraculously defeat the Philistines, but his story reveals how far Israel has gone away from their God by the end of his life.

The Epilogue and No King in Israel: Judges 17–21

▓ READ JUDGES 17–18 ▓

Judges 17–21 crystallizes Israel's descent with stories of idolatry, murder, rape, and horrors. The refrain "In those days Israel had no king; everyone did as they saw fit" (17:6; 21:25; cf. 18:1; 19:1) clarifies the problem. Israel did what they thought was right in their own eyes, irrespective of God's demands. But what of the statement that there was no king in Israel? Is the problem a lack of kingship? Some do argue that Israel's rebellion is due to the fact that they had no human king leading them. The book opens with a leadership challenge and concludes with repetition about the need for

LITERARY NOTES

Repetition in Judges

In the Old Testament repetition is a literary technique designed to (1) reinforce a point, (2) elaborate on a point, or (3) give nuance or ambiguity to a point. We see this in repeated refrains in Judges.

Reinforce	"The Israelites did evil in the eyes of the Lord" (2:11; 3:7, 12; 4:1; 6:1; 10:6; 13:1).
Elaborate	Israel "cried out to the Lord" for help, and God raised up a judge to lead them (see 3:9, 15; 4:3–4; 6:6–7; 10:10).
Reinforce	"The land had peace" (3:11, 30; 5:31; 8:28).
Nuance/ ambiguity	"In those days Israel had no king; everyone did as they saw fit" (17:6; 21:25; cf. 18:1; 19:1).

a king. Thus, a human king is what is longed for. However, internally, the book does not reinforce this idea. 📖

Gideon and Abimelech imitate kingship without being proper kings, and the narrative deconstructs the notion that their "kingship" is a blessing for Israel. Gideon's "kingship" leads to idolatry, and Abimelech's leads to murder and division. The narrative problematizes human kingship rather than elevating it.

A minority scholarly view, which we adopt here, is that the phrase points to the lack of a *divine kingship* among Israel. After all, Israel was doing what was right in their own eyes rather than in the sight of God. The judges gave Israel partially productive leadership, but as the narrative progresses, each judge is worse than the one before. Samson, the last judge, is indicative of the problem of all Israel: he does what is right in his own eyes rather than what is right in God's sight. "The problem was not so much that Israel lacked a king but that they had rejected YHWH's kingship and his rightful sovereignty over their lives."[5]

Implementation—Reading Judges as Christian Scripture Today

The apostle Paul concludes his letter to the Roman churches with a curious statement: "For everything that was written in the past was written to teach us, so that through the endurance taught in the Scriptures and the encouragement they provide we might have hope" (Rom. 15:4). For Paul, the Old Testament is written to help the church discern how to endure and experience hope.

Paul's words instruct us as we consider implementing Judges as Christian Scripture. Judges does not merely convey information; it is designed to facilitate examination and transformation. Its nuanced and subtle literary style draws us to reflect on Israel's core problems and why they go around in circles. Repetition enables us to recognize that Israel abandons YHWH, sinning against their covenant God. Sin leads to degradation and oppression. Thus, the stories do not just tell what happened in the past; they empower God's people to examine their own lives: Do we do what is right in *our* lives? Such self-centered egoism, living apart from the moral demands of God, is one further example of how humans attempt to throw off authority to find self-fulfillment. The outcome is the same. Humans oppress and exploit others for their own gains.

But apart from inviting readers to examine the reality of sin, Judges also instructs on transformation. What is needed is not an earthly king or political leader who will deliver us from our problems (a powerful word for the present day). Rather, what is needed is what Judges 17–21 points to: the true King of Israel, God himself. Living in communion with Israel's God, living by what is right in God's eyes, becomes a different way of life for thriving and joy.

It is dangerous to make the book of Judges about the lives of the judges. The goal of Judges is not encouraging readers to "be like Samson" or to "emulate the battle strategy of Gideon." Rather, the transformative potential of Judges comes in encountering the living God who has given readers the gift of the book to transform human moral vision and open an avenue for communion with that selfsame God.

KEY VERSES IN JUDGES

- After that whole generation had been gathered to their ancestors, another generation grew up who knew neither the LORD nor what he had done for Israel. Then the Israelites did evil in the eyes of the LORD and served the Baals. . . . In his anger against Israel the LORD gave them into the hands of raiders who plundered them. . . . Then the LORD raised up judges, who saved them out of the hands of these raiders. . . . But when the judge died, the people returned to ways even more corrupt than those of their ancestors, following other gods and serving and worshiping them. They refused to give up their evil practices and stubborn ways. 2:10–19
- The Israelites did evil in the eyes of the LORD; they forgot the LORD their God and served the Baals and the Asherahs. 3:7 (cf. 3:12; 4:1; 6:1; 10:6; 13:1)
- His father and mother replied, "Isn't there an acceptable woman among your relatives or among all our people? Must you go to the uncircumcised Philistines to get a wife?" But Samson said to his father, "Get her for me. She's the right one for me." 14:3
- In those days Israel had no king; everyone did as they saw fit. 17:6 (cf. 18:1; 19:1; 21:25)

Christian Reading Questions

1. Identify and explain the "cycle" in Judges and its significance for understanding the book of Judges.
2. Explain the function of a judge in the book of Judges. Why are the judges important in this phase of Israel's story?
3. Discuss the role of the Spirit in the book of Judges. Why is the Spirit important for the book?
4. What does the book of Judges teach us about ourselves? What does it teach us about God?

CHAPTER ELEVEN

1–2 Samuel

Orientation

Witches, warlords, wisdom, and weirdness characterize much of 1–2 Samuel. In its pages is a grand story connected to the stories of the patriarchs and Israel from Genesis through Judges, but this grand story moves forward to kingship and its failure and success.

The purpose of 1–2 Samuel is to recount the story of Israel's transformation from Israelite tribal confederacy (as we saw in Judges) to a monarchy under the reign of YHWH. As it achieves this purpose, 1–2 Samuel also sets an expectation of future Davidic kings anointed to reign in justice and righteousness. While monarchy, at least ideally, is good and prescribed under Israel's law (see Deut. 17:14–20), 1–2 Samuel exposes the shadow side to kingship, in the reigns of both Saul and David. The narrative teases the potential for poor kingship in 1 Samuel 8, where Israel wants a king "like all the nations" (1 Sam. 8:5 ESV). God says that if Israel settles for that kind of kingship, they will be disappointed (8:10–18). The negative example of Saul in the succeeding chapters proves God's words true in 1 Samuel 8. In the example of David, Israel has a better experience of what kingship can be when a human king rules under the authority of the divine King, YHWH (cf. Pss. 95–100).

In ancient times, 1–2 Samuel was recorded on a single scroll and read as one extended narrative. In modern

LITERARY NOTES

Hebrew Narrative

Dealing with story or, as it is commonly called, Hebrew narrative means we must recognize that it is literary art—a form of representation—rather than straightforward historical reporting of what happened in the past. Hebrew narrative is a story with a divine purpose: to disclose the purposes of God and the relation of God to the world. It does so by telling the stories of people, places, journeys, and actions that connect to other stories. So, we must be attentive to characterization, plot movements, repeated terms/patterns/scenes, ambiguity of presentation, and how the narrative displays characters' action without telling us what to think about it. These elements inform Hebrew narrative and help us understand the text.[a]

Bibles, this unified story is divided into two sections or "books" (1 and 2 Samuel). The books of 1–2 Kings, Ezra-Nehemiah, and 1–2 Chronicles in the Old Testament are similar. They are single books even though English translations divide them into two. Together, 1–2 Samuel offers an extended narrative that is marked by several transitions.

The most significant is the transition of kingship from Saul (Israel's first king) to David (Israel's second king). This story makes up much of the book (1 Sam. 9–2 Sam. 20) and is broken into smaller sections: the history of David's rise (1 Sam. 16–2 Sam. 5), the Davidic conquest of Jerusalem and the Davidic covenant (2 Sam. 6–8), and the succession narrative (2 Sam. 9–20). Beyond this, Israel's worship transitions from a shrine in Shiloh to YHWH's worship in the Jerusalem temple, which becomes the central sanctuary and the political center of the Davidic dynasty. But each of these plot movements occurs in a unified story. As a result, we read 1–2 Samuel together. In so doing, we neither imply that the combined text is seamless nor do we argue it emerged all at once. Still, different portions of the book, which may have come together at diverse times, at some point coalesced into a unified whole.

Figure 11.1. Detail of the anointing of David from "The Bible of Robert de Bello" (Canterbury?) (ca. 1240–53)

As with all Old Testament books, the primary focus of 1–2 Samuel is *theological* rather than *political* or *anthropological*. God's identity, character, and agency are the focus of the book. The primary actor and agent in the book is YHWH, the covenantal God of Israel. As God works through, by, and with the other actors in the book, he extends an invitation to see how he redeems by means of his work in and through the people of Israel and particularly Israel's early kings.

Although Israel's God, YHWH, is the central character, four other characters are fundamental to the story: Hannah (1 Sam. 1–2), Samuel (1 Sam. 2–12), Saul (1 Sam. 13–31), and David (1 Sam. 16–2 Sam. 24). When we look at the book from the opening presentation of Hannah, each character links forward and backward to the others, giving the narrative momentum.[1] Hannah births Samuel; Samuel anoints Saul as king; Saul's faulty kingship gives way to David; David's kingship proceeds forward, even if his reign has significant setbacks. 📖 📖

LITERARY NOTES

The Structure of 1–2 Samuel

1 Samuel 1–7: The rise of Samuel and the kingship of YHWH

1 Samuel 8–15: The rise and fall of Saul, king of Israel

1 Samuel 16–2 Samuel 4: The rise of David, king of Israel

2 Samuel 5–24: The reign of David, king of Israel (and the kingship of YHWH)

Theological Themes in 1–2 Samuel

Within the basic plot line of 1–2 Samuel, some aspects are important for understanding the book. First, David's story is part of the larger message in the book—the message that YHWH is the God who raises up and brings low, and the God with whom all kings must deal. God gives authority to his anointed king, but he can remove that authority as well. The lives of Saul and David depicted in the book remain secondary to what God is doing in and through his anointed king and people, Israel.

Second is the interweaving of divine judgment and salvation in 1–2 Samuel. God judges the priest Eli's household because of sin in 1 Samuel 1–3, but God promises salvation through Samuel in 1 Samuel 1–7. God judges Saul for his failure to follow God's requirements as king in 1 Samuel 10–15, but God establishes the dynasty of a future king "after his own heart" through David in 1 Samuel 16. Here, God's kingship is shown to be supreme over the authority of a human king.

Another way to understand the book is through a series of repeated elements in the narrative. Poetry at the beginning and end of the book frame it: the birth of Samuel (1 Sam. 1:1–2:11) and Hannah's song (1 Sam. 2:1–10) parallel David's poems (2 Sam. 22:1–23:7). Poetry also appears in David's **lament** over the deaths of Saul and Jonathan (2 Sam. 1:19–27).

The demise of Saul, the sinful first king of Israel, catalyzes David's rise to the throne. Different from Saul, David is the king who captures the heart of God. Still, there is some symmetry to the rise and fall of Saul (1 Sam. 8–15) and the rise and fall of David (2 Sam. 1–12). David, however, rises again after his fall, though not without turmoil (2 Sam. 13–20). The parallels between Saul and David also distinguish them, for God raises up the Davidic house, but Saul's dynasty is erased. Because YHWH is praised in the opening and closing of the book (1 Sam. 2 and 2 Sam. 22–23), we should remember that reading 1–2 Samuel requires us to hear what *God* might say to its hearers.

Exploration—Reading 1–2 Samuel

The Rise of Samuel and the Kingship of YHWH: 1 Samuel 1–7

■ READ 1 SAMUEL 1–7 ■

These first chapters contrast those God raises up and those God brings low. Hannah, forlorn for children with her husband and oppressed by her rival (her husband's other wife), turns to God for help. Eli, the priest at Shiloh who should perceive her pain and help her, is blind to her situation. He mistakes a forlorn Hannah for a drunk and does not understand her situation; eventually he comes to her aid. Further, we see in 1 Samuel 2 that although Eli enjoys one of the most revered positions in Israel, he cannot help the people of Israel from being defrauded at the place of worship . . . by his own sons! Eli's high position does not last terribly long in the narrative, for he and his sons are brought low at the word of YHWH (3:11–18). However, God raises up Hannah and grants her a son, whom she names

Samuel, which means "God hears." God has heard her cries for help and responded with a son. In gratitude, Hannah gives the boy back to YHWH to serve God at the tabernacle.

Because God has lifted her up, she offers a song of praise to God (2:1–10), a beautiful poem about the greatness of YHWH, who is high and holy and the source of all love, faithfulness, and salvation:

> There is no one holy like the Lord [YHWH];
>> there is no one besides you;
>> there is no Rock like our God. (2:2)

This poem concludes with an affirmation of the divine strength God provides for the king of Israel (2:10), which is strange because Israel has no king when Hannah utters these words. However, her words introduce the reality of kingship that will soon come in 1–2 Samuel.

Hannah's words are matched by David's final songs of praise in 2 Samuel 22:1–51 and 23:1–7, the final songs sung in 1–2 Samuel. Both Hannah's and David's songs share common themes, words, and phrases, providing "bookends" for the entire story of 1–2 Samuel and establishing the major theological themes of the book.

Hannah's and David's songs center on the incomparability of YHWH. Israel's God is king, and the book of Samuel remind readers that "human authority exists under Yhwh's reign, a theme that comes to prominence under David's closing songs (2 Sam. 22:1–23:7). Apart from Yhwh, Israel's kings have no authority."[2] This point about the primacy of YHWH's kingship provides a clear way to assess the leaders of Israel: Are they faithful to YHWH or not? First and Second Samuel depict the travails of Israel's kingship in the real world when compared against that standard.

Eli and Samuel are described as judges (1 Sam. 4:18; 7:15). As we learned in the book of Judges, a judge is a charismatic leader anointed and appointed by God to lead God's people, to settle disputes, and to deliver God's people from oppressors. In 1–2 Samuel, Eli and Samuel are judges/leaders who settle disputes and lead all of God's people.

First Samuel 1–3 presents Eli's waning prominence as Samuel's role as judge is waxing. Much of Eli's problem derives from his sons, who give the family a bad name. "Eli's sons were scoundrels; they had no regard for the Lord" (2:12). Eli did not restrain his

CANONICAL CONNECTIONS

1 Samuel 2 and 1 Samuel 22–23

God is Rock and Savior (1 Sam. 2:2; 2 Sam. 22:2–4, 32, 47).

God raises the lowly and brings down the exalted (1 Sam. 2:7–8; 2 Sam. 22:26–28).

God brings life out of death (1 Sam. 2:6; 2 Sam. 22:5–20).

God weighs action, decrees verdicts, and brings justice to the oppressed (1 Sam. 2:3, 9–10; 2 Sam. 22:7).

God strengthens his anointed king (1 Sam. 2:10; 2 Sam. 22:33–51; 23:2–7).

Hannah and Mary, Samuel and Jesus

The Gospel of Luke uses imagery and language from 1 Samuel 1–2 to point to Jesus, the true king who will succeed where Israel's kings failed. Hannah's song and Samuel's story help us understand both Mary and Jesus. Note parallels between Hannah's story and Mary's story.[b]

Hannah (1 Sam. 2:1–10)	Mary (Luke 1:46–55)
Childless	Childless
Divine intervention for Hannah	Divine intervention for Mary
Hannah's praise	Mary's praise
Praise for her Savior	Praise for her Savior

For Luke, Hannah and Samuel are figures that give flesh and meaning to God's blessing of Mary through the gift of Jesus. God raises up Hannah and Samuel and incorporates them into his redemptive purposes. They become a blessing to their own people in their own time and typify what the coming of Jesus will look like. Jesus will be the devoted son whose mother is the devoted servant of the Lord. This kind of figural interpretation is sometimes called typology. Both Hannah and Mary express hope in God for his gift of a child. Luke 1 records a song (Mary's "Magnificat") that uses language of Hannah's prayer (Luke 1:47, 52, cf. 1 Sam. 2:1, 4, 8). God provided a son in the past, leading to praise (Hannah's song), and God again miraculously provided a son who will be the Savior of the entire world, leading all to praise (Mary's song).

Luke also associates Jesus and Samuel. Hannah gave birth to Samuel, who would be both priest and prophet, a man who would anoint the king of Israel. Mary gave birth to the one who would be Priest, Prophet, and King of all kings. The maturation of Samuel becomes a blueprint for understanding the development of the Son of God, Jesus Christ; Luke's description of Jesus's growth echoes that of Samuel's growth (Luke 2:52; 1 Sam. 2:26; 3:19–20).

Samuel is the divine blessing to a childless mother just as Jesus is a divine blessing to a childless mother. Samuel is favored by God, as is Jesus. As Samuel grew, so Jesus grew. As Samuel was priest and prophet (and almost king; see 1 Sam. 8), so Jesus is the true priest, prophet, and king in Luke. For Luke, Samuel's life sets a pattern (figure) that testifies to Jesus. While Samuel is a great character in the story of the book of Samuel, for Luke his life looks toward one who will come: Jesus the Messiah.

children and is implicated in the family problems. The fall of Eli's household makes way for the rise of Samuel, who serves YHWH faithfully (unlike Eli's family).

More than just a judge, Samuel is a priest and prophet as well in a time when "the word of the LORD was rare; there were not many visions" (3:1). This is the first use of prophetic terminology in the book of Samuel ("word of the LORD" and "visions"). Samuel serves in the tabernacle from an early age, and in 1 Samuel 3 he hears the Lord's voice. God gives him a prophecy of judgment on Eli's family. In this call from YHWH, Samuel moves away from Eli's priestly family and toward his own priestly and prophetic duties.

First Samuel 4–7 is an unusual text with almost magical elements. The passage recounts the journey of the ark of the covenant, a golden box that represented the presence of God in the tabernacle. The Philistines capture the ark, which they consider divine, and place it in the shrine of their deity Dagon. Overnight YHWH topples Dagon's statue, revealing the Philistine god's impotence. While the ark is in Philistine lands, YHWH afflicts their people with tumors. After this affliction, the Philistines return the ark to Israel with a restitution offering. Some men from the Israelite village where the ark was taken look inside the ark (which is forbidden), and they die (1 Sam. 6:19–20). Then the ark is taken to Kiriath Jearim, where it sits for twenty years (7:1–2), and in time Samuel rallies Israel to proper worship and then victory over the Philistines (7:3–17).

The ark narrative highlights how YHWH's power will be revealed among all nations. The Philistines progressively realize the unrivaled authority of YHWH. At first, they believe that the ark of YHWH is powerful, thinking it was one of the other "gods" of the nations that they mistakenly thought plagued and killed the Egyptians (1 Sam. 4:6–8). According to the Philistines, the ark represented Israel's "gods." This is understandable because ancient peoples around Israel were polytheistic, meaning they worshiped many deities that represented the heavens, powers, and different natural phenomena.[3] In the narrative of 1 Samuel, the Philistines and Israel discover ever more deeply the identity of YHWH. YHWH is not like the deities of the nations: he is powerful over all gods and all nations.

The Rise and Fall of Saul, King of Israel: 1 Samuel 8–15

▓ READ 1 SAMUEL 12–15 ▓

First Samuel 8 focuses on the transition from the period of the judges to the period of monarchy in Israel. The transition itself, however, is ambiguous. On the one hand, it looks as though leadership should pass through the family of Samuel, but 1 Samuel 8:1–3 indicates that Samuel's sons were not good judges; they perverted justice and took bribes. This exposes how Samuel's sons flaunted the leadership bestowed on them and were judges unfaithful to YHWH (cf. Deut. 16:18–20). Because of this, the elders of the people look for another form of leadership. They ask Samuel for a king (1 Sam. 8:4–5) to lead the people. In light of Eli's sons, their request is perfectly sensible.

On the other hand, they ask for a king "such as all the other nations have" (8:5). Samuel is not pleased with the request and asks YHWH for guidance. YHWH approves the request but instructs Samuel to warn the people what a king will be like. The king will take Israel's children as servants and workers in his court. He will take the best of the fields and harvest. He will take a tenth of grain and wine for his court. He will take the best of the land for his own use. God's people will become the king's slaves (8:10–18).

The king will take more than he gives if he is a king like those of other nations. Contrasting this vision of kingship with kingship as presented in Deuteronomy 17:14–20 reveals the difference between the actual and ideal visions of kingship present in 1–2 Samuel. YHWH desires a king who obeys divine commands and honors fellow Israelites, as opposed to a king "such as all the

LITERARY NOTES

Saul: An Answer to the People's Request

The name of the first king of Israel, Saul, sounds like the Hebrew verb "to ask." Whenever Israel pronounces Saul's name, they are reminded that they got what they asked for! Saul is a Benjamite, which has negative connotations when read immediately after the book of Judges and its account of what happened within the tribe of Benjamin (Judg. 19–20). Saul's tribal affiliation sets an ominous tone to his reign. And yet this is the king that YHWH provides for the people.

other nations have." But YHWH gives them the king they want, even if it is not the king they need. 📖

The king is Saul. At Saul's anointing service to be king, Samuel proclaims to Saul the "word of God" (1 Sam. 9:27 NRSV)—namely, that YHWH has chosen Saul to be "*prince* over his heritage" (10:1 AT). Truly, Saul would deliver the people from the Philistines (9:16). But YHWH tells Samuel that Saul will do something else: "It is he who will restrain my people" (9:17 AT). When Israel pleads for a king like other nations have, they effectively reject their God (10:18–19). Nonetheless, YHWH grants their request and Saul is anointed. But where is Saul when Samuel calls on him to present himself? In an amusing scene, Saul is hiding among some baggage—not the best start to Israel's nascent monarchy! 📖 📖

After this inauspicious start, Saul leads Israel to military victory. The people attribute the victory to Saul (11:12). In one of the strongest statements in his reign, Saul boldly proclaims that YHWH has delivered Israel (11:13). Despite the positive presentation of 1 Samuel 11, the narrative presents Saul's victories and fidelity to YHWH unevenly in the remainder of 1 Samuel 9–14.

Things go badly for Saul in 1 Samuel 13–14. The Philistines were a great threat on the borders of Israel. They were people from the region of Greece and Crete that had sailed southeast across the Mediterranean and settled in the coastal plain in Israel. They held five major cities in the plain: Gaza, Ashdod, Ashkelon, Gath, and Ekron. The Philistines were a constant danger during the time of the judges, and they threatened Israel during the reigns of Saul and David.

In 1 Samuel 13 Saul is set to go to battle against the Philistines at Gilgal. Samuel had sent a message to Saul to wait to fight for seven days until he arrived at Gilgal to offer a sacrifice to YHWH (13:8–9). But Samuel does not come, and Saul offers the sacrifices himself instead. This act might seem expeditious, but it reveals Saul's greater concern for his own plan and timetable rather than following the word of the Lord, clearly given by the prophet.

Samuel's response to Saul's action is as clear as it is uncompromising: Saul had done a foolish thing by not obeying the commandments of God, and his kingdom will not endure. Samuel ominously tells Saul, "You have not kept the Lord's command" (13:14). Saul's action and Samuel's response expose a fissure in Saul's leadership and devotion. Although he might seem to be a worthy king, his lack of obedience to YHWH's word reveals his inability to lead well. Indeed, Saul appears more like a king of the other nations than a king devoted to YHWH.

A summary of Saul's reign appears in 1 Samuel 14:47–52. It details his family and victories against the Philistines but concludes that "the battle was strong against the Philistines all the days of Saul. So when Saul saw any valiant man or any brave man, he would gather him to himself" (14:52 AT). This verse could merely highlight Saul's leadership ability: he influenced warriors to his own side. However, in light of the narrative that follows, the verse subtly suggests that Saul enlists people into *his* army rather than *God's* army. Saul builds his name but "restrains" God's people from embracing God's name.

The idea that Saul is building his own name, not God's, emerges even more clearly in 1 Samuel 15. In this text, YHWH commands Saul to kill the Amalekites: "Now go, attack the Amalekites and totally destroy all that belongs to them. Do not spare them; put to death men and women, children and infants, cattle and sheep, camels and donkeys" (15:3). However we evaluate the command to devote the Amalekites to destruction (we will explore this more fully below), Saul does not obey God's command. He stops short, sparing the choice animals and the king of the Amalekites, Agag. Why would Saul do this? Because these represent the spoils of war, likely the spoils of war that go to a king "such as all the nations have." We can see the problem. Saul's failure was in his disobedience to YHWH's command and his tendency to mimic the kings of the nations. Although he feigns loyalty to YHWH, in fact, Saul prioritizes his royal prestige rather than obedience to YHWH's command. When Samuel arrives, Saul attempts to deceive him. The prophet will have none of it and drops the verdict:

> Does the Lord delight in burnt offerings and sacrifices
> as much as in obeying the Lord?
> To obey is better than sacrifice,
> and to heed is better than the fat of rams.
> For rebellion is like the sin of divination,
> and arrogance like the evil of idolatry.
> Because you have rejected the word of the Lord,
> he has rejected you as king. (15:22–23)

The Amalekites in Biblical Memory

Alongside the Philistines, the Amalekites are persistent enemies of Israel. Conflict between Israel and Amalek originates in the wilderness when Israel moves from Egypt to Canaan. When Israel was "weary and worn out" (Deut. 25:18), the Amalekites attacked and plundered them (Exod. 17:8–16; Deut. 25:17–19). The Amalekites are remembered for provoking and pillaging defenseless Israel.

Holy War in the Bible

1. Holy war is commanded with a concern for justice. Wars such as the one commanded in 1 Samuel 15 can only be rightly understood within the larger story that begins in Genesis, where God is committed to eradicating sin and renewing the broken world.

2. Holy war is limited and nonrepeatable. "Holy war" such as 1 Samuel 15 is confined to a particular time in Israel's history, and it is not to be repeated by the Christian church. Holy war is not justified for any people in the present world.

3. Holy war eliminates false worship, at least ideally. To get at the religious heart of an ancient people, one had to engage more than their "spirituality." The national identity of ancient peoples like Israel and Amalek consisted of three factors: their place, their god, and their kinship group. Moabites lived in the land southeast of the Jordan River and worshiped Chemosh. The Canaanites revered the storm god Baal, who governed the land of Canaan. The biblical text depicts the Philistines as worshiping the deity Dagon. The Israelites (obviously) worshiped YHWH in the promised land. Divine warfare breaks the bonds between deity-people-land: when the Amalekites were displaced and defeated, their gods were defeated and revealed as powerless and false.

4. Holy war in the Old Testament is not "holy war" at all. The term "holy war" was coined by German scholar Friedrich Schwally early in the twentieth century to describe wars in the Bible like the one in 1 Samuel 15. Schwally compared the wars of the Bible with Islamic jihad, as he understood it. When he uses the language of holy war to describe texts like 1 Samuel 15, he makes a faulty comparison. Biblical warfare is not primarily about people going out to fight in the name of God but rather God going to fight on behalf of his people. Most scholars today do not use "holy war" to describe this kind of war. Rather, they use the language of "divine warfare" instead.

Samuel then did what Saul did not do: he killed Agag (15:33). The importance of obeying YHWH's command is central in Deuteronomy (cf. Deut. 32:46), and it is central in Samuel's words as well. Saul's disobedience and its outcome are remembered later in the book of 1 Samuel, when Saul looks to gain a blessing in battle against the Philistines, and he summons Samuel's ghost via a witch from Endor (1 Sam. 28:18). Although mysterious and unusual, this story near the end of Saul's life reminds Saul (and the reader) of his failure to obey and the subsequent fall of Israel's first king.

But what of the divine command to kill the Amalekites? We return now to this question. No matter how bad the Amalekites are perceived to be, this command is difficult to reconcile with God's character. It is unwelcome especially in the modern world where this action is considered genocidal. The language "totally destroy" in English is better rendered from the Hebrew "devote to destruction." Either way, it sounds a lot like "holy war." Why would YHWH command something as brutal as this? What is going on with the command for "holy war"? Why would God command this?[4] ✠

When we reflect on warfare commands like 1 Samuel 15, it is important to remember that the ancients correlated military and religious life. In the ancient world, exposing the gods of the nations to be false, and protecting Israel from falling for these (false) gods, required more than general instruction. What was needed was a strong demonstration of the impotence of the gods of the nations and the supreme authority of YHWH. Much of this is in the background of 1 Samuel 15. The difficulty of the command, even understood in its ancient environment, stands out for modern readers.

What comes to the foreground in 1 Samuel 15 is the issue of obedience to YHWH: Will Saul build God's kingdom and obey YHWH's word, or will he build his own kingdom at the expense of YHWH's word? Saul's disobedience exposes his reticence to build YHWH's kingdom.

The Rise of David, King of Israel: 1 Samuel 16–2 Samuel 4

▦ READ 1 SAMUEL 16–19; 24–27; 2 SAMUEL 1–3 ▦

After Saul's disobedience at Gilgal, God sends Samuel on a mission to find the next king of Israel. At God's command, Samuel goes to Bethlehem to find Saul's successor from among Jesse's sons (1 Sam. 16:1). When Samuel arrives, Jesse parades his sons before the prophet. However, God rejected all of them.

> So he asked Jesse, "Are these all the sons you have?"
> "There is still the youngest," Jesse answered. "He is tending the sheep."
> Samuel said, "Send for him; we will not sit down until he arrives."
> So he sent for him and had him brought in. He was glowing with health and had a fine appearance and handsome features.
> Then the LORD said, "Rise and anoint him; this is the one."
> So Samuel took the horn of oil and anointed him in the presence of his brothers, and from that day on the Spirit of the LORD came powerfully upon David. Samuel then went to Ramah. (16:11–13)

From this point forward, the narrative shifts: Saul's reign, fame, and mental health diminish, and David's fame increases. David serves in Saul's court as a court singer and an armor bearer for the king (16:21–23).

One of the most famous events in David's rise to kingship is his defeat of the Philistine giant Goliath (1 Sam. 17). The encounter showcases David's bravery and, more importantly, his devotion to YHWH's very name (17:45). Taking smooth stones from a riverbed, David hurls a stone using his sling, and it strikes Goliath, killing him. David then cuts off Goliath's head.

Figure 11.2. *Saul and David* by Rembrandt (ca. 1651–54 and ca. 1655–58)

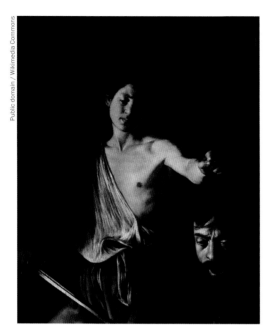

Figure 11.3. *David with the Head of Goliath* by Caravaggio (1610)

LITERARY NOTES

Reticence in Hebrew Narrative (2 Sam. 2–4)

In the war between the families of Saul and David in 2 Samuel 2–4, two leaders of raiding bands assassinate Saul's son Ish-Bosheth. They stab him in the stomach while he is alone and defenseless in his bed (2 Sam. 4). They then decapitate him and bring his head to David. Recognizing the humiliation of Saul's family, David has the assassins killed and then hung with their hands and feet cut off. These men wanted to shame Saul and his dynasty by severing Ish-Bosheth's head. David honors Saul and responds in kind by cutting off their hands and feet, thereby shaming them and their household.

Unlike in some Hebrew narratives, the text offers no explicit evaluation of these actions (cf. 1 Sam. 12:17), and we find no divine command for these actions, against either Ish-Bosheth or the two men. Furthermore, the narrator does not approve or decry these actions, which is important because sometimes the narrator's voice presents the perspective of God (e.g., 1 Kings 11:6; 14:22; 15:26, 34). The narrative opens a gap for the reader to evaluate the actions of David and the two assassins. It is possible to understand why these men did what they did, but it is equally possible to argue God does not approve of their actions. Although it tells the story, the narrative is reticent to approve or to prescribe their actions.[d]

For David, victory over Goliath is *not* David's triumph; it is YHWH's. David says, "All those gathered here will know that it is not by sword or spear that the LORD saves; for the battle is the LORD's, and he will give all of you into our hands" (17:47). This devotion to YHWH helps to distinguish David's nascent reign from Saul's established reign. This contrast is central to 1 Samuel 17–31, which details the demise of Saul and the rise of David. Saul and his son Jonathan perish in battle against the Philistines. Saul falls on his sword, taking his own life, further diminishing the legacy of the first king of Israel.

David's ascension to the throne in 2 Samuel 1–4 is not without conflict. Loyalists to Saul attempt to put Saul's son Ish-Bosheth on the throne. David, however, is YHWH's choice. War ensues (2 Sam. 2–4), but in the end David's forces win, clearing the path for his reign.

The Reign of David, King of Israel (and the Kingship of YHWH): 2 Samuel 5–24

▓ READ 2 SAMUEL 5–8, 11–15, 22–24 ▓

After David's rivals have been vanquished, David is installed as king (2 Sam. 5). Three steps to David's installation as king mirror the steps to Saul's installation:[5]

Action	Saul	David
Private anointing	1 Samuel 10:1–8	1 Samuel 16:1–13
Public acceptance	1 Samuel 10:17–27	2 Samuel 5:1–5
Military demonstration	1 Samuel 11	2 Samuel 5:6–25

As soon as he is accepted as king, David conquers the Jebusite city of Jerusalem as his capital (5:6–12). This act is a defining moment for David's reign, connecting the religious significance of Jerusalem (cf. Gen. 14:17–20) with the Davidic dynasty. David brings the ark of the covenant to Jerusalem (2 Sam. 6), legitimating Jerusalem as the permanent shrine to YHWH, even if the shrine is the temporary sanctuary rather than a permanent temple.

Dissatisfied that YHWH does not have a permanent dwelling, David expresses his desire to build a house for YHWH's name—in other words, a temple (7:1–2). He tells the prophet Nathan of his desire, and Nathan encourages him to do what God has put in his heart. However, that night God speaks to Nathan and gives him a word about the covenant God will make with David.

This covenant appears in 2 Samuel 7:8–16. David understands God's generosity toward him as a good thing (7:28), and the specific language of "covenant" appears in 2 Samuel 23:5, where David remembers how YHWH made an "everlasting covenant" with him, clearly referring to 2 Samuel 7. David's son Solomon reiterates the covenant of 2 Samuel 7:8–16 in 1 Kings 3:6–9 and 8:23–24. David and his successor believe the promise God makes in 2 Samuel 7 is an eternal covenant.

This everlasting covenant with David builds on the Abrahamic and Israelite covenants. As an Israelite, David is bound to the terms of the Israelite covenant (Exodus–Deuteronomy). And as a descendent of Abraham, David is an heir to the Abrahamic covenant. There are many similarities between the Davidic, Israelite, and Abrahamic covenants.[6]

The Davidic covenant is the next step in YHWH's covenant story. The reign of YHWH will be specially exerted through the reign of Israel's Davidic ruler. The king shall be the exemplar for the people, leading them to fidelity to YHWH. The king's faithfulness is determined, on a canonical read from Genesis through 1–2 Samuel, by the law of the king in Deuteronomy 17:14–20. Up to this point in the narrative of 1–2 Samuel, David's faithfulness to YHWH is portrayed in contrast to the faulty reign of Saul. In 2 Samuel 7, we find a new accent to David's faithfulness: he wants to build a temple where God's people can worship the Lord forever. Thus, kingship

THEOLOGICAL ISSUES

Similarities between the Covenants

Abrahamic Covenant	Davidic Covenant
Great name (Gen. 12:2)	Name (2 Sam. 7:9)
Children (Gen. 12:2–3)	Dynastic succession/"house" (2 Sam. 7:12)
Land (Gen. 15:7)	Land (2 Sam. 7:10)
Curse on enemies (Gen. 12:3)	Rest from enemies (2 Sam. 7:10–11)
Blessing (Gen. 12:3)	Blessing (2 Sam. 7:29)
Israelite Covenant	**Davidic Covenant**
God's "firstborn son" (Exod. 4:22)	King is God's son (2 Sam. 7:14)
Royal and holy nation (Exod. 19:4–6)	Priest-king (Ps. 110:2, 4)
Stipulations to follow (Exod. 20:2–17)	Stipulations to follow (Deut. 17:14–20)
Divine promises (Exod. 23:20–33)	Divine promises (2 Sam. 7:8–16)

and worship are bound in the reign of David, a point remembered later in the book of 1–2 Chronicles.

David's actions following the covenant are fitting to YHWH's commitment to him. First, he thanks YHWH for divine blessing and generosity (2 Sam. 7:18–29). He then wins victories in battle (2 Sam. 8 and 10). He exhibits generosity and kindness to Mephibosheth, the son of his friend Jonathan (2 Sam. 9).

However, in 2 Samuel 11, David's life takes a turn and moves downhill quickly—in only one chapter of narrative time—and the remainder of 2 Samuel 11–21 details David's decline. David's troubles begin when he decides to stay at home in Jerusalem instead of going to war with his men. From his palace, he perversely spies on a woman, Bathsheba, bathing. He has her brought to the palace and takes her to bed. She becomes pregnant. The matter is further complicated by the fact that Bathsheba is the wife of one of David's fighting men, Uriah. David has sinned against God, Bathsheba, and Uriah in the span of one chapter.

David's sin grows. First, he brings Uriah home from battle, hoping that he will sleep with his wife and never know the child is David's. The honorable Uriah refuses to enjoy time with his wife while his fellow soldiers are in battle. David then orders his general to put Uriah in the thick of battle where he is sure to be killed. The plan works, and David takes Bathsheba as a wife. The narrator concludes the story with clear disdain for David's serial sins: "But the thing David had done displeased the LORD" (11:27). Moreover, the prophet Nathan rebukes David for his sin, exposing the sin to the public and proclaiming that David's action will lead to unending strife in his household (12:7–12). David then recognizes his sin and admits it (12:13). However, the child conceived by the illicit affair dies.

True to Nathan's prophecy, the remainder of David's reign is characterized by disaster. David's son Amnon falls in love with Tamar, his sister (perhaps a half sister). The text says Tamar is the sister of David's son Absalom (13:1), which is important for the drama that ensues. Amnon, out of control with desire, rapes Tamar by preying on her kindness to him (13:1–22). When Absalom hears of Amnon's action, he schemes revenge against Amnon and justice for his sister. Two years later the opportune moment comes, and Absalom murders Amnon and flees Jerusalem (13:23–34). This is a pivotal moment in the Davidic dynasty, creating ripple effects through the remainder of David's life.

A key actor missing from the story of Tamar, Amnon, and Absalom is David. As Israel's king, David should enact and preserve justice among his people, but he is nowhere to be found in the narrative. His passivity in the face of his daughter's rape and his son's (Amnon's) sin exposes a general downward trajectory in David's life and reign. Absalom's rise in the succeeding chapters (2 Sam. 14–18) and the attempt he makes to usurp and depose his father can be traced back to David's inaction when Amnon violated Tamar.

Absalom conspires against his father, and the armies of David and Absalom go to war. Eventually, David's armies prevail, and Absalom dies in battle when his long hair gets caught in a tree and David's commander, Joab, skewers him to death with jav-

Figure 11.4. Illumination depicting the end of the story of David and Absolom from The Crusader Bible (ca. 1240)

elins (18:14–15). Absalom's gruesome end testifies again to the dark turn David's house takes after his sin with Bathsheba.

The book concludes with two poems of David. These poems echo themes begun in Hannah's prayer in 1 Samuel 2, especially Hannah's prayer about the coming anointed king: the messiah. David sings of this anointed king in 2 Samuel 22:51 and 23:1–7. YHWH trains the king's hands for war (22:35), but the final words of 2 Samuel 22 do not celebrate YHWH's preparation of the messiah for war. Rather, David concludes his psalm in praise: "He gives his king great victories; he shows unfailing kindness to his anointed, to David and his descendants forever" (22:51). David reveres YHWH's name throughout the long poem, extolling YHWH for his power and deliverance. In the final lines, David reveres YHWH because of the covenant kindness and loyalty YHWH demonstrates to the Davidic messiah and his dynasty. Despite the frailty of David and, therefore, the Davidic dynasty, the covenant YHWH makes with him means that YHWH will not forsake the dynasty. Although David's descendants might stray from YHWH (1–2 Kings), YHWH will not abandon them. The Davidic messiah is the one through whom YHWH will bless the world. David praises YHWH for his divine commitment to the anointed king in 2 Samuel 23:1–7.

The ending of 1–2 Samuel is mixed in its portrayal of David. On the one hand, David takes an ill-advised census of his people. It is not clear why he wanted to take the census, but it is clear that God did not want him to do it. Instead of obeying YHWH's voice, David carries out his own desire and enacts the census. As with his sin with Bathsheba, David is confronted by a prophet. And as with his previous sin, David repents (2 Sam. 24:17). However, the damage is done and judgment has come.

On the other hand, David then purchases the threshing floor of a man called Arunah, and this will be the place on which the temple will be built. David builds an altar there, offering sacrifices and worshiping YHWH. The book began at the tabernacle, the place of worship, and it concludes on a threshing floor in Jerusalem, a place of worship and the future home of Israel's temple. In this way, kingship and worship mark the faithful life of the Davidic king.

Implementation—Reading 1–2 Samuel as Christian Scripture Today

First and Second Samuel offers stories for God's people to stimulate thought, reflection, discussion, and deeper communion with God (Rom. 15:4). So 1–2 Samuel does not simply present information from the past, but it does invite participation from the reader to learn and grow with the subject matter of the text: God. But what specifically does 1–2 Samuel offer?

First, 1–2 Samuel instructs its readers about the glory of YHWH, the great King who raises the poor and brings low the proud. This was evident in the reversals of Eli and Samuel and then Saul and David. What distinguishes Samuel and David from Eli and Saul? Devotion to YHWH and the ability to embrace the plan of God.

Second, attending to the voice of God is central in the book. Hannah longs to hear from God (1 Sam. 1–2) and praises YHWH when he responds. Samuel's life, when he is both young and older, is founded on listening to YHWH's voice: "Speak, for your servant is listening" (1 Sam. 3:10). Samuel castigates Saul for failing to listen to the voice of God (15:14–29). David is identified as a person who has God's heart (13:14), whose loyalty contrasts with Saul's disobedience. YHWH's voice provides life for David and Israel, especially through the word of the prophet (Samuel for Israel, Nathan for David), so to obey YHWH's command is to choose life; neglecting YHWH's voice means choosing vice and death. YHWH's voice also reveals Israel's sin and judges it. Thus, attending to the voice of God remains vital for the continued communion with YHWH, and disregarding the divine voice leads to disaster. Judgment and salvation belong to YHWH. As the creator and covenant God, YHWH upholds justice and judgment. For this reason, YHWH can hold his people and the nations to account for any sin or breach of virtue.

Finally, this text instructs us on the once and future king, the Davidic messiah. The Davidic covenant (2 Sam. 7) details YHWH's plan to continue the covenantal story through the exemplar for Israel, the Davidic king. David is the contrast to Saul, but even David's rise meets conflict. He is the appointed and anointed king with whom YHWH enacts a covenant, but the very dynasty that YHWH builds from David's lineage points beyond itself to the coming messiah, the one presented in 2 Samuel 22:51. In this way, David becomes a figure of the coming of Jesus, the Messiah, whose lineage goes back to David. Whereas David falls short of the future messiah, he testifies about the coming king in 2 Samuel 23:1–7. The poem highlights several themes related to the messiah:

> The Holy Spirit inspires the messiah to speak good words (23:2).
> The messiah rules justly over his kingdom (23:3).
> The messiah's rule, like sun and rain, refreshes his kingdom (23:4).
> The messiah is incorporated into YHWH's everlasting covenant (23:5).
> The messiah's enemies will be cast away forever (23:6–7).

David, then, is a type of the coming messiah, Jesus. We echo what one scholar says of David and Jesus:

> The king described [in 2 Sam. 23:1–7] applies to some degree to David, but the idea of the king as the rising sun is ultimately applied to the Messiah. Second Samuel 23:1–7 is a full-length portrait of Jesus. He is the one who rules righteously and in the fear of the Lord, who brings the light of the new creation in His coming, who causes the land to flourish like a garden, and who takes up armor and spear against the thorns. But, as the next section makes clear, a righteous king also inspires imitation in his subordinates, and Jesus does the same, so that leaders of the church should aspire to approximate Him. All pastors and elders would do well to place 2 Samuel 23:1–7 on the doorposts of their houses, on their wrists, on the frontals of their foreheads.[7]

KEY VERSES IN 1–2 SAMUEL

- The Most High will thunder from heaven; the LORD will judge the ends of the earth. He will give strength to his king and exalt the horn of his anointed. 1 Sam. 2:10
- Does the LORD delight in burnt offerings and sacrifices as much as in obeying the LORD? To obey is better than sacrifice, and to heed is better than the fat of rams. For rebellion is like the sin of divination, and arrogance like the evil of idolatry. Because you have rejected the word of the LORD, he has rejected you as king. 1 Sam. 15:22–23

---

1. What do the books of 1–2 Samuel reveal about God? About people?
2. Describe the importance of the prophet Samuel in 1–2 Samuel.
3. How does the Davidic covenant fit with other Old Testament covenants?
4. How should we read 1–2 Samuel as Christian Scripture?

1–2 Kings

Orientation

The book of Kings is messy and dizzying. The plot line moves between the divided kingdoms of northern Israel and southern Judah without a great deal of hand-holding for the reader. The presentation of the kings could disorient you. Keeping track of the basic who, what, and when is a challenge. At one point, you may even encounter a grandmother trying to kill her own grandson, unsettling as that image is (2 Kings 11). Intrigue, corruption, reformation, and renewal are all ingredients of Kings.

The book begins with an unsettling portrait of the elderly King David on his deathbed. The scene creates a vacuum of power and an understandable uncertainty about the future. Transitions of power are vulnerable periods for most nations in past and current times. Within the royal dynasties of the ancient Near East, these transitional periods were especially charged. Political intrigue and personal ambition came to life when the throne was empty. The book of Kings, therefore, has a feel of transition and peril about it from beginning to end. King David is dying. Who will sit on his throne now? What will the kingdom look like with David gone? First and Second Kings extend the narrative of 1–2 Samuel past Saul and David, moving from one royal figure to the next. The royal history begins with the

Figure 12.1. David from the *Well of Moses* by Claus Sluter

The Regnal Formula in 1–2 Kings

The first eleven chapters of Kings focus on Solomon's reign. Then the book moves at a dizzying pace through forty kings. The regnal formula is a literary device that helps readers through this monarchical maze. The formula introduces the king and provides important information regarding his reign—namely, data about the date of the king's rule, his father or mother, the length of his rule, and an evaluation of his reign based on the Lord's perspective. Other elements may appear, such as a notice of his death or a reference to annals where more information on the king might be found.

The elements of the formula are basically the same for kings from the north and the south. Kings in the north are always negatively evaluated, and the explanation is typically the same: he followed the sins of Jeroboam, the first king of the Northern Kingdom. Negative evaluations of the southern kings are more complicated, with a variety of explanations offered. See 1 Kings 16:29–33 for an example from the Northern Kingdom of Israel and 2 Kings 12:1–3 for an example from the Southern Kingdom of Judah.

Figure 12.2. *The Prophet Elijah* in the Greek Orthodox Church and Museum, Miskolc, Hungary

THEOLOGICAL ISSUES

The "Old Testament God" in Kings

A common sentiment in the church and our culture is that the God of the Old Testament is a crank, a kind of grumpy old man whose trigger finger of judgment is quick. However, nothing is further from the truth. The patience and long-suffering of YHWH throughout the story of Kings should overwhelm readers.

end of David's reign and the beginning of his son Solomon's reign (ca. 960 BC). It continues to the dividing of the kingdom between north (Israel) and south (Judah), and it ends with Judean king Jehoiachin's release from prison during the Babylonian exile of Judah (ca. 560 BC). Kings covers a lot of historical ground.

While the book moves from king to king, a stable element remains throughout: the character of Israel's God is unchanged. From the earliest days of the Northern and Southern Kingdoms, Israel's idolatrous tendencies are manifest. The Northern Kingdom of Israel with its capital at Samaria *never* has a king who walks in the ways of the Lord. Yet God in his kindness sends Elijah and Elisha and other prophets as covenantal gifts to remind those in religious and political power of YHWH's exclusive claims on them. The story of the Southern Kingdom is a bit longer and more complex, but it ultimately follows the path of its northern neighbor. God's anger is fierce in Kings (1 Kings 14:9, 15; 15:30) yet God extends the people mercy and kindness despite their covenant infidelity.

As with the book of Samuel, the book of Kings is prophetic literature. This may surprise readers who consider Kings a historical book. The English Bible tradition places Kings within a collection of historical books, together with Joshua, Judges, Ruth, Samuel, Chronicles, Ezra, Nehemiah, and Esther. Given the content of Kings, it surely is history. The question is, What kind of history is it? No historical work is neutral in its engagement with historical sources and presentation of the findings. Most modern readers of history understand this dynamic. Still, Kings does not provide the kind of detailed historical information readers might want in order to understand the broader historical, cultural, and geopolitical context of Israel's history. In fact, Kings is often uninterested in providing the kind of details modern historians would find necessary to write a history of anything.

Historical Sources in 1–2 Kings

The compiler or editor of Kings drew from various historical sources. For example, toward the end of the Solomon narrative, the narrator says, "As for the other events of Solomon's reign . . . are they not written in the book of the annals of Solomon?" (1 Kings 11:41). If the king is a northern king or a southern king, the narrator might refer to the book of the annals of the kings of Judah or the book of the annals of the kings of Israel. As the reference to the annals of Solomon suggests, these sources contained much more material than is present in our canonical texts, which indicates the selective nature of the history telling in Kings. Information is gathered to support a history of Israel that focuses on God's covenant relation with Israel and Judah that in time comes undone because of the people's unfaithfulness.

For example, King Josiah ranks as one of Judah's greatest and most faithful kings (2 Kings 22–23). We will return to him in due course, but it is enough here to say he brought religious reform to Judah by reintroducing the torah to God's people and cleansing the temple from its idolatry. He was one of Judah's last kings "to do what was right in the sight of the Lord," and the narrative of Kings allots significant space to telling his story. Josiah and his rule are important to Judah's historical and religious memory. Yet consider how the book of Kings describes Josiah's death: "While Josiah was king, Pharaoh Necho king of Egypt went up to the Euphrates River to help the king of Assyria. King Josiah marched out to meet him in battle, but Necho faced him and killed him at Megiddo" (2 Kings 23:29). This brief account leaves all kinds of nagging questions. What geopolitical circumstances led to this moment? Why is Pharaoh Necho helping the Assyrians? Is there bad blood between Necho and Josiah? Why would Josiah travel so far to Megiddo—northwest Israel—to have this showdown with Necho? These questions and others are important, but Kings does not answer any of them.

Why is this the case? Because Kings is selective history. The book takes a theological or prophetic angle on Israel's history and is uninterested in providing all the historical details readers might wish to know. Remember, in the Hebrew canon, Kings is part of the Prophets, along with Joshua, Judges, and Samuel, and as such, it attests to the action of God's *word* in time.

Deuteronomy's Themes in 1–2 Kings

The formula "doing good/evil in the eyes of YHWH" appears throughout Deuteronomy (e.g., Deut. 4:25; 12:25; 17:2; 24:4). Kings uses this formula in its evaluations of the kings of Israel and Judah. Other themes in Deuteronomy appear in Kings as well—namely, exclusive devotion to YHWH alone and seeking the Lord with "all of one's heart" (cf. Deut. 4:15–25; 6:4).

RECEPTION HISTORY

A Perspective on Israel's History

Karl Barth describes the challenges of Israel's history, especially the history of the Davidic monarchy and all of its attendant problems: for example, the exile leaves the throne empty or there's no unbroken continuity from David forward toward some fulfilled end. All we appear to have is a "beginning without the corresponding development." Barth wonders out loud about this problem in the canonical portrayal of Israel's history and its kings. He surmises, "It is only eschatologically and therefore only as prophecy that they [Israel] can read and understand these texts, if at all, as the texts of revelation which for them they certainly were." He then concludes, "The kingship of Jesus Christ is the actuality, the subject which they attest—but which they can only attest. . . . The Israelite monarchy set up on the day of Ramah is the prototype or copy of the kingship of Jesus Christ."[a]

The book of Kings does present history. There is no reason to dismiss these books as historically inaccurate or untrue. But it is important to recognize the *kind* of history offered in Kings. It is prophetic history, and it provides an account of Israel's history from the standpoint of God's covenant relationship with them. This history orders itself to God's word and how it shapes human history. The covenant theology of Deuteronomy with its promise of life or death is a significant guiding norm in the narrating of Israel's history. These covenantal dynamics provide the interpretive lens for the author(s) of Kings and for readers like you and me. Both Israel and Judah experienced national tragedies of foreign domination and exile. The book of Kings provides a prophetic account of why these horrific events occurred.

Exploration—Reading 1–2 Kings

The differences between the books of Samuel and Kings are hard to miss. First and Second Samuel concern only two kings, Saul and David. These two kings are the focus of the narrative, although the privileged center and objective of 1–2 Samuel is the rise of the Davidic monarchy: King David, his accession to the throne, and the long-term promises God makes to his royal offspring. This clear thematic focus remains throughout the book. The book of Kings is much more varied and challenging, covering an enormous amount of time and a vast array of royal and prophetic personalities. The bulk of the narrative is devoted to King Solomon and the prophet Elijah, and their stories are some of the best known in Israel's history. Still, the casual reader of the book will likely experience some disorientation, given the sprawling content of Kings.

The following sections will give you a sense of the book's overall movement, structure, and principal figures. After Solomon, the kingdom of Israel divides between kingdoms in the north and south. The book of Kings weaves its narrative back and forth between these two kingdoms. For the sake of clarity and simplicity, this chapter will separate the material of the Northern and Southern Kingdoms.

The Passing of David and Solomon's Rise to Power: 1 Kings 1–11

■ READ 1 KINGS 1–11 ■

Kings begins with the aged King David in his bed, unable to keep himself warm. His attendants search for a young virgin to serve the frail king, and they bring in the "very beautiful" Abishag to take care of the king. Part of Abishag's duties include lying next to David at night to keep him warm. The narrator tells us that "the king did not know her sexually" (1 Kings 1:4 NRSV), drawing attention to the fact that David is no longer the powerful and virile leader of the Samuel narrative. The narrator highlights this moment in Israel's history for what it is: David is impotent. In modern political terms, he's a lame duck.

David's condition leaves a leadership vacuum. With all the drama of a Shakespearean political tragedy, the scenes that follow are filled with intrigue. David's son Adonijah makes his move to take the throne of Israel. Like Absalom before him, Adonijah's desire for the throne stems from his own self-exaltation (1 Kings 1:5). The phrase "put himself forward" in the NIV is "exalted himself" in the KJV. One modern translator suggests the following translation: "was giving himself airs."[1] Deuteronomy's instructions for the kings of Israel are clear: the kings of Israel are not to exalt themselves; they are not to "give themselves airs" (Deut. 17). In Israel's history self-exaltation always leads to disastrous ends in political and religious affairs. Back in 1–2 Samuel, Absalom ends up hanging from a tree by his hair. In time, Adonijah will meet a gloomy fate as well. 🔲 👥

The political pieces on the chessboard are moving. Adonijah gathers his supporters, including David's general Joab and Abiathar the priest (1 Kings 1:7). A sacrificial ceremony is held where, presumably, they will anoint Adonijah as king. Nathan the prophet catches wind of the plan and reports the news to Bathsheba, the mother of Solomon. King David is unaware and unknowing. In an interesting turn of phrase, Nathan reports to Bathsheba that "our lord David knows nothing about it" (1:11). Just as David did not "know"

THEOLOGICAL ISSUES

The Sin of Self-Exaltation

"You shall be like gods" (Gen. 3:5 AT). In the original sin of humanity was the desire for self-exaltation. Pride is a defining theme in Scripture's portrayal of humanity's deepest problem and need. To abandon oneself to God in devotion and obedience is the exact opposite of pride, for pride by its very nature seeks the exaltation of the self (2 Pet. 2:10). Pride is the act of making myself my own neighbor. Whether we admit it or not, all humanity is caught in its vice. There is a bit of Adonijah in all of us. The gospel brings an end to humanity's attempt to applaud or establish itself apart from the grace of God in Jesus Christ.

RECEPTION HISTORY

The Humiliation of Jesus and the Cure for Pride

Saint Augustine proclaims the glory of God's wisdom in the face of humanity's ills: "So because man had fallen through pride, she applied humility to its cure."[b] In the incarnation of Jesus Christ, the pride of humanity is dealt a death blow by the humility of God (Phil. 2:3–10). True humility stems from the knowledge of God's actions in Christ on behalf of sinful humanity. At this critical juncture alone can humanity know freedom from the tyranny of the self for the sake of a life lived *soli Deo gloria* ("to the glory of God alone"). Because of God's actions on our behalf in Christ, C. S. Lewis can offer the following words of hope in the practical affairs of our daily living: "The work of Beethoven and the work of a charwoman become spiritual on precisely the same condition, that of being offered to God, of being done humbly 'as to the Lord.'"[c]

Women in 1–2 Kings

Women did not enjoy the power men had in the biblical world. Despite these patriarchal realities, Kings depicts several women as key players and witnesses to God's providential and redeeming activity. Bathsheba plays a central role in securing the throne for Solomon (1 Kings 1:11–31). The queen of Sheba pays tribute to Solomon's wisdom and in turn praises YHWH, Israel's God (10:1–13). Later in 2 Kings, the wicked queen Athaliah tries to destroy the whole Davidic line, but an unknown princess by the name of Jehosheba rescues little Joash and hides him in the temple. Her action saves the Davidic line (2 Kings 11:2–3). Under the reforms of Josiah, Huldah the prophetess interprets the rediscovered law for a repentant Josiah (22:11–20). The list of faithful women in Kings also includes Naaman's servant girl (2 Kings 5:1–5) and the widow of Zarephath (1 Kings 17:8–15).

Abishag in 1:4, now David "knows" nothing about the plot to usurp his throne.

Bathsheba moves in swift and calculated action to secure the throne for her son Solomon. The chapter follows a series of momentous events. King David announces Solomon as his heir, Zadok the priest anoints him, and by the end of chapter one, Adonijah is begging King Solomon to spare his life. Solomon responds that if Adonijah acts in a worthy manner, he has nothing to fear, but "if evil is found in him, he will die" (1 Kings 1:52). 📖

The political dust settles for the moment as Solomon's accession to the throne is secure. From his deathbed, David challenges Solomon to keep God's law. The command to keep God's law (2:1–4) reminds readers of the admonition in Deuteronomy 17 that kings should keep God's law near them, read it regularly, and avoid the temptations to self-exaltation.

David also challenges Solomon to deal wisely with those whose power and presence are a threat to the kingdom, those who had shown themselves to be enemies of David. What may feel like a scene from *The Godfather* may be more than the settling of old scores, even though some old scores

Figure 12.3. *Visit of the Queen of Sheba to King Solomon* by Edward Poynter

are in fact settled. These enemies stand in the way of peace, which is necessary for the building of YHWH's temple. When Adonijah asks Solomon for Abishag—the young woman who helped keep the aged King David warm—Solomon receives the request as a back door attempt to reclaim David's throne. It was the last question Adonijah ever asked in this world. Solomon deals with his enemies, and his rule is "firmly established" (2:12).

Solomon's kingdom is a cresting wave that peaks and eventually flattens. At the beginning of his reign, Solomon has a dream in which God tells him to "ask for whatever you want me to give you" (3:5). Solomon asks for discernment in matters pertaining to justice. God is pleased and grants Solomon his request. Before the chapter ends, Solomon demonstrates his judicial wisdom before the whole kingdom when two prostitutes come before him, each claiming that a single baby is theirs. Solomon orders that the baby be cut in half and a piece given to each woman. One woman agrees, saying, "Cut him in two!" (3:26). The real mother, however, begs Solomon to spare the child and give it to the other woman. The whole nation marvels at Solomon's wisdom.

The book of Proverbs, often associated with Solomon, says that the fear or worship of the Lord is the beginning of wisdom. Early in his reign, Solomon—the wisest of all—links worship and wisdom together as he makes plans to build YHWH's temple. The heart of the Solomonic history (1 Kings 5–8) contains the planning, building, and dedication of this temple, the heartbeat of Israel's worshiping life before God. The details and numbers are staggering, and the craftsmanship and beauty would have been overwhelming. Cedar paneling carved with flowers, an inner sanctuary overlaid with pure gold, cherubim statues carved of cedar, outer walls carved with palm trees, cherubim, and flowers.

Public domain / Wikimedia Commons / Photo by Andreas Praefcke

Figure 12.4. *Temple Plans Explained to King Solomon*, ceiling fresco by Andreas Brugger at Church of St. Verena, Bad Wurzach, Germany

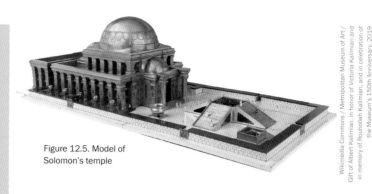

Figure 12.5. Model of Solomon's temple

THEOLOGICAL ISSUES

The Presence of God in the Temple

As a physical place, the temple took space within Israel's everyday life: walking to market, drawing water, cooking meals, and commerce. There in the midst of ordinary life, the very presence of God resided because of God's promise to be with his people. The temple promised life in the midst of death's dark shadow. Ezekiel's prophetic word attests to the gracious and free character of God and his relation to the people via the temple. Human sin and covenant unfaithfulness can temporarily harm the relation between God and his people. God's presence can leave the temple (Ezek. 10:1–19), and the consequences are dire. To be near God's presence is to be near life itself. To be without God's presence is to move toward the darkness of death.

The New Testament attests to Jesus's self-understanding as the true temple of God (John 1:14). "Destroy this temple, and in three days I will raise it up" (2:19 NRSV). Jesus was and is the very presence of God in our midst. To be with and in Jesus is to be alive; it is to live. "I am the resurrection and the life" (11:25). The presence of the temple in Israel's midst witnessed to the coming Christ who would bring God's presence to us and, in so doing, bring us the very gift of life itself (17:3).

The temple was furnished with a golden altar, golden table, lampstands of pure gold, gold floral work and lamps and tongs, golden wick trimmers, sprinkling bowls, dishes, censers, and door sockets (7:48–50). No imaginative reproduction or image could do justice to the temple's glory.

The construction of the temple is Solomon's great achievement, his lasting imprint on the kingdom of Israel. David's unrealized dream of building a house for God now stands complete and resplendent in Israel's midst (1 Kings 8:17–19; cf. 2 Sam. 7). Upon completion of the temple, Solomon dedicates it in a grand ceremony. His prayer of dedication is one of the Bible's most majestic prayers: "There is no God like you in heaven above or on earth below" (8:23). Solomon understands that no temple can contain YHWH (8:27). Even the heavens cannot hem in the Lord. Yet Solomon appeals to God's promises: "My Name shall be there" (8:29). Where God's name resides, God's very person resides as well. Where the name of YHWH rests, there his praying and repenting people will be heard and forgiven.

Solomon's admonition to the people after his dedicatory prayer is a kind of spoiler about how his own course would go, as well as how Israel's history would unfold. He summons the people: "And may your hearts be fully committed to the LORD our God, to live by his decrees and obey his commandments, as at this time" (8:61). In the next chapter, the Lord appears to Solomon and calls him to similar devotion: "If you walk before me faithfully with integrity of heart and uprightness, . . . I will establish your royal throne over Israel forever" (9:4–5). Unfortunately, even the great Solomon was susceptible to the power of sin. Chapter 11 reveals that "Solomon loved many foreign women" (11:1). Although the Lord had instructed the Israelites—including Solomon—not to intermarry, Solomon disobeys, "and his wives led him astray. . . . So Solomon did evil in the eyes of the

LORD. . . . The LORD became angry with Solomon" (11:3, 6, 9). A long shadow is cast over the whole of Solomon's person and kingdom. "It's not how you start; it's how you finish," goes the old saying. Solomon finishes in faithlessness, and the Lord says part of Solomon's kingdom will go to one of his servants.

In addition to the stories of the kings, the book of Kings includes accounts of prophetic figures. Nathan appears in the narrative of Solomon's succession in 1 Kings 1, but beginning in 1 Kings 11, several named and unnamed prophets appear. Elijah and Elisha are the most prominent. Unlike the so-called writing prophets—Isaiah, Jeremiah, Ezekiel, and the authors of the Minor Prophets— the prophets in Kings left no collection of written prophetic messages. Rather, these figures function as covenant emissaries whose presence, proclamations, and future predictions witness to a gracious and long-suffering God. The prophets demonstrate YHWH's continued claim on and love for his people in both the Northern and Southern Kingdoms.

The prophets called forth the judgment of God in light of God's covenant claims on his people. Elijah's showdown with the prophets of Baal on Mount Carmel reveal YHWH's uniqueness and singularity (1 Kings 18). Israel's God does not share his lordship with any other (Deut. 6:4). "I will be your God and you will be my people." This is the covenant formula from Deuteronomy, and the inverse threat is true as well: if you will not have me as your God and your *only* God, then your status

The Unnamed Prophet of 1 Kings 13

A troubling account of an unnamed prophet from Judah appears in 1 Kings 13. A young prophet from Judah is called to deliver a word of warning to King Jeroboam in Israel. God's instructions are clear: deliver the word and return home; do not eat, drink, or sleep in Israel. But the young prophet is hoodwinked by an older prophet in Israel who bids him to stay. When the young prophet returns home to Judah the next day, a lion kills him on the road. This story feels unfair from beginning to end, but a few points are worth highlighting. First, the prophetic word of the Lord will accomplish what it promises. Second, God's word is to be taken seriously; it is not an instrument for personal advancement or advantage. Third, Judah is to take note of what happened to its prophet. Beware of lying prophets and take heed to God's word lest you meet the lion of God's judgment as well.

Leviticus, Lions, and 1–2 Kings

Leviticus 26:21–22 makes a frightening prediction: if the people of Israel do not obey the Lord, then he will send wild animals to harm them. Three lion attacks take place in Kings. One is against an unnamed Judean prophet (1 Kings 13). The second attack also involves a disobedient prophet (20:35–36). The final attack takes place when the Assyrian expatriates who have settled in the land of the freshly exiled Northern Kingdom refuse to worship YHWH (2 Kings 17:25–28). All of these scenes indicate a fulfillment of the harrowing threat of Leviticus.

as *my people* is under threat. Elijah and Elisha as well as other lesser-known prophets—such as Ahijah, Huldah, and the unnamed prophet of 1 Kings 13—are gifts of God's relational grace to his people. Though their words are often hard, the prophets' role is to help people see the truth of God's Word and God's understanding of history and time. In the prophets of Israel and Judah, God speaks and gives himself to his people in communicative address. YHWH does not leave his people with direction but time and time again offers his word through his agents, the prophets.

The Kingdom Divided: 1 Kings 12–2 Kings 25

READ 1 KINGS 12:25–33; 18:16–46; 21; 2 KINGS 2; 22–24; 25:27–29

Near the end of Solomon's reign, an official named Jeroboam appears in the text for the first time (1 Kings 11:26). He will be the first king of the Northern Kingdom, and his name becomes a byword for the narrator of Kings, a figurehead for the kings after him who do *not* walk in the ways of the Lord. Remember, no Northern Kingdom monarch "did what was right in the eyes of the Lord."

But Jeroboam's story, like Solomon's, did not begin this way. It began with a promise from the Lord. The conditions of the promise are similar to conditions elsewhere in Samuel and Kings: "If you do whatever I command you," the Lord tells Jeroboam, "I will build you a dynasty as enduring as the one I build for David and will give Israel to you" (11:38). The Lord says he will humble David's descendants—Solomon's sins have generational consequences—"but not forever" (11:39). The promise to David and his offspring remains intact. For now, however, the glory of the kingdom is open for Jeroboam's taking.

Solomon's son Rehoboam is the heir to the Davidic throne, and he ascends the throne with all the skill of a dancing elephant. Refusing the advice of his elders—an attribute of a fool in Proverbs—Rehoboam doubles down with a heavy hand of power against the people. His petty approach to leadership leads to the schism of the north and south. Rehoboam remains on the throne in Judah with Jerusalem as its capital, but it is a pale shadow of its former glory.

Jeroboam takes the more promising and powerful Northern Kingdom with Samaria now as its capital (930 BC). On his way north from Jerusalem, he encounters a prophet named Ahijah. In a symbolic action, Ahijah tears his new cloak into twelve pieces. He gives Jeroboam ten pieces representing the ten tribes of Israel God now promises to Jeroboam. Solomon's offspring will retain the tribe of Judah, and Jeroboam's kingdom will consist of all the other tribes except Benjamin. (Chronicles clarifies that the Southern Kingdom included Judah and Benjamin.) Israel would never be the same after the golden era in the united monarchy of David and Solomon.

The division of the kingdom was the Lord's doing, and Rehoboam obeys the Lord's instructions not to fight against Jeroboam to retake the ten tribes (12:24). Jeroboam settles in the hill country of the north. Rehoboam remains in the south.

Then Jeroboam makes a political and religious decision with disastrous consequences that remain with the Northern Kingdom until the Assyrians sack them some two hundred years later. The logic of his decision makes sense on the surface. Israel is a religious people whose relation to the Lord centers on temple and sacrifice. With the temple located in the Southern Kingdom, Jeroboam perceives a very real threat. The lure of the temple will draw people's loyalty back to Jerusalem. To prevent this, Jeroboam has two golden calves made. He places one at the religious center of Dan and the other at Bethel—cities at the northern and southern end of his kingdom. He then announces to the people, "Here are your gods, Israel, who brought you up out of the land of Egypt" (12:28). The people could worship without traveling to the Jerusalem temple. "This thing," the narrator of Kings says, "became a sin" (12:30).

THE NORTHERN KINGDOM: ISRAEL

Jeroboam looms large in the history of the Northern Kingdom. In 722 BC, the imperial machine of the Neo-Assyrian Empire would bring Israel to an end. Before then, however, king after king after king is guilty of "doing evil in the eyes of the LORD and following the

CANONICAL CONNECTIONS

Jeroboam's Golden Calves

The language Jeroboam uses to describe his golden calves is stunning. "Here are your gods, Israel, who brought you up out of the land of Egypt" (1 Kings 12:28) is almost an exact replica of Aaron's description of the golden calf in Exodus 32:4. The allusion is intentional and near impossible to miss.

Readers can get hung up on the plural "gods" in most translations, but the Hebrew word *Elohim* can be translated as "God" or "gods." It's likely that Jeroboam, like Aaron, is not displacing the worship of YHWH for other gods. Calves or bulls were often used to depict the throne of God. The presenting "sin" is the desire to manage, shape, and coerce the worship of YHWH by human ingenuity and self-projection rather than on God's own revealed will. Whatever Jeroboam's intentions, the narrator of Kings understands his golden calves as the catalyst for generations of idolatry in the Northern Kingdom.

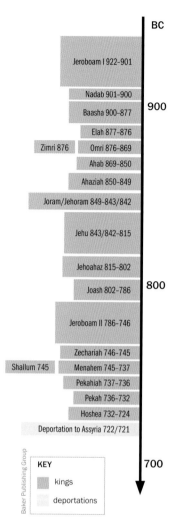

BC

Jeroboam I 922–901

900

Nadab 901–900

Baasha 900–877

Elah 877–876

Zimri 876   Omri 876–869

Ahab 869–850

Ahaziah 850–849

Joram/Jehoram 849–843/842

Jehu 843/842–815

Jehoahaz 815–802

800

Joash 802–786

Jeroboam II 786–746

Zechariah 746–745

Shallum 745   Menahem 745–737

Pekahiah 737–736

Pekah 736–732

Hoshea 732–724

Deportation to Assyria 722/721

700

KEY

kings

deportations

Baker Publishing Group

Figure 12.6. The kings of Israel

CANONICAL CONNECTIONS

A Biblical Illustration of Injustice

When the prophets speak about leaders who abuse their power by preying on those in inferior positions, few narratives of the Bible illustrate their prophetic concern as poignantly as Ahab and Naboth's vineyard. Micah the prophet describes those who abuse their power as "build[ing] Zion with blood" (Mic. 3:10). He even goes so far as to describe their injustice as a cannibalistic act of boiling others in a cauldron and eating them (3:1–3).

ways of Jeroboam" (e.g., 1 Kings 16:19). The history of the northern kings is one of idolatry, murder, and abuse of power. Israel's third king, Baasha, comes to the throne by killing Jeroboam's son Nadab, who was the sitting king of Israel. Then "as soon as he began to reign, he killed Jeroboam's whole family" (15:29). Baasha's actions fulfill the prophecy of Ahijah the prophet, the same prophet who had promised the Northern Kingdom to Jeroboam. Before Jeroboam's death, Ahijah prophesies against him for his idolatrous actions: "You have done more evil than all who lived before you. You have made for yourself other gods. . . . Because of this, I am going to bring disaster on the house of Jeroboam" (14:9–10). Jeroboam refuses to meet the conditions of God's blessings and promise, and his dynasty comes to an end with the assassination of his son Nadab.

Jeroboam's dynasty is short-lived, but two dynasties of the Northern Kingdom have a long reach: the dynasties of Omri (four kings) and Jehu (five kings). The Omride dynasty is a significant geopolitical player during the ninth century BC, even being mentioned on the Mesha or Moabite Stone. Politically speaking, Judah has limited power after the kingdom split, but Israel to the north is a key political player. The most notorious Omride king is Ahab, a name often associated with the worst kind of cunning. Ahab is evil **personified**, and his wife Jezebel is possibly worse. Ahab and Jezebel become a living gallery of idolatrous practices and abuse of power. Ahab's greedy fingers reach for the family vineyard of a man named Naboth (1 Kings 21). Naboth refuses to sell; his vineyard is his livelihood and, more importantly, his family inheritance. To sell his vineyard would be like selling his own identity. But Ahab wants it, so Jezebel schemes, and Naboth is murdered.

Ahab and Jezebel get their due. Ahab dies in battle, the dogs licking away his blood. Jezebel is thrown from a window by the direct order of Jehu, Israel's new king. The description of her death is ugly, much like the character of her life (2 Kings 9:30–37).

Jehu stands at the head of Israel's longest ruling dynasty and is a complicated figure. He is praised by the Lord for bringing judgment against the house of Ahab, yet he continues in the "sins of Jeroboam" (2 Kings 10:31). These sins of Jeroboam haunt the Northern Kingdom up through the reign of its final king, Hoshea.

In terms of history, the cause of Israel's demise was the Neo-Assyrian Empire bringing retribution against Hoshea and Israel for their failure to pay tribute to Shalmaneser V, the king of Assyria. The Assyrians march against the capital city of Samaria and lay siege to it for three years before finally capturing it, bringing the Northern Kingdom of Israel to an end. Assyria, however, was the agent of God's judging action. The narrator of Kings is quick to clarify that "all this took place because the Israelites had sinned against the LORD their God" (2 Kings 17:7). They had refused to follow the stipulations of God's law to worship YHWH and YHWH alone. They had refused to listen to the prophets God sent to warn them. The prophets were a gift of God's long-suffering mercy. Still, the Israelites "persisted" in the sins of Jeroboam right up until the point Shalmaneser destroyed their capital city (17:21–23). 🏺

Figure 12.7. The Mesha Stele, or Moabite Stone, details the exploits of King Mesha of Moab against Israel. The stone dates to the ninth century BC.

Figure 12.8. *Jezebel Eaten by Dogs* by Luca Giordano

The Neo-Assyrian Empire

The Neo-Assyrian Empire sat along the banks of the Tigris River in the northern region of modern-day Iraq. Three cities featured prominently in this kingdom: Assur (present-day Qal'at Sherqat), Kalhu or Calah (present-day Nimrud), and Nineveh (present-day Mosul). Assyrian culture and Babylonian culture were essentially the same. They spoke a dialect of Akkadian and worshiped both Marduk (Babylon's principal deity) and Assur (Assyria's primary god). Neo-Assyria was a military powerhouse with a kingdom extending from the reign of Ashurnasirpal II (883–859 BC) to its fall at the hands of the Medes and Babylonians in 612 BC. The expansive nature of Assyria's empire began with the reign of Tiglath-pileser III (744–727 BC). Under his rule, the reach of Assyria's power extended throughout the Fertile Crescent and surrounding regions. In 734 BC, the Northern Kingdom of Israel formed a coalition with several surrounding nations (Aram/Syria, Moab, and Philistia) against the swelling tide of Neo-Assyrian imperialism. This "Syro-Ephraimite" coalition pressured King Ahaz of Judah to join its efforts, but he refused. In response, these nations retaliated against Judah, though Ahaz appealed to Tiglath-pileser III for help. Assyria responded, and the Northern Kingdom was attacked in 734 BC. The final blow came in 722.

Asherah

Asherah was a female deity within the Canaanite religious myths. She was the wife of the god El and in a complicated relationship with Baal. Queen Jezebel had four hundred prophets of Asherah in 1 Kings 18:19, indicating that Asherah communicated through prophetic mediums. In the Old Testament "Asherah" also refers to a wood object—either a living tree, a stump, or a carved totem pole of some sort—that was used in worship (2 Kings 13:6; 21:3).

THE SOUTHERN KINGDOM: JUDAH

The history of the kings of Judah varies more than that of the northern kings. Some kings do "evil" in the sight of the Lord, while others do what is "right." The Davidic dynasty is the only dynasty to rule in Judah, though a queen named Athaliah makes a valiant effort at killing it off (2 Kings 11). The whole of Kings is told from the perspective of Judah's continuing importance and centrality. Jerusalem is still the location of the temple and the epicenter of Israel's worshiping life. Judah's capital city is also the place from which the Davidic promises endure and remain alive.

King Manasseh (696–642 BC; 2 Kings 21) stands at the top of the list of kings who do what is "evil" in the sight of the Lord. His father, Hezekiah, was a leader who brought about religious reforms in Israel. He tore down the high places and cleared the way for Judah to worship YHWH in faithfulness. Manasseh undoes his father's reforms. His idolatry includes the worship of astral deities or the gods of the stars. He offers his own children to the fire god Molech in the Valley of Hinnom, a valley whose proximity to the royal palace and temple of the Lord only exacerbates the offense. He erects idols and Asherah poles in the courts of the temple. As is most often the case, when love of God fails, so too does love of neighbor. Kings reports that innocent blood filled the streets of Jerusalem (21:16). Because of Manasseh's great evil, the Lord promises judgment on Judah, just as he had already judged Samaria in the north. Manasseh's detestable acts of idolatry and injustice cast the die for Judah's eventual destruction. Like Israel before them, Judah is doomed.

The reform efforts of Judah's best kings never appear thorough enough. Kings who do what is right in the sight of the Lord—including Jehoshaphat (1 Kings 22:43), Joash (2 Kings 12:2–3), Amaziah (14:3–4), and Azariah/

Uzziah (15:3–4)—still allow the "high places" to remain within Judah. The "high places" become associated with aberrant and idolatrous practices. These descriptions of Judah's kings indicate that all is not well, even when it appears to be so. Two kings on the list of good kings are portrayed as Judah's greatest: Hezekiah and Josiah. Kings says of both of them that there was no king like them in Judah either before or after they reigned (18:5; 23:25). Hezekiah's religious reforms are total, including the tearing down of the high places and the destruction of Moses's bronze serpent that had become an idol. Josiah likewise gives himself totally to the Lord and seeks to eradicate all idolatry from Judah.

But the narratives of both Hezekiah and Josiah have clouds with their silver linings. Hezekiah exalts himself before a Babylonian envoy toward the end of his reign (2 Kings 20:12–19). He shows off his wealth, and God detests the self-exaltation of his kings. Hezekiah repents after the prophet Isaiah pronounces judgment, but God promises that these same Babylonians will in time bring judgment against Judah. Josiah, as remarkable as he is, lives under the shadow of his grandfather Manasseh's wicked legacy. The narrator of Kings says that no king ever turned to the Lord with all his heart and soul and strength like Josiah did (cf. Deut. 6:4). "Nevertheless," says the narrator (2 Kings 23:26), Judah cannot escape the damage done by Manasseh. The Lord is intent on Judah's destruction. By the end of Kings, the Davidic throne sits empty, the temple is destroyed, and Judah's existence has been threatened by Nebuchadnezzar and his Babylonian army. In the face of exile, can a hopeful future exist?

Implementation—Reading 1–2 Kings as Christian Scripture Today

Who writes a history of their own country like that contained in Kings? The history has tragic elements

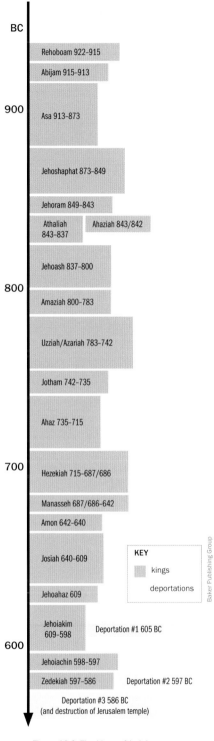

Figure 12.9. The kings of Judah

The Neo-Babylonian Empire

Ancient Babylon was the cultural and religious center in southern Mesopotamia. Babylon's neighbor to the north, Assyria, kept a watchful eye on Babylon for the many years of their regional dominance, even destroying the city in 689 and 648 BC. The rise of Nabopolassar as king of Babylon launched the Neo-Babylonian Empire (626 BC). There were many political alliances during this period. Assyrians allied themselves with the Egyptians against Babylonian advances. The Medes and the Babylonians entered an alliance against the Assyrians and Egyptians. By 610 BC Assyria had fallen from the heights of its power. Assyria's fall created a vacuum of control in the Syro-Palestinian region with the Egyptians and Babylonians vying for control. Nebuchadnezzar won a great victory against the Egyptians at Carchemish (a northern city of Syria) in 605 BC. By 597 BC, the first group of exiles were taken from Judah as Babylon established the region as one of its provinces. Zedekiah, Judah's puppet king installed by Nebuchadnezzar, rebelled against the Babylonians, resulting in the great destruction of Jerusalem, including its walls and temple, in 587–586 BC.

Jeremiah's Response to Jerusalem's Question

The prophet Jeremiah ministered within the city walls of Jerusalem during its most tumultuous time. His ministry extended from around 629 BC, during Josiah's reign, through the great Babylonian siege in 587–586 BC and into the exilic period. Jeremiah's message was simple: he reminds the religious and political leaders of Judah that Nebuchadnezzar and the advancing Babylonians are under the sovereign control of Israel's God. They are instruments of his judgment. To resist the Babylonians is to resist God himself. Why would this be happening to Jerusalem? Jeremiah answers repeatedly with the following refrain: "It is because they have forsaken my law, which I set before them; they have not obeyed me or followed my law" (Jer. 9:13). The covenantal threats of Deuteronomy arrive with the hoofbeats of Babylonian horses.

from beginning to end, but Kings presents God's prophetic view of that history. In life then as now, events in and of themselves often appear to be loosely connected and may be little understood. The prophetic account of history recorded in Kings connects the dots and provides an interpretive grid by which to understand complex historical phenomena. God chose Israel as his own, and with this choosing comes the responsibility of YHWH's people to worship and serve YHWH alone. When YHWH's people do not do this, their history unravels.

From this viewpoint, Kings may be gloomy, but it is not hopeless. The final chapter in Kings plants a seed of future redemptive hope. The new king of Babylon releases Jehoiachin, the exiled king of Judah, from prison and offers him a place of great honor among the nobles and others kings in Babylon (2 Kings 25:27–30). Jehoiachin, says the narrator, enjoyed regular meals at the king's table. This faint glimmer of light shows that what appeared to be lost—the Davidic promise—is in fact alive and well, open to the prophetic promises of God for the future. Kings calls for prophetic hope and trust that God can take what seems to be dead and make it alive again. As the empty tomb of Jesus attests, it is the very character of God to do so.

- "I am about to go the way of all the earth," he said. "So be strong, act like a man, and observe what the Lord your God requires: Walk in obedience to him, and keep his decrees and commands, his laws and regulations, as written in the Law of Moses. Do this so that you may prosper in all you do and wherever you go and that the Lord may keep his promise to me: 'If your descendants watch how they live, and if they walk faithfully before me with all their heart and soul, you will never fail to have a successor on the throne of Israel.'" 1 Kings 2:2–4
- Lord, the God of Israel, there is no God like you in heaven above or on earth below—you who keep your covenant of love with your servants who continue wholeheartedly in your way. 1 Kings 8:23
- When all the people saw this, they fell prostrate and cried, "The Lord—he is God! The Lord—he is God!" 1 Kings 18:39
- Then Isaiah said to Hezekiah, "Hear the word of the Lord: The time will surely come when everything in your palace, and all that your predecessors have stored up until this day, will be carried off to Babylon. Nothing will be left, says the Lord. And some of your descendants, your own flesh and blood who will be born to you, will be taken away, and they will become eunuchs in the palace of the king of Babylon." 2 Kings 20:16–18

Christian Reading Questions

1. What does the portrait of weak and elderly King David signify in the story? Why does this push us toward future hope?

2. Solomon loved the Lord in 1 Kings 3:3 and then many "foreign women" in 11:1. What does this portrait of Solomon say about the human heart?

3. How does the famous scene of Elijah on Mount Carmel fit with the claims of Deuteronomy 6:4?

4. Kings can be a gloomy book. How does its understated conclusion point toward future restoration and Christian hope?

CHAPTER THIRTEEN

Isaiah

Orientation

The prophets were the Lord's mouthpiece. Seized by a force outside of themselves, these inspired figures brought God's word to Israel and the world. The prophetic books, therefore, leave us with a legacy of God's speech to God's people, a treasure trove of divine direct address. But the Prophets are not easy reading. This word from the Lord to his people took place in a time far removed from our own. It is hard for today's readers not to feel somewhat paralyzed by the historical otherness of the Prophets. They are strange at times and not easy to follow. Even Martin Luther said the prophets tend to ramble on from one subject matter to the next. 📖

Yet the same divine speech given to the prophets continues to speak to God's people here and now, as it has throughout the centuries. The Prophets yield their fruits slowly, requiring great patience when reading them. Still, their canonical voices remain a stable and important feature of Christian confession and identity. "Thus *said* the Lord" and "Thus *says* the Lord" are flip sides of the same prophetic coin. God's prophetic word is God's direct address to his people of all ages. As the New Testament book of Hebrews says of the murdered Abel, though the prophets are dead, they still speak (Heb. 11:4). The Prophets may be hard, but they are worth the effort. 👥 🕊 📖

The prophetic literature comes out of particular moments in time. Identifying this history is not always easy or even possible. But we can identify certain historical features. Isaiah the prophet, for example, comes from the eighth century BC. The reign of King Hezekiah, the Syro-Ephraimite War, the imperial Assyrian threat, and the Babylonian exile all play a role in this literature and its development. Sorting through this background material and its importance presents numerous challenges, but two matters should remain front and center.

First, not all the prophetic material reveals its historical origin(s) or cause. If the primary goal of interpretation is to determine the material's historical setting, then the Prophets will often frustrate readers. A very simple principle is helpful: *the historical background of the text is as important as the text itself makes it.* The narrative portions of Isaiah 36–39 make the Assyrian threat from Sennacherib's army central. The text itself makes this historical event of some importance to interpretation. Isaiah 40–55, on the other hand, is widely understood to come out of the catastrophe of the Babylonian exile. The material suggests this historical background in various ways, but the Babylonian context of Isaiah 40–55 is not a central feature of this text. The text itself decides the importance of historical background.

Figure 13.1. Thirteenth-century depiction of the martyrdom of Isaiah from the Arundel manuscript 157

RECEPTION HISTORY

Augustine's Struggle with Isaiah

As a new convert, Saint Augustine tried to read Isaiah when preparing for his baptism. Augustine was a learned man, yet even he found Isaiah perplexing. He tells us he put the prophet to the side until he could better "learn the Lord's style of language." Students of all ages can take comfort in Augustine's struggle.[a]

HISTORICAL MATTERS

The Longevity of Prophets and Their Prophecies

Much work on the Prophets aims to uncover the historical person(s) behind the text. For example, Isaiah the man becomes a point of interest in order to press through the prophetic book to the man himself. Or Isaiah the book provides the entry point to a long editorial process by which the complete composition develops over time. Both of these approaches view the canonical form of Isaiah as a hurdle toward some other interpretive destination. While some good comes from these efforts, Christian reading practices tend to consider the prophetic book itself. Isaiah claims, "The grass withers and the flowers fall, but the word of our God endures forever" (Isa. 40:8). All flesh is grass. Just as we are here one day and gone the next, so too are the prophets as historical persons. Isaiah the prophet is dead. If tradition is true, he died a horrible death by order of wicked King Manasseh. While Isaiah hid in a hollow of a tree, Manasseh had the tree cut down with the prophet inside.[b] Isaiah the man is gone, but his words, his prophetic legacy, are alive and vital as God's word to humanity. The Word of the Lord endures forever. From the perspective of the biblical canon, Isaiah *is* his book.

LITERARY NOTES

Prophecy as Poetry

The Bible delivers much of biblical prophecy in the form of poetry. This may come as a surprise to English readers of the Bible because many of Isaiah's words, for example, do not sound like poetry. But in the Hebrew Bible, the poetic elements of biblical prophecy are evident. Robert Alter suggests two reasons for the poetic form of the prophetic literature. First, the prophetic formula repeated throughout the Prophets is "Thus says the Lord." Poetry is elevated discourse and serves the unique character of the prophetic word as God's direct address. Poetry sets itself off from prose, the language of ordinary experience. Second, poetry also aids in memory.[c]

Secondly, all the prophetical material has been "eschatologized" in its final form or final location in the Old Testament canon. What we mean by this clunky term is that the prophetic material exists for the sake of its future reception and hearing. The prophets spoke a meaningful word to their initial hearers, even when that word was misunderstood or even rejected. Yet the Prophets continue to exist in our Scriptures with an enduring word for future generations seeking to navigate the world from God's perspective. Isaiah demonstrates his own understanding of the importance of his prophetic legacy when he says, "Go now, write it on a tablet for them, inscribe it on a scroll, that for the days to come it may be an everlasting witness" (Isa. 30:8; cf. 8:16). The fact that you are reading this chapter and engaging the book of Isaiah attests to the fact that God's Word speaks to future generations.

Exploration—Reading Isaiah

From Judgment to Praise: Isaiah 1–39

JUDGMENT AND HOPE: ISAIAH 1–12

READ ISAIAH 1–2; 6–9; 11–12

"Don't bury the lede." This maxim for journalists and editors is clear enough: Don't keep your readers in suspense about your topic or your news story. Get the big idea out there right away so readers know what you're talking about and what to expect. Isaiah didn't write for the *Jerusalem Herald*, but he gets right to the point: Israel has rebelled against God (1:2).

The language of "rebellion" marks the beginning and the ending of this sixty-six chapter behemoth of a book. The editors responsible for Isaiah's final literary form made sure readers understood this central theme by bookending it to the front and the back. The book does not end on a cheery note, but it is a clear one: "And they will go out and look on the dead bodies of those who rebelled against me" (66:24). The beginning and ending of

LITERARY NOTES

The Authorship of Isaiah

Many critical scholars recognize the literary unity of Isaiah as a sixty-six chapter whole, though they do not think this requires a single author. That is, they do not think Isaiah wrote the entire book. Critical scholarship tends to divide the book into three parts: First Isaiah (chaps. 1–39), written during the time of the eighth-century-BC prophet Isaiah; Second Isaiah (chaps. 40–55), from the period of sixth-century-BC Babylonian exile; and Third Isaiah (chaps. 56–66), from the postexilic period. There are good reasons to question this tripartite structure of the book, especially the category of "Third

Isaiah." Wherever one lands on this issue, recognizing the unity of the book as Isaiah's prophetic witness is an important feature of the book's own internal claims and other canonical claims. For example, the images of blindness and deafness permeate the book as a whole, serving the themes of judgment (deafness and blindness) and restoration (the opening of the ears and eyes): Isaiah 6:9–10; 29:18; 35:5; 42:16–25; 44:18; 61:1 (where "release from darkness for the prisoners" is understood in the Septuagint as "opening the eyes of the blind"; cf. the quotation in Luke 4:18).

the book present ancient and modern readers with a pressing question about their relationship with the Lord, the Holy One of Israel: Are you my people or not? Are you among those who rebel against me or those who recognize me and me alone as Lord? 👥

Much of the prophetic writing in the Old Testament is poetry, which lends beauty and force to the prophets' pronouncements. Isaiah does not simply say, "You've rebelled!" He calls Israel a rebellious child (1:2), more rebellious than a stubborn mule (1:3). He says Israel's sins are like festering wounds and open sores (1:6). The corrupt Sodom and Gomorrah are twin sisters of **Daughter Zion**, a poetic name for Jerusalem (1:8). The faithful city (a feminine noun) becomes a prostitute (1:21). And on and on the literary deluge goes.

One of the more poignant opening chapters of Isaiah is chapter 5, with its Song of the Vineyard. Like a bard, Isaiah offers a simple song for those who can hear. The song seems harmless enough—and even lovely. *A lover plants a vineyard for his beloved. He clears a fertile hillside, plants choice vines, builds a watchtower for protection and a winepress for production. But*—change of musical key!—*instead of choice grapes, the vineyard produces bad fruit* (perhaps more literally, "stink fruit"). Lyrics that appear harmless shift abruptly as the bard interprets the song: "What more could have been done for my vineyard than I have done for it?" (5:4). Those listening to the song begin to squirm. Who's speaking now? Is this the singer or is something else going on? "Why bad grapes when I was looking for good grapes?" cries the wounded vintner. This question inspires a tirade of violence against the vineyard: walls destroyed, vines ripped out, trampled rows of grapes. What was once a promising vineyard is now a wasteland. The song's coup de grâce comes in verse 7: "The vineyard of the LORD Almighty is the nation of Israel, and the people of Judah are the vines he delighted in. And he looked for justice, but saw bloodshed; for righteousness, but heard cries of distress." Now all becomes clear; the Lord is the vintner and Judah is his vineyard.

The litany of pronouncements against Judah in these opening chapters can be summed up by Isaiah's own terms: "They have forsaken the LORD" (1:4). As the Song of the Vineyard makes clear, Israel's forsaking of the Lord is not an abstract idea. It is made concrete in two particular ways,

Jewish Tradition on Isaiah's Authorship

The rabbinic tradition presented in the Babylonian Talmud raises the question of Isaiah's authorship. When Baba Batra speaks of "writing" as it presses into the question of biblical authorship, the term "write" has a broader range of significance than our modern understanding of the term.[d] Moderns tend to limit the term to the "creative genius" behind the book. The answer the rabbis give to the question of Isaianic authorship is as follows: Hezekiah and his colleagues wrote Isaiah. Presumably, the Talmud understood the colleagues of Hezekiah as a scribal society who were responsible for putting Isaiah together in book form. Similarly, John Calvin imagined a situation where Isaiah's prophecies were publicly displayed at the temple and then stored in the temple treasury. In time these prophecies were collected and compiled into the whole we now know as Isaiah. However readers understand Isaiah's compositional history or how it came to be in its final form, the book itself understands Isaiah as its authorizing prophet from beginning to end.

ways already explicated in Israel's torah. Israel and Judah have forsaken the Lord by worshiping false gods (cf. "sacred oaks" in 1:29; see also the tree imagery in 2:6–22) and not loving their neighbors (cf. 10:1–4). Readers of Isaiah would be right to think in terms of the two tables of the law: love God and love your neighbor. God's people are the beneficiaries of his covenant kindness, and such divine grace should prompt people to worship the Lord, the Holy One of Israel, alone and to love their neighbors through righteous acts of justice. The two tables of the law form an axis: vertically, love of God; horizontally, love of neighbor. They are inseparable. The prophets make clear that Israel has failed along both lines of this covenantal axis.

The first twelve chapters of Isaiah find their center at chapter 6. Isaiah experiences a profound vision of the Lord, and he also receives his prophetic call. Typically, prophetic calls appear at the beginning of the prophetic books. Jeremiah is a good example (Jer. 1). The positioning of Isaiah's "call" in the sixth chapter leaves space for some interpretive debate. Is this actually Isaiah's initial call narrative or is it a commissioning to a new kind of prophetic ministry? John Calvin compares and contrasts Isaiah 1:1 with 6:1 and notes that the superscription of the book places Isaiah's ministry during the time of Uzziah's reign, and now

Figure 13.2. *Prophet Isaiah* by Antonio Alestra

De Agostini Picture Library / A. Dagli Orti / public domain / Wikimedia Commons

Uzziah has died.[1] So, it appears Isaiah's temple vision is a recommissioning, though it is not necessary to be certain about this. The death of Uzziah—a good king according to Kings and Chronicles—creates a perilous vacuum of political and religious leadership.

Isaiah 6 lays a foundation for much of the book of Isaiah. It echoes throughout the book, presenting a dire situation that is nonetheless open to God's redemptive intervention, which appears in Isaiah 40: "Comfort, comfort my people, says your God" (40:1). In his vision, Isaiah sees the Lord "high and lifted up" (6:1 ESV), terms reserved for the Lord alone in Isaiah. When Israel raises and exalts itself (cf. 2:12), it demonstrates arrogance in a space reserved for the Lord. While the earthly king Uzziah has died, the Lord remains on his kingly throne. Seraphim—terrifying beings more like flying serpents than cute cherubs—hover above YHWH's throne and exclaim the perfection of God's holiness: "Holy, holy, holy is the LORD Almighty; the whole earth is full of his glory" (6:3). The room shakes; smoke fills the space. Aware of his sinfulness and the sinfulness of the nation, Isaiah cries out that he is ruined (6:5). One of the angels places a burning coal on his lips to cleanse him.

Then Isaiah hears the Lord speaking among his divine council: "Who will go for us?" Cleansed and purified, Isaiah jumps at the task—"Here am I. Send me!" (6:8). Then God tells Isaiah the terms of his task: his words will be the instrument of God's judgment against the people, but his words will make their eyes blind and their ears deaf. Troubled, Isaiah asks, "How long?" (6:11). God replies with another hard word; Judah will become a wasteland, her inhabitants scattered. Isaiah's words of judgment will leave Judah like a tree cut down. But even cut-down trees are open to the possibility of new growth: "Holy seed is its new growth" (6:13 AT).

While much of Isaiah 1–12 contains judgment, it also contains words of hope. For example, Isaiah 2:1–4 paints a remarkable portrait of Mount Zion raised and exalted among all the nations as the highest of mountains. This future-oriented scene of hope depicts the

Call Narratives in the Old Testament

Scholars identify two types of call narratives in the Old Testament. The first is associated with the divine word (e.g., Jeremiah in Jer. 1) and the second with a theophany, an appearance of God. In the latter type, the one called encounters God's actual presence within the context of God's divine council (e.g., Micaiah ben Imlah in 1 Kings 22). Isaiah's call or commission narrative occurs by means of a theophany. He sees the exalted Lord, the King on his throne, among his heavenly council.

Blind Eyes and Deaf Ears

The blinding of eyes and the deafening of ears are two primary metaphors of God's judgment in Isaiah. By contrast, the opening of blind eyes and the unplugging of the ears portray God's forgiveness and redemption (cf. Isa. 35:5 and 40:5—"The glory of the LORD will be revealed" and "All people will see it together"). When Jesus gives his parable of the sower, he provides the logic of his parables. They are meant to both reveal and conceal. "Let anyone with ears to hear listen" (Luke 8:8 NRSV). Jesus says this because no one understood the meaning of the parable. The disciples ask Jesus to explain, and he quotes Isaiah 6:9: "Looking they may not perceive, and listening they may not understand" (Luke 8:10 NRSV). Jesus explains the parable to his disciples, opening their eyes and ears, so that they may understand the mysteries of God's kingdom. When Jesus does this, he is stepping into a prophetic framework already built in Isaiah. God's word revealed and explained is God's gracious move to love, forgive, and redeem.

peoples of the world streaming to Mount Zion, receiving instruction from the Lord, and enjoying an era of universal peace where instruments of war become agricultural tools: "They will beat their swords into plowshares and theirs spears into pruning hooks" (2:4). Similarly in Isaiah 4, Zion is promised a glorious future beyond the devastation of its current judgment.

Perhaps the most famous words of hope in Isaiah 1–12 are in chapters 7–9 with the promise of Immanuel. King Ahaz of Judah faces a political crisis in what's often called the Syro-Ephraimite War. In the midst of this crisis, Isaiah offers Ahaz a sign to bolster his faith in God's promises. The sign God offers to a reluctant Ahaz is the promise of a son named Immanuel, "God with us," born to a young woman or virgin (7:14). The term for this woman focuses on a young woman of marriageable age and would not typically be used for married women, thus "virginity" is assumed. The birth of this son is the promise of God's saving presence even in the midst of judgment (cf. 8:8, 10).

Against Isaiah's words, Ahaz follows the path of unbelief, and the promise of the coming son in Isaiah 7:14 becomes part of a larger messianic portrait in chapters 7–9 (see again 8:8, 10). Like a swelling tide, the Immanuel hopes of these chapters in Isaiah culminate in the oft-repeated words of Isaiah 9:6, "For to us a child is born, to us a son is given, and the government will be on his shoulders. And he will be called Wonderful Counselor, Mighty God, Everlasting Father, Prince of Peace." God's saving presence is

THEOLOGICAL ISSUES

Who Is "Immanuel"?

Who is Immanuel? Readers of Isaiah often struggle to identify the Immanuel figure with a historical referent. Medieval Jewish interpreters like Rashi and Ibn Ezra thought Immanuel in the immediate context of Isaiah 7:14 could be Isaiah's own son, Maher-Shalal-Hash-Baz (8:3). Modern readers often identify King Hezekiah as Immanuel's immediate referent. Hezekiah, the immediate successor to the unbelieving King Ahaz, was a faithful and righteous contrast to Ahaz.

Christians know that Matthew 1:23 identifies Immanuel with Jesus Christ. Two issues are involved in this interpretation. First, how does Matthew think of "fulfillment"? It appears fulfillment does not necessitate one referent but means a filling to the fullest. Jesus Christ fills out the Immanuel promises to their fullest, including what appears to be the exaggerated language of Isaiah 9:6—"Mighty God." Second, whoever may be the immediate referent of the Immanuel promise in Isaiah's historical context, the Immanuel imagery within chapters 7–9 points toward a future or eschatological hope beyond the Syro-Ephraimite crisis of Ahaz's day. Matthew's identification of Jesus as the fulfillment of Isaiah 7:14 assumes both of these biblical truths.

HISTORICAL MATTERS

The Syro-Ephraimite Crisis

The Syro-Ephraimite War (734–731 BC) was an attempt to pressure Judah to join an anti-Assyrian coalition of Israel (King Pekah of the Northern Kingdom) and the nation to Israel's north, Aram/Syria (King Rezin; cf. 2 Kings 15:27–31). The situation left Judah, particularly King Ahaz, in a vulnerable position. The countries of the coalition intended to divide Judah among themselves and replace Ahaz with another ruler (the son of Tabeel, a ruler whose identity is difficult to determine but whose name means "good for nothing"), leaving Judah vulnerable to the Edomites and Philistines as well (cf. 16:6; 2 Chron. 28:17–18). Isaiah advises Ahaz against joining this Syro-Ephraimite coalition.

fixed to God's messianic promise of a king who, unlike Ahaz, operates in faithfulness as a Wonderful Counselor, Mighty God, Everlasting Father, and Prince of Peace. 📖 ✋

Figure 13.3. *The Holy Family* by Nicolas Poussin

God's word in Isaiah 1–12 effects injury and healing, judgment and redemptive hope. Isaiah 10 presents the Lord as the great tree-feller, lopping off the boughs and limbs of Israel's prideful tree. "The lofty trees will be felled" (10:33). Yet even this terrifying prophecy opens to the hope of God's future dealings with his people. "A shoot will come up from the stump of Jesse" (11:1). From the cut down tree, a shoot of new life springs up as God promises a future Davidic king who will rule in wisdom, might, knowledge, and the fear of the Lord (11:2). Isaiah 1–12 begins in judgment and ends in praise (chap. 12). The night of mourning and loss gives way to the morning of praise and singing: "Sing to the LORD, for he has done glorious things; let this be known to all the world" (12:5).

THE LORD'S SOVEREIGNTY AND HARD WORDS FOR THE NATIONS: ISAIAH 13–23

■ READ ISAIAH 18 ■

Isaiah presents a cosmic view of the Lord's authority and rule. The Lord's redemptive focus is directed at his covenant people Israel. Readers of the Old Testament learn these truths early in the books of the Pentateuch. At the same time, Israel's God is the God who spoke the whole world into existence. His sovereign reach extends to all the nations, and chapters 13–23 attest to the extent of the Lord's rule and the authority of his word.

The prophet levels judgment oracles against Babylon, Philistia, Moab, Damascus (Syria), Cush (near Ethiopia), Egypt, and Tyre. The human arrogance the Lord

Figure 13.4. *The Tree of Jesse* by Victor of Crete

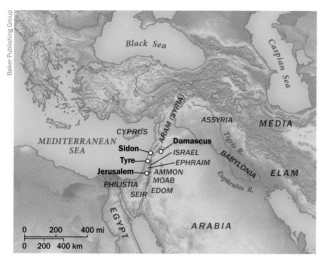

Figure 13.5. Map of the nations named in Isaiah 13–23

detests among his people in chapters 1–12 is the same trait leading to his judgment against the nations as well. Although it may be tempting to read these oracles against foreign nations as oracles of salvation for Israel—something akin to, "I am going after your enemies, Israel, take heart"—however, a close reading suggests otherwise. Jerusalem, representative of Judah, is one of the nations under the Lord's sovereign judgment (chap. 22).

The Lord has a plan in the book of Isaiah (cf. 19:12), and it includes the nations (cf. 14:26). This plan declares a coming "day of the LORD" when the Lord's outstretched hand will leave the whole earth in fear and trembling (cf. 19:16). Yet the character of the Lord to heal as well as wound also appears in these chapters. On that terrible day, an altar to the Lord will be in the very "heart of Egypt" (19:19). Even the Egyptians, Israel's archenemies, will cry out to the Lord, and he will send them a deliverer (19:20). Isaiah 19:19–22 is a stunning portrayal of the nations turning to the Lord in repentance and worship (cf. 2:1–4). These chapters clarify the worldwide scope of the Lord's sovereign reach.

COSMIC JUDGMENT AND REDEMPTION: ISAIAH 24–27

■ READ ISAIAH 24–27 ■

Isaiah targets Judah's rebellion in chapters 1–12, expands the scope of the Lord's sovereignty to include all nations in chapters 13–23, and widens the lens even more in chapters 24–27 to address God's cosmological judgment of the world and its ultimate restoration. Some interpreters refer to this portion of Isaiah as "the little **apocalypse**" because of its heightened imagery, cosmic viewpoint, and eschatological focus. Others dismiss the **apocalyptic** label because these chapters are tethered to history and are not characterized by heavenly mysteries or secrets, features of the apocalyptic genre.

Literary labels aside, these chapters portray the entrance of God's kingdom into the world. The coming

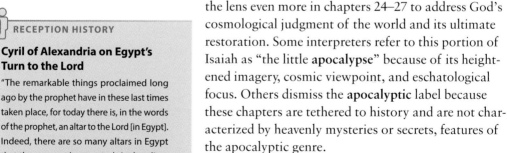

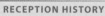

RECEPTION HISTORY

Cyril of Alexandria on Egypt's Turn to the Lord

"The remarkable things proclaimed long ago by the prophet have in these last times taken place, for today there is, in the words of the prophet, an altar to the Lord [in Egypt]. Indeed, there are so many altars in Egypt that they cannot be counted. And replicas of the cross are venerated by the inhabitants of Egypt, for they have believed our Lord Jesus Christ."[e]

day of the Lord brings both terror and renewal. The opening chapter (Isa. 24) recalls the flood narrative in Genesis 6 with its description of the guilt of the whole earth. The whole earth is laid low by devastation and loss, but these are not allowed the final word. Death leads to life. Destruction to renewal. Even the "islands of the sea" will "exalt in the name of the LORD" (24:15).

The glorious day of the Lord results in praise and thanksgiving in the songs of Judah, God's covenantal people (Isa. 26). But God's redemptive scope includes the whole of the cosmos. When Israel's God swallows up death forever and wipes away tears from faces, he does so for "all peoples," "all nations," and "all faces" (25:7–8). When death is dealt its final blow in this portion of Isaiah, "the little apocalypse," it sounds much like the book of Revelation. There, too, the Lord Jesus Christ wipes away tears from everyone's eyes and banishes death forever (Rev. 21:4). There, too, persons from every tribe and language and kingdom are the objects of God's cosmic redemptive action (5:9–10).

A PROMISED RIGHTEOUS KING: ISAIAH 28–39

■ READ ISAIAH 35; 36–39 ■

"Woe, woe, woe," cries the prophet in chapters 28–33 (28:1; 29:1, 15; 30:1; 31:1; 33:1). "Woe to . . . Ephraim [the Northern Kingdom]" (28:1 NRSV). "Woe to you, Ariel, Ariel" (29:1; "Ariel" may refer to the altar hearth in the temple and represents Jerusalem here). These are examples of the six "woe" oracles against Israel, Judah, those who deal secretly and deceptively with the Lord, those who trust Egypt instead of Israel's God, and the treacherous. Perhaps these six "woe oracles" mirror the six "woe oracles" of Isaiah 5 with the seventh woe Isaiah levels against himself in chapter 6. As Isaiah is cleansed on the far side of his "woe," so too is the royal household of Zion, which is promised a coming king who will reign in righteousness and justice (32:1).

This promise of a coming righteous and just king ties to the portrayal of King Hezekiah in chapters 36–39. These chapters contain a narrative of the Assyrian king Sennacherib's invasion of Judah in 701 BC (cf. 2 Kings 18:13–19:37). Besides the eventual destruction and exile of Judah in the

> CANONICAL CONNECTIONS
>
> **The Lasting Prophetic Word**
>
> Isaiah 8:16 and 30:8 make important statements about the longevity of the prophetic word for future generations.
>
> Bind up this testimony of warning
> and seal up God's instruction among my
> disciples. (8:16)
>
> Go now, write it on a tablet for them,
> inscribe it on a scroll,
> that for the days to come
> it may be an everlasting witness. (30:8)
>
> These statements are easy to overlook in a large book like Isaiah, but in both verses the prophet encourages his followers to store his words for future generations to hear. The prophets speak to their times, yet their words are not limited to their times. Isaiah's words are "an everlasting witness" and will be read by future generations as a divine witness (cf. Rom. 15:4).

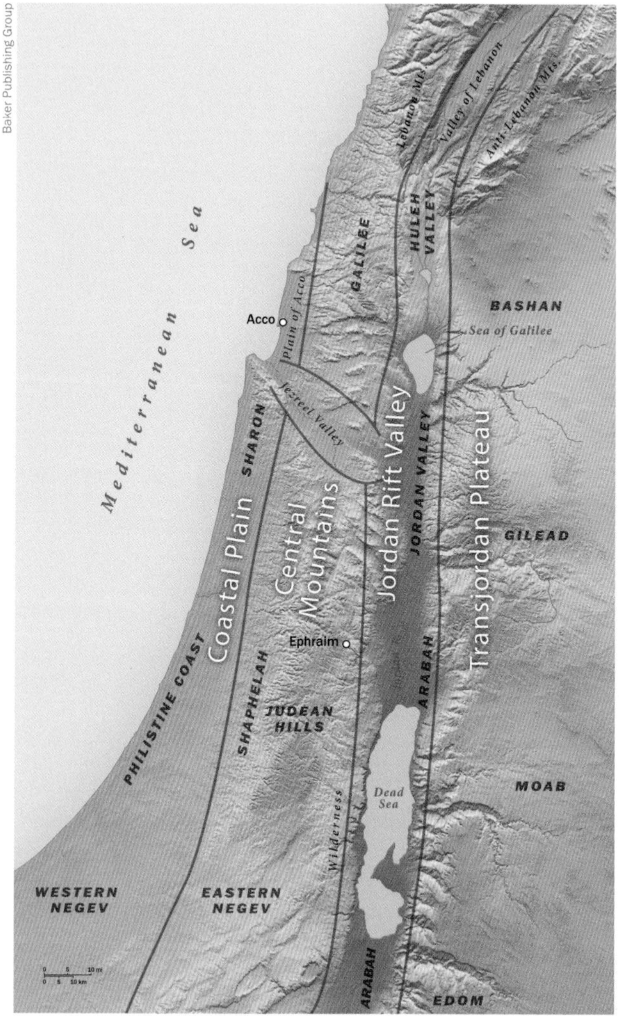

Figure 13.6. Map of the regions of Israel

sixth century BC by the Babylonians, this Assyrian invasion was one of Judah's most devastating historical events. The fortress city of Lachish along with many other cities in the Judean foothills (the Shephelah) suffered. From the captured Lachish, Sennacherib sent his field commander (the *Rabshakeh*) to Jerusalem to threaten the people and undercut their trust in King Hezekiah: "Do not let Hezekiah mislead you when he says, 'The LORD will deliver us'" (Isa. 36:18).

The scene is chaotic and desperate. Hezekiah rips his clothing in anguish. The people face certain destruction before a ruthless and overpowering army. Yet the word of the Lord from Isaiah to Hezekiah is one of simple trust: "Do not be afraid" (37:6). Hezekiah prays for deliverance (37:14–20), and the Lord answers through Isaiah (37:21–35). The final words of the prophecy summarize its message: "I will defend this city and save it, for my sake and for the sake of David my servant" (37:35). The next verses recount that the angel of the Lord put to death 185,000 of Sennacherib's troops. It was as simple as that: Hezekiah prayed for deliverance, the Lord promised deliverance, and the Lord delivered.

Hezekiah then experiences his own personal version of what the whole nation had just gone through (Isa. 38). He is on the verge of death, and death is sure to come. Hezekiah prays and weeps, and the Lord hears and adds fifteen years to his life. The king exemplifies a pattern evident in the Psalms: the psalmist waits patiently for the Lord; the Lord hears; the Lord delivers;

CANONICAL CONNECTIONS

Micah and the Assyrian Invasion

Micah, a contemporary of Isaiah, was from the lowland region devastated by the Assyrian army. He recounts the Assyrian havoc on these cities in Micah 1:10–16. The prophetic response to this onslaught is one of ritual repentance and mourning (1:16).

the psalmist praises and proclaims the Lord's salvation (e.g., Ps. 40:1–5).

Unfortunately, Hezekiah concludes his reign with an act of self-serving pride before a Babylonian envoy (cf. 2 Chron. 32:25). In Isaiah 39 he gives them a tour of the royal treasury and storehouses to show off his wealth. Hezekiah keeps nothing back from them, falling prey to the temptations Israel's kings were warned against in Deuteronomy 17—beware of the pride of power and the deceit of wealth. A king's honor comes from his dependence on the Lord, not his acquisition of power and wealth. Isaiah then tells Hezekiah of Judah's eventual destruction by the Babylonians. This prophecy creates a link to the following chapters of Isaiah (40–66).

Isaiah 39 is not the only link to Isaiah 40–66. Chapter 35, before the Hezekiah narrative (chaps. 36–39), builds another literary and prophetic bridge to chapters 40–66. This chapter anticipates the great day when the Lord will overturn the time of judgment. Deaf ears will hear again. Blind eyes will see (cf. 6:10). There will be a "highway" called the Way of Holiness for those making their way back to God and for God making his way back to his people (35:8). This "highway" will appear again in Isaiah 40, the prophetic chapter of renewal or "new things" on the far side of judgment.

Divine Comfort, Salvation, and a New World Order: Isaiah 40–66

■ READ ISAIAH 40–55; 60–61; 65–66 ■

Isaiah 40 marks a seismic shift in the book. Modern scholars often associate this shift with a change in authorship and setting—namely, an anonymous author during the Babylonian exile of the early sixth century BC. Recognizing a significant literary seam at chapter 40 does not necessitate this critical view. Even Thomas Aquinas in the thirteenth century, predating critical scholarship, recognized that "the second principal part" of Isaiah's prophecy begins at chapter 40. The intention of the second part of the book, according to Aquinas, is to bring comfort to a people wearied by the heavy hand of God's just judgment.

The opening words of chapter 40 make the matter clear: "Comfort, comfort my people, says your God." Even the pronouns speak to the tenderness of the reconciling moment. Back in chapter 6, Isaiah was told to go to "this people" (6:9). The distancing use of the pronoun "this" is similar to the kind of distancing in the name of Hosea's second child: Lo-Ammi, "not my

RECEPTION HISTORY

The Prophets and "I Have a Dream"

On August 28, 1963, Martin Luther King Jr. stood before an enormous crowd on the steps of the Lincoln Memorial and delivered his most famous speech, paving the way for the Civil Rights Bill of 1964. The timeless words of "I Have a Dream" ring with prophetic echoes of Amos and Isaiah. King's call for justice takes its cue from Amos—let justice roll down like waters, and righteousness like a mighty stream (Amos 5:24). His hope for racial equality resembles Isaiah's prophetic portrayal of Zion's forgiveness: "I have a dream that one day every valley shall be exalted, and every hill and mountain shall be made low, the rough places will be made plain, and the crooked places will be made straight; and the glory of the Lord shall be revealed and all flesh shall see it together" (cf. Isa. 40:4–5).[f]

CANONICAL CONNECTIONS

The New Testament and Isaiah 40–55

This portion of Isaiah, especially chapters 40–55, plays a significant role in the New Testament's explanation of the person and work of Jesus Christ. The Gospels are filled with allusions and references to Isaiah 40–55, which provides a Scripture-saturated language and grammar for the eschatological events of the life, death, and resurrection of Jesus Christ. Paul also quotes Isaiah 49:8 and its promise of a coming time of favor, a day of salvation. When is that day? Paul answers, "Now is the time of God's favor, now is the day of salvation" (2 Cor. 6:2).

people" (Hosea 1:9). The covenant formula—I will be *your* God and you will be *my* people—indicates the importance of these pronouns: "*your* God" and "*my* people." Sin ruptured the covenant relation between God and his people. But now, Isaiah's word brings comfort. "This people" becomes "my people" with a highway opening up for the Lord's return to his people.

Chapters 40–66 do not include the name of any prophets. The emphasis of the chapters is the centrality of the prophetic word of the Lord, not the prophet speaking them. "The grass withers and the flowers fall, but the word of our God endures forever" (40:8). Prophetic personalities come and go, but the word of the Lord endures forever and accomplishes its "gospel" or "good news" purposes (40:9; 52:7). The central agents of God's salvation in these chapters are the servant of the Lord and his offspring, the servants.

Four sections of Isaiah 40–55 reveal the enigmatic redemptive figure of the servant of the Lord: 42:1–4; 49:1–6; 50:4–9; and 52:13–53:12. These Servant Songs are situated to their literary surroundings and clarify who the offspring of Abraham really are. Before the first of these songs, there is little doubt about the identity of the servant (cf. 41:8–9). Who is the servant of the Lord? Answer: Israel. When, therefore, readers encounter the first of the Servant Songs (42:1–4), it seems clear that Israel is the servant of the Lord. Israel is God's elect and covenantal instrument. The Spirit empowers the servant for the sake of bringing justice to the nations (42:1). The servant is gentle and patient: "A bruised reed he will not break, and a smoldering wick he will not snuff out" (42:3). He is also faithful and perseveres in the role given to him.

A shift occurs in the servant theme with the promise of something new in Isaiah 48. "From now on I will tell you of new things, of hidden things unknown to you. They are created now, and not long ago" (48:6–7). What are these "new things"? In part, the new things center on the developing description of the servant of the Lord. While the servant is clearly identified with Israel in Isaiah 40–48, a challenge arises with this simple identification in chapter 49, the second Servant Song. The servant is identified as

Israel in verse 3, but in verse 6 the servant is also given a mission *to* Israel: "to restore the tribes of Jacob." How can that be? How can the servant be Israel and at the same time be given a mission to Israel? In this redemptive development, the servant of the Lord is identified as Israel and at the same time is distinct from the nation. The servant figure takes on Israel's election and mission for the sake of both Israel and the nations: "I will also make you a light for the Gentiles" (49:6).

The servant's mission culminates in the haunting descriptions of the suffering servant in Isaiah 53. The servant suffers in the place of others and as their representative. Rejected and reviled, the suffering servant bears a guilt and punishment that was not his to bear for the healing of all (53:5–6).

The description of the servant is increasingly personalized in these chapters, creating questions about the servant's identity. Who is this figure whose identity is forged together with Israel's yet cannot be identified simply as the nation? Christianity, from its inception, has understood Isaiah 53 as a witness to the suffering of Jesus Christ. Jesus embodies Israel's election and endures the judgment of its rejection for the sake of the whole world. Little wonder Matthew's Gospel describes Jesus in terms of the history of Israel: Jesus goes down to Egypt as a child and then returns; Jesus enters the wilderness for forty days and nights as Israel wandered forty years in the wilderness; Jesus sits atop a mountain and delivers the torah (Matt. 5–7). Jesus's actions and words make one thing very clear. He embodies Israel's election, mission, and rejection for the sake of Israel and the whole world.

Figure 13.7. *Isenheim Altarpiece* depicting Isaiah 53 and crucifixion scene by Matthais Grünewald

Public domain / Wikimedia Commons

Isaiah 52:7 proclaims the "good news" in terms of the reign of God. God's coming kingdom is indeed good news for those eagerly awaiting his appearing. The shock of Isaiah, however, is the means by which God's kingdom rule takes place. The message of the kingdom is wrapped up in the message of Isaiah 53—"Who has believed our message?" (53:1)—and its description of the suffering servant. The final Servant Song follows right on the heels of Isaiah 52:7, making clear the kind of rule God will bring into the world by the suffering of his servant. The outcome of the servant's suffering is a righteous offspring or "the many who are made righteous by the knowledge of him" (53:11 AT). As the prophecy moves on, the servant's offspring take center stage in the book's final section (chaps. 54–66). These offspring are not left nameless. They are the *servants* (plural): "This is the heritage of the servants of the LORD, and this is their vindication from me" (54:17). The move from the servant (singular) to the servants (plural) is a central element of Isaiah's redemptive drama.

The servants of the servant appear in Isaiah 54–66 as those who share in the sufferings of the servant and his hope for future vindication (65:13–16). As they live into the tension of faithfulness and suffering, the servants act as heralds of the good news (61:1–3). A key feature of the book entails this dynamic of servant to servants, especially with the way the terms "righteousness" and "justice" appear. In Isaiah 1–39, righteousness and justice are used in reference to Israel's guilt. They lack righteousness and justice and as a result incur God's judgment. In Isaiah 40–55, righteousness and justice are gifts given to the guilty through the servant's suffering on their behalf (cf. 53:11). In Isaiah 56–66, the terms "righteousness" and "justice" combine again. In Isaiah 1–39, the lack of righteousness is the justification for judgment. In Isaiah 40–55, righteousness is often linked to "salvation"—righteousness becomes a gift given on the basis of God's own righteous and saving acts (53:11). Now in Isaiah 56:1 we see righteousness, justice, and salvation coming together. In the midst of continuing wickedness, the servants respond in faithfulness to the righteousness provided for them by the servant.

CANONICAL CONNECTIONS

Paul and the Servant(s) of Isaiah

Much of Paul's logic in Galatians 3–4, including his allegory of Sarah and Hagar, trades on the movement of Israel–servant–servants in Isaiah 40–55. It is no accident that Paul quotes Isaiah 54:1—"Sing, barren woman"—as in his Sarah/Hagar allegory. The apostle wrestles with the question of Abraham's true offspring in Galatians, and Isaiah has provided for him a scriptural answer. Abraham's true offspring are those who have been made righteous by the Servant (Jesus Christ) and recognize their true identity and salvation in him and him alone.

THEOLOGICAL ISSUES

Justification, Sanctification, and Jesus

The Reformers made a distinction between justification and sanctification—being "saved" and becoming Christlike. This distinction is still a helpful one. Both components of our salvation are accomplished completely by the righteous actions of Jesus Christ in his life and death. Justification highlights the character of our salvation in terms of a declared act. We are given a right standing before God because of Jesus alone and are given a righteousness originating outside ourselves in Christ. Sanctification highlights Jesus Christ's making us holy. This facet of our salvation is a gift too, yet it also emphasizes the importance of a faithful response to the righteousness and holiness that is already completely ours in Jesus. As the Anglican Articles of Religion claim, good works done in faith are pleasing to God.

Figure 13.8. *The Peaceable Kingdom* by Edward Hicks (1834)

Public domain / National Gallery of Art / Gift of Edgar and Bernice Chrysler Garbisch

The book of Isaiah ends with a cosmic portrait of a new heavens and a new earth (Isa. 65:17–25). This is good news for the servants but devastating news for those who continue to reject Israel's God. Zion's future brims with hope: "The sound of weeping and of crying will be heard in it no more" (65:19). The book ends where it begins: with a harsh description of those who rebel against God (66:24). Yet even this harsh word is preceded by words of hope for a new heavens and a new earth (66:22).

Implementation—Reading Isaiah as Christian Scripture Today

The aim of this chapter is to give readers some handles for reading the book of Isaiah as a whole. Isaiah is like the Blue Ridge Mountains. There is always something more around the bend in the road, sure to surprise and perhaps even make you catch your breath. A cursory chapter like this leaves much important material unexplored, but readers can still grasp something of the whole of Isaiah and its prophetic legacy.

Isaiah leaves readers with a big question, and it is a question from God: *Are you my people, and am I your God?* The tendency for God's people to stray in terms of loving God and loving our neighbors remains perennial. We battle these tendencies individually and corporately till the day we die. A Christian's hope, however, in Isaiah's terms is the effective power of God's word to accomplish its redeeming work and the self-giving faithfulness of the suffering servant who gives his life for the salvation of the many.

Little wonder that Isaiah often takes center stage in the public reading of Scripture when Christians around the world find themselves in the seasons of Advent, Christmas, and Epiphany. "Arise, shine, for your light has come, and the glory of the LORD rises upon you" (Isa. 60:1).

KEY VERSES IN ISAIAH

- Hear me, you heavens! Listen, earth! For the Lord has spoken: I reared up children and brought them up, but they have rebelled against me. 1:2
- Go and tell this people: "Be ever hearing, but never understanding; be ever seeing, but never perceiving." 6:9
- Comfort, comfort my people, says your God. 40:1
- It is too small a thing for you to be my servant to restore the tribes of Jacob and bring back those of Israel I have kept. I will also make you a light for the Gentiles, that my salvation may reach to the ends of the earth. 49:6
- Yet it was the Lord's will to crush him and cause him to suffer, and though the Lord makes his life an offering for sin, he will see his offspring and prolong his days, and the will of the Lord will prosper in his hand. 53:10
- This is the heritage of the servants of the Lord, and this is their vindication from me. 54:17
- See, I will create new heavens and a new earth. The former things will not be remembered, nor will they come to mind. 65:17

Christian Reading Questions

1. In what ways are the people of God rebellious in the book of Isaiah, and how does God rescue them from their own sinfulness?
2. What is the significance of the description of God's people as "this" people in Isaiah 6 and "my" people in Isaiah 40?
3. How do the word of the Lord and the servant of the Lord serve as agents of redemption?
4. The servants of the servant follow him in obedience, future vindication, and shared suffering. What might this portrayal say to us about the Christian life of faith?

Jeremiah

Orientation

"See, today I appoint you over nations and kingdoms to uproot and tear down, to destroy and overthrow, to build and to plant" (Jer. 1:10). YHWH's commission to the prophet Jeremiah discloses the focus of the book: God's judgment and restoration of his people, Israel. Because of divine judgment, God's people will experience exile from their homeland. However, true to his covenant promises, YHWH offers future hope, particularly exemplified in the inspiring vision of Jeremiah 30–33. Nonetheless, the overarching feel of the book is one of divine wrath, reiterated by the prevalence of negative divine action toward Israel. In the commissioning of the prophet for his service to YHWH, Jeremiah 1:10 captures the central theme of the book: to uproot, to tear down, to destroy, and to overthrow. Only after divine judgment comes divine comfort: to build and to plant. The thematically central language of Jeremiah 1:10 finds its way into all other portions of the book: Jeremiah 12:14–17; 18:7–9; 24:6; 29:5, 28; 31:28–40; 42:10; 45:4. As YHWH's prophet, Jeremiah will preach a troubling message. 🏺🏺🏺

The historical setting of Jeremiah is the Neo-Babylonian invasion of Judah and subsequent exile of Jerusalem's inhabitants. These events occurred in

Figure 14.1. Icon of Jeremiah

Public domain / Wikimedia Commons

HISTORICAL MATTERS

Jeremiah's Context

The setting of Jeremiah begins in the latter third of the seventh century BC and extends through the Neo-Babylonian destruction of Jerusalem (ca. 626–586 BC). This time frame presents the waxing of the Neo-Babylonian Empire and the waning of the Judahite state. God raises up the Babylonians to punish Judah, much as described in the book of Habakkuk.

Greek Translations of Hebrew Texts

After the rise of Alexander the Great and the process of **Helleniza-tion** in the fourth century BC, Greek became the lingua franca—the common language—of the ancient world. Jewish scribes over a long period of time began translating the Hebrew Old Testament into Greek to maintain its relevance in new contexts. These Greek translations are often referred to as the **Septuagint, or LXX**, but in fact there are several ancient Greek translations of Old Testament books from the third century BC onward. These Greek translations are often compared to Hebrew texts (e.g., Codex Leningradensis, the Aleppo Codex, and Hebrew texts discovered at Qumran near the Dead Sea) to see how they are similar and different.

Hebrew and Greek Versions of Jeremiah

Hebrew Jeremiah (MT)	Greek Jeremiah (LXX)
Written in Hebrew	Written in Greek
Longer by about 2,700 words	About 2,700 words shorter
Oracles against nations in Jeremiah 46–51	Oracles against nations after Jeremiah 25:13 LXX
Two Qumran texts follow the Hebrew ordering of text	One Qumran text follows the Greek ordering of text
Later sources like Codex Leningradensis follow Hebrew ordering of text	

For a long time, scholars believed the Hebrew text of Jeremiah in the Masoretic Text was earlier than the Greek version. However, due to manuscript discoveries in and around the Qumran caves by the Dead Sea, most scholars now believe the Greek version of Jeremiah reflects an earlier Hebrew text of Jeremiah that was translated into Greek, while the MT represents a Hebrew edition with roughly 2,700 more words. The Qumran scrolls range in time from 300 BC to AD 300.

Recent questions center on how to assess these differences. Is the Greek edition paraphrasing a Hebrew text, thereby giving a rationale for its relative brevity? Is the longer Hebrew edition responding to the earlier Hebrew edition reflected in the Greek, expanding on it? Do the two Hebrew editions point to two authoritative Hebrew editions, one reflected by the MT and the other by the LXX? These questions and others are still being explored today.[a]

Figure 14.2. Qumran caves where ancient scrolls were discovered

stages.[1] As a result, Judah experienced a kind of serial trauma from Babylon for decades. Each of these phases is reflected in one way or another throughout the book of Jeremiah. 🏺 📖 📖

Exploration—Reading Jeremiah

Divine Judgment: Jeremiah 1–10

▪ READ JEREMIAH 1–4; 7 ▪

Oracles of divine judgment, accompanied by brief glimpses of hope, characterize this section. Judgment and its rationale are introduced in Jeremiah 1:14–16. God will be raising up a nation from the north to pour out disaster on Judah. By this time in history, the seventh century BC, Judah stands alone. Israel, the Northern Kingdom, was destroyed in 722 BC.

Babylon's Staged Invasion of Judah

By 597 BC, Babylon had invaded Judah, deposed Jehoiachin, and set Zedekiah on the throne as a puppet king to make Judah a vassal state (cf. 2 Kings 24:8–17). During this period, Babylon deports and exiles the literati of Judah (like Ezekiel the prophet), its leadership, and gifted Judahite young men like Daniel, Hananiah, Azariah, and Mishael. Zedekiah later revolted against Babylon, and Nebuchadnezzar marched on Jerusalem and laid siege to it. In 586 BC the Babylonian Empire crushed Jerusalem, razing it and forcibly exiling additional Judahites to Babylon. Finally, the Babylonians facilitated another round of deportations from Judah to populate the Babylonian homeland and provide workers for the empire after a failed attempt at Judean independence, which was put down by Nebuzaradan (582 BC).[b]

Now the Southern Kingdom will go the way of its northern neighbor. God's judgment is coming upon them.

Why would God do such a thing? YHWH rehearses the story of his people wandering in the wilderness, how he cared for his covenant people despite their waywardness. He brings charges against his people once again, particularly for idolatry (Jer. 2:1–3:5), in a memorable way: "My people have committed two sins: They have forsaken me, the spring of living water, and have dug their own cisterns, broken cisterns that cannot hold water" (2:13). Forsaking YHWH is tantamount to rejecting God's purpose with his covenant people. They have exchanged their covenant relationship for false worship, or digging worthless cisterns. Instead of experiencing life (water), Judah's idolatry will bring futility as their worship is empty. The implication is that Judah has chosen death. By contrast, YHWH is a never-ending stream of water for his people, but they have rejected him.

YHWH's commitment to Judah contrasts with Judah's sin and betrayal. Yet God (or the prophet) appeals to the people to return to their covenant partner (Jer. 3:14–4:4). This call to return to YHWH culminates in the evocative image of circumcision: "Circumcise yourselves to the LORD, circumcise your hearts" (4:4). Highly unusual, this phrase intends a covenant commitment to God from the inmost depths of the human soul. God's desire for and appeal to repentance is a bright ray of hope in the darkness of disaster. Sadly, the call is met with recalcitrance among the people. Only divine intervention to circumcise the heart of the people will accomplish God's purpose with his covenant people (Jer. 31:31–34).[2]

The Structure of Jeremiah

The book of Jeremiah is complex, containing oracles of judgment, oracles of salvation, letters, confessional prayers, historical reports, prose, poetry, and more. The material falls into five main blocks:

1. Divine judgment, Jeremiah's confessions, divine hope (Jer. 1–24)
2. Present recalcitrance, future hope, Jeremiah's pain (Jer. 25–38)
3. Jerusalem's fall and aftermath (Jer. 39–45)
4. Oracles against the nations (Jer. 46–51)
5. Jerusalem's fall and exile (Jer. 52)

Chronology in Jeremiah

The general flow of the book of Jeremiah leads to Jerusalem's fall and the inhabitants' exile. However, this overall structural progression is not a simple chronological development from 626 to 586 BC in the fifty-two chapters of the book. The book is organized by theme and focus rather than simple chronology. Some chapters are out of chronological order to highlight theological foci, themes, or concepts important in the book.

Jeremiah and Deuteronomy

The imagery of the circumcised heart first appears in the Torah: Leviticus 26:41; Deuteronomy 10:16; 30:6. Leviticus 26:41 depicts Israel's uncircumcised hearts in exile that are humbled and return to YHWH. Deuteronomy 10:16 calls on Israel to circumcise their hearts in complete covenant devotion to God. Deuteronomy 30:6 indicates a future restoration after exile when God's people will experience divine restoration and a divine circumcision of the heart: "The Lord your God will circumcise your hearts and the hearts of your descendants, so that you may love him with all your heart and with all your soul, and live." In these texts, God's appeal in Jeremiah 4:4 mirrors the appeal in Deuteronomy 10:16.

The Creative Suffering of God

Theologian Terence Fretheim explores the suffering of God in the Prophets. God suffers because, with, and for his people. God suffers because Israel rejects him (Isa. 1:2–3; 54:6; 63:7–10; 65:1–2; Jer. 2; 18:13–15; Hosea 9–11; 13:4–6). In divine laments (Jer. 9:9; 12:7–12; 15:5–9; 48:29–33; Ezek. 27:3–11, 26–36), God suffers pain as Israel sins against YHWH, which then leads God to enforce judgment against them. God also suffers with those who are suffering (Isa. 15:5; 16:9–11; Jer. 9:10, 17–18; 12:7; 31:20; 48:30–36), coming alongside the hurting and suffering with them. Finally, God suffers for humanity's sin, and he suffers the "weariness" of restraining divine judgment (Isa. 48:9; 57:11; Jer. 15:6; Ezek. 20:21–22; 24:12; Mal. 2:17).[c]

Figure 14.3. The prophet Jeremiah

By Jeremiah 7, the prophet has proclaimed clearly that destruction is coming for the people of Judah and Jerusalem. The people do not want to hear this message. They claim that because the temple of YHWH is standing, surely God is on their side and nothing bad will happen to them. Their optimism likely derives from traditional ideas about God's protection of Jerusalem, sometimes called "Zion theology" (see, e.g., Ps. 46).[3] However, Jeremiah reminds the people that God's desolation of the Shiloh sanctuary illustrates divine commitment to his just rule rather than any obligation to a geographical place like Jerusalem. In Jeremiah's famous "temple sermon," the prophet tells the people that holy sites do not guarantee YHWH's presence in Judah, but holy people do (7:3–11). He will return to this theme in his second temple sermon (26:1–6). Jeremiah assures Judah that God will protect his people and place, but only if God's people remain committed to him in that place.

Jeremiah 9 introduces a divine lament as God weeps because of his people's sin (9:1–2). Other prophetic texts present divine laments as well (12:7–12; 15:5–9; 48:29–33; Ezek. 27:3–11, 26–36). Often it is hard to distinguish the voice of God from the voice of the prophet in these verses, but divine suffering is heard in this merging of voices. 📖

Jeremiah's Confessions: Jeremiah 11–20

■ READ JEREMIAH 11–12; 18–19 ■

Alongside YHWH's suffering over the people's sin, Jeremiah 11–20 presents the prophet suffering through his divine calling. Sometimes called Jeremiah's "confessions," these raw prayers are protestations against God's call (12:1–6; 15:10–14, 15–21; 17:14–18; 18:18–23; 20:7–13, 14–18; cf. 23:9–10). The prophet experiences tension over God's commission and the pain of living out that calling. Jeremiah's vivid internal struggle over his own call and preaching, the people's rebellion, and divine judgment culminates with a cry of self-loathing. Jeremiah directs his confessions to YHWH in prayer, demonstrating, as Job and Lamentations do, that prayer is a means

Figure 14.4. *Jeremiah* by Michelangelo, Sistine Chapel (1512)

to navigate pain in the Old Testament. The instinct in the life of faith before YHWH is to pray and protest in pain and suffering.

Jeremiah 11:11–17 highlights how Israel's sin culminates in a "broken covenant" that God established with the people of Israel (11:3). In broad strokes, YHWH rehearses the Israelite covenant (Exod. 20–23; Leviticus; Deuteronomy), only to detail how Israel has broken the covenant stipulations. Leviticus 26 and Deuteronomy 28 promised that if Israel fails to uphold their commitment to YHWH, curses ensue, including exile from the land YHWH has given Israel. Jeremiah is instructed to proclaim that covenant curses are on their way to Judah.

Jeremiah's extensive prophetic sign acts emphasize the certainty of exile and disaster (see "Sign Acts of the Prophets" in chap. 8 above). Each sign act reinforces the certainty of disaster. In one sign act, Jeremiah is instructed to go to a potter's house and break pottery to signify the certainty of destruction (Jer. 18–19). In the thematic language from Jeremiah 1:10, YHWH tells Jeremiah that destruction of pottery and people is his prerogative: uprooting, tearing down, destroying, building, and planting (18:7–10).

Repentance is a possibility, but God's people will not choose it. As soon as Jeremiah pronounces judgment, particularly in Jeremiah 19, Pashhur, a priest at the temple in Jerusalem, hears Jeremiah's word of judgment and has him beaten and thrown in prison for his preaching (20:1–6). Pashhur's response to YHWH's word is emblematic of Israel's problem of disobedience. They cannot hear YHWH's word, and they rebel against it.

The Weeping Prophet

Jeremiah's prayers and tears, as well as grief from Judah's impending demise, lead John of Damascus (AD 645–749) to illustrate Jeremiah lamenting and weeping in his work on the book of Lamentations, which he also attributes to Jeremiah. Both Lamentations and the mourning of Jeremiah associate the prophet with weeping and mourning. Jeremiah is represented with forlorn visage and downcast state. The visual representation of Jeremiah as weeping creates pathos and a sense of loss and longing that is associated with most of the book.

LITERARY NOTES

"Sword, Famine and Plague"

One hallmark phrase in Jeremiah is "sword, famine and plague" (14:12; 24:10; 27:8, 13; 29:17–18; 32:24, 26; 42:17, 22; 44:13; cf. Ezek. 6:11; 12:16). Poetic in its imagery, the "sword" is a metonymy for warfare; "famine" is a metonymy for the experience of a city besieged and undergoing starvation; and "plague" indicates the disease and death that invade a besieged city once food supplies are gone, leaving the populace unable to fight off sickness. This short, punchy phrase paints a horrific picture of Jerusalem's impending doom. They will experience the invading Babylonian army ("sword"), flee into their city and suffer through the Babylonian siege ("famine"), and slowly die as the life of the community ebbs away ("plague"). No more terrifying phrase could portray what lies in store for Judah.

Jeremiah is broken by his experiences and his people's rebellion. He responds by turning to YHWH with an inflammatory prayer: "You deceived me, Lord, and I was deceived, you overpowered me and prevailed" (20:7) and "Why did I ever come out of the womb to see trouble and sorrow and to end my days in shame?" (20:18). It is for good reason Jeremiah is known as the "weeping prophet."

It may be easy to criticize Jeremiah as being faithless or weak because of his harsh words to God and his emotional turmoil. But Jeremiah's is a deep and rich spirituality. True spirituality in the Prophets maintains honesty before God in the midst of confusion and pain, even contending boldly with God. Jeremiah's complex interaction with God reveals extraordinary psychological depth and honesty as he faces a watershed event in the life of his nation and people. His prayers exemplify how lament fuels conversation with God in times of pain and struggle.

Divine Hope: Jeremiah 21–24

■ READ JEREMIAH 21–24 ■

Jeremiah 21–23 addresses failures of the leadership structures in Judah, particularly the king (Jer. 21–22) and prophets (23:9–40). These are contrasted by the righteous king that YHWH brings in the future in Jeremiah 23:1–8. God will bring his exiled and dispersed people (described as YHWH's flock) back to the land of Judah and resettle them after judgment. He will appoint a king to rule with justice, wisdom, and devotion to YHWH. God gives this future king a name: "YHWH is our righteousness" (23:6 AT). This brief ray of light in the darkness of the book reminds God's people that there is hope beyond exile.

God's covenant purposes with Israel will not be thwarted, even though the nation will be exiled because of its sin. The certainty of impending exile is reinforced by the strange vision Jeremiah receives concerning good and bad figs (Jer. 24). The "good" figs represent God's people going into exile. The "bad" figs represent those remaining in the land. Rather than being a purely historical statement about the people of Judah who remain in the land, this vision emphasizes the judgment, particularly exile, that is coming.

Present Recalcitrance: Jeremiah 25–29

■ READ JEREMIAH 26 ■

Jeremiah 25–29 expounds on the reality of exile in a variety of ways. In chapter 25, Jeremiah prophesies about invasion, exile, and return, and he has a prophetic vision of giving a "cup" of wrath to the nations to pour out on Jerusalem. Chapter 26 includes Jeremiah's second sermon about the temple. He prophesies disaster, which leads to death threats against him. Jeremiah then wears a yoke in chapter 27, a sign act illustrating the coming Babylonian invasion and exile of Judah. Then the false prophet Hananiah refutes Jeremiah's words (Jer. 28). In chapter 29, Jeremiah writes a letter to the exilic community, indicating that exile

Figure 14.5. *Jeremiah Lamenting the Destruction of Jerusalem* by Rembrandt (1630)

has already happened for some (29:2). Ezekiel, Daniel and his three friends, and other elites from Jerusalem would have been taken in 597 BC.

Future Hope: Jeremiah 30–33

■ READ JEREMIAH 30–33 ■

From the dark judgment of Jeremiah 1–29, a ray of light appears in Jeremiah 30–33. Often called the "little book of comfort" in Jeremiah's prophecies, these chapters offer the divine response to the broken covenant depicted in Jeremiah 11:1–17. Whereas God's people forsake their covenant with YHWH, their Lord is nonetheless committed to them. He will not break the covenant he has made with his people and act as they have. He will renew in them covenant fidelity, reign among them as their God, and settle them in their land.

Jeremiah 32 presents the message of hope in the life of the prophet. Jeremiah is told to buy a field during Babylonian siege. This action is absurd because land has no real value in this situation. But the purpose of the sign act is to show God's desire to make the land desirable and fertile once again after the horrors of exile. Jeremiah's purchase of the field exemplifies God's message of hope beyond exile. This is central to the new covenant message in Jeremiah 31. 👥 👥

The phrase "new covenant" occurs in Jeremiah 31:31–40, which lay within the promises of restoration in Jeremiah 30–33.[4] Every previous Old Testament covenant finds its fulfillment in the new covenant. Jeremiah 31:35–37 presents the new covenant as a future new creation unhindered

Augustine, the New Covenant, and a Salvific Contrast

Augustine (ca. 354–430) understood the new covenant as not simply a new era in God's work. Rather, the new covenant marks a salvific contrast. The old covenant equates to unbelief in God, and the new covenant equates to faith in God. Moses, Joshua, David, and others follow the law given to Moses (Leviticus–Deuteronomy) because of their faith in the Lord and, therein, experience divine grace. In this way, these Old Testament figures are new-covenant believers because they embrace God by faith. Their faith and allegiance to God typify what it means to experience new-covenant membership. This con- trasts with a view that simply sees an era of law (old-covenant Israel) versus an era of grace (new-covenant church). In this way, an Augustinian reading of the new covenant indicates a salvific contrast so that any believer of any era (from Noah to the apostle Paul to those who embrace Christ by faith today) is a new-covenant member. Their faith had always been in Christ.[d] Nonetheless, Augustine recognizes that the Mosaic law depicted in the Old Testament is fulfilled in Jesus and therefore not (entirely) applicable to followers of Jesus after his resurrection and ascension.[e]

Figure 14.6. *Saint Augustine* by Phillipe de Champaigne (ca. 1645)

Jerome, the New Covenant and Two Eras

Jerome (ca. 345–420) understood the new covenant in terms of two successive eras in the history of God's work with his people. In the first era (the old covenant), God engaged his people, Israel. Israel's failure to live up to the standards of the covenant opened the horizon of God's new work in Jesus, who brings the new-covenant era. Thus, the old covenant is no more, and the new-covenant era has begun in Christ and, thereby, the church. For Jerome, the new covenant presents two historical eras of God's divine action in the world, with the old-covenant era breaking into the new-covenant era in Christ. This distinguishes his reading from Augustine.

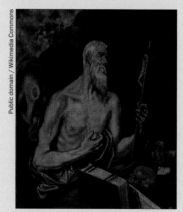
Figure 14.7. *Saint Jerome* by El Greco (Domenikos Theotokopoulos, ca. 1600)

by sin (affirming God's covenant at creation and with Noah). It proclaims that Abraham's descendants will be blessed by God (fulfilling the Abrahamic covenant). Jeremiah 31:33–34 shows that God changes the hearts of his people so that they love God and obey his law (fulfilling God's call in the Israelite covenant). Jeremiah 33:14–18 presents the Davidic king ruling over God's people in God's land (fulfilling the Davidic covenant).[5] So it is appropriate to say that although we find several covenants in the Old Testament, in the full canonical development of the text these covenants are related and coordinated to disclose God's purposes with the world. Each covenant leads toward the new covenant in which peace with God in his world is actualized. The new covenant projects a future in which all will be well in the relationship between God and Israel as the people dwell in God's land. Sin will no longer be operative in God's people, and they will live in perfect peace with their God and in the world.

How should we think about the new covenant? We have seen two options in Augustine and Jerome (see the sidebars). In terms of its structure, the new covenant is not new at all. 📜

The new covenant is deeply connected to the covenants we have witnessed in Genesis through

Divinely Initiated Covenants in the Old Testament

God's Unconditional Acts of Provision

Acts by which God establishes the covenant relationship (the blessings of the covenant given as an act of grace in the *past*)

Creation	Noah	Abraham	Israel	David	New Covenant
• Creation itself as a habitat for human-ity (Gen. 1:1–2:3; 2:4–25) • Divine blessing (Gen. 1:22, 28) • *Imago Dei* (Gen. 1:26–28) • The goal of creation: promised rest where the King will rule over his kingdom (Gen. 2:1–3)	• God "remembers" Noah and his family (Gen. 8:1) • Divine blessing (Gen. 9:1) • *Imago Dei* (Gen. 9:6) • Reaffirming the cre-ational order (Gen. 8:22) • Food (Gen. 9:3)	• God calls Abram (Gen. 12:1–3) • God blesses Abram (Gen. 12:2) • God appears to Abram (Gen. 12:7) • God will be Abram's "shield" (Gen. 15:1)	• God calls Israel (on the basis of the pa-triarchs) (Exod. 19:3; see also 3:7–16) • God blesses Israel with being fruitful and multiplying (Exod. 1:7, 12, 20; cf. Gen. 1:28; 9:1) and then rescues Israel (Exod. 19:4) • God delivers Israel from the land of Egypt / house of slavery (Exod. 20:2)	• God calls David to be "prince" over Israel (2 Sam. 7:8) • God is with David (2 Sam. 7:9) • God's blessing (2 Sam. 7:29) • *Note:* Another un-conditional act of God's provision is that David is an Is-raelite and so is part of God's redemptive work through Israel (and Abraham and Noah), as David recognizes in 2 Sam. 7:22–24.	• God's blessing based on God's faithful-ness in the past (Jer. 31:23–25) • God's commitment to creation (Jer. 31:35–37) • God's covenant with Abraham (Jer. 31:36; 33:25–27) • God's covenant with Israel at Sinai and Moab (Jer. 31:27–28; 33:25–26) • God's covenant with David (Jer. 33:14–23)

Covenant Stipulations

Commands by which the covenant relationship is maintained (the commands of the covenant, to be kept in the *present*)

Creation	Noah	Abraham	Israel	David	New Covenant
• Be fruitful, multiply, rule, subdue, exert dominion, tend and till the ground (Gen 1:28; 2:15) • Adam and Eve may eat from any of the trees in the Garden of Eden (Gen. 2:16) • Adam and Eve may not eat from the tree of the knowledge of good and evil (Gen. 2:17)	• Be fruitful, multiply, fill the earth (Gen. 9:1, 7) (note that Noah tends and tills the ground [Gen. 9:2] as a reaffirma-tion of Gen. 2:15) • Do not eat blood (Gen. 9:4)	• "Walk before" God and "be blameless" (Gen. 17:1) • Keep the covenant of circumcision as an everlasting covenant (Gen. 17:9–13)	• Carefully listen to God's voice (Deut. 30:15–20); keep his covenant (Exod. 19:5) • Keep the Ten Com-mandments (Exod. 20:2–17; Deut. 5:6–21) • Keep circumstan-tial laws (Exod. 20:22–23:33; Deut. 6:1–26:19)	• (Implied) Follow the instruction of the Lord given to all of Israel at Sinai and Moab, especially the law of the king in Deut. 17:14–20 • (Implied) Do not turn aside from the instruction of the Lord given to all of Israel, especially to the king, otherwise there will be divine punishment (see 2 Sam. 7:14)	• None given, but pre-sumably the stipula-tions are an inter-nalization of God's torah (the totality of God's instruction) in the "heart" of God's people, so that they will love God and fol-low him without fear or threat of punish-ment (cf. Jer. 31:33; 32:38–41); God's people will follow both the letter and spirit of the law

Covenant Promises

Results of keeping or not keeping the covenant (the consequences of the covenant, to be fulfilled in the *future*)

Creation	Noah	Abraham	Israel	David	New Covenant
• (Implied) If Adam and Eve eat from the plants in the garden, they will live • (Curse) If they eat from the tree of the knowledge of good and evil, they will die (Gen. 2:17)	• God will never again curse the earth or destroy every living creature (Gen. 8:21) • God will never again destroy the earth with water (Gen. 8:21; 9:11)	• God will uncondi-tionally bless Abram with a name, fam-ily, and land (Gen. 12:2–3, 7; 15:5–7, 13–16; 17:2–8; cf. 2 Sam. 7:9–13)	• Israel will be God's special possession among all nations on earth (Exod. 19:5) • Israel will be God's priestly kingdom and holy nation (Exod. 19:6)	• God will uncondi-tionally bless David with a great name (2 Sam. 7:9; cf. Gen. 12:2–3), a land for Israel (2 Sam. 7:10; cf. Gen. 12:2–3), and a dynastic "house" (2 Sam. 7:11–12; cf. Gen. 15:5, 13–16; 17:2–8)	• Restoration of the houses of Judah and Israel (Jer. 31:27; 32:36–41) • Fertility of flora and fauna in the land of Israel (Jer. 31:12)

(continued)

Covenant Promises *(continued)*

Creation	Noah	Abraham	Israel	David	New Covenant
	• God will remember his covenant and the rainbow will be a sign (Gen. 9:11–16) so that he will never destroy the earth (this is an everlasting covenant, v. 16) • (Curse) If humans take life, their lives will be required of them (Gen. 9:5)	• (Curse) Any descendant who is not circumcised will be "cut off" (Gen. 17:14)	• If Israel obeys, then God will fight *for* Israel rather than against Israel; he will bless Israel's food and water, take away sickness, remove barrenness, and fulfill the number of Israel's days; God will send terror before Israel against enemies and drive out Israel's enemies (little by little) and establish Israel's borders (Exod. 23:22–33) • (Curse) If Israel does not obey, they will not receive pardon and will be punished (Exod. 23:20–21)	• God will establish the Davidic throne and kingdom forever (2 Sam. 7:13–16) • (Curse) Divine punishment for "iniquity" against God, presumably from disobedience to God's stipulations of the Israelite covenant, given at Sinai and reiterated at Moab (see Deut. 5–30; esp. 17:14–20) • God will not take his *hesed* (steadfast covenant love) away from David (2 Sam. 7:15)	• New covenant that is rooted in the former covenant (given at Sinai/Moab), but the torah will be internal, on the hearts of God's people so they will know it and follow it explicitly (Jer. 31:31–34) • God will forgive iniquity and remember sin no more (Jer. 31:34; 33:8) • God reaffirms offspring for Israel (Jer. 31:36; cf. Gen. 12:2–3; 2 Sam. 7:13–16) • Restored city, temple, and sacrifices (Jer. 31:38–40; 33:9–18; cf. Ezek. 40–48) • Restored Davidic kingship and Levitical priesthood (Jer. 33:19–26) • Restored land (Jer. 32:41–44) • God will give his people a new heart that they will fear him for all time in an everlasting covenant (Jer. 32:39–40)

Note: We agree with Scott J. Hafemann that covenants are divinely initiated unconditional acts of provision and blessing by which God establishes his covenant with various parties. These covenants are not "earned" but always come with stipulations through which the relationship is maintained. See Scott J. Hafemann, *The God of Promise and the Life of Faith: Understanding the Heart of the Bible* (Wheaton: Crossway, 2001), 56.

Kings. The Abrahamic, Israelite, and Davidic covenants find their fulfillment in the new covenant. Nonetheless, the new covenant is different from previous covenants. First, the new covenant is a work of God in which he will "restore the fortunes" of a judged people (Jer. 29:14; 30:18; 31:23; 32:44; 33:7, 11, 26). This phrase depicts a renewed relationship between YHWH and his people, in a renewed land, under God's renewed rule. The new covenant is unique in its restoration in the following ways:

1. Divine forgiveness is characteristic of the new covenant, and sin is not managed for a brief period only to require further sacrifices. In the new covenant, God forgives sin completely (31:34; 33:8). We find no process by which God will forgive his people. It is simply a divine act of grace. One assumes it could be a special or unique sin offering, perhaps, but the change that accompanies divine forgiveness is not stipulated, only the fact that divine forgiveness will be perpetual: "I will forgive their wickedness and will remember their sins no more" (31:34).

2. The new covenant stresses the internal change of God's people for covenantal obedience to YHWH from the heart (31:31–34). God's law, then, becomes part of the interior life of God's people. Their hearts become internally imprinted, as it were, with God's virtues and

values: God's law is written on the hearts of his people and thus will not need to be read from tablets of stone.

3. Restored and revivified covenant relationship is central to the new covenant. Jeremiah 31:33 uses the covenant formula "I will be their God, and they will be my people," reaffirming the covenant relationship and the divine presence among Israel. Divine presence will expand so that *all* will know God in this covenant relationship, from the least to the greatest (31:34).

4. The new covenant envisions God's people in God's land under God's rule. YHWH will remove landlessness and dishonor and will resettle and honor his people in the land. The faithful king will reign once again (cf.23:1–8), and lost worship will again ensue in the temple (31:38–40; 33:9–26). The divided kingdom will be united again (31:27; 32:36–41). The city of Jerusalem will be restored (31:38–40; 33:9). The desolated land will be replenished and renewed (31:27–28; 33:12–13). God's people will live in God's land under God's rule.

5. YHWH renews the hearts of his people, and they return to YHWH in the new covenant (Jer. 31:18; cf. Lam. 5:21). When God turns to his people in renewal, they return to him (30:20; 31:18; Ezek. 36:11). The resulting covenant relationship between God and his people is no longer marked by sin.[6] YHWH, in effect, transforms their hearts to love their God (Jer. 31:33–34).

In summary, the new covenant is the climactic work of God's redemption of his people. The new covenant is grand and beautiful. It is a complete restoration whereby God offers forgiveness of sin, life, and hope (Jer. 32:37–41).

But when will this take place, and how? In Jeremiah's horizon, the new covenant lies beyond the exilic era. Seventy years of exile must be met for there to be a homecoming. But beyond this time frame, the full vision of the new covenant lies in an unspecified future, perhaps with some partial fulfillment of the new-covenant promises along the way.[7] But the hope of the new covenant was never fully realized until the advent of Jesus into the world. As we are told in Hebrews 8, Jesus is the mediator of this new covenant (vv. 6, 13). Jesus's coming changes everything. This is extraordinarily good news!

Jeremiah's Pain: Jeremiah 34–38

■ READ JEREMIAH 37–38 ■

After the beautiful vision of a new covenant, Jeremiah 34–38 reverts to words of impending doom and details the prophet's ongoing struggle with a rebellious royal house and people. Judah's king Zedekiah is warned of coming judgment at the hand of Nebuchadnezzar (Jer. 34). Jeremiah prophesies that YHWH will preserve the Rekabites for their obedience to God's word, but Judah will fall because of their disobedience to God (Jer. 35). The prophecy describes King Jehoiakim's rebellion against God, and he burns the scroll of Jeremiah's warning. As a result, God speaks a word of judgment against Jehoiakim (Jer. 36). The text returns to focus on Zedekiah in chapters 37–38, where Jeremiah is arrested, thrown in prison, and then thrown into a cistern as his words fall on deaf ears. Jeremiah 37–38 depicts the impending siege of Jerusalem in which the inhabitants will be slowly starved to death (37:21). By combining these passages into a unit, it is as if the sins of the grandfather (Jehoiakim) permeate the sins of the grandson (Zedekiah). Both together reinforce the message of the inability of God's people to hear and obey his voice: it has been this way for years! They need the new-covenant transformation but can experience it only after the exile.

Jerusalem's Fall and Aftermath: Jeremiah 39–45

▨ READ JEREMIAH 42–44 ▨

Inevitably, the city falls to the Babylonians. God's word of judgment comes to fruition. Chapter 39 tells how the city is taken. After a two-year siege, Jerusalem is starved and broken, and the Babylonian army invades and captures it in 587 BC (cf. 2 Kings 25:1–12; Jer. 52:4–16). Zedekiah attempts to escape but is overtaken at Jericho (39:4–7), while some of the people are exiled (39:9). The poorest people of the land are left alone, without protection or care. Nonetheless, the commander of the Babylonian army (Nebuzaradan) gives them vineyards and fields to cultivate (39:10).

The section concludes with Jeremiah's experience: he is freed from captivity and then is urged to flee to Egypt along with some of the survivors. God tells him to remain in the land of Judah rather than flee (Jer. 42). Jeremiah advises the survivors to stay in Judah, but they reject his words and travel to Egypt in hopes of security there. Jeremiah 43:6–7 records their disastrous move: "And they took Jeremiah the prophet and Baruch son of Neriah along with them. So they entered Egypt in disobedience to the LORD and went as far as Tahpanhes." That they took Jeremiah and his scribe, Baruch, further exacerbates the prophetic rejection and suffering elaborated throughout the book. Truly, a prophet has no honor among his own people (cf. Matt. 13:57). The disasters the survivors experienced should have drawn them to repent and turn back to YHWH, but Jeremiah 44 records their faithlessness in terms of fleeing to Egypt and burning incense to Egyptian deities (44:8). YHWH will bring disaster on the Judahite survivors in Egypt just as he did with the people of Judah and Jerusalem. Egypt cannot protect the people from divine judgment. In fact, instead of providing them with good, God gives them harm (44:27; cf. 21:10). 🗨

This section concludes with Jeremiah's letter to Baruch (Jer. 45). Although disaster is certain, God will preserve Baruch's life even as things disintegrate and judgment comes. All that God preserves is Baruch's life. Why? It is a glimmer of hope for YHWH's preservation of a remnant among the nations of the world.

Oracles against the Nations: Jeremiah 46–51

■ READ JEREMIAH 49–50 ■

The oracles against foreign nations fill Jeremiah 46–51. Different from where they appear in the Greek versions of Jeremiah, the oracles against the nations (OAN) follow Jeremiah's denunciation of survivors in Egypt and serve as a climactic word of judgment against Babylon, the instrument of divine wrath throughout the book. There are nine oracles in this section of Jeremiah:

1. Egypt (46:2–28)
2. Philistia (47:1–7)
3. Moab (48:1–47)
4. Ammon (49:1–6)
5. Edom (49:7–22)
6. Damascus (49:23–27)
7. Kedar and Hazor (49:28–33)
8. Elam (49:34–39)
9. Babylon (50:1–51:58)

Fascinatingly, as God will "restore the fortunes" of his people in the new covenant, the OAN proclaim that YHWH will also "restore the fortunes" of some judged peoples/cities/nations (Moab, Ammon, Elam). Other OAN do not employ this phrase (Egypt, Philistia, Edom, Damascus, Kedar and Hazor, Babylon). It is unclear why divine restoration is available for some and not for others. The emphasis, however, is on divine prerogative for judgment against the nations for various sins.

Jerusalem's Fall and Exile: Jeremiah 52

■ READ JEREMIAH 52 ■

As if to put an exclamation point on the doom depicted in the book, the final chapter of Jeremiah reiterates the action of Jeremiah 39. Jerusalem, the city of peace, falls in war. Zedekiah falls to Nebuchadnezzar. The city is burned to the ground, and Nebuchadnezzar and his army destroy the temple dedicated to YHWH, taking the precious bronze, silver, and golden temple implements back to Babylon. "So Judah went into captivity, away from her land" (52:27).

Implementation—Reading Jeremiah as Christian Scripture Today

If ever a text highlights divine wrath, Jeremiah is it. The prophet Jeremiah presents God's wrath through sign acts, language of doom, and detailed reports of invasion, siege, and ultimate destruction and exile. Jeremiah paints a picture of terror authorized by the hand of YHWH for his people's sins. How should we read this text as Christian Scripture?

Divine judgment. In the first place, we can see God's divine judgment for human sin. Although this is a prominent theme in other prophetic texts, Jeremiah depicts God as the prosecutor and judge of sinners. This is true for his own people, Judah (Jer. 1–2), but the OAN also testify that YHWH is more than the covenantal God of Israel. He is the cosmic Lord. His power as Creator authorizes his sovereignty over all nations. As such, he can judge the nations for their sins, but he can also restore their fortunes.

The suffering of God and prophet. We briefly saw the way in which both God and the prophet suffer because of the people and their sin. God grieves the ways in which his people refuse his care and concern. The prophet grieves the sins of the people and weeps a fountain of tears over it (Jer. 9:1). The suffering of both God and prophet coalesces in the way Jesus grieves over the city of Jerusalem and its rejection of his lordship and messiahship in Matthew 23.

Suffering of God, Suffering of Christ

"Jerusalem, Jerusalem, you who kill the prophets and stone those sent to you, how often I have longed to gather your children together, as a hen gathers her chicks under her wings, and you were not willing. Look, your house is left to you desolate" (Matt. 23:37–38). Jesus grieves over his people's resistance to God. One could interpret these words as those of the true prophet whose words are rejected or as the divine Son of God who grieves the people's sin and rejection. Or both. The book of Jeremiah reveals a pattern of prophetic and divine suffering that shows up in the life and ministry of Jesus.

Divine forgiveness and the new covenant.[8] Jeremiah's new-covenant prophecy depicts extraordinary divine forgiveness and compassion (Jer. 31). The new covenant highlights God's restored and forgiven people, living in God's renewed land under God's eternal rule with God's eternal law inscribed on their hearts. The new covenant is a radical expression of divine grace. God, true to his covenantal nature (cf. Exod. 34:6–7), proves to be compassionate in the covenant relationship with his people. Divine forgiveness is a significant part of the new covenant reality, but the new covenant is somewhat vague in its timeline for actualization. Of course, we know from the book of Jeremiah that seventy years of exile must occur before God will restore his people's fortunes (25:11–12; 29:10). However, the full vison of the new covenant where God will "remember their sins no more" exceeds any historical moment of restoration in the Old Testament. When will the new covenant occur, and how will divine forgiveness be established?

We find answers to these questions in the life and ministry of Jesus. In the Gospels Jesus inaugurates the anticipated kingdom of God and the new-covenant vision.[9] The connection between Jesus, divine forgiveness, and the new covenant is crucial to understanding how we can read Jeremiah as Christian Scripture.

Jesus correlates the new covenant and the coming of the kingdom in his final meal with his disciples (Matt. 26:27–29; Mark 14:24–25; Luke 22:15–20). Just prior to his betrayal, torture, and crucifixion, Jesus shares a Passover meal with his followers. Ritualized in every detail according to the stipulations of Old Testament law (Exod. 12:1–20), the Passover meal celebrated the memory of God's deliverance of his people from Egyptian slavery. The Passover gave God's people opportunity to remember and reexperience (ritually) divine rescue from generation to generation. The ritual remembers how God "passed over" divine wrath through spreading blood on the lintels of the doors of every Israelite home (12:21–27). Where YHWH's death angel saw the blood, God "passed over" divine judgment on that house. Where there was no blood, the death of the firstborn son ensued, for both Israel and Egypt. This is the context for Passover celebration.

From this context, Jesus instills significance to the Passover meal with his disciples. He tells his followers that the bread they eat in the Passover meal is his body: "This is my body given for you" (Luke 22:19). The gift of the bread to Jesus's followers signifies the breaking of his body in death, as the narrative reveals, by crucifixion. Jesus also took a cup of wine at the meal, and the Gospel of Mark presents Jesus's proclamation: "This is my blood of the covenant, which is poured out for many. . . . Truly I tell you, I will not drink again from the fruit of the vine until that day when I drink it new in the kingdom of God" (Mark 14:24–25). In Mark's presentation, Jesus's body and blood will satisfy God so that he will pass over his judgment. References to Jesus's broken body and shed blood point to the cross, which is central for understanding Jesus's Passover meal.

Further, Jesus's blood brings into effect the new covenant as well. Luke presents Jesus's words: "This cup is the new covenant in my blood, which is poured out for you" (Luke 22:20). Mark identifies it as "my blood of the covenant" (Mark 14:24), with some ancient manuscripts adding the adjective "new." With the body and the blood of Jesus, the new covenant is broken open into the world. Jesus's words indicate that the pouring out of his blood is central to enacting the new covenant, with Matthew adding that the shed blood is for the "forgiveness of sins" (Matt. 26:28).

Hebrews 9 and the New Covenant

The blood of goats and bulls and the ashes of a heifer sprinkled on those who are ceremonially unclean sanctify them so that they are outwardly clean. How much more, then, will the blood of Christ, who through the eternal Spirit offered himself unblemished to God, cleanse our consciences from acts that lead to death, so that we may serve the living God! For this reason Christ is the mediator of a new covenant, that those who are called may receive the promised eternal inheritance—now that he has died as a ransom to set them free from the sins committed under the first covenant. (Heb. 9:13–15)

For the writer of Hebrews, Jesus's blood becomes the mechanism by which God granted "cleansing" of consciences from acts that lead to death. Hebrews helps us to understand how and when the sacrifice of Jesus is the means and time of the new covenant, building from Jeremiah's prophecy. Jesus's death effects the long-promised hope for forgiveness in Jeremiah's new covenant (Jer. 31:34).

vali.lung / Shutterstock

Figure 14.8. Statue of Jeremiah by Rodo, Geneva, Switzerland (1913)

These Gospel cues together indicate that God sets right the sin problem of Israel in the new-covenant blood of Jesus. Jesus offers his body and sheds his blood for sacrificial atonement and for the forgiveness of sin. "In an acted parable Jesus interprets the passover 'bread' and 'wine' of his coming death. He thereby declares his death to be the means by which the redemptive significance of the passover will be fulfilled. His shed 'blood' brings into being a new covenant and accomplishes a new Exodus, an Exodus from sin and death."[10]

KEY VERSES IN JEREMIAH

- See, today I appoint you over nations and kingdoms to uproot and tear down, to destroy and overthrow, to build and to plant. 1:10
- "This is the covenant I will make with the people of Israel after that time," declares the Lord. "I will put my law in their minds and write it on their hearts. I will be their God, and they will be my people. No longer will they teach their neighbor, or say to one another, 'Know the Lord,' because they will all know me, from the least of them to the greatest," declares the Lord. "For I will forgive their wickedness and will remember their sins no more." 31:33–34

Christian Reading Questions

1. What is the theological message, or what are the theological messages, of Jeremiah?
2. Explain how the new covenant fits with the message of the book. Relate the new covenant to Jeremiah 1:10.
3. What is Jeremiah's great burden? How does it relate to Jeremiah's complaints?
4. In what ways can we read this book as Christian Scripture? Obviously one considers the new covenant, but do other pathways emerge as we read Jeremiah as Christian Scripture?

CHAPTER FIFTEEN

Ezekiel

Orientation

The book of Ezekiel may be the most bizarre of the prophetic books. It is riddled with mysteries and symbols, strange creatures and haunting scenes. Ezekiel does strange things, like lying on his side for over a year in order to bear the sins of the people (Ezek. 4). He bakes bread over a manure pile for all his neighbors to see (Ezek. 4). In an emotionally charged episode, God commands Ezekiel not to mourn the death of his wife (Ezek. 24). In chapter 16 Ezekiel compares the "house of Israel" to an abandoned infant who turns into a whoring bride. Readers will wince and squirm when reading the prophecies of the prophet-priest Ezekiel. It is not surprising that certain quarters of Jewish tradition kept parts of this book from being read until a person turned thirty. Other rabbinic streams link Ezekiel with Song of Songs as a book that risks bringing its readers into close proximity with the divine mysteries of the universe.

Ezekiel may startle and even offend readers, but it does so to reorient the wayward back to the covenant-keeping God of Israel. The shifting geopolitics of the ancient Near East left Judah vulnerable to the Neo-Babylonian Empire. Ancient Assyria had deported entire populations of conquered nations, but the Babylonians exiled select members of the defeated country's elite class. In 586 BC Nebuchadnezzar's army

Figure 15.1. *Ezekiel and the Hand of God* fresco from the synagogue in Dura Europas, near Salhiyah, Syria (third century AD)

conquered Judah and its capital city, Jerusalem. They destroyed the temple and the city walls. The Davidic throne sat empty. While 586 BC is an important date, the history with Babylon is more textured than a single date allows. About ten years before this cataclysmic moment (597 BC), the Babylonians deported key members of Judah's elite class, including the Davidic king, Jehoiachin. Daniel and his three friends—Shadrach, Meshach, and Abednego—were among these deportees, as was Ezekiel. The book of Ezekiel clearly situates the prophet-priest Ezekiel among this early exilic community in Babylon: "while I was among the exiles by the Kebar River" (Ezek. 1:1).

Ancient sources suggest that the Babylonians made use of various exiled peoples as land tenants for the king. The exiles of Judah settled at Tel Abib in a Babylonian region near Nippur on the Euphrates River (Ezek. 3:15). Other exiled peoples were also given land in Nippur and its surrounding districts. The book of Ezekiel indicates that the Jewish community at Tel Abib enjoyed some autonomy and self-government, as attested by the "elders" who make appearances throughout the book. Despite the benefits of such autonomy, the traumatic events of forced exile—including the loss of any status enjoyed in Jerusalem—must have shaped the social psychology of the Jews in exile. News from Jerusalem would have only reinforced their newly marginalized status, as those still in Judah, including the new king Zedekiah, considered themselves the rightful benefactors of the exiles' hardships. While there is much we do not know about the exilic community in Babylon, their world had certainly been turned upside down. Despair and even defeatism were present (Ezek. 18). Ezekiel issues harsh words for Jerusalem and hopeful words of future restoration for the exiles. He makes it clear that the Lord is not done with his people or his redemptive purposes for the world.

The setting for Ezekiel's prophecy outside the land of Judah raises interesting questions about Israel's God and his covenant commitments to his people. Ezekiel's vision in chapter 1—a vision that shares some features with Isaiah's vision in Isaiah 6—does not take place in the temple. The temple has become a problematic place for the exilic prophet. Many

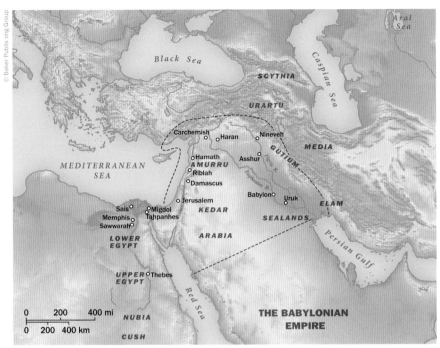

Figure 15.3. Ancient Babylon

of Ezekiel's sharp words of judgment against Jerusalem are leveled at the temple, particularly the idolatrous abuses taking place there (Ezek. 8–11). In one of Ezekiel's more troubling visions, the prophet sees the glory of the Lord depart from the temple (Ezek. 10). What was once a symbol of God's promised presence among his people is empty of all it had signified. Ezekiel receives the Lord's word outside Judah and, more importantly, far from the temple.

This basic observation about Ezekiel's location outside Jerusalem is testimony to God's covenantal promises to regather the lost sheep of Israel despite their catastrophic circumstances. What appears as death is in fact an opportunity for restoration and resurrection (Ezek. 37). The character of Israel's God to restore the repentant sinner is a fixed feature of his relationship with his people, even outside the parameters of the promised land. Because of the Lord's unchanging character, Ezekiel joins his voice to the whole company of faithful prophets when he calls on the exilic community to repent. The offer of repentance rests on the character of Israel's God to forgive.

It may seem odd that Ezekiel speaks judgment against Jerusalem from far away in Babylon. Who would hear him? Why would he do this? Ezekiel's primary audience is the exilic community in Babylon and future readers of all time. God's forthcoming judgment against Jerusalem by the Babylonians is a fait accompli in terms of divine determination. Jeremiah is giving the

"You Will Know That I Am the Lord"

Variations on a phrase appear so often in Ezekiel that it can feel redundant: "Then you will know that I am the Lord." Ezekiel clarifies the purpose of God's judging and redeeming actions: so that the exiles will know who the Lord is. A similar turn of phrase occurs repeatedly in the Exodus account of the plagues in Egypt. Why these harsh plagues? So that the people will know the character of the Lord (e.g., Exod. 10:2). God is severe in the face of rebellion and sin's deadly effects. God is also abundantly merciful to those who repent and turn back to the God whose very character is to forgive. Ezekiel is helping God's people come to know the true character of Israel's God. As Jesus prays in his high priestly prayer before the disciples, "This is eternal life: that they may know you, the only true God, and the one you have sent—Jesus Christ" (John 17:3 CSB).

THEOLOGICAL ISSUES

Repentance as a Way of Life

Many within the Christian tradition, especially its Reformational stream, have understood the life of Christian faith in its entirety as a life of repentance. Repentance recognizes our true identity as sinners in need of God's saving grace, turning from the former to the latter. "Lord, have mercy on me." This prayer is not just a onetime prayer for Christians but the prayer that marks their entire existence before God. As such, repentance becomes a state of being for a Christian, always turning to the Lord Jesus and his saving grace: away from sin and death toward God's immeasurable grace and promise of life.

The Structure of Ezekiel

The book of Ezekiel has a clearly identifiable structure:

- Chapters 1–24: Judgment against Jerusalem
- Chapters 25–32: Oracles against the nations
- Chapters 33–48: Future promises for God's people

same harsh—and unpopular—message back in Jerusalem, but the religious and political leaders in Jerusalem are done listening to the Lord's word. They have prophets for hire who tell them what they want to hear; they do not want to hear what Jeremiah and Ezekiel are preaching. But even this act of the Lord, sending prophets to his people despite their stubbornness, attests to God's character to forgive. Ezekiel's primary concern is the religious renewal of the despondent exilic community in Tel Abib. Even in the **diaspora**, God calls his people back to himself and promises life for those who turn to him from their rebellion. This is the God on display in Ezekiel. God's repentant people always have a future with the Lord.

Exploration—Reading Ezekiel

Judgment against Jerusalem: Ezekiel 1–24

■ READ EZEKIEL 1–4; 8–10; 16; 18; 24 ■

Ezekiel makes a startling claim in the opening verse of the book: while he was with the exiles, "the heavens were opened and I saw visions of God" (1:1). Ezekiel's prophetic ministry begins in an unusual setting: outside the promised land and away from the temple. This may seem to put him away from God's promised presence. For example, when Jonah fled from the land of Israel to Tarshish, he did so, in part, to remove himself from close proximity to God. Ezekiel receives his prophetic call and vision of God in an unlikely place: by the Kebar River in faraway Babylon.

Ezekiel 1 is a strange chapter, but it sets the whole tone of Ezekiel's prophecy. Ezekiel sees a gathering storm coming from the north. In this coming storm—"an immense cloud with flashing lightning" (1:4)—is a divine chariot composed of four creatures upholding what appears to be the divine throne. Repetition of the phrases "what looked like" or "the appearance of" throughout the chapter indicates the difficulty Ezekiel has describing the glorious vision he sees. The mysteries of God's rule come before him in visionary form, and Ezekiel can only relay the vision with all the limitations of his humanity. The real thing far exceeded Ezekiel's ability to describe it.

The center of the storm glows like metal out of a furnace. In the middle of this glowing brightness, Ezekiel sees four winged creatures, like the seraphim in Isaiah 6. Instead of the seraphim's six wings, these creatures each have four wings, but their wings do not appear to relate to their motion or flying. In Ezekiel 10, the prophet has a similar vision and identifies these creatures as "cherubim" (10:1). Here, he simply calls them "living beings" (1:5). These living beings appear human in form, though instead of a single face they each have four: a human face, a lion face, an ox face, and an eagle face. Their feet are bovine but with a burnished bronze appearance. The description of the creatures' legs and feet suggests that these creatures, though human in appearance, do not move according to the same rules of locomotion. Knees do not bend and feet do not roll from heel to toe to propel these beings forward. They move according to different laws of motions. With their wings stretched above them, touching each other in what appears as an angelic square, the beings move in any direction without turning. In other words, as best as we can describe this, the angelic base of this divine chariot throne moves without the creatures ever having to turn.

Then the prophet describes a set of wheels within wheels that sit on the ground beside each creature. Again, Ezekiel struggles to describe these wheels. Are they wheels like wagon wheels with one wheel inside another wheel? Or are they wheels set within other wheels so that the whole structure

Figure 15.4. Ezekiel, Byzantine icon

Figure 15.5. *Ezekiel's Vision* by Robert Pranker (1761)

The Four Faces of the Living Creatures

Ezekiel describes the living creatures as having four faces. The significance of these faces is somewhat ambiguous. Some have suggested they represent the apex creatures of the created order: human beings—made in God's image; lions—king of nondomesticated animals; oxen—king of domesticated animals; eagles—king of the air. Within the Christian interpretive tradition, these faces are linked at times with the four Gospels: Matthew, Mark, Luke, and John. William Greenhill's seventeenth-century commentary on Ezekiel notes that some think the four creatures signify the four covenants: Adamic, Noahic, Mosaic, and apostolic.[a] Or perhaps they represent the four monarchies of Assyria, Persia, Greece, and Rome. John Calvin may have been a bit too hasty in describing these readings as "fables," but he does offer some insight when he links the four creatures with their four faces to the four corners of the globe, highlighting the vision's intent: God's glorious overseeing of his divine plan in the providential affairs of the whole world.[b]

The Four Faces and the Gospels

Pope Gregory the Great (sixth century) wrote a collection of homilies on Ezekiel. He identifies the four faces of the four creatures with the Gospels. "For because he began from the generations of men, Matthew is justly represented as a man; because of the crying in the wilderness, Mark is rightly indicated by a lion; because he started from a sacrifice, Luke is well described as an ox; John is worthily signified by an eagle, he who says, 'In the beginning was the Word, and the Word was with God and the Word was God.'"[c] Because our Savior is the head of elect humanity, Gregory continues, there is no reason to limit the imagery to the fourfold Gospels. The creatures signify Christ because he became a man, died like an ox for our salvation, rose as a lion from the dead, and ascended into heaven like an eagle.

appears like a sphere able to move in any direction at any moment? We tend to like the latter option, though the limitations of our imaginations are hard to overcome. Whatever the wheels actually look like, they are bejeweled and sparkling. There are eyes on the wheels, and the creatures move at the express intent of the Spirit of God. The eyes reveal the all-seeing omniscience and omnipotence of the God of Israel, who created the whole world and oversees its four corners in the splendor of his majesty. Wherever the living creatures move, the four wheels move. Wherever the four wheels move, the living creatures move—all by the propulsion of the Spirit of God's will.

In this glorious vision, the creatures and their wheels move like flashes of lightning at a speed that is nothing but streaming light to the naked eye, like a twirling sparkler on the Fourth of July. Yet the creatures, their wheels, and the accompanying laser show are just accessories to the vision's central piece. Above these creatures and above their wings, Ezekiel sees a crystalline platform opening to a great expanse. Ezekiel describes this platform as "awesome" (Ezek. 1:22), but a more literal translation might be "fear inspiring." On top of the platform sits a throne, and on the throne Ezekiel sees one whose appearance was "like that of a man" (1:26).

The divine chariot with brilliant glory illuminating the northern sky has a throne on it. Sitting on the throne

Jonathan Edwards on Christ and a Great Wheel

"The space of time from Christ to the end of the world is as the revolution of a great wheel. In the beginning of it, Christ comes into the world, and the wicked Jews were judged as the destruction of Jerusalem, and after them the wicked heathen world in Constantine's time; and the old world comes to an end, and the church's glory follows. And then things in the Christ church gradually sink, till they come to the ground in the darkest times of Antichrist, and then gradually rise again, till Christ comes again, and judges the world, and destroys the church's enemies, and destroys the old heaven and earth; and then the church's glory follows."[d]

is one who looks like a man. What Ezekiel sees in this divine vision of omnipotent and omniscient glory is nothing less than the glory of God revealed in human form. Ezekiel peers into the mysteries of the universe with this vision, and in so doing, he sees the form of Christ slain before the foundations of the world.

The narrative of Ezekiel's call (chaps. 2–3) follows his vision of chapter 1. The Lord addresses Ezekiel as "the son of man," a title that appears regularly throughout the book. While this term has significant christological importance in other settings, here its role is more modest. It functions to keep perspective on Ezekiel's humanity in view of the glorious nature of Israel's God. The term also reminds Ezekiel of his dependence on the Spirit of the Lord, who sends and empowers him. Hence the reminder "Do not be afraid" appears three times in Ezekiel's call narrative.

Ezekiel's prophetic charge is similar to that of the other prophets. He is commissioned to the Israelites, whose identity is summed up with the word "rebellious" (cf. Isa. 1:2). They may not listen to Ezekiel, but they will surely know a prophet has been among them. Ezekiel's prophetic ministry rests on one command by which faithfulness is measured: "You must speak my words to them" (Ezek. 2:7).

In the midst of this call, an outstretched hand appears before Ezekiel. The narrative does not say so, but it is safe to assume this outstretched hand comes from the one sitting on the throne in chapter 1. The hand holds a papyrus scroll with writing on the front and back, unusual because scrolls normally had writing only on the front. Ezekiel saw the scroll's contents: lamentations, mourning, and woes. What happens next is bizarre, even by standards of biblical prophecy. The Lord tells Ezekiel to eat the scroll, and he does. A scroll filled with bitter words might be expected to taste bitter, but Ezekiel describes it as sweet as honey (3:1). The encounter with God's word brings pleasure; it is a delight even in its heaviness. Ezekiel ingests God's word so that his whole person is given to the purposes God has for him: "Son of man, go now to the people of Israel and speak my words to them" (3:4).

Then the text clarifies the shape of Ezekiel's prophetic ministry. He is to be a "watchman" or a "sentinel" (3:16–21). His role as a watchman entails two

Figure 15.6. Illumination of Ezekiel eating the scroll (1150–1200)

tasks: (1) announcing the coming destruction of Jerusalem and (2) warning the exiles of their complicity in Jerusalem's judgment while calling them to repent.

During Ezekiel's call narrative, he is struck mute and is confined to his house so that he cannot go out among the people (3:24–27). This muteness presents obvious challenges, given Ezekiel's call as a watchman to warn the people. The event may intend to emphasize the written legacy of Ezekiel's prophetic ministry, though the text itself does not say this explicitly. Most likely, Ezekiel's muteness attests to the Lord's complete control over the prophet's ministry. He does not speak at his own will but only when God has a message for him to deliver. Ezekiel's entire existence, including his ability to speak, is under the governance of God's divine hand. He has swallowed the scroll of God's word, and in a larger sense, God's word has also swallowed Ezekiel.

Ezekiel's prophetic ministry begins in chapter 4 with a series of sign acts (chaps. 4–5). Ezekiel draws a picture of Jerusalem on a brick and places various utensils around it to symbolize the coming siege. He then lies on his left side for 390 days, one day for each year of the people's sin. This period of time may represent the time from Solomon's unfaithfulness to Ezekiel's time. Then Ezekiel is instructed to lie on his right side for an additional forty days to represent a generation's worth of judgment facing the exiles. This act also relates the exilic experience to the forty years of wilderness wandering after the exodus. Sin (left side) and judgment (right side) come together to form this one sign act. During this period of lying on his side, Ezekiel is commanded to bake bread over a fire of human excrement. He protests, and the Lord allows him to cook his bread over cow manure instead. The defilement involved in this process represents the defilement God's people will face living in exile. In the final sign act of Ezekiel's initial ministry, he shaves off his hair. He burns a third of it, slashes at a third of it with a sword, and scatters a third to the wind. The sign's significance is that God's people will face widespread destruction by the sword. God's judgment has been unleashed on the "house of Israel."

The Lord makes clear to Ezekiel in chapter 6 the primary cause of the people's rebellion: their idolatry. This breach of the first commandment— have no gods besides me—is at the heart of Israel's rebellion and leads to God's judgment against them (chap. 7). In chapters 8–11, Ezekiel is taken by the Spirit to Jerusalem and is allowed to peer into the very inner chambers of the temple. Ezekiel sees "wicked and detestable" things taking place within that most sacred of spaces. In religious desperation, God's people are worshiping foreign gods within the temple walls. They believe the Lord has abandoned them (8:12). However, the irony becomes clear when, in chapter 10, God departs from the temple *because of* their idolatry. Ezekiel, by the Spirit, sees this departure of the Lord's glory. The saving health of God's people is always God's presence. His absence leaves them open to his judgment.

One of the more troubling chapters in the entire Bible is Ezekiel 16. The chapter is an allegory of God's covenantal relation with his people, and it depicts Israel's election as an act of the Lord rescuing Israel from infanticide. Israel's national forebearers left her for dead in the wilderness, but the Lord passed by and gave her life (16:6). Israel had no strong attraction for any god, much less the God who created the heavens and the earth. Yet God set his electing affection on Israel, redeeming her from the clutches of death and eventually doting on her with the lavish affection of a smitten lover and husband (16:1–14). But Israel trusted in her beauty and eventually played the prostitute (16:15–34; cf. chap. 23). The description of Israel's harlotry in this chapter is profane and shameful and sad. Israel's wanton acts of debauchery are worse than those of the famed Sodom (16:48).

Nonetheless, hope glimmers in this turbulent chapter. Against the backdrop of an appalling depiction of covenantal infidelity, God promises to reestablish his covenant with his people (16:62). Why would he do this? Because the people get their religious life in order? No. The motivating impulse of God's reconciling activity is his own self-determined commitment to keep the covenant relationship with his people. He will atone for their sins in a reconciling action intended to restore the broken relationship. Ezekiel understands the goodness of Israel's God leading them to repentance (cf. Rom. 2:4). As typical in Ezekiel, the Lord displays his reconciling grace to his people for a single purpose: "You will know that I am the Lord" (Ezek. 16:62).

The people believe their future fate is sealed, and they quote a **proverb** to prove their point: "The parents eat sour grapes, and the children's teeth are set on edge" (18:2). In other words, our parents have sinned against the Lord, and we suffer the consequences. Ezekiel implores the people to stop saying this proverb. It is not true and rests on a misunderstanding of who the Lord is. Who is the Lord? He is the one who will always forgive the repentant sinner. It is his very character to do so. "Repent and live!" declares the Lord to the exiles at Tel Abib and to all who would turn from their sins and believe in the truth of God's saving grace (18:32).

The first major section of Ezekiel ends with a deeply personal and difficult sign act for the prophet to enact. In Ezekiel 24, the Lord tells Ezekiel that his wife is going to die that very evening. When she dies, Ezekiel must not mourn her death. He can grieve inwardly but is to make no audible lament, cry no public tears, perform no ritual acts of mourning. When the events unfold as the Lord has said, Ezekiel obeys God's command and remains publicly stoic about his wife's death. The people plead with Ezekiel to tell them the meaning of his disturbing action. He gives them the Lord's answer: When the people hear of the destruction of Jerusalem, its temple, and its inhabitants, they are to act as Ezekiel. They are not to grieve or mourn but to see the hand of the Lord's judgment at work (24:21–23). This difficult prophecy concludes the first section of Ezekiel's prophecy.

Oracles against the Nations: Ezekiel 25–32

■ READ EZEKIEL 25 AND 32 ■

In chapters 25–32 Ezekiel's prophecies concern the surrounding nations. These nations were a perennial threat to Israel's national and religious sovereignty, and oracles against them appear throughout the Prophets (cf. Isa. 13–23; Amos 1–2). In these oracles the Lord makes clear his authority over all the nations of the earth. Though Israel enjoys a special status with the Lord as his elect, the God of Israel is not a national deity vying for authority in some cosmic conflict with the gods of the surrounding nations. As Jonah reminded the foreign sailors, the God of Israel is the Creator, the one who made the sea and the dry land. Enemy nations are under the sovereign

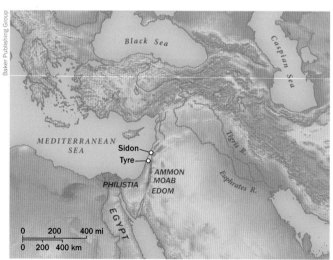

Figure 15.7. The seven nations of Ezekiel 25–32

hand of the Lord. Even the juggernaut Babylon serves the larger purposes of God's covenantal judgments against his people.

In these chapters seven nations come under judgment, most particularly for their injustice, hubris, and cruelty toward Judah. These nations are Ammon, Moab, Edom, Philistia, Tyre, Sidon, and Egypt. Apart from Egypt, the movement from Ammon to Sidon works in a clockwise direction around Israel.

In the midst of these prophetic oracles against the nations is a word of hope for Israel's future (Ezek. 28:24–26). The promise of God's judgment against the surrounding nations means the removal of Israel's perennial threats. Ezekiel describes them as "painful briers and sharp thorns" (28:24). The promised land as a covenantal blessing of God to his people entails living in peace and rest. Rarely did Israel ever know such conditions. God's promise in these verses is similar to those made in Isaiah 2:2–4 and Micah 4:1–3, where the latter days will be a time of universal peace. When God gathers his scattered people, they will live in the land God has promised them. Moreover, they will live there peacefully, building houses and planting vineyards. As in Isaiah's and Micah's portraits of this era, warfare will be a distant memory while God's people enjoy the idyllic setting of their own homes and vineyards.

Future Promises for God's People: Ezekiel 33–48

■ READ EZEKIEL 34 AND 37 ■

The book of Ezekiel shifts dramatically at chapter 33. Once again Ezekiel takes the role of watchman for the city of Jerusalem. His task here is only to warn of God's coming judgment by means of Nebuchadnezzar's army. Nothing can thwart it, and in verse 21 word comes of Jerusalem's fall in the twelfth year of exile. A man from the city escapes the terror and makes his way to the exilic community in Babylon. When the man arrives, God opens Ezekiel's mouth to speak. The words God gives Ezekiel in this moment are words of future hope. God's judgment against his people comes with a strong force, but it is not God's final word. He offers hope in the midst of the ruins, life in the midst of death. Ezekiel's task as a watchman after the fall of Jerusalem is to warn the exilic community away from future judgment: a call for God's people to embrace life rather than death.

The Good Shepherd

When Jesus describes himself as the good shepherd in the Gospel of John, his words reflect the future hope Ezekiel describes in chapter 34. However, Jesus takes the shepherd imagery even further. Not only is the Lord our shepherd in the person of Jesus Christ, making good on the promises from Ezekiel, he is the shepherd who lays down his life for the sheep (John 10:11).

Calvin's Christological Triad

John Calvin made much of the prophet, priest, and king offices in the Old Testament and their promissory character. Calvin offered the triad as a means of holding together the single covenant of grace in the Old and New Testaments centered on the person and work of Jesus Christ. Each of these offices also includes promises, and the promises are fulfilled in the person of Christ. He is our final prophet, God's definitive Word (Heb. 1:1–4). Christ continues to function as our high priest, presenting the perfection of his obedience to the Father by the Spirit on our behalf (Heb. 7). He is also our king, but not only our king; he's the King of kings, the Lord and Creator of all things visible and invisible (Col. 1:15–23; Rev. 19:16).

The Valley of Dry Bones

"Dem bones, dem bones gonna walk around," pulses the famous African American spiritual "Dry Bones." Ezekiel 37 is spooky and has all the trappings of a scene from *The Night of the Living Dead*. Yet from the vision come some of the greatest words of hope in all of Scripture. In the midst of all the faithless squandering of God's people, the promise of unconditioned grace and new life comes over bones representing the dead and long gone. Ezekiel 37 joins the chorus of Christians who confess their belief in the resurrection of the dead and the life of the world to come.

Ezekiel levels a strong warning against the "shepherds of Israel" (chap. 34). "Woe to the shepherds" is a refrain Ezekiel and Jeremiah share in common (cf. Jer. 23). "Shepherds" is a metaphor for those given the responsibility of leadership within Judah. The king and his officials are in view, but so are prophets and priests who shepherd the religious life of God's people. Those in leadership often come under heavy scrutiny in the Prophets (cf. Mic. 2–3), because a trickle-down economy of divine benevolence shaped the order of God's people. Those in anointed positions of leadership—prophet, priest, and king—were tasked with mediating God's kingship, Word, and the benefits of temple rituals and worship to the people. When the leaders served themselves, the whole divine order came undone, leading to disorder and chaos. Ezekiel speaks of future hope where God himself will be the people's shepherd instead: "For this is what the Sovereign LORD says: I myself will search for my sheep and look after them" (34:11). The result of God's shepherding his people is a restored and holy nation: a ruined people fully restored and filled with the saving knowledge of the Lord (ch. 36).

In chapter 37 the Spirit transports Ezekiel through space and time to a valley littered with dry bones: a valley of skeletal remains. The question comes, "Son of man, can these bones live?" Ezekiel answers, "Sovereign LORD, you alone know" (37:3). Then the Lord tells Ezekiel to preach, to prophesy to the lifeless bones in front of him. What message is Ezekiel to deliver to the dead bones? Live! Come to life! Ezekiel obeys, delivers the Word, and then hears the rattling of lifeless bones coming to attention as bones clack together to form human skeletons—"Ankle bone connected to the leg bone," goes the old spiritual. Then the skeletons develop tendons and muscles and skin until Ezekiel sees an army of bodies without life. The Lord tells Ezekiel to prophesy again for the breath (*ruach*) of God to animate the bodies, and when he does, they come to life and a vast army stands on its feet (37:10).

What is the purpose of this memorable vision? It offers hope to the exiles who thought all hope was lost. They were nothing but dried-up bones and lifeless corpses. But the character of Israel's God is to take that which is dead and make it alive again.

In chapters 38 and 39, Ezekiel describes God's vindication of his people against the threat of "Gog, of the land of Magog" (38:2). Who is Gog? And where is the land of Magog? Gog is called the prince of Meshek and Tubal, two cities that appear in Genesis 10:2–5 as coastland peoples near the Black Sea. Gog is the prince of a strange and violent people known for their barbaric ways. Magog may be a made-up name for the land of Gog. The idea

Figure 15.8. *Vision of the Valley of Dry Bones* by Gustave Doré (1866)

THEOLOGICAL ISSUES

Bringing Death to Life

God took dead Israel out of Egypt and brought it to life. He took the lifeless body of Jesus Christ from the tomb and brought it back to life again for the salvation of the whole world. The apostle Paul says we were dead in our trespasses and sins, but God, being rich in mercy, made us alive in Christ (Eph. 2:1–10). The Lord reveals his character to Ezekiel in the vision of dry bones. Our God takes the hopeless dead and makes them alive again. Both the Apostles' Creed and the Nicene Creed conclude with affirmation of the Christian's belief in the resurrection of the dead and life everlasting in the world to come.

CANONICAL CONNECTIONS

The Down Payment of Jesus's Resurrection

Matthew's Gospel includes an event associated with Jesus's crucifixion that is absent in the other Gospels. When Jesus dies on the cross, Matthew reports, "The tombs also were opened, and many bodies of the saints who had fallen asleep were raised. After his resurrection they came out of the tombs and entered the holy city and appeared to many" (Matt. 27:52–53 NRSV). This remarkable story is something of a "mini" resurrection of the dead. It is as if the power of Jesus's resurrection had an immediate effect on some of the dead around him: a kind of down payment on the future and final resurrection of the dead. The Christian tradition has read Ezekiel 37 and these verses in Matthew together, and understandably so. The Greek iconographic tradition at times portrays the death and resurrection of Jesus together with these other dead coming out of their tombs.

THEOLOGICAL ISSUES

Ruach—Spirit, Breath, Wind

Ezekiel 37 plays with the term "spirit," *ruach* in Hebrew. Ezekiel is brought to the valley by the "Spirit" (*ruach*). In verse 5 the Lord tells the bones that he will make "breath" (*ruach*) enter them, and they will come to life. Then Ezekiel prophesies to the "breath" (*ruach*) in verse 9. The "breath" enters the lifeless bodies and gives them life.

Is Ezekiel talking about the Holy Spirit or about "breath" as that which gives life or about the wind? The answer is yes. When Paul makes a distinction between fleshly bodies and spiritual bodies in 1 Corinthians 15, he is not setting physicality against immaterial existence: floating spirits. Rather, he is depicting two kinds of physicality: one animated by the flesh and one by the Holy Spirit. Our resurrected bodies, mysterious as they are to us now, will be bodies of the latter kind: bodies animated by the life-giving Holy Spirit and in no contest with the weakness of our earthly flesh or the destructive forces of sin.

Figure 15.9. Greek icon with the dead coming out of their tombs

in these chapters is that God will deal with the enemies of his people and with evil in one fell swoop at the end of the ages (cf. Rev. 19–20). God will display his glory for all the nations to see as he vindicates his people and eradicates the forces of evil in this world.

The book of Ezekiel concludes with nine chapters describing the details of the renewed temple (chaps. 40–48). The instructions are precise and thorough, assuring God's people that his promises for the future are certain. The Lord will be king among his people. His saving presence in the temple will be in their midst. God will be with them, and they will know who the Lord is. In New Testament terms, "The Word became flesh and made his dwelling [tabernacled] among us. We have seen his glory, the glory of the one and only Son, who came from the Father, full of grace and truth" (John 1:14).

Implementation—Reading Ezekiel as Christian Scripture Today

Ezekiel's startling images and glorious depiction of future hope offered inspiring resources for the African American spiritual tradition. One song from this tradition is "Ezekiel Saw the Wheel" (Louis Armstrong's version is perhaps the most famous):

> Ezekiel saw the wheel
> Way up in the middle of the air
> Ezekiel saw the wheel
> Way up in the middle of the air
> And the little wheel run by faith
> And the big wheel run by the grace of God
> A wheel in a wheel
> Way up in the middle of the air[1]

Nineteenth-century African American camp meetings often included a "Ring Shout," where rings of people would move counterclockwise singing and praising the Lord. The Ring Shout had its genesis in the tribes of Africa before the rise of Christianity among the slaves in America. The tradition was augmented for Christian purposes, and these acts of prayer and praise linked these faithful followers of Jesus to the wheels of Ezekiel, to the very wheels by which God's good and hard providence moved all things to his intended purposes. The worshipers set their gaze heavenward and provide an exemplary and faithful model of Christian existence: a confident belief that the God of the living is the One who can take that which is dead and make it alive again.

Figure 15.10. *Ezekiel Saw the Wheel* by William H. Johnson

A great challenge believers of all times face is the conflict between the experiences of our lives and the confession of our faith. What we believe to be true based on God's Word and the teachings of the church often go against our own basic instincts or experiences. Ezekiel encourages believers of all time to trust in the promises of God's Word against all experiential evidence to the contrary. He reminds us that God does oversee the whole of creation and is moving both creation and time toward God's redemptive end. The wheels of providence are turning.

Ezekiel also reminds us of God's character to take the dead and make them alive again, a basic confession of Christianity. God did so with Israel in Egypt, with Jesus Christ in the tomb, with Christians in their being born again from the death of sin to new life in Christ, and finally, with the hope of the resurrection of the dead.

KEY VERSES IN EZEKIEL

- In my thirtieth year, in the fourth month of the fifth day, while I was among the exiles by the Kebar River, the heavens were opened and I saw visions of God. 1:1
- And he said to me, "Son of man, eat what is before you, eat this scroll; then go and speak to the people of Israel." So I opened my mouth, and he gave me the scroll to eat. 3:1–2
- Your altars will be demolished and your incense altars will be smashed; and I will slay your people in front of your idols. 6:4
- He asked me, "Son of man, can these bones live?" I said, "Sovereign LORD, you alone know." . . . So I prophesied as he commanded me, and breath entered them; they came to life and stood up on their feet—a vast army. 37:3, 10

---

1. Ezekiel's primary audience from a historical perspective was the exiles in Babylon. How might Ezekiel's prophetic words speak to believers of all times, including ours?

2. Ezekiel ate a bitter scroll but it tasted like honey. How can God's Word, which contains difficult words, be received as something sweet and nourishing? For example, the Scriptures tell us very difficult things about our human nature, sin, and the consequences of our sin. How can these truths be received as sweet, as good news?

3. Ezekiel 16 is a difficult chapter in many ways. How would you describe the covenantal character of God on display in this chapter? How does this chapter relate to the character of God revealed in Christ and on display in the gospel?

4. God takes dead things and makes them alive again in Ezekiel 37. Think about the implications of this central feature of God's character as it is revealed in the death and resurrection of our Lord Jesus and in our Christian confession that we await the resurrection of the dead and the life of the world to come.

The Minor Prophets or the Book of the Twelve— Hosea through Malachi

Orientation

The Prophets can feel like a maze for many readers. Isaiah looms large with its sweeping historical scope and numerous twists and turns. Jeremiah moves from one historical period to the next and then back again with little to no orientation or explanation. Ezekiel is strange and provocative. If you have made it through these books—and we hope you have!—then come the challenges and joys of the Minor Prophets. They are "minor" in size only, not in substance. These twelve prophetic voices offer rich treasures to those willing and patient enough to mine their depths.

The first six Minor Prophets (Hosea–Micah) include prophets to the Northern Kingdom (Israel) and prophets to the Southern Kingdom (Judah).

Figure 16.1. *Jonah and the Whale* folio from a Jami al-Tavarikd (Compendium of Chronicles)

The books follow a rough chronology of Israel's and Judah's history, from a preexilic situation to exile and then to the postexilic period. The chronology is not neat and tidy, however. Hosea, for example, is the anchor of the Minor Prophets, but Amos predates Hosea. Micah is in the middle of the twelve Minor Prophets, when from a strictly historical perspective it should be nearer Hosea and Amos. The chronology is somewhat loose and flexible.

The final six Minor Prophets (Nahum–Malachi) consider YHWH's rule over Israel and the nations. Nahum, Habakkuk, and Zephaniah highlight God's activity with his people under the threat of Assyria and Babylon. Haggai, Zechariah, and Malachi close the Minor Prophets with a focus on God's work among his people in the Persian period and beyond. Thus, the last six books of the Minor Prophets span hundreds of years and three major world empires:

Nahum	Assyria
Habakkuk	Babylon
Zephaniah	Assyria
Haggai	Persia
Zechariah	Persia
Malachi	Persia

The Minor Prophets fit onto a single scroll much like Isaiah, Jeremiah, and Ezekiel did. Since at least the time of Ben Sira in the second century BC, this prophetic corpus was linked together as "the twelve prophets" (cf. Sirach 49:10) and understood as a single book among the Latter Prophets: Isaiah, Jeremiah, Ezekiel, and the Twelve. Both the early Jewish and Christian receptions attest to this view of the Minor Prophets as a single prophetic book—Josephus, the Babylonian Talmud, and Jerome's preface to the Vulgate are examples of this understanding. What emerges in the history of these books and their reception is the following principle: the Minor Prophets are treated collectively as a whole (often identified as the "Twelve") and as individual books with their own literary integrity.

There are several indications of their "wholeness" or the intention of their shaping in a single corpus. First, the ending and beginning of certain books link to each other. For example, Joel ends with the Lord roaring in Zion, while Amos begins with the Lord roaring in Zion. Second, Jonah, Micah, and Nahum illustrate a range of options for the nations and their future relation to Israel's God. Together these three books make the following claims: nations that turn to Israel's God will know the grace and forgiveness shown to the Ninevites in Jonah; nations that do not will experience the Lord's fierce judgment, as in Nahum and Micah 4:11–13. Third, little gems of canonical unity appear throughout the Twelve. For example, the attributes of the Lord's name listed in Exodus 34:6–7 occur at crucial junctures in the Minor Prophets. When Joel calls on God's people to repent in Joel 2, when the king of Ninevah calls his people to repent in Jonah 3, when Jonah complains to God in Jonah 4, when Micah reflects on God's character in Micah 7, and when Nahum appeals to God in Nahum 1, they all echo the words of Exodus 34:6–7: "For he is gracious and compassionate, slow to anger and abounding in love, . . . yet he does not leave the guilty unpunished" (AT).

These repeated appeals to Exodus 34:6–7 in the Twelve reveal something about the overall intent of these books. Readers through time are drawn into a set of life-and-death theological questions about God and his ways in the world. These questions are not abstract but are rooted deeply in a lived faith before the God of Israel. In other words, the stakes were and are high. Hosea's prophecy ends by raising these questions and laying out the journey readers of all time are to take when engaging the Twelve. Hosea asks, "Who is wise? Let them realize these things. Who is discerning? Let them understand. The ways of the LORD are right; the righteous walk in them, but the rebellious stumble in them" (Hosea 14:9). Readers of the Twelve are brought into a living encounter with the God of Israel, who is gracious to those who repent and severe with those who refuse him.

Exploration—Reading the Minor Prophets

Hosea: Prophet of the Covenant

■ READ HOSEA 1–3; 12–14 ■

Hosea has the first position among the Twelve not because it is the oldest book but because of the message the prophet delivers. Augustine describes Hosea as difficult to understand yet profound in what it has to say.[1] It sets the tone for the whole of the prophetic collection.

CANONICAL CONNECTIONS

Name Theology and Exodus 34:6–7

Exodus 34:6–7 plays a crucial role in the "name theology" of the book of Exodus. "What is your name?" Moses asks the Lord at the burning bush. God replies, "I AM WHO I AM," or "I WILL BE WHO I WILL BE" (see Exod. 3:13–14). The Lord's name, his character and identity, is manifest in his saving actions. God's name—the LORD or YHWH—is the gift of his saving and holy self to his people. After the golden calf encounter at Mount Sinai, the relationship between God and his people is strained to the point of potential annihilation. But God forgives his people and relents from total destruction. In the midst of these events, God reveals the character of his name in Exodus 34:6–7. These attributes of God's name reveal his character as merciful and severe.

CANONICAL CONNECTIONS

The "Bride of Christ"

When Paul speaks of the church as the "bride of Christ," he is not picking a random metaphor to make his point. Paul draws from the Scriptures of Israel and its primary metaphor for describing the Lord and his people in terms of groom and bride. It is little wonder that both the synagogue and the church have, for most of their history, read Song of Songs as erotic poetry in service of describing the marital relation between the Lord and his people, Jesus and his church.

Hosea begins with Yahweh's command that the prophet take an adulterous wife. He obeys, and she bears him children (or at least bears children; whether Gomer's three children in chap. 1 are all Hosea's is unclear in the text). The children's names are symbolic just as Hosea's marriage is: Jezreel, the place of Israel's rebellion; Lo-Ruhamah, "no mercy"; and Lo-Ammi, "not my people" (Hosea 1:4–9). The last name, especially, speaks to the deep relational rupture between the Lord and his people. Israel is no longer "my people." The name undoes the covenantal formula: "I will be your God and you will be my people."

But this is not the end of the story. The beauty rising out of the ugliness of the first three chapters is the Lord's unrelenting love toward his unfaithful wife. He commands Hosea to buy back his unfaithful wife, just as the Lord buys back his people at his own expense (chap. 3). The Lord can and must act in judgment but is unable to allow judgment as his final word. His love and loyalty run too deep; they are part of God's character and being. He must love and does love in the way that Jesus will love his disciples in the Gospels: "Having loved his own . . . , he loved them to the end" (John 13:1).

Hosea 4–14 moves from Hosea's symbolic marriage to his prophetic speech. The prophet leaves little doubt as to the scope of Israel's faithlessness: "There is no faithfulness, no love, no acknowledgment of God in the land" (4:1). Instead, "there is only cursing, lying and murder, stealing and adultery; they break all bounds [illicit behavior], and bloodshed follows bloodshed" (4:2). Priests come under special scrutiny because they ignore God's law in acts of willful ignorance. The result of this priestly failure is disastrous: "My people are destroyed from lack of knowledge" (4:6). Instead of having proper knowledge of God, based on God's revealed will to them in his law, the people and the land fester in idolatrous disorder and disease.

In spite of this covenantal chaos, the Lord refuses to let go of his people. Like Hosea in his marriage to Gomer, the Lord in his faithfulness refuses to give Israel up. God's electing love of Israel is based on his own determination to love them (cf. Deut. 7:7–8). Though God's judgment is real, bringing with it the sting of his rejection, the Lord cannot and will not ultimately abandon his people. His judgment intends to bring the people to repentance. The book of Hosea ends with a moving account of repentance: "Return, Israel, to the LORD your God. Your sins have been your downfall. Take words with you and return to the LORD. Say to him: 'Forgive all

Figure 16.2. Archaeologists have discovered many figurines and other religious symbols that indicate the widespread idolatry of the people of Israel during the preexilic period.

The Meaning of Repentance

"Repentance" as a term means to turn away from sin and toward God. The elements of repentance in Hosea include the following:

1. The recognition of sin and its consequences
2. Repentance or turning from sin
3. Confession and appeal to mercy
4. Rejection of past practices with a determination not to engage in those practices anymore

These facets of repentance are demonstrated in the prayer of confession from the Book of Common Prayer.

Almighty and most merciful Father,
we have erred and strayed from your ways like lost sheep.
We have followed too much the devices and desires
of our own hearts.
We have offended against your holy laws.
We have left undone those things which we ought to have done,
and we have done those things which we ought not
to have done;
and apart from your grace, there is no health in us.
O Lord, have mercy upon us.
Spare all those who confess their faults.
Restore all those who are penitent, according to your promises
declared to all people in Christ Jesus our Lord.
And grant, O most merciful Father, for his sake,
that we may now live a godly, righteous, and sober life,
to the glory of your holy Name. Amen.[a]

---

our sins and receive us graciously, that we may offer the fruit of our lips'" (14:2–3).

Joel: Locusts and the Day of the Lord

■ READ JOEL ■

Joel is a small book between Hosea and Amos. Dating the book is a challenge because its title (1:1) offers no information on the matter. In comparison, titles in Hosea and Amos include names of kings and even significant events (Hosea 1:1; Amos 1:1). However, the date of Joel is not of paramount importance to the book's message, a message whose principal concern is genuine repentance from God's people. The book of Hosea ended with a call to repentance—"Take words with you" (Hosea 14:2)—and the book of Joel demonstrates what this repentance should look like.

Joel introduces an important theme in the Minor Prophets: the day of the Lord (Joel 1:15). The day of the Lord announces the coming of God to judge and to save (2:1–2). This means it is good news for some and bad news for others. In the first chapter of Joel, the prophet illustrates the day of the Lord by appealing to a plague of locusts (1:4) that devastated the land's grain, oil, and wine production. This locust plague is a small picture of the greater plagues God will bring on his people if they continue to defy him (2:1–2). In this case, the day of the Lord is a dreadful terror. "Who can endure it?" Joel asks (2:11).

CANONICAL CONNECTIONS

Hosea Fulfilled in Matthew

In the nativity story, Jesus escapes Herod's slaughter of baby boys by fleeing to Egypt. Yet Matthew says he went to Egypt "to fulfill what had been spoken by the Lord through the prophet: 'Out of Egypt I have called my son'" (Matt. 2:15 NRSV). Matthew appeals to Hosea 11:1 as a prophecy fulfilled in Christ. However, Hosea is not making a prophetic prediction but is speaking of Israel's election out of Egypt. How can Jesus be "fulfilling" Hosea 11:1? What Jesus fulfills in Matthew's Gospel has to do with the whole history of Israel as God's elect. Jesus embodies Israel's election for the sake of Israel's and the whole world's salvation. In time, Jesus will also experience the rejection and judgment of Israel in his sufferings on the cross—again, for the sake of Israel and the whole world.

CANONICAL CONNECTIONS

Locusts in Exodus and Joel

Locusts is one of the ten plagues against Pharaoh in Exodus (Exod. 10). The purpose of the plagues, or signs, in Exodus is "that you may know that I am the Lord" (10:2). Joel echoes Exodus by making a similar claim. The intent of God's judgment is the knowledge of the Lord (Joel 2:27).

Joel identifies the only group of people who can endure the terrible heat of God's appearing: the repentant. "'Even now,' declares the LORD, 'return to me with all your heart, with fasting and weeping and mourning'" (Joel 2:12). Why would Joel bank everything on God's mercy for the repentant? Because God's name, his very character, promises this gracious outcome. Joel appeals to Exodus 34:6–7, where the Lord explains his name and highlights his mercy, patience, loving-kindness, and grace (Joel 2:13–14). When God appears, all who call on his name will be saved (2:32). Chapter 3 makes clear the scope of the day of the Lord. God's judging and redeeming activities are for all nations and all people.

Amos and Obadiah: Let Justice Roll Down

 READ AMOS 1–3; 5; 9; OBADIAH ■

The prophet Amos is from the region of Tekoa in the Southern Kingdom, but he was a prophet to the Northern Kingdom of Israel. Although called by God to prophesy, Amos denies that he is a prophet: "I am not a prophet, nor am I the son of a prophet" (Amos 7:14 NASB). Rather, he says he worked with sheep and sycamores. His prophetic ministry took place during the middle of the eighth century BC. From Amos's prophecies, it appears the people had an unfounded optimism; they longed for the day of the Lord because they thought it would make their lives better. Amos counters, "Woe to you who long for the day of the LORD! Why do you long for the day of the

LORD? That day will be darkness, not light" (5:18). Amos goes on to name the sins of Israel, many of which involve the exploitation of vulnerable people (5:10–13). Although God's people still offer sacrifices and celebrate religious festivals, Amos says these rituals do not make up for injustices against one's neighbors (5:21–24).

Hosea, Amos's younger contemporary, aimed his prophetic ministry against the religious sins of the people, while Amos takes special concern with the people's failure to love their neighbor, what we might call social sins or sins of injustice. Amos makes it clear that God is not interested in religious lip service. In terms of the Ten Commandments, the two tables of the law—love God and love your neighbor—cannot be separated from each other. Performing religious acts without justice or love of neighbor infuriates God. Amos does not say religious observances or liturgy are unimportant; he says authentic worship involves love of God and love of neighbor. 📖

LITERARY NOTES

3 + 4 = 7

In the oracles against the nations in Amos 1–2, the prophet repeats the phrase "For three sins of _____, even for four" (1:3, 6, 9, 11, 13; 2:1, 4, 6). It is not immediately clear what the prophet intends with this phrase, though the emphasis appears to focus on the manifold character of the nations' sins. In other words, they have sinned abundantly against God. It is possible the numbers are meant to be taken together: 3 + 4 = 7. Seven is the number of perfection or completion and in this context suggests the "perfection" of the nations' rebellion against God. In Amos 1–2, the number 7 is also the number of nations listed plus one, Israel. The surprise in the list is the addition of Israel among the nations coming under God's judgment.

Amos contains a list of oracles against the nations, and he includes Israel among God's enemies (1:2–2:16). Chapters 3–6 outline Israel's rebellion in terms of injustice and complacency. The heartfelt cry of these chapters is found in chapter 5: seek the Lord. Again, the character of God to forgive the repentant has already been established in the Minor Prophets, and Amos operates under the same theological assumptions. The hard word is intended to draw God's people back in repentance. A series of visions depicting the Lord's coming wrath appears in chapters 7–8. The book ends with a promise of coming judgment in chapter 9 and a singular word of hope: "I will restore David's fallen shelter" (Amos 9:11).

Amos ends with a warning against the Edomites, a perpetual enemy of God's people. Obadiah follows on the heels of Amos with a single chapter of a prophecy against the Edomites, Israel's neighbors to the east. The Edomites were the offspring of Esau, Jacob's twin brother. Just as Jacob and Esau had struggled against each other, so had their descendants, the Israelites and the Edomites. The Edomites were a constant thorn in the side of ancient Israel and are a paradigm of all nations who set themselves against Israel's God and his people. Obadiah says God will judge Edom for their pride and mistreatment of God's people (Obad. 3).

Jonah: The Prodigal Prophet

■ READ JONAH 1–4 ■

Few books of the Bible capture the imagination like Jonah. While the book's contents are serious, its humorous elements are also obvious. In Anne Rice's novels on the life of Jesus, Joseph, Jesus's father, tells the story of Jonah to his children, who roll on the ground in laughter as they listen. While Jonah is not a bust-your-gut comedy, it is comedic nonetheless. For example, even

Figure 16.3. *Jonah and the Whale* by Peter Lastman (1621)

YHWH's Care for All Nations

In the Old Testament the name Elohim—God—often speaks to the universal character of Israel's God outside the national and religious boundaries of Israel. In the context of God's interaction with his covenant people, his personal name "YHWH" is used most often. It is not insignificant that the "pagan" sailors with Jonah first cry out to their gods (elohim), but at the end of chapter 1, they cry out to and then fear (worship), vow, and sacrifice to YHWH (Jon. 1:14, 16). Again, God's covenantal care for all nations is evident in this chapter and the following chapters with the Ninevites—Israel's dreaded and ruthless enemy from Assyria.

The Sea in the Ancient World

In ancient times, people considered the sea a pernicious and perilous force. Sea monsters like Rahab and Leviathan roamed these waters (cf. Job 26:12; Ps. 74:14), and in Genesis 1, for example, the sea has to be tamed by the word of God so its hostile forces do not overtake the land. The unleashing of the waters is a metaphor for God's judgment in the Old Testament. The great flood in Genesis shows the power of the primordial waters when they are unleashed by God.

The Sign of Jonah

In Matthew 12:38–41 and Luke 11:29–32, Jesus responds to requests for signs or visible demonstrations of his unique powers. Jesus says no sign will be given except the sign of Jonah. In both Matthew and Luke, Jesus tells his audience that the Ninevites, who heard and believed what Jonah said, will stand in judgment of them at the final day. It appears that the sign of Jonah relates to Jesus's person and his work. What signs did Jonah do? None. The sign of Jonah is Jonah himself and his message. Matthew draws special attention to the three days and nights Jonah spent in the fish's belly. Here the work of Christ appears as Jesus draws attention to his future death and resurrection.

the cows in the fields of Ninevah participate in ritual acts of repentance: fasting and wearing sackcloth. The comedic elements draw us in and leave us with questions, not just about Jonah but about ourselves.

In a four-part drama that corresponds to the chapter divisions of the book, Jonah acts unlike any other prophet. Other prophets may lament and protest their calling, but Jonah rejects God's call and flees from "the presence of the LORD" (1:3 NRSV). Jonah believes the farther he can get from God's presence in the temple, the safer he is from God and God's call. There is no such good fortune for the prophet, who receives a crash course on the omnipresence of God.

Jonah flees to Tarshish with pagan sailors. From an ancient perspective, Tarshish represented the end of the world to the west. Yet Jonah could not outrun God. The Lord hurls a storm so perilous that the sailors all cry out to their representative gods and have to wake the deep-sleeping Jonah to cry out to his. When the sailors realize Jonah is the source of their distress, the prophet identifies himself as a Hebrew who worships the God who made the sea and the land. Jonah demands to be thrown overboard, and as he sinks to certain death, the storm stops. Then a great fish swallows Jonah, making his death appear even more certain.

Jonah 2 breaks up the narrative of this fast-paced and adventure-filled story by introducing a psalm of thanksgiving. The fish appears to be the end of Jonah, but it is in fact the instrument of his salvation. Jonah 2 locates Jonah's prayer in the belly of the fish, but it is told from the perspective of his deliverance. "In my distress I called to the Lord, and he answered me" (2:2). Jonah is in dire straits, heading to "sheol" or the land of the dead. In his distress he yearns for the temple, for the presence and deliverance of the Lord. The Lord answers his plea for mercy and delivers him when the fish "vomited Jonah onto dry land" (2:10). Jonah 2 and Jonah 4 now relate to each other as mirror prayers. In the first, we find Jonah pleading for God's mercy and receiving it. In the second, we discover Jonah aghast and vehemently opposed to God's mercy to undeserving sinners.

Chapter 3 begins by repeating Jonah's call from 1:1, adding "a second time" (3:1). Jonah obeys and preaches perhaps the shortest and most effective sermon ever recorded: "Forty more days and Ninevah will be overthrown" (3:4). The response is mass national repentance from the king of Ninevah all the way to the animals. This repentance is based on an appeal to the Lord's character as one who forgives the repentant: "Who knows? God may yet relent," says the king of Ninevah (3:9; cf. Joel 2:13–14). And God does indeed relent. Remarkably, the king of Ninevah appeals to Israel's God in the covenantal terms of God's people (cf. Joel 2:14), a potentially offensive act. Ninevites are not Israelites; they exist outside the covenant boundaries of Israel. Yet they are using the covenantal language of the elect.

Jesus and Jonah

Much of Jesus's earthly ministry follows the plot of Jonah, with Jesus's identity overlapping with the forgiving God of Jonah and the Pharisees acting like Jonah. Jesus announces the kingdom of God and participates in kingdom feasts in celebration of God's return to his people. Yet Jesus eats with all the wrong kinds of people: sinners, tax collectors, prostitutes, even a Samaritan woman. Jesus came to seek and save the lost, and the whole of the Gospels reveal Jesus's gracious and forgiving identity to be one with the God of Israel.

Chapter 4 shows Jonah at perhaps his worst. In chapters 1–2 he is a prodigal son (cf. Luke 15) and receives forgiveness. In chapter 4, Jonah is the elder brother, sulking and blustering in the face of God's grace given to the wrong people. Jonah also reveals why he fled in the first place: because he knew that God is gracious, compassionate, slow to anger, abounding in love, and quick to forgive (Exod. 34:6–7 again). Jonah is furious because God acted in accord with his character but did so with the "wrong" people.

The Lord provides Jonah with a hard object lesson. In the blistering heat, the Lord gives Jonah a little tree for shelter. Then he sends a worm to destroy the shady bush. In deep despair, Jonah pleads with God to take his life, and the Lord asks Jonah a penetrating question: "Is it right for you to be angry?" (Jon. 4:9; cf. 4:4). Jonah looks silly as he despairs over his little tree, while God demonstrates his gracious concern for the multitude in Ninevah. The story ends abruptly, inviting readers to see themselves in Jonah. Do we view ourselves as objects of God's undeserved grace (the prodigal son), or are we the elder brother, frustrated that God gives grace to the wrong kind of people?

Figure 16.4. *The Return of the Prodigal Son* by Rembrandt (1669)

Public domain / Wikimedia Commons

Micah: Love God and Love Your Neighbor

■ READ MICAH 1–3; 4:1–5; 6:1–8; 7:18–20 ■

The prophet Micah ministered during the same time as Isaiah, and both were prophets in Judah. Unlike Isaiah, Micah did not come from the capital at Jerusalem. His home was the lowland region between the Judean hills to the east and the Mediterranean coast on the west. This area, often called the Shephelah, experienced great destruction when the Assyrian armies made their way from the north through the region and then on to Jerusalem. Something of this tumult appears in Micah 1:10–16 as Micah lists cities from the Shephelah that experienced great suffering. We are told in Kings and Isaiah that Assyria left Jerusalem untouched because of the Lord's saving intervention, but the negative impact on Judah outside Jerusalem was significant.

Micah 1–3 reveals the book's main concerns. In these chapters, Judah breaks the first and second tables of the law—love God exclusively and love your neighbor as yourself. Both Samaria and Jerusalem, capitals of the Northern and Southern Kingdoms, practice idolatry and exploit their neighbors by abusing positions of power. Because of this, God's judgment is coming: "The mountains melt beneath him and the valleys split apart" (1:4).

Chapters 2 and 3 address the wealthy and political and religious authorities who abuse their positions by exploiting the vulnerable. Micah uses the metaphor of cannibalism to describe the kinds of injustice taking place. He says the leaders "tear the skin from my people and the flesh from their bones" and "chop them up like meat for the pan, like flesh for the pot" (3:3–4 AT). Even priests are happy to adjust their message depending on how they are compensated (3:11).

Micah 3:12 and 4:1 form something of the center crease of the Minor Prophets. Micah 3:12 speaks of death and destruction and Jerusalem becoming a heap of rubble. God acts as the judge in these first three chapters, but the story shifts in Micah 4:1, which speaks of God's power to redeem and restore. With chapter 5, Micah 4 reveals the future possibilities for the nations of the world. They can, like the Ninevites of Jonah, turn to God in repentance and experience the blessings of deliverance and peace he offers (4:1–5). Or they

HISTORICAL MATTERS

Lachish and the Shephelah

Lachish was a fortress city that served as an outpost and protective barrier for Jerusalem. It is listed among the cities of the Shephelah that suffered under Sennacherib's imperial assault in 701 BC. A relief of Sennacherib's defeat of Lachish hangs in the British Museum.

THEOLOGICAL ISSUES

Micah 5:2 and the Son's Eternality

Micah 5:2 says the promised and future Davidic king has "origins . . . from of old, from ancient times." The expression "ancient times" may best be understood as "from eternity." Such language might be dismissed as inflated royal imagery from the ancient world, or it could be read within the broad sweep of Scripture, reflecting the humanity and divinity of this coming king revealed in the person and work of Jesus Christ. The technical phrase theologians use to describe the Son's eternal identity and divinity is "the eternal generation of the Son." Throughout the church's history, Micah 5:2 has served this Trinitarian doctrine.

can, like the Ninevites of Nahum, defile God and his people, and then be trampled under the Lord's judgment (4:11–13). Micah 5 promises a coming Davidic king who operates in the strength of the Lord and brings God's peace. 🔼

Micah 6 and 7 return to the major themes of chapters 1–3. The Lord speaks against those in positions of power practicing injustices against the people. One of the best known verses of the Minor Prophets is Micah 6:8: "He has shown you, O mortal, what is good. And what does the LORD require of you? To act justly and to love mercy and to walk humbly with your God." Micah laments the people's broken relationship with the Lord and their misplaced confidence in religious rituals (6:1–7). The people have forgotten the Lord's deliverance from Egypt; they have forgotten their status as the people of the Lord. Micah calls them back to a life where God is at the center and concern for one's neighbor has a privileged place.

Micah ends with a play on the prophet's name, which means "Who is like the Lord?" Micah 7:18 begins, "Who is a God like you . . . ?" What kind of God is the Lord, the God of Israel? The response includes language of Exodus 34:6–7. He is a God who is quick to forgive and show love to his people.

Nahum: The Demise of Nineveh

■ READ NAHUM 1 ■

A small book of only three chapters, Nahum exults in the violent overthrow of Assyria. The book's judgment oracles focus on Nineveh, Assyria's capital, which was sacked by the Babylonians in 612 BC. The book anticipates and celebrates this destruction of God's enemy.

Nahum's oracles portray an imperial war machine doomed for judgment. Chapter 1 shows Nineveh's fall to be YHWH's judgment against Assyria as well as divine salvation for his people. Chapter 2 details the enemy invasion against Nineveh, in which the city walls are breached and Assyrian infantry is swept away. Chapter 3 offers a woe oracle for the "city of blood," whose lies and exploitation are doomed for destruction. The oracle mentions Nineveh's whips, chariots, war horses, cavalry, swords, spears, heaps of dead, and human enslavement—a horrific war machine that will be undone: "'I am against you,' declares the LORD Almighty. . . . 'All who see you will flee from you and say, "Nineveh is in ruins—who will mourn for her?"'" (3:5, 7).

But Assyria's demise is counterbalanced by the salvation of God's people: "The LORD is good, a refuge in times of trouble. He cares for those who trust in him, but with an overwhelming flood he will make an end of

Scholars note similarities in how the theophanies in Nahum 1:2–8 and Habakkuk 3:3–15 announce God's action to deliver his people and judge enemy nations. In both texts, God is on the move to save his people and judge the oppressing nation, and creation turns upside down as God manifests divine power. Some scholars explain these similarities as editorial (called "redactional") action by later editors of the Minor Prophets. The thought is that these editors received an earlier text of Nahum and Habakkuk and then edited/redacted it, in order to connect the texts together. By this redaction, the texts testify together to Israel's divine deliverance and to divine judgment against those who would oppress Israel. Other scholars explain the connection between texts differently: as the books were incorporated into the Minor Prophets, it made sense for Nahum and Habakkuk to complement Zephaniah, revealing God's sovereignty over all earthly empires: Assyria is judged with the nations in Nahum and Zephaniah, Babylon is judged in Habakkuk. The two great empires of the eighth to sixth centuries, Assyria and Babylon, respectively, cannot stand before YHWH's power.

Nahum 1:15; Isaiah 52:7; and Romans 10:14–15 all say the feet of those who bring good news are beautiful. Nahum and Isaiah both speak of an end of enemy oppression and divine deliverance of God's people. The "good news" for both prophets is that peace from enemies and divine salvation has come! This message of good news must be shared by a messenger, someone to advance this gospel for those who need to hear it. The apostle Paul recognized the theological freight of the good news: divine peace and salvation from the Old Testament prophets point to their ultimate fulfillment in the gospel of Jesus, the Messiah. Divine deliverance from sin and death is found in Jesus, and that message should be proclaimed to both Jew and gentile.

Nineveh" (1:7–8). Divine grace for Jacob/Israel reappears in Nahum 1:15 and 2:2. Thus, salvation is offered to Israel even as judgment is pronounced on the nations. The theophany of Nahum 1 offers a glimpse of YHWH's judgment and salvation.

Judgment and salvation make up the two-step rhythm of YHWH's action for Israel and the nations. For Nineveh, the blood-soaked city, divine action means judgment against sins of exploitation, murder, and abuse. Nineveh's demise means salvation for Israel, and the "good news" proclaimed in Nahum is that God will deliver and provide peace for his people by judging the enemy nation.

Nahum 1:3 echoes Exodus 34:6–7, a text we have seen elsewhere in the Minor Prophets.[2] Nahum draws the covenant character of YHWH into God's broader activity against Nineveh. Nahum 1:3 agrees that YHWH is slow to anger but by no means clears the guilty, but the language of divine wrath piles up in 1:2–3. Any nation that willfully breaches God's commands awaits his judgment. Nahum uses language directed to Israel after their sin of forming the golden calf, particularly Exodus 34:7, and applies it to Nineveh (the capital city of the nation of Assyria) in Nahum 1:3: God will not clear the guilty—they will be judged. The poetry thus emphasizes divine judgment, despite divine patience, revealing that YHWH's patience has limits: at a certain point God's anger breaks forth to deliver the oppressed from the oppressor. By drawing together Israel's salvation and Nineveh's demise in the book, Nahum confirms that YHWH is the imperial Lord over all nations.

Habakkuk: Faith in the Faithful God

■ READ HABAKKUK 1:2–4; 2:1–20; 3:16–19 ■

How do people of faith respond when confronting confusing and dangerous times? This is a central question that occupies the book of Habakkuk. The poetry opens with a set of questions to God about situations of injustice among the people of Judah.

The prophet identifies the following issues in his prayer to God: (1) God is unresponsive to cries of help; (2) God causes Habakkuk to gaze on injustice; (3) God tolerates wrongdoing; (4) God's law is ineffective, leading to further situations of injustice. In these protests, the prophet offers a lament to God. Lament is a kind of prayer that voices a complaint to God about distress, and it is uttered to persuade God to act on the sufferer's behalf.[3] Habakkuk's prayer is neither petulant nor petty. Whenever injustice arises in the world, God's people should cry out, "Why is this happening?" and "How long is this injustice going to go on?" These twin prayers of "Why?" and "How long?" are the most prevalent questions, for instance, in the book of Psalms. The reason Habakkuk asks these questions is because, as a human being, he *does not know* the reason for his experience, and he *does not know* how long the situation will last. How could he? He is merely a human being, like the rest of us!

However, the prophet's prayer offers a model of faithful response whenever times of confusion or pain, frustration or loss emerge in life. He does not wish to "fix" things immediately; the prophet's first response is to turn to God, who *does know* why the prophet is experiencing what he is and who *does know* how long the situation will last. Prayer to God, even protesting prayer, is common in the life of faith.

In Habakkuk, the source of injustice, at least on the face of it, derives from God's own people—in Judah! The law God gave to provide his people a way to live well in the land and to restrain them from doing evil is shown to be ineffective (Hab. 1:4; "paralyzed," NIV), and therefore wickedness multiplies unchecked.

YHWH responds to the prophet in Habakkuk 1:5–11. Habakkuk had asked God for deliverance from oppression and injustice among his people. Instead of providing answers or miraculous deliverance, God says he is bringing judgment on his people through the Babylonians (the "Chaldeans").

The idea that God would raise up the Babylonians to judge Judah is offensive to Habakkuk. The prophet responds to God in Habakkuk 1:12–17. His basic questions are, Will not raising up the Babylonians

Radomir Vrbovsky / CC BY-SA 4.0 / Wikimedia Commons

Figure 16.5. The Ishtar Gate of Babylon, reconstructed

The Righteous Will Live by Faith

The New Testament interprets the statement in Habakkuk 2:4 that "the righteous person will live by his faithfulness" in different ways, with different emphases. Romans 1:16–17 focuses on the righteousness of God and the faith of God's followers. Galatians 3:11 focuses on the faith (rather than works) of the righteous, and Hebrews 10:36–39 speaks to the righteousness of Christ and the faithfulness of his deliverance. Central to all these affirmations, however understood, is the person and work of Jesus Christ.

to judge Judah lead to Judah's ultimate destruction? How can God use the Babylonians for judgment? They will not give God glory; they will devote their spoils to an idol!

God responds in Habakkuk 2:2–20. This section falls into two parts: 2:2–5 and 2:6–20. In the first part, YHWH instructs the prophet (and likely the people) to wait for the vision or revelation of divine deliverance and judgment to come to pass (2:2). This revelation is written down on tablets to encourage those who read it. Although God is using the Babylonians, he will also judge them for their arrogance (2:5) and injustice (2:6–19). Divine justice, then, is secured, and God is trustworthy. What is needed now is the people's faith in the faithful God (2:4).

A series of five woe oracles round out the vision described in Habakkuk 2:2–3. Each in its own way reveals the retributive principle: you reap what you sow. As Babylon has sown injustice and wickedness, so their wickedness will be turned back on them. The nations they have pillaged will pillage them. This principle of equal measure reveals YHWH's order in a just world.

The book concludes with a theophany and prayer (3:3–15, 16–19). From the initial questions raised in the book, Habakkuk now is transformed. The prophet prays for the day of distress to come and, even in the face of it, can affirm in praise to YHWH, "I will rejoice in the Lord, I will be joyful in God my Savior. The Sovereign Lord is my strength" (3:18–19).

Zephaniah: The Great Day of the Lord

■ READ ZEPHANIAH 1–2; 3:9–20 ■

In this third successive prophetic book with three chapters, the focus returns to the sins of Judah and the nations. The prophet Zephaniah is a social critic of the powerful in Jerusalem and Judah. Based on the superscription in Zephaniah 1:1, he ministers in the first half of Josiah's reign (639–609 BC), just prior to the young king's reform movement (ca. 622 BC; see 2 Kings 22:3–23:23). The book opens with a shocking divine pronouncement: "I will sweep away both man and beast; I will sweep away the birds in the sky and the fish in the sea—and the idols that cause the wicked to stumble" (1:3). This prophecy echoes the creation account from Genesis 1, drawing attention to YHWH as the creator God. However, the poetry abruptly inverts this vision, introducing YHWH as the destroyer of creation.

YHWH's universal action of destruction in Zephaniah 1:2–3 narrows to a particular focus on Judah and Jerusalem (v. 4), but verse 2 interrelates the fate of Israel and the nations (Gen. 12:2–3). How is this possible? God is not simply the patron deity of Israel; YHWH exercises an imperial rule over all nations.

For a myriad of sins expressed in Zephaniah 1, God's response is the day of the Lord, an event of divine judgment and/or salvation, for Israel and/or the nations, in accordance with the justice and mercy of YHWH. For Zephaniah 1, the day of the Lord is a day of terrible judgment, even described with YHWH's offer of a sacrifice.

On the day of the Lord, YHWH acts as "Mighty Warrior" (1:14–16). The idea of YHWH as a warrior goes back to the Song of the Sea in Exodus 15:3: "The LORD is a warrior; the LORD is his name." Whereas in Exodus YHWH battles Egyptian forces, in Zephaniah YHWH battles his own people in judgment and wrath (Zeph. 1:18).

The appropriate response to impending judgment should be repentance, as in Joel and Jonah. Accordingly, Zephaniah 2:1–3 calls on God's people to "seek the LORD" instead of perpetuating evil. Verse 3 repeats the command to "seek" three times, commanding the hearers to seek YHWH, righteousness, and humility. Israel should pursue YHWH and covenantal faithfulness and devotion to their God and to one another.

The remainder of chapter 2 is a set of oracles against the nations: Philistia (2:4–7), Moab and Ammon (2:8–11), Cush (2:12), and Assyria (2:13–15). It is unclear why these nations are mentioned, but divine judgment seems to move geographically from the west (Philistia) to the east (Moab and Ammon) and then to the south (Cush) and then the north (Assyria). The nations surrounding Judah and Jerusalem sit under the judgment of YHWH.

Chapter 3 continues the theme of judgment but focuses on Jerusalem, which continues to oppress others (3:1) and be unrepentant (3:1–3). Jerusalem's leaders, priests, and prophets are predatory, and Zephaniah calls them "roaring lions" and "evening wolves" (3:3). YHWH's righteousness contrasts with their wickedness (3:5). As a just God, YHWH will eradicate injustice and sin, among Israel and the nations (3:8).

However, Zephaniah concludes not in wrath but in mercy (3:9). YHWH reestablishes the nations through a radical act of grace in which all people call on YHWH's name, indicating their devotion and allegiance to him. As it is in the nations, so YHWH will do with his people, and the book

Restoration of Fortunes in the Prophets

The phrase in Zephaniah 3:20 that YHWH restores the fortunes of his people is a theological term that is found in the Minor Prophets as well as in other prophetic texts. In the Minor Prophets, the language occurs in Hosea 6:11, Joel 3:1, Amos 9:14, and Zephaniah 2:7 and 3:20. This restoration of his people's fortunes does not mean a simple return to the status quo—that is, the relationship God, people, and land enjoyed prior to the act of judgment. Rather, restoring the fortunes of Israel indicates a divinely initiated future beyond judgment, in which the covenant relationship between God and his people is realized in its ideal potential. Sin is no longer operative when God restores the fortunes of Israel. The language of restoration derives from the repeated Hebrew root *shuv*, which occurs throughout the Minor Prophets.[c]

concludes with the restoration of God's city and God's people ("Daughter Zion," 3:14). This restoration appears in the future, beyond the day of judgment:

> YHWH will reign in their midst as king (3:15).
>
> YHWH's people will not fear (3:16).
>
> YHWH will rejoice in his people and sing over them (3:17).
>
> YHWH will turn mourning to joy (3:18).
>
> YHWH will vindicate the oppressed and needy (3:19).
>
> YHWH will end exile and restore Israel's fortunes (3:20).

This expansive restoration vision is eschatological in focus, meaning that it presents a time beyond divine wrath in which the world will be scrubbed of sin and shame, the righteous will be vindicated, and the wicked shall be judged. 📖

Haggai: Restoring the Temple and the People

■ READ HAGGAI ■

The book of Haggai focuses on the restoration of the temple and how God's people should live in the Persian period (roughly 539–338 BC). Israel in this era is a Persian province (a satrapy) and is administered by a Persian governor. One of the local provinces in the satrapy is called "Yehud," which approximates the same space as the Northern and Southern Kingdoms of Israel prior to the exile. Haggai's message revolves around the validity and significance of the new temple built in Jerusalem. Some in Haggai's time thought the reconstructed temple would be inferior to the glory of the temple destroyed by the Neo-Babylonian king in 586 BC. To this, YHWH says, "The glory of this present house will be greater than the glory of the former house" (Hag. 2:9).

YHWH moves the heart of Haggai to help build this new temple in the second year of Persian king Darius I (521–486 BC). He prophesied during a period of fifteen weeks in 520 BC, according to dates in the book (see table 16.1).

Table 16.1. Dates in Haggai

The twenty-first day of the sixth month (1:1)	August 29, 520
The twenty-fourth day of the sixth month (1:15)	September 21, 520
The twenty-first day of the seventh month (2:1)	October 17, 520
The twenty-fourth day of the ninth month (2:10, 18, 20)	December 18, 520

Alongside Zerubbabel and the high priest Joshua, Haggai was an influential leader in Yehud. Together they restored the temple complex. Within fifteen weeks, Haggai ushered in a new period of Jewish history: the nearly six hundred years that we now describe as the Second Temple period, from 515 BC to the first century AD.

Haggai 1 identifies the problem at the heart of the book. The temple is in ruins, and God's people are content with this fact. Haggai is not. The prophet is given the message to rebuild along with Zerubbabel and Joshua. To encourage the people, Haggai speaks YHWH's word of divine comfort and presence: "I am with you" (1:13; 2:4). This phrase recurs throughout the Old Testament to indicate YHWH's presence among his covenant people. Even though they are living under Persian rule, God is able to empower them to do the work of rebuilding. God empowers Joshua, Zerubbabel, and Haggai to lead. Whether Israel is free or under foreign occupation, YHWH still exerts his empowering presence. Empires hold no sway over his authority.

Then YHWH promises Zerubbabel he will be God's "signet ring" (2:23), a rare designation in the Old Testament. Ancient Near Eastern kings used signet rings to seal various objects to indicate their possession of the object. YHWH presents himself as the king over all, and Zerubbabel becomes the living exemplar of the king's royal seal. Zerubbabel is the "seal" of YHWH; his leadership is under the auspices of the divine king. Zerubbabel is chosen and favored by YHWH, who calls Zerubbabel "my servant," "my signet ring," and "chosen" one (2:23).

As the leader who belongs to YHWH, Zerubbabel represents even more. According to 1 Chronicles 3:17–19, Zerubbabel is a descendant of King David. Haggai 2:20–23 suggests the restoration of the Davidic house through Zerubbabel without explicitly calling him the king. This conclusion to Haggai connects the temple restoration with the restoration of the Davidic king, echoing the divine promises in the Davidic covenant (2 Sam. 7:12–14).

Zechariah: Israel's Return and YHWH's Restoration

■ READ ZECHARIAH 1–3; 7–8; 9–12 ■

Alongside Haggai, Zechariah is a prophet of the Persian period. He is the son of Berekiah, son of Iddo (Zech. 1:1, 7; Ezra 5:1; 6:14). The book of Nehemiah identifies Iddo as being from a priestly clan (Neh. 12:4) and also indicates a person called Zechariah took the leadership of the clan (12:16). From these texts, it appears Zechariah was a priest in the sixth century BC. As in Haggai, Zechariah also includes specific dates of the prophet's ministry (see table 16.2). These dates indicate that Zechariah was active in Persian Yehud just prior to the dedication of the temple, completed in 515 BC.

Zechariah's concern is to highlight the return of God's people to Judah, especially in Zechariah 1–2. God has exiled his people and disciplined them, but that judgment is not the final word. Instead, God calls his people to "return" to him, and he, in turn, will "return" to them (1:3). Zechariah then has a series of night visions that concern God's promise of restoration for the people of Israel, their temple, and their land (visions 1, 3, 4, 5), and judgment for Israel's enemies (visions 2, 6, 7, 8):

Table 16.2. Dates in Zechariah

The eighth month of Darius's second year (1:1)	October/November 520
The twenty-fourth day of the eleventh month (of same year) (1:7)	February 14–15, 519
The fourth day of the ninth month of Darius's fourth year (7:1)	December 7, 518

1. A horseman (1:8–17)
2. Horns and craftsmen (1:18–21)
3. A surveyor (2:1–13)
4. A high priest (3:1–10)
5. The gold menorah (4:1–14)
6. A flying scroll (5:1–4)
7. A woman in a basket (5:5–11)
8. Four chariots (6:1–8)

In these visions, the book of Zechariah depicts divine salvation and judgment in YHWH's sovereignty. Even the powerful Persian nation is nothing compared to the might of YHWH, who can restore and resettle his scattered people or topple mighty empires.

Zechariah 7–8 contains sermons that rehearse the reason for Judah's destruction in 586 BC (and, for that matter, Israel in 722 BC). These sermons also promise divine blessing beyond exile, from 539 BC and beyond. Restoration is central to these sermons, particularly restoration of the temple and city of Jerusalem, so the prophet encourages the people to complete the work. YHWH urges the people not only to remember the justice of the exile (Zech. 7) but also to recognize the renewal that lay before them by the mercy of God (Zech. 8). The renewal of Zion will encompass a restoration of Israel, but it will incorporate the nations as well (8:20–23).

Zechariah 9–14 does not have specific dates as Zechariah 1–7 does. Rather, this section is future oriented, pointing to a time in which YHWH will defeat all enemies (12:1–9) and reign in justice after great battle (14:1–21). The messianic king will reign

THEOLOGICAL ISSUES

The Remnant

God preserves Israel through judgment. But those who remain after judgment are a "remnant" (Zech. 8:6) that God will restore. The notion of a remnant is common in the Old Testament prophetic material, especially in the Minor Prophets (Mic. 2:12; 4:7; 5:7–8; 7:18; Zeph. 2:7, 9; 3:12; Hag. 1:12, 14; 2:2; Zech. 8:11–12) as well as in Isaiah and Jeremiah. It is the idea that God preserves his covenant people and will establish his reign among them. The remnant testifies to God's covenantal love and commitment to Israel and to his ongoing devotion to fulfill his promises to Israel to bless the nations through them (Gen. 12:2–3).

under the authority of God (9:9–17). These chapters also provide justification for the future rule of this coming king: the sin of God's people who "pierced" God needs to be addressed (12:10–14), and bad leadership in Israel's past must be replaced with YHWH's king and his divine reign (11:4–17). YHWH promises future miraculous cleansing and purification so that he can reign among his people (13:1–9). This future restoration is portrayed as a kind of new exodus out of bondage and a new creation in which Zion will be refashioned as completely holy to the Lord (14:20).[4] YHWH is confirmed as the king and shepherd of Israel but also the "king over the whole earth" (14:9). Zechariah 9–14 confirms the covenantal and cosmic reign of YHWH. YHWH exerts lordship over all nations through the covenantal purposes with Israel and particularly through Israel's messianic and coming king (9:9–13). The last chapter of Zechariah depicts a final restoration and judgment on the day of the Lord (14:1). The future-oriented vision in these chapters pushes far beyond the sixth century BC.

CANONICAL CONNECTIONS

Zechariah 9–14 in the New Testament

Because of Zechariah 9–14's central vision of YHWH's reign, the messianic king, and YHWH's defeat of enemies, the New Testament authors understood these chapters to testify about God's work in Jesus, the Messiah. One of the Gospels' most recognized images is Jesus's triumphal entry into Jerusalem on the week of his crucifixion. He rides on a donkey from the Mount of Olives through the eastern gate of the city in fulfillment of Zechariah's prophecy (Zech. 9:9–11; Matt. 21:2–7). Zechariah 9–14 was vital for the New Testament authors as they understood the messianic work and mission of Jesus. They saw it as connected to YHWH's renewal of Israel and his restoration of all things, connected to messianic suffering, and foundational for understanding the scope and direction of divine judgment.[d]

Malachi: The Message of the Great King

■ READ MALACHI 2–3 ■

Malachi presents the message of the great king, YHWH (Mal. 1:14). Malachi also provides instruction on how God's people ought to live under Persian imperial rule. With a less glorious temple and diminished freedom, Israel wonders if following YHWH is worth it.

To this, Malachi speaks for the great king, and he calls God's people back to faithfulness. He reminds Israel that YHWH is their father and they are his children (Mal. 1:6; 2:10). Moreover, as the great king, YHWH holds his people/family to the terms of his reign—namely, the covenant.

In the Persian period, royal messengers brought messages to various parties on behalf of the king. It is possible that the message and structure of Malachi were influenced by Persian royal emissary texts. On this understanding, the prophet expresses the message of Israel's God, who is portrayed as the great king in the book (Mal. 1:14). The message of the great king must be delivered to the people.[5]

Some wonder whether Malachi was an actual person. The Hebrew name Malachi (*mal'aki*) is translated "my messenger." Malachi 3:1 uses the same term (*mal'aki*) where "my messenger" is intended, not a proper name.

Figure 16.6.
Persian king
Darius I seated
with attendants

Whether one believes Malachi to be a royal emissary or a literary figure, there is no question that the book of Malachi is filled with Scripture. In only four chapters, it interacts with the story of Jacob and Esau (Gen. 25–36), the account of Edom's offense against Israel (Num. 20:14–21), and several prophetic texts (Isa. 34:14; Jer. 49:12–13, 17; Ezek. 25:13; 32:29; 35:3–4, 7, 9, 14–15; 36:33–36; Amos 1:11; Obad. 1:7, 10, 12). The book's emphasis on covenantal faithfulness resonates with the "love" language of Deuteronomy (Deut. 6:5). Malachi closes the Minor Prophets with a theme begun in Hosea: YHWH's love and covenant relationship with Israel.

Malachi begins with God's declaration to his people, "I have loved you" (Mal. 1:2). This opening statement invites Israel to consider God's continuing covenant love for his people, despite the challenges they face in the postexilic period. YHWH affirms his covenant commitment with the startling pronouncement, "I have loved Jacob, but Esau I have hated" (1:2–3). This language is not about God expressing the emotion of hate or manifesting xenophobia. It expresses YHWH's covenant relationship with Israel, following the usage of "love" language in Deuteronomy (4:37; 7:8–9, 13; 10:12, 14–15, 18–19; 11:1, 12, 22; 13:3; 19:9; 23:5; 30:16), as well as in Hosea (Hosea 11:1, 4; 14:4). YHWH's "hate" for Esau is not hatred as we might think of it. Rather "hate" indicates that YHWH is not in a covenant relationship with Esau as he is with Jacob/Israel.

Despite YHWH's faithfulness to his people, they do not reciprocate. Chapters 1–2 detail their unfaithfulness. The priests and the people offend God by giving improper and inadequate sacrifices and offerings (Mal. 1:6–14). The priests do not follow YHWH's covenant relationship with Levi (2:1–9). Israel has profaned the holy sanctuary "by marrying women who worship a foreign god" (2:11). When YHWH does not accept their tainted offerings, the people lament and weep, even though their offerings are not acceptable (2:13). As elsewhere in the Old Testament, YHWH speaks of Israel's unfaithfulness in terms of marriage and divorce (2:14–16). And finally, the people question whether there is divine justice in light of all the ways YHWH has not accepted them (2:17). Yet God's people rob God by not contributing offerings at the temple (3:8–9) and say that it is futile to serve God at all (3:13–15). Israel does not embrace YHWH in their way of life, so they do not give offerings to YHWH at the altar or devote themselves to him.

YHWH responds to the people's rebellion with a salvation oracle that depicts the day of the Lord (3:2), a day of judgment *and* salvation. YHWH's "messenger" (*mal'aki*) will prepare the way before YHWH's entry into the world for judgment of the wicked and salvation for those faithful to him. The messenger is associated with two other figures: "the lord" (*ha'adon*) and "the messenger of the covenant" (*mal'ak habberit*). Their identity is vague (angels?), but they represent God in some way. The messenger brings a word of salvation for the Levites and for those who seek YHWH, delight in his covenant, and fear him (3:2–4). But the converse is also true. For those who reject YHWH, refuse their covenant commitments, and do not fear YHWH, the day of the Lord will be a time of judgment.

The end of the book (4:1–6) offers two conclusions, conjoined at some point in the editing of the book or the collection of the Minor Prophets. The first ending is in Malachi 4:4, where God calls his people to remember the instruction of Moses given at Horeb. This echoes the second giving of the law in Deuteronomy ("Horeb" is Deuteronomy's name for Sinai). This first ending draws the rhetorical audience to Sinai once again. Moses's instruction looms large: like the first (Exodus) and second (Deuteronomy) generations instructed by Moses, the generation of the faithful in Malachi's time are bound in covenant to the "statutes" and "ordinances" given by God. The first generation failed to keep their obligations (cf. Deut. 5:2–5), so what will the generation living under Persian rule do? They are to remember God's covenant and obey in faith.

The second ending in Malachi 4:5–6 envisions future hope with the advent of "Elijah" before the day of the Lord comes. Elijah will "turn the hearts of the parents to their children, and the hearts of the children to their parents" (4:6). Instead of being divided, families of Israelites from across generations will be unified in their fear of the Lord and devotion to him.

Moses and Elijah represent the great prophets of the periods of the exodus (Moses) and the early monarchy (Elijah). The first and second conclusion of Malachi, then, close the Law and the Prophets by drawing together the "Torah of Moses" and "Elijah, the prophet." A forward-looking, eschatological emphasis is offered at Malachi's conclusion, which is also the conclusion of the Prophets. YHWH's day of judgment and salvation is coming. The new Elijah will appear, and then the day of the Lord is not far behind.

Implementation—Reading the Minor Prophets as Christian Scripture Today

In what ways are the books of Hosea–Malachi understood as Christian Scripture? Perhaps undervalued in today's world, the Minor Prophets testify to a different way of understanding history. Whereas modern readers may think of history as events that happened in the past, the Minor Prophets present history as a steady presentation of horrors—past and present—confronted and overcome by the God of Israel. Thus, history is neither neutral nor natural but is subject to the purposes of God. The overall chronological development from the Assyrian period to the Persian period and beyond in Hosea–Malachi shows God is not aloof from human struggle and pain. Rather, God set the world aright in times past and ensures that it will be refitted and remade so human corruption and greed will no longer blight it.

YHWH's "day" in the Minor Prophets, then, becomes a way of understanding divine judgment and salvation that will be our future hope. The day of the Lord in the twelve Minor Prophets emphasizes that Israel's God will not abide injustice and sin. Judgment is a purification of the world from the stain and pollution that sin brings to families and communities. God is a God of justice, and in the day of the Lord, YHWH will set things right. Thus, humanity should repent of sin and follow the ways of YHWH. They should seek YHWH, justice, and righteousness (Zeph. 2:1–3).

The complementary action of divine justice is divine salvation, which YHWH offers in the day of the Lord. In God's judgment of sin, he

Figure 16.7. *The Great Day of His Wrath* by John Martin (1851–53)

Figure 16.8. *The Plains of Heaven* by John Martin (1851–53)

vindicates the righteous—namely, those who resist the persistent pull to fall away from God (exemplified in Malachi's prophecy). God's compassion and divine patience empower restoration (Zeph. 3:9–20). Divine grace is operative in and through divine justice. God's final word on human destiny is restoration, purification, and rejoicing: "Sing aloud, O Daughter of Zion; Rejoice and exult with all your heart, O Daughter of Jerusalem! The Lord has taken away the judgments against you; he has cleared away your enemies. The King of Israel, the Lord, is in your midst; you shall never again fear evil" (3:14–15 ESV).

The day of the Lord in the Minor Prophets traces judgment and salvation through different periods of time, which finally culminate in Jesus Christ, according to the New Testament. For the apostle Paul, the day of the Lord is a day of divine interruption, wherein Jesus comes into the world and judges it. Paul envisions Jesus's ascension after his crucifixion to be complemented by Jesus's return to earth to vindicate the righteous and judge the wicked. Paul describes the day of the Lord as the "day of Jesus Christ" (Phil. 1:6), or elsewhere the "day of Christ" (Phil. 1:10; 2:16) or "day of our Lord Jesus Christ" (1 Cor. 1:8). Paul affirms that when Jesus returns, like YHWH on his "day," he will judge the world and pronounce judgment on all wickedness (Acts 17:31; 2 Tim. 4:1). The Minor Prophets' declarations of judgment on the day of the Lord find their exclamation point in the return of Jesus. Further, Jesus will bring freedom from death, transforming the old order of sin and decay when he comes on his "day" (Phil. 3:20–21). Jesus is the vindicator of the righteous who comes to judge the living and the dead (2 Tim. 4:1; 1 Pet. 4:5).

Christian Reading Questions

1. What is the importance of the day of the Lord in the Minor Prophets?
2. In what ways is the statement in Habakkuk 2:4 that "the righteous person will live by his faithfulness" understood? How does the New Testament's reception of Habakkuk 2:4 fit?
3. How do the nations fit into God's plan in the Minor Prophets?
4. What does it mean for Malachi to feature YHWH as a "great king"?
5. The last verse of Hosea, the first book of the Minor Prophets, says, "Who is wise? Let them realize these things. Who is discerning? Let them understand. The ways of the Lord are right; the righteous walk in them, but the rebellious stumble in them" (Hosea 14:9). How does this verse prepare you to read all of the Minor Prophets?
6. How does Exodus 34:6–7 influence the theology and structure of the Minor Prophets? In what ways does the character of God's name revealed in Exodus 34:6–7 serve as a major theme of the Minor Prophets?

CHAPTER SEVENTEEN

Introduction to the Writings

Life on the Ground

The Writings, or the Ketuvim, is the third part of the Old Testament in the Hebrew canon. As a collection, the Writings are looser in their structure than the Law and the Prophets. The order of the books in the Writings varies more widely in their reception history than the order of books in the Law and the Prophets. The significance of the Writings is not so much their order as in their relation to what precedes them: the Law and the Prophets.

A wide range of literature appears in the Writings, from poetry and wise sayings to laments to narratives. In a sense, the Writings are a kind of grab bag of materials that are not identified as Law or Prophets. One could read the Writings with the descriptor "and this is what remains." But it would be a mistake to separate the Writings from the Law and the Prophets in terms of scriptural relations. As the third and final part of the Old Testament canon, the Writings build on the foundation of the Law and the Prophets,

LITERARY NOTES

Order of the Writings

The Hebrew text most students of the language are familiar with, the Masoretic Text (ca. AD 1000), orders the Writings in three sections: (1) poetic books (Psalms, Job, and Proverbs); (2) the Megilloth, or the scrolls (Ruth, Song of Songs, Lamentations, Ecclesiastes, Esther); and (3) Daniel, Ezra-Nehemiah, and Chronicles.

The Babylonian Talmud (ca. AD 500) provides a different order: Ruth, Psalms, Job, Proverbs, Ecclesiastes, Song of Songs, Lamentations, Daniel, Esther, Ezra, and Chronicles.

Another Masoretic tradition, linked with the Aleppo Codex and the Leningrad Codex (Masoretes from the region of Tiberius in Galilee), offers a slightly different order: Chronicles, Psalms, Job, Proverbs, Ruth, Song of Songs, Ecclesiastes, Lamentations, Esther, Daniel, Ezra-Nehemiah.

In other words, the ancient sources show that the books in the Writings do not have as fixed an order as those in the Law and the Prophets do.

Public domain / Wikimedia Commons

Figure 17.1. Psalms page from the Aleppo Codex (tenth century)

CANONICAL CONNECTIONS

The Law, the Prophets, and the Psalms

When Jesus meets with the disciples after his resurrection, he teaches them about himself in the Law, the Prophets, and the Psalms (Luke 24:44). Jesus's reference to "the Psalms" may refer not only to the book of Psalms but to Psalms as the head of the Writings. So when Jesus refers to "the Psalms," he does so in terms of Psalms' signal position in the Writings and as a title for the whole section of Israel's Scripture.

THEOLOGICAL ISSUES

How Should We Then Live?

In his classic work *How Should We Then Live?* Francis Schaeffer discusses how a culture's art reflects that culture's ideals and ethics. For example, Michelangelo's stunning sculpture of David reveals the paradigmatic human whose hands are disproportionate to the body. Schaeffer claims these hands reveal something of Michelangelo's humanist ideals, ideals centered on the abilities of humans to think and create. People have questioned aspects of Schaeffer's work, but the question he raises about living in the real world in light of the truths of God's revelation remains a question worth pondering and pressing among every generation of the faithful.

assuming their presence and authority. The Writings show us what life looks when lived under the authority of the Law and the Prophets.

An example of the Writings assuming the authority of the Law and the Prophets appears notably in Psalms 1 and 2. (In fact, the whole book of Psalms assumes the authority of the Law by mirroring the Torah in its five-book shape; see the chapter on Psalms.) Not every ancient canonical list puts Psalms first in the Writings, but a notable tradition does, and most Hebrew Bibles today begin the Writings with the book of Psalms. Students can observe this "Psalms-first" structure in the Tanakh, the Bible of the Jewish Publication Society, on a shelf in their college or university library. Psalm 1 begins with an overt reference to the Torah: "Blessed is the one who does not walk in step with the wicked or stand in the way that sinners take or sit in the company of mockers, but whose delight is in the law [Torah] of the Lord" (Ps. 1:1–2). Psalms begins, therefore, by describing the blessed person or the person living in the fullness of God's presence and favor as the one who delights in God's Torah. For Psalms, the centrality and authority of the Law are necessary conditions for a happy life lived before God.

Psalm 2 follows and intends to be read with Psalm 1. Psalm 2 ends much as Psalm 1 begins: "Blessed is the one" and "Blessed are all" (Pss. 1:1; 2:12). The phrase "how blessed" or "blessed is/are" bookends the content of both psalms read together. In Psalm 2, the kingdom of God and the reign of his anointed king extend over the whole world. True human flourishing, the "blessed" state, occurs when God and his king are recognized as Lord over all. The prophetic books, including the Former Prophets (Joshua–Kings), show the historical tensions ancient Israel experienced as **Lady Zion** sought to live under God's rule and reign. Many of the main issues of faithlessness Israel experienced in the Former and Latter Prophets relate to the claims of Psalm 2.

Psalm 1 reaches back to the Law, and Psalm 2 recalls the legacy of the Prophets. In their own ways, these opening psalms serve as a gateway to the book of Psalms and the rest of the Writings. As such, they assume and build on the legacy of the Law and the Prophets.

The Writings raise questions for ancient Israel and all readers of Holy Scripture about how to live. How do we pray and navigate life before God in a complex world? Welcome to the book of Psalms. How can we live well in the world? Enter Proverbs. Does marital sex touch the transcendent? Is sex more than sex? Hello, Song of Songs. Does anything matter? Can we really flourish in this senseless world? Can our desires be rightly ordered? Here comes Ecclesiastes. Does wisdom have

Figure 17.2. Hand of the *David* by Michelangelo

its limitations? Can the righteous suffer? Is God bigger than our suffering? Are God's thoughts and ways infinitely beyond ours? The haunting book of Job wades into these difficult and treacherous waters. Is there really a smiling face behind the frowning providence of human suffering? Two extraordinary women can help answer this question: Ruth and Esther. Will history move toward God's redemptive purposes, or can circumstances thwart God's will? Hello, Daniel, Ezra-Nehemiah, and Chronicles. The questions continue with the Writings as they engage the messiness of embodied life. For today's Christian seeking to navigate a complex world, the Writings offer perhaps Scripture's most hospitable welcome.

Wisdom

Few sections of the Old Testament are under as much scrutiny these days as the so-called wisdom literature of the Writings. These books include Proverbs, Job, Ecclesiastes, and, at times, Song of Songs. The question is not whether "wisdom" is a biblical theme or biblical concept. This is not disputed. Rather, the concerns today relate to the limitations this genre classification places on interpreting or reading these books. Genre describes a type of literature. Genre categories emerge as texts that share similar features, say "wisdom," are grouped together. Genre analysis can be helpful, but only so far as genre does not become the primary key to understanding biblical texts. In the case of wisdom literature, the use of genre analysis has come under important critical scrutiny.

For some time, scholars engaged the wisdom literature as an independent category (genre) of the Old Testament. A good deal of interpretive baggage came along with this practice. One general example is the idea

Solomon and Wisdom Literature

Linking Solomon to Proverbs, Ecclesiastes, and Song of Songs has a history in certain Jewish and Christian traditions. These traditions considered these books in terms of Solomon's age. Jewish tradition thought Solomon wrote Song of Songs when he was young, Proverbs in middle age, and Ecclesiastes as an older man. Christian readers associated Song of Songs with the bliss of the heavenly life, and so they thought in these terms: Proverbs came first, followed by Ecclesiastes, and then Song of Songs depicting heavenly bliss.

CANONICAL CONNECTIONS

The Megilloth and Jewish Feasts

The Megilloth or "scrolls" refers to five small books in the Writings that have been received together in a somewhat stable order: Ruth, Song of Songs, Ecclesiastes, Lamentations, Esther. Ruth's signal position in the Megilloth appears to be part of its own history of writing because of the term "virtuous woman." Proverbs 31 ends with the description of the virtuous woman, and Boaz describes Ruth as a virtuous woman in Ruth 3. The relation becomes apparent: Ruth is the model of the virtuous woman of Proverbs 31.

These five books, in time, become linked to particular festivals and liturgies in rabbinic Judaism, perhaps formalized in the fifteenth or sixteenth century though likely stemming from a tradition before this time. Song of Songs is read at Passover, Ruth at the Festival of Weeks (Shavuot, celebrating when God gave Torah to Moses), Lamentations on the Ninth of Ab (memorial day for the destruction of the temple), Ecclesiastes/Qoheleth on the Feast of Tabernacles (Sukkoth, celebrated in the fall to commemorate the huts Israel lived in during the wilderness wanderings), Esther at Purim (celebrating the Jews' deliverance from Haman's plot to destroy them).

that wisdom literature operated outside of the normal scope of the Old Testament's religious particularity. Instead, the literature was thought to draw from the wisdom traditions of the ancient Near Eastern world and appeal to general and shared/universal principles for effective living. For example, many proverbs in the book of Proverbs (esp. Prov. 22:17–24:22) are very similar to the wise sayings of an Egyptian named Amenemope (twelfth century BC). Other scholars have shown the influence of ancient Ugaritic and Babylonian sources on biblical wisdom literature, particularly in their comparing and contrasting of righteousness and wickedness.

While none of these background features are controversial in themselves, it may be more useful to read Proverbs, Job, and Ecclesiastes in association with other books of the Old Testament. As biblical texts, these books have significance that goes far beyond reading them as "nonreligious" literature. For example, the wisdom sayings of Proverbs are received and understood within a comprehensive religious commitment: "The fear of the LORD is the beginning of wisdom" (Prov. 1:7). Proverbs may borrow material from any source where wisdom is to be found, but it filters these treasures through the ultimate commitment to fearing the Lord. How does one fear the Lord? By attending to the first commandment or the Shema of Deuteronomy 6:4: the Lord and the Lord alone! From this vantage point, wisdom functions as a servant of Torah and does not operate outside its authority. Similarly, Ecclesiastes concludes its survey of challenging questions by returning to the basic matters of Israel's religious identity. When all is said and done, "fear God and keep his commandments" (Eccles. 12:13). Reading Job in relation to the book of Genesis opens a biblical storehouse of profound insights about what it means for God to be God and humans to be human. Like righteousness, justice, holiness, and loving-kindness, wisdom takes its rightful place under the gracious and sovereign hand of Israel's God.

Conclusion

The Old Testament Writings are a diverse body of literature. Daniel, Ezra, and Nehemiah pick up on the historical timeline where Kings left off: exile into the postexilic return of Israel. Chronicles shares much in common with Samuel and Kings, covering roughly the same historical period but from a different perspective. While Samuel, for example, offers us the unvarnished version of David, Chronicles portrays a squeaky-clean David. Why would Chronicles omit the Bathsheba affair? There are at least two reasons. First, the author of Chronicles knows readers are familiar with Samuel and Kings, so Chronicles is not trying to deceive. Second, in Chronicles' postexilic setting, the portrait of David elicits confidence in God's original promises to David and his throne. Chronicles offers a hopeful motivation for those rebuilding the royal and religious institutions of a postexilic Judah.

Perhaps more importantly, Chronicles begins with nine chapters of genealogies, tedious reading that nonetheless serves a larger theological purpose. Chronicles, like Genesis, roots God's redemptive purposes in the world by means of genealogies. Recall that the whole book of Genesis builds on a genealogical structure: "These are the generations of . . ." (*toledoth*). God works his saving purposes on the stage of real history. Chronicles, in relation to Genesis, moves us from Adam to King Saul in order to launch the narrative of King David. In time these genealogies open to the final redemptive purposes revealed in Jesus Christ, Son of David and Son of God (Rom. 1:3). It is no accident that Matthew, the first of the fourfold Gospels, begins with a genealogy. Genesis and then Chronicles pave a genealogical path, and Matthew walks this path straight to Jesus Christ.

Christian Reading Questions

1. In what ways do the Writings relate to the Law and the Prophets? How does this help you understand the importance of this section of the Old Testament?
2. Why might the Writings be especially pertinent to today's Christian, especially as we view the Writings' concern for the question "How shall we live?"
3. What are the potential interpretive limitations for identifying certain books in the Writings as wisdom literature?

CHAPTER EIGHTEEN

Psalms

Orientation

Psalms is the prayer book of the Bible. In it God teaches his children how to speak to him and how to live their lives in his presence. For well over a century now, the human ability to reason and to shape our own identities has been central. We determine who we are, what we want to be, and how to achieve this identity. The Enlightenment challenge of "Dare to reason" threw off the constraints of previous authorities and moved the human mind and its ability to reason to center stage. Human progress could accomplish anything! Today, the mantra has shifted from "Dare to reason" to "Dare to be yourself" or "Dare to discover your true self" or "Dare to define yourself as you wish." The individual self is the lens through which reality is understood and experienced.

Figure 18.1. Medieval manuscript of Psalms

The book of Psalms operates from a completely different worldview. It moves Christians away from the self-focus of modern humanity and presses them to understand themselves in light of the all-encompassing and all-enveloping presence of God. Psalms addresses our humanity in terms of God's presence and goodness. The book defines our lives in a simple yet complex way: our humanity comes most clearly into view in God's presence. John Calvin famously described the Psalter as "an anatomy of all the parts of our souls."[1] Readers are laid bare before the Psalms and discover the glory of God's goodness and the truth about what it means to be human.

The Shape of the Psalms

The word "Psalms" is from the Greek word *psalmos*, which means "song" or "hymn." The Hebrew title for the book is *Tehillim* or "praises." The Hebrew title is more appropriate because the entirety of the book of Psalms has a shape, and that shape is directed toward praise. Praise occurs throughout the collection, but the book's ending especially turns to praise, beginning at Psalm 144. Everything is called on to praise the Lord—angels, sun, moon, stars, and the limitless galaxies of the universe. All are summoned to praise. This call to praise runs throughout the book.

Gregory of Nyssa, a fourth-century theologian, saw the book's shape toward praise as an indication of the Christian life itself. Christians encounter the complexities of human life, its ups and downs, joys and sorrows, as they are ever moving toward heaven itself, where God's presence and beauty overwhelm these human struggles. How do humans respond when lost in wonder, love, and grace? Praise. Praise is breath to the lungs for Christian pilgrims. It enables us to see the world more clearly, ourselves more modestly, and our God more gloriously. From the perspective of Psalms, living and praising are both essential elements of our being.

The shape of Psalms moves us toward praise, but the book has another shape as well. Psalms consists of five books; it is a collection. The Old Testament begins with a five-book structure: the Torah or Pentateuch. The book of Psalms mirrors these five books of Moses in its overall shape and structure. This "canonical shape" of Psalms makes an important point and informs interpretation of the book.

First, while Psalms reveals the complexity of human life, the book is essentially torah, instruction. Psalms instructs us in the character of a life lived in its totality before the living God. In this sense, Psalms is catechetical. It provides an instructional manual for Christians along

LITERARY NOTES

The Structure of Psalms

Book 1: Psalms 1–41
Book 2: Psalms 42–72
Book 3: Psalms 73–89
Book 4: Psalms 90–106
Book 5: Psalms 107–150

CANONICAL CONNECTIONS

Psalms and the Davidic Covenant

The five-book structure of Psalms leads some to suggest deeper patterns or developing themes across the books. One perspective sees the shape of the Davidic covenant, so important in Israel's lived experience, in the book. Books 1 and 2 reveal the main subject of Psalms, King David, along with the promises made to David and his offspring (the terms of the Davidic covenant). In Book 3, the Davidic covenant appears to come undone (Book 3 is the darkest section of Psalms; see, e.g., Ps. 88). During Israel's history, the exile threatened the Davidic covenant. Book 4 provides a renewed perspective as it highlights the Lord as king (Pss. 93–100). Book 5 reintroduces the messianic hope of the Davidic covenant with its two David collections geared toward the future (Pss. 108–10; 138–45).

their pilgrim journey. The individual psalms provide Christians with language suited to the variety of human experiences: prayers for disorientation and confusion, prayers seeking wisdom, prayers seeking forgiveness, prayers thanking God for his saving power. A believing existence is not static but dynamic: movement before the living God.

Secondly, Psalms as Torah instructs us in the character of God. The book invites readers to think in theological terms. Who is God, and what does he reveal about himself and the world? Psalms instructs those who pray to understand the character of the One to whom they pray. "Surely God is good to Israel, to those who are pure in heart" (73:1). Such a basic confession of faith reveals the character of God as good—God is goodness itself—even when life's trials and confusion suggest otherwise.

Psalms testifies to the truth of an ancient phrase used by the church: *Lex orandi, lex credendi*, which means "The law of prayer [*lex orandi*] is the law of belief [*lex credendi*]." What we believe and how we pray are interrelated; believing and praying/worshiping cannot be separated. Christians confess certain things to be true about God, about Jesus Christ, sin, repentance and forgiveness, and our hope for a future shaped by the saving promises of a good God. The content of our faith, however, cannot be detached from the lived reality of Christian existence. We pray as the gathered community of the redeemed so we can know the truths of God's revelation, and we know the truths of God's revelation by his Spirit so we can pray in accord with God's will. The heartbeat of the book of Psalms pulses the rhythm of *Lex orandi, lex credendi*. Psalms testifies to the way Christians come to know and to know rightly. We do so in the communal life of prayer before the living God who speaks to us and shapes us by his Word. 📖

Psalm Titles

Many psalms have titles that provide information about authorship (e.g., "A psalm of David"), musical/liturgical directions (e.g., "For pipes" or "For the director of music"), and at times, the historical circumstances behind the psalm's composition. For example, the title of Psalm 18 identifies David as the psalm's author along with the historical circumstances of the psalm—"when the Lord delivered him from the hand of all his enemies and from the hand of Saul." In our English Bibles, these titles are typically found in an italicized font just above the psalm itself, appearing like editorial insertions.

The Hebrew Bible, on the other hand, marks psalm titles as verse 1 of the psalm. They are not separated from the body of the psalm as a header, and so are not easily dismissed in importance. When Psalm 51—a **penitential psalm**—provides a title describing the Bathsheba affair as the historical event behind the psalm's composition, the Hebrew Bible sees that title as a feature of the psalm itself, not an editorial aside. The history and

Figure 18.2. *David and Saul* by Ernst Josephson (1878)

function of these titles is still a matter of some controversy. Complicating matters is a comparison of the Hebrew Bible to the Greek Septuagint. The latter has more psalm titles than the former, indicating that the fixing of titles to particular psalms was still an active feature of the reception history of Psalms. What are readers to make of these titles?

Dating the titles or relating them to the actual writing of individual psalms remains difficult. Many scholars believe these titles are later additions, though there is no compelling reason to doubt the Davidic authorship of the psalms that claim it. Some scholars dismiss the titles because they hold a particular theory about the psalms and their history—for example, all psalms are the product of Israel's worship and should not be read in light of any particular circumstances, such as the Bathsheba affair or David hiding in the caves of En Gedi. Others argue for or against the inspiration of these titles on the basis of their later insertion. In our view, there appears little reason for readers of Psalms to dismiss the titles, whether they are later additions or not. They are a part of the canonical text and inherent to their earliest reception.

Reading certain texts in light of other texts—what the Jewish tradition calls midrash—adds to a psalm's depth and texture. It brings the Bible into conversation with itself, which allows deeper—and more interesting—readings! The title of Psalm 3, for example, links the psalm with David's flight from his son Absalom. The events of 2 Samuel 15–18 overlap with the concepts of Psalm 3. Enemies have risen against David (Ps. 3:1). Many consider his situation hopeless; God has abandoned him (3:2). Nevertheless, David places his trust in the Lord (3:3–8). In fairness, many psalms follow these same themes, though the particular language in Psalm 3 of lying down, sleeping, and waking (v. 5) reflects the Absalom narrative. David arrived at the Jordan River, slept there, and then rose before daybreak to cross it (2 Sam. 17:22). Psalm 3 and the Absalom narrative share in a mutual relationship. David's lament, distress, and loss—elements of the tragic Absalom narrative—are given the shape of prayer in Psalm 3. Psalm 3 gives readers access to the piety of King David and, to borrow an idea from George Eliot's *Middlemarch*, his hidden life. The particularity of David's distress turns him heavenward in the hard period of the Absalom tragedy—and it does the same for the covenant community in all times as believers enter into David's shared loss and ultimate hope.

A few concluding comments are in order regarding the psalm titles. First, while the historical designations of psalm titles play an important role in their interpretation, psalms themselves are not limited to their historical origins. In other words, the historical titles are not exhaustive accounts of psalms' meanings. Psalms is ready-made for believers of all times to enter into lament and praise. Second, where a psalm lacks a historical title—and most of them do—interpreters should not try to identify the particular historical occasion behind the psalm. Psalms as a whole is happy to remain open to all times and places.

Exploration—Reading Psalms

The book of Psalms is impressive in its scope and sweep. Exploring its content can easily become challenging. Students of Scripture would do well simply to dive into the book and read it, frequently. As the prayer book of the Bible, Psalms remains a companion for the faithful believer for all times and places. The psalms accompany the pilgrim along the way. In the words of Eugene Peterson's classic treatment of the Psalms of Ascent (Pss. 120–34), the psalms support "a long obedience in the same direction."[2]

This exploration section explains the various kinds of psalms in the book. These categories can prove helpful for turning to the psalms themselves. This section also considers a few key psalms: Psalms 1, 2, and 73. These psalms serve as important markers for those in pursuit of a "long obedience."

Recognizing the different types of psalms can be helpful, but it is also important to remember that the whole of Psalms is titled *Tehillim* or "praises." The shape of Psalms with all its internal variety moves intentionally toward praise. Yet within this larger movement toward praise are various kinds of psalms.

Psalm types or forms are determined by considering together various psalms (and authors) that share common themes. Psalms, for example, that highlight the Torah (Pss. 1, 19, and 119) are called Torah psalms. Interpreters often disagree as to the number and variety of types, but the list below is somewhat standard. These psalm types are constructions, labels given from outside the text itself, and therefore should serve a reading of psalms, not dominate it.

Hymns

▓ READ PSALM 103 ▓

A hymn expresses praise to God. The focus of a hymn is external to the worshiper; the focus is Godward. In the midst of life's complexities, the character of God comes into clear view, and the psalmist exults in God's goodness. Hymns reveal humanity at its fullest: not with a focus on the self but with a clear view of the goodness of God and the peace that comes from taking refuge in him. These psalms sparkle with joy.

Lament Psalms

▓ READ PSALM 13 ▓

The Bible is honest about the human condition. It is not escapist literature that removes us from the burdens of having a body and living in the material world. Believers suffer, experience loss, and can enter seasons of deep disorientation before God. The history of the church is filled with faithful followers who experienced seasons of deep lament before the Lord. Lament psalms open the door of prayer for those suffering because of life and because of God.

Lament psalms move from a place of despair toward praise. These prayers reorient worshipers to their ultimate end and hope. Rarely do the lament psalms speak to the alleviation of difficult circumstances. There are other types of psalms that offer this kind of perspective. Lament psalms move

Ellen Davis on Biblical Lament

"Whining is empty self-expression, annoyingly repetitive, as every parent knows. But lament is an art form, and the presence of the lament in the Bible means that for Jews and Christians, it is initially a sort of scripted performance of the difficult journey through trouble to God."[f]

A Lament to Christ

Gregory of Nazianzus (a fourth-century church father) pens a poem patterned on the laments of Psalms.

A Prayer to Christ

Where's the injustice? I was born
   human—well and good!
But why am I so battered by life's tidal
   waves?
I'll speak my mind—harshly perhaps,
   yet I will speak:
Were I not yours, my Christ, this life
   would be a crime!
We're born, we age, we reach the measure of our days;
I sleep, I rest, I awake again, I go my way
With health and sickness, joys and
   struggles as my fare,
Sharing the seasons of the sun, the
   fruits of the earth,
And death, and then corruption—just
   like any beast,
Whose life, though lowly, still is inno-
   cent of sin!
What more do I have? Nothing more,
   except for God!
Were I not yours, my Christ, this life
   would be a crime![g]

toward praise because of God's unchanging character even in the midst of life's greatest sorrows. The psalmist appears to have an internal conversation reorienting the self toward God as creator and redeemer.

Thanksgiving Psalms

READ PSALM 40

Thanksgiving psalms express praise and gratitude for God's deliverance from sorrow or trouble. Their exultation in God's great deliverance speaks to the alleviation of suffering, sickness, and loss. Grateful hearts and mouths are the opposite of idolatry in the Bible; the apostle Paul encourages his churches to always rejoice, pray without ceasing, and be thankful (Phil. 4:4–6; 1 Thess. 4:16–18). Gratitude for God's grace motivates a life of obedience. We do not obey to earn God's favor or pay a debt—Jesus did that for us completely. We obey because of our deep gratitude for God's redeeming deliverance in Jesus Christ. Thanksgiving psalms reflect this gratitude.

Remembrance Psalms or Salvation-History Psalms

READ PSALM 77

Remembering God's mighty acts of deliverance provides psalmists the key to navigating the life of faith. "Remembering" is a covenantal term that entails an active participation in events long ago even though God's people are now removed from those moments in time. The Passover, for example, involves a kind of reenactment of the exodus that reinforces for God's people their presence then and there. How could they be present back then when removed from those moments by generations? Because their very existence is due to God's work "back then" and his application of that work to the current moment "now." He acted then in powerful and miraculous ways, sustains his people in the present, and will fulfill his kingdom promises in the future once and for all. Believers find comfort, encouragement, and hope for the future by recalling God's powerful deeds of the past.

Royal Psalms

■ READ PSALM 2 ■

Royal psalms celebrate the king of Israel and, within Psalms, focus specifically on King David and his offspring. These psalms are especially rich for messianic interpretation, though, as we will discuss at the end of this chapter, the entire book of Psalms should be understood as properly messianic.

Wisdom Psalms

■ READ PSALM 49 ■

Wisdom psalms share features with wisdom literature. While some suggest that "wisdom" in Israel's religious history operated in a kind of secular space outside the sphere of the religious, the Old Testament canon resists this move. It links wisdom with Solomon and links the monarchy of Israel with worship of YHWH. Even Proverbs states that wisdom's proper foundation is "the fear of the LORD" (Prov. 1:7). Finding "wisdom" psalms in the prayer book of Israel and of the church also indicates wisdom's proper context in a life lived before the God of Israel, the Lord who is Father, Son, and Holy Spirit.

Torah Psalms

■ READ PSALM 19 ■

Torah psalms celebrate God's torah or God's law. "Law" often connotes a narrow view of torah, focusing on legal matters, the "thou shalt nots" of the law. While these do exist and are torah, torah has a broader range that includes all God's instruction. Torah might be understood as another way of saying God's "revelation." The fact that God has spoken and revealed himself to humanity should lead to praise. It is a remarkable feature of our faith. Christians believe God has not left them in the dark about God's identity, his creative and redemptive purposes, and his desires for humanity and its flourishing. The longest psalm is a torah psalm: Psalm 119, with 176 verses attesting to the beauty, power, and grace of God's torah. This psalm is an acrostic—each of the twenty-two stanzas is titled with a consecutive letter of the Hebrew alphabet, and each line in a given stanza begins with that same Hebrew letter. A to B to C to D all the way to Z. The form itself attests

THEOLOGICAL ISSUES

"Remembering" and the Lord's Table

"Do this in remembrance of me" is an invitation from our Lord to table fellowship with him (Luke 22:19; 1 Cor. 11:24). When it comes to the Lord's Table or the Eucharist, Christians disagree over many theological details. We will not settle those matters here, but on one matter the Old Testament helps. "Remembering" is not merely calling something to mind but is active participation by God's Spirit in the saving events of history. When Christians on Good Friday sing "Were you there when they crucified my Lord?" the biblical and theological response to that question is, "Undoubtedly and unreservedly yes."

THEOLOGICAL ISSUES

A Homily on Delighting in Scripture

"Let every man, woman and child therefore, with all their heart, thirst and desire God's Holy Scriptures, love them, embrace them, have their delight and pleasure in hearing and reading them, so as at length we may be transformed and changed into them. For the Holy Scriptures are God's treasure house wherein are found all things needful for us to see, to hear, to learn and to believe, necessary for the attaining of eternal life."[h]

Jeremiah and the Zion Psalms

The prophet Jeremiah clashes with false prophets over the security of Jerusalem as projected in the Zion psalms. Jeremiah warns that God is bringing judgment on Jerusalem, and the false prophets—with support of biblical traditions—reject Jeremiah's doom and gloom message. How could what he says be right? "Zion cannot be shaken" (e.g., Ps. 125:1). The psalms declare it. Yet the false prophets highlighted the Zion tradition at the expense of other clear voices in the tradition, like the book of Deuteronomy. Zion's indestructability was not a promise without qualifications. It rested on the foundation of Zion's covenant fidelity to love the Lord their God and him alone.

to the perfection of God's Word and the way in which it shapes the totality of created existence from A to Z, or from *aleph* (א) to *tav* (ת).

Zion Psalms

■ READ PSALM 46 ■

Zion psalms celebrate God's holy city. Mount Zion is the location of the temple, and the whole of Jerusalem takes the title Zion as well. The extension of the name Zion from the Temple Mount alone to Jerusalem itself speaks to the way the temple and God's promised presence in the people's midst define the city and its inhabitants. The Zion psalms highlight God's presence within the city and its indestructability because of Zion's favored status in God's eyes.

Penitential Psalms

■ READ PSALM 32 ■

Penitential psalms are psalms of repentance born out of the brokenness of sin and its devastating consequences. They portray a physical and spiritual heaviness of guilt: "When I kept silent, my bones wasted away" (32:3). These psalms move the worshiper through sin's guilt and heaviness to honest confession of sin—naming the thing for what it is—to the great relief of God's forgiveness. Much like the Prophets, the penitential psalms assure believers of all time of God's merciful character. For those who turn to Christ in honest confession and repentance, the Lord will always extend his mercy. God can do nothing else because he operates from the stability of his character.

Figure 18.3. Illuminated manuscript page from the penitential psalms

The psalm types listed here could be expanded or divided in different ways, but these provide a helpful handle on the various kinds of psalms in the book. They illustrate the worshiping community and the individual believer in the multifaceted reality of life before God—from joy to grief to reflection to repentance and beyond. In all these experiences, Psalms invites us to live every moment of life in God's presence and en route to praise.

The book of Psalms waits for us as these moments of our lives unfold.

A Gateway to a Life Lived before God: Psalms 1 and 2

▓ READ PSALMS 1–2 ▓

On the Ocoee River in East Tennessee, a river guide will give instructions about what is expected and how best to navigate the rapids ahead. "When I say left, paddle

Figure 18.4. *Saint Jerome Writing* by Caravaggio (1605–6)

hard left. . . . When I say 'stop' . . ." The guide's instructions are important. They set expectations and let participants know what is needed for a safe and successful trip. In effect, the river guide is saying, "If you want to survive, you might listen up." Psalms 1 and 2 are like a river guide's speech before entering the wild river of life in God's presence that begins with Psalm 3.

The church father Jerome describes Psalms as a large house with many rooms, each requiring different keys. The Holy Spirit provides the keys to these rooms, and Psalm 1 functions as the front door of the large house. The difference in form between Psalms 1–2 and then Psalm 3 is clear. Psalms 1 and 2 are instructive, while Psalm 3 begins with the language of prayer, direct address to God: "LORD, how many are my foes!" (3:1). The instruction of Psalms 1–2 opens the door to the large house and many rooms of the book of Psalms.

The focus of these introductory psalms is the "blessed" or "happy" life. The term "blessed" bookends Psalm 1 and Psalm 2.

Blessed is the one who does not walk in step with the wicked or stand in the way that sinners take or sit in the company of mockers. (1:1)

Blessed are all who take refuge in him. (2:12)

The question of human happiness is one that philosophers have asked for a long time. Is life worth living? If so, how might one live a happy life? Aristotle famously answered this question by appealing to intellectual and moral virtue. The good life is, in part, the virtuous life that exists in that happy space between two extremes; courage, for example, hovers between fear and naive bravado. In its own way, the Bible also concerns itself with human happiness, or better put, human flourishing in the blessed state of God's presence and favor. Psalms 1 and 2 address one of life's greatest and most enduring questions: Is happiness possible, and if so, how might I find it?

Psalm 1 makes it clear that the blessed or happy person is the one who loves God's Word. They do not walk or stand or sit with ungodliness; they do not grow comfortable with evil and its rejection of God and his ways. Rather, their existence is Godward and marked by a deep affection and commitment to God's law or God's Word. The blessed person hungers and thirsts after God's direction day and night. They strive to live every moment within the view of God's being and his voice. Their attitude toward God's Word is one of "delight" or affection and hard work, meditating on it day and night (1:2). Those who love God's Word experience the promise of God's blessing. The fruit of their lives is always in season.

Psalm 2 reveals the power of God's kingdom and God's anointed king. In its ancient Israelite context, Psalm 2 witnesses to the election of the Davidic king as God's representative on earth. From the standpoint of the whole Bible, Psalm 2 speaks beyond the range of King David to include and highlight David's greater son, Jesus Christ. "You are my son," God says to his messianic king (2:7). These words, read with Isaiah 42:1, shape God's declaration about Jesus Christ at his baptism: "This is My beloved Son, with whom I am well pleased" (Matt. 3:17 NASB). The "blessed" or happy person finds refuge in God and his anointed king. The promise of refuge or safe harbor underneath God's wings is a theme that weaves throughout the book of Psalms. The happy person takes refuge from the hostilities of the world in God and under his wings.

Psalms 1 and 2 speak of the blessed state and lay the foundation for a life in God's favor. This life includes a deep devotion to and affection for God's Word, a recognition of God's kingdom rule and his anointed King, and the deep peace that comes from resting in him. These are conditions for a robust and full life of prayer before the living God.

Life at the Seams—A Psalm of Disorientation: Psalm 73

▓ READ PSALM 73 ▓

Psalm 73 is the first psalm of the somber Book 3 and lies at the center of the book of Psalms. From this position, it looks back to the claims of Books 1 and 2 and forward to the challenges and darkness of Book 3, along with the promises of Books 4 and 5. Psalm 73 holds together the bigger themes and religious challenges of Psalms.

Asaph, the psalm's author, was a priest. His vocation entailed holy things, and the concerns of temple worship

THEOLOGICAL ISSUES

The Son within the Godhead

Christian theologians speak of "the eternal generation of the Son." The Son as a distinct person within the Godhead relates to his eternal generation from the Father. The early church fathers spoke clearly about there never being a time when the Son was not. When humans beget or have children, children come into existence that once were not. This, naturally, makes sense because humans make other humans, and human beings are not eternal creatures. So, there is a time when we were not. But for God the Father to beget God the Son requires an eternal relation or shared essence between the Father and the Son that had no beginning.

occupied his days. Yet he exhibits for the faithful of all times the great angst that can result when faith and life experience collide. Asaph begins with the confession that "God certainly is good to Israel, to those who are pure in heart" (73:1 AT). In terms of Psalms, Asaph is saying, "I know Psalm 1 and confess what it says is true. God is good to those who devote themselves to torah, to the Israelite who is pure in heart." Yet there is a problem, and Asaph identifies the problem in verse 2 with the contrast word "but": "But as for me, my feet came close to stumbling" (AT).

What causes Asaph's crisis of faith? From one angle, the answer appears straightforward. The wicked prosper while the righteous suffer (73:3–12). It troubles Asaph to see the godless enjoy easy lives while they mock God. These incongruities of life are challenges for good people of all times and places: "Why do we struggle so much to make ends meet, when those selfish tycoons out there enjoy their summer yachts?" These sentiments are understandable and nothing new. But the problems for Asaph go deeper. Asaph joins the company of all righteous sufferers, Job most especially, because his deepest problem is not with his circumstances but with God: "Surely in vain I have kept my heart pure and washed my hands in innocence" (73:13). God, you made promises, and life is not adding up.

Asaph's honesty offers great comfort. The psalm does not describe a change in Asaph's circumstances, nor do we know the particularities that occasioned this psalm. Instead, the psalm highlights a shift in focus, bringing God and his future promises back to the center: "When I tried to understand all this, it troubled me deeply till I entered the sanctuary of God; then I understood their final destiny" (73:16). Asaph realigns his perspective to the things of God, and he is able to conclude, "Whom do I have in heaven but you? And with you, I desire nothing on earth" (73:25 AT). The sum of reality is never defined or exhausted by my experience now, Asaph realizes. God's purposes, goodness, and promise for the future stand firm despite the challenges of any current experiences.

Implementation: Reading Psalms as Christian Scripture Today

The book of Psalms leaves Christians waiting, opening them to the future hope of God's promises, much like the shape of the book itself in its movement toward final praise. The waiting has a clear object in Psalms: the psalmists wait on God. "I waited patiently for the LORD," or "Wait for the LORD" (40:1; 27:14). The psalmists redirect Christians along their way to wait on the Lord, even when life rages and roars.

Psalms is the prayer book of Israel, and it is also the prayer book of Jesus. There are multiple entry points for understanding the relation of

Psalms as the Standard for Prayer

Dietrich Bonhoeffer offered a stirring lecture on Christ in the book of Psalms to his students at Finkenwalde Seminary (an unofficial seminary of the Confessing Church in Nazi Germany). In the lecture he made a claim about how Christians can come to understand the book of Psalms. His counsel is instructive. "There is no access to a psalm other than through prayer. . . . The answer to the question: How am I to pray something that is still so incomprehensible to me? is: How are you to understand what you have not yet prayed? Rather than our own prayer being the standard for the psalm, it is rather the psalm that is the proper standard for our prayer."[i]

Jesus Christ to the book of Psalms. Jesus as David's heir and the fulfillment of the Davidic covenant is one such entry. The whole history of Israel in its election and rejection by Israel's God witnesses to Christ. He is the elect one and the one who bears all of Israel's and the world's rejection of and subsequent judgment by God. Another entry point is Christ's role as mediator. As the risen Lord who learned obedience through suffering, he intercedes for us now in a fitting way before the Father by the Spirit (Heb. 4:14–16). Jesus prays Psalms on our behalf and as our advocate. All prayer to the Father is mediated by the Son, and few Christian truths are as comforting as Jesus praying for his own. ☩

KEY VERSES IN PSALMS

- Blessed is the one who does not walk in step with the wicked, or stand in the way that sinners take or sit in the company of mockers, but whose delight is in the law of the LORD, and who meditates on his law day and night. 1:1–2
- Blessed are all who take refuge in him. 2:12
- Whom have I in heaven but you? And earth has nothing I desire besides you. 73:25
- For the LORD is the great God, the great King above all gods. 95:3
- Praise the LORD. 150:6

Christian Reading Questions

1. How do Psalms 1 and 2 present the blessed/happy life? How does this differ from the way your culture understands happiness?

2. How does the shape of Psalms as torah influence one's approach to reading them?

3. What does it mean that we were created to praise? How might Augustine help us understand this facet of our being?

4. Bonhoeffer suggests we put Psalms on the lips of Jesus first before we put it on ours. How might this help you understand how Jesus is praying for you and the church? How might this influence your approach to prayer?

CHAPTER NINETEEN

Job

Orientation

If the book of Proverbs teaches what might be considered the basic curriculum about biblical wisdom, then the book of Job is the advanced curriculum. Job explores what happens when a righteous and blameless person suffers for no apparent reason. Proverbs teaches that a life lived well before God will lead to divine blessing and a life of foolishness will lead to destruction. The book of Job seems to counter this basic claim in Proverbs, or at least expose an example where these things do not seem to play out.

The book of Job has perennial fascination precisely because of the way it presents life and faith at the extreme—human suffering in excruciating detail. The story is about a man named Job who, the first two chapters of the book make clear, is upright and blameless before God but has everything taken from him: his health, his family, his wealth. All that remains is Job's wife, who instructs her husband to curse God and die (not the most encouraging of partners!). So, what benefit is there to being upright if his life ends in disaster? How is his suffering just? 📖

Figure 19.1. *The Magdalen, or Sorrow* by Paul Cézanne (1869)

THEOLOGICAL ISSUES

Theodicy

The book of Job has some similarities with ancient Near Eastern tales of suffering, often called "theodicies," a term derived from the Greek words *theos* ("God") and *dikē* ("justice"). So a **theodicy** is an exploration of the relationship between God and justice. Usually such explorations center on how bad things—even horrors—can happen to humanity if there is a good and powerful God who orders the world. If ever there was one who experienced horrors, it would be this man called Job.

HISTORICAL MATTERS

The Poem of the Righteous Sufferer

Ludlul bēl nēmeqi (ca. 1400 BC), translated "The Poem of the Righteous Sufferer," or in other versions "Dialogue between a Man and His God," is a Babylonian poem that is related to an ancient Sumerian poem, which was received and adapted in Babylonian literature. It is an extended poem that focuses on the theme of unjust or undeserved suffering. Like the book of Job, it concerns a man who undergoes extraordinary suffering, and it explores how it is that righteous people suffer terrible things in life. As in Job, the protagonist cannot see why the deity does not intervene to help or save his life. By the end of the poem, the deity (Marduk, the Babylonian patron god) grants the sufferer relief. As in Job, the poem's conclusion culminates with divine restoration.[a]

LITERARY NOTES

The Structure of Job

Job is organized by a frame narrative, which means narrative opens the book (Job 1–2) and concludes the book (42:7–17). The poetic core (3:1–42:6) sits within this narrative frame.

Narrative frame	Prologue: The earthly and heavenly scenes (Job 1–2)
Poetic core	First series of speeches: Job and friends (Job 3–14)
	Second series of speeches: Job and friends (Job 15–21)
	Third series of speeches: Job and friends (Job 22–27)
	Job's wisdom poem (Job 28)
	Job's speeches (Job 29–31)
	Elihu's speeches (Job 32–37)
	God's speeches (Job 38–41)
	Job's response (Job 42:1–6)
Narrative frame	Epilogue: The restoration of Job (Job 42:7–17)

What makes Job's experience more complicated is that it results from a divine wager between God and a figure called the *satan* in the heavenly council (1:6–12; 2:1–6). Job's world turns upside down, and he has no idea why! This is the position of all human sufferers, whether ancient or modern.

Exploration—Reading Job

Prologue—The Earthly and Heavenly Scenes: Job 1–2

■ READ JOB 1–2 ■

The prologue introduces Job's reversal of fortunes as a result of heavenly discussion and a sort of wager. The *satan* comes before YHWH with the "sons of God" in the heavenly council, and YHWH asks him what he has been doing. The identity of the *satan* is debated, but clearly it is a figure who has access to God and can roam about the earth. At the very least, this figure is antagonistic to Job and challenges God. The *satan* simply says that he has been going to and fro over the earth. God then asks, "Have you considered my servant Job? There is no one on earth like him; he is blameless and upright, a man who fears God and shuns evil" (1:8). God pronounces and affirms Job's piety and devotion, with honorific description: "my servant," "blameless," "upright," and "a man who fears God and shuns evil." This piling up of descriptors shows us that God is pleased with Job. The *satan* then argues that Job fears YHWH only because of the prosperity that he has experienced: Job honors God because of the "stuff" YHWH gives him (1:9–11). If YHWH took it all away, then,

Figure 19.2. Bronze statue *Job* by Gerhard Marcks (ca. 1957), Saint Klara Church in Nürnberg, Germany

Settings in the Prologue and Complexity in Suffering

Job's prologue distinguishes between two settings: in the heavens and on the earth. The only actor to traverse the heavenly and earthly settings is the *satan*. Corresponding to these two settings, Job 1–2 plays on two levels of knowledge: human and divine, earthly and heavenly. The prologue establishes the earthly experience of the protagonist Job, a non-Israelite YHWH-fearer from the land of Uz (a region associated with Edom, southeast of the Dead Sea) who experiences a tragic reversal of fortunes as he loses his livelihood/ flocks and his children (1:13–19), his health (2:7–8), and even his wife, as she seemingly turns against Job (2:9–10). As Job experiences this serial trauma, his friends and wife provide a "down-to-earth" perspective on the events. They try to understand what is going on and why, just like Job does. The second level of knowledge is the heavenly perspective, where God—as well as the other major figure, the *satan*—knows what is going on in Job's life and why. Both settings and levels of knowledge interrelate, creating complexity and depth both in how we understand Job's life and experience and (more fundamentally) how we navigate trauma, suffering, and loss from a human perspective, looking for divine insight that may be hidden to us.

Gregory the Great on the *Satan*

The figure of the *satan* is with the Lord in the heavenly scenes with the "sons of God" who present themselves to God. The "sons of God" are often thought to be angels in Christian tradition, and the *satan* has been interpreted as Satan, the great adversary to humanity and God. Christian tradition views Satan as the fallen angel Lucifer. Obviously, this creates a real challenge: What is Satan doing in heaven among the angels with God? Pope Gregory the Great (ca. 540–604) wrestled with this question in his famous allegorical and moral interpretation of the book of Job in *Moralia in Job*.[b] Gregory explains:

He [Satan] was in the Lord's sight, but the Lord was not in his sight; as when a blind man stands in the sun, he is himself bathed indeed in the rays of light, yet he sees nothing of the light, by which he is brightened. In like manner then Satan also appeared in the Lord's sight among the Angels. For the Power of God, which by a look penetrates all objects, beheld the impure spirit, who saw not Him.[c]

the *satan* says, Job would abandon YHWH. Thus, the wager between YHWH and the *satan* ensues.

The Hebrew text of Job does not explain in detail the identity of the "sons of God" or the *satan* in Job 1:6. In the NIV of 1:6, "angels" present themselves before God in the heavens, "and Satan also came with them." The Hebrew phrase the NIV translates as "angels" is "the sons of God," a Hebrew phrase that *may* indicate angels but also may refer to a divine assembly in the heavens. The ancient hearers may well have interpreted "sons of God" as divine beings in the heavenly council, as we find in Canaanite theology. If this is the case, then God is holding court with the divine beings in heaven.

Figure 19.3. Detail of a miniature of Gregory the Great writing, inspired by the Holy Spirit (represented as a dove), by the scribe Teodericus (twelfth century)

The *satan*'s accusations appear in Job 1:9–11 and 2:4–5. He accuses Job of not really honoring God regardless of what happens to him: he honors God only because of divine blessing, either the blessing of family and wealth (1:9–11) or health (2:4–5). The *satan* believes if God takes away these blessings, then Job will "curse" God. Although the *satan* thinks Job will abandon God, God is willing to bet that Job will worship him no matter what.[1]

The *Satan*'s Identity and Purpose

There is some ambiguity as to the purpose and identity of the *satan*. First, it is difficult to exactly correlate the biblical Satan (from the New Testament) with the *satan* in Job because of the Hebrew language. A definite article precedes the word *satan*, which is strange if it is the proper name or title "Satan." It would be like introducing ourselves as "the Heath" or "the Mark" rather than "Heath" or "Mark." So "the *satan*" may not intend the proper name "Satan," nor does it clarify the *satan*'s purpose.

Second, we may think of the *satan* as a member of the divine assembly in the heavens who serves as a divine agent roaming "throughout the earth" (Job 1:7; 2:2) to assess the devotion of hu-

manity to God. When the *satan* finds faulty faith among humanity, he makes an accusation against that party before God for God to then make judgment. Thus, the *satan* could be interpreted as a divine agent in the heavenly council, who makes accusations against, or is adversarial to, human beings.

Finally, recent research suggests that as an agent of the heavenly assembly, the *satan* is not an accuser but an attacker or executioner of humanity. On this understanding, the *satan* attacks those deemed to be guilty of wrongdoing. In the prologue of Job, the *satan* attacks righteous Job in his flesh. His wrongful attack on Job and Job's faithfulness in spite of it prove God's verdict about Job correct.[d]

Who Is the *Satan* Accusing?

The idea of the *satan* accusing Job of wrongdoing seems straightforward enough, but when we look a bit deeper, the *satan* may be accusing God of improperly ordering the world. After all, it was God who created this world, so the *satan* accuses God of making a world where people worship God only for what he gives. That is why the *satan* is in the heavenly assembly: to accuse God. Thus, the people God has made do not really revere him with a heart of devotion. Take away their health, wealth, and freedom through suffering, and God's people will fail in their devotion to him. Thus, the *satan* accuses God of being a weak, faulty, or imperfect creator.

For our part, we tend to agree with this perspective, that the *satan* is accusing God of being a weak or imperfect creator and uses

Job as his prime piece of evidence. If Job fails in the test, then God is proven to be an imperfect creator. If Job maintains his integrity, then God wins the bet and the *satan* is proven wrong.

Whether you think the *satan*'s accusation is directed against God or Job, we can all recognize that the accusation provides the catalyst to move the narrative forward, to prove God (and Job) right in what God says: "Have you considered my servant Job? There is no one on earth like him; he is blameless and upright, a man who fears God and shuns evil. And he still maintains his integrity, though you incited me against him to ruin him without any reason" (2:3).

LITERARY NOTES

Levels of Knowledge in Job

The prologue of Job is brilliant in the levels of knowledge and perspectives it generates as well as how humans embody these levels of knowledge throughout the rest of the book:

The reader's knowledge	The reader knows what Job and the other characters cannot know: that the wager in the divine council has taken place.
Job's knowledge	Job knows what his comforters do not: that he is, in fact, innocent of sin and did not "do" anything to deserve tragedy. Job does not know his predicament is a result of a wager in the heavenly council.
Job's friends' knowledge	Job's comforters (and later Elihu) do not know that Job is innocent and his predicament is a result of a heavenly wager between YHWH and the *satan*.*
YHWH's knowledge	Job is upright and does not simply worship YHWH because of divine blessings. YHWH knows he is the perfect creator.
The *satan*'s knowledge	He does not know if Job is upright, worshiping YHWH regardless of physical state or only because of divine blessings.

* Christopher R. Seitz, "Job: Full-Structure, Movement, and Interpretation," *Interpretation* 43, no. 1 (1989): 10.

Job has no knowledge of either the cause or rationale behind his experience. By contrast, the reader gains access to a heavenly perspective on Job's suffering. In response to his calamity, Job maintains his faithfulness to YHWH and does not sin (1:22).

Biblical Mourning

As a ritual, mourning symbolically inverts the normal order of living and associates the mourner with the world of the dead. The mourner moves from normal "life" (a premourning stage), to symbolic "death" (mourning enacted), to renewed "life" (rejoicing). Outward actions (cutting hair, tearing robes, throwing dust on oneself, sitting on the ground, sitting in silence, weeping, fasting, avoiding sex, and abstaining from worship) signify symbolic death. The mourner expects to move beyond this ritual state, and mourning is not complete until the mourner enacts the requisite restorative actions—washing, dressing, and reintegrating into normal life. If this is accurate, Job's mourning acts (descending to the ground, tearing his clothes, sitting on the ash heap, etc.) are not simply expressions of emotions or deep sadness, as modern readers tend to view them. The action of Job 2:8–42:6 takes place in a mourning ritual, anticipating a traverse from Job's mourning to renewed joy.

At the end of the prologue, Job's friends enter the story to perform the appropriate service to Job within an ancient cultural mourning rite (2:11–13). The mourning rite serves as the major ritual context for the entire book. The remainder of the book anticipates Job's movement *out of* mourning.

Poetic Core: Job 3:1–42:6

FIRST SPEECH CYCLE: JOB 3–14

■ READ JOB 3; 7; 9–14 ■

Job introduces the problem, as he sees it, in a dark poem in which he recounts the misery of living and the peace that would come by dying (Job 3). With similarities to Genesis 1, the lament of Job 3 reconsiders Job's place in creation, and in so doing it raises questions about YHWH's ordering of the world. Job's words are a **lament**, a kind of prayer that voices a complaint to God about distress in order to persuade God to act on the sufferer's behalf.[2] A lament is not petulant or faithless; it is an honest prayer to God from a place of deep pain.

Beginning in Job 4, we find the varied advice Job's "comforters" (Eliphaz, Bildad, and Zophar) offer to help him. Their words of comfort may attempt to end the mourning Job experiences. However, their words have the opposite effect. Instead of liberating Job, they oppress him and perpetuate his mourning. Their poor comfort leads Job into deeper discontent. Exasperated, Job will exclaim, "You are miserable comforters, all of you!" (16:2).

Eliphaz speaks for the first time in Job 4–5. He is a Temanite and assesses life by what he can observe in the world. His viewpoint is not far from the wisdom of the book of Proverbs. His mode of analysis is *empirical*— that is, knowledge and wisdom about the nature of suffering come by what he observes in life. By Job 5, Eliphaz

CANONICAL CONNECTIONS

Job 3 and Genesis 1

Creation in Genesis 1:1–2:3	Job's Lament in Job 3
Day 1: light/darkness (Gen. 1:3–5)	Light/darkness (Job 3:4a)
Day 2: heaven (Gen. 1:6–8)	(Without parallel)
Day 3: land/vegetation (Gen. 1:9–13)	(Without parallel)
Day 4: lights (Gen. 1:14–19)	Darkness (Job 3:6)
Day 5: fish/birds (Gen. 1:20–23)	Leviathan (Job 3:8)
Day 6: humans (Gen. 1:26–31)	Perish at birth (Job 3:11)
Day 7: Sabbath (rest) (Gen. 2:1–3)	Peace of death (Job 3:13)

has encouraged Job in his piety, reminded him that no one can discern fully the ways of God, and suggested that if Job is that upset he should take his case to God in prayer (5:8). Finally, he connects suffering and divine correction: "Blessed is the one whom God corrects; so do not despise the discipline of the Almighty. For he wounds, but he also binds up; he injures, but his hands also heal" (5:17–18). Eliphaz's instruction sounds a good bit like Proverbs 3:12, where YHWH "disciplines those he loves." Although he assesses Job's situation by what he observes, he has *not* observed the heavenly scenes in Job 1–2. Eliphaz misapplies a proverb (a general truth garnered after lifelong reflection) and uses it as a specific rubric to assess Job's situation. Proverbs are meant to form character and wisdom; Eliphaz uses proverbial and retributive wisdom to evaluate Job's innocence or guilt.

Job responds to Eliphaz in chapters 6–7, affirming his innocence before YHWH. Job turns directly to YHWH in prayer: "If I have sinned, what have I done to you, you who see everything we do? Why have you made me your target? Have I become a burden to you? Why do you not pardon my offenses and forgive my sins? For I will soon lie down in the dust; you will search for me, but I will be no more" (7:20–21).

Bildad responds to Job in Job 8, unable to keep quiet over Job's complaint. Job's lament to God is unpalatable to him. Bildad argues that God is just, and so God justly punishes those who do evil. Job's children died as just punishment from God, Bildad argues (8:4), and if Job is not careful, he will be next! Bildad is harsher than Eliphaz, to say the least!

Job responds (Job 9–10) and affirms that God is just and right (9:1–13). No one is purely innocent before God. However, in this case, Job knows he is innocent of willful wrongdoing that warrants divine punishment. He challenges God to lay out the charges against him (10:2).

Zophar speaks in Job 11, and his perspective is highly theoretical: there are many sides to the issue (11:6), and God is unfathomable. Zophar affirms with Eliphaz and Bildad (and Job) that YHWH rightly punishes wicked people. But Zophar applies this truth to Job's situation and considers Job wicked (11:14). Moreover, Zophar says that when and if distress comes, and one is innocent, then the suffering will eventually pass (11:15–20). This is theory with no practical understanding of real suffering.

Job rebuts this argumentation as ridiculous. The issue is not that calamity will pass but that God has authored the calamity (12:7–25). By Job 13, Job prepares his "case," a legal disputation to God (13:18), and insists on "arguing" it (13:3, 15). He really wants to see God in person (13:15) so that he can speak to God and they can dialogue rather than his current experience, that of monologue (14:15). Job's longing for a call-and-response interaction foreshadows what he will experience in actuality later in the book.

SECOND AND THIRD SPEECH CYCLES: JOB 15–21 AND 22–27

■ READ JOB 16; 19; 21; 27 ■

The first speech cycle is followed by two more: Job 15–21 and Job 22–27. Whereas Job's friends began with gentle conversation, by the second and third speech cycles, they are increasingly indignant at Job's professed innocence and impudence. The fact that Job would like to speak to God or see him to plead his case is just too much for the friends. They are working on the assumption that if someone suffers, then God has laid it on them because of sin (cf. Lam. 3:39). Because Job is suffering, God has laid it on him because of some (unknown or unclear or unstated) sin. Job simply cannot understand that. Job says that if the roles were reversed, he would bring proper comfort as opposed to windy words that his friends are giving (16:2–5).

Job calls on his friends not to rebuke but rather to have pity on him. He argues that it is God who has struck him, for no good reason (19:21). Still Job expresses hope that his redeemer lives and in the end will rise on the earth, presumably to redeem, defend, and rescue Job from his plight (19:25–27). And it is Job's plea that God would stand before him, and he would see him with his eyes. This plea rhetorically functions to persuade God to act on Job's behalf, and it gives us information about his faith and hope.

WISDOM HYMN: JOB 28

■ READ JOB 28 ■

A hymn to wisdom in Job 28 interrupts the flow of the speech cycles in Job. The speaker of this poem is unknown. It does not appear to be Job. Rather, the poem is an insertion to the flow of the text that extols wisdom and affirms the difficulty of attaining it. As in Proverbs, wisdom is discerning the ways of God in all of life. Wisdom is the ability to discern the design of the universe that God has created. At the deepest level, wisdom is the ability to understand our world, how it fits together, and humanity's place in it. Those who acquire wisdom achieve success.

But, of course, wisdom is hard to find, and the difficulty of attaining it is the theme of the poem. People cannot find it; one cannot dig it out of the ground. The animals and ancients could not find it. God alone can find where wisdom dwells since he alone sees everything in heaven and earth (28:23). Wisdom's mystery belongs to God, who perceives and understands its end and beginning. If wisdom belongs to God, then it makes sense that a pursuit of wisdom is a pursuit of God. The poem concludes: "And he said to the human race, 'The fear of the Lord—that is wisdom, and to shun evil is understanding'" (28:28).

Wisdom and the Fear of the Lord

The declaration in Job 28:28 that the fear of the Lord is wisdom echoes other texts in the Writings (cf. Prov. 1:7; 9:10; 31:30; Eccles. 12:13). The fear of the Lord does not refer to terror but rather to the awe and reverence of God in all of life. Thus, fearing God in this way sets one on the path of wisdom.

How do we interpret Job 28? Does it serve as an antithesis to Job's questions about the divine order? If so, there is a dispute within the book about how the world works and how humanity should engage God in the light of its confusing realities. In this case, the poem is a corrective to Job's questions. Or does the poem encourage Job to trust in God, who holds wisdom and who knows the created order, despite divine inscrutability? In this case, the poem encourages rather than rebukes, inspiring trust in YHWH's care amid calamity. We prefer this second option without foreclosing on the first.

As a responsible human being, Job *should* trust in YHWH, even if he does not understand his situation. Why? Because Job 28 affirms there *is* order and direction in creation because God upholds the world. Even if the order is hidden to Job, it is not hidden to God. Of course, the problem with this interpretation is the hard reality of Job's present suffering, an existential threat that looms large and is in need of resolution. The divine wager at the beginning of the book is still not resolved either. The theme of divine inscrutability and human responsibility reappears in the whirlwind speeches of Job 38–41.

JOB'S FINAL SPEECHES: JOB 29–31

■ READ JOB 31 ■

Job offers his final defense in Job 29–31. Job remembers his life before disaster (Job 29) and contrasts that life with his present existence. He now is dishonored, disgraced, and downcast. God does not listen to him, and his body is wasting away (Job 30). Finally, he argues for his innocence, listing the ways he has upheld devotion to YHWH by living a way that is honest, true, and faithful. He feels so strongly, his concluding words are almost introspective as he pleads for God to hear his defense: "Oh, that I had someone to hear me! I sign now my defense—let the Almighty answer me; let my accuser put his indictment in writing. Surely I would wear it on my shoulder, I would put it on like a crown. I would give him an account of my every step; I would present it to him as to a ruler" (31:35–37).

ELIHU'S SPEECHES: JOB 32–37

■ READ JOB 32–35 ■

Although Job's friends no longer speak in the book, in Job 32–37 a new character appears: Elihu. He has not been introduced prior to this point in the book, and we do not know what to do with him as he speaks. It is as if this final soliloquy signals an end to the speeches of outside voices in the earthy scenes.

God will show up in Job 38–41, but before he does, Elihu stands up and (impetuously?) defends God. A young man, Elihu appears as if he has been sitting around, not as a comforter to Job but rather as a bystander. In Job 32–33 Elihu attacks Job's comforters for not putting Job in his place theologically. He also critiques Job for a lack of theological understanding of justice. In Job 34 Elihu defends God's government of the universe. In Job 35, Elihu dismisses the notion that God will appear to Job, as Job stated of YHWH (19:25–27). And then finally, in Job 36–37, Elihu describes God, providence, and God's wonders of creation. He is a bit of a young blowhard. He rebukes Job's friends.

He rebukes Job. He speaks for God and declares the mysteries of God are clear and comprehensible. Readers know, as Job does, that things are infinitely more complex than Elihu describes them.

Even more troubling, Elihu, with all his bravado, claims to speak under divine inspiration (32:8), as the Spirit of God has given him understanding. However, nothing in the text confirms Elihu's claim. Elihu's words do

Figure 19.4. *Job and His Friends* by Kristian Zahrtmann (1887)

not conform to traditional prophetic speech where the "word of the LORD came upon X," as we have seen with the Prophets. He claims to speak for God and enjoy divine understanding regarding Job's situation, but what he says in his speeches does not comport with the reality of Job's experience. Elihu claims too much.

GOD'S SPEECHES: JOB 38–41

■ READ JOB 38–41 ■

From Elihu's speeches, the poetry transitions to God's speech in two soliloquies. Throughout the speech cycles, Job pleaded for God to show up, to hear him, and to answer his prayers (9:32–35; 10:2–22; 13:17–28; 14:1–22; 17:3; 30:20; 31:35–37). Now God does just that: he answers Job. YHWH says, "Who is this that obscures my plans with words without knowledge?

"After these also, Eliu, a younger person, is joined to them in their reproaches of blessed Job. In his person is represented a class of teachers, who are faithful, but yet arrogant. Nor do we easily understand his words, unless we consider them by the help of the subsequent reproof of the Lord."[e]

Behemoth and Leviathan

These two creatures are interpreted as primordial beasts in the ancient literature. For instance, in 2 Esdras 6:49–52, the creatures are said to be created by God on the fifth day of creation. Behemoth is associated with the land and Leviathan with the sea. In later rabbinic literature, particularly the Babylonian Talmud, Baba Batra 75a–b, the beasts are killed and served as the banqueting meat at the messianic banquet. Modern scholars associate them with the hippo (Behemoth) and crocodile (Leviathan).

Figure 19.5. *Gathering Storm* by Georges Michel (1830–39)

Brace yourself like a man; I will question you, and you shall answer me" (38:2–3).

The speeches, then, should respond to Job's questions and pain, at least in the perspective of the reader. But the reader's point of view might not be shared by YHWH! In the first speech (Job 38–39) God speaks to Job about the marvels of animate and inanimate creation. In Job 40–41, God describes the two great powers (Behemoth and Leviathan), asking if Job can subdue them or understand them. The poetry is grand and majestic, and God speaks directly to Job "out of the storm" (38:1). This is another example of a theophany in the Old Testament, a visible manifestation of the divine, apprehensible by human senses. 👥

Why does God speak from the storm? On the one hand, the storm is a powerful analogy to Job's life. The storm created Job's first experience of loss in Job 1. His children were killed by a mighty wind, and his flocks and wealth were taken as well. His experience is tumultuous and terrifying. So Job is facing a storm of life, literally, when God shows up in the storm. On the other hand, the storm is not just an analogy of Job's experience. In the Old Testament, the storm is the place where God works and speaks, as at Mount Sinai (Exod. 19). In Old Testament theophanies like Job 38–41, storm, thunder, and lightning often accompany God's presence, and thunder and lightning are heard as the very voice of God, as in the Sinai theophany. The storm, although terrifying, also indicates divine presence and divine speech. God speaks in and through the storm.

On the face of it, God's response is somewhat dissatisfying. He does not provide a point-by-point rebuttal of Job's claims. Nor does YHWH offer a clear response to Job's questions from earlier in the speech cycles. Instead, God redirects Job to the order and direction of creation and the authority and control YHWH holds over the created order. He asks a series of rhetorical questions throughout the divine speeches: Was Job present at creation (38:4)? Does Job understand how the constellations cohere (38:32–33)? Can

Job divine the mysteries of the world or hold the world together? These questions anticipate a negative response: there is no way that Job knows what God knows. Job responds to God's first speech: "I am unworthy—how can I reply to you? I put my hand over my mouth. I spoke once, but I have no answer—twice, but I will say no more" (40:4–5).

Despite Job's declaration, YHWH speaks again. This second speech exposes even more of Job's limited perspective, his partial knowledge of God, and his lack of understanding of divine control over creation. YHWH knows the ways of Behemoth and Leviathan, two beasts that could be interpreted as two great primordial beasts of creation or as a hippopotamus and a crocodile. Either way, YHWH demonstrates Job's lack of understanding of their ways and contrasts that with

Figure 19.6. *Behemoth and Leviathan* by William Blake (1825, reprinted 1874)

his own divine knowledge of their ways. Of course, Job could not know these things! Job is human, but God is divine. His perspective and control are limited, while YHWH's knowledge and control are limitless.

JOB'S RESPONSE: JOB 42:1–6

■ READ JOB 42 ■

By the end of the speeches, Job responds to God in chapter 42. In verses 1–6, Job has come to a deeper understanding of his situation, but more specifically, he has come to a deeper trust in YHWH. He gains two specific insights from God's speeches: the first is the wonders in creation that come from the hand of God (v. 3), and the second is a deeper understanding of God's perspective (v. 5). When all is said and done, Job is satisfied with God's address to him, even if modern readers have more questions.

But what do we make of the key verse of Job 42:6: "Therefore I despise myself and repent in dust and ashes," as translated in the NIV? On the face of it, it sounds as though Job repents of some unspecified sin and remains in dust and ashes, perpetuating a kind of mourning.

The problem connecting Job's repentance and some kind of sin is that it does not follow the grammar or semantics of

THEOLOGICAL ISSUES

Why Does Job Repent?

Both Jewish and Christian tradition have questioned the nature of Job's repentance in Job 42:6. Jewish scholar Tur-Sinai indicates Job has sinned and repents of "unjust words and unjust thoughts."[f] What those words and thoughts could have been, however, is unclear. Others believe Job repents of false pride, elevating his just grievances above his trust in God.[g] Job's repentance, however, may have nothing to do with sin at all.

the Hebrew very well. And from the standpoint of the book, leaving Job in mourning creates problems. If Job's plea is to move *out* of mourning, then God's speeches perpetuate his ritual state rather than leading him out of it.

More than that, this interpretation creates a real problem in the book: God has allowed the *satan* to afflict Job, and as a result, Job sins against God and needs to repent. If this is true, then the *satan* has won the wager begun in the prologue, and YHWH has lost. Thus, we tend to push against this interpretation. Rather, we believe the verse indicates Job's movement out of the mourning ritual.

Following the logic of Hebrew grammar and semantics, the verse in question should be translated "Therefore, I reject and am comforted regarding dust and ashes."[3] The NIV translation, then, is probably not the best. The meaning of the verse, in paraphrase, is as follows: "[On account of God's revelation that he affirmed in 42:2–5,] Job says, 'I reject and I am comforted regarding the mourning process I have undergone. I can now move to a renewed sense of life.'" In this interpretation, Job refuses mourning and turns away from it. He is "comforted." Job's declaration of comfort represents both a rejection of mourning and movement toward a renewed vitality in life.

Epilogue—The Restoration of Job: Job 42:7–17

The narrative epilogue in Job 42 complements the prologue. Worship, eating, and sex reappear, behaviors seen in the prologue. Note the concentric pattern: eating (1:4, 13 // 42:11); sacrifice, prayer, and worship (1:5, 20–21 // 42:8–10); livestock and children (1:2–3 // 42:12–15); health lost and regained (2:7–8 // 42:16). When understood in light of the mourning ritual identified above, these behaviors reflect a movement out of mourning into restored joy. God's presence has provided for Job what both Job's friends and Elihu could not provide: a way out of mourning into renewed life.

We also see God castigate Job's friends. In Job 42:8 YHWH states he is angry with Job's friends for not speaking the truth about him. The Hebrew text of this verse indicates that it is not the content of the friends' speeches that is particularly offensive to God. Rather, the problem is that they spoke *about* God, but Job spoke *to* God. Job is the only character in the book who speaks directly to God: Job prays to God directly (e.g., 9:32–35; 10:2–22; 13:17–28; 14:1–22; 17:3; 30:20; 31:35–37). In this we find a major emphasis on prayer in the book. Like all humans, Job does not know everything about God or about his situation, but when he prays, God shows up.

Above all, God's knowledge of the entire situation is affirmed but nonetheless mysterious for humans. The wisdom poem (Job 28) and whirlwind speeches (Job 38–41) indicate that the majesty, wisdom, and knowledge of God go beyond normal human understanding. But fear of God remains the key to any human understanding (e.g., 28:28). Although God's world is created and orderly (at least in the whirlwind speeches), the text provides at best an indirect response to queries raised by Job, his friends, or the reader—questions such as, What is humanity? Is the world sensible and ordered? Do the righteous suffer in vain? How should the righteous respond to suffering? Is God just in his dealings with the world? Will the righteous always be blessed and the wicked always be punished? Where is God in suffering? What constitutes truthful speech in a time of trouble? These questions are interrelated and demand attention; attempts to encapsulate the meaning of Job within only one of them will prove deficient. Further, indirect response (or perhaps nonresponse) to these questions does not imply the futility of human understanding but elicits deeper reflection on God and his ways with humanity in his ordered creation.

Figure 19.7. *Printed Book of Hours* (folio 78r, Job) by Guillaume le Rouge (1510)

The logic of this remains sensible in that it provides a wisdom theology deeply invested in the ambiguities of existence, and it refuses to provide easy or rationally simplistic answers to difficult and profound issues of the human condition. The epilogue cannot suffice for either a denouement or resolution to a tragic situation. Why? Because Job's children still are dead. Although he gains more wealth and has more children, this is not a story of "All's well that ends well." Only a heartless person would call new children suitable replacements for those who have died. Rather, it is better to understand the epilogue as marking Job's restoration to renewed life out of the symbolic death of mourning.

Implementation—Reading Job as Christian Scripture Today

Job does not reveal the mysteries of divine justice and human suffering, at least not in full. The book goes so far as to say that God is in control and has wisdom beyond human understanding. The book confirms that God holds the mysteries of human pain. However, there is so much that the book does not explain, or explain fully. Readers understand that God has allowed the heavenly wager with the *satan* to go forward, but we do not fully understand why. From the epilogue, we know that Job has remained faithful to YHWH, YHWH is proved right, and the *satan* is wrong. In this sense, God has created a good moral order.

Job teaches what it looks like to follow God even when life becomes unbearably confusing, unimaginably painful, and horribly cold. It does not offer the "whys" of human experience (the direction of explanation Zophar, Bildad, and Eliphaz take) as much as it provides a way to understand the "hows" of bearing up and surviving when life gets extreme.

The book of Job offers a pathway for hope. Job moves from faith to deeper faith in and through prayer. Job is the only one who prays in the book. He prays in the prologue, interceding for his children. He prays in the speech cycles, in contrast to his friends. He prays to God for relief, help, explanation, and presence. And God does provide divine presence in the midst of his suffering. From this experience, Job is satisfied and can move out of mourning. It is Job's prayers that YHWH extols to Job's friends, who did not pray at all in the book (Job 42:7–8). Prayer is the first and best reflex when life turns upside down. Prayer is an affirmation of trust in God even as the petitioner questions, cries, pleads, and protests divine action. Prayer is offered to God from the perspective of human experience in the hopes that God will hear and respond with a divine perspective.

The exemplary faith of Job and his innocent suffering, as well as the text's depiction of him as a person of prayer, prefigure the life of Jesus and the life of faith. Job's prayers throughout the book anticipate the prayer life of Jesus. Job's prayers in unimaginable suffering prepare us for Jesus's prayers in the garden of Gethsemane (Matt. 26:36–46) and his prayers from the cross (27:45–50). Gregory the Great sees God's declaration in Job 1:8 as a type of Jesus's purity and righteousness, echoing the language of Isaiah 53:9.[4] Job, then, serves as an exemplar of faith and blamelessness that will be fulfilled in Jesus's faith and blamelessness. Moreover, Job's innocent suffering anticipates Jesus's innocent suffering. Although undeserving of affliction, Jesus bears it as does Job. However, the contrast between Job and Jesus is crucial: Job's suffering and vindication does not mediate for his friends; Jesus's suffering and vindication mediates forgiveness for the world. In all, Job prepares us for Jesus. It is no wonder that theologian Karl Barth describes the Old Testament as a kind of prototype for Jesus. In its story, we see the Christ. 👥 -

Christian Reading Questions

1. What is a frame narrative, and how does it function in the book of Job?

2. What is the mourning ritual, and how does it affect the interpretation of the book?

3. What do each of the friends argue in their speeches to Job? Are they the same arguments, or are they different?

4. What does the book of Job contribute to the idea of spiritual formation?

5. How can we read the book of Job as Christian Scripture? In what ways does it inform our understanding of Jesus in the New Testament?

CHAPTER TWENTY

Proverbs

Orientation

The book of Proverbs is a collection of sayings, aphorisms, and poetry exploring what it means to navigate life with wisdom. The book is an edited composition. Its introduction associates the proverbs (Hebrew *meshalim*) with Solomon, son of David (Prov. 1:1), affording authority and royal identity to the book (see how he is identified with the wisdom sayings in two other places in the book, 10:1; 25:1). Solomon is known in the biblical material for his wisdom (1 Kings 5:12), even if he is a complex figure in the Old Testament.[1] So it is unsurprising that the book derives in some manner from Solomon, the son of David.

It might be tempting to exclude Proverbs from the redemptive story of the Old Testament, particularly the covenantal development from creation (Gen. 1–2) to Noah (Gen. 6–9) to Abraham (Gen. 12, 15, 18, 24) to Israel (Exodus–Deuteronomy) to David (2 Sam. 7) to the new covenant (Jer. 31). After all, the themes of covenant or redemption, the stories of the exodus from Egypt, or the events from the wilderness to the promised land do not seem to appear in the pages of Proverbs.

However, it is vital to read this book in the context of the Old Testament's covenant story. The reason is simple: the canon invites us to do so. The association of Solomon with Proverbs links the book to royal wisdom and the Davidic covenant. More importantly, in Proverbs wisdom begins and ends with the fear of YHWH, the covenant Lord of Israel. Thus, Proverbs should not be loosened from this theological mooring if we want to understand it rightly.

Proverbs contains wisdom, or at least the influence of wisdom, from other sources, including Egyptian wisdom and wisdom of men named Agur and Lemuel, but this does not detract from the theological vision that Proverbs offers. And theological vision is what is offered in Proverbs: the vision of a life lived along the grain of the universe. But how is a life of wisdom achieved? In short: the fear of YHWH (Prov. 1:7; 9:10; 31:30). 📖 📖

Figure 20.1. Egyptian scribe

Exploration—Reading Proverbs

Proverbs is designed to enculturate its hearers to wisdom. Proverbs 1:2–7, the introduction to the book, reminds its hearers that those who are inexperienced may gain wisdom, and those who are wise can be wiser still. The ability to tease out riddles, gain insight, enact justice and prudence, exert discretion, and then grow in these skills is available to those who read and embrace the book of Proverbs.

The culmination to the book's introduction is Proverbs 1:7, which teaches that there is a foundation to wisdom, and it is "the fear of the LORD." Proverbs 9:10 returns to this idea, and Proverbs 31:30 closes the book with a focus on fearing the Lord. Without this foundation, one cannot be wise or grow in wisdom.

But "the fear of the LORD" is also the beginning point and returning point of wisdom. That is to say, if one wants to *begin* on the journey toward wisdom, then one must start with fearing God. If one wants to *advance* in wisdom in the journey of life, then one must return to the fear of the Lord again and again. Fear of the Lord is not simply an idea; it is a journey of discovery in relationship with the creator God as one pursues wisdom.[2]

With this foundation in mind, we can ask the basic question, What does it mean to fear the Lord? Fearing God does not mean to live in terror of the divine, wondering if God is going to get us whenever we do something wrong. Rather, fearing the Lord is gaining an ever-deepening sense of the God-ness of God, who is creator, sustainer, and redeemer. Fearing the Lord means living

HISTORICAL MATTERS

Proverbs and Egyptian Wisdom

Proverbs has a section of wisdom sayings known as the thirty sayings of the wise (Prov. 22:17–24:22). This collection displays striking similarities to the Egyptian wisdom text Instruction of Amenemope (ca. 1100–1000 BC). This leads some to argue that the Instruction of Amenemope has either influenced the thirty sayings or been incorporated into the biblical text. With the thirty sayings of the wise mentioned in Proverbs 22:20, it is interesting that the Instruction of Amenemope contains thirty chapters![a]

LITERARY NOTES

Inclusio in Hebrew Poetry

Proverbs emphasizes the fear of YHWH as being central to wisdom. This emphasis is evident in the structure of the book. Repetition is central to understanding how biblical texts mean, especially poetic books. When certain themes, phrases, or ideas repeat at key junctures in the book, then we have a sense that the repetition is there to guide us in what is important to remember. "The fear of YHWH" is repeated at key junctures in the book: to conclude the introduction and begin instruction on the world of wisdom and folly, to conclude the worldview section and introduce the pithy proverbs, and finally to conclude the book. We call this repetition an *inclusio* structure.

The Structure of Proverbs

in and returning to the awe and wonder of *this* God in all of life. Fearing God is not merely about attending religious services or reading the Bible or promising not to swear. Rather, it is discovering the presence of God in every sphere of life: home, work, agriculture, social spheres, economics, politics, and so on.

Proverbs trains its readers to discover and grow in what it means to be wise. Wisdom in Proverbs is a "totality concept," meaning that it touches everything in life.[3] But what is wisdom? Biblical wisdom is the ability or skill to navigate God's world in a way that accords with God's purposes and direction. Thus, wisdom should not be considered "secular," even if Proverbs deals with ordinary kinds of things: how to speak to others, how to cultivate the land, how to work hard, how to relate with others, how to be a friend, how to have integrity, how to live honestly, and how to avoid troubles. Often, we might think of these things as secular, but in Proverbs, these relate to living well before God. Everyday realities for Proverbs are bound up and held together in relationship with God, or "fearing" God. Because God has established everything by wisdom (8:22–31), everything matters to God. The very grain of the universe is shot through with the glories of God.

Biblical wisdom discerns general patterns to the good life and to an unhappy life, and it exhibits these patterns in general antitheses: the fool versus the wise, the greedy versus the generous, the righteous versus the wicked, the industrious versus the sluggard. These general patterns of life are important because they show how God has made the world and how God's ways produce good things in life. Further, biblical wisdom shows how these patterns can be traditionally taught, especially in a home setting: a father or mother teaches a child wisdom, and the child should listen to the parent who is wise.[4]

When Israel grows in wisdom, they grow in their understanding and skill to live along, rather than against, the grain of the universe. "Human wisdom is a correlate of the wisdom by which

Figure 20.2. *The Gleaners* by Jean-Francois Millet (1857)

the world has been made."[5] This truth about biblical wisdom reveals that all of life belongs to God and is holy, even if Proverbs does not generally address things we might consider more religious, such as sacrifice, temple, priesthood, and prophets.

Worldview and Wisdom: Proverbs 1–9

■ READ PROVERBS 1; 7–9 ■

Proverbs 1–9 introduces its hearers to wisdom by providing a general way of looking at the world. Proverbs 1–9 teaches that God has ordered the world in such a way that pursuing wisdom leads to life, but pursuing folly (some translations render the Hebrew with "fool" or "foolishness") leads to death.

This general worldview of Proverbs 1–9 is the kind of instruction a parent might offer a child. The instruction in this section sets boundaries and introduces its hearer to the world of opportunity. In a real sense, the child being instructed in wisdom is a naive youth (called the "simple"; e.g., 7:7) who needs to grow in wisdom and understand the way of the world.

To instruct with clarity, Proverbs 1–9 intro-duces the child to three governing metaphors: (1) two ways—namely, the path of life (wis-dom) and the path of death (folly); (2) the two women—namely, Lady Wisdom and Lady Folly; and (3) the two houses—namely, the house of wisdom and the house of folly. From these meta-phors, the reader can envision, in practical terms, what it might look like to be wise or to be a fool.

The metaphors of two women, Lady Wisdom and Lady Folly, are really **personifications**, where an inanimate object or concept is given human features or characteristics. In this case, foolishness and wisdom are portrayed as women. These la-dies take their stand in the markets and gates and in the city, calling out to the simple youths. Lady Wisdom invites the simple youths to take her path, to inhabit her house, and to dine with her. Lady Folly does the same. Each woman appears

Figure 20.3. *Wisdom Hath Builded Her House* by Novgorod (1548)

to make her call from the same places. And they make the same call to the simple: follow me, and I will give you the good life. Lady Wisdom's words are proved true: those who find wisdom find life and God's favor. Those who reject wisdom embrace death (Prov. 8:35–36). Lady Folly's promises, by contrast, are deceptive and death-dealing for the simple (7:21–22).

By polarizing wisdom and folly through these metaphors, the book shows youth (and readers of Proverbs) that wisdom is not simply about gaining information; wisdom is about life—embodied existence—in the real world of work, commerce, relationships, and politics. Wisdom is discovering *how* to live well in this world in a way that accords with the good life that God affords to those who fear him.

Proverbs and Wise Sayings: Proverbs 10–29

▓ READ PROVERBS 11–12; 19; 22; 24 ▓

Whereas Proverbs 1–9 introduces the reader to the *worldview* of wisdom, Proverbs 10–29 offers wise sayings that touch every aspect of life. Proverbs 10–15 gives basic patterns of what it means to live well, and Proverbs 16–29 exposes the contradictions in life. In this way, the book of Proverbs moves from (1) the general (Prov. 1–9) to (2) the more advanced and specific (Prov. 10–15) to (3) the most advanced, with contradictions (Prov. 16–29). Like any good instruction, an increasing scale of rigor marks the development of Proverbs.

Proverbs 10–29 introduces the reader to what we understand as "proverbs," short poetic sayings that give a general truth. The point of a proverb is to provide a truism about life in God's world so that we begin to understand how God has ordered the world in wisdom. Further, a proverb intends to build the character of its readers so they become wise. In Proverbs 10:4 (see the sidebar "What Is a Proverb?"), the goal of the proverb is to help readers understand that hard work is a gift from God and to form readers into people who value hard work and cast aside sloth. Character formation is essential for properly embodying the instruction of the proverbs.

Unsurprisingly, Proverbs 10–29 engages many of the challenges humans deal with in life. Many themes recur in these chapters:

Working in a way that is wise	Honesty and integrity in work
Speaking in a way that is wise	The virtue of a harmonious home

Gossip and slander as vice

Generosity as a virtue

Greed as a vice

The virtue of accepting correction and discipline

Lying and deception as vice, both in commerce and at home

The virtue of contentment and humility

The vice of pride

The virtue of peace

The vice of being quarrelsome

Of course, there are variations on these themes, and Proverbs 10–29 explores them in detail. 📖 📖

Some think Proverbs presents a naive view of retribution and reward: If people follow the instruction of YHWH, then they will experience blessing and prosperity. If people do *not* follow the instruction of YHWH, then they will experience curse and destitution. It is sometimes thought that the books of Job and Ecclesiastes give countertestimony to the naivety of this simple principle. Job shows that even if you follow YHWH, you might encounter disaster, and Ecclesiastes exposes the inner contradictions of life's search for meaning. In this way, Job and Ecclesiastes present traditional retributive wisdom in revolt.

This view, however, misunderstands the purpose of the book of Proverbs, which is *not* to provide a mechanistic or naive view of faithfulness and reward. Rather, Proverbs recognizes that not all people who are faithful to God will experience prosperity. Proverbs is not blind to the fact that some lazy people might be wealthy (especially if that wealth is inherited!). Rather, the purpose of Proverbs is to build and form a life of character and wisdom through the fear of YHWH. It presents a worldview of wisdom and invites its hearers to inhabit that house.

A key example of the complexity (rather than naivety) of the poetry is found in its contradictory proverbs. A striking example is Proverbs 26:4–5: "Do not answer a fool according to his folly, or you yourself will be just like him. Answer a fool according to his folly, or he will be wise in his own eyes."

Well, which is it? Should the person pursuing wisdom answer a fool or not? If we follow the idea that (1) proverbs are promises or (2) proverbs are naive presentations of retribution, then we run into serious problems with these verses. The reader is unable to decide what to do in the real world: if I answer a fool, then I will rightly rebuke him, but if I don't answer a fool, then I'll be like him! The text presents an impossible dilemma.

However, if the proverbs (even the contradictory proverbs) intend to build character and wisdom in the life of the YHWH-fearer, then one understands that sometimes it is wise to answer a fool and sometimes it is not. When does one know the difference? The wise will know! In this way, Proverbs provides a range of possible and appropriate actions in life without simple or mechanistic application. A person must go to school in the house of wisdom and continually grow and develop in understanding.

Growing in the school of wisdom means understanding the complexities of life and being able to evaluate lesser or greater goods. We see this point as well when we look at the seemingly contradictory proverbs regarding righteousness and prosperity and wickedness and destruction. The most common teaching in Proverbs is that righteous living brings the good life: "The integrity of the upright guides them, but the unfaithful are destroyed by their duplicity" (11:3). This antithesis is straightforward. However, note Proverbs 11:16: "A kindhearted woman gains honor, but ruthless men gain only wealth." Being kind brings honor and respect, but sometimes the opposite of being kind (being ruthless) brings a good (wealth), but of a lower quality than honor and respect. The problem is not with wealth per se. In the traditional teaching, diligence and wisdom bring prosperity, but in Proverbs 11:16 it is possible to affirm the complexities of life and assign different value to different goods. Wealth is valuable but not nearly as valuable as respect and honor. Dishonest gain is really no gain at all when one thinks hard about it.

Taking individual clusters of sayings together, Proverbs beckons its readers to absorb its wisdom *as a whole* rather than simply by a "verse-a-day" approach. The individual proverbs are incorporated into the full vision of the book, and then the individual proverbs are assessed alongside other proverbs in a never-ending recursive movement. Indeed, reading Proverbs ushers its reader to a lifetime of discovery (1:5).

Prayer of Agur: Proverbs 30

◼ READ PROVERBS 30 ◼

Proverbs 30 introduces us to an unknown figure named Agur, who is the son of Jakeh (30:1). We know nothing of this figure, but he speaks an "inspired utterance," phrasing that echoes prophetic language. The apparent point is that wise sayings derive from God just as do prophetic utterances. What follows is a series of reflections on the limits of human knowledge and understanding and the incomparability of the wisdom of God (30:1–6). Agur prays for contentment with moderation and truthfulness in his life (30:7–9) and then reflects on unethical behavior in life (30:10–14). The sayings of Agur conclude with a series of numerical proverbs about the created order, wisdom, and folly (30:15–33).

Conclusion—The Sayings of King Lemuel and the Song of the Valiant Woman: Proverbs 31

■ READ PROVERBS 31 ■

The book concludes with a royal instruction and a song. Following the wisdom of Agur in Proverbs 30, 31:1–9 presents the wisdom of another unknown figure: King Lemuel. Lemuel actually repeats divine wisdom his mother taught him (31:1), wisdom focused on the just and appropriate behavior of kings (31:2–9). The instruction of Lemuel's mother precedes the Song of the Valiant Woman (31:10–31), which schools all readers in wisdom.[6] This song is a hymn, of sorts, praising the valiant woman for the incredible industry and wisdom that she exhibits. She is extolled for her "noble character" (31:10), and the remainder of the song details what noble character looks like:

- working hard from morning to night
- evaluating good purchases and assessing the value of property
- being shrewd with resources
- providing for her family and household
- exhibiting generosity toward the destitute
- bringing honor to her family
- speaking with wisdom and faithful instruction
- engaging in profitable business

Proverbs 31:30 summarizes her character: "Charm is deceptive, and beauty is fleeting; but a woman who fears the Lord is to be praised." The woman's character in action shows fear of God to be a public demonstration of the awe and wonder of God in all of life. Wisdom touches every segment of human existence: family, community, government, commerce, and so on.

The identity of this woman has been a point of discussion for millennia. Jewish interpreters understood her to be the collective vison of the people

CANONICAL CONNECTIONS

Proverbs and Jesus

Jesus has adapted the doctrine of the two ways in Proverbs into the doctrine of the two "gates": one is wide, and its road leads to destruction (folly); the other is small, and its narrow road leads to life, where only few will enter (wisdom). "Enter through the narrow gate; for the gate is wide and the road is easy that leads to destruction, and there are many who take it. For the gate is narrow and the road is hard that leads to life, and there are few who find it" (Matt. 7:13–14 NRSV).

of Israel. Christian interpreters considered her to be the collective vision of the church. It is possible, however, to see this incredible woman as wisdom herself. Thus, when this woman embodies the virtues and values depicted throughout Proverbs 10–29, she personifies wisdom. Recent interpreters have understood this hymn to be a hymn to wisdom personified.[7] Too often Proverbs 31 has been narrowly applied to a woman's life of faith and relegated to special occasions in churches, such as Mother's Day, but there is good reason for women *and* men to embrace the holistic vision of life offered by the valiant woman!

Implementation—Reading Proverbs as Christian Scripture Today

While it is possible to embrace Proverbs as a text of biblical wisdom, it may be harder to view this text as Christian Scripture. However, there are several ways in which Proverbs connects to the Christian life.

First, Proverbs is God's wisdom for all of life. All of life belongs to God, and Proverbs provides pathways to live well in God's world. Thus, to read Proverbs is to grow in God's wisdom and to live along the grain of the universe. We can discover what it means to be wise and live well because God makes it possible when humans fear and follow the Lord.

Second, Jesus is an example of one who has gone to the house of wisdom. In his own teaching he embraces traditional wisdom teaching. People around Jesus recognized that he taught in parables, just as found in biblical wisdom (Matt. 13:1–52, esp. 13:3). Jesus also incorporates the basic antithetical teaching of wisdom and folly in his parables. In Jesus's parable of the wise and foolish builders, he reshapes the houses of wisdom and folly (Matt. 7:24–29). There was one builder who established his house on the sand (folly) and one who established his house on the rock (wisdom). When the storm came, the one who built on the rock saw his house remain and the other saw his house destroyed.

Jesus's teaching on wisdom and folly sharpens to a new focus in the Sermon on the Mount, as his teaching is oriented toward human flourishing.[8] This focus for wisdom is found in following and pursuing the way of Jesus, a way of life focused on God and his divine reign in Christ. This is the way

Figure 20.4. *Sermon on the Mount*, altarpiece in the Franciscan church of St. Francis Xavier in Zagreb, Croatia

to wisdom, life, and human flourishing (i.e., "the good life") rather than any other pursuit, which is folly. Jesus embodies and provides biblical wisdom that can be pursued and embraced. In this way, the doctrine of the two ways/houses/women in Proverbs prefigures Jesus and his teaching on the kingdom of God.

But Jesus is not just a wisdom teacher, and the Sermon on the Mount is not just a new wisdom text. The claim of the New Testament is much grander. Jesus is wisdom incarnate. He is the one who frustrates the wisdom of this world. In 1 Corinthians 1, Paul does not claim that Jesus is a sage, or a wisdom teacher; he is the very power and *wisdom* of God.

In Christian tradition, Jesus is both God (who is eternally Word/Logos with the Father and the Spirit) and the Son (who is eternally begotten). Christians recognize Jesus also is wisdom incarnate (Col. 1:15). Thus, the entire created order, following the logic of Proverbs 8:22, is made through the Son of God, Jesus the Messiah. Jesus is

THEOLOGICAL ISSUES

Christ, the Wisdom of God

"For since in the wisdom of God the world through its wisdom did not know him, God was pleased through the foolishness of what was preached to save those who believe. Jews demand signs and Greeks look for wisdom, but we preach Christ crucified: a stumbling block to Jews and foolishness to Gentiles, but to those whom God has called, both Jews and Greeks, Christ the power of God and the wisdom of God" (1 Cor. 1:21–24).

HISTORICAL MATTERS

Athenagoras of Athens on Jesus, the Son

"If in your great wisdom you would like to know what 'Son' means, I will tell you in a few brief words: it means that he is the first begotten of the Father. The term is used not because he came into existence (for God, who is eternal mind, had in himself his Word or Reason from the beginning, since he was eternally rational) but because he came forth to serve as Ideal Form and Energizing Power for everything material. . . . The prophetic Spirit also agrees with this account. 'For the Lord,' it says, 'made me the beginning of his ways for his works.' (Proverbs 8.22) Further, this same holy Spirit, which is active in those who speak prophetically, we regard as an effluence of God (cf. Wisdom 7.25) which flows forth from him and returns like a ray of the sun."[f]

the wisdom of God that confounds the wise of this world (1 Cor. 1:18–20). Moreover, recognizing the identity and mission of Jesus is tantamount to gaining wisdom, or having one's eyes "opened" (Luke 24:13–35, esp. v. 31).[9] This line of theological reasoning persists from the second century AD to the present.

KEY VERSES IN PROVERBS

- The fear of the Lord is the beginning of knowledge, but fools despise wisdom and instruction. 1:7
- The Lord brought me forth as the first of his works, before his deeds of old; I was formed long ages ago, at the very beginning, when the world came to be. 8:22–23
- The fear of the Lord is the beginning of wisdom, and knowledge of the Holy One is understanding. 9:10

Christian Reading Questions

1. What is the doctrine of the two ways in Proverbs, and how does this presentation of the doctrine serve the theology of the book?
2. What is biblical wisdom, and why is it essential for navigating life?
3. Do proverbs teach promises? Universal principles? Something else?
4. In what ways does Proverbs 8 relate to Jesus Christ in Christian tradition?

CHAPTER TWENTY-ONE

Ruth

Orientation

Long novels require patience. Plots and characters develop over time, thickening the story and the experience of the reader. But they require a high level of commitment. Readers must commit to the long haul and may discover something wonderful in the process—whether they read C. S. Lewis's Narnia series or classic novels such as Charles Dickens's *Bleak House* or John Steinbeck's *East of Eden*. Many generations of readers have experienced the joy and insight such novels can bring.

Short stories offer a different kind of reading experience than the novel. Because they are shorter, the complexity of their plots is limited. They are pithy and to the point, highly artistic and selective as the story drives toward its climax. O. Henry was the master of the twisted fate, evident in his "The Gift of the Magi," a moving tale about a young couple who sell their most precious possessions to give each other gifts. Edgar Allan Poe can make the hairs on your arms stand up straight. Flannery O'Connor's "A Good Man Is Hard to Find" has left many readers squirming in their seats. Short stories are clean and tight, but they can also leave readers with quite an impression.

The book of Ruth is a short story or novella of this type, and a marvelous one at that. The book follows Naomi and her daughter-in-law through great loss and suffering to redemption and resolution. Along the

> **CANONICAL CONNECTIONS**
>
> **The Canonical Location of Ruth**
>
> Much like its namesake, the book of Ruth can migrate in its location. In canonical traditions, the book falls in two places. In the English Bible tradition, Ruth is between Judges and Samuel, aligning with Ruth's historical setting in the time of the judges and before Israel's monarchy (Ruth 1:1). Ruth also links easily to Proverbs, and in the Hebrew Bible, it often follows Proverbs as the first book of the Megilloth (see chap. 17 above). Proverbs 31 describes the virtuous woman, and Boaz calls Ruth a "virtuous" woman in Ruth 3:11 (AT). Identifying Ruth as a primary example of the virtuous woman in Proverbs 31 comes as a bit of a gracious surprise, given her identity as a Moabite woman.

way, the foreigner Ruth becomes the direct ancestor of King David and, of course, King Jesus as well. The story has loss and suffering along with the beauty of loyalty and affection. The book of Ruth draws the reader in and captivates the imagination from the first scene to its last.

Exploration—Reading Ruth

The book of Ruth is like a four-act play that unfolds in four chapters. Each chapter carries the plot forward, complicating life for Naomi and Ruth and then moving them toward resolution and redemption.

Act 1—Disaster Strikes: Ruth 1

▓ READ RUTH 1 ▓

The book of Ruth forces its readers to face the hard providence of God. In the story's first act, a cascade of disaster befalls Naomi, Ruth's mother-in-law. As the book's central character, Naomi suffers what William Cowper describes as a "frowning providence."[1] A famine hit the land of Judah, and Naomi travels with her husband, Elimelek, and sons away from Bethlehem to the region of Moab. The story offers no assessment of Elimelek's

LITERARY NOTES

The Structure of Ruth

Chapter 1: Naomi's world turns upside down

Chapter 2: Ruth's happy providence

Chapter 3: An evening plan

Chapter 4: A marriage and a child: hope restored

HISTORICAL MATTERS

The Moabites

The Moabites are the descendants of Lot and are often depicted negatively in Scripture. Their chief god was Chemosh, and they were forbidden to enter the assembly of the Lord (Deut. 23:3). Genesis 19 traces the beginning of the Moabites to Lot's incestuous relations with his daughters. The word *mo'ab* means "from a father" and testifies to the nation's less than virtuous beginnings. Ruth's status as a Moabite woman speaks of God's great grace and redemptive power.

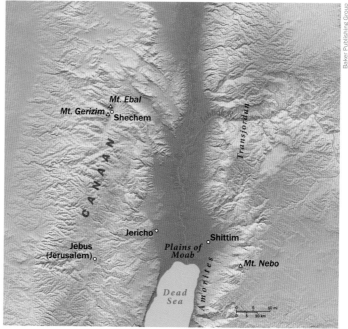
Figure 21.1. Map of the region of Moab and Israel

decision to leave Judah for Moab; the events that follow are not linked to this decision as an act of God's judgment. Nevertheless, what follows is a hard providence for Naomi: Elimelek dies in Moab, and Naomi's two sons also die, leaving as widows the Moabite women they had married. Naomi's situation is dire; a woman with no husband and no male offspring to support her was among the most vulnerable in the ancient world. To be "left without her two sons and her husband" was a devastating loss (1:5).

Naomi hears of God's provision back in the land of Bethlehem and decides to return home. Her Moabite daughters-in-law, Orpah and Ruth, intend to go with her, but Naomi urges both women to return to their homes. This is wise advice given the circumstances, but they do not want to leave her. In an emotional scene, Naomi argues that she is too old to have children, and even if she could, were they going to wait around until her new sons grew up? Her speech strikes a chord with Orpah, who returns to her familial roots. There is no reason to think ill of Orpah's decision. From a certain vantage point, she is certainly the more sensible of the two daughters-in-law. Yet it is her sensible act that provides such a contrast for the courage of Ruth, who demonstrates relentless loyalty to Naomi.

Ruth refuses to leave her mother-in-law, and in one of the greatest oaths of loyalty ever recorded in Scripture, Ruth claims, "Where you go I will go, and where you stay I will stay. Your people will be my people and your God my God. Where you die I will die, and there I will be buried. May the LORD deal with me, be it ever so severely, if even death separates you and me" (1:16–17).

When the penniless and vulnerable Naomi and Ruth arrive in Bethlehem, the whole town is abuzz. "Can this be Naomi?" the women of the town ask (1:19). Naomi answers, "Don't call me Naomi [my delight]. . . . Call me Mara [bitterness]. . . . I went away full, but the LORD has brought me back empty" (1:20–21). Naomi says she is not the same woman who left Bethlehem all those years ago with her husband and sons. Naomi is under the heavy hand of a frowning providence: "The LORD has afflicted me" (1:21).

Figure 21.2. *Ruth and Naomi* by Laurits Tuxen

RECEPTION HISTORY

Ruth and the Harvest

The first act in the book of Ruth concludes with a statement about the time of year Naomi and Ruth arrived back in Bethlehem. It was "the beginning of the barley harvest" (1:22 NRSV). In Jewish tradition, Ruth is read during the festival of Shavuot, a festival that combines the celebration of harvest and the giving of the law to Moses at Sinai. Shavuot highlights the link between the law and the land or between faithfulness and the gift of land, place, and sustenance.

Act 2—A "Chance" Encounter: Ruth 2

■ READ RUTH 2 ■

"As it turned out" (NIV) or "she happened to come upon" (ESV) marks the events of act 2 in the story of Ruth (2:3). The Hebrew of this verse is, roughly, "her chance chanced." The storyteller's point is straightforward: Ruth stumbles onto a field to glean without any prior knowledge of its owner or its significance. The narrator introduces Boaz in 2:1, giving the reader information Ruth does not yet have. Divine providence is moving over the waters of chaos to bring order and redemption to these two suffering women, Naomi and Ruth.

The economic system of ancient Israel was generous and, to borrow a phrase from Marilynne Robinson, had an open hand of generosity to the needy.[2] The law stipulated that fields should not be completely harvested but were to remain open at the edges so the needy could glean grain for their own subsistence. It was a remarkable system that both provided for the poor and protected their dignity at the same time; they had to come and work alongside the professional gleaners for their livelihood. Ruth is among the needy at the margins of the field, gleaning grain to keep herself and Naomi alive. Ruth works hard and garners the attention of the overseer and eventually of Boaz himself: "Who does that young woman belong to?" Boaz queries (2:5).

Boaz quickly moves into the position of Ruth's protector. While the story never clarifies the dangers posed to a young woman like Ruth in this time, it is highly suggestive. Boaz encourages Ruth to work in his field and his field alone. He presses her to stay close to the women in the field and gives explicit instruction for no man to "lay a hand on" her (2:9). He provides for her physical needs as well by giving her a free pass to the water jars and feeding her before the day ends. Naomi comments at the end of the chapter about the danger of being harmed in someone else's field (2:22). What becomes apparent is Ruth's courage. A young woman in an open field was a vulnerable target, but Ruth puts herself in harm's way for the sake of Naomi, and the Lord provides Ruth with a protector in a field she just "happened upon."

Boaz tells Ruth why he has taken an interest in her: "I've been told all about what you have done for your mother-in-law since the death of your husband" (2:11). Boaz understands the great risks Ruth has embraced for the sake of loyalty to Naomi. In response, he blesses her in the name of the Lord and provides for her material needs, even encouraging the young men to pull out extra for her when she gleans. When Ruth returns to Naomi that evening, carrying the abundance of her day's work, Naomi peppers her with questions. Where did you go today? How did you glean all of this? Ruth names Boaz as the source of this great kindness, and the wheels of the story

Figure 21.3. *Ruth in the Field with Boaz* by Julius Schnorr von Carolsfeld

begin to move toward their ultimate destination. The plot is set, and the characters are revealed. The Lord will show his great kindness to three principal actors: Naomi, Ruth, and Boaz.

Act 3—The Threshing Floor: Ruth 3

▓ READ RUTH 3 ▓

In chapter 3, Ruth's and Naomi's roles reverse. Ruth left her homeland in Moab, including the potential of a second marriage, as an act of loyalty to Naomi and, more importantly, Naomi's God. Now, Naomi plots how to care for Ruth: "My daughter, I must find a home for you, where you will be well provided for" (3:1). Naomi provides Ruth with her plan, and it is a risky one.

Ruth is to wash, perfume, and put on her best clothes and go to Boaz under the cover of night. After Boaz is well fed and filled with drink, Ruth positions herself at his feet while he sleeps on the threshing floor. The scene is provocative, and denying some level of romantic tension appears unwarranted. Ruth uncovers Boaz's feet in the night, the two of them alone with Ruth's perfume wafting through the air. The episode may be risqué but goes nowhere sexually. In retrospect it could not go in this direction. Both Boaz and Ruth are virtuous and act accordingly.

Public domain / Wikimedia Commons / National Gallery, London

HISTORICAL MATTERS

Pentateuchal Customs in Ruth

Naomi identifies Boaz as a *go'el*, one of their "guardian-redeemers" (NIV) or "kinsmen redeemers" (2:20). The term *go'el* comes with some mystery in Ruth. The word links to a tradition in Leviticus that designates a kinsman-redeemer as one who recovers family members sold into slavery because of their poverty (Lev. 25:47–55). In Deuteronomy, a "levirate marriage" (Deut. 25:5–10) obligates a widow's brother-in-law to marry her for the sake of providing her children. As the story of Ruth unfolds, the levirate tradition appears at play, though unlike anything that Deuteronomy suggests. Naomi is the widow in the family, and the application of levirate customs to Ruth is an extension of this law at best. These customs in chapter 2 and in chapter 4—where the nearer relative is told he will have to marry Ruth before he can claim Naomi's land—bespeak a network of customs known at the time but unknown to us. The *go'el* of Leviticus and the levirate marriage of Deuteronomy inform the book of Ruth, but they do so in ways that are indirect and unknown to us now.

Startled, Boaz awakens to discover a woman lying at his feet. "Who are you?" he asks. She responds, "I am your servant Ruth" (3:9). This exchange leads to a tender moment, in which Ruth makes herself available to Boaz in marriage and Boaz responds with the kindness, grace, and gratitude of a man overwhelmed by the Lord's blessing: "And now, my daughter, don't be afraid. I will do for you all you ask" (3:11). A blood relative with a closer claim on Naomi and Ruth lives in the region, and Boaz will have to address this potential hurdle, but as Naomi says at the end of the chapter, he will not rest until the matter is settled.

Act 4—A Deal, a Wedding, and a Child for Naomi: Ruth 4

■ READ RUTH 4 ■

The city gates were the business districts of ancient Israel. Boaz makes his way to this district, bringing along with him ten elders of the town. The setting feels official, and it is. Boaz addresses the other kinsman-redeemer (a character who remains unnamed), and he does so with the shrewdness of a deft deal-maker. He asks the man if he would like to claim Naomi's land. Well, who would not want land with its potential for capital return? The nearer relation says he'll take it. Then Boaz provides more context. The land comes along with a wife, and the implication of Boaz's words is, no wife, no land. And if you take the deal and Ruth has offspring, eventually the land will be theirs and no longer yours. The sweet deal does not appear as sweet anymore, and the nearer relation backs out. Boaz announces the final claims of the deal in front of the whole assembly. He will take the widow Ruth as his wife in order to carry on the family name.

Throughout, the book describes Ruth as a Moabite (1:22; 2:2, 6, 21; 4:5, 10). At the end, she is no longer described as a Moabite (4:13). Ruth is now Boaz's wife and a daughter of Judah, compared to Rachel and Leah in the blessing pronounced on her by the elders and the people of Bethlehem. Also, the story ends with Naomi holding Ruth's firstborn child, Obed. The women of the town bless Ruth for providing an offspring, and they bless Naomi by saying, "Naomi has a son!" (4:17). Naomi enters into the company of the barren women of the Old Testament: Sarah, Rebekah, Rachel, Hannah, and even Lady Zion (e.g., Isa. 54:1) are without hope in this world because their ability to bear offspring is hindered by age, health, or tragedy. Yet the Lord in his kindness grants all of them, even Lady Zion, offspring in a hopeless situation. Naomi's words to Ruth and Orpah

CANONICAL CONNECTIONS

Tamar, Naomi, Ruth, and Lady Wisdom

The elders of the city bless Boaz publicly by linking his union with Ruth to the offspring of Tamar and Judah. The story of Tamar and Judah in Genesis is a scandalous one (Gen. 38). Yet Tamar embodies the shrewd actions of Lady Wisdom much as Naomi and Ruth do in this story. By the women's actions, the providence of God works itself out in the history of redemption. God uses human agents in all of their brokenness to further his work in the world.

in chapter 1 ring true at every human level: "Even if I thought there was still hope for me . . ." (Ruth 1:12). She was without hope in this world. Now, with a child in Naomi's arms, the story ends with abundance of grace for Naomi.

Implementation—Reading Ruth as Christian Scripture Today

A narrative like Ruth is open to many layers of interpretation. The book and its main characters—David's direct ancestors—embody something of the exilic pattern that David's offspring will know in time under the Babylonians. Naomi and Ruth return from exile and experience the blessing of the Lord in dire circumstances. The narrative of Abraham also foreshadows this, as the founder of the nation wandered outside his homeland, trusting in the saving promises of the Lord.

Figure 21.4. *Naomi, Ruth and Obed* by Thomas Rooke

The principal agent of the story, however, is the Lord. God is the real actor as he demonstrates his loving-kindness (*hesed*) to Naomi, Ruth, and Boaz. He does so in the course of normal human affairs. Nothing miraculous occurs in this book in terms of the grandiose ceasing of normal acts of creation. The sun does not stop. Waters do not part. No axe heads float to the surface. Rather, we follow a woman who loses everything and in the face of her great loss receives loving-kindness from her daughter-in-law and from the Lord. How does God show his blessing? By ordering Naomi's steps back to her homeland and through the "chance" encounter Ruth has with Boaz, a kinsman-redeemer. God was orchestrating the whole affair, yet his view was not merely on the book's three main characters. The Lord had the whole of Judah's future in view. Even more broadly, the Lord had the redemption of the whole world in view.

The book ends with a genealogy that plays an important role in redemptive history. Through the course of humans' marrying and bearing children, God works out the redemption of his people and the whole world. The last word of the book is "David," and rightly so. David is Judah's greatest king and the instrument of promise for God's people. More than this, David's greater Son stands in view, even though history must wait for him. Yet even in the waiting, the Son's presence is already there in the figure of the great redeemer Boaz

The Heidelberg Catechism on Providence

27. Q. What do you understand by the providence of God?

A. God's providence is
his almighty and ever present power,
whereby, as with his hand, he still upholds
heaven and earth and all creatures,
and so governs them that
leaf and blade,
rain and drought,
fruitful and barren years,
food and drink,
health and sickness,
riches and poverty,
indeed, all things,
come to us not by chance
but by his fatherly hand.

28. Q. What does it benefit us to know
that God has created all things
and still upholds them by his providence?

A. We can be patient in adversity,
thankful in prosperity,
and with a view to the future
we can have a firm confidence
in our faithful God and Father
that no creature shall separate us
from his love;
for all creatures are so completely in his hand
that without his will
they cannot so much as move.[b]

and his great-grandson David, the king of Judah. How remarkable that the wheels of redemptive providence begin with a virtuous man noticing a foreign woman in his field and making sure she's taken care of.

KEY VERSES IN RUTH

- But Ruth replied, "Don't urge me to leave you or to turn back from you. Where you go I will go, and where you stay I will stay. Your people will be my people and your God my God. Where you die I will die, and there I will be buried. May the LORD deal with me, be it ever so severely, if even death separates you and me." When Naomi realized that Ruth was determined to go with her, she stopped urging her. 1:16–18
- So she went out, entered a field and began to glean behind the harvesters. As it turned out, she was working in a field belonging to Boaz, who was from the clan of Elimelek. 2:3
- The women said to Naomi: "Praise be to the LORD, who this day has not left you without a guardian-redeemer. May he become famous throughout Israel!" 4:14

Christian Reading Questions

1. What is providence, and how does the book of Ruth illustrate it?

2. Where does the book of Ruth appear in different canonical traditions? What accounts for these different orderings, and what is the significance of the differences?

3. How is God's grace on display with Ruth the Moabitess?

4. How does the book of Ruth fit within the larger frame of redemptive history?

CHAPTER TWENTY-TWO

Song of Songs

Orientation

Song of Songs has stunned readers for generations, both ancient and modern, its presence in the canon something of a shock. Its poems are filled with erotic imagery and energy, making the book something of a scandal.

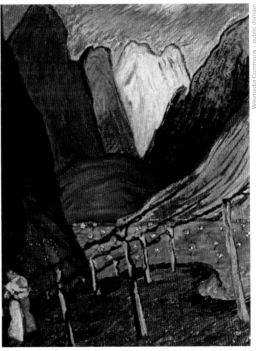

How does a book like this fit within the pages of Holy Scripture? Is the book about sex and young marital passion, or is there something more at play? Why does God not appear in the poems? All these questions and more have challenged interpreters for generations.

The book is titled "Song of Songs," and sometimes it is called "Song of Solomon" because of its first verse: "The Song of Songs, which is Solomon's" (Song 1:1, e.g., NRSV). The title "Song of Songs" shares something with another Solomonic theme from the book of Ecclesiastes: "vanity of vanities" (Eccles. 1:2, e.g., NRSV). In both these phrases, a singular noun (song, vanity)—is combined with a plural noun (songs, vanities). The grammatical force of this kind of phrase is elevation to a high status. This book is not merely a collection of songs; it is the "best of songs" or

Figure 22.1. *Lovers Vineyard* by Marianne von Werefkin (1915)

Wikimedia Commons / public domain

Bernard of Clairvaux on Love and the Song of Songs

"Here Love Speaks Everywhere!"

If anyone desires to grasp these writings, let him love! For anyone who does not love, it is vain to listen to this song of love—or to read it, for a cold heart cannot catch fire from its eloquence. The one who does not know Greek cannot understand Greek, nor can one ignorant of Latin understand another speaking Latin, etc. So, too, the language of love will be meaningless jangle, like sounding brass or tinkling cymbal, to anyone who does not love.[a]

Books Associated with Solomon

As we noted in the introduction to the Writings in chapter 17, the rabbinic and Christian traditions link Song of Songs with Proverbs and Ecclesiastes, the other two books associated with King Solomon. These three books reflect the various stages of King Solomon's life and wisdom. Within the Jewish tradition, Solomon writes Song of Songs as a young man, Proverbs in midlife, and Ecclesiastes as an elderly man: passion, wisdom, and reflection mark this pattern of personal development. The Christian tradition understands Proverbs as Solomon's first writing, Ecclesiastes as his second, and Song of Songs as his third. Proverbs brings with it the structure of a well-lived life; Ecclesiastes claims the limits of human wisdom; and Song of Songs reveals the heavenly life of song and love.

Lyrical Poetry

The poet Mary Oliver defines "lyrical poetry" as simple poems composed normally of no more than sixty lines with a single subject matter and single voice.[b] They tend to be highly personal and emotional. Theologian Robert Jenson describes Song of Songs as lyrical "sensual love poems."[c]

the "supreme song." Rabbi Akiva (ca. AD 100) calls Song of Songs the most sacred of all books in the Writings, identifying it as the holy of holies.[1] In a similar vein, the third-century theologian Origen claims, "Blessed too is he who enters holy places, but much more blessed is he who enters 'the Holy of Holies!' . . . Blessed likewise is he who understands songs and sings them,...but much more blessed is he who sings 'the Song of Songs.'"[2] Whatever one makes of these poems, both the Jewish and Christian interpretive traditions place a high value on them.

Song of Songs is poetry, but can we be more specific about the kind of literature it is? Some think it contains wedding songs, songs intended for use at wedding festivities. Others see a developing drama between two lovers, the Shulamite woman and a shepherd, with Solomon coming in as a third party like Don Juan seeking to bring the Shulamite woman into his herem.[3] Still others see a relation between these poems and pagan liturgies—namely, Song of Songs mimics poems for a love goddess. Most of these attempts fail at some level to hold the whole book together. A less ambitious but safer approach to identifying the literature of Song of Songs is that it is an anthology of sensual lyrical poetry.

The poems highlight the perspective of the female lover, though the male lover crafts his own perspective as well. The book begins, "Let him kiss me with the kisses of his mouth—for your love is more delightful than wine" (1:2). Readers immediately get a sense of the character and imagery of the poetic verse. The Song's simple poems link the natural world and the emotional/physical character of love. Wine both satisfies and intoxicates those who put their lips to it. So too the lover's kiss. The poems are lighthearted and expressive as the two young lovers wander the countryside together, their love playing out in the evocative scenes of the natural world around them. The poems offer a master class in metaphoric imagery. Plants and orchards, gazelles and sheep, gardens and grapes—all provide the poet with a rich palette for portraying the depth, beauty, and pure joy of young love. While older readers may roll their eyes at such sentimentality, the Scriptures do not. They celebrate the intensity of love and its erotic fulfillment.

Is Song of Songs Saying Something More?

Is Song of Songs about human love and sexual self-giving and satisfaction? Yes, but this "yes" has significant addendums attached to it. The poems, especially in their Jewish and Christian reception history, are not *merely* about human sexuality. The poems speak about human sexuality insofar as human sexuality touches something of the transcendent, something that goes beyond the physicality of human sex to the very love of God for his people. For centuries Jewish readers have understood Song of Songs primarily as love poetry between God and his chosen people, Israel, his bride. The Christian interpretive tradition follows this course by identifying the book's primary referent as Christ's love for his bride, the church. So, is the book about human love and sexuality, or is it about God's love shown in Christ for his church? Yes.

The nineteenth-century Scottish preacher Robert Murray M'Cheyne says, "There is no book of the Bible which affords a better test of the depth of a man's Christianity than the Song of Solomon."[4] For M'Cheyne, who represents something of the best of the Christian tradition, Christian faith is never merely intellectual or the assent of the will. It is highly affectionate and filled with wonder, praise, and adoration. All these elements ripple through the imagery of Song of Songs. The book is a collection of erotic lyrical poetry for sure, celebrating as it does the mysteries and profundities of human sexuality. At the same time, the book is so much more, just as human sexuality is so much more. The material things of poetry and sexuality touch on the transcendent. They witness beyond themselves to the depths of something more—or, better, Someone more.

When the Christian tradition extends these poems into the realm of Christ and his church or the affections of the Christian for Christ, they pull together the whole of the Christian Bible. Hosea was a prophet whose very existence embodied the dynamics of love, marriage, infidelity, and unrequited love. His words as well as his marriage to Gomer, along with all its relational complexity, spoke to the covenantal relationship between God and his people

THEOLOGICAL ISSUES

A Christian Sexual Ethic

A Christian sexual ethic rests on the assumption that sex has its origins in God's gracious and loving provision for humanity and the whole world. Christianity as a faith embraces the body and physicality. Far from encouraging an escapist faith that seeks to overcome human embodiment, Christianity understands creation and embodiment as a gift. This also leads to a fundamental Christian principle: our bodies are not detached from our identities, nor are they merely tools for human self-gratification. Human sexuality with all of its attendant pleasure becomes disordered and destructive when it occurs outside the created framework God intended in the marriage bed of a man and a woman.

Robert Murray M'Cheyne and the Song

Robert Murray M'Cheyne was among the great Scottish preachers of the early nineteenth century. His *Memoir and Remains* is a classic of Christian spirituality. In it are several sermons by M'Cheyne on Song of Songs. For M'Cheyne the poems in the Song reveal the depth of intimacy between the Christian and Jesus Christ. For example, in his sermon on the tender words of Song of Songs 2:3—"As the apple tree among the trees of the wood, so is my beloved among the sons" (KJV)—M'Cheyne discovers the following doctrine: "The believer is unspeakably precious in the eyes of Christ, and Christ is unspeakably precious in the eyes of the believer."[d] Readers gain a sense of the Christian interpretive move to associate the subject matter of these poems with the greatest of all loves, Christ and his people.

The Structure of Song of Songs

Song of Songs 1:2–6	Love's delight
Song of Songs 1:7–2:7	A lovers' dialogue
Song of Songs 2:8–17	Love's season
Song of Songs 3:1–5	Love lost and found
Song of Songs 3:6–11	Solomon's glory
Song of Songs 4:1–5:1	Love: A ripe and fruitful garden
Song of Songs 5:2–6:3	A lovers' dialogue
Song of Songs 6:4–6:12	The woman's beauty
Song of Songs 7:1–8:4	Consummated love
Song of Songs 8:5–14	Love's final thoughts

Genres of the Poems

Friedrich Horst provided specific categories or genres for the poems of Song of Songs. He calls them songs of yearning, self-description, tease, admiration, description of experience, description of physical charms, and boasting.[e] These categories may help when reading the poems, but it is good to remember that genres are constructs intended to serve reading/interpretation, not lord over it.

(Hosea 1–3; cf. Ezek. 16). Jesus himself honored marriage by attending a wedding in John 2 and beginning his public ministry there with the great miracle of turning water to wine. In the Bible, human love and sexuality in the bonds of marriage witness beyond themselves to God's transcendence and his great self-giving demonstrated in the life and death of his Son.

Exploration—Reading Song of Songs

The lyrical poems of Song of Songs are simple in their structure and streamlined in their theme. They celebrate love and especially the enthusiasm of young love. Rather than engage every poem, this chapter highlights just a few but encourages readers to explore them all.

Love's Delight: Song of Songs 1:2–6

■ READ SONG OF SONGS 1:2–6 ■

The first set of poems begins with yearning, particularly the yearning of the woman. Kisses and the bed chambers set the scene (1:2, 4). The senses are fully engaged. Love is better than the taste and experience of wine. Perfume wafts through the air. The setting evokes adoration and delight from other maidens attending in the background and interacting with the woman's language of love. She teases the king with self-deprecation, describing herself as "dark . . . yet lovely" (1:5). Unlike today where people pay to tan their bodies, in this era, a dark tan showed someone to be a common laborer. The woman makes use of the vineyard as a metaphor. While she worked in her brother's vineyard, she was unable to attend to her own vineyard—namely, her body. Naturally, the description of the woman's body as a vineyard or a garden elicits desire for the precious fruits of vineyards and gardens.

A Lovers' Dialogue: Song of Songs 1:7–2:7

▓ READ SONG OF SONGS 1:7–2:7 ▓

The second set of poems is a playful back-and-forth between the two lovers. She asks, "Where can I find you as you graze your flocks?" (see 1:7). He retorts, "Just follow the tracks of the sheep, most beautiful of women" (see 1:8). These poems are passionate and intimate. This is the language of the bedroom, the kind of communication best kept private. The man praises the woman's physical features, and the woman describes the alluring effects of her perfume, leading the man to lie in intimate repose with her (1:12–13). The poem moves back and forth between their praises of each other's physical charms.

The woman playfully describes herself as "a rose of Sharon, a lily of the valleys" (2:1), metaphors that suggest the woman's coy modesty. These flowers were "a dime a dozen." There was nothing special about them per se. Yet the man responds, "Like a lily among thorns is my darling among the young women" (2:2). In other words, you are no simple lily among a field of lilies. You are a singular flower among the thorns of all the other maidens: no one is like you. The poem ends with a sensual love scene, filled with the passion of the moment (2:3–6).

"Do not arouse or awaken love until it so desires," the woman charges the maidens (2:7). As the poems unfold, love becomes something of a personified agent (cf. 8:6). The woman speaks a word of wisdom here, and this charge carries throughout the poems (cf. 3:5; 8:4). Love follows its own course and cannot be artificially generated. When the timing is right and love has awakened, then the fruits of what she has experienced with the king are proper and in order. In other words, when love, whose true source is the Creator, follows its own course and its own proper timing and setting, then its delights are ordered toward their true purpose and meaning. Outside of love's created purpose, "aroused love" can lead to disorder and destruction. It is the awakening of love before it so desires. ⬆

Love, a Ripe and Fruitful Garden: Song of Songs 4:1–5:1

▓ READ SONG OF SONGS 4:1–5:1 ▓

The description of love and its delights in this poem is over the top yet endearing. "Your eyes behind your veil are doves" (4:1). "Your temples behind your veil are like the halves of a pomegranate" (4:3). The adulation is fawning yet sincere. "You are altogether beautiful, my darling; there is no flaw in you" (4:7). The poem ends

THEOLOGICAL ISSUES

C. S. Lewis on Disordered Love

C. S. Lewis's classic take on demons in *The Screwtape Letters* speaks to the devastating effects of disordered human love and sexuality on the Christian. When Uncle Screwtape writes to his nephew demon Wormwood, he warns the young demon not to allow the young Christian he is tempting to enjoy real pleasure—the kind of pleasure we see on display in Song of Songs—because "real pleasure" is the territory of the Enemy (God). Distorted pleasure is the territory of the demonic and the path to destruction.

Figure 22.2. Minstrel playing before King Solomon from the Rothschild Mahzor

with a walk through the garden as the lovers draw attention to all they see as fitting images of their love: choice fruits, cinnamon and spices, a flowing fountain (4:13–15). This poem is a smorgasbord of delightful images describing the passion of love.

Love in Full Bloom: Song of Songs 5:2–8:14

■ READ SONG OF SONGS 8:1–7 ■

Song of Songs ends with one of the greatest descriptions of love in all of literature: "Place me like a seal over your heart, like a seal on your arm; for love is as strong as death, its jealousy unyielding as the grave. It burns like blazing fire, like a mighty flame. Many waters cannot quench love; rivers cannot sweep it away. If one were to give all the wealth of one's house for love, it would be utterly scorned" (8:6–7). We can only begin to plumb the depths of this description here. These poetic verses of the Song are best memorized and sung, repeated and passed on to the next generation of lovers. Lovers seal each other's hearts and become enmeshed with each other's bodies. They become one flesh; their identity is no longer their own possession. Each individual's identity is bound up with the other. To speak of the one requires the presence of the other. Love is as strong as death. It is intense; it clarifies our finitude. The ending of love is like death; it is absolute. Love is zealous and refuses to yield. Graves do not relinquish their dead, and love holds on to its object with ferocity. "Love is not love which alters when it alterations finds," said the lofty Shakespeare.[5] Song of Songs could not agree more. Love burns. It consumes. It is an unquenchable flame. If a person stood before an offer of true love or the wealth of the world, only a fool would take the wealth.

Implementation—Reading Song of Songs as Christian Scripture Today

The subject matter of Song of Songs is love and all the attendant human experiences of it: anticipation, disorientation, delight, loss, reunion, and the thunder of sexual intimacy. This chapter offered a sampling of the poems in the Song.

The phrase "Do not arouse or awaken love until it so desires" is an elusive phrase yet appears with some frequency in the poems (2:7; 3:5; 8:4). We discussed it already in terms of love's proper place and order. The phrase presents love as a personified agent and highlights the importance of its time/timing. True love, marital love, takes time. Christian marriages are covenanted acts, including vows between the man and woman before a congregation including family, friends, and, most importantly, God. What these vows affirm is that marriages need time. What the Song of Songs demonstrates is that marital love is passionate and also complicated, unique to each couple as they seek to love and know the other as an act of loving and serving God. A dynamic relationship as profound and mysterious as marriage demands time: lots and lots of time.

A book like Song of Songs should be handled like a diamond—held to the sun to capture some of the ways it bends and refracts the light. The book's subject matter cannot be fully grasped, just like light cannot be grasped. It lets us know that the joys and losses of human love are real and concrete. They are grounded in the physical and emotional engagement of human lovers. At the same time, this love is caught up in something much more, something transcendent. To enter into true love and ordered sexual pleasure is to taste something of the divine. These human experiences are lightning flashes on a dark hillside revealing a glimpse of the great love God has shown to his people in Christ. This kind of love burns like an eternal flame.

KEY VERSES IN SONG OF SONGS

- Let him kiss me with the kisses of his mouth—for your love is more delightful than wine. 1:2
- Place me like a seal over your heart, like a seal on your arm; for love is as strong as death, its jealousy unyielding as the grave. It burns like blazing fire, like a mighty flame. Many waters cannot quench love; rivers cannot sweep it away. If one were to give all the wealth of one's house for love, it would be utterly scorned. 8:6–7

Christian Reading Questions

1. How does Song of Songs help us think about the relation between human sexuality and the divine?
2. How does properly ordered desire and pleasure operate in the Christian life? Why does Uncle Screwtape—the great demon mentor in C. S.

Lewis's *The Screwtape Letters*—see true pleasure as God's playing field, not his?

3. How does human, marital love witness to the greater love that Christ has for his church?

4. What is the significance of the phrase "Do not arouse or awaken love until it so desires"? How does such a phrase inform a Christian understanding of human love?

CHAPTER TWENTY-THREE

Ecclesiastes

Orientation

Ecclesiastes has historically been one of the more contested books of the Bible. Its difficulty does not lie with basic interpretive questions (though these exist), such as who wrote the book and when. The challenge of the book is its central claims and message, what the book is about. A range of options have been offered, some of which are not mutually exclusive and some of which are.

Does Ecclesiastes require its readers to join in its apparent contempt for this world, abandoning the goods of this world and instead longing for the "unseen and eternal" (cf. 2 Cor. 4:18)? Many within the Christian interpretive tradition read Ecclesiastes this way, including Origen and Jerome. Is Ecclesiastes the despair literature of the Bible? Did Solomon in his old age become someone like Franz Kafka or Albert Camus? Does the book reflect the absurdity of human existence, leaving readers adrift in terms of life's joys and purpose? Do Solomon and the German philosopher Friedrich Nietzsche shake hands in agreement over this book? Yes, indeed, Herr Nietzsche, the "nauseous" character of humanity's existence includes only pain and absurdity (cf. *The Birth of Tragedy*). Again, some think so. Could Solomon be a precursor to the great yet gloomy philosopher Arthur Schopenhauer? For Schopenhauer, the question "Is life worth living?"—a question asked by philosophers of all time—must be answered "No." Life is suffering. Full stop. Therefore, it is not worth living. Would the elder Solomon concur?

Figure 23.1. King Solomon as depicted on the ceiling of the Lutheran Ascension Church, Jerusalem

Does Ecclesiastes enter the ranks of the great pessimist tradition? Again, some think so.

The reading of Ecclesiastes here differs from the above options. Admittedly, Ecclesiastes is open to these reading strategies, but such readings focus on the book's clouds and not its silver lining. Ecclesiastes does contain dark, despairing clouds, but they are set against a bright backdrop that celebrates the goodness of God's creation and the freedom found in the fear of the Lord. Far from offering despair, Ecclesiastes speaks with the wisdom of an elder. It guides readers through the stormy seas of life while pointing out the safe harbors along the way. Readers of all time do well to engage Ecclesiastes and to engage it often.

Exploration—Reading Ecclesiastes

The Hebrew title of Ecclesiastes is *Qoheleth*, the word in the book's first verse that is often translated "Teacher" or "Preacher." *Qoheleth* stems from the Hebrew word for "assembly" or "gathering," and the basic term—*qahal*—is often translated as *ekklēsia* in Greek. Our English word "church" shares in this translation history. Thus, the English title of the book is Ecclesiastes, and the main speaker of the book is Qoheleth or one from the assembly who instructs the gathering. Solomon is not named in the first verse, but his presence is implied. Ecclesiastes is a book within the Solomonic tradition, with the aged son of David offering sage counsel to those wise enough to listen.

Part 1—Chasing Wind: Ecclesiastes 1–6

■ READ ECCLESIASTES 1–3; 5 ■

So much of the meaning of Ecclesiastes depends on the translation of the Hebrew word *hevel*. First appearing in Ecclesiastes 1:2, the word captures the book's purpose: "'Meaningless! Meaningless!' says the Teacher. 'Utterly meaningless! Everything is meaningless.'" The NIV's "meaningless" is the

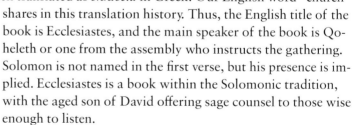

word *hevel*. Readers of almost every other translation will be familiar with the word "vanity." "Vanity of vanities" is a familiar phrase in the English-speaking world.

But what exactly does *hevel* mean? Answering this question is harder than it first appears. *Hevel* means "breath" or "wind." In Ecclesiastes it is a metaphor, and metaphors make translations difficult. Metaphors are suggestive and associative by their very nature, but a translation has to decide what they understand the metaphor to signify. Still, metaphors can be slippery when we try to nail them down to one thing. Qoheleth speaks clearly, even if painfully, about the incongruities of life. What we think about life—even the good life—does not always add up. Making sense of everything under the sun can lead a person to despair at the apparent "meaninglessness" of it all. This explains the NIV's choice of "meaningless" for the metaphor of "breath" or "wind."

The translation "meaningless" highlights something true about the book. It would be strange to say, "Wind of wind, everything is breath." No one would be sure what it means, so a translation that interprets the meaning is necessary. Both the content of Ecclesiastes as a whole and the metaphor of "breath" or "wind" are necessary for understanding what the book is about and what the term *hevel* suggests. The NIV settles on "meaningless."

We do not pretend to offer a final reading on Ecclesiastes. Nevertheless, considering the metaphor of *hevel* a bit more may be helpful. Consider "breath" or "smoke." (Smoke offers a helpful visual for what "breath" or "wind" are like.) What do these images bring to mind? What experiences do they suggest? Think of a kindly old man, sitting on a park bench with a lit cigar between his fingers. Watch him puff out that smoke, and watch it fade away. It is here, and then it is gone. What you see in your mind's eye with the man and his cigar is *hevel*. In this light, *hevel* illustrates two things: (1) the fleeting character of our lives and (2) our inability to grasp and understand life and to extract from it all it has to offer; it is like wind or smoke through our fingers.

While not exhaustive, this reading of *hevel* helps make sense of the book's brooding character. Life *is* fleeting, and the goods of this life do resist our taking hold of them. Even the meaning of life presents challenges for the human mind, especially when our brief existence is set against the enduring character of creation. Just think of the trees that were around before your grandparents and will be around long after your time as well. Those trees humble us. The moments of our lives come and go. Even when the good moments come, our ability to savor them confronts the limitations of our smoke-like existence. Life can run right through our hands. In

Figure 23.2. *Self Portrait with Vanitas Symbols* by David Bailly

Qoheleth's terms, "It's a chasing after the wind" (e.g., Eccles. 1:14). At its very basic level, *hevel* speaks to human limitations against the stable backdrop of creation and Israel's God, but it does not necessarily mean everything is meaningless. "Generations come and generations go, but the earth remains forever" (1:4).

Qoheleth aims at three particular targets where the *hevel* character of our existence is most evident: the search for wisdom, the toil of our hands, and the pleasures of this life. At the end of chapter 1 (1:12–18; cf. 2:12–17), Qoheleth describes his studious efforts to gain wisdom and knowledge. The Teacher devoted his rational faculties to understand the world, to categorize and differentiate all the varieties of matter and motion under the sun, and to gain expertise in the practical art of living well. Even though the king of Jerusalem increased in wisdom beyond all of his royal predecessors, he recognizes the limitations of his pursuit. If the wisdom of this world flows from the mind and intent of its Creator, then human beings will always face the limitations of their knowledge. Just when we think we understand the mechanisms and movements of this world, that knowledge becomes wind through the fingers: "For with much wisdom comes much sorrow; the more knowledge, the more grief" (1:18). This proverb from Qoheleth contains layers of truth. The more one knows, the more one recognizes what they do not yet know. The end of wisdom in Ecclesiastes is a recognition of human finitude.

RECEPTION HISTORY

From Womb to Tomb

The English poet and cleric John Donne (1572–1631) wrote,

> Earth is the womb from
>   whence all living came,
> So is't the tomb, all go unto
>   the same.[c]

The knowledge of our mortality and of life's fleeting character brings with it an existential weight for all who take the time to reflect on it. Wisdom does indeed bring sorrow and grief.

Qoheleth also laments the *hevel* nature of pleasure in this world (2:1–11). He gave himself to laughter, wine, possessions, and entertainment. Nothing in this list is inherently evil. In other words, Qoheleth is not describing a fraternity party gone wild per se, though excesses are imaginable. In fact, many of the pleasures he describes in chapter 2 will be praised later in the book as the reception of God's lot or portion in this life. What Qoheleth laments is the inability of pleasure to provide humans with ultimate satisfaction. Even these things are like smoke in the air. Even the good things of this world can leave us empty. "Laughter," Qoheleth says, "is madness" (2:2).

The Teacher of Ecclesiastes also laments the achievements of human labor or work as breath or smoke (2:17–23). He describes his work as *hevel* and grievous (2:17) because his work in the context of his finitude loses its luster and promise. All this building and making something out of nothing, all of this industry, will outlast me. Once I am gone, who then will oversee the labors of my fleeting life? There is no guarantee, Qoheleth laments, that person will be wise. In fact, they might be a fool (2:19). For Qoheleth, the weight of these truths—his *hevel* existence—leaves him with "grief and pain" (2:23).

Who does not sympathize with Qoheleth as he muses over these heavy facts of life under the sun? Scholars might give their whole career to a particular branch of knowledge, writing a summative piece of work in their field. They then place their research in a solitary place among the host of other books on the same subject either already written or waiting to be written. These kinds of thoughts—legitimate ones we might add—bring with them a heaviness. Novels are full of such figures like the lamentable Mr. Casaubon in *Middlemarch*, a pompous pseudoscholar whose magnum opus, *Key to Mythologies*, remains unfinished and unimportant at his death. Casaubon gives his every waking hour to a task that in retrospect impacts no one and means nothing. Readers of all ages do not have to work hard to feel the force of Qoheleth's lamentation. A man or woman gives their life to the building of a company or the creating of a product only to leave their life's work in the hands of another. There are no guarantees that the "another" has the skill or wisdom to carry on their life's work. These things are heavy.

THEOLOGICAL ISSUES

Arthur Schopenhauer and Ecclesiastes

Arthur Schopenhauer (1788–1860) was one of the most important philosophers of the nineteenth century. He understood the basic structures of the world in terms of will/desire and concluded that humanity is consigned to suffering because of this basic structure. Humans desire, and desire entails suffering. We suffer for lack of something we want. Yet, and here lies the cruelty of our world, when humans achieve that which they desire, they grow quickly bored with it. They recognize the desired thing does not live up to its promises: like a child the day after Christmas growing tired of their presents. In terms of Ecclesiastes, Schopenhauer is on to something about human existence, though his suggestions for how to escape this suffering differ radically from Qoheleth's.

Where does the full reality of *hevel* leave us? In despair? In a brooding sense of meaninglessness? Potentially yes. If people look at their lives within the framework of Qoheleth's understanding of *hevel*—and Qoheleth is most certainly right in what he claims—then despair or "meaninglessness" is a logical outcome. A whole sea of literature over the past century plus would concur. Nevertheless, Qoheleth does not leave us in despair. He leaves us with two monumental and life-altering truths, truths fit for those who believe in God as creator of heaven and earth.

First, Qoheleth moves us away from the despair over our pursuit of wisdom, pleasure, and work back to these very things understood as God's gift to us in our fleeting lives: "I know that there is nothing better for people than to be happy and to do good while they live. That each of them may eat and drink, and find satisfaction in all their toil—this is the gift of God" (Eccles. 3:12–13; cf. 2:24; 3:22).

Ecclesiastes 3 guides us through a tour de force of God's providence. "There is a time for everything, and a season for every activity under the heavens" (3:1). God's ordering of time and his governing purposes do not remove the sting of *hevel*. Finitude and the limitations of human capacity to grab hold of life force the faithful to refocus with some frequency: to cling to the purposes of God and embrace the good gifts he has given us in this life. In this respect, Qoheleth is so kind to his readers. He does not offer an escape from reality, but he shows God's kindness in the good gifts of this created world: a day on the lake, an evening out with friends, a walk-off home run in the ninth. Gifts, all of them. However, if we make these gifts final and ultimate, *hevel* bears down on us once again with all of its existential weight.

Second, in the light of *hevel*, Qoheleth brings God into central focus. Over against our finitude stands the eternality and magnitude of our heavenly Father. Fearing God—worshiping and serving him, ordering our existence in light of his being and his will—reveals humanity's reason for existence. As Ecclesiastes 3:11 reminds us, "He has also set eternity in the human heart."

"Much dreaming and many words are meaningless. Therefore fear God" (5:7). Qoheleth ends the whole book with a clear call to fear God; our attention will turn there in the next section (12:13–14). Yet the seeds for this epilogue are sown here in the first section. Without God in the world, *hevel* leaves us in meaningless absurdity. With God, however, our finitude is overshadowed by his being. God's good gifts— toil, pleasure, and wisdom—also take their proper role as means toward our final end, God himself. As Augustine famously says, "Our heart is restless until it rests in you."[1] We are restless in this world apart from God, and rest is only to be found in him.

Part 2—Human Limitations and Life's Greatest Good: Ecclesiastes 7–12

■ READ ECCLESIASTES 9–12 ■

The second half of Ecclesiastes elaborates on many themes of the first half. Qoheleth offers his wisdom on various matters in chapters 7–8, highlighting humanity's finitude in the process. All of us face death's chilling reality. No one escapes it, neither the wise nor the fool (9:1–10). Within the Christian tradition, the role of pastor and priest is aiding people in the "art of dying." The wise person lives in the full acknowledgment of their eventual death. In Ecclesiastes 9:11–11:6, Qoheleth offers more wisdom as he engages the incongruities of life. Life does not always make sense.

The book ends (11:7–12:14) by returning to the silver lining of *hevel*'s cloud: embrace life and fear God (cf. 5:7). "However many years anyone may live, let them enjoy them all" (11:8). Qoheleth encourages young men and women to "remember your Creator in the days of your youth" (12:1). Few instructions are better aimed at young people. If life is to be enjoyed, despite and in light of *hevel*, then our Creator must be in clear view. Otherwise, we are consigned to take God's good gifts and turn them into ultimate gifts, leaving us with smoke and wind. As Qoheleth concludes the whole book, "Now all has been heard; here is the conclusion of the matter: Fear God and keep his commandments, for this is the duty of all mankind. For God will bring every deed into judgment, including every hidden thing, whether it is good or evil" (12:13–14).

RECEPTION HISTORY

Meaning and Experience

"We had the experience but missed the meaning,
And approach to the meaning restores the experience
In a different form, beyond any meaning
We can assign to happiness."[e]

T. S. Eliot, *Four Quartets*

THEOLOGICAL ISSUES

Restless Hearts

In the opening paragraphs of *Confessions*, Augustine writes,

> You are mighty, Master, and to be praised with a powerful voice: great is your goodness, and of your wisdom there can be no reckoning. Yet to praise you is the desire of a human being, who is some part of what you created; a human hauling his deathliness in a circle, hauling in a circle the evidence of his sin, and the evidence that you stand against the arrogant.
>
> But still a mortal, a given portion of your creation, longs to extol you. In yourself you rouse us, giving us delight in glorifying you, because you made us with yourself as our goal, and our heart is restless until it rests in you.[f]

Implementation—Reading Ecclesiastes as Christian Scripture Today

The Christian tradition recognizes the limitations of human wisdom. The topsy-turvy world of Ecclesiastes is the very world the greatest Teacher, Jesus Christ, came to redeem. Early Christian approaches to Ecclesiastes identified the book's author as the king moving among his subjects, coming to understand their suffering. Jesus Christ in his incarnation moves among his people and comes to know their suffering and human limitations. The book of Hebrews says Jesus entered the school of human suffering in order to learn obedience and become a fitting High Priest for his people (Heb. 4:14–16). Jesus, therefore, is the embodiment of God's wisdom (1 Cor. 1:30) and brings the message of Ecclesiastes into proper focus. How a Christian lives and dies includes the full scope of life under the sun. For Christian faith, the question of living and dying begins and ends with the person and work of Jesus Christ.

THEOLOGICAL ISSUES

Feeling God's Pleasure

In the classic film *Chariots of Fire*, the great missionary Eric Liddell tells his concerned sister that God made him for a purpose, as a missionary to China. But God "also made me fast," he says, "and when I run, I feel his pleasure."[9]

Ecclesiastes forces humans to face our limitations and the certainty of our death. These, admittedly, are not happy topics, but they represent reality, and only fools avoid engaging them. In light of *hevel*, Ecclesiastes returns us to the good things of this earth as God's gifts. Embrace them, says the Preacher, and recognize in them God's kindness to us in this fallen world. These earthly pleasures are the legitimate gifts of God. Yet they are provisional and not final. They too are *hevel*. God, however, is not *hevel*. Fearing him and ordering our desires and affections toward him is the ultimate good. Only then can we know the purpose of our existence and find meaning. 🕮

KEY VERSES IN ECCLESIASTES

- Vanity of vanities, says the Teacher, vanity of vanities! All is vanity. 1:2 (NRSV)
- He has made everything beautiful in its time. 3:11
- This is what I have observed to be good: that it is appropriate for a person to eat, to drink and to find satisfaction in their toilsome labor under the sun during the few days of life God has given them—for this is their lot. Moreover, when God gives someone wealth and possessions, and the ability to enjoy them, to accept their lot and be happy in their toil—this is a gift of God. They seldom reflect on the days of their life, because God keeps them occupied with gladness of heart. 5:18–20
- Now all has been heard; here is the conclusion of the matter: Fear God and keep his commandments, for this is the duty of all mankind. For God will bring every deed into judgment, including every hidden thing, whether it is good or evil. 12:13–14

Christian Reading Questions

1. How can a book as brooding as Ecclesiastes be hopeful?
2. If life and what makes up a life are fleeting and ungraspable—breath and smoke—what gives humans any reason for living?
3. Ecclesiastes shows the limitations of wisdom, toil, and pleasure and then says they are God's good gifts. How do we make sense of this tension?
4. How does the person and work of Jesus, the great Teacher, redeem life lived under the sun?

CHAPTER TWENTY-FOUR

Lamentations

Orientation

If you invited all the books of the Bible to a dinner party, Lamentations would be the most difficult guest. How would you seat them in the room? Isaiah or Deuteronomy may get seats of honor, maybe Genesis as well. The other prophets would have their turn, Jeremiah to the left, Ezekiel to the right, but where to seat Lamentations? After all, *this* is the guest that would be howling in agony, covered in ashes, weeping uncontrollably, and leveling accusations against those who have caused hurt. Not an easy dinner . . . because Lamentations makes everyone uncomfortable.

This is because Lamentations *is* uncomfortable. Its poetry confronts its readers with pain and prayer. Its poets created a literary masterpiece that reflects, and reflects on, the horrors accompanying the desolation of Jerusalem in 586 BC. It wrestles theologically with that watershed event in which the Neo-Babylonian Empire destroyed Jerusalem and the surrounding environment, leaving a deep and abiding scar in the social memory of the people of God. Death, devastation, disease, and deprivation fill the pages of Lamentations.

Skilled poets crafted Lamentations sometime between 586 and 515 BC, just after Jerusalem had been sacked and obliterated by the Babylonians. The poems were a way for the remaining postwar Judahite people to relate to their God in a radically changed situation. Their religious center—the temple—was gone. Their leaders—prophets, priests, and king—were either dead, exiled, or impotent. And their social structure was strained as

LITERARY NOTES

The Structure of Lamentations

1. Zion's desolation, divine wrath, and Zion's prayer (Lam. 1–2)
2. The strongman's experience and communal prayer (Lam. 3)
3. Shame and sin (Lam. 4)
4. A community prayer (Lam. 5)

they lived under foreign occupation, first by Neo-Babylonia and then by Persia. Questions arise in this changed situation. How would life persist? How would they go on? How would they approach God—and themselves—in their humiliation, sin, and anger? 📖 📖 📖

Exploration—Reading Lamentations

Zion's Desolation, Divine Wrath, and Zion's Prayer: Lamentations 1–2

▨ READ LAMENTATIONS 1–2 ▨

The first two chapters of Lamentations introduce Lady Zion, or "the Daughter of Zion," who is one of the major speakers in the book. She introduces her experience in 1:9, 11–16, 18–22; 2:11, 20–22, and her voice continues in 2:20–22. The voice of a narrator in the first two chapters counterbalances that of Zion, commenting on her experience. Still, Zion is the central character in the first two poems as she cries out to God over her affliction.

Her words express her experience. She is the broken and battered voice of the mother of God's people. She cries out amid her suffering (1:9–13, 20) and experience of guilt (1:18). She prays and protests God's actions, calling out to him for the lives of her children and city (1:20–22; 2:20–22). She is fragmented and despondent.

As a whole, Lamentations 1 reveals the great reversal that overtakes the city and people of God. The reversal motif is common in **city laments**, and here Lamentations makes good use of it. Former glory to present shame is a common theme. This great reversal draws the reader's

Alphabetic Acrostic Structure

An alphabetic acrostic found in Lamentations 1–4 and the traces of an acrostic in Lamentations 5 structure the book. The first word of each verse in Lamentations 1, 2, and 4 begins with a successive letter of the Hebrew alphabet: *aleph, bet, gimel, dalet,* and so on. In Lamentations 3, sets of three lines begin with these successive letters: *aleph-aleph-aleph, bet-bet-bet,* and so on. And although Lamentations 5 does not follow this pattern, it has twenty-two lines, corresponding to the number of letters in the Hebrew alphabet.

Why the Acrostic Structure?

The alphabetic acrostic communicates comprehensive devastation. It expresses anguish "from A to Z." Because the poem moves through the alphabet, it resists pausing. The reader must keep moving: through *aleph,* then *bet, gimel,* and *dalet* until arriving at the Hebrew letter *taw.* This structure continues until Lamentations 5, which shatters the structure of the alphabetic acrostic, and only twenty-two lines remain. This poem is a communal prayer for help.

Figure 24.1. *Seated Nude* by Pablo Picasso (1909–10)

What Are City Laments?

Lamentations mourns the destruction and loss of the city of Jerusalem. Although not identical, Lamentations approximates Mesopotamian city laments. In these Mesopotamian laments, a patron deity (like the god Marduk in Babylon) could be defeated in battle by another deity (like the high god El), leading to the desecration and sacking of the patron god's shrine in the god's own city. Poets created city laments to commemorate the desecration of the shrine. The Lament for Ur, Lamentation for Sumer and Ur, the Lament for Nippur, and the Lament for Uruk are hallmark examples.[a] Similarly, Lamentations mourns the destruction of Jerusalem. Yet, despite destruction, Lamentations still points to hope in God. YHWH may have destroyed the city, but YHWH was not overpowered by another deity. YHWH takes away, and YHWH can restore.[b]

attention to two theological realities present in the poem: a theology of sin and punishment that is met with a theology of suffering.

SIN AND PUNISHMENT

A theology of sin and punishment, or retribution, is present in Lamentations 1, though some argue that sin is downplayed or even relatively insignificant in the book. Specifically, verses 5, 8–9, 14, 17–18 affirm that Zion's suffering is a result of divine punishment for her sin. The narrator says,

> Jerusalem has sinned greatly,
>   and so has become unclean.
> All who honored her despise her,
>   for they have all seen her naked;
> she herself groans
>   and turns away. (1:8)

Zion says,

> The LORD is righteous,
>   yet I rebelled against his command.
> Listen, all you peoples;
>   look on my suffering.
> My young men and young women
>   have gone into exile. (1:18)

This theology of divine retribution affirms Zion's sinfulness and the validity of divine punishment. This theme is so well attested in Lamentations 1 that it is reiterated in the reception of Lamentations in Jewish tradition. The midrash on Lamentations was composed by the sixth century AD to reinforce for the Jews that divine punishment over Israel's sin was entirely justified, and this theological perspective provided a way for the Jewish people to move forward with God. Although punishment was necessary according to the midrash, repentance and obedience to YHWH's word offer a pathway to renewed life.

THEOLOGY OF SUFFERING

However, this reality of sin and punishment is complemented by a theology of suffering. That is, the poetry of Lamentations 1 highlights suffering without explicitly linking the experience to the people's sin. Rather, the poetry highlights human suffering *as* suffering. As it does so, the poetry casts a light on the experience of pain: pain because of loss and bereavement, pain as a result of enemy action against Zion, and pain as a result of God's activity. By doing this, the poetry engenders a sense of sympathy for Zion's loss and grief in verses 1–4, 6–7, 10–13, 15–16, and 19–22. Here Zion's suffering stands paramount, and we hear Zion call out to God because of her pain.

Lamentations 2 contains one of the most focused presentations of divine action against God's people and city in the entire Old Testament. This poem centers on divine wrath. In terms of speaking voices, the narrator reappears and speaks prominently throughout the poem. Whereas Zion spoke prominently in Lamentations 1, the narrator takes most of the space in chapter 2.

Zion only gains her voice in earnest in Lamentations 2:20–22, and there she draws into her prayer the language of the narrator from verses 1–19. Zion prays to God about his wrath, her mourning and ruin, and the work of enemies against her. As is fitting in prayer, Zion takes her distress to the Lord. In fact, prayer is a key component to understanding the book. Zion goes to God in prayer throughout the book (1:20–22; 2:20–22); the community prays (Lam. 5); and both the individual and communal voices pray in Lamentations 3.

The Strongman's Experience and Communal Prayer: Lamentations 3

■ READ LAMENTATIONS 3 ■

Next to Psalm 119, Lamentations is the most developed acrostic poem in the Old Testament. It is a literary masterpiece. The acrostic structure from Lamentations 1–2 gains intensity in the third poem, where sets of three poetic lines begin with the respective letter of the Hebrew alphabet rather than only the first poetic line, as in Lamentations 1–2. This difference catches our attention. A new speaker appears in Lamentations 3:1—the "man" or "strongman" (Hebrew *geber*). Understood to be various individuals, the

Lamentations 3:21–24 and Exodus 34:6–7

Lamentations is filled with echoes of other biblical texts. The echoes of Exodus 34:6–7 reverberate in Lamentations 3:21–24. Exodus 34:6–7 (NRSV) affirms YHWH to be "merciful" and gracious, slow to anger and abounding in "steadfast love" and "faithfulness." These characteristics recall how YHWH describes himself after Israel committed grave sin with the golden calf in the wilderness. YHWH's revelation highlights the fact that although Israel sins, God's mercy will remain. Lamentations 3:21–24 (NRSV) also speaks of God's "steadfast love," "mercies," and "faithfulness," using the language of Exodus 34 to comfort those who experience suffering and degradation. They are reminded that all is not lost. Divine mercies are new every morning because YHWH's steadfast love is still operative. YHWH is still the covenant Lord of Israel, and his mercies will break forth as the morning light.

"strongman" is ambiguous. Whatever his identity, he speaks about his situation of suffering in verses 1–18.

From there, he turns to his foundation for hope in 3:19–24, without a doubt the most famous section of the poetry—and with reason! These verses beautifully articulate the hope that comes in the covenantal relationship between God and his people. Echoing the revelation of divine character in Exodus 34:6–7, Lamentations 3:19–24 reveals that hope for the future is found in God and him alone! The bright light of God's covenantal commitment shines beautifully in this affirmation of faith during suffering.

It would be fitting for the poem to conclude there: a bright light shining after two dark chapters. However, the poem continues, providing wisdom-like instruction on bearing up under suffering (3:25–39). And after this, the poetry turns to second-person address to God. The direct address to the Lord persists to the end of the chapter (v. 66). All told, the second half of the poem is prayer to God from the depths of pain. Interestingly, the first-person singular ("I") speech of the man from verse 1 intermingles with first person plural ("we") speech of the community throughout the latter half of the poem. Through the interplay of the community and individual voices in their repetition of language, we see that prayer for divine help becomes more and more prominent in the poem.

Shame and Sin: Lamentations 4

■ READ LAMENTATIONS 4 ■

Opening with the reversal motif from honor to shame (4:1–10), Lamentations 4 advances a theology of sin and punishment in a way not witnessed in the poetry until now. The emphasis on sin and suffering stands out, particularly in the way sin is attributed to priests and prophets (4:13–15). Leadership structures among the nation of Judah have failed the population. God's people have suffered because of their leaders' sin. There is also remorse over failed hope in foreign nations to deliver them from God's wrath and Babylon's terrors (4:17). The poem mentions the anointed of YHWH who was captured by enemies (4:20). This title refers to the king of Israel, and the Greek translator renders the Hebrew with "the messiah of the Lord." Because of this translation, early Christian interpreters saw the title as a reference to Jesus the Messiah, who was captured by those who crucified him. We will explore this a bit further in the comments below.

Finally, the poem concludes by turning to the nation of Edom and the reality of exile. Both are significant and related, as Edom likely helped facilitate the Neo-Babylonian invasion of Judah and Jerusalem. Parataxis, the poetic presentation of images that appear alongside one another without apparent logical connection, stands out in this poem. Each image and topic explored within the poem—whether sin, suffering, honor, nations, Edom, or exile—does not follow in a logical order. Rather, the reader negotiates a pastiche of images and topics that are bound together through the alphabetic acrostic.

A Community Prayer: Lamentations 5

▓ READ LAMENTATIONS 5 ▓

In Lamentations 5, the acrostic fades away, suggesting the end of the poem. There is a shift from three poetic lines per letter of the alphabet in Lamentations 1–3 (with exceptions in 1:7 and 2:18) to two poetic lines per letter in Lamentations 4 and to one poetic line per letter in Lamentations 5. In this way, the length of the poems diminishes in chapters 4 and 5, as does the intensity of the acrostic form. The strident cries of the Daughter of Zion in Lamentations 1–2 are not present in the final poem of the book. Nor is the pronounced voice of the "strongman" from Lamentations 3. Also missing is the confident expectation of Lamentations 4:22 that the exile will end. Rather, this final poem in the book is a communal lament that groans to God about persistent suffering under foreign oppression. It is like the voice of those who experience the hostility of God (3:43–45) and the mocking of enemies (3:46–54). The community mourns loss of honor and presence of shame (5:1–5). They cry out to God for help, with no guarantee that he will answer (5:19–22). But their prayer goes up to YHWH, their only hope in a time of trouble.

The poem concludes with a question mark. God's silence and lack of

Figure 24.2. *The Maiden's Lament* by Horace Vernet

engagement with the situation of his people are clear in some of the final words: "Why do you always forget us? Why do you forsake us so long?" (5:20). The closing verses of the poem echo the language of Jeremiah's call for restoration: "Restore us to yourself, LORD, that we may return; renew our days as of old" (5:21; cf. Jer. 15:19; 31:18; and cf. Ezek. 36:11). Only God can change the situation of his people because only he can restore and renew. If God's people are to experience a future life beyond their present death, then the poet recognizes only God can raise them from their grave. The poetry concludes mysteriously: "unless you have utterly rejected us and are angry with us beyond measure" (Lam. 5:22). There is no certainty as to what God will do: Will he restore or reject? Will divine anger or compassion hold sway? It is unclear. No wonder Lamentations leaves us uncomfortable!

Implementation—Reading Lamentations as Christian Scripture Today

"In Lamentations (this is the merciless mercy that shines in the poetry) we are spared nothing; nothing of flailing curses and denunciations. Ourselves, under winds of catastrophe wildly veering, like weather vanes in a tornado."[1] Lamentations burns as an eternal flame that marks the persistence of human suffering, but readers may embrace its light as a beacon that draws those who mourn to discover comfort in its words. Readers recognize the beckoning call of Lamentations, particularly in terms of the book's value as a tool to wrestle with grief and pain.

In recent years, scholars have mined the psychological insights on grief and then correlated these insights with the perspectives on suffering, grief, bereavement, and loss in Lamentations. The book has also been used as a way to understand the psychology of prayer. Reading Lamentations through the lens of psychological study opens the book into the modern world.

In addition, scholars recognize the value of Lamentations as postwar literature and connect this ancient text to recent literature of warfare. In the comparative analysis, the human devastation, reversal from honor to shame, and catastrophic effect on the environment present in Lamentations resonate with human expression in the wars of Sarajevo, Kabul, China, and elsewhere. As ancient postwar literature, Lamentations still speaks in a wartorn world.

Jews and Christians have used Lamentations for centuries as a liturgical text to commemorate some of the most important aspects of their traditions. For Jews, Lamentations is part of the Tishah b'Ab services, which commemorate major disasters in Jewish memory, including the destruction of the first and second temples, and the Shoah (the Holocaust), for example. The Christian church has employed Lamentations primarily during Holy Week, as it commemorates the passion and death of Jesus Christ. Lamentations is often part of the liturgy of the Tenebrae (or "shadows") services on Maundy Thursday, Good Friday, and Holy Saturday. This has been the case since the Middle Ages.

Although Lamentations is important in Catholic tradition in the Tenebrae services, Protestant worship has not resourced the book to the same extent. However, in either Catholic or Protestant traditions, the connections between Jesus and figures of Lamentations are useful for reflecting on the work of Christ by way of analogy: the suffering Jesus and the suffering individual (Lam. 3:1–19), the passion of Jesus and the suffering community (3:40–66; Lam. 5), the death of Jesus and the destroyed temple (Lam. 2), the laments of Jesus and Lady Zion (Lam. 1–2), and the arrest and capture of Jesus and the captured Messiah (4:20). Each theme enables pious reflection in the context of praise, repentance, and corporate prayer.

Soong-Chan Rah employs Lamentations as a tool for the American church to encounter the suffering of the world. Lamentations provides a critique against success-centered triumphalism of the Western church and a call to lament and repent. Rah sees in Lamentations a gift that must be opened for the church to face its future well. He calls the church to integrate a theology of suffering alongside a theology of celebration: both lament and praise, suffering and triumph. For Rah, Lamentations is a glimpse of what the church should seek.[2]

Figure 24.3. *Christ on the Cross* by El Greco (Domenikos Theotokopoulos, 1578–1610)

Christian Reading Questions

1. Describe the poetic structure of Lamentations, particularly the poetic structure as it relates to the alphabetic acrostic.

2. How does Lamentations 3 fit within the book as a whole? In what ways does Lamentations 3 serve as a climax to the book, and in what ways does it not serve in that capacity?

3. How is prayer important in Lamentations, and what does this contribute to Christian theology?

CHAPTER TWENTY-FIVE

Esther

Orientation

The book of Esther presents the story of the Jewish woman Esther as she rises to prominence in the Persian court. Her ascension is complemented by the rise of one of her relatives and countrymen, Mordecai, after he endures great trouble. Through the leadership and devotion of Esther and Mordecai to each other and their people, Israel endures as God's people against all odds.

The book's historical context is somewhat unclear, but it is reasonable to see it in the reign of Xerxes I, who reigned from 485 to 465 BC. He is called "Ahasuerus" in Hebrew, but English translations often render this as "Xerxes" (cf. Ezra 4:6). This sounds simple enough, but the ancient Greek translation of Esther (LXX) identifies the king as Artaxerxes, possibly Artaxerxes I, who reigned from 465 to 425 BC. We consider the book's setting to be the reign of Xerxes I / Ahasuerus.

Intriguingly, the book never explicitly mentions God's name or divine action, leading some to question whether Esther is a secular narrative. Perhaps God is absent from the book. Esther does diverge from other biblical books in the Old Testament when it comes to divine action; God does not speak or act directly in the book in Esther. However, the many happy "coincidences" throughout the book lead us to recognize God at work "behind the scenes" to protect and provide for his covenant people. 📖

LITERARY NOTES

The Structure of Esther

Esther 1–2: The rise of Esther

Esther 3–4: The rise of Haman and the threat of genocide

Esther 5–6: Esther's plan and Mordecai's honor

Esther 7–8: Haman's execution and Esther's intervention

Esther 9–10: Jewish victory and Mordecai's leadership

Exploration—Reading Esther

The Rise of Esther: Esther 1–2

■ READ ESTHER 1–2 ■

Esther's story unfolds during the reign of the Persian king Ahasuerus, whose reign encompassed the whole known world (1:1). This vast imperial authority and the perceived strength of Ahasuerus contrast with the weakness of the Jewish people. To showcase his wealth and power (looted from conquered nations!), Ahasuerus holds a banquet for the nobility of Persia. Deep into the party and fully intoxicated, Ahasuerus commands his queen, Vashti, to appear before the nobility so he can show off her beauty as he has his wealth. She refuses and, as a result, is forbidden from coming before Ahasuerus again. Further, Vashti's position is stripped from her, and an opportunity is open to replace her in the court.

Interestingly, the stated need for Ahasuerus's punishment of Vashti stems from the concern that wives across the empire, emboldened by Vashti's actions, will no longer respect their husbands (1:16–18). The problem, of course, with this supposed threat to patriarchal rule is that it was unjust in the first place, but Ahasuerus creates a law to support an exploitative exercise of power over those who had no power. This asymmetrical power dynamic between the whims of Persian royalty and those without power is a theme that recurs in Esther.

Chapter 2 introduces Ahasuerus's scheme to replace Vashti: a kind of perverse beauty pageant to find an attractive young virgin for his harem and then to be his new queen. One of the women he finds appealing is the young Jewish woman called Esther (2:9, 17).

Esther's cousin, Mordecai, positions her to be in the beauty pageant but warns her not to expose her Jewish ethnicity. It is not clear why this is the case, other than the fact that the Jewish people had immigrant status in the empire. As the narrative of Esther progresses, some Persian officials express racist hatred for the Jews, so perhaps that was a motivating factor as well. At any rate, Esther abides by her cousin's instructions, and she finds greater favor than any other concubine in the royal harem. With much fanfare, Ahasuerus makes her queen in the place of Vashti (2:17).

CANONICAL CONNECTIONS

The Law of the Medes and Persians

Esther 1:19 reads, "Therefore, if it pleases the king, let him issue a royal decree and let it be written in the laws of Persia and Media, which cannot be repealed." The notion of the unimpeachable law held among the Persians and Medians is something that also appears in the book of Daniel (Dan. 6:8, 15).

HISTORICAL MATTERS

Esther or Hadassah?

Esther 2 introduces us to Mordecai's cousin, Esther, who is also called Hadassah. What is the difference between the two names? Esther, which sounds like the Persian word for "star," may also echo the name of the Babylonian fertility goddess, Ishtar. By contrast, her Hebrew name, Hadassah, is the Aramaic word for the evergreen shrub called a myrtle. The myrtle is an evergreen flowering shrub that exists throughout the Mediterranean world. Like Daniel and his three friends in Daniel 1, as an exile living in a distant land, Hadassah receives a new name to reflect the new geopolitical realities she faces. This new name also reflects the contested space she will occupy throughout the book: navigating her Jewish identity and heritage within the Persian homeland.

The narrative does not evaluate the actions of the characters in Esther 1–2. Esther hides her ethnicity. Mordecai, it seems, pimps out his cousin. Ahasuerus is exploitative and manipulative. And yet the narrative does not explicitly tell us how to think about the actions of *any* of the characters! The storytelling in Esther is subtler than that; the narrative *shows* character action and invites evaluation from the reader.

In this way, the story does not display the same kind of narrative techniques that we see in 1–2 Kings or 1–2 Samuel, where the omniscient narrator unambiguously proclaims that "character X did evil in the sight of YHWH." One way we can begin to evaluate the virtue or vice of the action in the narrative is to assess how the story echoes earlier actions, phrases, and scenes we find in other books of the Old Testament.

For example, the beauty contest in Esther 2 echoes the body contest in Daniel 1, where wicked royal power exploits God's people only to find that they flourish. Mordecai's and Esther's actions are neither affirmed nor rejected, but the echoes of Daniel 1 in the text open the possibility of God's favor to be shown to his people living in a distant land under an exploitative power.

Esther and Human Trafficking

Recent research into Esther has explored the connections between Esther's experience and human trafficking, particularly sexual trafficking. The harem in Esther 1–2, on this reckoning, would be made up of women from other nations who were abducted and then sexually trafficked in the royal court. The narrative neither explains nor explains away the horrors of this possibility. It leaves open the reader's imagination to the horrific reality of sexual trafficking and the commonplace way in which imperial rule can exploit others, particularly women.[a]

Figure 25.1. *The Festival of Esther* by Edward Armitage (1865)

David Firth asserts, "More than any other text in the Old Testament, Esther asks us to read it in the light of the canon of Scripture."[1] Esther echoes other biblical texts with similar language, storytelling, and type scenes (type scenes are repeated scenes within or across a piece of literature). Esther effectively retells other Old Testament stories with variation and nuance that give meaning to the action of the book of Esther. Esther retells Joseph's story of reversal from dishonor to honor of God's people. The story of Nabal is retold with the life of Haman. The story of Saul is retold through the life of Mordecai. The story of God's deliverance for Hezekiah is retold with the story of God's deliverance for Mordecai. The experiences of Daniel and his friends are retold through the experiences of Mordecai and Esther. While God is conspicuously absent as a speaker and actor in the book of Esther, God shows up in the way the narrative retells Israel's story in the story of Mordecai and Esther.

The Rise of Haman and the Threat of Genocide: Esther 3–4

■ READ ESTHER 4 ■

Esther 3–8 details a plot, hatched by Haman the "Agagite," to destroy the Jews living in Persia. It begins when Ahasuerus elevates Haman, but Mordecai refuses to honor him. Instead of focusing his rage directly on Mordecai, Haman determines to exterminate the entire Jewish populace living in the empire (3:6). The king approves and issues a royal decree to ensure the action is carried through. Enemies begin assembling to kill the Jews throughout the empire, and Haman casts lots (Hebrew *purim*) to determine the date of their annihilation.

Mordecai learns of Haman's scheme and leans on Esther, who is the queen in the royal palace, to persuade Ahasuerus to alter his decree. In a series of exchanges, Mordecai offers Esther a powerful word, that she is where she is for just this moment in the story of God's people (4:13–14).

Whereas in Esther 2 Mordecai had instructed Esther to hide her Jewish ethnicity, he now encourages her to advocate for her people and deliver them from distress. Esther conceals her Jewish identity in the beginning of her story, but by the end of chapter 4, she mourns alongside her fellow Jews and determines to act on their behalf (4:16).[2] Esther will be the means of deliverance for her people.

CANONICAL CONNECTIONS

Haman, Mordecai, Agag, and Saul

Throughout the book of Esther, the text emphasizes the role of Haman the "Agagite," which is a strange designation. The identity of this people group is unclear. The ambiguity opens the possibility of interpreting the kinship of Haman with a non-Israelite king in 1 Samuel 15—Agag, the Amalekite. This makes sense because Mordecai is depicted as a Benjamite, from the same kinship group as Saul, who was commanded by God to kill Agag. Saul does not obey, and it costs him his kingship. By establishing the relationship between Haman and Mordecai along the lines of Agag and Saul, the narrative exposes the possibility of Mordecai closing the loop on unfinished family business! Which, of course, by the end of the book of Esther, he does.

Esther and the Old Testament

Esther	Canonical Connection	Explanation
Joseph's Story		
Esther 3:4	Genesis 39:10	Speaking "day after day" and not listening
Esther 2:3–4	Genesis 41:34–37	Appointing officials; gathering food for storehouses // gathering women for harem
Esther 6:11; 8:2	Genesis 41:42–43	Joseph/Mordecai dressed in honor and given signet ring
Esther 4:16	Genesis 43:14	"If I perish, I perish" // "If I am bereaved, I am bereaved" (using similar grammatical construction)
Esther 8:6	Genesis 44:34	Similar use of interrogative
The Exodus		
Esther 6:1	Exodus 12:42	Ahasuerus's sleepless night is thought to be on the "night of watching," the night of Israel's exodus from Egypt, according to Jewish tradition. Esther's narrative foreshadows another miraculous deliverance.
The Book of Samuel*		
Esther 1:10; 5:9	1 Samuel 25:36; 2 Samuel 13:28	Ahasuerus, Nabal, and Amnon have "high spirits" from wine that foreshadow unwise actions and bad outcomes. Haman has "high spirits," leading the reader to understand that he, too, is about to have a bad outcome for unwise action.
Esther 3:1, 10; 8:3, 5; 9:24	1 Samuel 15; 2 Samuel 1:1–16	Haman is an Agagite. Saul does not kill Agag, the Amalekite king. Esther retells the story of the Amalekite problem in Israel's history through Haman's life in Persia.
Esther 2:5–6	1 Samuel 9:1	Mordecai's genealogy proceeds from Saul, Israel's first king. Mordecai (Saul's line) gains victory over Haman (the Agagite), reversing Saul's former failure with the Amalekites (whose king was Agag).
The Book of Kings		
Esther 3:1	1 Kings 1:5	"And he *exalted him* and placed his authority over the princes who were with him" (AT). // "Now Adonijah son of Haggith *exalted himself*, saying, 'I will be king'; he prepared for himself chariots and horsemen, and fifty men to run before him" (NRSV).
Esther 5:3	1 Kings 1:16	King Ahasuerus said to Esther, "What do you want?" (AT) // King David said to Bathsheba, "What do you want?" (AT)
Esther 2:6	2 Kings 24:11–15	King Nebuchadnezzar exiles Jerusalem and Judah during Jehoiachin's reign and takes captives to Babylon.
Isaiah†		
Esther 4:1	Isaiah 37:1 // 2 Kings 19:1	Mordecai "tore his clothes, put on sackcloth and ashes, and went out into the city, wailing loudly and bitterly." // "When King Hezekiah heard this, he tore his clothes and put on sackcloth and went into the temple of the LORD."
Esther 4:1	Isaiah 58:5	"sackcloth and ashes" // "sackcloth and ashes"
Esther 4:1–17	Isaiah 37:2–35	Interaction between Esther and Mordecai through intermediaries (Hathak, Esther's maidservants, and her eunuchs) // interaction between Isaiah/God and Hezekiah through intermediaries (Eliakim, Shebna, and priests).
		Climax in Esther 4 with Mordecai's request (Esther 4:13–14) and Esther's response (4:15–16) // Climax in Isaiah 37 with Hezekiah's prayer (Isa. 37:14–20) and God's response (37:21–35).
		Mordecai goes to the outer court of the palace (Esther 4:1–2) in his ritual state of mourning // Hezekiah mourns in the "temple of the LORD" (Isa. 37:1). Spatial differences give hints at expected response. If God delivered through the prophecy of Isaiah when Hezekiah went to the temple, then how will God deliver his people in Persia?

(continued)

Esther	Canonical Connection	Explanation
	Joel‡	
Esther 4:3	Joel 2:12	"There was great mourning among the Jews, with fasting, weeping and wailing. Many lay in sackcloth and ashes." // "Return to me with all your heart, with fasting and weeping and mourning."
Esther 4:14	Joel 2:14	"Who knows?" // "Who knows?"
	Daniel 1–6**	
Esther 1:1–12	Daniel 5:1–4	Ahasuerus's banquet // Belshazzar's banquet
Esther 2:1–18	Daniel 1:8–16	beauty contest // body contest
Esther 3:1–6	Daniel 3	not bowing to Haman // not bowing to the statue
Esther 3	Daniel 6:1–24	Plots of royal administrators
Esther 6	Daniel 2:1; 6:18	Sleepless kings

Note: This extended chart of canonical connections is adapted from charts in David G. Firth, Brittany N. Melton, and Heath A. Thomas, "Under the Intertextual Umbrella: An Introduction," in *Reading Esther Intertextually*, ed. David G. Firth and Brittany N. Melton, The Library of Hebrew Bible/Old Testament Studies 725 (London: T&T Clark, 2022), 3. This chart builds on the extensive canonical connections mentioned in the groundbreaking work of Adele Berlin, *Esther*, JPS Commentary (Philadelphia: Jewish Publication Society, 2001), xxxvii.

* David G. Firth, "When Samuel Met Esther: Narrative Focalisation, Intertextuality, and Theology," *Southeastern Theological Review* 1, no. 1 (2010): 22–27.

† Heath A. Thomas, "The Fruit of Mourning: Esther Enriched by the Latter Prophets," in *Reading Esther Intertextually*, ed. David G. Firth and Brittany N. Melton, The Library of Hebrew Bible/Old Testament Studies 725 (London: T&T Clark, 2022), 92–93.

‡ Thomas, "The Fruit of Mourning," 90.

** Berlin, *Esther*, xxxiv–xli; Matthew Michael, "Daniel at the Beauty Pageant and Esther in the Lion's Den: Literary Intertextuality and Shared Motifs between the Books of Daniel and Esther," *Old Testament Essays* 29, no. 1 (2016): 116–32 (esp. 124–27).

Esther's Plan and Mordecai's Honor, Haman's Execution and Esther's Intervention: Esther 5–8

■ READ ESTHER 6–8 ■

Esther goes to the king and develops a ruse to expose Haman's wickedness and preserve her people. Because Ahasuerus is so entranced with Esther, he tells her that she can make any request she chooses, and he will grant it. Instead of making her request immediately, she invites Ahasuerus and Haman to a banquet (Esther 7). There, she states, "If I have found favor with you, Your Majesty, and if it pleases you, grant me my life—this is my petition. And spare my people—this is my request. For I and my people have been sold to be destroyed, killed and annihilated. If we had merely been sold as male and female slaves, I would have kept quiet, because no such distress would justify disturbing the king" (7:3–4).

At this, Haman's scheme is exposed. Through a series of events, Ahasuerus punishes Haman by impaling him on a pole that Haman had originally set up to kill Mordecai (5:11–14; 7:9–10). Esther then asks Ahasuerus to write a royal decree to reverse his decree of Jewish destruction. The king does just that, and the Jewish people are saved from annihilation (8:11–14).

Instead of being defeated by enemies, the Jewish people are empowered to defend their lives in the Persian Empire. They celebrate their victory over

Figure 25.2. *Esther Denouncing Haman to King Ahasuerus* by Ernest Normand (1888)

Haman's plan with a festival called Purim ("lots"), an ironic remembering of the lots that Haman cast to determine the date of the Jews' demise. The celebration of Purim becomes an annual ritual in which God's people remember the defeat of Haman and their deliverance at the hand of Mordecai and Esther. Purim is celebrated on the fourteenth and fifteenth of the month of Adar, roughly March/April.

Jewish Victory and Mordecai's Leadership: Esther 9–10

■ READ ESTHER 9–10 ■

Because of the obedience of Mordecai and Esther, Haman's plan was upended and the Jewish people experienced victory instead of death (Esther 9:23–26). The story concludes with not only Esther's elevation and affirmation as Persian queen and faithful Jew but also Mordecai's elevation to the second-in-command of the Persian Empire (Esther 10). The book ends with a hopeful tone and a call to virtue through the example of Mordecai: "He worked for the good of his people and spoke up for the welfare of all the Jews" (10:3).

Implementation—Reading Esther as Christian Scripture Today

As one considers reading Esther as Christian Scripture, one finds the New Testament echoes the language of Esther (at least the Greek version) in the story of Herod Antipas and Herodias's daughter (Mark 6:17–29). Mark incorporates language from the banquet scene of Esther to show how Herod is willing to give up to half of his kingdom (6:23) to please Herodius's daughter. Her only request? The death—more specifically, the head—of John the Baptist. In Esther (5:3, 6; 7:2), Ahasuerus offers Esther up to half of his kingdom if that is her desire. But Esther's desire is life for her people, not death. The contrast between Esther and Herodius's daughter exposes the wicked character of the latter and the virtue of the former.[3]

God's response to exploitation and power also rises as a theme in Esther. Unjust exercise of power and exploitation of ethnic groups and women are common in the history of humanity. Modern societies are afflicted with power-hungry leaders just as much as ancient societies were. Thus, it is comforting to see that God still cares for those who are downcast and destitute, that Israel's God raises up the lowly and humbles the proud. The book of Esther serves as resistance literature to the powers of the present world. Whenever naked power seems to be greater than anything else, Esther reminds us that even though God may be quiet, he is not silent. Although God may seem immobile, he is on the move.

The subtle, quiet power of God's reign provides countertestimony to the loud and audacious powers that exploit and oppress, annihilate and exterminate, and crush weakness for their gain. But the countertestimony gives greater detail about *how* God's reign is exercised in everyday realities. The subtle, quiet power of God's reign exerts itself through *God's people*. Esther and Mordecai must step into their moment before God for the good of all, despite risking their lives. Esther's commitment captures the idea: "If I perish, I perish" (4:16). Esther and Mordecai risk much to serve greatly. So, too, must those who follow Christ step into their moment in life for the good of all. As Jesus taught, "Whoever wants to be my disciple must deny themselves and take up their cross and follow me. For whoever wants to save their life will lose it, but whoever loses their life for me and for the gospel will save it" (Mark 8:34–35).

Esther reminds us that God's kingdom is exercised—in the real world—when God's people risk much to love their neighbor as themselves. God's people are not perfect people, just ordinary people. The ordinary powerlessness of Esther and Mordecai, contrasted against the authority of Ahasuerus and Haman, testifies that God likes to take the weakest of the world and empower them to be positive agents for the good of all—in the manner of Jesus: "For he was crucified in weakness, but he lives by the power of God. For we also are weak in him, but in dealing with you we live with him by God's power" (2 Cor. 13:4 CSB).

Christian Reading Questions

1. What is significant about the absence of God's name or explicit action in the book of Esther? How does this shape its theology?

2. How does Esther fit in the theology of the Old Testament?

3. Although God's name is not mentioned in the book, is it appropriate to consider Esther as secular Jewish literature? Why or why not?

4. Why do you think God is not mentioned as a primary named actor in the book? Does this diminish its theological voice within the Old Testament? Why or why not?

5. When you consider the two major protagonists in the book (Mordecai and Esther), who do you consider to be the hero of the narrative?

CHAPTER TWENTY-SIX

Daniel

Orientation

The book of Daniel provides hope for God's people as they face an uncertain world, especially when they are seemingly powerless amid world powers. This encouraging message is dressed in strange clothing, however, as the book offers puzzling imagery, difficult tests of faith, and the rise and fall of world kingdoms. In all of it, Israel's God is promised to be the one who defeats the powers and ushers in an eternal reign of peace and joy.

Daniel's structure is organized in two basic blocks: Daniel 1–6, where the experiences of Daniel and his friends are recorded (in third-person speech), and Daniel 7–12, where Daniel recounts his visions and offers his prayer (in first-person speech). Three tests highlight God's call for faithfulness amid suffering (Dan. 1, 3, and 6). Two visions of four kingdoms signify the failure of rival powers before God's reign (Dan. 2 and 7). Two stories of royal pride—that of Nebuchadnezzar and Belshazzar—reveal the different ways kingdoms may survive: in Nebuchadnezzar's story, humility and penitence is the way to restoration for the nations (Dan. 4), but in Belshazzar's story, pride is the way to their fall (Dan. 5). Daniel 8 and 10–12 give additional information on how the four kingdoms described in Daniel 2 and 7 will fall and be replaced with the reign of God. Finally, Daniel 9 reveals how God's people may experience restoration, as Daniel's prayer for repentance models the way for God's people to experience an end to exile. 📖 🏺

Exploration—Reading Daniel

Daniel and His Friends: Daniel 1–6

▓ READ DANIEL 1; 3; 6 ▓

The opening chapter of Daniel depicts forcible migration for Daniel and his friends. The Babylonians transferred young men of noble standing in Judah to a land they did not know, to live in an empire that viewed them as powerless slaves (1:3–5). In place of their own language and learning of Israel's God, they were subjected to the language and learning of Babylon (1:4–5). This new reality threatened their commitment to Israel's God. Even their names were changed. Their Hebrew names, which testified to something about Israel's God, were exchanged for something to do with Babylonian culture or deities.

Daniel (God is judge) → Belteshazzar (Bel protect the king)

Hananiah (YHWH is gracious) → Shadrach (associated with the deity Marduk)

Mishael (Who is like God?) → Meshach (Who is like Aku?)

Azariah (YHWH has helped) → Abednego (servant of Nebo)

They were also required to eat the food given to them by the royal palace. However, "Daniel resolved not to defile himself with the royal food and wine, and he asked the chief official for permission not to defile himself this way" (1:8). The text does not specify what about the food would lead to some sort of defilement, but for whatever reason, Daniel drew a line in the sand that he and his friends would not cross.[1]

"Defilement" is language from the context of purity and impurity that we saw in Leviticus. Being defiled meant being unfit for service as the people of God. If this is true, Daniel saw his life in the service

The Structure of Daniel

Daniel and His Friends: Daniel 1–6	Daniel 1: The food test	
		Daniel 2: Nebuchadnezzar's vision of four kingdoms
	Daniel 3: The fire test	
		Daniel 4–5: Royal pride
	Daniel 6: The lions' den test	
Daniel's Visions: Daniel 7–12	Daniel 7–8: Daniel's vision of four kingdoms; Daniel's vision of the ram and goat	
		Daniel 9: Penitential prayer
	Daniel 10–12: Daniel's vision	

HISTORICAL MATTERS

Hebrew and Aramaic in Daniel

The Old Testament is predominantly written in Hebrew, but a unique feature of Daniel is that it contains two Semitic languages—Hebrew and Aramaic. The Hebrew portions are in Daniel 1:1–2:4a and 8:1–12:13. The Aramaic portion is in Daniel 2:4b–7:28. Why are there two languages in this book? Aramaic was the official language of the Persian Empire by 500 BC, but Assyria and Babylon also used the language in earlier times. The shift from Hebrew to Aramaic in Daniel 2:4b begins when Nebuchadnezzar's wise men speak up, and then it concludes after Daniel's vision of the four kingdoms and the eternal kingdom of God in Daniel 7. Aramaic usage in the book has the effect of situating Daniel's experience in the Persian context, using the Persian imperial language.

LITERARY NOTES

Daniel   361

Royal Advisers and Diviners

King Nebuchadnezzar brought Daniel and his friends into his royal courts to be part of the retinue of advisers. Daniel 1:20 describes these advisers as "magicians and enchanters," which raises questions about what kind of service they provide. It was not uncommon in the ancient world for advisers or diviners to be part of the "brain trust" of the royal court. These diviners would advise the palace on various matters and would often serve prophetic functions in examining celestial phenomena (astrology), interpreting dreams, or the like to determine the will of the gods. Daniel and his friends were placed within this retinue of advisers and displayed greater wisdom than them all.

of Israel's God, and he and his friends would not do anything to jeopardize their relationship with their covenant Lord. This account details the first of three tests in the book. The first is the food test, in which Daniel and his friends are faithful to God no matter the cost. Their faithfulness brought them blessing and favor in the king's palace. They become trusted advisers, wise above all other advisers in the kingdom (1:19–20).

The second test focuses on Daniel's three friends, Shadrach, Meshach, and Abednego (Dan. 3). The question is whether they will worship the state-mandated golden idol made by Nebuchadnezzar. True to their covenant God, the three remain faithful to YHWH even if it costs them their lives. They are thrown into a blazing furnace as punishment for their civil disobedience, but God miraculously delivers them in the flames, and a heavenly being appears with them in the furnace. The flames do not harm them, and when they come out of the furnace, they do not even smell of smoke! Shadrach, Meshach, and Abednego's faithfulness to God leads Nebuchadnezzar to praise Israel's God (3:28–29) and to promote the three men to positions of power.

Figure 26.1. *Daniel in the Lions' Den* by Peter Paul Rubens (1615)

The final test appears in Daniel 6, and it focuses on the experience of Daniel. The kingdom has shifted from Babylonian rule to Median rule under the authority of Darius the king (5:31; 6:1). Daniel is a trusted adviser and leader in the kingdom, but Darius's administrative leadership wants to subvert Daniel's influence. Because Daniel was faithful to God in daily prayer, they concoct a plan that uses that prayer to trap him. They convince Darius to approve a law that makes it illegal to pray to anyone but the king for the next thirty days. If one breaks this law, they will be thrown to the lions. The administrators set the trap, and the test proceeds. Daniel prays to Israel's God, as is his habit, and they catch him. The king is trapped as well, recognizing that he approved the law that leads to Daniel's death sentence. He says to Daniel, "May your God, whom you serve continually, rescue you" (6:16). As in the other tests, God delivers. Daniel is preserved in the lions' den. As in Daniel 3, when the king sees this divine deliverance, he praises Israel's God, and Daniel prospers. In Darius's closing words, he issues a decree for his people to fear and revere Daniel's God, and he lifts high Israel's God among the nations (6:26–27).

Darius's affirmation of God's sovereign power to deliver when the faithful persevere in testing is matched with his affirmation of God's vital power among the nations. Further, Darius speaks of God's kingdom, which will not be destroyed, and God's rule that will never end. The permanence of God's dominion is contrasted with earthly rule, which is the topic of Daniel 2, 4, and 5.

Daniel 2 depicts a bad dream King Nebuchadnezzar has. The dream is about world kingdoms, which we will discuss in our analysis of Daniel 7. Here, it is enough to say that God grants Daniel the ability to interpret Nebuchadnezzar's vision of four world powers, represented by a massive statue made of four materials: gold, silver, bronze, and iron. These materials represent kingdoms that will all end. By contrast, another kingdom will emerge, different from the others, and this kingdom will be established by Israel's God: "In the time of those kings, the God of heaven will set up a kingdom that will never be destroyed, nor will it be left to another people. It will crush all those kingdoms and bring them to an end, but it will itself endure forever" (2:44). God's eternal kingdom contrasts with the ephemeral nature of the other world powers. [image]

The ephemeral nature of earthly kingdoms becomes important when we turn to Daniel 4–5, which reveals the pride of kings (Nebuchadnezzar in Dan. 4; Nebuchadnezzar's successor Belshazzar in Dan. 5). Nebuchadnezzar has a troubling dream about a vast tree that is cut

Figure 26.2. *Nebuchadnezzar* by William Blake (1795–1805)

down. Daniel interprets the dream and tells Nebuchadnezzar that he will be brought low (cut down) and wander like a beast until he acknowledges the sovereignty of Israel's God over all nations (4:25). Nebuchadnezzar's dream is fulfilled, and his reign is stripped from him until he acknowledges God's might and power, an act of humility and deference to God (4:34). This reversal from honor to shame, from glory to ignominy, reveals that even the nations' apparent power is given and taken away by God. Only God's power is absolute, and only God's reign is forever.

Nebuchadnezzar's reversal is effected by his response to God. When he responds with humility and repentance, God restores him. Restoration is possible when one recognizes God's power and authority over all.

Belshazzar does not have the same experience of transformation. Daniel 5 tells of a great feast put on by the king in which he uses the looted implements from Jerusalem's temple. As the king and his guests drink wine from the sacred vessels, they praise gods other than Israel's God. When they do, a hand appears, writing a mysterious message on the wall. No one is able to interpret the writing, and Daniel is summoned. He interprets the writing, which says Belshazzar's kingdom will be taken from him because he has not humbled himself (5:22), he set himself up to rival God (5:23), and he failed to honor "the God who holds in his hand your life and all your ways" (5:23). Thus, Belshazzar's ruin is certain, his story demonstrating that humility before Israel's God is essential for kings.

In Daniel 1–6, God gives Daniel the ability to interpret dreams and wonders (Dan. 2; 4–5), and God gives Daniel and his friends the strength to persevere through tests (Dan. 1; 3; 6). After the tests, both

Figure 26.3. *Belshazzar's Feast* by Rembrandt

Nebuchadnezzar and Darius admit the power and majesty of God (2:47; 4:1–3, 34–37; 6:26–27). Further, we see the virtues of humility and penitence accented for kings of the nations: Nebuchadnezzar praises God after humiliation and restoration, and Darius praises God after discovering God's power in deliverance. This theme of royal humility in the face of YHWH's power will reemerge in Daniel 9.

Figure 26.4. *Hand-Writing on the Wall* by James Gillray (1851)

In the first half of the book, God preserves Daniel and his friends and blesses them to be a blessing to the nations. Their covenantal identity as God's people hovers in the background of the book. Their very lives bear the name of God. Their obedience even in the midst of suffering is not ignored by God. God provides for them as they suffer, and God turns evil intentions to good. Thus, Daniel 1–6 demonstrates God's faithfulness, power, and goodness in the face of imperial powers. God's people can endure no matter what earthly powers inflict on them. God is trustworthy.

Daniel's Visions: Daniel 7–12

Central to Daniel 7–12 is the message of divine power and God's ability to set the world to rights, even when it appears that evil will win the day. God's demonstrated ability to turn around the worst of circumstances for his own glory is as important in the second half of the book as in the first half, even if the style of the second half of the book is vastly different.

In Daniel 7–12, the book shifts from narrative accounts to what is known as apocalyptic literature. Imagine this shift in the book as being a bit like the change from a close-up action shot in a movie (Dan. 1–6) to a wide-angle shot of the broader landscape (Dan. 7–12). In the close-up, God demonstrates goodness and power to Daniel and his friends while they live as exiles in Babylon. In Daniel 7–12, God displays his power at a global and cosmic scale. God moves in the heavens and on the earth, both in the present and in the future.

Public domain / Wikimedia Commons

LITERARY NOTES

Imagery in Apocalyptic Literature

Daniel 7–12 includes many strange and mysterious images. This is a feature of apocalyptic literature. Human beings, for instance, do not appear always as normal human beings, for one is associated with "the clouds of heaven" in Daniel 7:13. The beasts we see in Daniel 7 don't look or sound like anything we have seen before, as they exhibit characteristics of many animals at once. Otherworldly visions are characteristic of apocalyptic literature. Two of Daniel's visions include imagery of beasts. Various people and beings are described: angels (Gabriel/Michael), humans ("son of man"), humanlike people (one "like a son of man"), "people of the Most High," and "Ancient of Days." These titles point to the fact that the language itself is designed not merely to describe events and people but also to make the reader reflect on how things are described and why they are described as they are. The symbolism used in these chapters is as significant as what is said in them.

Time in Apocalyptic Literature

Daniel's visions in Daniel 7–12 are dated according to the reign of specific kings (7:1; 8:1; 9:1; 10:1; cf. 11:1), but the visions themselves incorporate several opaque chronological terms that are common in apocalyptic literature. In Daniel 9, the expressions "weeks" and "weeks of years" describe what is likely seven years (1 "week" = 7 years; e.g., NRSV). The visions themselves focus on "the end" or the "time of the end" (8:17, 19; 9:26–27; 11:35–40; 12:4–13) or what people sometimes call "end times" in popular language. The "time of the end" is grand in scale. While this period can refer to the overthrow of Persia (Dan. 8), it also stretches beyond these historical confines (Dan. 9–12) to the time when God will reign unchallenged. So time itself is a broad category in apocalyptic literature.

Visions and Apocalyptic Literature

Daniel 7–12 consists of otherworldly visions given by God in dreams. Apocalyptic literature often presents visions or dreams as a mode of discourse. The visions are recounted through the perception of the one receiving them. Since Daniel receives these visions, the text relates his perspective on them in first-person speech. Whereas Daniel could interpret dreams in Daniel 1–6, in Daniel 7–12 the prophet needs someone else to interpret his visions. A heavenly being explains what Daniel sees, specifically an angel named Gabriel (8:16; 9:21). Another angel is mentioned in these visions as well, Michael, who protects God's people (12:1). These figures unpack Daniel's visions and convey their heavenly portents.

Figure 26.5. Commentary on the Apocalypse (The Silos Apocalypse) by Beatus of Liébana, including Beatus's world map (AD 1091–1109)

The distinctive use of imagery, time, and visions we find in Daniel 7–12 represents an opportunity to embrace. Daniel 7–12, like other apocalyptic literature, creatively presents a different reality for its hearers in which they can envision the certainty of the coming divine reign. Within this horizon of expectation, Daniel 7–12 becomes a comfort for those who are suffering and a catalyst for God's people to serve faithfully in a hostile world of oppressive empires.

DANIEL'S VISION OF THE FOUR KINGDOMS: DANIEL 7

■ READ DANIEL 7 ■

In Daniel 7, Daniel has a vision of beasts rising from the sea and of the heavenly throne room in which "one like a son of man" receives an everlasting dominion (7:13–14). Verses 1–8 introduce the four beasts from the sea. Traditionally, these beasts are aligned with the four kingdoms of Nebuchadnezzar's dream in Daniel 2, but there is a lack of consensus on the historical identity of these kingdoms. Two views are prominent and are detailed in the chart "The Empires in Daniel 2 and 7."[2]

The Empires in Daniel 2 and 7

Image	Traditional Identities of the Empires	More Recent Identities of the Empires
Daniel 2		
Head of Gold	Neo-Babylonian Empire (605–539 BC)	Neo-Babylonian Empire (605–539 BC)
Arms and chest of silver	Medo-Persian Empire (539–331 BC)	Media (unknown)
Belly and thighs of bronze	Greek Empire (331–146 BC)	Persian Empire (539–331 BC)
Legs of iron	Roman Empire (146 BC–AD 395)	Greek Empire (331–146 BC)
Daniel 7		
Lion	Neo-Babylonian Empire (605–539 BC)	Neo-Babylonian Empire (605–539 BC)
Bear	Medo-Persian Empire (539–331 BC)	Media (unknown)
Leopard	Greek Empire (331–146 BC)	Persian Empire (539–331 BC)
Iron-toothed beast	Roman Empire (146 BC–AD 395)	Greek Empire (331–146 BC)

One key challenge in unpacking the meaning of the empires is the identity of the "Medes" or the "Medo-Persian" Empire. There can be no doubt that a people called "Medes" lived in the Zagros mountains from the tenth century to the sixth century BC. According to the ancient Greek historian Herodotus, the Medes formed an empire in the Zagros mountains sometime in the eighth to seventh century BC, but this claim is disputed by modern scholars. It is clear the Medes conquered the city of Assur (the original home city of the Assyrian empire) in 614 BC, and after this, they joined forces with the Babylonians under the leadership of Babylonian king Nebopolassar. It also is clear the Medes were subsumed in the Persian Empire under the reign of Persian king Cyrus, which is why the title "Medo-Persian" Empire makes some sense. What remains difficult is that archaeological evidence to date does not support the reality of an extended Median Empire, analogous to Babylon or Persia, at any point in their history. So, interpreting the Medes as the second empire with arms and chest of silver presents some difficulty.

Some prefer not to assign the four kingdoms to a specific set of historical kingdoms but instead argue that the kingdoms represent "all the kingdoms of history."[3] On this reading, the vision's portrayal of the "one like a son of man" represents the ultimate defeat of all earthly kingdoms opposed to the reign of the God of Israel, whomever they may represent in whatever time. For our purposes, it is possible to affirm that whatever the kingdoms' identification, God's kingdom wins out in the end.

In the vision of Daniel 7, Daniel sees a strange set of animals rise from the sea, representing kingdoms of the earth. These animals are violent, indicating their intent as earthly kingdoms: they will be violent and oppressive. The final beast that rises from the sea is an iron-toothed beast with ten horns. The horns represent, most likely, the extended power and authority of this kingdom compared with the kingdoms that preceded it. As he observes the horns, Daniel witnesses a little horn emerge from the midst of the horns and uproot three of them. Stranger still, this final horn has the eyes of a human being and speaks arrogantly!

As one reflects on the narrative presentation of strange beasts, it is worth noticing how the beasts appear in the vision. They rise from the sea. Normally, leopards, lions, and bears do not live in the sea! The sea in some Old Testament texts indicates the waters of chaos, places of disharmony and danger (think of the sea in Jonah or Pss. 46:1–3; 93:3–4). From this perspective, the four beasts are very strange indeed. The beasts are also unusual because they are hybrid creatures. Normally, lions and leopards do not have wings, and leopards do not have four heads. For ancient readers, these images would be terrifying. More importantly, they are theologically significant because the beasts are aberrations of the created order.

In Genesis 1, God creates each animal group according to its kind. There is an order and symmetry to creation. The beasts and kingdoms they represent transgress this order: animals should fill the land, fish fill the sea, and birds fill the sky. Furthermore, their hybrid natures—lions and leopards with wings, and so on—defy the order of creation "according to their kinds." These beasts and kingdoms are violent and destructive, living in rebellion against God. How shall God respond? Do these kingdoms threaten God's authority or upend creation?

In Daniel 7:9–10, the vision transitions to disclose God, here described as the "Ancient of Days" who takes his seat alone among thrones. That the "Ancient of Days" sits alone signifies God's unrivaled power. Further, his hair and clothing are white, signifying his purity of governance, which contrasts with the violent kingdoms presented in 7:1–8, whose governance is depicted as predatory. Fire accompanies the throne of the "Ancient of Days," which reinforces the purity and holiness of God's reign. Finally, in this vision, millions attend the "Ancient of Days," and he opens the "books" in the "court" (v. 10). This last revelation helps us understand the "Ancient of Days" is not only royal, pure, holy, and sovereign; he is also the judge who weighs the character and deeds of those recorded in the book. Most immediately, his judgment goes to the beastly kingdoms that Daniel sees in 7:1–8.

The "Ancient of Days" deals with the boastful and arrogant horn mentioned in verse 8 and strips the authority of the four beastly kingdoms. Daniel 7:13–14 introduces one "like a son of man," which could be translated one "like a human being." The figure in verse 13 is humanlike, and in context this description is important and contrastive. This "one like a human being" is distinct from the beastly figures in the vision. That is, this figure fits creational design. He is not a lawless, transgressive beast. Rather, he is like a human. But verse 13 also reveals his uniqueness. This figure comes with the clouds of heaven and is ushered into the presence of the "Ancient of Days." This image, well known in Canaanite mythic tales, is the image of a God-man riding the clouds. Here Daniel sees this figure as a God-man, receiving authority and a kingdom from God himself. All nations and peoples worship him, and his kingdom and authority will never fade. Rather than striving for royal authority and oppressing others to obtain it, as witnessed in the beastly kingdoms, the "one like a human being" receives his kingdom from God, and all worship him eternally.

In the presentation of the kingdom of the "one like a human being," one finds a powerful divine response to evil and violent

Figure 26.6. Fresco showing Revelation 1:12 (the Son of Man and the seven golden candlesticks), Kretzulescu Church, Bucharest (ca. 1722)

kingdoms—namely, judgment. God's divine "No!" to exploitation, oppression, and injustice in earthly kingdoms is met with a divine "Yes!" to his establishment of a kingdom of peace and everlasting harmony.

The New Testament understands this individual to be Jesus (Matt. 16:27–28; 19:28; 24:30–31; Mark 13:26; Luke 21:27; John 3:13). He is a man, but equally he is God. The point in Daniel's description of the "one like a son of man" is that to *this* figure God will give an everlasting kingdom. Unlike the beasts, which are vile and bloody and strive for power, the "one like a son of man" receives power from on high.

Those allied with the "one like a son of man" and devoted to the Ancient of Days are called the "saints of the Most High" (Dan. 7:22, 27 ESV). To these God gives judgment/justice (v. 22), and they reign in God's kingdom (v. 27). While it is unclear who this group is in the prophecy of Daniel, the text opens various possibilities: exiles, people restored in the land of Israel, or some other restored group. In Daniel's context, for those for whom the book was written, this word would have been an incredible encouragement. Those who were suffering in Babylon would not be left by the wayside.

Their God would remember them. He would give them a kingdom of peace and justice and would annihilate evil—because that is who God is!

DANIEL'S SECOND VISION AND PENITENTIAL PRAYER: DANIEL 8–9

■ READ DANIEL 8–9 ■

Daniel's expansive vision in chapter 7 moves to a more focused one in chapter 8, where a ram and goat represent kingdoms of the earth, sometimes understood as Persia (ram) and Greece (goat). Daniel watches the ram expand its territory, and he sees the goat destroy the ram to establish its own authority. The text describes the ram's campaign toward the west and the north, befitting a move from southern Persia up the Tigris-Euphrates River valley, and then toward the south through Palestine. The description of the goat's campaign "from the west" fits the notion of Alexander the Great's campaign from the west to the east, conquering the world as no one had witnessed before.

This vision leaves Daniel perplexed. The vision of the future depicted violence and power grabbing. And yet God gave the vision to Daniel to reaffirm both the divine plan and divine control.

In Daniel 9, Daniel offers a **penitential prayer**, the answer to which is a vision of "seventy 'sevens' [weeks]" (9:24–27). Daniel's prayer reinforces that Israel considered exile to be a punishment for sin (cf. 9:11; Ezra 9; Neh. 9; cf. Deut. 28–30). Daniel knew the prophets had warned of this disaster as well, as

HISTORICAL MATTERS

Kings and Kingdoms in Daniel

Nebuchadnezzar (Neo-Babylonia)

Cyrus (Persia)

Darius the Mede (appointed by Cyrus)

Alexander (Greece, four kingdoms of Thrace, Macedonia, Ptolemaia [Egypt], Seleucia [Syria]; mentioned in Dan. 8:8, 22 as the "horns" in Daniel's vision of the goat)

Antiochus IV Epiphanes (Seleucid) (likely the "master of intrigue" mentioned in 8:23–25)

THEOLOGICAL ISSUES

Penitential Prayer

Daniel's prayer teaches theology. Other significant penitential prayers are found in Nehemiah 9 and Ezra 9. They pray the tradition of Israel in a way that tells the story of God's people, confesses sin, and returns to God for forgiveness. Daniel's prayer teaches several truths about Israel's God:

- A gracious God. The God to whom Daniel prays is gracious and merciful. Daniel's words indicate that he understands God not as a cosmic killjoy but as a loving and gracious God (9:4, 9). The language he uses is rooted in Exodus 34:6–7.
- A covenant God. The God to whom Daniel prays is in relationship with his people by covenant. As such, God is committed to this people and that they be a light to the nations. The exile of God's people (anticipated long ago in Deut. 28) is not the final word but a dark night of discipline before the dawn of

reconciliation. The covenant stipulates that exile is not punitive for its own sake but rather is corrective and rehabilitative.
- A forgiving God. Daniel prays to the One he knows will forgive because that is his nature (9:9). Daniel knows that God's forgiveness is certain for those who repent from their sin and turn to him.
- A listening God. Daniel prays to a God who hears the cries of his people. God is compassionate. He hears because of his great mercy and love (9:18). This gives confidence to those who read Daniel to pray to this God and trust him to hear their cries of suffering and to deliver them as he sees fit.

Daniel 9:24–27 is God's response to Daniel's prayer, and it is a strange response. But it shows us that God does answer prayer, although not always the way we think he should.

his mention of Jeremiah in Daniel 9:2 indicates. Jeremiah 29:10 records the pronouncement of a seventy-year exile. Daniel admits the people's sin, and in so doing, draws his readers to turn to God and repent as well. As they do, they express their faith in God. ⬚

DANIEL'S FINAL VISION: DANIEL 10–12

⬚ READ DANIEL 10–12 ⬚

Daniel 10:1–12:13 is an extended unit comprising the final vision. Daniel 10 introduces the vision, Daniel 11 presents the vision, and Daniel 12 resolves the vision, in which God vindicates both himself and his people.

In Daniel 9 the prophet prayed a prayer of repentance in response to God's Word, and he heard a response from heaven (literally). Chapter 10 takes up this theme again. As with other introductions to the prophet's visions, Daniel 10:1 includes a formula that identifies the year of the king's reign (third), the king (Cyrus), and the recipient of the vision (Daniel). In chapter 9, Daniel is reading the prophet Jeremiah and responding to God's Word, but Daniel 10:1 says he receives a "true" message about a "great war."

Now of course the message was true, so why bother to say so? This statement emphasizes again the truthfulness of God and his plan to defeat evil and bring about ultimate peace. This plan was also evident in Daniel 7, but here the statement about the truth of this message would be very comforting to a people oppressed—as God's people often are.

The speaker of the message is a figure that Daniel alone sees, and it is very much like the figures in Ezekiel 1 and 8–11. It may be God himself speaking, or it may be an angel. The text does not definitively say. The figure offers words of encouragement to Daniel:

- Daniel is highly esteemed (10:11).
- The angelic being is sent to Daniel to speak to him (10:11).
- Daniel should not be afraid (10:12).
- God responds to Daniel's prayer through this being (10:12).
- Daniel is to hear what God is doing with his people (10:14).

But verse 13 says something very curious (which leads us away from thinking that the person speaking is God himself). The being says that he would have come sooner, but the "prince of the Persian kingdom" detained him for some days. This speaker likely is a major angelic figure. He says the angel Michael came to help him in this fight and then remained in battle against the Persian demonic force so the figure speaking to Daniel could deliver God's message (v. 21). This angel of God has been battling an angel of darkness, against whom he will soon battle again (v. 20). Daniel perceives a cosmic battle that is happening alongside a human conflict between human kings and kingdoms.

Daniel 10 concludes with the speaker's comment about the "Book of Truth" (v. 21). This book is probably the shaping of world activity by God's hand, the history of the world according to God's plan. In this plan, human and heavenly powers are at work, but they are all supported and guided by the sovereign hand of God—his ways, plans, and ultimate victory over evil are reliable and true.

The king mentioned in Daniel 11 may be Antiochus IV Epiphanes or the indulgent, idolatrous antichrist (Rev. 13). The two may be related, at least to a degree, depending on how one understands biblical prophecy. If biblical prophecy is fulfilled one and only one time, then the king is *either* Antiochus IV *or* the antichrist. Sometimes this is how biblical prophecy works. For example, the vision in Daniel 7 of "one like a son of man" receiving an eternal kingdom has one and only one fulfillment: Jesus. But other prophecies have more than one fulfillment. This appears to be the case with Daniel 11, which is fulfilled by Antiochus IV Epiphanes but is fulfilled in a more extensive way by the later antichrist. However understood, it is clear that this king is horrible but gets his due punishment—and no one helps him (v. 45).

Chapter 12 counters the demise of this idolatrous and wicked king with the glory of God. The angel Michael once again rises up to fight for God's people. God will judge the peoples of the earth in a final sense through, on the logic of Daniel 7, his appointed king. This king judges "some to everlasting life, others to shame and everlasting contempt" (12:2). This is the most explicit statement about resurrection in the Old Testament. Clearly, at the end of history as we know it, there is a general resurrection for both the wicked and the righteous. Those whose names are "written in the book" receive eternal, resurrected, embodied life (12:1; the book of life, the record of those who have lived with their faith and hope in the salvation of God, in Christ). Those whom God in Christ judges as being not written in the book live, but to eternal shame and contempt (hell).

In the theology and message of Daniel, these verses highlight the finality of God's dealing with the wicked. They will be eternally shamed—at individual, communal, kingdom, and spiritual levels. Yet those who place their faith and hope in God's salvation will find eternal life as their reward in a resurrected body.

In verse 3, the angel tells Daniel, "Those who are wise will shine like the brightness of the heavens, and those who lead many to righteousness, like the stars for ever and ever." These words are a climactic key to the book.

They highlight why the book was written. By accepting the book's teaching of God's power and sovereignty, the way God deals with the wicked, his divine vindication of the faithful, and his ultimate defeat of sin and sinful kingdoms, a person becomes "wise." Readers are to embrace this teaching and teach others as well. God's word and God's plan are clear for those who will see it. Those who reject this message (fools, in the language of Proverbs) go about trying to find other kinds of knowledge, but their search (as well as their lives) is doomed from the start (v. 4). Wisdom begins with knowing and fearing the Lord and what he is doing in the world (Prov. 1:7; 9:10). Daniel provides God's plan. The wise will see and embrace it to eternal life. The fool will look elsewhere to eternal death.

Daniel's vision that began in chapter 10 concludes as it began: with a description of the location of the vision in 12:4–9. It provides a bookend to the vision and a suitable conclusion to the book. 👥

Implementation—Reading Daniel as Christian Scripture Today

For a Christian implementation of Daniel, it is appropriate to reflect on the "one like a son of man" and Jesus, the Son of Man. Scholars puzzle over the identity of the figure described in the Aramaic as *kebar enash*, alternatively translated "one like a human being" (7:13). The simile at work here is that one who is *like* a human being is also *unlike* a human being. He is like a human being and thereby unlike the creation-defying kingdoms that preceded him. Therefore, as a human being, the horizontal aspects of this Son's creational participation are affirmed. Also, as one who rides on clouds, this Son is associated with heaven. He is associated (in some way) with divinity. He goes on the clouds *unto* (Aramaic *'ad*) the Ancient of Days. This figure goes up to the divine assembly to receive the authority and dominion granted him by the Most High God, affirming the vertical aspects of the Son's creational participation.

The figure in Daniel 7 who receives authority from the Ancient of Days is associated with both heaven and earth, uniting the two. The Son of Man

RECEPTION HISTORY 👥

The Tribulation Depicted in Daniel 12?

Interestingly, the final verses of chapter 12 (esp. Dan. 12:7, 11) have been interpreted sometimes as referring particularly and specifically to the three and a half years of the tribulation period in dispensational theology. While this is possible, there are other possibilities: (1) The time periods are not as strict as years (the Hebrew says "time, times and half a time" in v. 7). It may be multiple years or an ambiguous time. (2) The time refers to the reign of Antiochus IV Epiphanes, whose activity at the temple in Jerusalem was idolatrous and abominable (congruent with the "abomination of desolation" language in Dan. 12:11 NASB). (3) The time frames were intentionally unclear to drive home the point of verse 9: "Go about your business being faithful to God, Daniel. These words are sealed up and preserved until the end. Your responsibility is not to know all the details in exactitude but rather to trust God as you have learned in this book and in your life with the Lord" (author's paraphrase). On this last point, Daniel teaches its readers that suffering may occur in the present, but it is not the final story. God's plan is true and reliable. Followers of God can be patient and trust in God and his divine plan to overthrow evil. God will bring comfort and an end to suffering. Evil is horrific, but in the end God wins.

brings the authority of heaven to earth. The ambiguity of the simile and its concomitant description contribute to the significance of the whole scene. In the context of Daniel 7, what matters most is that a heavenly and earthly Messiah receives God's dominion that brings peace on earth.

With these realities in view, it is not surprising that Jesus uses the title "Son of Man" to describe his identity and ministry. This is a favorite title of Jesus in Matthew (used more than two dozen times). When Jesus stands on trial before the Sanhedrin, he alludes clearly to Daniel 7:13, affirming he is that individual: "From now on you will see the Son of Man sitting at the right hand of the Mighty One and coming on the clouds of heaven" (Matt. 26:64; cf. Mark 14:62; Luke 22:69). The point is that Jesus understood himself to be the one who unites heaven and earth. He is human and divine and brings in the dominion of God.

Whenever Christians receive the body and blood of Jesus, we are reminded that he has shed his blood to usher in God's reign and reconcile humanity back to God. He brings heaven to earth and draws his followers into his reign. With Christ, Christians await the time when he will reign consummately in his kingdom. Upon receiving the body and blood of Christ, Christians respond with gratitude, "Thanks be to God." This worship is a foretaste of Christ's eternal reign on this earth, to which Daniel testifies. Our worship reminds us once again that the Lord reigns and his reign will never end!

Moreover, Jesus's reign reminds us of Daniel's emphasis on hope and patience amid suffering. As Jesus's reign is secure, followers of Jesus can stand firm in the trials of life, patient that God's power will preserve, rescue, or deliver. Even when the powers of evil seem to be ascendant, God's reign will put the world to rights.

RECEPTION HISTORY

John Calvin on Jesus in Daniel

"Christ was set forth as the Son of man, although he was then the eternal Word of God."[b]

KEY VERSES IN DANIEL

- But Daniel resolved not to defile himself with the royal food and wine, and he asked the chief official for permission not to defile himself this way. 1:8
- The king said to Daniel, "Surely your God is the God of gods and the Lord of kings and a revealer of mysteries, for you were able to reveal this mystery." 2:47
- In my vision at night I looked, and there before me was one like a son of man, coming with the clouds of heaven. He approached the Ancient of Days and was led into his presence. He was given authority, glory and sovereign power; all nations and peoples of every language worshiped him. His dominion is an everlasting dominion that will not pass away, and his kingdom is one that will never be destroyed. 7:13–14

Christian Reading Questions

1. Explain how Daniel and his friends preserve their missional identity, living within the world of Babylon while preserving their faithfulness to Israel's God.
2. What is apocalyptic literature and how is it distinctive from other prophetic texts?
3. Explain Daniel's purpose and message. Give special attention to specific texts and themes.
4. What does the theme of God's sovereignty have to do with Daniel?
5. How does Jesus relate with the Son of Man in Daniel 7?

CHAPTER TWENTY-SEVEN

Ezra-Nehemiah

Orientation

In the ancient world, Ezra-Nehemiah was understood as one complete work rather than two. The Jewish scribes who interpreted the Old Testament (called Masoretes) understood the unity of the corpus to the degree that they marked the "middle" of the book at Nehemiah 3:32. English Bibles today split Ezra and Nehemiah, but their story is one story rather than two. Thus, we read these books together in this chapter. 👥

Ezra-Nehemiah portrays the time frame from the Persian reign of Cyrus the Great in 539 BC to Artaxerxes I in 425 BC. Likely, some portions were composed close to the events described, and the book was compiled by 400 BC, although Ezra 1–6 may have been affixed as late as 300 BC.[1] 📖

Exploration—Ezra-Nehemiah

The Goal Initiated—Cyrus's Decree: Ezra 1:1–4

▓ READ EZRA 1 ▓

Ezra-Nehemiah begins by characterizing the action of the book as a fulfillment of prophecy: "In the first year of Cyrus king of Persia, in order to fulfill the word of the LORD spoken by Jeremiah, the LORD moved the heart of Cyrus king of Persia to make a proclamation throughout his realm and also to put it in writing" (Ezra 1:1). What is likely intended here is the prophetic word of Jeremiah 25:1–14 or 29:10–14, which foretell the seventy-year exile and subsequent return. God is bringing his people back to the land. It is a kind of "second exodus": from exile in Persia to homecoming in the land of promise.

The means of divine restoration, however, is unique: a royal decree. This famous decree is from Cyrus, the Persian king who defeated Babylonian opposition and took control of the former Babylonian kingdom. During his reign, he consolidated his authority and fostered goodwill among the people by allowing captured and exiled prisoners of war from Babylonian invasions to return to their homelands. His decree enabled these vanquished peoples to rebuild their gods' shrines. Ezra 1:1–4 identifies four elements of Cyrus's edict:

1. YHWH has given Cyrus the authority over all kingdoms.
2. YHWH appointed Cyrus to rebuild Jerusalem's temple.
3. Any Israelite can return (or "go up") to Jerusalem to work on rebuilding the temple.
4. Local Persians are to equip the Israelites with silver and gold, goods and livestock, and offerings to fund the rebuilding effort.

For Ezra-Nehemiah, Cyrus's reign is determined by YHWH rather than royal strategy

RECEPTION HISTORY

Origen and Jerome on Ezra and Nehemiah

If Ezra-Nehemiah is really one composition, then how did we get two books in our modern Bibles? The two books were disjointed into Ezra and Nehemiah notably by Origen (third century AD). In the late fourth century Jerome translated the Bible from the Hebrew and Greek into Latin and divided Ezra-Nehemiah into two books. His Latin translation, the Vulgate, became the Bible of the Western church, and so dividing Ezra and Nehemiah into two books was codified.

Public domain / Uffizi Gallery

Figure 27.1. *St. Jerome in the Desert* by Giovanni Bellini (ca. 1480)

LITERARY NOTES

The Structure of Ezra-Nehemiah

The structure of Ezra-Nehemiah makes clear why the books should be read together. Together, the books move toward the initial goal of returning to Judah to build God's house, offer steps along the way amid conflict, introduce major protagonists (Ezra and Nehemiah), and then conclude with the achieved goal of temple celebration. Thus, it is sensible to see the whole of the composition as a unity.[a]

I. The goal initiated: Cyrus's decree (Ezra 1:1–4)

II. The community rebuilds God's house (Ezra 1:5–Neh. 7:72)

   1. Introduction: The people prepare for return (Ezra 1:5–6)

   2. The community returns and rebuilds altar with opposition (Ezra 1:7–6:22)

   3. Ezra and the people return to build community with conflict (intermarriage) (Ezra 7:1–10:44)

   4. Nehemiah returns to rebuild city wall with opposition (Neh. 1:1–7:4)

   5. Closure: Repopulating the city (Neh. 7:5–72; reiterating Ezra 2, binding the composition)

III. The goal reached: Celebration of God's house according to Torah (Neh. 7:73–13:31)

Figure 27.2. Ezra works on a copy of the Bible, Codex Amiatinus (ca. eighth century), Biblioteca Medicea-Laurenziana, Florence, Italy.

or imperial power. Further, the idea that YHWH appoints Cyrus depicts Israel's God not merely as a local deity but rather as an imperial Lord over all nations and peoples. This is fitting to YHWH's power as the creator of heaven and earth. Thus, Cyrus affirms YHWH is the "God of Israel" but also the "God of heaven" who has given all kingdoms to Cyrus.

Archaeological evidence of Cyrus's edict was discovered in Babylon in 1879. A monumental inscription, now known as the Cyrus Cylinder, presents Cyrus's resettlement policy for his conquered regions. Although there are general similarities between the content of the Cyrus Cylinder and Ezra 1:2–4, there are differences as well. This discrepancy leads some to argue that the Bible is historically imprecise and, therefore, an unreliable guide to understanding what happened in the past.

We take a different approach. That both the Cyrus Cylinder and Ezra 1:2–4 present Cyrus's decree to enable conquered peoples to return to their homelands and rebuild their shrines represents a core historical fact that both texts share. Ezra, however, is concerned primarily with what God is doing with his people Israel, not other nations. Ezra's recounting of Cyrus's decree reveals the theological power at work in the decree: YHWH has done this. The omission of other nations' shrines

HISTORICAL MATTERS

The Edict of Cyrus and the Cyrus Cylinder

The decree written on the Cyrus Cylinder is sometimes called the edict or decree of Cyrus. Its content approximates some of Ezra 1:1–4 and 2 Chronicles 36:23. The relevant content on the cylinder reads as follows:

From [Ninev]eh(?), Ashur and Susa, Agade, Eshunna, Zamban, Meturnu, Der, as far as the region of the Gutium, I returned the (images of) the gods to the sacred centers [on the other side of] the Tigris whose sanctuaries have been abandoned for a long time, and I let them dwell in eternal abodes. I gathered all their inhabitants and returned (to them) their dwellings.[b]

This selection indicates that Cyrus did, in fact, decree that conquered peoples were free to return to their homelands and take care of their religious shrines (the gods of the nations). Ezra 1:1–4 and 2 Chronicles 36:23 record that decree as it related to the people of Judah living in the Persian period.

Figure 27.3. The Cyrus Cylinder

and deities fits Ezra-Nehemiah's focus on the primacy of YHWH's power over all gods, kings, and kingdoms. Thus, for Ezra-Nehemiah, Cyrus issued this decree not from the abundance of his beneficence but rather because of the providential movement of God in history. Theologically, Ezra-Nehemiah presents divine action as the primary driver of imperial action, subverting and subsuming the authority of empire under the authority of YHWH, Israel's God. Thus, the Israelites who lived in the ghettos of Persia or the contested land of Israel could take comfort that their God is high above all powers and could be trusted with their tenuous state.

The Community Rebuilds God's House: Ezra 1:5–Nehemiah 7:72

THE COMMUNITY RETURNS TO BUILD: EZRA 1:5–6:22

▓ READ EZRA 4–6 ▓

After presenting the decree of Cyrus, the book presents the challenges and opportunities of the rebuilding effort. Temple personnel take center stage, as the list of returnees in Ezra 2 focuses on the priests and Levites especially. Also listed are the descendants of Parosh, likely stonemasons and builders (cf. Neh. 3:25), as well as the men of Bethlehem, who may have served as builders like the family of Parosh. Mention of the men of Bethlehem may be a subtle nod to the Davidic dynasty, which also came from Bethlehem. Similarly, descendants of the "servants of Solomon" are in the returnee list (Ezra 2:55–57), perhaps hinting at the return of the Davidic throne.

Jeshua (sometimes translated "Joshua") and Zerubbabel are the two leaders who will engage the rebuilding effort. They begin with the altar of the Lord, followed by the building of the temple complex. Ezra 3:10–11 records that as the temple foundation is laid, the Levites and priests praise God with the language of the book of Psalms: "He is good; his love toward Israel endures forever" (3:10).

This great moment for the returnees is a time of sadness for those old enough to remember

CANONICAL CONNECTIONS

Exodus and Ezra-Nehemiah

Exodus 12:31–32 and Ezra 1:2–4	Release of Israelites by imperial decree
Exodus 12:35–36 and Ezra 1:4–6	Israelites receive aid from gentile neighbors
Exodus 12:31 and Ezra 1:4	Release for purpose of worship

If Ezra depicts a kind of second exodus from Persia in accord with the historical exodus from Egypt, then we may assume that the relationship between Persia and the Jews was not as rosy as may first appear. God is on the move delivering his people from slavery, but the fact that Persia and Egypt are correlates in the texts tells us that Israel needs divine deliverance. Thus, Ezra-Nehemiah does view Persia as a beneficent overlord, taking into account the freedom of return to rebuild the temple.

CANONICAL CONNECTIONS

Psalmic Language in Ezra

"He is good, his love toward Israel endures forever" (3:10). This language echoes without exactly repeating the language of Psalms 100:5; 106:1; 107:1; 117:2; 118:1–4, 29; 138:8. However, Psalm 136 features, in every verse, the language of God's love that endures forever. The returnees celebrate the steadfast love of YHWH because they have just experienced the first major step of God's restoration of his people in the land. Worship and sacrifice are possible once again because the altar stone has been laid.

Solomon's temple prior to its destruction by Nebuchadnezzar. Compared with the glory of that structure, the present moment is a distinct letdown (3:12). The narrator comments, "No one could distinguish the sound of the shouts of joy from the sound of weeping, because the people made so much noise. And the sound was heard far away" (3:13). These words capture the ambiguity of the return. On the one hand, God has been gracious and compassionate to his people in facilitating their return and restoration effort. God has fulfilled, in part, the prophecy of Jeremiah's new covenant for their day. The exile is over, and the restoration is at hand! On the other hand, the restoration cannot be fully realized because of its partial nature. Partial in the sense that those who return are only those "whose heart God had moved" (1:5) rather than the full populace. Partial in the sense that the former glory was greater than the latter. Partial in the sense that God's people live in their own land but under foreign occupation and rule (which Ezra 9 and Neh. 9 characterize as being in slavery). Partial in the sense that, as the book will reveal, God's people are already implicated in sin by their intermingling with the peoples of the land. And finally, partial in the sense that Nehemiah 13 concludes the Ezra-Nehemiah corpus with the need for reform action. If restoration is accomplished in Ezra-Nehemiah along the contours of Jeremiah's vision, then it can only be a tenuous and partial fulfillment of prophecy awaiting its full expression at a future time.

Table 27.1. Reign of Persian Kings and Biblical References

Persian King	Timeline of Reign	Biblical Reference
Cyrus II (the Great)	539–530 BC	Ezra 1:1–4; 6:3–5
Cambyses II	529–522 BC	not mentioned
Darius I	521–486 BC	Ezra 4:24; 5:5–7 (Haggai and Zechariah's ministry); Ezra 6:13–15 (Zerubbabel completes temple building, 515 BC)
Xerxes I	485–465 BC	Ezra 4:6 (Hebrew "Ahasuerus"; may be Ahasuerus of the book of Esther)
Artaxerxes I	465–425 BC	Ezra 7:7 (possibly Ezra's mission in 458 BC); Neh. 2:1; 13:6 (cupbearer to king in 444 BC)
Xerxes II	423 BC	not mentioned
Darius II	423–404 BC	not mentioned
Artaxerxes II	404–359 BC	Ezra 7:7 (some place Ezra's mission here in 398 BC)
Artaxerxes III	358–338 BC	not mentioned

Note: For a full discussion of the chronology of Ezra-Nehemiah, see Andrew E. Steinmann, *Ezra and Nehemiah*, Concordia Commentary (St. Louis: Concordia, 2010), 29–63.

Ezra 4–6 presents the ongoing battle to rebuild in the face of opposition and new leadership. In Ezra 4, some people of the land frustrate and complicate the temple project, bribing regional governors and attempting to impede progress. Undeterred, Jeshua and Zerubbabel lead the people toward their goal. The prophets Haggai and Zechariah encourage and support the people in the midst of this opposition (Ezra 5:1), a point reflected in the Minor Prophets Haggai and Zechariah. Comfort and support were needed; Ezra 5 presents regional leadership (Tattenai and Shethar-Bozenai) contesting the rebuilding work. These opponents write Darius I to challenge the claim that Cyrus II actually issued a decree enabling the Jews to rebuild the temple. The letter is delivered, a search of the Persian royal archives is made, and Darius locates a scroll with Cyrus's edict, confirming royal authorization for the work. Further, Darius blesses the work, pays for the rebuilding out of the royal coffers, and threatens punishment for anyone who prevents it (Ezra 6). The section concludes with completion of the temple, its dedication in 515 BC, and the celebration of the Passover (6:13–22).

With the names of regional governors and Persian kings mentioned, we might begin to wonder how these leaders fit within the action of the book.[2] With this in mind we thought it might be helpful to see the possibilities and how it all fits together (see table 27.1).

EZRA'S LEADERSHIP IN JERUSALEM: EZRA 7–10

▓ READ EZRA 9 ▓

After the completion and dedication of the temple, Ezra the chief priest (a descendant in the line of Aaron) comes to Jerusalem from Babylon. This section is known as "Ezra's Memoir" because of the first-person speech of Ezra throughout as he details his experience with the returnees in the land. Ezra 7:6 describes Ezra as having royal favor ("The king had granted him anything he asked") and divine favor ("The hand of the Lord his God was on him"; cf. v. 9). The text also describes Ezra in the following ways:

Ezra is a teacher (7:6).
Ezra is "well-versed in the Law of Moses" (7:6).
Ezra devotes himself to "the study and observance of the Law of the Lord" (7:10).
Ezra devotes himself to "teaching its decrees and laws in Israel" (7:10).

Ezra is a priest, and his work has a distinct focus on reading, interpretation, and instruction in "the Law of Moses" or "the Law of the Lord."

Foreign Peoples in Ezra 9:1, Exodus, and Deuteronomy

The list of nations in Ezra 9:1 is curious. Mention of Jebusites is anachronistic, as this people did not even exist by this time in history.[c] Further, Ezra's list differs from descriptions of the peoples of the land in Exodus (e.g., Exod. 3:8, 17; 34:11): Moabites, Ammonites, and Egyptians are not included in those texts. Finally, Moabites and Ammonites are excluded from the sanctuary because of their oppression of Israel in the wilderness wandering (Deut. 23:3). Egypt is Israel's historic oppressor. So, the descriptions of the peoples of the land with whom Israel intermarries is theologically combustive. Israel has intermarried with those whom God has displaced from the land in Exodus–Deuteronomy (Canaanites, Hittites, Perizzites, Jebusites, and Amorites); those God has forbidden from entering the temple (Moabites and Ammonites); and those with whom Israel experienced its greatest oppression (Egypt).

Interpretation of God's Word and giving rulings on it become more and more important in the postexilic period down to the time of Jesus.

Ezra discovers God's people have intermarried with the people of the land: "Canaanites, Hittites, Perizzites, Jebusites, Ammonites, Moabites, Egyptians and Amorites" (9:1). When Ezra learns this, he mourns and grieves his people's sin. He offers a penitential prayer to God, recognizing that such intermarriage is sinful (9:3–15). In chapter 10, he leads his people to confess and repent as well. The memoir concludes with a list of those guilty of intermarriage (10:18–44). Israel's intermarriage with the people of the land reveals their spiritual compromise and disobedience to God's Word.

Ezra's prayer is a penitential prayer, and it can be compared with the prayers in Daniel 9 and Nehemiah 9. The overall content is the same in each of these prayers: (1) God's people have sinned and violated the terms of YHWH's covenant with Israel in various ways (particularly in terms of intermarriage with foreign peoples in Ezra-Nehemiah); (2) YHWH has rightly punished his people in accordance with the terms of the covenant; (3) God's people now repent and ask for divine favor and restoration. Ezra also thanks YHWH for the way that he has done what he had promised to do: return the people to the land of promise. Ezra's

Ezra-Nehemiah and the Fulfillment of Prophecy

In accordance with the intertextual nature of the Old Testament, Ezra 7–9 recalls the language of Jeremiah's new covenant, particularly Jeremiah 31.[d]

Jeremiah 31	Ezra 7–9
"remnant of Israel" (v. 7)	"remnant" (9:14)
"I will . . . gather them" (v. 8) "He will . . . gather them" (v. 10)	"I gathered them" (8:15 NRSV)
"over the goodness of the LORD" (v. 12 NRSV) "I will saturate my people with goodness (tubah)" (v. 14)	"The hand of our God is upon all those who seek Him, for good (tobah)" (Ezra 8:22 AT)
"enemy" (v. 16)	"from enemies" (8:22, 31)
"I was ashamed and humiliated" (v. 19)	"I was ashamed to ask" (8:22) "I am too ashamed" (9:6)

Jeremiah 31	Ezra 7–9
"straight path" (v. 9 NRSV)	"straight path" (8:21 AT)
"holy to the LORD" (v. 40)	"in his holy place" (9:8 NRSV)
"Let us go up to Zion" (v. 6)	"Journey up from Babylon . . . to Jerusalem" (7:9 NRSV)

The language from the new covenant appearing in Ezra's reflections on the experience of Israel subtly affirms a fulfillment of Jeremiah's prophecy. In Israel's return from Persia to the promised land, the exodus experience is revived in the postexilic period, and God's prophetic promise to gather a remnant and bring his people back has been fulfilled. And yet, in Ezra's penitential prayer (Ezra 9), the fulfillment is seen to be only partial. God's people still live under oppression and do not enjoy full possession of the land. God's people still have a prevalent sin problem that manifests in their very heart.

perspective on their return to the land is favorable, as he uses language that resonates with that of Jeremiah's new covenant (Jer. 31). 𝒮

Although Ezra thanks God for (partly) fulfilling the terms of the new covenant, not all is fulfilled. Ezra says that they are experiencing freedom only for a (brief) moment (9:8). The peaceful flash of time is not the eternal fulfillment of the land belonging to Israel in the new covenant. Persian rule can only be a stopgap in God's plan. Ezra longs for something greater. Ezra thanks God for the "little relief" Israel experiences, but nonetheless they remain in "bondage" (9:8). Ezra draws attention to the fact that God's people do not live in their land free, as they live under the authority of Persian rule in their homeland, hence Ezra's reference to "bondage" in 9:8. The reason for this penitential prayer is to request God's forgiveness and to motivate divine deliverance from Persian rule to Israel's freedom. Ezra's prayer reinforces that the author of goodness in their current situation is not *Persia* but rather YHWH! Israel's God is Lord over Persia and orchestrates the events in which the people find themselves. As such, Israel's loyalty belongs to the Lord rather than Persia.

Ezra considers their intermarriage with foreign peoples to be rebellion. He enjoins Israel: "You have been unfaithful; you have married foreign women, adding to Israel's guilt. Now honor the LORD, the God of your ancestors, and do his will. Separate yourselves from the peoples around you and from your foreign wives" (10:10–11). The people respond in the affirmative, but they demur as to the process and timing of the divorces. Still, the text indicates that Ezra's work is complete, reforming the people's compromise, effectively sending non-Israelite women and children away from their husbands and fathers. The listing of the men who intermarried concludes the section.

NEHEMIAH'S MEMOIR AND REPOPULATING THE CITY: NEHEMIAH 1–7

▧ READ NEHEMIAH 1–6 ▧

Nehemiah 1–6, known as "Nehemiah's Memoir," depicts the experience of Nehemiah, the cupbearer to King Artaxerxes I. Nehemiah feels the weight of Jerusalem's plight, vulnerable to attack because the walls that protect it are in ruins, destroyed by Nebuchadnezzar's invasion over a century earlier (Neh. 1:3). Nehemiah offers a prayer to God that both confesses sin and recites a history of God's covenantal faithfulness, in some ways similar to Ezra 9. Nehemiah prays God's Word to God in order to persuade God to act in the moment.

God's means of deliverance is the Persian king. Just as Joseph received favor in the royal house of Pharaoh, Nehemiah receives the favor of

Artaxerxes I and is given permission to go rebuild the walls (Neh. 2:6). The antagonists in Nehemiah's story are Sanballat the Horonite, Tobiah the Ammonite, and Geshem the Arab. These officials want to keep the Jews in and around Jerusalem poor and uncomfortable. Nehemiah speaks of mocking, oppression, and ridicule (4:1–3) and even a plot to kill the workers (4:11). Sanballat accuses Nehemiah and the people of insurrection against Persia to prevent their progress (6:5–7). Despite this opposition, the work on the walls is completed in fifty-two days (6:15).

Nehemiah 7 rehearses how God's people would protect, fill, and live in the city that Nehemiah has preserved. A completed wall with gates and towers requires guards to ensure the city will be safe. Nehemiah 7 describes the guards appointed to protect the city. A completed city wall facilitated protection, and more exiles could return home. Nehemiah 7:4–73 details the mass migration of Israelites returning to Jerusalem to worship and live there.

The Goal Reached—Celebration of God's House according to Torah: Nehemiah 7:73–13:31

■ READ NEHEMIAH 9–11 ■

The renewed people and place require governing laws for the common good, and Nehemiah 8 shows that this people will be governed by God's law. Ezra reads aloud God's law before the city and people, and at each turn, when they hear the instruction, they respond with obedience. Chapter 8 concludes: "Day after day, from the first day to the last, Ezra read from the Book of the Law of God. They celebrated the festival for seven days, and on the eighth day, in accordance with the regulation, there was an assembly" (8:18). This gives the impression that God's law would govern God's people in God's land.

However, Nehemiah 9 reveals the persistent problem of sin among the returnees. Like Daniel 9 and Ezra 9, Nehemiah 9 is a penitential prayer that confesses sin, repents of it, and requests divine forgiveness. The prayers in Ezra-Nehemiah tend to depict the Jews' situation as essentially burdensome. They are grateful to God for returning them to the promised land even as they express consternation about living under foreign rule.[4] Nehemiah concludes the prayer by stating to God that the returnees are not liberated under Persian rule but are oppressed as slaves (Neh. 9:36). The reason for their slavery? YHWH has punished them for sin, and so the goodness of the land does not go to God's people but rather to the kingdom YHWH has set over them (9:37). Nehemiah says Persia rules over the body of Israel, and they are in deep distress. From Nehemiah's perspective, YHWH rightly placed the Jewish people in this terrible situation because of their sin. Therefore, divine control over Israel provides the foundation for his penitential prayer to God: if God can punish sin, God can relent over disaster as well. The key to the change, of course, is repentance. If God's people confess and repent, then God can deliver his people from Persian rule.

Nehemiah 10 parallels the reforms that are also detailed at the end of the book, in Nehemiah 13. In Nehemiah 10, God's people solemnly vow to keep God's law (10:29). The passage also details which of the returnees have vowed to be obedient (10:1–27) alongside the Levites, who also enjoin themselves to obedience (10:28–39).

Figure 27.4. A model of the wall and palace of the second-temple complex in Jerusalem, viewed from the south to the north. The eastern wall and towers that protect the royal palace are visible.

Nehemiah 11–12 describes the leaders of Israel who resettle Jerusalem, with an emphasis on the temple personnel who would ensure proper worship at the sanctuary (11:1–23; 12:1–25). Why are there two lists of priestly and Levitical returnees? Most likely, these represent two sources of material from two different time periods (the return to Jerusalem in the sixth century BC as well as the time of rebuilding in Ezra and Nehemiah's fifth-century time frame). These sources have been combined in the text's final form to emphasize the way in which temple worship was restored.[5] A strong emphasis on the proper restoration of temple worship is important for the Second Temple period, where proper worship in the proper place was essential for the continued vitality of God's

HISTORICAL MATTERS

Nehemiah 10 and 13

Nehemiah 10 and 13 seem to repeat one another in content. Williamson notes the following parallels:[e]

Mixed marriages	10:30	13:23–30
Sabbath	10:31	13:15–22
Wood offering	10:34	13:31
Firstfruits	10:35–36	13:31
Levitical tithes	10:37–38	13:10–14
Neglect of the temple	10:39	13:11

Why do these texts mirror one another? There are two possibilities: (1) It may be that the people of God commit to follow God's law on the items listed in the chart above (Neh. 10), only to stray from those commitments and then recommit to them point by point in Nehemiah's second term as governor (Neh. 13). If this is the case, then the action of Nehemiah 10 precedes the action of Nehemiah 13, and they are chronological. Alternatively, (2) the action of Nehemiah 13 could occur prior to Nehemiah 10, and the reforms happened first and Nehemiah 10 has been inserted into the narrative dischronologically as a narrative technique to pique the reader's attention. Williamson prefers the latter option, making Nehemiah 10 and 13 dischronological. The question, of course, is why. Perhaps to set the failure of the people and the need for reform in the forefront of later readers. God's people still stray from the path and need continual reform to keep them on track.

What Happened to the Ark of the Covenant?

The details of what happened to the ark of the covenant after the Babylonian invasion are lost to history. Some believe Nebuchadnezzar took it along with the other temple implements when he destroyed Jerusalem in 586 BC. However, Jewish tradition describes how Jeremiah took the ark and hid it on Mount Nebo, where it has been hidden since (2 Maccabees 2:4–10). The ark will be revealed, according to Maccabees, when God restores his people and kingdom.

people in God's land. There is one notable exception to the restoration. The sanctuary does not contain the ark of the covenant, which was taken by Nebuchadnezzar and lost to history. Nehemiah 11 also includes a note on other settlers, indicating that the resettlement did not solely focus on Jerusalem but also included cities to the north as well as cities in the south.

Nehemiah 13 indicates need for reform once again. Sin still sits too close to God's people. This chapter details the various reforms of Nehemiah in his second term as governor, and the chapter is interspersed with Nehemiah's prayer:

- that God remember his reforms (13:14)
- that God remember his Sabbath reform (13:22)
- for divine retribution against sinful Levites (13:29)
- for divine favor (13:31)

We have seen similar prayers in Nehemiah's memoirs. Short, focused prayers of Nehemiah interrupt the narrative flow at key points, enjoining God to act on behalf of the people:

- for divine favor to rebuild (1:5–11)
- for retribution against enemies (4:4–5)
- for divine favor for his care for his people (5:19)

Israelites, Judahites, and Jews

Sometimes students identify the ancient people of Israel as the "Jewish" people. While we understand what students mean, their categories are a bit off, and technically they are thinking anachronistically. The term "Jew" comes from the postexilic Persian period. Prior to Persian rule, the people of Israel in the Southern Kingdom were identified as Judahites, and the people of Israel in the Northern Kingdom were called Israelites. When Israel fell in 722 BC, only Judah remained, even if sometimes the Old Testament uses "Israel" to describe the theological, covenantal people of God rather than the Northern or Southern Kingdoms. After the Southern Kingdom of Judah fell in 586 BC, they were under Babylonian rule, and then once Babylon was defeated by Persia in the mid-sixth century BC, Judah became a Persian province (or "satrapy"). One of the local districts in the Persian Empire was "Yehud," which was made up of (roughly) the old Southern Kingdom of Judah. The name "Jew"—or "Yehudi"— derives from this Persian designation. Thus, it is anachronistic to label Abraham, Moses, Israelites in Egypt, or Israelites in Joshua– Kings as "Jews." The term "Jew" technically only becomes a term for people who live in the Persian governance within the district of Yehud. (Yehud was translated as "Judea" by the Greeks and, later, the Romans.) In the postexilic period moving into the Second Temple period, the term "Jew" was crystallized in common parlance as a descriptor for those who lived with distinctive religious and social identifiers that distinguished them from Hellenized culture after the reign of Alexander the Great and then the rise of the Roman Empire. The Jewish people, then, are understood as historically connected to the people of Israel, identified as an exiled and restored people in the region of Yehud in the Persian period, and distinguished as those who practiced social and religious customs distinct from others in the Greco-Roman world. This broad context informs how we come to understand the term "Jew" in the New Testament.

- for strength to complete the work (6:9)
- for divine retribution for Sanballat and false prophets (6:14)

These prayers give a glimpse into the theocentric focus of Nehemiah and provide a picture of the life of faith. At every obstacle, prayer is on Nehemiah's lips. He prays for divine favor, divine retribution, and strength to complete the work of rebuilding Jerusalem's walls. In this way, Nehemiah models for God's people a life of prayer.

Implementation—Reading Ezra-Nehemiah as Christian Scripture Today

Ezra-Nehemiah illustrates faithful prayer. Whenever Ezra and Nehemiah confront challenges or opportunities, they pray. Prayer is the first and best reflex in the life of faith. Their example becomes a model for the faithful follower of YHWH and, by extension, a picture of Jesus, whose life was governed by prayer.[6] Prayer, especially for Nehemiah, focused on provision of divine strength (for work), divine retribution against enemies (divine justice), and divine favor for God's people. The point of prayer, then, is to open the petitioner to God's activity in their life.

Ezra-Nehemiah also shows the struggle to live faithfully in trying times. This is especially evident in the difficult issue of divorce at crucial moments in the book (Ezra 9–10; Neh. 9–13). Ezra-Nehemiah authorizes divorce in the community of God, which included sending women and children away from the father and family (Ezra 9:1–3; 10:1–44; Neh. 9:2; 10:28, 30; 13:1–3). The book depicts separation of non-Israelite peoples from among the people of Israel. This would have certainly meant mass divorces.

What motivated these divorces? It was an attempt to live faithfully in trying times, when navigating the way forward was difficult. We feel compassion for the leaders facing such difficult obstacles. The community's compliance with the divorces represents the people's deep commitment to living faithfully, and we feel compassion for the people in this difficult spot, even if we may disagree with the decisions that were made. The best-made plans, or at least the best-intended plans, are still made in a context east of Eden. Still, why would they do it?

It may be that the Israelite returnees were divorcing their Israelite wives to intermarry with peoples of the nations. The prophet Malachi, a rough contemporary of this time frame, addresses this problem (Mal. 2:10–16). If this was the case, then it would be understandable that Ezra and Nehemiah were concerned to separate these folk as second wives/children from the primary marriage. Mixed marriages could have meant a second wife from a non-Israelite nation. The divorce of the Israelite wife and remarriage to a non-Israelite was considered compromise and sin. Faithfulness meant divorcing and sending away the non-Israelite as a kind of purgation for Israel's people and land.

However, another explanation is possible. From the text, it appears that Ezra and Nehemiah see their world under threat from outside influences, where "outside" means not just non-Israelites but those who are not faithful to YHWH. In this, we must reckon with the theocentric worldview of ancient peoples. Ancient peoples envisioned themselves as being a people of a deity. For Israel, ideally it was YHWH who was revered. For Moab, it was Chemosh. For Canaan, it was Baal. For the Babylonians, it was Marduk. The national deity was the focus of the people's identity and worship. The admixture of peoples interspersed with the Israelites indicates a theological concern not for racial purity as much as purity of devotion to YHWH. These nations did not worship YHWH alone; their worship may well have been compromised with worship of other deities as well.

The danger is that intermarriage among the nations would dilute devotion to Israel's God, compromising their covenantal commitments. Israel is still called to be "a kingdom of priests and a holy nation" (Exod. 19:6) in this Persian context. From the perspective of Ezra and Nehemiah, Israel ministering to the nations meant that they must be holy. And holiness meant they must protect themselves from the worship of other gods (Deut. 13:1–18). Intermarriage with the nations is a danger that distracts God's people from pure and undefiled worship. Ezra and Nehemiah's concern is that Jewish faith would be diluted and watered down beyond the point of recognition. Again, faithfulness meant divorcing and sending away the non-Israelites as a kind of purgation for Israel's people and land.

This explanation for mandated divorce on the basis of theological fidelity is possible even if tragic. Because of the work of Ezra and Nehemiah, we know that children are left fatherless, and there is no sense of provision for those sent away (Ezra 10:44). Reading Ezra-Nehemiah as Christian Scripture is not easy.

We can affirm that Ezra and Nehemiah's instinct for purity is vital for the faithful life even if we are less than positive about their execution of their purity ideal. The concern for purity of worship and life is witnessed in the early church, where Paul urges the Corinthians not to be "unequally yoked" in 2 Corinthians 6:14 (ESV). This certainly means that the church should not be improperly joined with *any* venture in which devotion to Christ

THEOLOGICAL ISSUES

Jesus and Divorce

In Matthew 19, religious leaders press Jesus on whether divorce is lawful for any reason. Jesus replies that divorce is a concession due to the hardness of human hearts. While permissible, divorce is not God's ideal. Even if divorce is mandated in Ezra and Nehemiah, it is not ideal, reflecting the brokenness of life and a community in need of divine help.

might be impeded by an asymmetrical commitment with people or worship that leads believers away from Christ. In other words, purity of devotion to Christ is essential for identity as a follower of Christ.

However, Paul supplements this teaching with explicit instruction regarding marriage and divorce between believers and unbelievers in 1 Corinthians 7:12–16. There he instructs that the Christian husband or wife who is married to a non-Christian should stay in the marriage as a witness to lead the unbelieving spouse to Christ. The background for this text is that one spouse came to faith in Christ, while the other did not. Instead of divorcing and sending away (as in Ezra-Nehemiah), the Christian spouse should stay in the marriage as a loving witness to Jesus's love. "How do you know, wife, whether you will save your husband? Or how do you know, husband, whether you will save your wife?" (1 Cor. 7:16 ESV). If the non-Christian spouse leaves, then so be it. But the believer is not to send the nonbeliever away.

KEY VERSES IN EZRA-NEHEMIAH

- The LORD, the God of heaven, has given me all the kingdoms of the earth and he has appointed me to build a temple for him at Jerusalem in Judah. Any of his people among you may go up to Jerusalem in Judah and build the temple of the LORD, the God of Israel, the God who is in Jerusalem, and may their God be with them. And in any locality where survivors may now be living, the people are to provide them with silver and gold, with goods and livestock, and with freewill offerings for the temple of God in Jerusalem. Ezra 1:2–4
- Many of the older priests and Levites and family heads, who had seen the former temple, wept aloud when they saw the foundation of this temple being laid, while many others shouted for joy. Ezra 3:12
- Ezra had devoted his life to the study and observance of the Law of the LORD, and to teaching its decrees and laws in Israel. Ezra 7:10
- In all that has happened to us, you have remained righteous; you have acted faithfully, while we acted wickedly. Neh. 9:33

Christian Reading Questions

1. How would you describe the theology of Ezra-Nehemiah? What theological themes stand out in the books?

2. How does Ezra-Nehemiah fulfill the new covenant prophecy of Jeremiah 31? How does Ezra-Nehemiah leave the new covenant prophecy unfulfilled?

3. What was the purpose of divorce in Ezra-Nehemiah? Does Ezra-Nehemiah advocate divorce? How does Ezra-Nehemiah cohere with other biblical teaching on divorce?

4. In what ways does Ezra-Nehemiah relate to the Pentateuch (particularly the books of Exodus and Deuteronomy)? How do these connections with the Pentateuch inform the theological messages in Ezra-Nehemiah?

5. What is the significance of prayer in Ezra-Nehemiah? Is penitential prayer like we find in Ezra-Nehemiah important for Christian spirituality? Why or why not?

CHAPTER TWENTY-EIGHT

1–2 Chronicles

Orientation

It may come as a bit of a surprise to find Chronicles at the end of Israel's Scriptures. In English Bible traditions Chronicles is part of the Old Testament collection of history books: Joshua, Judges, Ruth, Samuel, Kings, Chronicles, Ezra, Nehemiah, Esther. It's a familiar order for many, and it makes good sense. This ordering provides a tight history of Israel from the conquest of the land, to the united monarchy, to the division of the kingdom into north and south, on to exile and ends with the postexilic hope for a reconstructed Judah.

By contrast, the Hebrew canon tends to place Chronicles at the end of its third section, the Writings. Placed here, Chronicles testifies to the ongoing validity of God's promises to David, Judah's hope for God's future redemptive actions, and the importance of the temple. Chronicles brings an end to the Old Testament Scriptures yet at the same time it stands open to God's continuing work based on his promises to David's offspring and the temple's unique role to mediate God's presence to the covenant people.

Chronicles is challenging because most of its material also appears in Samuel and Kings. Interpreters situate the authorship of Chronicles in the postexilic setting. The book's reference to the edict of Cyrus (2 Chron. 36:22–23) dates the book after the destruction of the Neo-Babylonian Empire and during the time of the Persian Empire.

CANONICAL CONNECTIONS

Chronicles and the Gospels

The placement of Chronicles at the end of the Writings makes for a rich preparation for the Gospel of Matthew. The whole of Chronicles centers on the promises made to David and his offspring. Matthew begins with a genealogy that links Jesus to the Davidic line and shows him to be in continuity with messianic promises of Chronicles.

Davide Troli / Shutterstock

Figure 28.1. *David* by Michelangelo (1501–4)

The challenge is particularly acute when its presentation of the material is compared to Samuel and Kings. Chronicles offers a selective retelling of Israel's history for a particular purpose. In particular, King David comes off looking as polished and clean as Michelangelo's statue of him. The Bathsheba affair and the subsequent murder of her husband Uriah are absent. Readers also encounter a sterilized form of Solomon, the great builder of Israel's temple. In Kings, Solomon loved the Lord at the beginning of his reign (1 Kings 3:3). Near his end, he loved "many foreign women" (11:1) and dishonored God by allowing their gods into the land. This account is not in Chronicles. How do readers navigate these challenges?

First, it is important to recognize that the Chronicler, the narrator of this book, is not trying to deceive readers. The ancients did not think of history as a hard-and-fast category where precision reigned supreme. History also played an exhortative role and was meant to instruct and inspire. This is true of Chronicles. Chronicles assumes readers are aware of the traditions present in Samuel and Kings (cf. 1 Chron. 29:29). Those books tell Israel's history from the standpoint of Deuteronomy's theology, where covenantal blessings of land, king, and worship could be forfeited by the infidelity of God's people. Chronicles is not supplanting this tradition. In fact, Judah had just lived through the gut-wrenching implications of it. Rather, Chronicles is telling Israel's history from the standpoint of God's commitment to maintain the covenant relationship with his people, despite their unfaithfulness.

Chronicles is written to inspire God's people to hope in the Lord's kingdom promises, promises linked to the Davidic throne and the temple. The Chronicler's intent is the unification of Israel under a singular throne and temple, and his selective use of Israel's history serves this purpose. If you have attended a fiftieth wedding anniversary, you will know something of this dynamic. Pictures display the young couple smiling at their wedding. Other pictures show family vacations, Christmases shared, children growing, grandchildren laughing, and on and on. No one at the anniversary

party believes these pictures are lying. They tell a selective and beautiful truth about the long-term joy of
a committed marital relationship. But neither would
anyone think those pictures tell the full story: fussy
arguments on the way to church, marital disappoint-
ments, the grief of great loss—the sorrows of life. These
pictures typically do not appear at celebrations, but
everyone knows they are present even in their absence.
Chronicles operates in a similar way. The "full story"
from Kings is present even in its absence. 🗍

CANONICAL CONNECTIONS

Chronicles and the Gospel of John

Just as Chronicles assumes the material
in Samuel and Kings, the Gospel of John
assumes Mark's Gospel. John shapes the
historical life of Jesus in a theological
and colorful way but not in order to sup-
plant the other Gospels, Matthew, Mark,
and Luke. John and the Synoptics complement each other in much the same
way as Chronicles and Samuel/Kings do.

Second, Chronicles draws from earlier biblical traditions to serve its
theological purposes. Brevard Childs offers several ways the Chronicler
engages the tradition, including harmonization, supplementation, and typology. With harmonization, for example, readers find the Chronicler harmonizing Deuteronomy 10:8 and 2 Samuel 6. The former makes clear that
only the Levites were allowed to carry the ark of the covenant. In 2 Samuel
6, the ark is moved from Kiriath Jearim to Jerusalem with no mention of
who is carrying the ark. In the Chronicles account (1 Chron. 15:26–27), the
Levites are named as the ones carrying the ark, thus harmonizing these two
traditions.

The Chronicler also supplements his canonical sources by making
use of other material as well. For example, the account of Hezekiah in
2 Chronicles 29:3–30:27 includes material not found in the Kings account
of Hezekiah, such as details of the Passover celebration. Typology also
plays a role for the Chronicler. This literary and theological device links
together people and events separated by time. For example, Chronicles
describes Solomon in ways that are similar to Joshua. As Joshua extended
the leadership of Moses into a new generation, so too does Solomon extend David's leadership. Similar associative patterns are found between
Moses and David. With these devices and more, the Chronicler engages the
traditions of Israel for the sake of the current as well as future generations
of readers.

The people of God had suffered a great blow of judgment from the Neo-
Babylonian Empire. With city walls in disrepair, the temple in ruins, and
an empty Davidic throne, the postexilic community suffered under God's
mighty hand of judgment. From an earthly vantage point, they had every
reason to despair. Yet the Chronicler calls the people to hope and to unite
as a single Israel. Three major themes of Chronicles are the means by which
the people could both unite and hope in God's future for them: the Davidic
covenant, a renewed temple, and a priesthood ready and able to establish
and maintain faithful worship of the Lord.

Exploration—Reading 1–2 Chronicles

The Genealogies: 1 Chronicles 1–9

■ READ 1 CHRONICLES 2 ■

Chronicles lingers over genealogies. Readers are forgiven when they encounter the book and find its first nine chapters tedious. Why so much attention to so-and-so begetting so-and-so? Recall that the structure of Genesis is built on the *toledoth* pattern—"These are the generations of . . ." The foundational book of the entire Bible thinks genealogies are important. Genealogies matter because they reveal something of the continuity of God's people through time, and more importantly the continuity of God's covenantal promises. Creation and redemption relate to each other in necessary ways: creation is the stage for redemption, and redemption restores a fallen creation to its original, divine intent. The genealogies of Chronicles begin with Adam, linking God's dealings with the postexilic people to creation itself. All of human history moves toward God's redemptive purposes for his people Israel, and the implications of these purposes are for the redemption of the whole world.

Beginning with Adam, the genealogies take a wide-angle view and then tighten the frame on the sons of Israel ("Jacob"). As would be expected, Judah comes first in the detailed list of Israel's sons, with special attention given to Judah's most famous son: King David (1 Chron. 2:1–4:23). Then the other tribes follow, beginning with Simeon (4:24) and ending with Asher (7:30–40). Chapter 8 provides a more extensive genealogy of Benjamin because of the importance of King Saul, a Benjaminite. Beginning in chapter 9, the genealogies list those who returned to Judah from exile in Babylon. Again, continuity of people, place, and history is of paramount importance for the postexilic community. Finally, the genealogies conclude by repeating Saul's family line to transition to the narrative itself, a narrative that begins with Saul and moves very quickly to David.

The genealogies emphasize Judah and Levi, and in this emphasis the purpose of Chronicles is clear. Israel's whole history (beginning as it does with Adam at creation), its reason for existence, and its future hopes rest with God's promises to David and the centrality of the temple for Israel's religious identity.

The Reign of King David and the Building of the Temple: 1 Chronicles 10–29

■ READ 1 CHRONICLES 16–17; 28–29 ■

After the genealogies 1 Chronicles makes clear its main subject matter: King David. Israel's first king, the great Benjaminite Saul, had died. The

Chronicler does not make as much fuss over Saul as the book of Samuel does. The only Saul narrative in Chronicles is that of his tragic death. Saul is mortally wounded by Philistine arrows but has not yet died. He commands his armor bearer to run him through with a sword so that the king of Israel could avoid the torture and humiliation of his enemies. The armor bearer refuses to kill the Lord's anointed, as David had also done (1 Sam. 24), so Saul sees to the task himself, falling on his sword. The mighty has fallen, and the Chronicler leaves no doubt about why Saul came to such a tragic end: "Saul died because he was unfaithful to the LORD" (1 Chron. 10:13). The rest of the book turns to King David.

The Chronicler paints David as a man after God's own heart. David is resolute in his commitment to the Lord, especially evident in his commitment to plan for the temple's construction. The link between the Davidic throne and temple worship is indissoluble. The Chronicler presents David's political ambitions in terms of his religious devotion. The center of the narrative describes David's return of the ark of the covenant to Jerusalem (1 Chron. 13–16; cf. 1 Sam. 6:1–7:1). The story details the ill-fated first attempt to move the ark, when God's instructions for moving the sacred object are disregarded and an attendant is struck dead for touching the ark (1 Chron. 13:9–14). In 1 Chronicles 15 the ark successfully arrives in Jerusalem, and David "appointed Asaph and his associates to give praise to the LORD" (16:7). What follows is a long psalm of praise (16:7–36), as the Chronicler links David to the book of Psalms (esp. Pss. 96:1–13; 105:1–15; 106:1, 47–48) and also highlights Asaph's priestly role in the worship of Israel. The link between temple worship and Davidic kingship is clear. 📜

Much of the Chronicler's focus is on David's preparation for the construction of the temple. Readers can easily get lost in the details, though the details are part of the larger point. The temple and all of its details were of singular importance to David, to the people under his leadership, and, most importantly, to the Lord. It was not God's plan for David to build the temple, but David gave all his energies toward preparing for its construction. Solomon would build it, but David, noting Solomon's youth and inexperience (22:5), provides the plans and materials for the grand undertaking (chaps. 22–29). The Chronicler outlines various families of Levites, the guild of musicians, gatekeepers, and other political and military officials. The effect of these details and the interconnecting of religious and political activities link throne and temple. Throne and temple were integral to the covenant that gave Israel its basis for unity and hope.

David's life ends in praise, worship, and sacrifice (29:10–22). For the Chronicler, David's final royal act is prayer. He offers a prayer that links the loyalty of the heart with the external rituals of Israel's temple worship. The authority of the crown moves seamlessly from David to Solomon, and David passes off the scene "having enjoyed long life, wealth and honor" (29:28). The Chronicler bypasses the account of the elderly, impotent David being warmed in his bed by Abishag the virgin (2 Kings 1) and offers no hint of the weakness and vulnerability of old age. Rather, David "died at a good old age" (1 Chron. 29:28). King David represents more than himself. He symbolizes the future Davidic throne and the promises of a messianic era where kingship, worship, and priesthood bloom into the fullness of their promises.

CANONICAL CONNECTIONS

Torah and Temple

David's prayer in 1 Chronicles 29:10–22 links together Mount Sinai and Mount Zion. David's prayer reaches back to the language of Sinai as he prays for his son Solomon to attend to the Lord's commands and statutes, all the while linking Solomon's faithfulness to Torah with the temple's construction (29:19). Temple worship serves the purposes of Sinai as it calls for the people to order their loyal devotion to Israel's God and no other. Naturally, Israel's idealized history and its real history do not sit comfortably next to each other. The tension of these two realities opens the messianic and temple promises to the future of God's kingdom actions in the world.

CANONICAL CONNECTIONS

Bezalel and Solomon

The Chronicler notes that the tabernacle Moses constructed was housed in Gibeon, along with the bronze altar built by Bezalel, son of Uri, son of Hur (2 Chron. 1:5). Not much is said of Bezalel outside Exodus (Exod. 31:1–11; 36:1–2). He makes no appearance in the Kings account of the temple's construction. His presence here in Chronicles provides an important link. Exodus 31:3 describes Bezalel as filled "with the Spirit of God, with wisdom, with understanding, with knowledge and with all kinds of skill." The association of Bezalel and Solomon appears intentional. Both were filled with God's Spirit and abundant in wisdom/skill for the sake of constructing God's tabernacle and temple, respectively.

Solomonic Glory: 2 Chronicles 1–9

◼ READ 2 CHRONICLES 1; 3–7; 9 ◼

Solomon's accession to Israel's throne extends the legacy of his father, David. "The LORD his God was with him," and everything Solomon touches turned to gold (2 Chron. 1:1). Solomon's extraordinary gifts of leadership and wisdom are not the product of his own giftedness. The Chronicler makes clear that Solomon begin his reign in worship before the living God (1:2–6) and in a dependent posture before the Lord. "Ask for whatever you want me to give you," the Lord declares (1:7). Solomon asks for wisdom and knowledge and in so doing unlocks the Lord's generosity toward him. Because Solomon does not ask for wealth, possessions, or honor but wisdom and knowledge in order to serve God's people well, the Lord blesses him with material wealth as well (1:12).

From the Chronicler's telling, the purpose of Solomon's reign is the construction of the temple. Details, details, and more details are given: from cedar, juniper, and algum logs to stonecutters and goldsmiths, no detail is left unattended (2 Chron. 1–2). Second Chronicles 3 describes the temple's actual construction, from the dimensions of the whole edifice to the color of the curtains (blue, purple, and crimson) to decorative palm trees on top of fine gold along with juniper paneling of the main hall. No artistic detail is left to chance.

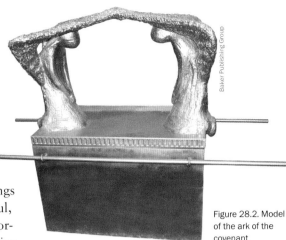

Figure 28.2. Model of the ark of the covenant

The temple is magnificent. Its furnishings (chap. 4) are resplendent and purposeful, serving the priests and the rituals of worship. Finally, in preparation for the dedication of the temple, the ark of the covenant is brought to its proper location in the holy of holies, that inner sanctuary of the temple where God's presence is manifest and his mercies are bestowed (chap. 5).

HISTORICAL MATTERS

The Contents of the Ark

The ark of the covenant, according to the Chronicler, contained only the two tablets of Moses (2 Chron. 5:10). Earlier descriptions of its contents include a jar of manna (Exod. 16:32–34) and Aaron's staff (Num. 17:10–11). The Chronicler offers no explanation about the missing elements, though it may be that these items were lost when the Philistines had control of the ark (1 Sam. 4–5).

The whole scene exudes celebration and joy. The priests are dressed in their fine linen. Scores of musicians lift their trumpets, cymbals, and instruments of praise. Their song is simple: "He is good; his love endures forever" (5:13). In the midst of this praise and thanksgiving, God's Shekinah presence falls on the place, and the glory of the Lord fills the whole temple: "The LORD is in his holy temple; let all the earth be silent before him" (Hab. 2:20).

Solomon's long prayer of dedication (2 Chron. 6) reveals something of the theology of the temple. The temple cannot "contain" God's presence (6:18). The works of human hands do not constrain the living God, who knows no spatial or temporal boundaries. Yet God gives his presence to this material structure as a promise to dwell among his people. When the people sin, lose a battle, forget their way, wrong a neighbor, suffer drought—when any of these or a host of other unfortunate events of providence or unfaithfulness take hold—there sits the temple. The temple offers a perpetual reminder of the hope of God's forgiveness and the healing power of his presence. "If they have a change of heart" (6:37) and "if they turn back . . . with all their heart and soul" (6:38), then the Lord will hear their prayers again and forgive their sins. The temple is a perpetual reminder of God's covenant loyalty to his people and his quickness to forgive those who turn to him with all their hearts.

Solomon's renown reaches the queen of Sheba, who is amazed at the king's wisdom and accomplishments. Yet even the queen of Sheba recognizes the true reason for Solomon's splendor: "Praise be to the LORD your God, who has delighted in you and placed you on his throne as king to rule for the LORD your God" (9:8). Solomon grows in wisdom and wealth, reigning for forty years until he too follows his father, David, to the grave (9:31). The legacy of Solomon's temple remains for generations until Judah's faithlessness and rebellion lead to its destruction.

A Kingdom Split, Fallen, and Restored: 2 Chronicles 10–36

■ READ 2 CHRONICLES 33–36 ■

Chronicles follows the reign of Solomon with the kingdom's split into northern and southern parts. Solomon's son Rehoboam rejects wise counsel and instead chooses heavy-handed and abusive leadership. Jeroboam establishes his rule in the Northern Kingdom, though Chronicles does not dwell much on him or it. After Solomon's reign, the fate of the Northern Kingdom is all but sealed. After the Northern Kingdom's fall to the Assyrians, the Southern Kingdom lives under the threat of its own coming demise. Much of this section of Chronicles overlaps with its counterpart in Kings. English Bibles often provide references to the corresponding Kings narratives in the margins or section titles.

A few matters are worth highlighting in this section of Chronicles. First, the religious reforms of King Hezekiah in chapters 29–31 link Hezekiah, one of Judah's greatest kings, to David and Solomon before him. As they focused their attention on religious renewal and temple worship, so too does Hezekiah. "The service of the temple of the LORD was reestablished" (29:35). Hezekiah is faithful to the worship of the Lord. In Chronicles Hezekiah also celebrates the Passover. This episode is not found in Kings and raises the question of why Chronicles includes it. The details of the chapter are complex, but of special importance is Hezekiah's invitation for the northern tribes of Israel to attend. Many "scorned and ridiculed" the invitation (30:10). But some came (30:11). Chronicles appears to instruct its audience about the goal of national unity for all Israel, north and south. Chronicles also clarifies how such unity might be achieved—namely, through the faithful worship of Israel's God in accord with his torah (30:12).

Second, the Chronicler's account of Manasseh provides a fascinating counterpoint when compared with the account in Kings. The kings of Judah follow a roller coaster of ups and downs. One king walks in the ways of the Lord, only to be followed by one who does not. Manasseh is the latter kind of king, his wickedness unparalleled by other Judahite kings: "But Manasseh led Judah and the people of Jerusalem astray, so that they did more evil than the nations the Lord had destroyed before the Israelites" (2 Chron. 33:9). Manasseh rebuilt the high places (locations for idolatrous practices) destroyed by Hezekiah, reinstated the worship of Baal and Asherah, built altars to idols in the temple itself, and even placed an image of a foreign god in the temple (33:2–7). As if it could not get worse, Manasseh also sacrificed his own children in the valley of Ben Hinnom. There is evil and then there is evil. Manasseh was really evil.

None of these descriptions of Manasseh are new. Kings lays them out with a similar level of horrific detail. Yet Chronicles takes Manasseh's story in a very different direction. Manasseh suffers a blow under the armies of Assyria, who take him captive to "Babylon" (2 Chron. 33:11). While suffering there in shame, Manasseh "sought the favor of the Lord his God and humbled himself greatly before the God of his ancestors" (33:12). The Lord responds like the prodigal's father, who runs off the porch to embrace his rebellious son (Luke 15). The Lord restores Manasseh, and Manasseh returns to Jerusalem a changed man. He rebuilds the city walls and gates and restores the military infrastructure of Judah. More than this, he gets rid of all the foreign gods and the sacrileges in the temple. Manasseh, like his father Hezekiah, restores the true worship of the Lord. Manasseh becomes a model of the exiled Israelite who repents of sin and returns to the promised land with a renewed sense of purpose and determination to worship the Lord in accord with his word.

Chronicles moves toward its end with the high note of Josiah's reign and religious reforms (2 Chron. 34–35). However, the narrative fades after Josiah because his offspring and successors, Jehoiakim, Jehoiachin, and Zedekiah, do "evil in the eyes of the Lord" (36:5, 9, 12). These three rule in Judah during the tumultuous decade of Babylonian incursion and eventual destruction of Jerusalem (596–586 BC). Unlike Kings, however, Chronicles ends with a word of hope. The Persians destroy the Babylonian Empire, and Cyrus the Great is sovereign over Judah and all the lands of the Near East. Cyrus makes a decree that allows the exiles of Judah to return to their land and rebuild their temple. The description of Cyrus in the last two verses of Chronicles is of special importance. First, Cyrus's heart is moved to make this proclamation for Judah "in order to fulfill the word of the LORD spoken by Jeremiah" (36:22). Second, Cyrus recognizes the God of Judah, the Lord, as the one who has given him the rule over the kingdoms of this earth.

Implementation—Reading Chronicles as Christian Scripture Today

Chronicles is easy to overlook in the Scriptures of Israel. In its early chapters, readers encounter lengthy genealogies—difficult material to read and understand. Yet even in these challenging lists, the Chronicler reveals God's redemptive actions in the history of human affairs. The Lord oversees the tribes of his people and royal line of his Davidic king in order to propel his people to hope and faithfulness.

The temple and the crown are the principal means of Israel's worship, the instruments of the covenant relation with the Lord who promises, "I will be your God and you will be my people" (Jer. 7:23). The Gospel narratives of our Lord Jesus highlight these features of his person and work. They use genealogies to link Jesus to David's line. His status as David's royal son is a feature of Christmas nativity scenes: the wise men bow before infant Jesus as the king of the Jews. The Gospels reveal that Jesus was and is King of the Jews. Moreover, Jesus understands himself as God's presence

Figure 28.3. *Crucifixion* showing Christ on the cross with INRI above him, by Andrea Mantegna (1456–59)

and temple among his people. John's Gospel pays special attention to this feature of Jesus's identity. The Gospel opens with John's declaration that "the Word became flesh, and dwelt [tabernacled] among us" (John 1:14 NASB). Then when Jesus cleanses the temple, he announces, "'Destroy this temple, and in three days I will raise it up.' . . . But he was speaking about the temple of His body" (2:19, 21 NASB). Crown and temple combine in the person and work of Jesus Christ. He is God's presence in our midst, and he is the royal ruler we so desperately need.

KEY VERSES IN 1–2 CHRONICLES

- And David became more and more powerful, because the LORD Almighty was with him. 1 Chron. 11:9
- And you, my son Solomon, acknowledge the God of your father, and serve him with wholehearted devotion and with a willing mind, for the LORD searches every heart and understands every desire and every thought. If you seek him, he will be found by you; but if you forsake him, he will reject you forever. Consider now, for the LORD has chosen you to build a house as the sanctuary. Be strong and do the work. 1 Chron. 28:9–10
- LORD, the God of Israel, there is no God like you in heaven or on earth—you who keep your covenant of love with your servants who continue wholeheartedly in your way. You have kept your promise to your servant David my father; with your mouth you have promised and with your hand you have fulfilled it—as it is today. 2 Chron. 6:14–15

Christian Reading Questions

1. What is the significance of the long genealogies in Chronicles?
2. Why would the Chronicler present David in such squeaky-clean terms? How does it contribute to the purpose of the book?
3. How does the link between crown and temple help us read the Gospels better?
4. What gospel hope does Chronicles offer in the story of Manasseh?

Glossary

apocalypse A genre of literature with a narrative framework in which YHWH discloses divine realities in time and space via an otherworldly being (angel) to a human recipient. Especially found in the book of Daniel in the Old Testament.

apocalyptic A worldview anticipating YHWH's intervention in history at the end of time. Appears especially in the book of Daniel in the Old Testament.

apodictic law A direct prohibition in biblical law ("Thou shalt not . . ."), especially found in the Ten Commandments.

Assyria/Assyrian *See* Neo-Assyria (also: Assyria/Assyrian).

atonement A sacrifice that makes (1) a payment or ransom for sin and (2) a purification from uncleanness or impurity (e.g., Lev. 4:26).

Babylon/Babylonian (and Neo-Babylonia) The eastern Semitic nation in the southern Tigris-Euphrates River valley. The capital of the Old Babylonian (and later, Neo-Babylonian) Empire was Babylon. The Old Babylonian Empire spanned from the nineteenth to sixteenth centuries BC, and the Neo-Babylonian Empire spanned from 626 to 539 BC. The Neo-Babylonian Empire was the great threat in the times of the prophets Jeremiah, Habakkuk, and Ezekiel.

Canaanites A broad designation for the inhabitants of Palestine prior to the settlement of ancient Israel.

canon Derived from the Greek word for "rule." Canon as a theological concept relates to the authoritative character of Christian Scripture, an authority that emerges from within the biblical texts themselves and is recognized by Christ's church.

casuistic law   Case law in biblical law, especially following the pattern "if this . . . then that . . ."

city lament   A form of ancient Near Eastern poem that mourns and commemorates the destruction of a city.

clean   A common person or thing that is pure and qualified for normal ritual use. Its polar opposite is unclean. *See also* common.

common   A person or object in the neutral ritual state, which can be subdivided into two common types, the clean and the unclean. A basic category in Leviticus.

cosmogony   An explanation about how the world came to be. *See also* primeval history.

cosmology   External and internal logic for why our world is the way it is.

covenant   A special bond between parties, often in the form of a treaty. The most significant covenants in the Old Testament are promissory between Israel's God, YHWH, and the people of Israel. YHWH promises to be Israel's God, and Israel promises to be YHWH's people. Thus, stipulations ensue in the relationship, and YHWH guarantees its success. Covenants in the biblical material express similarities to and differences from other ancient Near Eastern covenants.

Daughter Zion   *See* Lady Zion / Daughter Zion.

defilement/defile   A condition of impurity or uncleanness that prevents someone or something from being fit for use in Israelite worship.

diaspora   The dispersal of ancient Jews from their ancestral homeland in Israel; often specifically refers to the exiled community of Judah in Babylon (and later, Persia) after 586 BC.

Enuma Elish   An Old Babylonian creation myth with some similarities to the biblical creation account.

Epic of Gilgamesh   An ancient Mesopotamian story about Gilgamesh, king of the ancient city-state of Uruk.

eschatology/eschatological   The doctrine of last things or end times.

Hellenization   The spread of Greek culture in the Mediterranean region and beyond after the conquest by Alexander the Great in the fourth century BC.

higher criticism/critical   A kind of biblical study that emerged from German scholarship in the eighteenth and nineteenth centuries that seeks to determine a text's originating contexts, including its literary history and authorial purpose. This is to be distinguished from *lower criticism*, which is the study that attempts to establish the biblical text from biblical manuscripts, sometimes called "textual criticism."

holy/holiness   A property that belongs solely to God but can be conferred on people and things through specialized rituals. A holy person, place, or thing is set apart by YHWH for a particular task or function. "Holy" objects and people (which are fit for special divine service) are distinguished from "common" people and things (which are not fit for divine service). Holiness is also distinct from uncleanness and defilement, ritual categories that bar common and unclean objects from divine service and require rites of purification or atonement to be ritually fit once again.

judge   An ancient Israelite who provided justice to parties in dispute. Judges were to emulate the justice of God. A judge in the book of Judges was a charismatic deliverer appointed by God to deliver Israel from an oppressor.

judgment oracle   A primarily negative pronouncement of God's action against individuals, groups, or nations.

Ketuvim   *See* Writings (Ketuvim).

king   The premier leader of a nation in the ancient Near East, including Israel. A king governs the people, often as a representative of the nation-state's deity. The king in Israel governed under the authority of YHWH.

Lady Zion / Daughter Zion   Personification of the city and people of Jerusalem as a woman.

lament   A kind of prayer that voices a complaint to God about distress in order to persuade him to act on the sufferer's behalf.

Law/Torah   The first five books of the Old Testament (Genesis–Deuteronomy). Also called the Pentateuch.

lawsuit text   A text in the form of a legal accusation against a party, with YHWH as prosecutor and judge. These often function with judgment oracles.

Marduk   Patron deity of the Babylonians.

messenger speech   Prophetic speech that suggests a word-for-word disclosure of God's message through the prophet. The phrase "thus says the LORD" or "says the LORD" often accompanies it to signify God's speech to the prophet and the prophet's self-identification as the spokesperson/messenger for God.

messiah   A divinely anointed and appointed leader for a particular task. In the Old Testament, the messiah came to be understood as the Davidic king and eventually as an eschatological Davidic ruler who restores all things and brings peace.

messianic oracle   A kind of salvation oracle that offers hope in terms of a future anointed king appointed by YHWH for justice and deliverance.

metanarrative   An all-encompassing theory or explanation about the complexities of human life, thought, and behavior.

middoth   Hebrew word for the thirteen attributes of YHWH from Exodus 34:6–7.

Midian/Midianite   People group that lived west of the Gulf of Aqaba in the Arabian Peninsula. Moses lived with the Midianites after fleeing Egypt, and he married a Midianite. Thus, the Midianites are kin to Israelite ancestors.

Mount Moriah   The highest point in Jerusalem, the place where Abraham offered Isaac and the eventual location of the temple itself. Sometimes associated with Zion in the Old Testament books.

myth of Atrahasis   An epic poem from ancient Akkad that tells the story of a great flood that has some similarities to the Genesis flood account.

Neo-Assyria (also: Assyria/Assyrian)   The Neo-Assyrian Empire (912–612 BC) was the final stage in the powerful rule of the Assyrians in history. With its capital in Nineveh, the Neo-Assyrian Empire included the northern and southern Tigris-Euphrates River valley, Syria, Anatolia, Persia, and even parts of Arabia. The Neo-Assyrian Empire was the great threat for the eighth-century-BC prophets Isaiah, Hosea, Amos, and Micah.

Neo-Babylonia   *See* Babylon/Babylonian (and Neo-Babylonia).

Nevi'im   The second major division in the Hebrew canon of the Old Testament. It follows the Torah and contains the books of Joshua–Malachi. *Nevi'im* is the Hebrew word for "prophets."

oracles against the nations (OAN)   Judgment oracles directed against foreign nations that threatened Israel or Judah.

Passover   Annual celebration of God's gracious act of restraining judgment against Israelites whose houses displayed blood over the doorposts; divine judgment was enacted against the firstborn children of Egypt (Exod. 12). The Passover celebrates grace and judgment.

penitential prayer/psalm   Prayers that rehearse the tradition of Israel, confess sin, and turn to YHWH for forgiveness; Daniel 9, Ezra 9, and Nehemiah 9 are examples.

Persia/Persian   The ancient empire that defeated the Neo-Babylonian Empire, conquering Babylon in 539 BC. Cyrus the Great founded the Achaemenid Empire, and Persia reigned supreme until Greek Alexander the Great defeated Persia at the Battle of Gaugamela (331 BC). The Persian Empire is the context of the books of Daniel, Haggai, Malachi, Zechariah, and Ezra-Nehemiah.

personification/personified   An inanimate object or concept given human features or characteristics.

pharaoh   The title of the Egyptian king. The pharaoh plays a significant role in the book of Exodus.

polytheism/polytheistic   The worship of many deities that represented the heavens, powers, and different natural phenomena. Related to *henotheism*, the worship of one high deity while recognizing the existence of other deities.

priest/priestly   A person in ancient Israel from the tribe of Levi who mediated between YHWH and the people in worship and sacrifice. Priests taught the instruction of YHWH and interceded before YHWH for the people.

primeval history   The overarching story in Genesis 1–11 that provides explanations for the big questions of human existence. *See also* cosmogony.

prophet   A spokesperson for YHWH in Israel and Judah.

prophetic utterance   A basic form of speech from a prophet that often includes the phrase "utterance of YHWH."

Prophets (Nevi'im)   The Hebrew designation for the Old Testament texts that span from Joshua through Malachi; includes the Former Prophets (Joshua–Kings) and Latter Prophets (Isaiah–Malachi).

protology   The doctrine of initial things.

proverb   A short, pithy saying that teaches general truths about life gained after lifelong reflection.

rabbinic Judaism   The period of Jewish history that spans from roughly the first to the sixth centuries AD; this period follows the completion of the Babylonian Talmud. Rabbinic Judaism holds that two forms of torah, or divine instruction, were given by God at Sinai: the Oral Torah and Written Torah. *See also* Talmud.

Reformation/Reformer   A period of church history characterized by a reform movement in the Catholic Church, initiated by Martin Luther in Germany. The Swiss Reformation (Huldrych Zwingli; John Calvin) and the English Reformation followed the German Reformation. The Reformation marks a fragmentation of the Catholic Church.

revelation God's disclosure of the divine self through the Bible, creation, and Jesus.

ritual A regular symbolic action designed to communicate or inculcate something about reality.

rule of faith A guide for proper reading of the Bible's total witness, particularly as it relates to identity of God as Father, Son, and Holy Spirit.

salvation oracle A message of restoration or salvation by YHWH; counterpart to the judgment oracle.

Septuagint, or LXX Greek translations of the Hebrew versions of the Old Testament that were accomplished by various translators in the third century BC.

Shekinah A term that describes the manifest presence of YHWH dwelling with Israel, building from the Hebrew verb *shakan* (Exod. 25:8; 29:45).

source criticism A field of study that tries to determine the separate documents that make up a larger document (e.g., JEDP for the Pentateuch).

synagogue Jewish house of worship used for assembly of the community as well as study. Synagogues developed at least by the third century BC but are probably older. Synagogues remain fundamental to Judaism to the present day.

Talmud The collection of oral teachings (Oral Torah) of the rabbis from the Second Temple period (fifth century BC through first century AD); from the Hebrew verb *lamad*, "to teach." Judaism has two versions of the Talmud: the Babylonian Talmud and the Palestinian Talmud. Each exhibits different styles and concerns of rabbis from Babylon and Palestine, respectively.

TaNaK The acronym for the three-part division of the Hebrew Bible: Torah (Law), Nevi'im (Prophets), and Ketuvim (Writings).

theodicy An exploration of the relationship between God and justice, usually deriving from the question of how bad things—even horrors—can happen if there is a good and powerful God who orders the world.

theophany A visible manifestation of the divine, apprehensible by human senses.

Tiamat The goddess who represents the sea and chaos in Mesopotamian mythology.

toledoth A formula in Hebrew appearing in Genesis, translated "These are the generations of . . ."

Torah *See* Law/Torah.

Trinity/Trinitarian In Christian faith, the reality of God being three-in-one: Father, Son, and Holy Spirit.

unclean A common person, place, or object that is unqualified for normal usage as it depicts some sort of abnormality when compared with normal function or usage. Uncleanness is contagious, and whatever comes into contact with an unclean thing becomes unclean. Clean is the inverse of unclean. *See also* clean; common.

wisdom The ability/skill to navigate God's world in a way that accords with God's purposes and direction. Wisdom in the Old Testament begins with the fear of YHWH, the awe and reverence of YHWH in all of life.

Writings (Ketuvim) The third and final section of the Hebrew Old Testament, with texts that span from Psalms through Chronicles.

Zion The chosen place of worship for YHWH, associated with the sanctuary in Jerusalem. Zion is also the place where YHWH's worshipers make pilgrimage to revere YHWH. Zion is associated with the Davidic dynasty in the monarchical period of Israel.

Notes

The endnotes for each chapter appear first, followed by the notes to the sidebars for that chapter.

Chapter 1 Introduction to the Old Testament as Christian Scripture

1. Friedrich Nietzsche, *Twilight of the Idols and The Anti-Christ*, trans. R. J. Hollingdale (London: Penguin Books, 2003), 148.

2. Flannery O'Connor, *Mystery and Manners: Occasional Prose* (New York: Farrar, Straus & Giroux, 1969), 34.

3. Ira Gershwin and George Gershwin, "Let's Call the Whole Thing Off."

4. Gerhard von Rad, *Old Testament Theology*, trans. D. M. G. Stalker (San Francisco: HarperSanFrancisco, 1962), 1:105.

5. Karl Barth, *Church Dogmatics*, vol. I/2, *The Doctrine of the Word of God*, trans. G. T. Thomson and Harold Knight, ed. G. W. Bromiley and T. F. Torrance (London: T&T Clark, 1956), 58.

a. Augustine, *Confessions*, trans. Henry Chadwick (Oxford: Oxford University Press, 1991), 9.13, p. 163.

b. Irenaeus, *Against Heresies* 1.8.

c. T. S. Eliot, "Religion and Literature," in *Selected Prose of T. S. Eliot*, ed. F. Kermode (New York: Farrar, Straus & Giroux, 1975), 98.

d. Francis Turretin, *Institutes of Elenctic Theology*, ed. James T. Dennison, trans. G. M. Giger (Phillipsburg, NJ: P&R, 1992), 1:102–3.

e. Hugh of St. Victor, *On the Sacraments of the Church* 1.7.

f. Heidelberg Catechism, in *Creeds, Confessions, & Catechisms: A Readers Edition*, ed. Chad Van Dixhoorn (Wheaton: Crossway, 2022), 298.

g. Herman Bavinck, *Our Reasonable Faith: A Survey of Christian Doctrine* (Grand Rapids: Eerdmans, 1957), 103.

h. Johann Georg Hamann, *Über die Auslegung der Heiligen Schrift*, vol. 1 of *Sämtliche Werke*, ed. Josef Nadler (Wien: Thomas-Morus-Presse, 1949), 5.

Chapter 3 Genesis

1. T. S. Eliot, "The Hollow Men," in *Collected Poems, 1909–1962* (New York: Harcourt, Brace & World, 1963), 82.

Chapter 3 Sidebar Notes

a. Dietrich Bonhoeffer, *Creation and Fall: A Theological Exposition of Genesis 1–3*, ed. John W. de Gruchy, trans. Douglas Stephen Bax, Dietrich Bonhoeffer Works 3 (Minneapolis: Fortress, 2004), 25.

b. "The Creation Epic," trans. E. A. Speiser, in *Ancient Near Eastern Texts Relating to the Old Testament*, 3rd ed., ed. James B. Pritchard (Princeton: Princeton University Press, 1969), 67.

c. J. R. R. Tolkien, "Mythopoeia," https://www.tolkien.ro/text/JRR%20Tolkien%20-%20Mythopoeia.pdf.

d. Bonhoeffer, *Creation and Fall*, 64.

e. See Luther's comments in *Lectures on Genesis: Chapters 1–5*, vol. 1 of *Luther's Works*, ed. J. Pelikan (Saint Louis: Concordia, 1958).

f. Augustine, *The Trinity*, trans. E. Hill, The Works of Saint Augustine I/5 (New York: New City, 2015), 2.19, p. 34; Martin Luther, *Lectures on Genesis: Chapters 15–20*, vol. 3 of *Luther's Works*, ed. J. Pelikan (Saint Louis: Concordia, 1961), 192–95; John Calvin, *Commentaries on the First Book of Moses Called Genesis*, trans. J. King (Grand Rapids: Baker Books, 2005), 468–70.

g. Søren Kierkegaard, *Fear and Trembling*, trans. Alistair Hannay (London: Penguin Books, 1985), 146.

h. John Calvin, *Commentaries on the Book of Genesis*, vol. 1, trans. J. King (Grand Rapids: Baker Books, 2005), 199–200.

Chapter 4 Exodus

1. Benno Jacob, *The Second Book of the Bible: Exodus, Part 2*, trans. W. Jacob (Hoboken, NJ: KTAV Publishing House, 1992), 984–85.

Chapter 4 Sidebar Notes

a. Percy Bysshe Shelley, "Ozymandias," in *Selected Poems* (New York: Gramercy Books, 1994), 30.

b. Robert Jenson, *Systematic Theology: The Triune God*, vol. 1 (Oxford: Oxford University Press, 1997), 63.

c. Maximus the Confessor, "Ad Thalassium 17," in *On the Cosmic Mystery of Jesus Christ*, Popular Patristics Series 25 (New York: St. Vladimir's Press, 2003), 105–8.

d. Martin Luther, *The Large Catechism*, trans. F. Bente and W. H. T. Dau (St. Louis: Concordia, 1921), Project Gutenberg eBook, https://www.gutenberg.org/cache/epub/1722/pg1722-images.html.

e. Babylonian Talmud, Rosh Hashanah 17b, *The William Davidson Talmud*, Sefaria.org, https://www.sefaria.org/Rosh_Hashanah.17a.15?lang=bi, emphasis added.

Chapter 5 Leviticus

1. See Jay Sklar, *Leviticus: An Introduction and Commentary*, Tyndale Old Testament Commentary 3 (Downers Grove, IL: IVP Academic, 2014), 50. See also Sklar, *Sin, Impurity, Sacrifice, Atonement: The Priestly Conceptions*, Hebrew Bible Monographs 2 (Sheffield: Sheffield Academic, 2005), 80–101.

2. Sklar, *Leviticus*, 51–53.

a. Origen, *Homilies on Leviticus 1–16*, trans. Gary Wayne Barkley, Fathers of the Church 83 (Washington, DC: Catholic University of America Press, 1990), 29.

b. For a discussion of similarities and differences between holiness and purity in Hebrew, Sumerian, and Akkadian conceptualizations, see E. Jan Wilson, *"Holiness" and "Purity" in Mesopotamia*, Alter Orient und Altes Testament 237 (Neukirchen-Vluyn: Neukirchener Verlag, 1994).

c. See the discussion of Roy E. Gane, "Worship, Sacrifice, and Festivals in the Ancient Near East," in *Behind the Scenes of the Old Testament: Cultural, Social, and Historical Contexts*, ed. Jonathan S. Greer, John W. Hilber, and John H. Walton (Grand Rapids: Baker Academic, 2018), 361–67, esp. 363–64.

d. Tertullian, *The Five Books against Marcion* 3.7, in *The Ante-Nicene Fathers*, ed. Alexander Roberts and James Donaldson (repr., Grand Rapids: Eerdmans, 1978), 3:327.

e. Thomas Aquinas, *Summa Theologiae*, trans. Laurence Shapcote (Green Bay, WI: Aquinas Institute, 2012), I-II, 71–114, pp. 261–436.

f. Aquinas, *Summa Theologiae*, I-II, 71–114, Q. 102 A. 2, p. 319.

Chapter 6 Numbers

1. See the discussion of Carmen Joy Imes, *Bearing God's Name: Why Sinai Still Matters* (Downers Grove, IL: IVP Academic, 2019), 84–86.

2. Terence E. Fretheim, *Exodus*, Interpretation: A Bible Commentary for Teaching and Preaching (Louisville: John Knox, 1991), 315–16.

3. Fretheim, *Exodus*, 316.

4. In our translation, "my word" is literally "my mouth," indicating the close association between the command of God and the rebellion against his spoken command, which leads to death.

a. David L. Stubbs, *Numbers*, Brazos Theological Commentary on the Bible (Grand Rapids: Brazos, 2009), 20.

b. Origen, *Homily XXVII on Numbers*, in *An Exhortation to Martyrdom, Prayer, First Principles: Book IV, Prologue to the Commentary on the Song of Songs, Homily XXVII on Numbers*, trans. Rowan Greer (Mahwah, NJ: Paulist Press, 1979), 248.

c. Mark J. Boda, *A Severe Mercy: Sin and Its Remedy in the Old Testament*, Siphrut 1 (Winona Lake, IN: Eisenbrauns, 2009), 94–95.

d. Saint Irenaeus, *The Demonstration of the Apostolic Preaching*, trans. J. Armitage Robinson (London: SPCK, 1920), §58, 121–22.

e. For the transliteration of the text and its English translation, see Martti Nissinen, *Prophets and Prophecy in the Ancient Near East*, with contributions by C. L. Seow and Robert K. Ritner, Writings from the Ancient World 12 (Atlanta: Society of Biblical Literature, 2003), 207–12. For full discussion of the text, see Joel S. Burnett, "Prophecy in Transjordan: Balaam Son of Beor," in *Enemies and Friends of the State: Ancient Prophecy in Context*, ed. Christopher A. Rollston (Winona Lake, IN: Eisenbrauns, 2018), 135–204.

f. Émile Puech, "Balaam and Deir 'Alla," in *The Prestige of the Pagan Prophet Balaam in Judaism, Early Christianity and Islam*, ed. George H. van Kooten and Jacques van Ruiten, Themes in Biblical Narrative 11 (Leiden: Brill, 2008), 25–47.

g. See the stimulating study of Matthew Thiessen, *Jesus and the Forces of Death: The Gospels' Portrayal of Ritual Impurity within First-Century Judaism* (Grand Rapids: Baker Academic, 2020).

Chapter 7 Deuteronomy

1. See the discussion of Daniel I. Block, *Deuteronomy*, NIV Application Commentary (Grand Rapids: Zondervan, 2012), 305–6. For a full scholarly discussion on the Name theology and formula, see Sandra L. Richter, *The Deuteronomistic History and the Name Theology:* lᵉšakkēn šᵉmô šām *in the Bible and the Ancient Near East*, Beihefte zur Zeitschrift für die alttestamentliche Wissenschaft 318 (Berlin: de Gruyter, 2002).

2. For helpful discussions on Israel's leadership roles and their ancient Near Eastern counterparts, see Jonathan S. Greer, John W. Hilber, and John H. Walton, eds., *Behind the Scenes of the Old Testament: Cultural, Social, and Historical Contexts* (Grand Rapids: Baker Academic, 2018), esp. 355–60, 368–74, 475–81, 492–98.

3. Prophets in the ancient world had diverse functions, but clearly in Assyria and Babylonia prophets served the designs of kings. For further discussion, see Craig G. Bartholomew and Heath A. Thomas, *The Minor Prophets: A Theological Introduction* (Downers Grove, IL: IVP Academic, 2023), chapter 2: "The Ancient World of Prophecy."

Chapter 7 Sidebar Notes

a. Crispin Fletcher-Louis, *Jesus Monotheism*, vol. 1, *Christological Origins: The Emerging Consensus and Beyond* (Eugene, OR: Cascade Books, 2015), 11.

b. See the extensive discussion of Erik Waaler, *The Shema and the First Commandment in First Corinthians: An Intertextual Approach to Paul's Re-reading of Deuteronomy*, Wissenschaftliche Untersuchungen zum Neuen Testament 2/253 (Tübingen: Mohr Siebeck, 2008).

c. John Calvin, *Institutes of the Christian Religion*, trans. Henry Beveridge (Peabody, MA: Hendrickson, 2008), 2.7.7, p. 222.

d. Calvin, *Institutes*, 2.7.10, p. 224.

e. Calvin, *Institutes*, 2.7.12, p. 225.

f. See the excellent work of Carmen Joy Imes, *Bearing God's Name: Why Sinai Still Matters* (Downers Grove, IL: IVP Academic, 2019); Imes, *Bearing God's Name at Sinai: A Reexamination of the Name Command in the Decalogue*, Bulletin for Biblical Research Supplement 19 (University Park, PA: Eisenbrauns, 2018).

g. For translation and discussion, see "The Code of Hammurabi," trans. Theophile J. Meek, in *Ancient Near Eastern Texts Relating to the Old Testament*, ed. James B. Pritchard, 3rd ed. (Princeton: Princeton University Press, 1969), 163–80.

h. For a helpful discussion, with qualifications, on the meaning of the Akitu festival, see Benjamin D. Sommer, "The Babylonian Akitu Festival: Rectifying the King or Renewing the Cosmos?," *Journal of the Ancient Near Eastern Society* 27, no. 1 (2000): 81–95.

i. Gregory of Nyssa, *The Life of Moses*, trans. Abraham Malherbe and Everett Ferguson (Mahwah, NJ: Paulist Press, 1978), §305, §315, pp. 133, 135.

Chapter 8 Introduction to the Prophets

1. For full discussion of the twelve Minor Prophets, see Craig G. Bartholomew and Heath A. Thomas, *The Minor Prophets: A Theological Introduction* (Downers Grove, IL: IVP Academic, 2023).

2. For alternative timeframes, see Jonathan Stökl, *Prophecy in the Ancient Near East: A Philological and Sociological Comparison*, Culture and History of the Ancient Near East 56 (Leiden: Brill, 2012), 1. Stökl argues ancient Near Eastern prophecy concludes in the waning days of the sixth century BC.

3. For example, in the Minor Prophets alone, the "word of the Lord" occurs forty times, "thus says the Lord" occurs forty-three times, and "the Lord's declaration" occurs forty times.

4. Jeannette Mathews, *Prophets as Performers: Biblical Performance Criticism and Israel's Prophets* (Eugene, OR: Cascade Books, 2020), 1–6, 155–90.

5. This language is that of Ernest Lucas, "Prophets," in *IVP Introduction to the Bible*, ed. Philip S. Johnston (Downers Grove, IL: IVP Academic, 2006), 115–40, here 118.

a. J. Rabbinowitz, *Midrash Rabbah: Deuteronomy* (London: Soncino, 1939), 88.

b. Jakob Wöhrle, "So Many Cross-References! Methodological Reflections on the Problem of Intertextual Relationships and Their Significance for Redaction Critical Analysis," in *Perspectives on the Formation of the Book of the Twelve*, ed. Ranier Albertz, James D. Nogalski, and Jakob Wöhrle, Beihefte zur Zeitschrift für die alttestamentliche Wissenschaft 433 (Berlin: de Gruyter, 2012), 14.

c. This chart is adapted from Stökl, *Prophecy in the Ancient Near East*, 10. I (Heath) have used this same adapted chart in "The Ancient World of Prophecy," chap. 3 in *Minor Prophets* by Craig G. Bartholomew and Heath A. Thomas. Copyright © 2023. Used by permission of InterVarsity Press, P.O. Box 1400, Downers Grove, IL 60515, USA. www.ivpress .com. Martti Nissinen uses the terminology "inductive" and "non-inductive" divination for intuitive and technical diviners in *Prophets and Prophecy in the Ancient Near East*, with contributions by C. L. Seow and Robert K. Ritner, Writings from the Ancient World 12 (Atlanta: Society of Biblical Literature, 2003), 1. John H. Walton distinguishes between the two types of divination as "inspired" (= intuitive diviner) and "deductive" (= technical diviner) in *Ancient Near Eastern Thought and the Old Testament: Introducing the Conceptual World of the Hebrew Bible* (Grand Rapids: Baker Academic, 2006), 240–41. He borrows these designators from Jean Bottéro, *Religion in Ancient Mesopotamia* (Chicago: University of Chicago Press, 2001), 170–71.

d. Mari letter 19, in Nissinen, *Prophets and Prophecy in the Ancient Near East*, 44.

e. For a thorough treatment of the etymology of these terms and the possibility that the term "prophet" (*nābî'*) represents a postexilic projection, indeed an all-encompassing term describing the various actions of diverse figures in the preexilic period, see Stökl, *Prophecy in the Ancient Near East*, 156–200.

f. Stökl, *Prophecy in the Ancient Near East*, 196–200.

g. Harriet Beecher Stowe, *Woman in Sacred History* (New York: Portland House, 1990), 85.

h. Kirsopp Lake, ed., *The Apostolic Fathers*, vol. 1, Loeb Classical Library (London: Harvard University Press, 1919), 7.2–9.2, pp. 246–49 (translation by authors).

Chapter 9 Joshua

a. This phrase comes from the Nicene Creed.

Chapter 10 Judges

1. See the fantastic analysis of David J. H. Beldman, *Judges*, Two Horizons Old Testament Commentary (Grand Rapids: Eerdmans, 2020), 222–30; Beldman, *Deserting the King: The Book of Judges*, Transformative Word (Bellingham, WA: Lexham, 2017), 34–41.

2. J. Clinton McCann, *Judges*, Interpretation: A Bible Commentary for Teaching and Preaching (Louisville: Westminster John Knox, 2011), 42.

3. For a close poetic study of the song, see Frank Moore Cross Jr. and David Noel Freedman, *Studies in Ancient Yahwistic Poetry*, Biblical Resource Series (Grand Rapids: Eerdmans, 1997), 8–14.

4. Beldman, *Judges*, 162–63.

5. Beldman, *Judges*, 190; Beldman, *Deserting the King*, 48–60; David J. H. Beldman, *The Completion of Judges: Strategies of Ending in Judges 17–21*, Siphrut 21 (University Park, PA: Eisenbrauns, 2018), 114–21.

Chapter 10 Sidebar Notes

a. For discussion on the Canaanite pantheon, see Gregorio del Olmo Lete, *Canaanite Religion according to the Liturgical Texts of Ugarit*, trans. Wilfred G. E. Watson (Winona Lake, IN: Eisenbrauns, 2004), 43–86; Jonathan N. Tubb, *Canaanites*, Peoples of the Past (Norman: University of Oklahoma Press, 1998), 73–75.

b. For a detailed study of characterization and the three types identified, see Adele Berlin, *Poetics and the Interpretation of Biblical Narrative* (Sheffield: Almond, 1983), 23–42.

c. There is some discussion as to whether this is really a human messenger appointed by God or a divine being from the heavenlies sent to earth to speak YHWH's words. See Beldman, *Judges*, 105; Daniel I. Block, *Judges, Ruth*, New American Commentary 6 (Nashville: Broadman & Holman, 1999), 259.

d. Cyril of Jerusalem, *The Catechetical Lectures of S. Cyril, Archbishop of Jerusalem* (Oxford: John Henry Parker, 1838), 16.28, p. 217.

Chapter 11 1–2 Samuel

1. Heath Thomas and J. D. Greear, *Exalting Jesus in 1–2 Samuel*, Christ-Centered Exposition Commentary (Nashville: Holman Reference, 2016), 9.

2. David G. Firth, *1 & 2 Samuel*, Apollos Old Testament Commentary 8 (Nottingham, UK: Apollos, 2009), 43.

3. For a helpful introduction to the religious views of other nations in the Old Testament, we recommend interested readers to consult Craig G. Bartholomew, *The Old Testament and God*, Old Testament Origins and the Question of God 1 (Grand Rapids: Baker Academic, 2022), 199–393.

4. The following discussion is influenced by Thomas and Greear, *Exalting Jesus in 1–2 Samuel*, 104–8. For a helpful overview of "holy war" and its problems, see Heath A. Thomas, Paul Copan, and Jeremy Evans, eds., *Holy War in the Bible: Christian Morality and an Old Testament Problem* (Downers Grove, IL: IVP Academic, 2013).

5. Firth, *1 & 2 Samuel*, 120–21.

6. Chart adapted from Thomas and Greear, *Exalting Jesus in 1–2 Samuel*, 195.

7. Peter J. Leithart, *A Son to Me: An Exposition of 1 & 2 Samuel* (Moscow, ID: Canon, 2003), 309.

Chapter 11 Sidebar Notes

a. See the classic work by Adele Berlin, *Poetics and the Interpretation of Biblical Narrative* (Sheffield: Almond Press, 1983).

b. Thomas and Greear, *Exalting Jesus in 1–2 Samuel*, 45–46, 64–65. See also E. Earle Ellis, *The Gospel of Luke*, New Century Bible (London: Marshall, Morgan and Scott, 1981), 74–75; Joel B. Green, *The Gospel of Luke*, New International Commentary on the New Testament (Grand Rapids: Eerdmans, 1997), 100–105.

c. Firth, *1 & 2 Samuel*, 119.

d. Thomas and Greear, *Exalting Jesus in 1–2 Samuel*, 179–82.

Chapter 12 1–2 Kings

1. Robert Alter, *The Hebrew Bible*, vol. 2, *Prophets: A Translation and Commentary* (New York: Doubleday, 2019).

Chapter 12 Sidebar Notes

a. Karl Barth, *Church Dogmatics*, vol. II/2, *The Doctrine of God*, trans. G. W. Bromiley et al. (Edinburgh: T&T Clark, 1994), 385–89.

b. Augustine, *Teaching Christianity* [*De Doctrina Christiana*], trans. E. Hill, The Works of Saint Augustine I/11 (New York: New City, 1995), 1.13.

c. C. S. Lewis, "Learning in War-Time," in *The Weight of Glory* (New York: HarperOne, 1980), 55–56.

d. Michel de Montaigne, "On the Inconsistency of Our Actions," in *The Complete Works*, trans. D. M. Frame, Everyman's Library 259 (New York: Knopf, 2003), 296.

Chapter 13 Isaiah

1. John Calvin, *Commentary on the Book of the Prophet Isaiah*, vol. 1, trans. W. Pringle (Grand Rapids: Baker Books, 2005), xxxii.

a. Augustine, *Confessions*, trans. Henry Chadwick (Oxford: Oxford University Press, 1991), 9.13, p. 163.

b. "The Martyrdom of Isaiah," trans. Robert Henry Charles, in *Pseudepigrapha of the Old Testament*, ed. R. H. Charles (Oxford: Clarendon, 1913), 5:1–15. Cf. Heb. 11:37.

c. Robert Alter, *The Hebrew Bible: A Translation and Commentary*, vol. 2, *Prophets* (New York: Norton, 2019), 618.

d. See Baba Batra 15a.

e. Cyril of Alexandria, quoted in *Isaiah: Interpreted by Early Christians and Medieval Commentators*, ed. and trans. R. L. Wilkin, The Church's Bible (Grand Rapids: Eerdmans, 2007), 196.

f. Martin Luther King Jr., "I Have a Dream," August 28, 1963, University of Minnesota Human Rights Library (website), http://hrlibrary.umn.edu/education/lutherspeech.html.

g. Karl Barth, *Church Dogmatics*, vol. II/1, *The Doctrine of God*, trans. T. H. L. Parker, W. B. Johnston, Harold Knight, and J. L. M. Haire, ed. G. W. Bromiley and T. F. Torrance (London: T&T Clark, 1957), 665.

Chapter 14 Jeremiah

1. For discussion of Babylonian engagement with Judah, see Bill T. Arnold, *Who Were the Babylonians?*, Society of Biblical Literature Archaeology and Biblical Studies 10 (Leiden: Brill, 2005), 87–105.

2. John D. Meade, "Circumcision of the Heart in Leviticus and Deuteronomy: Divine Means for Resolving Curse and Bringing Blessing," *Southern Baptist Journal of Theology* 18, no. 3 (2014): 59–85.

3. For discussion, see Heath A. Thomas, "Zion," in *Dictionary of the Old Testament: Prophets*, ed. J. Gordon McConville and Mark J. Boda (Downers Grove, IL: IVP Academic, 2012), 907–14.

4. The following discussion on the new covenant follows the logic and concepts of Bruce Riley Ashford and Heath A. Thomas, *The Gospel of Our King: Bible, Worldview, and the Mission of Every Christian* (Grand Rapids: Baker Academic, 2019), 82–84.

5. Note that the covenant with David conjoins the covenant at creation and the Abrahamic covenant in Jer. 33:19–22. See also Jer. 33:23–26.

6. J. Gordon McConville, *Judgment and Promise: An Interpretation of the Book of Jeremiah* (Winona Lake, IN: Eisenbrauns, 1993), 97: "His [Jeremiah's] 'bring me back that I may be restored' [Jer. 31:18] rests on a play on the verb *šûḇ* which is at the heart of the great solution, and indeed of all theological wrestling with the relationship of divine enabling and adequate human response to God."

7. See, e.g., the partial fulfillment of the new covenant in Ezra's words in Ezra 7–9. J. G. McConville, "Ezra-Nehemiah and the Fulfilment of Prophecy," *Vetus Testamentum* 36, no. 2 (1986): 205–24. See also our chapter on Ezra-Nehemiah in this volume.

8. The following discussion on divine forgiveness and the new covenant follows the thinking of Ashford and Thomas, *The Gospel of Our King*, 84–87.

9. "It is only through this obedient Son [Jesus], God the Son incarnate, that we have God's long-awaited kingdom inaugurated in this world (through the new covenant)." Peter J. Gentry and Stephen J. Wellum, *Kingdom through Covenant: A Biblical-Theological Understanding of the Covenants* (Wheaton: Crossway, 2012), 595.

10. E. Earle Ellis, *The Gospel of Luke*, New Century Bible (London: Marshall, Morgan and Scott, 1981), 251.

Chapter 14 Sidebar Notes

a. For a helpful introduction to the issues and discussion, see Leslie C. Allen, *Jeremiah*, Old Testament Library (Louisville: Westminster John Knox, 2008), 7–11.

b. For helpful discussion, see Oded Lipschits and Joseph Blenkinsopp, eds., *Judah and the Judeans in the Neo-Babylonian Period* (Winona Lake, IN: Eisenbrauns, 2003).

c. Terence E. Fretheim, *The Suffering of God: An Old Testament Perspective*, Overtures to Biblical Theology (Philadelphia: Fortress, 1984), 107–48. See also the discussion of Heath A. Thomas, "Suffering," *Dictionary of the Old Testament: Prophets*, ed. J. Gordon McConville and Mark J. Boda (Downers Grove, IL: IVP Academic, 2012).

d. There is much to unpack here. However, the most extensive and insightful study of this contrast is found in Joshua N. Moon, *Jeremiah's New Covenant: An Augustinian Reading*, Journal for Theological Interpretation, Supplements 3 (Winona Lake, IN: Eisenbrauns, 2011).

e. See, e.g., Augustine, "Against Two Letters of the Pelagians" in *Saint Augustine: Anti-Pelagian Writings*, vol. 5 of *Nicene and Post Nicene Fathers*, series 1, ed. Philip Schaff (New York: Christian Literature, 1887), esp. book 3, 402–15.

Chapter 15 Ezekiel

1. "Ezekiel Saw the Wheel," AZLyrics, https://www.azlyrics.com/lyrics/louisarmstrong/ezekielsawthewheel.html.

Chapter 15 Sidebar Notes

a. William Greenhill, *Ezekiel*, Geneva Series of Commentaries (Edinburgh: Banner of Truth, 1994), 46–48.

b. John Calvin, quoted in *Ezekiel, Daniel*, ed. Carl L. Beckwith, Reformation Commentary on Scripture (Downers Grove, IL: IVP Academic, 2012), 9.

c. Saint Gregory the Great, *Homilies on the Book of the Prophet Ezekiel*, trans. T. Tomkinson (Etna, CA: Center for Traditionalist Orthodox Studies, 2008), 71.

d. Jonathan Edwards, "Ezekiel 1," in *Notes on Scripture*, ed. Stephen J. Stein, vol. 15 of *Works of Jonathan Edwards* (New Haven: Yale University Press, 2008), 377.

e. Robert Jenson, *Ezekiel*, Brazos Theological Commentary on the Bible (Grand Rapids: Brazos, 2009), 42–43.

f. John Calvin, quoted in Beckwith, *Ezekiel, Daniel*, 16–17.

Chapter 16 The Minor Prophets or the Book of the Twelve—Hosea through Malachi

1. Augustine, *City of God* 18.28.

2. Hosea 1:6, the "mercy" of God is no longer operative; Joel 2:13, which calls people to repentance due to God's "compassion"; Jon. 3:9, where the king of Nineveh wonders about the compassion of God; and 4:2, where Jonah laments the mercy and grace of God and that Yahweh's character abounds in steadfast love; Mic. 7:18–20 presents Yahweh as forgiving, passing over transgression and showing steadfast love.

3. This definition derives from Heath A. Thomas, *Habakkuk*, Two Horizons Old Testament Commentary (Grand Rapids: Eerdmans, 2018), 67.

4. See the discussion of Craig G. Bartholomew and Heath A. Thomas, *The Minor Prophets: A Theological Introduction* (Downers Grove, IL: IVP Academic, 2023), 272–74.

5. R. Michael Fox, *A Message from the Great King: Reading Malachi in Light of Ancient Persian Royal Messenger Texts from the Time of Xerxes*, Shiphrut 17 (Winona Lake, IL: Eisenbrauns, 2015), 120–28.

Chapter 16 Sidebar Notes

a. Anglican Church in North America, *The Book of Common Prayer and Administration of the Sacraments* (Huntington Beach, CA: Anglican Liturgy Press, 2019), 12.

b. Theodoret of Cyrus, *Commentaries on the Prophets*, vol. 3, *Commentary on the Twelve Prophets*, trans. Robert Charles Hill (Bookline, MA: Holy Cross Orthodox, 2006), 209.

c. Hosea 3:5; 5:4; 6:1; 7:10; 11:5; 12:6; 14:1–2; Joel 2:12–13; 3:4, 7; Amos 4:6, 8–11; Obad. 1:15; Jon. 3:8; Mic. 2:8; 5:3; Nah. 2:2; Zech. 1:3, 16; 4:1; 8:3; 9:12; 10:6, 9; Mal. 3:7.

d. See the classic discussion of R. T. France, *Jesus and the Old Testament: His Application of Old Testament Passages to Himself and His Mission* (Vancouver: Regent College, 1998). Note also other connections from the Gospels: Zech. 2:10 and Mark 13:27; Zech. 9:11 and Mark 14:24; Zech. 11:12–13 and Matt. 27:9–10; Zech. 12:12 and Matt. 24:30; Zech. 13:7 and Matt. 26:31, Mark 14:27.

Chapter 18 Psalms

1. John Calvin, *Commentary on the Book of Psalms*, trans. J. Anderson, vol. 4 of *Calvin's Commentaries* (Grand Rapids: Baker Books, 2005), xxxvii.

2. Eugene H. Peterson, *A Long Obedience in the Same Direction: Discipleship in an Instant Society* (Downers Grove, IL: InterVarsity, 1980).

Chapter 18 Sidebar Notes

a. Athanasius, "The Letter of St. Athanasius to Marcellinus on the Interpretation of the Psalms," in *On the Incarnation*, Popular Patristics Series 3 (Crestwood, NY: St. Vladimir's Seminary Press, 1996), 105.

b. Sigmund Mowinckel, *The Psalms in Israel's Worship*, trans. D. R. Ap-Thomas (Grand Rapids: Eerdmans, 2004), 9.

c. Augustine, *Confessions*, trans. H. Chadwick (Oxford: Oxford University Press, 1998), 9.8, p. 160.

d. Martin Luther, "Preface to the Psalter," in *Luther's Works* (Philadelphia: Fortress, 1960), 35:253.

e. C. S. Lewis, *Reflections on the Psalms: The Celebrated Musings on One of the Most Intriguing Books of the Bible* (New York: Harcourt, 1958), 94–95.

f. Ellen Davis, *Opening Israel's Scriptures* (Oxford: Oxford University Press, 2019), 326.

g. Gregory of Nazianzus, "A Prayer to Christ," in *Gregory of Nazianzus*, ed. Brian E. Daley, SJ, The Early Church Fathers (New York: Routledge, 2006), 170.

h. "An Information for Them Which Take Offense at Certain Places of the Holy Scripture," The Second Book of Homilies 10, in *The Books of Homilies: A Critical Edition*, ed. G. Bray (Cambridge: James Clark, 2015), 368.

i. Dietrich Bonhoeffer, "Lecture on Christ in the Psalms," in *Theological Education at Finkenwalde: 1935–1937*, vol. 14 of *Dietrich Bonhoeffer Works* (Minneapolis: Fortress, 2013), 387.

Chapter 19 Job

1. Tremper Longman III, *Job*, Baker Commentary on the Old Testament Wisdom and Psalms (Grand Rapids: Baker Academic, 2012), 82–84.

2. This definition derives from Heath A. Thomas, *Habakkuk*, Two Horizons Old Testament Commentary (Grand Rapids: Eerdmans, 2018), 67.

3. For full discussion, see Heath A. Thomas, "Job's Rejection and Liminal Traverse: A Close (Re)reading of Job 42:6," in *The Unfolding of Your Words Gives Light: Studies in Biblical Hebrew in Honor of George L. Klein*, ed. Ethan C. Jones (University Park: Pennsylvania State University Press, 2018), 155–74. See also Lindsay Wilson, *Job*, Two Horizons Old Testament Commentary (Grand Rapids: Eerdmans, 2015), 206–7.

4. Gregory the Great, *Morals on the Book of Job*, vol. 1, *Parts 1 and 2*, trans. Charles Marriott (Oxford: John Henry Parker, 1844), book 2, §43, p. 97.

Chapter 19 Sidebar Notes

a. Takayoshi Oshima, *Babylonian Poems of Pious Sufferers:* Ludlul Bēl Nēmeqi *and the Babylonian Theodicy*, Orientalische Religionen in der Antike 14 (Tübingen: Mohr Siebeck, 2014); Alan Lenzi and Amar Annus, "A Six-Column Babylonian Tablet of *Ludlul Bēl Nēmeqi* and the Reconstruction of Tablet IV," *Journal of Near Eastern Studies* 70, no. 2 (2011): 181–205; Alan Lenzi and Amar Annus, *Ludlul bēl Nēmeqi: The Standard Babylonian Poem of the Righteous Sufferer*, State Archives of Assyria Cuneiform Texts 7 (Helsinki: Neo-Assyrian Text Corpus Project, 2010). For an online version, see https://www.ebl.lmu.de/corpus/L/2/2.

b. Gregory the Great, *Morals on the Book of Job*, vol. 1, *Parts 1 and 2*, book 2, §§3–4, pp. 69–71.

c. Gregory the Great, *Morals on the Book of Job*, book 2, §5, p. 71.

d. See, e.g., Ryan J. Stokes, *The Satan: How God's Executioner Became the Enemy* (Grand Rapids: Eerdmans, 2019).

e. Gregory the Great, *Morals on the Book of Job*, vol. 3, *Part 5*, trans. Charles Marriott (Oxford: John Henry Parker, 1844), book 23, §4, p. 5.

f. N. H. Tur-Sinai, *The Book of Job: A New Commentary* (Jerusalem: Kiryath Sepher, 1957), 578.

g. John E. Hartley, *The Book of Job*, New International Commentary on the Old Testament (Grand Rapids: Eerdmans, 1988), 537.

h. G. K. Chesterton, introduction to *The Book of Job* (London: Cecil Palmer and Hayward, 1916), xxii.

i. Karl Barth, Church Dogmatics, vol. III/1, *The Doctrine of Creation*, trans. J. W. Edwards, O. Bussey, and H. Knight, ed. G. W. Bromiley and T. F. Torrance (1958; repr., Peabody, MA: Hendrickson, 2010), 21–22.

Chapter 20 Proverbs

1. Lucas Glen Wisley, "Israel's Paradoxical King: The Characterization of Solomon in 1 Kings 1–11, 2 Chronicles 1–9, Proverbs, Ecclesiastes, and Song of Songs" (PhD diss., University of Cambridge, 2018).

2. Beautifully expounded by Craig Bartholomew, *Reading Proverbs with Integrity*, Guides to Biblical Scholarship (Cambridge: Grove Books, 2001), 8–9.

3. Raymond van Leeuwen, "Wisdom Literature," in *Dictionary for Theological Interpretation of the Bible*, ed. Kevin J. Vanhoozer (Grand Rapids: Baker Academic, 2005), 848.

4. Craig G. Bartholomew and Ryan P. O'Dowd, *Old Testament Wisdom Literature: A Theological Introduction* (Downers Grove, IL: IVP Academic, 2011), 25–30.

5. Bartholomew, *Reading Proverbs*, 9.

6. Following Al Wolters, *The Song of the Valiant Woman: Studies in the Interpretation of Proverbs 31:10–31* (Milton Keynes, UK: Paternoster, 2001).

7. See, *Song of the Valiant Woman*.

8. Jonathan T. Pennington, *The Sermon on the Mount and Human Flourishing: A Theological Commentary* (Grand Rapids: Baker Academic, 2017), 14–16.

9. David F. Ford, "Jesus Christ, the Wisdom of God (I)," in *Reading Texts, Seeking Wisdom*, ed. David F. Ford and Graham Stanton (London: SCM Press, 2003), 4–21 (esp. 13–15).

a. For the *Instruction of Amenemope*, see Miriam Lichtheim, *Ancient Egyptian Literature*, vol. 2, *The New Kingdom* (Berkeley: University of California Press, 1976), 146–63.

b. Aloys Grillmeier, *Christ in the Christian Tradition*, vol. 2, *From the Apostolic Age to Chalcedon (451)*, trans. John Bowden (Atlanta: John Knox, 1975), 26–32.

c. We are building on the insights of F. W. Dobbs-Allsopp, *On Biblical Poetry* (Oxford: Oxford University Press, 2015), 110–85.

d. For a good study of the poetry of Proverbs, see Knut Martin Heim, *Poetic Imagination in Proverbs: Variant Repetitions and the Nature of Poetry*, Bulletin for Biblical Research Supplements 4 (Winona Lake, IN: Eisenbrauns, 2013).

e. Augustine, "Sermon 37," in *Sermons*, vol. 2, Sermons 20–50, trans. Edmund Hill, ed. John E. Rotelle, The Works of Saint Augustine III/2 (New York: New City, 1990), 184.

f. English translation from Athenagoris, *Legatio and De Resurrectione*, ed. and trans. William R. Schoedel, Oxford Early Christian Texts (Oxford: Oxford University Press, 1972).

Chapter 21 Ruth

1. William Cowper, "God Moves in a Mysterious Way."

2. Marilynne Robinson, "Open Thy Hand Wide: Moses and the Origins of American Liberalism," in *When I Was a Child I Read Books* (New York: Farrar, Straus & Giroux, 2012), 59–83.

a. Jonathan Burnside, *God, Justice, and Society: Aspects of Law and Legality in the Bible* (Oxford: Oxford University Press, 2011), 241.

b. Heidelberg Catechism, Heidelberg-Catechism.com, accessed April 22, 2024, https://www.heidelberg-catechism.com/en/lords-days/10.html.

Chapter 22 Song of Songs

1. Rabbi Akiva, Mishnah Yadayim 3:5.

2. Origen, "The First Homily," in *The Song of Songs Commentary and Homilies*, trans. R. P. Lawson, Ancient Christian Writers 26 (New York: Newman Press, 1956), 266.

3. Franz Delitzsch, *Commentary on the Song of Songs and Ecclesiastes*, trans. M. G. Easton (Grand Rapids: Eerdmans, 1968), 6.

4. *Memoir and Remains of Robert Murray M'Cheyne*, ed. Andrew Bonar (Edinburgh: Banner of Truth Trust, 1995), 480.

5. William Shakespeare, "Sonnet 116."

a. Bernard of Clairvaux, Sermon 79.1, quoted in Roland E. Murphy, *The Song of Songs*, Hermeneia (Minneapolis: Fortress, 1990), xxiii.

b. Mary Oliver, *A Poetry Handbook: A Prose Guide to Understanding and Writing Poetry* (New York: Harcourt, 1994), 84–85.

c. Robert W. Jenson, *The Song of Songs*, Interpretation: A Bible Commentary for Teaching and Preaching (Louisville: Westminster John Knox, 2005), 1, 13.

d. *Memoir and Remains of Robert Murray M'Cheyne*, ed. Andrew Bonar (Edinburgh: Banner of Truth Trust, 1995), 351.

e. Murphy, *Song of Songs*, 60.

Chapter 23 Ecclesiastes

1. Augustine, *Confessions*, trans. Henry Chadwick (Oxford: Oxford University Press, 1991), 1.1, p. 3.

a. Martin Luther, *Notes on Ecclesiastes*, quoted in Eric S. Christianson, *Ecclesiastes through the Centuries*, Blackwell Bible Commentaries (Malden, MA: Blackwell, 2007), 2.

b. Thomas Wolfe, quoted in Christianson, *Ecclesiastes through the Centuries*, 70.

c. John Donne, *Donne's Satyr*, quoted in Christianson, *Ecclesiastes through the Centuries*, 116.

d. Bonaventure, *Commentary on Ecclesiastes*, quoted in Christianson, *Ecclesiastes through the Centuries*, 113.

e. T. S. Eliot, "Dry Salvages" (the third poem of *Four Quartets*), in *Collected Poems, 1909–1962* (New York: Harcourt, Brace & World, 1963), 194.

f. Augustine, *The Confessions*, trans. Sarah Ruden (New York: Modern Library, 2017), 1.1, p. 3.

g. *Chariots of Fire*, directed by Hugh Hudson (1981).

Chapter 24 Lamentations

1. Daniel Berrigan, *Lamentations: From New York to Kabul and Beyond* (Lanham: Sheed & Ward, 2002), xvii–xviii.

2. Soong-Chan Rah, *Prophetic Lament: A Call for Justice in Troubled Times* (Downers Grove, IL: InterVarsity, 2015), 203.

a. For critical editions of Mesopotamian city laments, see Jacob Klein, trans., "Lamentation over the Destruction of Sumer and Ur," in *The Context of Scripture: Canonical Compositions from the Biblical World*, ed. William W. Hallo and K. Lawson Younger Jr. (Leiden: Brill, 2003), 1.166:535–39. Much of the discussion here on city laments derives from Heath A. Thomas, *Poetry and Theology in the Book of Lamentations: The Aesthetics of an Open Text*, Hebrew Bible Monographs 47 (Sheffield: Sheffield Phoenix, 2013), 144–47.

b. As the Assyrian relief from the palace of Tiglath-pileser III at Nimrud reveals, the Assyrian warriors carry off the images of foreign gods away from a captured town, thereby exiling the deity. See F. F. Bruce, *Israel and the Nations: From the Exodus to the Fall of the Second Temple* (Exeter, UK: Paternoster, 1969), plate 6.

Chapter 25 Esther

1. David G. Firth, *The Message of Esther: God Present but Unseen*, The Bible Speaks Today (Nottingham, UK: Inter-Varsity Press, 2010), 33.

2. Heath A. Thomas, "The Fruit of Mourning: Esther Enriched by the Latter Prophets," in *Reading Esther Intertextually*, ed. David G. Firth and Brittany N. Melton, The Library of Hebrew Bible/Old Testament Studies 725 (London: T&T Clark, 2022), 92–93.

3. For full discussion, see Kara J. Lyons-Pardue, "Esther in Dialogue with Mark: Power, Vulnerability, and Kingship," in Firth and Melton, *Reading Esther Intertextually*, 159–68.

a. See, e.g., Ericka Shawndricka Dunbar, *Trafficking Hadassah: Collective Trauma, Cultural Memory, and Identity in the Book of Esther and in the African Diaspora* (London: Routledge, 2021).

Chapter 26 Daniel

1. The favor that they would find in the king's court came "not by capitulating to the lifestyle of the Babylonians epitomized by the king's food, attractive as that lifestyle may have been, but by remaining rigorously true to Torah and trusting in God." Paul L. Redditt, *Daniel*, New Century Bible Commentary (Sheffield: Sheffield Academic, 1999), 46.

2. For discussion, see C. L. Seow, *Daniel*, Westminster Bible Commentary (Louisville: Westminster John Knox, 2003), 44–47; Paul R. House, *Daniel*, Tyndale Old Testament Commentary 23 (Downers Grove, IL: IVP Academic, 2018), 3–7.

3. Greg Goswell, "The Visions of Daniel and Their Historical Specificity," *Restoration Quarterly* 58, no. 3 (2016): 129–42 (esp. 135).

a. Irenaeus, *Against Heresies*, trans. John Keble (London: James Parker, 1872), 5.2, p. 512.

b. John Calvin, *Commentaries on the Book of the Prophet Daniel*, vol. 2, trans. Thomas Myers (Edinburgh, Scotland: Calvin Translation Society; Grand Rapids: Baker Books, 2009), 41.

Chapter 27 Ezra-Nehemiah

1. H. G. M. Williamson, *Ezra, Nehemiah*, Word Biblical Commentary 16 (Waco: Word, 1985), xxxvi; Sara Japhet, "Sheshbazzar and Zerubbabel—Against the Background of the Historical and Religious Tendencies of Ezra-Nehemiah," *Zeitschrift für die alttestamentliche Wissenschaft* 94 (1982): 66–98, esp. 88.

2. For further study and for the dates of Persian kings, see Marc Van De Mieroop, *A History of the Ancient Near East, ca. 3000–323 BC*, 3rd ed., Blackwell History of the Ancient World (London: Wiley Blackwell, 2016), 308–412.

3. Lena-Sofia Tiemeyer, *Ezra-Nehemiah: Israel's Quest for Identity*, T&T Clark Study Guides to the Old Testament (London: T&T Clark, 2020), 15–16.

4. See H. G. M. Williamson, *Ezra and Nehemiah*, Old Testament Guides (Sheffield: Sheffield Academic, 1987), 26–27; J. G. McConville, "Ezra-Nehemiah and the Fulfillment of Prophecy," *Vetus Testamentum* 36, no. 2 (1986): 205–24.

5. For further discussion, see Williamson, *Ezra, Nehemiah*, 341–66.

6. See, e.g., Geir O. Holmas, *Prayer and Vindication in Luke Acts: The Theme of Prayer within the Context of the Legitimating and Edifying Objective of the Lukan Narrative* (London: T&T Clark, 2011).

a. T. C. Ezkenazi, *In an Age of Prose: A Literary Approach to Ezra-Nehemiah* (Atlanta: Scholars Press, 1988), 38.

b. Mordechai Cogan, "Cyrus Cylinder (2.124)," in *The Context of Scripture*, vol. 2, *Monumental Inscriptions from the Biblical World*, ed. William W. Hallo (Leiden: Brill, 2003), 315.

c. Lena-Sofia Tiemeyer, *Ezra-Nehemiah: Israel's Quest for Identity*, T&T Clark Study Guides to the Old Testament (London: T&T Clark, 2020).

d. For the full exploration of the intertexts and the original correlation via a helpful chart, see J. G. McConville, "Ezra-Nehemiah and the Fulfilment of Prophecy," *Vetus Testamentum* 36, no. 2 (1986): 205–24, esp. 213–18.

e. H. G. M. Williamson, *Ezra and Nehemiah*, Old Testament Guides (Sheffield: Sheffield Academic, 1987), 27, alerts us to these parallels. We adapt his insights for the chart and what follows.

Index

Aaron, 60, 68, 79, 86, 88–89, 92–95, 97–98, 133–34, 193, 381, 397
Aaronic blessing, 101
Abraham, 13, 21–22, 24–26, 30, 34–47, 49, 51, 64, 81–82, 89, 101, 103, 105, 134, 141, 149–50, 177, 212, 214, 224–26, 306, 323, 386, 406
adultery, 58–59, 112, 178, 252
agriculture, 28, 72, 81, 206, 308
Ahab, 147, 194–95
Ahaz, 133, 196–97, 206–7
Akkadian, 28, 71, 104, 196, 413 note b (chap. 5)
allegory, 53, 214, 241
Amos, 7–8, 126, 133–35, 137–38, 212, 242–43, 250, 253–55, 264, 268, 406
analogy, 29, 96, 300, 349
ancient Near East, 12, 25, 27–28, 30, 55, 75, 99, 102, 104, 111, 114, 115, 117, 118, 122, 130–31, 138, 183, 233, 265, 276, 291, 404–5, 414n2 (chap. 7), 414n2 (chap. 8)
angel, 13, 33, 38, 41–43, 50, 52–53, 140, 154, 159–60, 205, 210, 231, 237, 269, 279, 293, 365–66, 371–72, 403
apocalypse, 208–9
apocalyptic, 208, 365–66, 375, 403
Aquinas, Thomas, 83, 211
Aramaic, 4, 345, 352, 361, 373
archaeological evidence, 12, 98, 130, 252, 367, 378
Assyria, 103–4, 115, 118, 185, 192–96, 198, 208–11, 258–61
Athanasius, 279
atonement, 67–68, 70, 73–77, 79–81, 83, 85, 87, 117, 232, 403, 405
Augustine, 1, 3, 29, 38, 187, 201, 224, 251, 282, 290, 314, 339

Baal, 55, 154, 156, 165, 174, 191, 196, 204, 388, 399
Babylon/Babylonia/Neo-Babylonia, 115, 118, 130, 196–99, 217–19, 233–36, 259–64
Babylonian Talmud, 203, 250, 273, 300, 407–8
Balaam, 97–98

Barth, Karl, 12, 186, 213, 304
Bavinck, Herman, 12
blessing, 41–45, 77, 81, 88–90, 119–20, 311, 322–23
blood, 31, 41, 53–54, 68, 74–76, 79, 83–84, 94, 99, 100–101, 157, 185, 194, 196, 199, 203–4, 225, 231–32, 252, 259–60, 322, 369, 374, 406

Calvin, John, 38, 43, 110, 142, 145, 203–4, 238–39, 244, 278, 374, 399, 407
captivity, 37, 228, 230
children, 41, 48, 53–54, 143, 145, 321–23, 399
circumcision, 34, 219–20, 225
clean/unclean, 70–79, 94
conquest, 18, 115–16, 141, 147–48, 167, 391, 404
cosmic, 28, 38, 207–9, 215, 230, 242–43, 267, 365, 370, 372
covenant, 21–22, 34, 81, 104–5, 136–37, 224–26
  Abrahamic, 36, 177, 224, 417n5
  Davidic, 167, 177–79, 181–82, 224–26, 265, 279, 290, 306, 393, 395, 417n5
  Mosaic or Israelite, 58, 144, 177, 221, 224–26
  new, 83, 101, 137, 223–32, 306, 380, 382–83, 389
  Noahic, 34–35, 225–26
critical approach, 17
curse, 31, 35, 37, 81, 97–98, 104, 109–10, 112, 119, 128, 158, 177, 221, 225–26, 291, 293, 311, 348
Cyril of Alexandria, 208, 263
Cyrus, 263, 367, 370–71, 376–81, 391, 399, 400, 407

Daniel, 7, 8, 129, 131, 219, 223, 234, 273, 275, 277, 352–54, 356, 360–75, 382, 384, 403, 406–7
David, 167–80, 281, 323, 394–96. *See also* covenant: Davidic
day of the Lord, 125, 128, 208–9, 253–54, 262–63, 267, 269–72
Dead Sea Scrolls, 98. *See also* Qumran
demon, 33, 329, 331, 371
Deuteronomist, 17

425

divination, 118, 131, 132, 172, 181, 415 note c
divine council, 205, 294
Documentary Hypothesis, 17
doubt, 31, 93
dream, 41, 131, 133, 189, 190, 212, 338, 362–64, 366

Eden, 30–31, 56, 81, 225, 280, 317, 387
Edom, 88, 95, 130, 148, 155, 206, 208, 210, 229, 242–43, 255, 269, 293, 347
Egypt, 48, 115, 117, 198, 208, 228, 307
Elijah, 50, 124–25, 128, 138, 184, 186, 191–92, 199, 269, 272
Elisha, 124, 184, 191–92
Elohim, 25, 36, 143, 193, 256
Enuma Elish, 28, 404
Ephraim, 43, 68, 89, 148, 155, 196, 201, 206, 208–10
Esau, 41–42, 255, 268
eschatology/eschatological, 29, 63, 128, 149, 186, 202, 206, 208, 212, 264, 269, 404
ethics, 59, 109, 112, 274, 313, 327
exile, 37, 81–82, 122–23, 217–19, 234

false prophets, 223, 286, 387
figural representation/interpretation, 38, 43, 48, 101, 170
flood, 24, 27–28, 30, 33–35, 55–56, 209, 256, 259, 406
fool, 114, 172, 192, 291, 308–9, 311–12, 314–16, 330, 337–40, 373
form criticism, 283

garden, 29–32, 181, 225, 283, 304, 327–30
genre, 208, 275, 328, 403
grace formula, 130
Gregory of Nazianzus, 284
Gregory of Nyssa, 53, 121, 279
Gregory the Great, 238, 293, 299, 304

Hamann, Johann Georg, 12
heaven, 41, 50, 90, 215, 292–94, 366, 369
Hezekiah, 196–97, 199, 201, 203, 206, 209–11, 306, 354–55, 393, 398–99
higher criticism, 12
Hittite, 103–4, 116, 156, 382
holy/holiness, 66, 69–72, 87, 205, 388
Holy Spirit, 6, 26, 36, 44, 75, 181, 245, 285, 287, 293, 315, 408–9
Hugh of St. Victor, 9

idolatry, 56, 61, 83, 98, 108–9, 112, 124, 154, 161, 163–64, 173, 181, 185, 193–94, 196–97, 219, 234, 240–41, 252, 258, 284
incense, 68–69, 76, 228–29, 247
inspiration, 3, 12, 281, 299
Irenaeus, 6, 363
irony, 49, 241, 357
Isaac, 12–13, 26, 37–42, 44, 49, 51, 64, 82, 103, 406

Jacob, 26, 30, 40–44, 46, 49–51, 61, 64, 82, 93, 98, 102–3, 145, 149, 213, 216, 255, 260, 268, 394
Jericho, 99, 142–48, 155, 228, 318
Jerome, 9, 100, 224, 241, 250, 263, 287, 333, 377
Josiah, 13, 17, 133, 151, 185, 188, 197–98, 262, 399
judge, 110–14, 153
  charismatic saviors, 126, 153
  courts, 153
  law of the judge, 114
justice, 114, 130, 137, 178–80, 194, 214, 255

King, Martin Luther, Jr., 137, 212
kings
  of Assyria, 196
  of Babylonia, 198
  in Daniel, 363–64, 370
  of Israel, 194
  of Judah, 194–97
  law of the king, 114–16
  and messiah, 98, 168, 170, 179–81, 267
  of Persia, 380

lamb, 40–41, 53, 117
lament, 130, 168, 220, 222–23, 239, 242, 256, 259, 261, 268, 273, 382–84, 295–96, 337, 343–44, 347, 349, 404–5, 418n2
latter days, 243
law, 7–8, 17–19, 21–22, 57–60, 65, 72, 74–75, 82, 101–2
  apodictic, 59
  atonement, 73–75
  Calvin's three uses of, 110
  casuistic, 59
  clean and unclean, 70–72, 75–79
  dietary laws, 75–78
  forgiveness, 74, 76–77
  holy times and festivals, 81, 106
  lex talionis, 100
  love, 80, 107–8
  leadership laws, 113–18
  Mosaic law / law of Moses, 20, 65, 81–83, 148–49, 224, 381
  rejoicing, 109–12
  rituals, 87–88, 94
  sacrifice, 75–80, 101–2
  Ten Commandments, 58–60, 61, 106–7, 112
  torah, 16, 109, 111
  two tables of, 59, 82, 204
levirate marriage, 321
Luther, Martin, 29, 38, 42–43, 59, 200, 333

Maccabees, 386
Marcion, 65
marriage, 31, 42, 47, 115, 206, 241, 252, 268, 318, 321–22, 327–28, 331, 377, 382–83, 385, 388–89
Mesopotamia, 75, 117, 130, 132, 157, 198, 344, 399, 404, 408
Messiah, 44, 75, 98, 128, 170, 179, 181, 230, 260, 267, 304, 315, 346, 349, 374, 406

middoth, 61

Moab, 44, 86–88, 95, 97, 99, 102–3, 105–6, 122, 127, 136, 144, 148, 155, 157, 174, 195–96, 207–8, 210, 225–26, 229, 242–43, 263, 317–19, 321–22, 324, 382, 388

moon, 25, 28, 106, 156, 279

mystery, 31, 36, 56, 297, 321, 374

Nebuchadnezzar, 126, 197–98, 219, 228–29, 233, 243, 255, 360–66, 370, 380, 383, 386

Origen, 18, 66, 86, 326, 333, 377

parable, 48, 52, 204–5, 232, 250, 314, 338

parallelism, 280

Persia, 17, 22, 128, 135, 157, 234, 238, 250, 264–70, 343, 351–52, 354–57, 361, 366–67, 370–71, 376–86, 388, 391, 399, 404, 406–7

personification, 309, 405, 407

Philistine, 96, 156–57, 162–63, 165, 170–76, 206, 395, 397

plague, 53–54, 96–97, 171, 222, 236, 253

priests, 58, 66–84, 90, 116–17
    and atonement, 73–74
    and holiness, 70–72
    Israel as kingdom of priests, 66, 81
    and Jesus, 52, 84, 340
    law of, 116–17
    offerings and sacrifices, 76–77
    and the sanctuary, 67–70

prophets, 117–18, 125–36, 191–92, 201–2. See also false prophets
    in the ancient Near East, 118
    canonical grouping, 125–28
    and covenant, 136–37
    and gender, 132–34
    in Israel's history, 130–32
    and Jesus, 3, 137–38
    law of, 117–18
    prophetic books, 128–30
    and sign acts, 135

providence, 10, 22, 38, 42, 44, 49, 247, 275, 299, 318–20, 322, 324, 338, 397

queen of heaven, 229

Qumran, 218. See also Dead Sea Scrolls

rabbinic Judaism, 6, 125, 203, 233, 276, 300, 326

redeemer, 45, 51, 55, 284, 297, 305, 307, 321–24

redemption, 16, 29, 32, 34, 45, 48–49, 51, 53, 55–56, 58, 64, 84, 90, 123, 135, 137, 205, 208, 216, 227, 306, 317–18, 320, 322–23, 394

remnant, 229, 266, 382

resurrection, 3, 22, 53, 56, 83, 101, 138, 141, 190, 212, 215, 224, 235, 244–45, 247–48, 256, 274, 372

revelation, 6, 12–13, 47, 51–52, 57, 60–62, 64, 130, 186, 191, 209, 215, 262, 272, 274, 280, 285, 302, 346, 367, 408

righteousness, 22, 37, 110, 120, 136, 166, 203, 209, 212, 214, 222, 255, 262–63, 270, 276, 304, 312, 372

Sabbath, 29, 34, 58, 63, 69, 81, 106–7, 112, 295

Satan, 292–94, 302, 304–5

Saul, 134, 140, 166–68, 171–77, 180–81, 183, 186, 258, 277, 280–81, 354–55, 394–94

Sennacherib, 201, 209–10, 258

sexuality, 110, 327–29, 331

sign act, 134–35, 221, 223, 230, 240, 242

signet ring, 265, 355

Solomon, 28, 47, 126, 140, 151, 171, 184–94, 199, 240, 276, 285, 306, 325–28, 330, 333–34, 379–80, 392–93, 395–98, 401

Tarshish, 236, 256

textual criticism, 405

Theodore of Mopsuestia, 263

Theodoret of Cyrus, 263

Thomas Aquinas, 83, 211

Torah, 7–8, 16, 20–21, 23, 46, 55, 58–59, 81, 109, 111, 120, 124–25, 127–28, 139–41, 185, 204, 213, 220, 225–26, 269, 274, 276, 279–80, 283, 285, 289–90, 377, 384, 396, 398, 405–9

Trinity, 25, 38–39, 239, 409

Turretin, Francis, 9

typology, 170, 393

united monarchy, 17, 193, 391

vineyard, 194, 203, 228, 243, 328

virgin, 187, 206, 352, 396

vision (prophetic), 98, 131–34, 204–5, 222–23, 234–39, 266–67, 365–68, 370–74

von Rad, Gerhard, 12

warrior, divine, 54, 145, 158

watchman, 239–40, 243

wisdom literature, 275–77, 285

woe, 209, 239, 244, 254, 259, 262

Writings, 326, 391
    in canonical lists, 274
    canonical ordering, 273
    as Christian Scripture, 277
    and wisdom, 275–76

Yehud, 264–66, 386

Zechariah, 7–8, 126, 131, 136, 194, 250, 265–67, 380–81, 407

Zephaniah, 7–8, 126, 133, 250, 260, 262–64

Zerubbabel, 265, 379, 380–81

Zion, 194, 203, 205–6, 209, 212, 215, 220, 250, 264, 266–67, 271–72, 274, 286, 322, 342–45, 347, 349, 382, 396, 404–6, 409